FIVE STRAIGHT LINES

ALSO BY ANDREW GANT

Christmas Carols: From Village Green to Church Choir

O Sing Unto the Lord: A History of English Church Music

Music: Ideas in Profile

FIVE STRAIGHT LINES

A History of Music

ANDREW GANT

P

PROFILE BOOKS

First published in Great Britain in 2021 by
Profile Books Ltd
29 Cloth Fair
London
ECIA 7JQ
www.profilebooks.com

Copyright © Andrew Gant, 2021

1 3 5 7 9 10 8 6 4 2

Typeset in Dante by MacGuru Ltd
Printed by Aquatint Ltd

The moral right of the author has been asserted.

All rights reserved. Without limiting the rights under copyright reserved above, no part of this publication may be reproduced, stored or introduced into a retrieval system, or transmitted, in any form or by any means (electronic, mechanical, photocopying, recording or otherwise), without the prior written permission of both the copyright owner and the publisher of this book.

A CIP catalogue record for this book is available from the British Library.

ISBN 978 1 78125 777 7
eISBN 978 1 78283 325 3

'I've tried to read a few history books myself, and ... the main problem with them is this: they all assume you've read most of the other history books already. It's a closed system. There's nowhere to start.'

Jeff, in *England, England* by Julian Barnes

In memory of John Davey, who loved books and music

Contents

Introduction ... 1
Prologue: The First Million Years ... 14

Part One: Music in the Ancient World (40,000 BCE–500 CE) ... 17
1. Bone Flutes and Magic, Far East and Middle Earth: Prehistory and the Music of the Ancient Civilisations ... 19

Part Two: The Medieval World (500–1400) ... 29
Introduction ... 31
2. Love and Astronomy: Art and Science in the Medieval Age ... 37
3. The Sound of the Sacred ... 45

Part Three: Renaissance (1400–1600) ... 57
Introduction ... 59
4. 'To Rome for Everything …': Music in the Catholic World ... 66
5. Reformation ... 85

Part Four: Baroque (1600–1759) ... 99
Introduction ... 101
6. Vespers and Vivaldi: The Catholic South ... 112
7. Violins and Versailles: France ... 140
8. Purcell, Handel, Bach and the Bachs: Baroque Music in Protestant Northern Europe ... 157

Part Five: Classicism (1740–90) ... 175
Introduction ... 177

9. 'Bach is the Father, We are the Children': Enlightenment and the Birth of the Classical Age	197
10. 'Let There be Light': Haydn, Mozart and Vienna	214

Part Six: The Romantic Century (1770–1914) — 233
Introduction — 235
11. I, Genius: Weber, Beethoven, Schubert and Their World — 250
12. 1812: Overture — 273
13. A Tradition Fulfilled: Symphony, Symphonists and Sonata — 299
14. Elephants, Arias and the Gods at Twilight: Opera — 330

Part Seven: The Age of Anxiety (1888–1975) — 405
Introduction — 407
15. A Tradition Renewed: Mahler and Sibelius — 416
16. The Challenge of Modernism: Schoenberg, Stravinsky and How to Avoid Them — 426
17. America and the Jazz Era — 480
18. Ways Ahead: Britten, Messiaen, Copland, Shostakovich and Their World — 498

Part Eight: Stockhausen and *Sgt. Pepper* (1945–2000) — 513
Introduction — 515
19. Moderner Than Thou: Darmstadt, Electronic and Experimental Music, and the Legacy of Schoenberg — 522
20. Industry and Artistry: Pop Music — 541

Part Nine: The Way We Live Now (2000–∞) — 553
21. World Music, Girl Power and White Men in White Ties — 555

Epilogue: The Next Million Years — 563

Notes — 565
List of Illustrations — 603
Acknowledgements — 604
Index — 605

INTRODUCTION

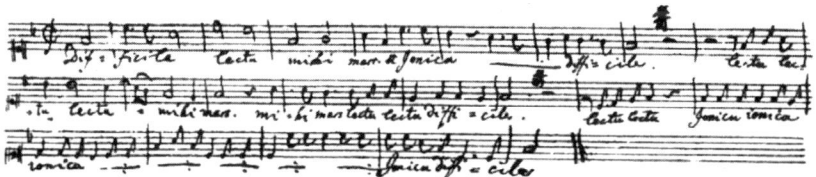

This is a song by one of the most sublime musical geniuses of all time.

The Latin is made up. If you pronounce it with a thick Bavarian accent, it comes out as 'Lick my arse'.

It's a joke, written by Mozart to poke fun at a friend.

There are lots of sublime geniuses in this book. But there's lots of other music, too.

Inevitably, this story leads on the great works and the great lives. But it also attempts to put those lives in context. Who were these musicians? What were they like? How did they make a living (or more often, in Mozart's case, not)? How does their music fit into the intellectual, social and technological tenor of their times? What other music did they hear? What did they sing in the pub when the concert was over? (Purcell's rounds are even ruder than Mozart's.)

Music and Words

One question facing the nervous writer of a book of this kind is whether there is in fact any point in using words to describe a non-verbal creature like music. Elvis Costello famously remarked that 'writing about music is like dancing about architecture'.[1]

Words are all we have.

But while some musical terms have a fairly precise, even scientific definition (an octave is the distance between two sounds created by dividing the frequency of a vibrating wave into two equal parts – a fact known and unchallenged since at least the age of Pythagoras), most do not. The word 'sonata' (literally, 'sounded', or 'played', as opposed to 'sung') can refer to a noisy early seventeenth-century ensemble piece by the Venetian composer Giovanni Gabrieli or the knotty innards of a movement by Haydn or Brahms. A 'symphony' could be a little snatch of strings in an anthem by Purcell, a three-movement curtain-raiser to an opera by J. C. Bach, or to Mahler the outpouring of the whole world. Spellings, and borrowings between languages, can set up some ambiguities, too: the familiar old favourite in your front room or school hall is known as a piano, but *piano* is simply the Italian word for 'quiet', borrowed as a name for the new instrument because of its ability to grade volume. The Australian composer Percy Grainger waged a one-man war on Italian terms, refusing to use even the humble Italian-derived 'violin', preferring the more Anglo-Saxon 'fiddle' (to the extent of calling the cello the 'bass fiddle', and the viola, rather pleasingly, the 'middle fiddle').[2]

Words move through time. The word just used to describe Grainger is 'composer'. Usage of that word has come to imply inspired thought, spontaneous utterance: making things up. In fact, its etymology also contains ideas of assembly, of putting things together, of placing working parts next to each other. It's about artifice as well as art, engineering as much as hearing secret harmonies. Stravinsky once told a French border guard he was an 'inventor of music' rather than a composer.[3]

The English language, that rich, shifting, many-layered creature, has other words for people who make things. Someone who works with words is a wordsmith, like a blacksmith. The person who makes plays is a playwright, like a wheelwright or a shipwright. Could the composer who fashions sounds into shapes be a notesmith, or a notewright? Not just a dreamer of dreams, but a maker of things.

Names shift in time, too. The sixteenth-century English composers William Byrd and Thomas Tallis were spelt Bird, Birde, Byrde, Byrdd and Talles, Talliss, Talless, Taliss, and other variants, in contemporary documents. Mozart, like any well-educated eighteenth-century polyglot, translated his name depending on where he was, turning his baptismal 'Johannes Chrysostomus Wolfgangus Theophilus' into 'Gottlieb', 'Amadeus' and hybrids like 'Wolfgang Amadè Mozart'. Other names changed through travel, politics and local usage: Roland de Lassus became Orlando di Lasso, Israel Beilin became Irving Berlin, Fritz Delius became Frederick, Gustav von Holst lost his 'von' and Schönberg his umlaut. Some musicians are known after the place they came from (Palestrina, Viadana, Gilles de Bins *dit* Binchois); others by nicknames or stage names (Heinrich 'In Praise of Women' Frauenlob, William 'Count' Basie, Jacob Clemens 'Not the Father' non Papa, which seems to be an obscure Renaissance in-joke). Some names still haven't quite settled into an accepted usage: scholars tussle politely over whether the celebrated fifteenth-century English polymath John Dunstable was actually Dunstaple. Suffice to say that the composer himself wouldn't have given a quilisma one way or the other.

There is, inevitably, technical language in this account. This raises the question of how we write about music. We can do this:

> ... the first subject is presented in the minor tonality before being developed through modal shift, retrograde, and fully worked-out triple invertible counterpoint.

Or we can do this:

> I took the theme for a walk, then in the middle I changed it to major and came up with a very sprightly little tune, but in the same tempo, then I played the theme again, but this time ass-backwards; in the end, I wondered whether I couldn't use this merry little thing as a theme for the fugue? – Well, I didn't stop to inquire, I just went ahead and did it, it fit so well as if it had been measured by [my tailor].[4]

The first is an amalgam of the kind of instruction handed down by harmony and counterpoint tutors since time immemorial. The second is by Mozart.

Is one or the other what the writer and pianist Charles Rosen loftily described as 'a failure of critical decorum'?[5]

Actually, both are indispensable and unavoidable. As the lyricist Sammy Cahn said, 'You can't have one without the other.'[6] The trick is to get the balance right.

The question of how much knowledge to assume is, of course, a matter of judgement. I hope I have flattered my reader just enough.

In any event, the cautious author can take some comfort from the fact that this is not a new problem. In the preface to his admirable *History of Music* of 1776, Sir John Hawkins forewarned his readers:

> For the style, it will be found to be uniformly narratory; as little encumbered with technical terms, and as free from didactic forms of speech, as could consist with the design of explaining doctrines and systems; and it may also be said that care has been taken not to degrade the work by the use of fantastical phrases and modes of expression, that, comparatively speaking, were invented yesterday, and will die tomorrow; these make no part of any language, they conduce nothing to information, and are in truth nonsense sublimated.[7]

I will leave it to my readers to nominate the modern equivalents of Hawkins' 'fantastical phrases' and 'nonsense sublimated'. In any case, the best way to use this guidebook through the myriad mysteries of music is to have a good sound system and streaming service to hand (or, even better, a ticket for a concert or a gig), rather than rely on the slippery, insignificant and unreliable stand-ins which fill these pages, words.

And, besides, why shouldn't you dance about architecture if you want to?

The Long View

Another question facing a historian of music is: how much history, and how much music? How much about the people, and how much about the notes? The attempt to tie pretty much all of Western music together in one volume has sometimes seemed a bit like Mr Casaubon drily embarking on his 'Key to All Mythologies' in *Middlemarch*, or Monty Python's 'Summarise Proust' competition. But there are advantages in the method, as well as madness.

Taking the long view of musical history allows connections to emerge. It also invites consideration of how, and why, musical style changes over time.

All music is born in its own local context. Some transcends that context. Looking back, we tend to see the standout work more clearly than the vernacular hinterland which surrounds it and from which it grew. The work which begins as the exception becomes the exemplar: the unique becomes the paradigm.

As well as looking at how the music changes, the long view can also allow us to look over time at how context changes. That's not just a question of performance style, crucial though that is. It's also about how listening changes. Listening has a social, aesthetic, intellectual, moral and spiritual dimension. People listen differently, as well as write and perform differently, in different eras. We need to try to understand how they did it, and what they thought they were listening for. A Mass by Palestrina reminds its congregation where they stand in relation to their God and His church. A modest little minuet by Lully is not just a pretty tune, it tickles the listener's *amour propre* by flattering him that he knows the steps, not just of the dance but of the whole ritual of precious society. A quartet by Mozart lays out the sense of order, balance and rationality underpinning eighteenth-century thought. Art had to be smuggled into a compact already signed and sealed between composer and listener, and not be allowed to show too much.

Beethoven changed all that. Beethoven told his listeners that he was ahead of them; their job was to catch up. If we don't get his meaning, it's our fault, not his.

That works if you're Beethoven.

But rolling forward the presumptions of one age into the next is an error of logic. It can lead us to look for a top genius in each generation, even if, like Macavity, he's not really there. Books like this one end up inviting you to read about composers you've heard of and like alongside composers you haven't or don't, and treat those impostors just the same.

We need to get over it. All music needs, and deserves, to be treated on its intrinsic merits. Schools and styles are not equal, successive and equivalent. Even more pernicious and damaging is the idea that popular or inherently simple music is by definition less interesting than self-appointed serious or complex music. Distinctions of that kind don't help, and have to go.

Musicians just do what they do. Some know instinctively that they are pushing music in important new directions. Others think that they are (but actually aren't). Most are just doing their job as well as they can.

The *Musikgemälde* and the Musome

As with other fields, some have turned to the insights of Charles Darwin as a way into how music changes and grows (despite being warned by one eminent musical historian about the pitfalls of 'the pestilential analogy with biological evolution', fit only for 'simple minds').[8] Another model from natural history provides a different view of musical style spread out over time.

The German naturalist Alexander von Humboldt observed that nature exhibits similar responses when subjected to similar pressures, despite being separated in time and space. He charted these areas of similarity on a beautiful diagram which he called his *Naturgemälde*, 'an untranslatable German term that can mean a "painting of nature" but which also implies a sense of unity or wholeness', according to his biographer.[9] Areas of similarity, or 'long bands' as Humboldt called them, are shown together on a schematic of the slopes of the Andean volcano Mount Chimborazo. Modern science calls Humboldt's long bands 'biomes': classes of living things which show features in common because they are responding to similar pressures and stimuli.

Could Humboldt's insight into nature work as a way of observing music across history? Arnold Schoenberg and Charlie Parker both found their inherited language obsolescent; both responded by deconstructing its harmony and scales. They exist in the same musical equivalent of a biome (could we call it a 'musome'?), responding to the same forces in ways which share characteristics. Seventeenth-century court opera, nineteenth-century French grand opera, big Broadway musicals and stadium glam rock all answer the call for costly, mass live entertainment with tunes, tights, flashing lights and flummery: same requirements, same 'musome'. The modern singer songwriter with a guitar is like the troubadour with a lute. A courtly passepied by the Baroque composer Michel Richard Delalande and Irving Berlin's 'Cheek to Cheek' answer the same need: handing a beautifully dressed celebrity couple a toe-tapping tune to show off their moves, while everybody else looks on admiringly. *West Side Story*, on the other hand, comes from the same stable as *Rigoletto*: sophisticated technique allied to a tuneful style for serious purpose. William Byrd's 'captivity' motets go with Shostakovich's string quartets. Late fourteenth-century French ars subtilior is highly seasoned sensuality in the last days of a dying tradition; so are the late nineteenth-century songs of Hugo Wolf and Reynaldo Hahn.

Humboldt insisted on seeing life on earth in its entirety. Maybe his methodology can help us to see music in time as he saw nature in space, as a 'living whole', not a 'dead aggregate'.

Genus: Human; Species: Composer

Genius is, by definition, individual. But great musical creators do, broadly, have some things in common; not least, sheer hard work.

Early training is key: Benjamin Britten learnt exactly the same things from his mentor Frank Bridge as Mozart did from his father and Thomas Morley did from William Byrd (as well as some things unknown to them, of course). Music was often (though not always) the family business, surrounding the young neophyte composer not just with sounds but with the day-to-day practicalities of practice and professionalism.

All artists need routine: while ideas flow continuously (like 'a faucet', said Aaron Copland),[10] working them into shape requires discipline at desk or piano – many have found early mornings best for this.

Employment is another constant. Most of music's greatest minds had to waste energy on tussles with their paymasters, and many came off worse. Lesser talents have often been better at the worldly side of things – for every Purcell there's a Nicholas Staggins, for every Shostakovich a Nicolas Nabokov. The extent to which commercial reality can be bent to meet artistic imperative (or vice versa) is another thread. Stravinsky said that 'the trick, of course, is to choose one's commission, to compose what one wants to compose and get it commissioned afterwards', as he often did.[11] Many, indeed most, composers still did their share of teaching and performing to help keep themselves in paper and pencil sharpeners. Britten recalled a society lady at a village tennis party asking him what he intended to do for a living. 'I want to be a composer,' the young man replied. 'Oh yes,' said the lady; 'and what else?'[12] The story is usually read as elderly incomprehension of the artistic imperative. Actually the lady was making an entirely sensible point.

As performers, composers are responsible for realising what they dreamed of at their desk. Haydn 'learned in general how musicians must be handled and thus succeeded by much modesty, by appropriate praise and careful indulgence of artistic pride so to win over

[the] orchestra';[13] Bernstein didn't. (Though few have treated their collaborators quite as badly as Charles Mingus, who punched trombonist Jimmy Knepper in the mouth during a rehearsal, ruining his embouchure and taking a full octave off his range.)

Composers make style, but style also makes composers. Composers need technique. The job requires them to master their inheritance so that they can contribute to, build on, or kick away what they have learnt, according to their lights. What they learn is craft, grammar, manners: rules. Stravinsky liked working 'in chains', believing that 'An artist's individuality stands out more clearly ... when he has to create within definite limits of a convention.'[14] Haydn's biographer Georg August Griesinger said that he 'convinced himself that a narrow adherence to the rules oftentimes yields works devoid of taste and feeling ... in music only what offends a discriminating ear is absolutely forbidden'. Rules, to Haydn, were 'like tight clothes and shoes, in which a man can neither move nor breathe'.[15] But this doesn't mean the composer can kick his clothes and shoes off altogether: Haydn's young friend Mozart thought that a piece of music should be 'like a well-tailored dress', and 'must always be pleasing, in other words must always remain Music'.[16] Technical analysis tells us how that is done (usually described after composers have already brought a style to full maturity). In the phrase of the pianist and music critic Charles Rosen, 'the possibilities of art are infinite but not unlimited'.[17] In other words, its infinities are unfurled within deliberate limits.

What were they like? It's quite easy to come to glib conclusions about the link between personal characteristics and habits and creativity. In fact, taken as a whole, the corps of great composers shows a range of different ways of living a human life. They are, in fact, a bit like the rest of us. Some were happily married, like Bach and Purcell; others were not, like Haydn. Some exhibited a fairly intense sex drive alongside their creativity, like Mozart and Schumann; others didn't, like Handel. Some were self-absorbed and determined to the point of monomania, like Wagner; others were clearly agreeable and social creatures, loved and admired by a wide circle of friends, like Mendelssohn. All dealt with the physical realities of their times, including death, disease and dodgy medicine – between them, Bach, Purcell and Mozart buried no fewer than eighteen children in infancy. What musical potential did they bury alongside those little corpses? Where are the ghosts of these lost infants now? Do they show up in their fathers' music or letters? It is difficult to find them. Or was it really part of the manner of the times to treat death as an incidental inevitability, explained away in conventional religious phrases? It is hard to believe it.

History: Streams and Dams

The musicologist Friedrich Blume said: 'History is an ever-rolling stream: it is the historian who builds the dams.'[18] One of his precursors, Guido Adler, did much to transfer the concept of 'style-periods' from art history.[19]

This book is, broadly, a history of the Western, classical, art music tradition. It divides musical time into parts, varying in length from about fifty years (Classical) to about 100,000 years (prehistory), bookended by a prologue and an epilogue that peer speculatively backwards and forwards. Each part (except the first and the last) has an introduction, touching on generic issues such as the ideas and external forces acting on the music of the time; the place of the composer in society; some technical information about musical style; and a number of representative musical examples. This, then, allows the individual chapters to tell their story without having to keep stopping to explain what a fugue is: forms have a history, just like people and pieces.

The names used here for this division of musical time into strata are sanctioned by long usage. They are far from being historical fact. The borders between them can be slippery, too, which is why the dates in the part headings often overlap. But they work because they stand not just for the movement of musical style and technique, but also for the ideas, manners and beliefs which underpin it.

The novelist Henry James once said that 'we possess a great man most when we begin to look at him through the glass plate of death'.[20] Most of the people in this book are dead. However, the idea that a reputation is fixed and capable of being seen as a whole at the moment of its earthly accomplishment is wrong. A history of music is also a history of histories. Reputations move through time, revealing as much, or more, about the observer as the observed. Fine writers on music like Mattheson, Burney, Forkel, Griesinger and many others of their tribe confirm that the historian, like the composer, exists in context. This is largely about the intellectual environment within which they wrote. But it's also about the repertoire they heard. Scholars writing about Baroque and Renaissance music even half a century ago simply heard less of it than we do now. Conversely, I have of necessity written here about the operas of Marschner, Meyerbeer, Mercadante and Spontini, but have never seen a note of them in the theatre, inescapable as they were in their day. Here, their contemporaries hold the advantage.

When you survey a landscape, what you see depends to a large extent on where you stand.

Welcome to the Museum: Sources, Written and Not

A number of key ideas and questions underpin the writing of musical history: Is there such a thing as a canon of great works? How do we deal with pieces and composers famous in their day but since forgotten? Who was right? If Chopin played the same piece twice in succession, but differently each time (as is claimed anecdotally), which is the real piece? Is there, in fact, such a thing? How could he write such a piece down?

Notation both charts and directs history. The vast majority of human music is never written down at all. You know lots of nursery rhymes, folk songs, football chants and Christmas carols, but you never sat down and learnt them – they're just there. That's how oral traditions work. Within the separate, parallel tradition of written, authored art music, notation has gone through a series of distinct phases, each of which had limitations which the next phase sought to address. This raises the question of the extent to which the means of expression controls what is expressed, and vice versa. Does Renaissance music not have a symbol for double-dotted notes because the style didn't need them, or did composers not use them because they had no way of writing them down? Or both? How did practicalities like the composer working ideas out on a slate before transcribing them into individual part books (not a full score) affect the actual music? Music designed to be sung from memory need never be written down at all. Irving Berlin never learnt to read music. Nor did Paul McCartney. When he tried, several times, late in his career, he gave up because what he saw squiggling along the five straight lines on the page in front of him 'doesn't look like music';[21] for the Beatles, the finished object was a performance or a recording, not marks on a piece of paper. The jazz pianist Erroll Garner said, 'No one can hear you read.'[22]

Then there's that familiar old standby of human affairs, luck. Some music survived because the paper it was written on got used for something else – binding a set of accounts, or being stuffed into an organ pipe to stop it wheezing. Known unknowns include a complete missing cycle of Bach cantatas, or the musical riches of the royal library in Lisbon, listed in the surviving catalogue but destroyed in the devastating earthquake of 1755. Unknown unknowns remain out of reach, parallel historical universes which must exist but cannot be visited. Sources vary, too, not just because of practical things like the move from manuscript to printing but because some composers took great pains to preserve their legacy, while others did not. Relatives are inconsistent, as well: Vera Stravinsky cemented her husband's reputation after his death; Wilhelm Friedemann Bach sold his share of his father's manuscripts to pay off his debts. Written accounts have to acknowledge the context of the writer: family members like C. P. E. Bach and Max Maria von Weber write about their famous forebears with loyalty and affection; colourful characters like Mendelssohn's friend Eduard Devrient talk up their own role in significant events; witty wordsmiths like Johann Mattheson can enjoy a good story as much as historical accuracy; colleagues can be generous, rivals can be catty and jealous. Novelists have fictionalised events in composers' lives from the beginning: Eduard Mörike about Mozart, Romain Rolland on Beethoven, James R. Gaines re-inventing Bach, Elgar reimagined by James Hamilton-Paterson, who said, 'I have tried to be as factually accurate as was interesting.'[23] The English historian George Dangerfield reminds us that history 'reconciles incompatibles, it balances probabilities; and at last it attains the reality of fiction, which is the highest reality of all'.[24] All written sources are, to a greater or lesser extent, fictionalisations: a letter, even written the same day as the events it describes, makes choices and allowances.

Finally, a book of this kind can easily be critiqued for what it leaves out. Like a football manager reviewing his substitutions at the end of a game, I can only assess my choices when the shape of the completed whole becomes clear: should I have brought Alessandro Scarlatti on before half-time; would ten minutes of Turnage have added energy on the left wing in the closing passage of play? Enough, perhaps, to say that the choices are mine. This is *a* history of music, emphatically not *the* history.

Come, Hear the Music Play …

On a chilly evening in spring 1745, the petite, pretty, popular French soprano Élisabeth Duparc rose to her feet on the boards of the King's Theatre, Haymarket, to present to the fickle London public a brilliant and brooding new oratorio by George Frideric Handel: *Belshazzar*.

The words are by Handel's finest wordsmith, the gifted but grumpy Charles Jennens. Jennens begins by etching the rise and fall of human civilisations:

> Vain, fluctuating state of human empire!

Vividly, he compares their fate to the course of a human life:

> First, small and weak, it scarcely rears its head,
> Scarce stretching out its helpless infant arms …

Would the irascible Jennens mind a modern musical historian borrowing his sweeping imagery as a way into the history of music, both before and after that foggy spring day in London? Or would he think that the historian, as he once said of Handel, had 'Maggots in his Brain'?[25]

Probably. But his words provide one of many possible pathways through the story which follows.

The 'helpless infant … small and weak' is perhaps humankind's first stirrings of a feeling for pitch and rhythm. Jennens goes on:

> Anon, it strives
> For pow'r and wealth, and spurns at opposition …

much as music did in Handel's and Jennens' own day.

> Arriv'd to full maturity, it grasps
> At all within its reach,

'full maturity' being the masterful synthesis of Mozart;

o'erleaps all bounds (Beethoven);
Robs, ravages and wastes the frighted world' (a pretty good
    description of the shivering Romantic visions of Schubert
    and Berlioz);
At length, grown old and swell'd to bulk enormous (Wagner);
The monster in its proper bowels feeds
Pride (Mahler); luxury (Strauss); corruption, perfidy (the
    rotting death of the safe laws of tonality);
… Of her weakness
Some other rising pow'r advantage takes,
Unequal match! … (jazz, modernism, pop);
plies with repeated strokes
Her infirm aged trunk (punk, funk, take your pick …)
… she nods, she totters,
She falls, alas, never to rise again!

But, says Jennens, the story isn't over; it just starts again:

The victor state, upon her ruins rais'd,
Runs the same shadowy round of fancied greatness,
Meets the same certain end.

Is that the arc of the story of Albinoni and Al Jolson, of Byrd and the Byrds, of crumhorns, crab canons and Kraftwerk?

I don't know. This is a story without an end.

One of Verdi's farm labourers once expressed astonishment that his master could make money drawing little hooks on five straight lines.

Those lines haven't always been straight, and there haven't always been five of them. But they have hooked in their inky grasp some of the funniest, most profound, disturbing, moving and truthful insights into the human condition in all art.

This is their story.

Prologue

THE FIRST MILLION YEARS

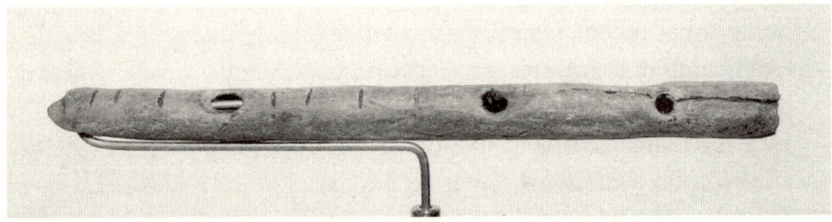

This is a story with no beginning.

When did two hominids first fall into step when walking, enjoying the subliminal sense of rhythm made by their footfall?

Activities which we would recognise as musical, involving the use of pitch, rhythm, heightened vocal expression and deliberately fashioned technologies, have been part of human behaviour since the advent of our species and before.

One-million-year-old tools allow us to imagine a mind in which we can, in the words of musicologist Gary Tomlinson, 'discern foundational capacities for human music', linking materials to the chains of gesture and social interaction required to fashion them.[1] The 'voicescape' of shared activities permits the idea of perhaps 500,000 years ago, a 'protolanguage', a concept rich in speculation and pitfalls. Tomlinson tells us that music is both related to and different from language: 'Song offers itself, in this complex relation to language, as a second modern behaviour.'[2] Our next ancestors, through the most recent quarter of a million years, continued the process of making patterns and hierarchies which form the embedded fundamentals of all music, though still a long way short of anything approaching a grammar: 'Neanderthals did not sing as modern humans do, and they did not speak a modern language; but their fashioning of the material world preserves traces of powerful cognitive patterns at once protomusical and protolingusitic.'[3] Sign and symbol in the era of *Homo sapiens* (where we talk of time in the tens, rather than hundreds, of thousands of years) provide 'glimpses of modernity' in which, potentially, 'the addition of discretized pitch leaves us still in the realms of protomusicking, if on the verge of these new, transformative possibilities'.[4] These possibilities included melodic building blocks and temporal patterns: tune and rhythm. Last in this reduction of a million years of music into a single short paragraph is the era of large-scale population movements, migrations and climate events, leading up to the first physical evidence for actual human music-making some 40,000 years ago, evidence which takes the astonishing form of real, recognisable musical instruments.

What makes Tomlinson's account so profound and so important is that it makes clear that music is not something added to human activity at a late stage of development, to 'colour in' the bits of discourse and behaviour which language or social interaction couldn't reach or didn't want. Music is not, to borrow a famous phrase from the linguist Steven Pinker, 'auditory cheesecake'.[5] Marches and lullabies were not written because somebody noticed the need for them, they are inherent in that need. They are that need. Music does things in and to the brain and the body that we cannot deny or ignore.

The natural foundations of music gave rise both to its basic musical units and its functions, both traceable through time: 'At this foundational level, not only basic capacities for music ... but also the general social uses to which it is put probably assumed familiar forms farther back in our deep history than we have thought,' says Tomlinson. 'Musical behaviours have changed, to be sure; but can we discern much fundamental difference between a church choir singing today and the music ... that must have resounded at [the 11,000-year-old settlement in Turkey] Göbekli Tepe?'[6] Composer Ralph Vaughan Williams also noted the natural, spontaneous occurrence of familiar musical shapes: 'I once heard a Gaelic preacher ... and when he got excited he recited on a fixed succession of notes:

Now this is the basis for much folk song.'[7]

We make music because we have to. Deep history confirms what it is about music that cements it at the heart of what it means to be human: it is social, technological, linked to but different from language and sign. It is hierarchical, not just underpinning but creating human institutions. It is transcendent, allowing us to explore things not available to the senses and logic: what Tomlinson calls 'thinking-at-a-distance',[8] the basis for all corporate and shared endeavour and ritual.

The significance of this chapter in this story is that these forces and insights embedded in our deepest past underpin all music. Sometimes they come close to the surface, without us having the slightest clue why.

And so history begins.

Part One

MUSIC IN THE ANCIENT WORLD (40,000 BCE–500 CE)

1

BONE FLUTES AND MAGIC, FAR EAST AND MIDDLE EARTH: PREHISTORY AND THE MUSIC OF THE ANCIENT CIVILISATIONS

A chronological account has to start somewhere.

The flutes of Hohle Fels and Geissenklösterle are about 40,000 years old.

After the twinkling of an eye comes the Cycladic civilisation of 3000 BCE, with its strange, blank-faced figurines playing lyres and pipes. Minoan Crete, captured in Sir Arthur Evans' Victorianised restorations at Knossos, sent the lyre and other instruments around the Mediterranean, including to the Mycenaean Greeks from around 1500 BCE. There's no doubt (though also no direct evidence) that significant texts were chanted, both epic poetry and ritual, religious texts: the kind of sing-song prose sometimes known as 'heroic recitative' can be identified from the Hebrew psalms through to Homer.

Greece

Many musical words were given to us by the Greeks: harmony, melody, orchestra, organ, chorus, tonic, symphony, polyphony, tone, baritone, rhythm, chromatic, syncopation, music. Many of these words are conceptual – describing ideas, rather than things – used by later ages to add authority to their own stage of musical development. Ancient thought developed the equally long-lasting concept of music as essentially two parallel disciplines: a philosophical science based on the mathematical order of the cosmos; and a practice.

Music fitted into ancient society in a wide range of contexts, including festivals, contests, drama of all kinds, symposia, recitation and ritual. The Greek word *mousike* embraced not just melody, but poetry, performance and dance. Population growth around the eighth century BCE fuelled social change which allowed the concept of the '*polis*', or notionally unified political entity, to emerge, with the time and capacity for intellectual and leisure activities like music and poetry. Later, the notion of the 'tyrant' (as yet without its malevolent later aspects) allowed artistic and intellectual activity to coalesce around an individual ruler: an early incarnation of the court as musical patron and employer, a key idea running through much of this story.

Aulos, cithara, phorminx, hydraulis: Greek instrument names have largely vanished along with their frail strings and wooden frames. But the instrumental families to which they belong are instantly recognisable. The aulos was a reed instrument, usually with two pipes, producing a melody over a kind of drone, like a bagpipe. The cithara was a small hand-held lyre or harp: the phorminx was one of many varieties of lyre, with four strings. There were no bows: strings were plucked. Percussion of all kinds included shells, bells, drums and rattles. The hydraulis was a kind of pipe organ powered by water pressure. Instruments evolved continuously: later harps had up to seven strings (occasionally more), allowing new kinds of mode and modulation to be added beyond established technical and artistic rules, to the horror of conservatives like Plato.

Instruments would often accompany singing. A citharode was a singer who accompanied himself on the cithara, while a citharist merely played. Similarly, an aulete played the aulos, while an aulode sang to its accompaniment (as a wind instrument, played, unlike the citharode, by someone else).

Greece was rich in musical theorising, at least from the time of Plato in the mid fourth century BCE. Aristotle's pupil Aristoxenus wrote on the two principal divisions of music theory, 'harmonics' and 'rhythmics', dealing with both in terms of the mathematical division of, respectively, pitch and duration.

For the singer and composer of vocal music, pitch and rhythm was fixed by the poetry. Greek syllables have fixed quantities, long or short (depending on the vowel and number of consonants). They also have rules about pitch, which are marked out by accents.

So the text:

πολιοὶ μὲν ἡμὶν ἤδη
κρόταφοι κάρη τε λευκόν

(*Polioi men hēmin ēdē*
Krotaphoi karē te leucon)

has a rhythm built in of:

short–short–long, short–long, short–long–long

But the pitch in each repetition is different. In the first line the raised pitch only appears in the penultimate syllable; in the second line there are three raised pitches (on the first, fourth and eighth syllable).

Greek writers such as Lasus of Hermione systematised and codified details like the names of the lyre strings (and, thus, notes of the scale) and, crucially, the modes or scales and how they fitted together, giving them the names rediscovered in the Renaissance and used ever since – Dorian, Phrygian, Ionian, Mixolydian, etc. – with all their variants, combinations, revisions and improvements.

Pythagoras was born around 570 BCE. His insights into the relationship between the mathematical ratios within music and the balance of nature and the human soul are captured in another Greek word, *harmonia*.

As always with the great names of antiquity, it is open to speculation as to what extent these detailed ideas originated with Pythagoras himself and how far they were developed by later followers like Philolaus of Croton. But the countless evocations of his name and speculative reproductions of his musico-celestial diagrams testify to the huge reach and influence of his ideas, right through to the time of scientists like Copernicus and Newton, 2,000 years after his death.

The Pythagoreans and their heirs through to Ptolemy in the first century CE analysed and demonstrated the mathematical ratios within pitch relationships in enormous detail. Pythagorean tuning bases all intervals on the frequency ratio 3:2. It involves tuning the fifths first, and produces the characteristic mixture of pure intervals and 'wolf' intervals. The discrepancy in pitch between twelve 'just' (i.e. perfectly tuned) perfect fifths and seven octaves is known as the Pythagorean comma. Pythagoras related these mathematical properties of music to the order of the cosmos, which in turn could be harnessed to promote 'soul adjustments' in the individual. (On the other side of the world, Pythagoras's contemporary Confucius was developing not dissimilar ideas about the function of good music in the satisfactory alignment of the human personality, extending this idea to encompass ideal forms of government and social order – as did some Greek communities, notably the Arcadians.)

The Greeks absorbed everything into their rich civilisation, including the cowhorn from their ancient Indo-European homelands, and the five-footed poetic rhythm also found in Finland. The oldest substantially complete example of written music comes not from Greece but from Canaan, in modern Syria. The Hurrian songs, as they are known, pair texts in a local dialect with musical symbols referring to intervals and a system of tuning, inscribed on clay. They date from about 1400 BCE. Some fragments name a composer. The longest (anonymous) song is a hymn to Nikkai, goddess of orchards and wife of the moon god. Neither words nor music can be definitively reconstructed. A first-century CE papyrus contains 100 lines of a partheneion or 'maiden song', probably dating back to seventh-century BCE Sparta, performed by ten girls who sing and dance to the accompaniment of a citharist (who laments that he is too old to join in the dance himself). An account of the mythical death of the sons of Hippocoön, the usurper of Sparta, with moralising comment, is followed by a passage in which the girls give their names, praise the beauty of their leader, describe their performance and refer to a rival choir – an indication of the role of competition in formal performance. This Archaic period, from around 700 BCE, saw innovations in song, musical theory and instrument design.

Greek musical writing appears in the surviving record about 2,000 years ago with the Seikilos Epitaph, a memorial carved on a stone column. Greek letters placed neatly above the syllables allow the tune to be read quite easily. Its maker added an inscription to his brief elegy for (possibly) his wife: 'I am a tombstone, an image. Seikilos placed me here as a long-lasting sign of deathless remembrance.' He certainly succeeded (despite the efforts of Mrs Purser, wife of the director of a firm of railway engineers in the 1890s, who sawed off the base so that, in the words of the archaeologist Sir W. M. Ramsay, 'it could stand and serve as a pedestal for Mrs Purser's flowerpots').[1]

The progress from the late Archaic to the early Classical period around 500 BCE brings some big names into view. The intimate lyrics of Sappho began to find a place in public music-making. Competitive art became a civic and political tool in the brief 'golden age' from the turn of the fifth century, separate from ritual, hastening the rise of the expert professional performer. Homer described music-making in many contexts, including the revealing story of Thamyris, a travelling virtuoso citharode, who offered to take on and defeat all comers in a singing contest, including the Muses themselves, for which temerity he was struck blind. Theory and practice continued to be debated and developed by thinkers like Epigonus and Lasus (author of 'the first book about music', according to the Classical scholar M. L. West),[2] and realised in sound by professional musicians like the prolific poet Pindar. Pindar describes music's role in the ideal society of the Hypoboreans, dwelling beyond the North Wind:

The Muse ...
does not forsake that land: dance-choruses of girls
are everywhere, and the assertive voices
of lyres and resounding shawms [a reed instrument] are ever
    astir[3]

By contrast, Aeschylus calls a society at war 'danceless, lyreless',[4] and Sappho tells us that a man in mourning for his wife banned all music from the town for a year. Here is Pythagoras's notion of the well-ordered soul in tune with music seen in daily life. It was a notion well-known to Shakespeare.

Classical Athens witnessed and nurtured music in all its forms. Great public festivals saw the dramatic performance of paeans, hymns and wild, choral 'dithyrambs', addressed to Dionysus. The Great Panathenaea, an annual festival in honour of Athena, hosted contests of playing and singing. In the 470s BCE Themistocles put up a special building for them, the Odeion, modified by Pericles in 446 BCE. At home, the leisured classes enjoyed the eternal 'symposium', a kind of club for intellectual discourse and sensual pleasure, with plenty of informal music. The singer poet Anacreon was a key player. Music featured in education, too: a beautiful painted cup of around 480 BCE shows a boy getting several different kinds of musical instruction in a schoolroom (the slave who took him to school sits at the back and listens). Religious ritual, with chanting, helped unite the *polis* in a corporate activity, involving an interplay between the aristocratic closed symposium and the open festivals.

A key role of music in society was in drama. Aristophanes' comedy *The Frogs*, written in 405 BCE, depicts the god Dionysus staging a subterranean contest between the styles of two of Aristophanes' recent contemporaries, the solemn choruses of Aeschylus against the fashionable fripperies of Euripides (Aeschylus won). The mature tragedies of Sophocles and others drew on an eclectic mix of influences, from masked ritual to folk art, converted by political fiat into set-piece civic and competitive events involving recitation and dancing as well as music. Running through the entire period, and well beyond, was the performance tradition of epic poetry.

Plato bitterly attacked the messy and ill-disciplined modern style, whose practitioners

> imitate all things, including ... claps of thunder, and the noise of wind and hail and axles and pulleys, and the notes of trumpets and flutes and pan-pipes, and the sounds of all instruments, and the cries of dogs, sheep, and birds; and so his style will depend wholly on imitation in voice and gesture, or will contain but a little of pure narration.[5]

He particularly disliked men imitating women. Plato and his student Aristotle distinguished between music as a liberal art, made by a man who is free (ἐλεύθερος, or *liber* in Latin), and music as a trade: 'no man can practise virtue who is living the life of a mechanic,' sniffed Aristotle haughtily.[6] One modern scholar sees in this disdain for the professional the historical roots of the 'antithesis ... between the ideal of a liberal arts college and a business school, between a gentleman and a tradesman'.[7] Another writer takes a different view, calling Plato's resistance to change 'pious twaddle'.[8]

Among celebrated singers of the new style towards the end of the fifth century BCE was Timotheus, who proudly said, 'I sing not the old songs, my new ones are better ... Away with the Muse of old.'[9] Aristoxenus countered: 'Music, like Africa, keeps producing some new kind of animal every year.'[10] The last few centuries BCE belonged to performers, not composers, at festivals and contests, in the newly formed artists' guilds, at athletic trials like the Pythian and Isthmian Games, and at royal events like the five-day festivities at Susa marking one of the three marriages of Alexander the Great.

Much of this account of music in Greek civilisation resonates throughout this book, not just in later Greek-inspired music like Ralph Vaughan Williams's youthful, buzzing overture to Aristophanes' *The*

Wasps, written in Cambridge twenty-five centuries after the play, or Handel's epic evocation of *Alexander's Feast*, complete with a part for Timotheus, but even more in the recurring ideas and debates about music and morals, old and new styles, tuning, education and music in society.

The Greeks did it all first.

Rome

Greece was certainly the most musically fertile of the ancient civilisations, but it wasn't the only one. Egyptian art is full of images of music and dancing. The Old Testament has music at the heart of many of its most vivid stories, from Jubal to Joshua to David and his psalms and Salome and her dance.

Rome, by contrast, is always seen as much less interested in music. Partly this is because not one note of Roman music has survived. Partly it's because the subsection of the literary culture of Rome that has come down to us is more interested in the written word than its Greek equivalent (which was more invested in the performance, and hence has a closer connection to music). Partly it's because Roman writers continued to treat music as two distinct disciplines: philosophical speculations on things like rhythm and metrics, completely divorced from everyday life; and snooty moralising about the tawdry hazards of actual music, especially new music (Seneca, Juvenal and Tacitus, like critics of all ages, only really got their juices flowing when writing about something they didn't like).

But there is a vast amount of literary and circumstantial evidence for the central place of music in Roman life, from interludes for the tibia (the Roman equivalent of the aulos) in the plays of Plautus and Terence, to military music using early kinds of brass instruments (some of them Etruscan in origin), a key role in religious ritual, big fees for popular professionals, music in the home, the hydraulis at the circus and tibia at the sacrifice, all fixed in fresco and mosaic.

Early Christian Music

The most important influence on the history of music in the centuries following Christ was the development of His church. St Paul's peregrinations around the Mediterranean provided the groundwork for structures which went on to support so much of the music in this book: the Christian liturgy, chant and monasticism.

Scriptural and Talmudic literature demonstrates that the great Temple of Jerusalem featured elaborate instrumentally accompanied psalmody in its ritual. A relief carved onto the triumphal Arch of Titus in Rome in 81 CE clearly shows a large silver trumpet among the loot pillaged from the temple following the siege, capture and sack of Jerusalem in 70 CE. Gatherings of the first Christians often centred around a meal, commemorating the Last Supper at which the disciples sang 'an hymn' (almost certainly a psalm). St Paul describes such a meeting (though the ever-prickly Paul famously used the phrase 'sounding brass, or a tinkling cymbal' to characterise vain speech, perhaps as an implied criticism of over-elaborate, temple-style music).[11] More organised early versions of the Christian Eucharist, such as that described by Justin Martyr in around 150, do not specify psalm-singing; though recited elements must surely have fallen into the form of semi-sung heightened speech known as 'cantillation'. Later, as the formal Eucharist moved to the morning, evening meal-time gatherings evolved to include the *agape*, or love feast, as described by Cyprian of Carthage in the third century:

> Now as the sun is sinking towards evening ... Let a psalm be heard at the sober banquet ... You will better nurture your friends, if you provide a spiritual recital for us and beguile our ears with sweet religious strains.[12]

The morning Eucharist, meanwhile, included psalm-singing as a regular element by the fourth century, with the discrete clerical role of cantor emerging to support and deliver it. The church musician was born.

Another, very different form of Christian practice emerged when men of strong faith and character took to communing with their god in isolation, often in the desert. Monasticism would provide a firm foundation for music for the next thousand years and more, partly through the opportunities for performance and education within its many and varied communities, partly though the music it engendered and employed: Latin liturgical chant, or plainsong. No single repertoire has exercised a longer or more important influence on the development of style and technique.

Early monastic music was very different from the highly specialised glories which were to follow. The fourth-century ascetic Palladius described the sound of psalm-singing emerging from several separate cells on the sides of Mount Nitria in Egypt as the monks within worked and worshipped – more as a kind of corporate act of meditation than a disciplined performance. As monasticism spread around the great cities of the Near East, its worship settled into the shape of eight daily services, or 'hours', finally formalised by Benedict in around 530. Importantly, it belonged to men and women equally. The distinction with the more public cathedral practice, led by a priest or a bishop, began to emerge. Both used psalms, hymns and antiphons (in this context, vaguer terms than in later usage). Psalms began to take their regular place at four main points within the formal structure of the Mass: an introit at the beginning; the gradual and alleluia surrounding the biblical readings; at the offertory; and at communion. Hymns began to be written in regular metre, notably, in the fourth century, by Ambrose, traditionally considered the author of the Te Deum, who also pioneered antiphonal chanting between the two sides of the choir. The architecture of a thousand years of sacred music is here. Movingly, the church historian Diarmaid MacCulloch tells us that we can find evidence for early Christian music-making not just from pictures, parchment, papyrus or paper, but in a surviving worshipping tradition in some churches in Turkey. Their music, says MacCulloch, is 'likely to represent a living tradition from the oldest known musical performance in Christian history'.[13] To our ears it sounds more 'Eastern' than 'Western', predating the great schism in Christianity by most of a millennium.

The doctors and fathers of the early church continued to wrestle with the role of music. Its moral perils weren't lost on them, as at all periods. The late fourth-century archbishop of Constantinople John Chrysostom said that 'where the aulos is, there Christ is not',[14] and called musical instruments, secular song and dancing 'the devil's rubbish'.[15] By far the best and subtlest exponent of these arguments was Augustine of Hippo. His six-volume *De Musica* restricts itself to the scientific aspects of rhythm, after the manner of Pythagoras and Plato: the sixth volume, following his conversion and baptism, draws its examples from Ambrosian hymns rather than Classical poetry. Augustine struggles to reconcile the celestial *numerositas*, or 'numberliness', which reveals the ordered changelessness of God through music, with his own keen sensitivity to its sensual beauties. Music in her daily dress of dance and timbrel was a dangerous temptress; clothed in academic gown she offered a gateway to the divine.

Constantine's Edict of Milan in 313 and Theodosius's Edict of Thessalonica in 380 aided the spread and codification of Christian practice, and its ability to absorb local influences into a range of regional practices. The key figures of the sixth century, St Benedict and Pope Gregory, moved music into its next phase, picked up and promoted by proselytisers like Alcuin and Augustine of Canterbury in distant England.

England reminds us that sacred music, though certainly the most important artistic form, wasn't the only one. The tradition of recited epic poetry, with instruments and some form of heightened declamation, must surely have filled the darkened halls of Wessex and Mercia in the centuries before Alfred and the unwelcome arrival of the Danes and Norsemen.

All later ages looked back to antiquity. Ensuing centuries tussled with and gnawed on its notions of theory, practice, study, morality and society. Classical antiquity became a sort of ready-made library of ideas, to be repackaged and reimagined: what one modern writer has called 'the age of potted knowledge'.[16] Learned later Italians like the seventeenth-century theorist Angelo Berardi endlessly justified their efforts with ego-enhancing evocations of 'what Plato said' and the '*parere* ['opinion'] *di Seneca*'.[17] Attempts to revisit the actual music of the Classical period faltered on the almost total lack of surviving source material. But it must surely have reached a significant level of sophistication – the double-piped aulos, and the keyed hydraulis (which, because it was powered by water, freed both hands to play) must have permitted a kind of drone-based polyphony.

Modern scholar M. L. West noted that 'in the end, Antiquity was destined to leave us far more musical theory than music'.[18] Today, Oxford academic Armand D'Angour has done much to reveal the actual sound of this ancient music. His reconstructed performances can easily be found online, an intriguing and moving insight into a living, ancient world.[19]

Part Two

THE MEDIEVAL WORLD (500–1400)

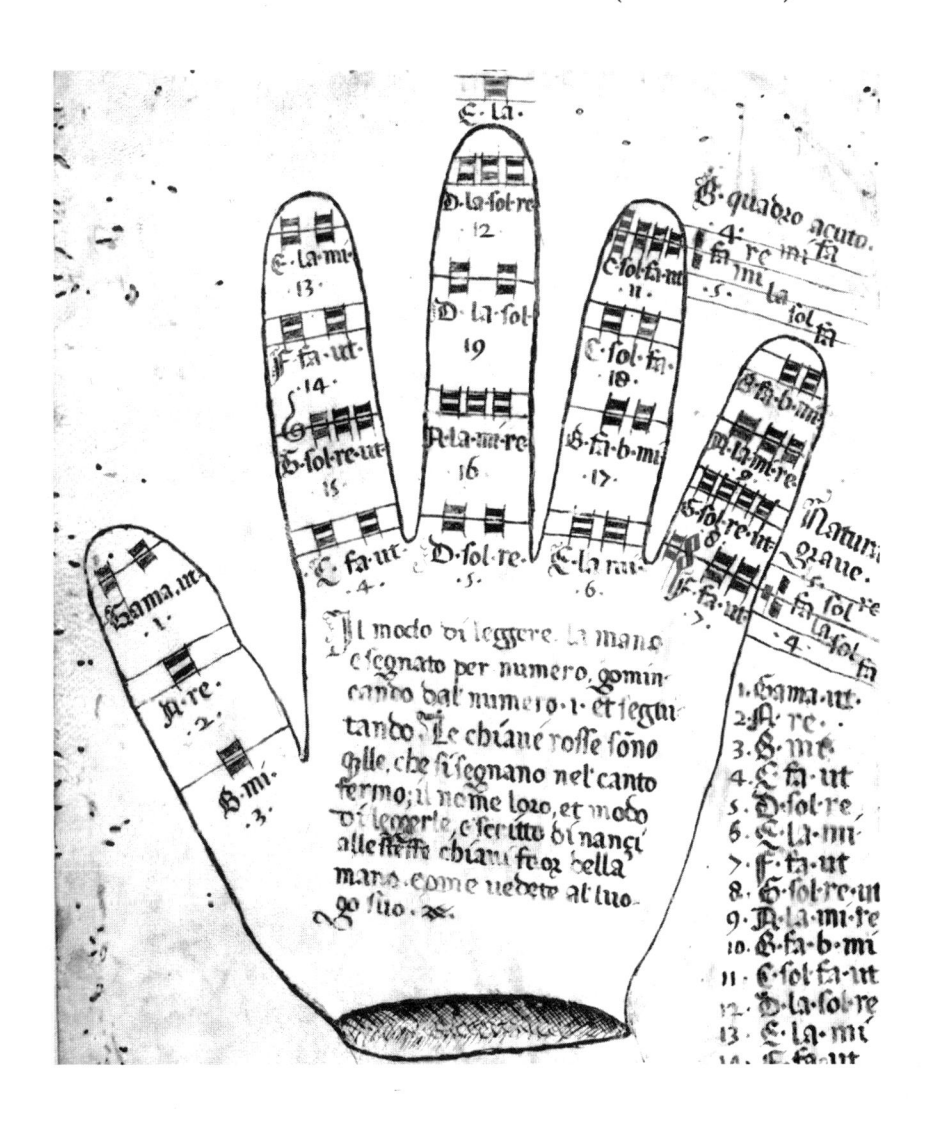

INTRODUCTION

Clausula and troubadour, prolatio and bumbulum ... The language and landscape of the medieval period are a foreign country. They predate things we have come to know and rely on: what a cadence sounds like; how to tell consonance from dissonance; how rhythm is written down; which musical instrument goes with which piece – even the idea that there is any such thing as a standardised form of a particular instrument. This music requires us to listen, and think, differently.

Primitive it most emphatically is not. Treatises of the time contain as much maths as music. Medieval music reached for the mind of God. Platonism (or one of the Platonisms) of the twelfth century led to Gothic cathedrals employing the perfect proportions, not only of the Golden Mean (or Golden Section), but also of 1:1, 2:3, and 3:4, because dividing a string in these proportions gives the octave, the fifth and the fourth – the perfect intervals in music. Thus if you wanted to reflect the mind of the Creator, expressed in His creation, you could do no better than use these proportions for the house of the Lord, and the music heard in it. The Italian historian Umberto Eco has said that medieval aesthetics involved 'an apprehension of all the relations, imaginative and supernatural, connecting the contemplated object with a cosmos opening on to the transcendent ... feelings of artistic beauty were converted at the moment of their occurrence into a sense of communion with God'.[1]

These chapters watch music move from one musical line, or voice, to many. A key identifier of the emerging medieval manner is that multi-voiced music came into existence by adding parts to an existing melody, almost always a plainsong, which could be treated in a variety of ways. This *cantus firmus* (or 'solid song') was sung by the tenor (from the Latin verb *tenere*, 'to hold', meaning the part which holds the plainsong). This tenor was the lowest part: higher voices could be *discantus* ('singing apart') or some other variant. It was also possible to add parts around or against (*contra*) the tenor (the contratenor). A part added above could be the contratenor altus, below the contratenor bassus. Even when later forms no longer relied on an existing melody, the sound of a slow-moving lower voice with more elaborate music above remained a characteristic feature.

Medieval music existed in a kaleidoscope of different forms, defined by performance context, scoring, words, technical preoccupations and other features. Among sacred forms were the clausula (polyphonic setting of a single word from a passage of plainsong), conductus (a song to accompany movement during the liturgy), motet (a word which has taken on all sorts of shades of meaning across the ages), and many others (with a certain amount of crossover – a three-part motet might turn up in a different manuscript without its tenor, thus turning it into a two-part conductus). Organum was the earliest, and simplest, way of making two-part sonority from a single melody. Rondellus and hocket (possibly from the same etymology as 'hiccup') are ways of chucking ideas, verbal and musical, from one voice part to another. Many pieces had different words (and often different languages) in the different voice parts. Tropes were extra passages of text – for example, for a particular saint's day – dropped into the fixed sections of the liturgy such as the Mass. Most of these forms had secular applications as well. Instruments could freely play an untexted line, but with no indication of which instrument – a whole world of buzzings and tootlings emerged when the passionate pioneers of the early music movement in the 1960s started recreating their rebecs, shawms and crumhorns from evidence available mainly in the form of images, literature and administrative records. When Ernoul de Halle, canon of Cambrai, died in 1417, his goods included a harp, a lute, a gittern, a rebec, two vielles and a psaltery – this canon clearly enjoyed his music outside church as well as in.

Secular forms included the chanson, identified by a distinctive scoring of two equal lower voices and one higher voice, and the rondeau, shaped by the particular form of its text with its inbuilt refrains and repeats (the rondeau quatrain, with a four-line refrain, the cinquain with three plus two, etc.), and many other types of love song, folk song, war song and party song, often with local or national characteristics. Some texts could be frankly earthy, embracing the cheerful vulgarity of a Rabelais or a Chaucer. Acrostics feature regularly, the first letter of each line spelling out the name of the composer or some other significant word – testament to the love among the educated of patterns, puzzles and word games. Song types where text and music stand in a fixed relationship to one another have come to be categorised as *'formes fixes'*, principally rondeau, virelai and ballade. Certain musical forms could fit any text in the same metre, much as psalm tunes were later to do.

Musical features include the distinctive under-third cadence (see the example given overleaf), completely different in sound and function from the later ways of moving to a final chord in modal and tonal practice. Harmony developed from treating fourths, fifths and octaves as consonances: the sweet sound of thirds and sixths came later, allowing in that modern thing, the triad.

A neat amalgam of some of the features referred to above appears in the technique known as faburden, a way of embellishing a plainsong by improvising an additional voice part a perfect fourth above the melody, and another a third below (moving to a fifth below at cadences and some other points). Once familiar with the principle, a well-trained group of clerics and choirboys could make sweet harmonies from just a single book of chant. The characteristic chains of 6/3 chords created by faburden became a signature of English music in particular. Another identifying feature of the medieval style is the default division of the beat into three rhythmic units, not two. Much of this repertoire sounds as if it's in what later eras would call compound time signatures: 6/8 or 9/8.

Notation, naturally, evolved over the long period travelled in these chapters. Its progress is key to understanding this music: at each stage, composers and theorists invented new ways to write down the new things they wanted to say.

The earliest two-part music outside of treatises comes down to us as musical symbols written above a line of text. There are no stave lines: the symbols, known as unheighted neumes, show the musical line rising and falling, but not when or by how much, a kind of memory aid for the singer of a tune they already know. A definitive reconstruction is, alas, impossible. Plainsong notation eventually (from around the twelfth century) placed the neumes on a four-line stave (though not always and everywhere to begin with), an entirely practical and adaptable way of transmitting a huge and varied body of repertoire, in use for many centuries (and, indeed, still).

The three-voice refrain to the fifteenth-century English carol 'There is no rose', preserved at Trinity College, Cambridge, showing the characteristic chains of triads in first inversion and the distinctive under-third cadence.

Plainsong does not require the precise notation of rhythm, because only one musical line is being sung. When two or more voices sing different lines at the same time (polyphonic music), notation must ensure that everyone sings at the same speed. The next phase was mensural, or measured, notation. Symbols similar to the old neumes are placed on a (usually) five-line stave, but they now have a specific duration in relation to each other: for example, the breve is divided into semibreves, which are further subdivided into minims (quick notes). Symbols roughly equivalent to modern time signatures (and, also, sometimes different colours of ink) were used to indicate if the division is into groups of two or three, or some combination of both, according to a pre-existing system of rhythmic 'modes'. The usual division was in threes, often equivalent to modern compound time signatures such as 6/8, giving medieval music its characteristic dance-like quality, full of jaunty syncopations and cross-rhythms. As the period progressed, note values got shorter, with a greater freedom of subdivision into smaller groupings. A ligature is a single symbol indicating two or more notes sung to a single syllable. Singers would usually read from a single part, like a modern orchestral player. Manuscripts could often be lavishly illustrated, works of visual as well as musical art. Instrumental music often used forms of tablature specific to the instrument – essentially, a kind of graphic fingering chart – gradually superseded by conventional stave notation (with the partial exception of music for the guitar family).

Of course, like all ages, the medieval era rang with all kinds of music. Chaucer's prim Prioress 'soong the service dyvyne, Entuned in hir nose ful semely'; but his Miller was 'a janglere ... A baggepipe wel koude he blowe and sowne, And therwithal he broghte us out of towne.'[2] These are the sounds which echo through the pages which follow.

Stages in the evolution of notation:

a)

Unheighted neumes (without stave lines), showing the rise and fall of the music, but not actual intervals or pitches.

b)

Plainsong notation: neumes on a four-line stave, with a C clef on the top line, giving pitch and relative note lengths (but not precise rhythm).

c)

Mensural notation, on five lines, using a G clef: precise rhythmic notation allows two or more lines to be sung together. The first two notes are a ligature. Modern transcription on the right.

d)

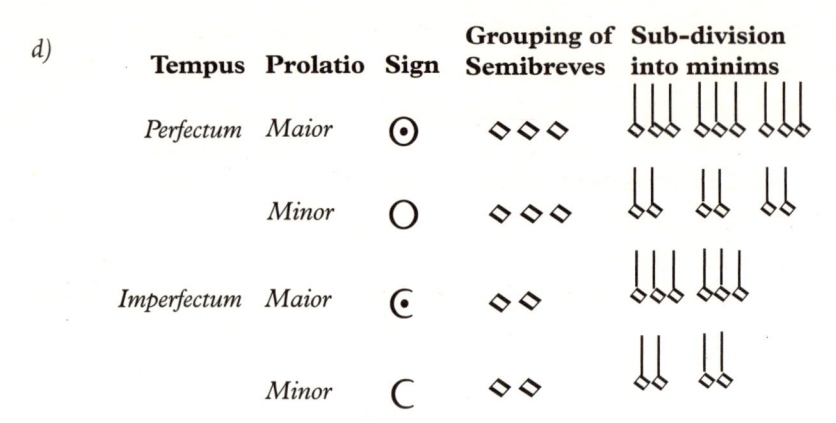

Tempus	Prolatio	Sign	Grouping of Semibreves	Sub-division into minims
Perfectum	Maior	⊙	◇ ◇ ◇	♦♦♦ ♦♦♦ ♦♦♦
	Minor	O	◇ ◇ ◇	♦♦ ♦♦ ♦♦
Imperfectum	Maior	₵	◇ ◇	♦♦♦ ♦♦♦
	Minor	C	◇ ◇	♦♦ ♦♦

Rhythmic modes. The 'tempus' determines whether the breve is divided into three semibreves ('perfectum') or two ('imperfectum'); the 'prolatio' whether the semibreve is further subdivided into three minims ('major') or two ('minor'). Other complex rhythmic relationships are conveyed by numbers, symbols and changes in the colour of the ink.

2

LOVE AND ASTRONOMY: ART AND SCIENCE IN THE MEDIEVAL AGE

Writing in the early sixth century, the Roman philosopher Boethius observed that 'Music is bound to us by nature: it can both encourage and destroy moral behaviour.' Elsewhere, he makes explicit the link between the search for harmony and the search for truth:

Why does a strange discordance break
The ordered scheme's fair harmony?
Hath God decreed 'twixt truth and truth
There may such lasting warfare be,
That truths, each severally plain,
We strive to reconcile in vain?[1]

Boethius was a true intellectual giant. In his musical writings he links an extraordinarily detailed technical and mathematical analysis of things like modes, scales and intervals with their place in the natural order and their role in achieving a just equilibrium in the human mind. Sometimes his thought seems to skip across the ages like time-travelling lightning: celestial bodies moving through space must have a music of their own, only we cannot hear it. All this is based on a rich understanding of his ancient forebears, particularly Aristotle and Plato.

The Athenian Academy finally closed after nine centuries in 529, just five years after Boethius fell from power and was executed for treason. But its spirit lived on into the Christian age, with many Classical texts continuing to be copied and read. Music emerged as one of the four subjects making up the 'quadrivium' of study (the others being arithmetic, astronomy and geometry). Medieval thinkers believed like Boethius that 'musica speculativa', the philosophical and mathematical examination of music's role in the cosmos, was a higher art than mere practical 'musica instrumentalis', which relied on those debased and unreliable guides, the senses.

Writing 800 years after Boethius, Dante echoed his elegant yearning to place music at the heart of the natural order:

> Diverse voices make sweet melodies here on earth below;
> So the blessed in heaven, though they occupy varying stations
>   according to their merits,
> Co-exist without envy and render sweet harmony among these
>   spheres.[2]

Carmina Burana

Our earliest surviving Western secular art music is Latin song from around the eleventh century. Like its sacred cousin, notation (where it exists at all) uses unheighted neumes, without stave lines, giving little more than a rough outline of the rise and fall of the melody. Tunes can be reconstructed if they reappear in a later source in a different form, usually with different words ('contrafacta'). Often, this second source will reveal the pitches, but leave a definitive account of rhythm out of reach.

Curiously, the already archaic and unhelpfully vague system of unheighted neumes was adopted as late as the early thirteenth century by the compilers of the collection known as *Carmina Burana* (so-called in the nineteenth century after the monastery where the manuscript was found). *Carmina Burana* is a wonderful document, bursting with the rich variety of medieval life. Written out by priests, some of its original authors may have been 'goliards', a modern term of uncertain origin used to describe disaffected worldly clerics, who used so-called 'goliardic metres' in the composition and performance of their scabrous anti-establishment verses. Some of the poets often described as goliardic were quite highly placed, such as Philip, the chancellor of Paris University. Others were itinerant clerics and students, younger sons with no money or responsibilities, who made it their business to satirise and poke malicious fun at everything, particularly the church. They wrote mostly in Latin, with High German, vernacular French and other regional dialects thrown in. A few of the poets can be identified, most cannot. All of the 254 poems in *Carmina Burana* were intended to be sung, though only about a quarter include musical notation on the manuscript. Alongside the bawdy fun and wicked satire is highbrow courtly entertainment and real learning. Stern Christian doctrine sits alongside pagan deities and Classical celebrities like Dido and Aeneas. Flagrant clerical abuse of the emerging money economy comes in for particular scorn. There is a brilliant gospel satire, 'Here Begins the Gospel of the Silver Coins' (a pun on Marcus the evangelist and marca the coin); there is the '*Officium usorum*', a liturgy for an order of lazy, gambling priests; there is a '*presbyter cum sua matrona*' ('a priest with his wife': priests, of course, were supposed to be celibate); and there are frankly pornographic songs like '*Sic mea fata canendo*' (which mentions the writer's '*rosa cum pudore/pulsatus amore*' and a number of other attributes which may perhaps be left untranslated). The manuscript also includes sacred plays with musical notation (in neumes). Tucked away among the 119 badly bound pages of parchment are several exquisite miniature illustrations showing a forest, a pair of lovers, scenes from Classical mythology, people drinking beer and playing chess, and the merciless goddess Fortuna with her wheel (a striking image, invented and first used by Boethius).

The Troubadours

The troubadour stands as the emblem and exemplar of medieval secular music. In the words of the modern scholar John Caldwell, 'in this repertory can be found in its purest and simplest form the essence of the whole of medieval lyricism'.[3]

The troubadours flourished from 1100 to around 1350, reaching a high stylistic peak in the fifty years or so around the beginning of the thirteenth century. Around 450 individual poets and composers can be identified, their accomplishments recorded in the many 'chansonniers' or songbooks, and in evocative (though doubtless romanticised) accounts of their lives known as 'vidas'. They wrote and sang in Occitan, the language of the region covering what is now the lower third of France and small parts of Spain and Italy. The troubadours came from all social classes – a notable early practitioner was Duke Guilhem IX of Aquitaine. They were not itinerant strolling players, but were typically employed in a noble or courtly household (though might have moved between such establishments), to entertain and indulge their lords' musings on the higher arts of love, the not-so-distant ancestors of Shakespeare's Feste and his many other fools, boys, clowns and jesters whose melancholy melodies give 'a very echo to the seat where Love is throned'.[4]

Troubadour poetry is lyric, not epic or dramatic. The three main styles of leu (light), ric (rich or elaborate) and clus (closed forms with much wordplay and verbal trickery) embrace many forms and subsets of rhyme, scansion, subject matter and metre, including the canso (a love song with five or six stanzas and a concluding envoi), the tenso (a poetical debate), laments, riddles, pastorals, and the gap (a boasting song presented as a challenge, like a modern football chant). As always, many of the poems survive as text only, maybe with the name of a tune appended as a tantalising hint. Musical sources are monophonic (single-lined), requiring creative speculation to recreate the sound of singers and instruments seen in contemporary images and descriptions.

A small but notable group of female troubadours were known as trobairitz. One, Azalais d'Altier from the Gévaudan, wrote a salut d'amour of 101 verses, *Tanz salutz e tantas amors*, to another, Clara d'Anduza.

Naturally, the style and manner of the troubadours changed as they moved around Europe, picking up local characteristics as they went. The most distinctive were the trouvères of northern France, and their lower-caste compatriots the jongleurs, rough and ready minstrels of the road, all-round entertainers who would dance, tumble and juggle as well as sing and play, despised by their courtly colleagues because they didn't write their own songs. The true trouvères were educated amateurs, including burghers or '*bourgeois*' who formed '*puis*' or musical societies such as that at Arras. This idea found fertile soil among the Minnesinger of Germany, who sang of '*Minne*' (courtly love) in their Frauenlob ('Praise of Women' – also the nickname given to one of the style's leading practitioners in the fourteenth century), leading to the great later tradition of musical guilds and civic music-making exemplified by Hans Sachs and the Meistersinger.

The Occitan repertoire was cultivated and performed in parts of present-day Italy and Spain, though Spain provides a reminder that the division of music, and indeed daily life and thought, into separate categories marked secular and sacred is anachronistic and artificial. The *Cantigas de Santa Maria*, collected (and very possibly written) by

Love and Astronomy: Art and Science in the Medieval Age 41

Alfonso X of Castile, employ the manner and vocabulary of the troubadour style to place the works and daily doings of the Virgin Mary at the heart of everyday life, as medieval man always did with his friends and familiars, the saints and martyrs of the church. '*Muito foi nóss' amigo/Gabriël, quando disse:/"María, Déus é contigo"*' translates from the original Portuguese/Galician as something like: 'You were a good friend to us, Gabriel, when you said, "Mary, God is with you."'

A song by the French trouvère Blondel de Nesle captures the timeless simplicity of the style: moonlight and love songs, never out of date.

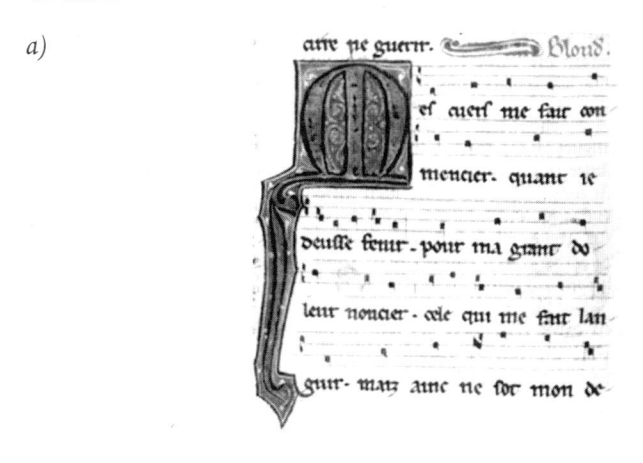

a)

b)

Mes cuers me fait con-men-cier, Quant je deüsse___ fe - nir
Pour ma grant do-leur non-cier, Cel qui me___ fait lan - guir.

maiy onc ne___ sens mon de - sir si ne me doi mer - veil-lier,

je sens ai an - goisse___ et i - - re

A song by the late twelfth-century trouvère Blondel de Nesle. a) The first two lines of the song in an original source; b) A modern transcription of the complete song. The poet sings of unrequited love in a melody of great freedom and beauty. The source notation leaves elements like the precise rhythm and the nature of the accompaniment (if any) to the performer.

The Drama

Music for dramatic and theatrical use grew out of sacred and liturgical drama. The English manuscripts known as the Winchester Tropers date from around 1000, and include music for the scene in the Easter gospel where the three Marys come to the garden of Gethsemane to honour the body of Jesus, only to find the tomb empty. The *Regularis Concordia* of *c*.980 describes the performance:

> While the third lesson (of Easter Day Matins) is being read, four of the brethren shall vest, one of whom, wearing an alb as though for some different purpose, shall enter and go stealthily to the place of the 'sepulchre', and sit there quietly, holding a palm in his hand. Then, while the third responsorium is being sung, the other three brethren, vested in copes and holding thuribles in their hands, shall enter in their turn and go to the place of the 'sepulchre' step by step, as though searching for something. Now these things are done in imitation of the angel seated on the tomb, and of the women coming with perfumes to anoint the body of Jesus. When, therefore, he that is seated shall see these three draw nigh, wandering about as it were and seeking something, he shall begin to sing softly and sweetly, '*Quem quaeritis.*' As soon as this has been sung right through, the three shall answer together, '*Ihesum Nazarenum.*' Then he that is seated shall say, '*Non est hic, Surrexit sicut praedixerat. Ite, nuntiate quia resurrexit a mortuis.*' At this command the three shall turn to the choir saying, '*Alleluia. Resurrexit Dominus.*'

The astonished conversation goes: 'Whom do ye seek?' 'Jesus of Nazareth.' 'He is not here, he is risen as he said. Go, announce that he is risen from the dead.' The liturgy has become a mini play, with music, movement and elements of staging. The idea became wildly popular: the *Quem quaeritis* ceremony alone generated many hundreds of versions over a period of about 650 years.

There are examples all over Europe. *Carmina Burana* contains two theatrical items on spiritual themes. The Fleury playbook of around 1200 contains ten sacred plays covering Christmas, Easter and episodes from the lives of St Nicholas and St Paul. The *Ludus Danielis*, the *Play of Daniel*, exists in two sources. The earliest has no extant music. The second was written by the young scholars of thirteenth-century

Beauvais, and uses monophonic music to add an extra element to the poetic rendering of Daniel's ill-fated encounters with kings and lions. But the text is full of other tantalising musical hints, too, like references to harps and hand-clapping and *'mille sonent modis'* ('a thousand different sounds'), as well as a 'conductus' for the progress of the queen and a repeated refrain, *'Rex in aeternum vive'* ('May the King live for ever!') The neophytes of Beauvais clearly intended to have some fun with their devotions.

Part of the appeal of the sacred drama is that it puts the people, stories and message of the Bible firmly into the context of everyday life. Mixed with ancient and mysterious things like parish processions, local legends and atavistic folk tales of sad saints and fiery dragons, the tradition gave rise to some of the most evocative emblems of medieval art: the mystery and passion plays. Guilds of players would trundle into market square and monastery steps on wheeled carts, which they would transform into the heavens, a stable, the gardens of Eden or Gethsemane, a flood for Noah to navigate with his doves and his nagging wife (who he calls a 'ramskyt', or 'ram shit', in one cycle), or the flaming jaws of hell (in Coventry a man was paid four pence to keep the infernal flames alight). Costumes were the daily dress of the players. Music was provided by the actors and the men and boys of the local monastery, putting familiar things like the Magnificat, Mary's song to the angel, in its rightful place in the story. Cosmic themes are given local colour: the Wakefield shepherds moan about the weather, their wives, robbers and taxes, and give the baby Jesus some cherries and a pet bird.

Morality plays, with music, were acted all over Europe. The French composer Guillaume Dufay may have seen the play *Tempio dell'Onore e delle Vertù* on a visit to Pinerolo, near Turin, at carnival time in 1439. As late as 1553 Mary I of England's Chapel Royal musicians (who included Thomas Tallis) put on a play to mark her coronation, featuring characters such as 'Genius Humann ... 5 virgins ... Sickenes, feblenes ... The bad angel'.[5] Shakespeare may have seen the last representatives of the English mystery players as a boy in Stratford, and perhaps remembered both their subject matter and their acting style when he has Hamlet tell the travelling player that his histrionic manner 'out-Herods Herod'.[6] The decennial Oberammergau passion play in Bavaria is the oldest continuously performed survivor of the tradition, but it is in truth a late example, assembled in the early seventeenth century from four manuscripts of the fifteenth and sixteenth centuries, with music added later still.

A number of other surviving works show the cheerful medieval habit of chucking all sorts of styles and influences in together. *Le Jeu de Robin et Marion*, by the late thirteenth-century trouvère, poet and member of the Confrérie des jongleurs et bourgeois d'Arras, Adam de la Halle, tells the kind of comical-pastoral tale of love, sheep and trials of fidelity familiar right through to the Renaissance and beyond. The *Chanson de Roland*, assembled between about 1040 and 1115, is the most famous chanson de geste, as they were called (and the earliest surviving work of French literature): a gory, chivalrous and entirely partisan account of the noble Franks' heroic struggles against the infidel Saracens and Muslims from *'d'oltre mer'* ('across the sea') during the reign of Charlemagne three centuries before. The *Roman de Fauvel* of around 1310 encompasses, among much else, 169 pieces of monophonic and polyphonic sacred and secular music in both Latin and French, many glorious illustrations, talk of dung and sex, word-play, puns, acronyms and in-jokes. The more than 3,000 lines of text tell the story of an ambitious horse called Fauvel, whose name is both an acronym and a verbal play on the names of the six vices – *'flaterie'*, *'avarice'*, *'vilanie'*, *'varieté'*, *'envie'* and *'lacheté'* – as well as the word for brown, 'fauve'. The name has given rise to the English expression 'to curry favour'; i.e. to 'curry' (groom) Fauvel.

Instrumental Music

Fiddling minstrels and wheezing bagpipers peer out at us from many medieval images, carvings and manuscripts. Very little written instrumental music has survived: the hundreds of different types of wind, string, percussion and keyboard instruments would have played music improvised from a songbook or from memory, with a drone or a descant added according to the capabilities of instrument and player. But there are some sources, including dances, which wouldn't have sounded out of place in an eighteenth-century dancing manual or at a modern-day folk festival in a muddy field in Sidmouth or the Appalachians.

3

THE SOUND OF THE SACRED

Plainsong

Some 500 years after the death of Christ, the Western branch of His church formalised its worship into the patterns which it has used, more or less, ever since.

St Benedict of Nursia wrote his 'Rule' around the mid sixth century. It provides a detailed prospectus for the enlightened and efficient running of a monastery, including the division of the day into eight services of prayer (the daily 'Office', also known as the monastic 'Hours'), with plenty of psalms *'cum Alleluia canendi'* ('sung with Alleluias') and items like the 'ambrosianum' (hymns in four-line stanzas in imitation of the style of Ambrose).[1] Although the Latin can be a bit ambiguous about the precise use of the verbs *dicere* ('to say') and *canere* ('to sing'), it is clear that, as one modern scholar puts it, 'the entire office was modulated with notes'.[2]

Half a century after Benedict wrote his Rule on the sun-baked slopes of Monte Cassino, the next major player in this story took up the staff and mitre of St Peter a hundred miles away, in Rome. Pope Gregory I reigned from 590 to 604. His precise personal involvement with liturgical and musical details is debated, but his importance in the codification of the chant was widely accepted in Francia from the eighth century onwards.

This liturgical practice went forth into all lands. In the seventh century, singers trained in Rome travelled as far as England: Putta, bishop of Rochester, was Gregory's grand-pupil, taught by his students. In 747 the Anglo-Saxon church resolved 'That all the most Sacred Festivals of Our Lord ... in the method of chanting, shall be celebrated in one and the same way, namely, according to the sample which we have received in writing from the Roman Church.'[3] The spread of the unified system of plainsong was intended to replace the regional variants – Gallican, Mozarabic, Ambrosian – with the

Roman-Frankish chant, now called 'Gregorian', adopted everywhere. In Rome it displaced the somewhat similar local Roman chant, found in sources from the eleventh to the thirteenth centuries, usually referred to as 'Old Roman'. The spread was spurred on by Charlemagne's edict of 789, the *Admonitio Generalis*, probably written by the English monk Alcuin of York. Charlemagne's chronicler, Notker the Stammerer, records that the early envoys of the new manner secretly agreed among themselves to teach different chants in different cathedrals and monasteries in order to thwart the centralising ambitions of Charlemagne, but this plot was foiled when the Pope sent out a new cohort of loyal monks to the abbeys at Metz and St Gall (now in south-eastern France and Switzerland respectively), from where Gregorian chant successfully made its way round monastic Europe.

The 'method of chanting' adopted at the Anglo-Saxon council of Clofesho (or Clovesho – the actual place cannot be identified) in the mid eighth century was plainsong. The plainsong repertoire is vast, covering the fixed parts of the liturgy such as the Mass, all the possible additional items like tracts, responds, antiphons and alleluias, daily bread like the Lord's Prayer and newly composed hymns like *Pange Lingua* and, later, the popular and expressive hymns to the Virgin Mary (comparing her to the moon, stars and sea in poetry which revels in her youth and femininity). Some of these later hymns, often by known authors, introduce rhyme and metre (like the thirteenth-century *Dies Irae*), allowing the plainsong tune to be interpreted using a regular rhythm.

Among the earliest and finest surviving books of liturgical plainsong are the manuscripts in the library of the Abbey of St Gall, dating from around 980. They include letters added as an instruction to the singer ('c' for *'celeriter'*, or 'quickly'; 't' for *'tenere'*, 'hold'), described by Notker.

Plainsong varies enormously in its level of sophistication, from simple tunes with a single reciting note to florid ornamental melodies. Many singers probably couldn't, or didn't, read: an abbey or large church might have just a couple of copies of a missal or psalter for the leaders, with everybody else joining in by ear or from memory.

Two-part Music

The next stage was to add colour by not having all the singers singing the same note at the same time: harmony. Polyphonic, or multi-voiced, music emerged. Like most innovations, this had certainly been going on, probably in a largely improvised form, long before scribes and theorists wrestled with ways of writing it down from around the ninth century.

The simplest way to create harmony was to add a second vocal line singing note for note against an existing plainsong. The main melody became known as the 'vox originalis', the added part as 'vox organalis'. The technique as a whole gained the catch-all name 'organum'. There are two basic types: the added part can sit on a single pitch below the main tune, like a drone (echoing the familiar sounds of bagpipes and the hurdy-gurdy); or it can shadow the plainsong at a fixed interval, singing the same tune in parallel. A musically literate singer with a basic grasp of the principle could add a part to a plainsong '*ex improviso*', by sight. More sophisticated organum combined elements of drone and parallel. Manuscripts from around 1100 show the added part becoming ever more elaborate, having two or more notes to a single syllable against the plainsong's one. This 'melismatic' part floats freely and expressively over a slow 'tenor': the world of later polyphony is beginning to come within earshot.

The rich mix of music and maths in the early medieval mind is vividly glimpsed in two treatises of the late ninth century, *Musica enchiriadis* and *Scolica enchiriadis*. The two works describe and notate polyphony in similar ways, the *Scolica* in the customary Socratic dialogue form. The philosophy and practice of organum are set out in magisterial depth and detail, defining pitch, scale, interval and ratio, leaning heavily (as usual) on the borrowed authority of Boethius and the Greeks. Master instructs Student how to avoid 'an infinity of disharmonies' through a proper understanding of things like the 'triple superquodpartiens' and the 'multiplex'.[4] Unfortunately, the letter-like symbols of the so-called Daseian system of musical notation used in these works leave plenty of ambiguity around, for example, the rather odd scale employed. But the modern traveller through these pages cannot miss the precision of ear and mind that created it, and can easily catch the 1,000-year-old echoes of monkish voices resounding in sturdy parallel round the unadorned pillars of ancient places like Aachen, Durham and Santiago de Compostela.

Unusually, England provides an example of innovation in the notation of two-part music in the early tenth century. In one volume,

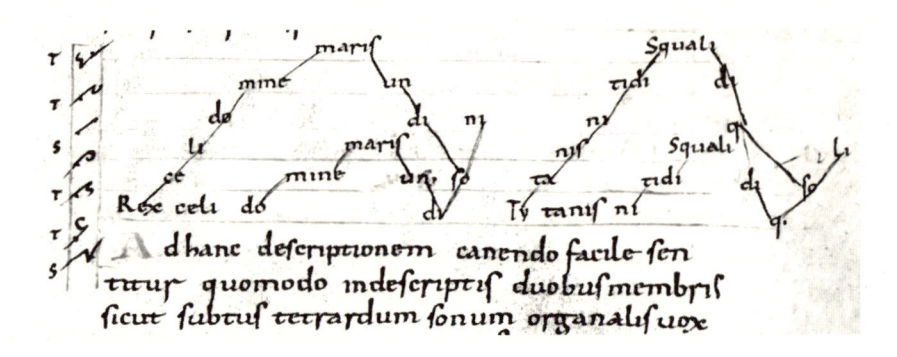

```
T                    marıſ              Squalı
                mmé      un         tıdı      di
T           do               di  nı     nı
S         lı      marıſ       nıſ      Squalı
T   ce       mıné   dıſ, ſc     tα    tıdı      lı
  Reẋ celı do            dı              di      q.
T
S    Ad hanc deſcrıptıonem canendo facıle ſen
    tıtur quomodo ındeſcrıptıſ duobuſ membrıſ
    ſıcut ſubtuſ tetrardum ſonum organalıſ uox
```

Rex   coe - li   Do - mi - ne   ma - ris   un - di - so - ni
Ti - ta - nis   ni - ti - di   squa - li - di - que so - li.

One of a number of types of organum, an early form of two-part polyphony, in Daseian notation from the ninth-century Musica enchiriadis, *and in modern notation. The Latin text points out that 'from this description' ('Ad hanc descriptionem') singers can 'easily' ('facile') make 'two elements' ('duobus membris') by adding the 'organum' ('sonum organalis vox').*

the handsomely coloured, beautifully clear pages of the Winchester Tropers show the added vox organalis achieving an elaboration and complexity worlds away from the comparative simplicity of the *Enchiriadis* treatises, even if the mysterious dashes and squiggles of the notation keep a definitive realisation tantalisingly out of reach.

The names of the key theorists of the tenth and eleventh centuries show the extent to which the intellectual life of the Middle Ages was genuinely international. Odo 'of Cluny' (a Frenchman), the German Hermannus Contractus (his name meaning 'the lame' or 'crippled'), John 'of Afflighem' (possibly an Englishman called John Cotton, then working in Switzerland) and the Italian Guido d'Arezzo described, debated and developed all aspects of their art. They discussed the different types of organum, and developed notation from the unsatisfactory models in the *Enchiriadis* texts – Guido is credited with inventing modern-style staff notation, in succession to the older 'neumatic' style using plainsong-style symbols, or 'neumes'. A key theoretical concern was around how to divide up the scale, giving rise to an ideal pattern of six notes, known as a hexachord, divided by the intervals of (in ascending order) two whole tones, one semitone, then two whole tones (equivalent to the first six notes of an ascending major scale, in modern parlance). If the starting note is moved to a different pitch, a note will need to be inflected: B becomes B flat; accidentals are born. Theory only allowed such inflections in certain circumstances: one flat was essentially the only possible 'key signature' throughout the Renaissance. Accidentals which lay outside the 'gamut', or permitted scale, were not written in. If required to avoid the forbidden tritone (the 'unnatural' sound of the diminished fifth) or to create the appropriate cadence for the mode, the trained singer would add them by ear according to the principles of *'musica ficta'*, or 'feigned music' (as opposed to *'recta'*, or 'correct' music, which is what is on the page in front of you). Alongside all this theorising came a strong dash of practical help for the working musician. 'Solmisation' is the system of associating pitches with verbal syllables to help learning and reading. An early version borrowed the first syllable of each line of the plainsong hymn *'Ut queant laxis'*, whose successive musical phrases happen to start on the ascending notes of a scale, producing the pattern ut–re–mi–fa–so–la. This was described in Guido's *Micrologus* of 1026. Another innovation also borrowed his name: the 'Guidonian hand', which puts pitches and intervals onto a schematic of hand and fingers, so the scale can be taught using hand gestures and movements. Both ideas have lasted a thousand years (so far), producing along the way such not-so-distant descendants as the early nineteenth-century sol–fa system.

Hildegard

Very little monophonic music can be confidently attributed to a particular composer (although Hermannus Contractus is credited with two of the four elegant antiphons addressed to the Virgin Mary). A striking exception is the twelfth-century German mystic Hildegard of Bingen. Hildegard has left us a huge body of work, preserved in stunningly beautiful manuscripts, on subjects including theology, natural history and medicine, as well as the earliest surviving sacred music drama not attached to a specific liturgy (*Ordo Virtutum*, the 'Play of the Virtues', a morality play in which the Devil gets no tunes but has to spit and snarl his words), a made-up language with its own notation (the *Lingua Ignota* or 'unknown language'), and sixty-nine monophonic musical compositions to her own texts. Much of her writing springs from the ecstatic visions she experienced from earliest childhood and throughout her long life as a nun, often associated with physical illness and vividly described:

> Listen: there was once a king sitting on his throne. Around him stood great and wonderfully beautiful columns ornamented with ivory, bearing the banners of the king with great honour. Then it pleased the king to raise a small feather from the ground and he commanded it to fly. The feather flew, not because of anything in itself but because the air bore it along. Thus am I 'A feather on the breath of God'.[5]

Her music shares this quality of rapt visionary enthusiasm, soaring in melismatic ecstasy unlike anything else of the time. It is perhaps the first music in which we can genuinely hear the voice and character of an individual composer: the sequence 'O, Jerusalem' is a beautiful example. Celebrated in her day, Hildegard has regained her rightful fame in the era of modern scholarship, historically informed performance and recording.

The Ars Antiqua

Monophonic music doesn't need precisely notated rhythm. Because everyone is singing the same thing, you can follow your neighbour, or the natural flow of the words. Organum, in its simpler forms, has the same quality: the separate vocal lines still pronounce the syllables of the text at the same time, and can draw rhythm and speed from that. The same applies to early, improvised forms of polyphony. Genuine polyphonic music, where different vocal lines have different iterations of text which nonetheless have to fit together, requires a whole new approach to codifying, and notating, rhythm. This is the key feature of the sacred art music of the period from around 1160 to 1310, known to history as the ars antiqua (as opposed to the later ars nova: like some other later pairs of time periods, the earlier only became known as 'old' once people began calling the later period 'new'; the term wasn't used at the time).

Two key theorists of the mid to late thirteenth century, Johannes de Garlandia and Franco of Cologne, described the transformative principle of differently shaped notes having different, and precise, rhythmic values, which can be read according to a detailed and complex system known as rhythmic modes: Franco said that '"modus" is the idea of sound measured in long and short note values'.[6] Both writers use the term 'mensurabilis' in the titles of their treatises: 'mensural', or 'measured', music held sway until the late fifteenth century evolved the simplified form of notation which we have used, essentially, ever since.

Polyphonic music would be sung mostly by groups of soloists. Partly this arises from the liturgy, where in certain texts a passage sung by one or more solo voices would be answered by a chorus in a form of call and response (for example, a gradual like the Christmas 'Viderunt Omnes', where the full body of singers joins in at the word 'omnes' ('all')). Partly it was practical: trained singers did the tricky bit, everybody else the familiar tunes in unison. Partly it was an aesthetic judgement: the early fourteenth-century Parisian theorist Johannes de Grocheio put polyphonic music in a sociological context (and his listeners firmly in their place) when he said that the motet was 'not intended for the vulgar who do not understand its finer points and derive no pleasure from hearing it: it is meant for educated people and those who look for refinement in art'.[7] The allocation of complex polyphony to a group of skilled soloists lasted well into the fifteenth century. There are examples of simplified forms of notation which appear to be an attempt to get musicians unversed in the mysteries of mensural notation to take part in a small amount of modest and unpretentious polyphony.

The ars antiqua flourished in France. An early centre was the Abbey of St Martial, in Limoges. Its repertoire of tropes, sequences and early organum were a significant and innovative precursor of the most important school of composers, centred not in a monastery but around the great secular (that is, run by priests rather than monks) cathedral of Notre Dame de Paris. This group worked from around 1160 to 1250 (thus making it permissible to take the term ars antiqua back this far), though it is important to note that most sources of the music, theoretical and biographical accounts of its practitioners, date from considerably later. Two such writers were (or may have been) English: Walter Odington described the rhythmic modes in around 1300; and a treatise dating from twenty or thirty years earlier is thought to have been written by an English student working in Paris who has left us no clue to his identity. He is known to history, following the designation adopted by the pioneering nineteenth-century French musicologist Edmond de Coussemaker, as Anonymous IV.

Most Notre Dame composers are as nameless as their recording angel. But Anonymous IV picked out two men working around the turn of the thirteenth century for special praise, who thus become the first composers whose names can be confidently ascribed to particular pieces of polyphonic music: Magister Leoninus and Magister Perotinus. We are told that Léonin compiled a 'great book of organum', later altered and added to by Pérotin (to use the French forms of their names), who was a fine composer and 'better than Léonin'.[8] Pérotin's *Viderunt omnes* reveals a real sense of musical architecture. Their work shows the remarkable reach of the Notre Dame style, developing and extending the principles of organum to make music not just in two parts but in three or four. Their relentless use of the harmonic intervals of the fifth and the fourth moving in parallel is related to the Platonist ideals of proportion: a sound roundly condemned by the later practice of the Renaissance and Baroque, and harsh and foreign to our modern ears. But these were sophisticated minds in full command of their technical resource.

Sources of Notre Dame-style music are found through the thirteenth century and beyond as far apart as Las Huelgas (just outside Burgos in northern Spain) and St Andrews in Scotland, all based on the great liturgical cycle of two-part organa from the Parisian *Magnus Liber*, ascribed to Léonin.

Sacred music as a whole shows many types, varieties and techniques. 'Ocketus', or 'hocket', makes rests in one voice part correspond with sounds in another. The effect can be an infectious jazzy vitality, as in the irresistibly jolly pieces over the characteristic repeated 'swung' bass (known as a '*pes*', or footprint) found in the English collection known as the Worcester Fragments. The famous English secular song 'Sumer is icumen in' from Reading Abbey catches the effervescent fizz of the style. Once again, the sacred and the secular turn out to sound the same. The thirteenth-century motet typically featured a tenor composed of phrases based on one of the six modes, sometimes repeated, sometimes in different rhythmic patterns (a pointer to the next phase of innovation), with upper parts moving with more freedom, still usually in some form of triple time. An intriguing development was giving the upper parts a different text from the tenor, combining Latin with French, the sacred with the secular or even the entirely profane. It can be a little odd listening to one singer venerating the Virgin in Latin while another sings of earthly love in French. The modern mind can find such pieces difficult to place: as the scholar John Caldwell notes, 'the whole question of the social function of the motet is one which has never been fully elucidated'.[9]

The Ars Nova

To mark the transition into the next, and last, major phase of medieval music we find ourselves back in the company of our friend Fauvel, the allegorical horse. The *Roman de Fauvel* of around 1310 contains a great many musical items. Many are composed in the older, thirteenth-century manner. There is also a series of motets demonstrating a new approach. They are thought to be the work of a leading musical progressive, Philippe de Vitry. De Vitry may also be the author of a shadowy treatise, identifiable only from later and variously corrupt and partial sources, which has given its name to the innovations which came to characterise art music of the fourteenth century: ars nova.

On a technical level, the ars nova extended and expanded the available range of note values and subdivisions within them. The 'tempus' (beat) was the division of the longest note into smaller, and could be 'perfectum' (divided into groups of three) or 'imperfectum' (two). The 'prolatio' was the further subdivision within the beat, and could be 'maior' or 'minor', also referring to further subdivisions into twos or threes. In practice, the effect was the gradual introduction of many shorter note values in the fourteenth century, with a concomitant slowing-down of longer notes which made the old 'long' and 'double long' obsolescent.

As always in medieval music, rhythm is key. De Vitry's new style allowed two minims in 'tempus perfectum' to be interpreted long–short, rather than short–long, allowing a more naturalistic, less syncopated style of delivery. Another significant use of rhythm was the technique of repeating a series of pitches (known as a 'color') using a series of rhythmic units called a 'talea', which also repeats, sometimes with different interpretations of the rhythmic subdivision of the beat at each repetition. 'Talea' and 'color' are not necessarily the same length and could thus overlap: the tenor of the Kyrie of

Machaut's *Messe de Nostre Dame* uses a color of twenty-eight pitches divided into seven repetitions of a talea of four rhythmic durations ($7 \times 4 = 28$). Modern scholarship has given the principle the name 'isorhythm'. It is a logical extension of the old rhythmic modes into a way of organising and unifying an entire piece.

As always, there were people who disliked and mistrusted the new. Church music in particular has always been vulnerable to the charge that singers and listeners alike are encouraged to pay more attention to the sensual appeal of the music than to the devotional demands of the text. Critics are often our best witnesses, because they know exactly what they don't like. In 1324/5, Pope John XXII issued a famous broadside which captures the neologisms of the ars nova well:

> Certain disciples of the new school, much occupying themselves with the measured dividing of beats, display their rhythm in notes new to us, preferring to devise new methods of their own rather than to continue singing in the old way. Therefore the music of the Divine Office is disturbed with these notes of quick duration. Moreover, they hinder the melody with hockets, they deprave it with discants, and sometimes they pad out the music with upper parts made out of secular songs. The result is that they often seem to be losing sight of the fundamental sources of our melodies in the Antiphoner and Gradual, and forget what it is that they are burying under such superstructures. They may become entirely ignorant of the ecclesiastical modes, which they have already ceased to distinguish, and the limits of which they abuse in the prolixity of their notes. The modest rise and temperate descents of plainsong are entirely obscured. The voices incessantly rock to and fro, intoxicating rather than soothing the ear, while the singers themselves try to convey the emotion of the music by their gestures. The consequence of all this is that devotion, the true aim of worship, is neglected, and wantonness, which ought to be eschewed, increases. We hasten to forbid these methods, or rather to drive them more effectively out of the house of God than has been done in the past.[10]

It made little difference.

The ars nova had various regional incarnations around Europe, including the Trecento style of Landini in Italy. A curious footnote is the highly mannered subset of secular songs dating from late fourteenth-century southern France and northern Spain, concerned with complexity, refinement, experimentation and affected utterance, known as the ars subtilior. Many pieces appear to be written to look good as much as to sound good, on staves arranged on the page in the shape of a circle or a heart.

Machaut

This account of sacred and secular music in the Middle Ages ends with a musical poet who produced both. Guillaume de Machaut lived from 1300 to 1377. He was a churchman and diplomat as well as a composer and poet. He has left us examples of the highest art in many forms: monophonic secular songs known as 'lais'; isorhythmic motets in the manner of de Vitry; 'ballades' in from one to four parts, employing regular rhyme schemes and repeating refrains; rondeaux and virelais. The *Messe de Nostre Dame* of around 1360 is the first complete setting known to be by a single composer. It represents a huge leap in expressivity, technique and degree of unity on the few earlier complete settings, and points the way to the emergence of the Mass as the principal sacred musical form in the following century.

Machaut sings to us of courtly as well as divine love, with skill and grace. His is the authentic voice of the late Middle Ages.

Part Three

RENAISSANCE (1400–1600)

INTRODUCTION

In February 1456 Guillaume Dufay wrote from Geneva to Piero and Giovanni de' Medici in Florence. As well as revealing his cosmopolitan ease in corresponding on equal terms with the most potent nobles, the letter shows the composer pushing his latest efforts: 'I have composed this past year four lamentations about Constantinople, which are rather good.'[1] The fall of Constantinople to the Turks in 1453 was one of the events which helped unleash the intellectual and artistic realignment known to us as the Renaissance.

More than most such descriptors, 'renaissance' (literally, 'rebirth') is a troublesome word. Its application to art, history and music mean different things, and don't completely coincide in time. It's also important to remember that there wasn't just one: twelfth-century Gothic art was a renaissance; so, in a different way, was eighteenth-century Enlightenment thought. Dividing the musical renaissance into distinct phases is also historically hazardous. Like all such words, it's a shorthand; but a shorthand mustn't become a shortcut.

Like all ages, the Renaissance involved a good deal of conscious myth-making. In the words of the historian Peter Frankopan, 'artists, writers and architects went to work, borrowing themes, ideas and texts from antiquity to provide a narrative that chose selectively from the past to create a story which over time became not only increasingly plausible but standard'.[2] The strand of thought which became known as renaissance humanism accorded a new respect to the works of man, but it emphatically still regarded those works as part of God's creation and design. The theorist Johannes Tinctoris made the link explicit, referring to Christ as 'that greatest musician ... who made [God and man] one in duple proportion'.[3]

Like all forms of organic growth, external circumstances had to be propitious. The social organisation of the Italian city states and the Roman church provided status, employment and reputation to the creative artist. Travel brought influences in from the east and out to the west. Trade and conquest pushed boundaries ever further afield. People, books and ideas moved around Europe and beyond with comparative freedom. Historians have begun to think about the extent to which trading contact with the older and more advanced civilisations to the east kickstarted the European Renaissance. The great harbour fortifications on the south coast of Crete stand witness to that idea, a stern mixture in stone of Venetian cultural imperialism and Byzantine curlicues, the lions of St Mark gazing confidently from their columns across the sea towards Mesopotamia and on to India and China. Musically, these factors encouraged a period of popular transmission and dissemination of international repertoire: the Venetian sailor and trumpeter Zorzi Trombetta da Modon travelled widely, noting down counterpoints to a number of contemporary pieces, including works by the Englishman John Dunstable, in his shipping notebook, using a simplified form of notation of his own.

Printing

Technology, as always, played a part, and by far the most important technology of the period was printing. Music found its way into print right from the very dawn of the new science, beginning with woodcuts of liturgical chant in the 1460s and 1470s, not long after the Gutenberg Bible itself was printed. Movable type was first used to print music by Ulrich Han in his *Missale Romanum* of 1476, but the real pioneer of this revolutionary development was Ottaviano Petrucci, an able and ambitious young man, educated in the culturally enlightened city of Urbino in the Marche.

All artistic movements need their entrepreneurs and artisans. Petrucci was both of these and more. In him met all the talents required for a successful career in the manner of the times – a sort of ultimate Renaissance backroom boy. As a discerning musical 'cognoscento' he was able to appreciate and accurately reproduce the music of the best and most modern composers; as an artisan and engineer he expanded the technical capabilities of his trade with method and skill; as a businessman he knew his market and fed it wisely; as an operator he had the judgement and ability to secure lengthy monopolies on the printing of music not just from the Venetian Doge but from the Pope as well. His name is not as familiar today as those of the composers he promoted. But his importance (and of others like him) to the history of music cannot be overstated.

Petrucci used the triple-impression method of printing: each sheet goes through the presses three times, once for the stave lines, once more for the notes, and a final time for the words. He was a genius at it: his imprints are laser sharp, and perfectly legible five hundred years after they emerged inkily from the press. But the method caused problems for less fastidious practitioners – lines and notes could easily slip out of alignment, rendering the results useless. The solution was the technique developed in England by another Renaissance polymath (and Thomas More's brother-in-law), John Rastell. Each note, together with the short section of stave lines on which it sits, is set up separately on a succession of single-note blocks. The printer has, for example, a block with a minim on the bottom line of the stave (or, by turning it upside down, the top line), which he can use to give whatever note the clef specifies for that line. Words are set up underneath. It requires only one impression per page. A potential problem is assembling the stave from a large number of short sections, presenting a challenge in keeping the lines straight. But skilful practitioners like John Day in England and Pierre Attaingnant in France quickly turned the method into an art form, complete with immensely detailed illustrations, full of light and shade, all carved in wood.

Music in Context

Performing resources evolved, too. Critically, the 1460–90s revolutionised the way music could be performed. In well-resourced church settings, professional singers and masters of choristers were appointed and choir schools founded. In the early fifteenth century, complex polyphony was the preserve of small groups of soloists, mostly priests. A hundred years later, the finest sacred choral music could call for huge choirs, in many parts with lots of use of sectional subgroups and further division (known as 'gimmell'). High treble and low bass parts soared and grumbled at the extremes of their range (a favourite device of English composers). Intriguingly, we have some examples of the laity singing. In the 1480s the Nieuwe Kerk in Delft appointed lay singers as professional musicians, even if they were married. The divide between sacred and secular music, which were increasingly sharing personnel, narrowed to an extent.

As in all ages, ordinary people had their music, too. In the middle of the sixteenth century, if you'd been strolling through Whip-Ma-Whop-Ma-Gate in York, or down a hillside in Provence, or across the Plaza de Santa María in Burgos, you might have heard church bells measuring out the eternal cycle of the church's year, lute songs warbled through the window of a merchant's house or drinking songs bellowed through the open door of an inn, a viol consort tuning up in a nobleman's chamber, counting songs from the schoolroom, ballad-sellers peddling tales of saints and murder, the sweet voices of choirboys rising as if from heaven from behind the rood screen and stained glass of the cathedral, a tabor tapping out a dance in the town square, the night watchman sounding the knell of parting day, a troupe of travelling players rehearsing a mystery play. You might perhaps also have caught a hint of a tune you might recognise today, such as 'Greensleeves', or 'La Folia', or a little French shepherd boy with his bagpipes made from a cow's stomach playing something which would resurface centuries later as a Victorianised Christmas carol: 'Ding, Dong, Merrily on High' or 'Angels from the Realms of Glory'.

This was the musical world in which the trained composer lived and moved. It was a thorough training, most likely beginning at home (music, like other trades, often ran in families), and continuing as a choirboy in the local cathedral or monastery, immersed in the newest music and the company of like-minded older boys and accomplished adults. Technical instruction was delivered in the schoolroom – modes, cadences, counterpoint, improvisation based on rules, singing at sight and playing the lute, viol and keyboard. Musical examples might be painted up on the wall as a teaching aid, a sort of fifteenth-century whiteboard: an example can still be seen in Windsor Castle, as legible now as it was to the head-scratching young scholars of the 1470s.

Society was changing, too. Monasteries were reducing in importance. Women were still kept off the stage and out of the choir stalls. But music at home involved everybody: the first female composer to have had a single publication dedicated entirely to her own music was the Italian Maddalena Casulana, associate of Isabella de' Medici, praised and performed by fellow composers Orlande de Lassus and Philippe de Monte, author of several books of madrigals printed at Venice in the 1560s and 1570s; expressive, assured music, matching words to music with some of the theatricality and emotion of contemporaries like Luca Marenzio.

The composer was an employee. Music was his job. This meant he was employed by the church, or by a noble family. Socially, he was perhaps about halfway up the scale: more than a servant, but less than a second son. The job description might include singing, playing, instructing the children of the family in 'fingering of organs and virginals' and running the choir, as well as writing music.[4]

The Music: Modes, Counterpoint, Dissonance, Form

One of the features of the period is that composers, very broadly, shared a similar style. A group of talented musicians emerged in fourteenth-century France, Flanders and Burgundy. Many found their way south, and in the sixteenth century the stylistic centre shifted to Rome. Style and technique was shared through proximity and printing. Technically, sacred and secular music drew on the same resources.

Those resources included modal scales, imitative counterpoint, and dissonance – things a composer had to learn, like an apprentice painter patiently poring over a corpse in a marbled mortuary before making his attempt on the muscled torso of St Sebastian or Christ on the cross.

'Modes' are scales. If you base a composition on the scale between C and C, it has a particular character. If, instead, you use D as the starting note of your scale, the music has a quite different character, because the tones and semitones are in different places within the scale.

'Imitative counterpoint', or 'imitation', means writing a short tune to each phrase of a text, then presenting that tune in each voice part one after the other, sometimes transposed to different pitches, building up and varying the texture by introducing the voices one at a time. The piece falls naturally into sections as each section of the text gets a new snatch of melody, treated imitatively in its turn. (There may also have been a practical consideration behind this division into sections: there was no full score, so the composer could only work out each point of imitation for as long as he could hold the passage of music in his head, or write it on a slate with stave lines painted on it.) A well-worked piece of counterpoint could be sung, played, or both: a letter of around 1502 refers to 'a song by [the French composer] Josquin also suitable for performance on instruments'.[5] Many compositions turn up with alternative sets of words for different uses, often in different languages (known as 'contrafacta').

The opening of a motet by Palestrina. The music is in the Dorian mode, uses a point of imitation to introduce the words 'Ad Dominium' etc., in each voice part successively, and builds to a dissonance in the alto on the third beat of bar 8.

'Dissonance' is a particular kind of sound made by two notes sounding together which, according to the prevailing theory, had to be approached in a certain way and then resolved to form a 'consonance'. A piece, or section, cannot stop (or begin) on a dissonance. Careful use of dissonance therefore creates momentum, a feeling of expectation in the listener's mind that a resolution will follow. Composers, and nationalities, varied in the extent and character of their use of dissonance. Late in the period the theorist Artusi compared dissonance to the use of spices in cooking.

These were the building blocks of the ars perfecta of Giovanni Pierluigi da Palestrina, the mature Renaissance style. The composer was no longer adding parts one by one to a plainsong, as his medieval forebear did, like the master builder of old, adding rooms to a half-timbered hall house as and when they were needed so that the finished building seems to tumble upwards and outwards almost at random. Now he wrote (or adapted from an existing source) all the music himself, so the piece could be imagined all at once, like the gorgeous prodigy houses of Smythson or Palladio, conceived complete in a glitter of glass and pale stone. As for the Renaissance idea that its arts were based on models from Classical antiquity, music has less of a claim than other art forms, for the simple reason that those models didn't exist. But musical theorists were just as keen as everyone else to lend their brand an authentically antique patina: the eight modes were given Greek names from their earliest use, names which they partly share with the architecture around which they echoed: Ionic and Ionian, Dorian and Doric. Notation evolved quickly from medieval mensural writing to reach essentially its modern form – easily readable today with a little practice.

Very often, the composer wouldn't actually write his own new tunes and themes for a Mass or other polyphonic work, but simply borrowed them from an existing source, which might be a plainsong, a folk song, or another piece of sacred or secular music written either by himself or by someone else. It wasn't plagiarism, still less a breach of copyright (a concept which didn't exist), it was a kind of homage; the skill was in turning the original music into something else, with different words, mood, and probably also a different number of voices. There were Masses based on war songs like 'L'Homme armé', folk songs like 'Western Wind' and secular part songs like 'Triste départ'. Composers found all sorts of inventive ways of reworking a tune or a model, including some highly mathematical procedures for carving up a plainsong, like the early sixteenth-century English Masses 'on a square', full of complex number patterns and relationships, rooted in medieval Platonism. This is why so many Mass settings have names: Palestrina's *Missa Assumpta est Maria* (unpublished in his lifetime and probably composed in the 1580s or 1590s) is based on the music of the composer's own motet of that name (which is in turn based on a short section of plainsong). Some Mass names are unblushingly secular: Lassus based his *Missa je ne menge point du porc* of 1570 on a song by Claudin de Sermisy about the eating habits of pigs. Many songs of the time deal with eating, drinking and wenching, some of them cheerfully obscene.

The Renaissance style is one of the polished glories of musical time. Its masters applied it with an infinitely subtle and fluid mixture of grace and engineering, and fascinated theorists have pored lovingly over its inner workings ever since. In the words of its first and finest analyst, the eighteenth-century Austrian composer and analyst Johann Joseph Fux, '*ita quoque musica tempori accommodanda est*' ('thus the music presents itself anew to every age and accommodates itself to the times').[6]

4

'TO ROME FOR EVERYTHING ...': MUSIC IN THE CATHOLIC WORLD[1]

In the late fourteenth century the Flemish composer Johannes Ciconia headed to Rome to pursue his musical career. Stylistically, he provides a bridge between the ars nova and the new Italian ways. Geographically, he pioneered a trend of musical geopolitics that persisted throughout the Renaissance.

The great councils of the church continued to provide the background for the professional composer, not just by addressing questions of style (usually as a kind of footnote to more important considerations like vestments, liturgy and who got to be Pope), but also by establishing centres of employment at rival ecclesiastical courts, and at the councils themselves. Among the 18,000 clerics who descended on the town of Constance, now in south-western Germany, for the council of 1414–18 were singers from Lichfield and Norwich, who, in a key moment in introducing the English manner to Europe, sang the feast of their own St Thomas of Canterbury 'beautifully with a great noise, with great burning candles, and with angelically sweet singing at Vespers'.[2] The period was thoroughly overpopulated with popes, partly because they kept dying (three in one year), partly because schism and power politics set up several rival papacies (three at the same time from 1409).

Most surviving music of the period is sacred. As the style approached full maturity the long-running Council of Trent of 1545–63 and its various subgroups continued the slightly half-hearted attempt to come up with a distinctively Catholic response to the artistic and intellectual currents of the Protestant reformations in northern Europe, with little discernible effect. By the late sixteenth century, the great musical masters around Europe essentially wrote in the same style for the same mistress: holy church and her liturgies, sent from Rome.

The Era of Burgundian Pre-eminence

The early musical Renaissance can be captured in the names of a place and three geniuses: Burgundy, Binchois, Dufay and Dunstable.

In around 1440 the poet Martin le Franc devoted a couple of the 24,000 verses of his poem *Le Champion des dames* to describing how the Burgundian court composers Binchois and Dufay developed a *'nouvelle pratique / De faire frisque concordance ... / Et ont prins de la contenance / Angloise et ensuy Dunstable'* ('a new method of making fresh harmony ... and have adopted the English countenance and followed Dunstable').[3]

Exactly what le Franc might have meant by his evocatively ambiguous phrase *'la contenance Angloise'* can be gleaned from features of English music of the time. Sweet-sounding harmonies using the intervals of thirds and sixths add new colours to the older, more rugged sounds of the Worcester Fragments. One treatise advises that up to five such intervals in succession produce an effect 'fayre and meri'.[4] Here, perhaps, is le Franc's *'frisque concordance'*.

The largest collection of early fifteenth-century English sacred music is the Old Hall manuscript, compiled probably over the twenty years or so to 1421. Leading composers represented include Leonel Power and 'Roy Henry', a pun in courtly French which identifies this clearly highly able musician as 'King Henry', probably Henry V himself.[5] Both names confirm the collection as the property of the Chapel Royal, which, in true late medieval grandstanding style, actually accompanied Henry onto the battlefield of Agincourt in 1415, singing Mass before battle and thanksgiving after. There is also a wedding motet by Thomas Byttering for Henry's marriage to Catherine of Valois in 1420 (battle and marriage were both later mentioned by Shakespeare).

John Dunstable has no pieces in the main part of the Old Hall collection. Dunstable was a true polymath. His epitaph (lost, but reconstructed) records his 'secret knowledge of the stars'.[6] In a striking testament to his reach and influence, his name appears in sources across Europe more than in his native country. The Abbot of St Albans in his native Hertfordshire referred to his knowledge of medicine as well as music and astronomy.[7] His music adds a uniquely personal lyricism to the last flowering of isorhythmic techniques and old-fashioned cadences. For example, Dunstable's *Magnificat secundi toni* shows him freely working his plainsong model into music full of rhythmic and textual variety, enjoying the sweet harmonies noted and imitated by his admirers across the Channel.

English musical style exerted a powerful influence on the richly artistic early fifteenth-century Burgundian court, home to many who were *'excellens en art de musique'*, as a contemporary account of the wedding of Duke Philip the Good to the Infanta Isabella of Portugal in 1430 put it.[8]

Gilles de Bins, known as Binchois, was probably born around 1400, in Mons, Hainault. He was employed briefly as an organist in Lille (and, possibly, as a soldier) before taking up a post in Duke Philip's chapel some time in the 1420s. Politically, northern Europe was tied to its English neighbour in the years following the Agincourt campaign, and an intriguing reminiscence of events in 1424–5 has Binchois being handsomely paid for a composition by a visiting English earl, and taking part in a spirited defence of his Burgundian master in the context of an alleged assassination attempt by the English. He left court in 1453 with a substantial pension and a comfortable job as provost of the church of Saint-Vincent in Soignies, Belgium. He died in 1460. Binchois has been described as 'a rather shallow composer' by comparison with his contemporaries, specialising in tuneful but lightweight rondeaux.[9] Songs like *'Mon seul et souverain desir'* certainly have immense lyrical charm and considerable harmonic and rhythmic subtlety. But emerging scholarship has revealed that his corpus of church music is large, varied, innovative and inventive. *Nove cantum melodie* is a multi-texted motet written to celebrate the birth of Philip and Isabella's first child in 1431, using old-style isorhythmic procedures in its complex structure. There are many Mass movements, motets and Marian antiphons. The wide-ranging theorist and composer Johannes Tinctoris believed that by the time of his death Binchois had won himself a 'name eternal' by his 'delightful compositions'.[10] Modern performers and audiences are, gradually, coming to agree.

Binchois and Dufay worked alongside each other in one of those close, symbiotic artistic relationships (possibly dating from early childhood) which are a notable feature of musical history. An exquisite miniature portrait in the manuscript of le Franc's poem shows the two musicians chatting amiably, instruments to hand.

The biography of Guillaume Dufay includes much shuttling between Cambrai (now in north-eastern France) and important parts of Italy, following the demands and distractions of career, family, schism, pope and antipope.

Born around 1397, Dufay was a choirboy and 'altarista' (clerical assistant) at Cambrai's richly musical cathedral from 1409. He became a priest, then served in the papal choir from 1428 and the court of Savoy from 1433 (just in time for the lavish marriage of Louis of Savoy to the sister of the king of Cyprus). Visits home to his mother combined with the never-ending papal politics saw him shuffling between courts and countries, including a period back in the papal chapel, temporarily based in Florence, at the heart of the Medici Renaissance.

A mid-career moment at the end of the 1430s found him back in Cambrai, forty, famous, accomplished and rich, living in a big house on the proceeds of patronage and employment from pope, antipope, the antipope's son, and several paid prebends. He was in Rome again in 1450. Back home he met the celebrated younger composer Johannes Ockeghem. In 1472 his Mass *Ave regina caelorum* was sung at the dedication of Cambrai cathedral (a ceremony which lasted from 3.00 a.m. to midday). Two years later his will touchingly requested the singing of a hymn '*submissima voce*' (literally, 'in a low voice', rendered by his executors as '*en fausset*' or 'in falsetto') at his last moments, followed by an antiphon sung by the cathedral choirboys and three men 'if time permits'.[11] It did not: the antiphon was added to his requiem the day after his death in November 1474.

Dufay took older stylistic devices like isorhythm and the underthird cadence to their final level, helping to work through what his modern biographer David Fallows calls 'the fall from favour of intricate gothicism and the increased desire for clarity on a large scale' (a trend discernible in other arts).[12] His output is huge, including Mass settings based on secular tunes (e.g. the 'cantus firmus' *L'Homme armé* Mass, dating from the 1460s) and ballades of his own (e.g. Mass *Se la face ay pale*, composed in the 1450s on musical material from a chanson written in 1434–5), motets, songs and liturgical items.

Many of these composers display a range of activities and intellectual sympathies. Dunstable was read and admired across Europe, not just, or even principally, as a musician. Binchois's modern biographers call him 'a highly political animal'.[13] Dufay held a degree in canon law, worked alongside the architect Filippo Brunelleschi in Florence, and wrote an isorhythmic motet based on the mathematical proportions of Florence's cathedral and Brunelleschi's crowning dome. In 1467 Piero de' Medici called him 'the greatest ornament of our age'.[14]

In the 1470s, as the era of Dunstable, Binchois and Dufay was coming to an end, Tinctoris noted and applauded the international influences flowing between the three composers, praising them alongside younger talents of his own generation. Among modern scholars, David Fallows regards Dufay as 'unchallenged as the leading composer of the Middle Ages', and 'by far the most interesting and fulfilling medieval composer'.[15] Margaret Bent goes further for her man, calling John Dunstable 'probably the most influential English composer of all time' – a bold claim, but not unwarranted.[16]

Into the Sixteenth Century

Composers of this period developed the touching habit of writing musical memorials, known as *'déplorations'*, for each other. When Johannes Ockeghem hymned his late friend Binchois, *'patron de bonté'* ('paragon of goodness'), in a mournful French elegy over a semi-liturgical Latin text in the lower voices,[17] he was perhaps turning the page into the next phase of the musical Renaissance (despite being Binchois's junior by just ten or twenty years).

Musical trends from around 1450 include the Mass supplanting the motet as the main musical utterance, less frequent use of the old motet-style cantus firmus tenor with a different text, a shift in the default rhythmic division (the 'tactus', or beat) from three to two (with passages in three time used as an exception to add variety rather than the other way round, as typically, for example, in the dance-like Osanna sections of Mass settings by Lassus and Palestrina), a move towards equally spaced voice parts replacing the older top line over tenor and contratenor with the same range, and modes with their distinctive, new-sounding cadences. All of this encouraged the flowing, free, varied vocal lines of the later sixteenth century.

Antoine Busnois rose from being a self-styled 'unworthy musician of the illustrious Count of Charolais', according to his motet *In hydraulis*,[18] to fame and fortune when the 'illustrious Count' became Duke Charles the Bold of Burgundy in 1467. In 1470 Busnois secured permanent employment as a singer at Charles's court. His most celebrated work, the latest in a series of Mass settings based on the

a) The first phrases of the song 'L'homme armé', and b) the opening of the 'Missa L'homme armé' by the mid-fifteenth-century French composer Antoine Busnois. Busnois uses the tune straight in his tenor part, weaving elaborate references to it in the other, more florid voice parts, for example the opening interval of a rising fourth in the upper two voices.

secular song *'L'Homme armé'*, dates from around this time. Tinctoris ranked him among Europe's finest.

Johannes Ockeghem's birth date is even more uncertain than most: probably some time between 1410 and 1425. In 1443 he was a 'left-hand singer' ('left-handers' on one side of the church sang polyphony, while 'right-handers' on the other side sang chant – complex music was still for small groups of experts, not the full choir) at the Onze-Lieve-Vrouwe cathedral in Antwerp. He worked in France, including at Notre Dame de Paris, and travelled widely, including on a diplomatic mission to Spain in 1470. He died in 1497, at an advanced age, mourned by many in music and words. His music moves from the style of his probable teacher Binchois to something combining technical wizardry with real feeling. The *Missa Prolationum* is an old-fashioned essay in 'mensural canon' (in which the canons move at different speeds in the different voice parts). His beautiful, ascetic

Requiem is the first surviving polyphonic setting (Dufay's is lost). Modern scholar John Caldwell remarks that 'in his concern for the purely sonorous aspect of the art Ockeghem was a true romantic'.[19]

Like other periods of musical history, the era of Burgundian pre-eminence demonstrates that, as one modern writer puts it, 'the European musical world could be very small for those who lived in the right place and operated in the right circles'.[20] A truly international group of musicians born in the middle of the fifteenth century met, mingled, moved around, made music, and took style forward towards the future. Netherlanders Alexander Agricola and Heinrich Isaac served the Hapsburg/Burgundian Grande Chapelle around the time of the accession of Duke Philip the Handsome in 1482. Pierre de la Rue inadvertently picked up three months of English influence at the court of Henry VII when he was shipwrecked in the English Channel on his way to Spain in 1506. Spanish music exerted influence on papal music, audible, for example, in penitential items like the *Lamentations of Jeremiah* and settings of the Passion Gospels. The Spanish composer Francisco de Peñalosa spent some time in Rome, as did others. Loyset Compère brought the lighter Italian manner to France. The Frenchman Antoine Brumel worked in Paris, Chartres and Italy. His musically refined compatriot Jean Mouton taught the Dutchman Adrian Willaert, who provided a link into the later landscape of Venetian music.

In 1502, two courtiers corresponded with their duke, Ercole d'Este of Ferrara, urging the rival claims of two potential recruits to the duke's chapel: 'by having Josquin in our chapel I wish to place a crown upon this chapel of ours,' wrote one; the other urges the claims of Isaac: 'It is true that Josquin composes better, but he composes when he wants to, and not when one wants him to, and he is asking 200 ducats in salary while Isaac will come for 120. But Your Lordship will decide what should be done …' The duke was advised to consider not just the rival claimants' musical skills but the lustre they would bring to his reputation: 'there is neither Lord nor King who will now have a better chapel than yours'.[21] Josquin was appointed.

Josquin's eventual successor at Ferrara was another of this tight little group of northerners, Jacob Obrecht. The son of a Ghent city trumpeter, he was born around 1457/8, and died of plague in Ferrara in 1505. The titles of his many Mass settings hint at his searching creativity and taste for variety: the early *Caput* and *L'Homme armé*

Masses, middle-period settings *Grecorum*, *Je ne demande* and *Pfauenschwanz* ('Peacock Tail'), the flowering of a unique mature style from the 1490s in the Masses *Fortuna desperata* and *Rose playsante*. His striking approach to things like unifying a vocal line through repeated rhythmic units, dropping the long note cantus firmus in and out of the texture, and long-range planning of blocks of chord and key left little immediate legacy. Among his contemporaries, the writer Paolo Cortese considered him 'mighty in varied subtlety, but in his overall style of composition rather rough';[22] the Swiss music theorist Henricus Glareanus noted that Obrecht's music was found 'everywhere' in southern Europe and praised its 'grandeur'[23] – an opinion shared by Obrecht's former choirboy, the Dutch humanist Erasmus.

The biggest name of this period is Josquin des Prés.

Josquin was born around 1440 in the musically fertile Franco-Flemish north-eastern corner of France. By 1459 he was a 'biscantor', or singer, in well-resourced Milan cathedral. He was in the service of the Sforza family (alongside fellow composers Gaspar van Weerbecke and Loyset Compère) when the cultured but cruel Galeazzo Sforza was murdered in 1476 and succeeded by his brother Ascanio, who (typically for the sanguinary ecclesiastical power politics of the period) became a cardinal in 1484. Josquin was in the papal chapel for around a decade to probably 1495, then went back to France, possibly to the royal court, before returning to Italy and service with Duke Ercole of Ferrara, leaving in 1503 to escape the plague which sadly saw off his successor, Obrecht. By 1504 he was provost of Condé, in his native north-eastern France, where he died in 1521.

Josquin was richly famous in his day. He was the only composer to have more than one book exclusively of his own work published by Petrucci, who issued his Mass settings on three separate occasions. His music was often reprinted through to the mid sixteenth century, a rare accolade in an age which preferred the new. His name often appeared on other men's music, another (less welcome) mark of his reputation. He was praised by writers as diverse as Glareanus, Baldassare Castiglione and François Rabelais; Martin Luther was, perhaps surprisingly, a huge admirer. Josquin earned many musical memorials from fellow composers: Nicolas Gombert used a deliberately archaic element in his own elegy for Josquin, *Musae Jovis*, in the form of an old-style long note cantus firmus, as a clear tribute to the older musician; a full three decades after Josquin's death, Jacquet of

Mantua composed a motet which weaves titles of pieces by Josquin into its text and uses variants of Josquin's own music, a unique act of homage.

Like other early sixteenth-century figures, Josquin was 'an outstanding exponent of new techniques as well as a summarizer'.[24] The still-new resource of the motet, with its virtually infinite choice of texts drawn from the Psalms, the Bible, devotional poetry and elsewhere, offered greater range and freedom to his creativity than the naturally more conservative Mass with its fixed text and established techniques. He loved canons, puzzles and intricate games where notes, melodies and even things like solmisation syllables (ut, re, mi, etc.) are made to work forwards, backwards and upside down. *Qui habitat* (c.1520) rolls four canons across twenty-four voice parts, an essay in sheer sound. Penitential pieces like *Miserere* and *Absalon, fili mi* match almost obsessive vocal motifs with carefully controlled chord changes. Josquin is perhaps the first composer to speak to us in a voice we recognise as part of a tradition which leads directly to us, no longer distanced by the remoteness of medieval manners and thought.

Other parts of Europe produced their own varied glories: the intricate Masses and motets of Peñalosa in Spain, where the printing industry lagged behind Italy and northern Europe; England lost her earlier leadership in musical aesthetics (noted with regret by Tinctoris), but she did produce the distinctive form of the fifteenth-century carol in the ancient 'burden and refrain' ('verse and chorus') form, with much use of the characteristic chains of 6/3 chords (triads spaced as a fourth placed above a third, or what later ages would call first inversion chords) derived from the improvised faburden technique, as described on page 33.

At the beginning of the sixteenth century there were still only very few institutions supporting large-scale polyphony. Most of the singing was done by priests, supported by a few professional singers. The music they sang looks both forwards and backwards: Ockeghem's Requiem employs parallel fifths as if in an echo of Pérotin; Obrecht's *Missa Fortuna desperata* moulds the music of its model into melodic motifs and imitative points like a sketchbook for the later Palestrina style; the second Agnus Dei of Josquin's *L'Homme armé* Mass sends soaring scale passages pursuing each other around the texture, full of plangent passing notes, like Lassus.

Josquin wrote a déploration on the death of Ockeghem in 1497.

It's in French, with a tenor singing words and melody from the Latin Mass for the dead. Halfway through, the old-style cantus firmus stops, giving way to a freely composed roll-call of composers lamenting the loss of their *'bon père'*, as if the medieval period had finally run out of road, right here, in the middle of this piece. The song has been described as 'a Requiem for the Middle Ages'.[25] It closes with Josquin's trademark – a few simple chords.

The Ars Perfecta: Towards Palestrina

The sixteenth century brought the maturing and perfection of the Renaissance style.

At its start, in England, where the majority of sources were destroyed by the iconoclasm of the Reformation, the magnificent Eton Choirbook survives as an indication of style and scope in the two decades or so leading up to its compilation around 1520: soaring, complex, many-voiced, difficult music by composers including Gilbert Banester, John Browne, Walter Lambe and others, much of it addressed to the Virgin Mary. Stylistic features cross the boundaries between its three main periods of music, introducing elements of imitation, high treble and low bass, while also taking in the distinctive 'false relation' and 'English cadence' – a particular kind of dissonant harmonic clash much used by the next generation of Englishmen, Thomas Tallis, John Sheppard and William Byrd. Many of the Eton composers, principally Robert Fayrfax and William Cornyshe, earned their daily bread at the Chapel Royal and both were also active in masques, 'disguisings' and theatricals of all kinds at court. The Eton books are visually spectacular, richly coloured and lavishly studded with squat Tudor faces, no doubt friends and neighbours of the skilful scribes. The Eton Choirbook is perhaps the last hurrah of the medieval manuscript: the more business-like later Tudors preferred their music printed – more practical, but less pretty.

The big names of the middle of the century are another international crew with an essentially common style, drawn from the demands of the Roman church immediately before the Reformation challenged the established order.

The Frenchman Philippe Verdelot was present at the cosmic stand-off between the Medicis and the reformist monk Girolamo Savonarola in Florence in 1498. Like Byrd in England (though less dangerously), he flagged his allegiance by using texts and music associated with the martyred monk in his own work. Nicolas Gombert pushed the late Franco-Flemish interest in imitation even deeper into his music than Josquin. The Dutchman Adrian Willaert holds a key place in the story as a pioneer of the Venetian style, using separate choirs echoing each other from the distant galleries of St Mark's – a technique clearly visible in some works by Lassus, Palestrina and others, and absolutely central to the next phase of musical development in the seventeenth century. In England, the last major composer to be largely unaffected by the Protestant Reformation was John Taverner, who died in 1545, just before his increasingly unstable monarch, Henry VIII (though he did lose his job at the former Cardinal College in Oxford when Henry appropriated it from his disgraced former minister, Cardinal Thomas Wolsey). Taverner's counterpoint rejoices in the kind of naggingly repeated figures loved by Josquin, and provides the key link between the music of Eton and the world of Tallis. The Spaniard Cristóbal de Morales gave the mid-century style his country's familiar spark of Iberian fire: his motet *Emendemus in Melius* (though of uncertain attribution) draws morbid drama from the choir patiently praying to be allowed to amend their sinful lives in penitential counterpoint, while the tenor bellows a different thought to a repeated snatch of melody, medieval-style: *'memento, homo, quia pulvis es, et in pulverum reverteris'* ('remember, O man, that thou art dust, and unto dust thou shalt return').

The generation of English composers who lived through the rapid changes of monarchs and religion in the middle of the century included both Protestants like Christopher Tye and Catholics like John Sheppard and one of several musicians called William Mundy: fine composers, trained under the old dispensation. In the Low Countries Jacob Clemens, nicknamed 'non Papa', used his own religious hinterland to produce the first polyphonic setting of the complete psalter in Dutch, a key indicator of how established style could meet new orthodoxies. The hugely prolific Dutchman Philippe de Monte wrote pieces in German, Latin, Italian and French, lived in Italy, visited England with the chapel of Philip II of Spain when he married Mary Tudor in 1554, and corresponded with William Byrd on a joint setting of verses from Psalm 137, *'Super flumina Babylonis'* ('By the Waters of Babylon'), an under-the-radar lament for the repression of the Catholic church in England, aligning it with the psalmist's account of the sufferings of the captivity of the Jews in Babylon in the sixth century BCE. Among notable composers towards the end of the century was the Spanish-based Frenchman Philippe Rogier, whose splendid six-voice *Laboravi* was lifted wholesale by the English composer Thomas Morley and passed off as his own, with minimal changes (a deception only uncovered in 1982).[26] A group of English composers continued to write Latin music which was in many ways more interesting than the restricted fare for the new church. Osbert Parsley produced a fine set of the Catholic composer's calling card, the *Lamentations of Jeremiah*. So did Robert White, who died along with his entire family in an outbreak of plague at his place of work, Westminster Abbey, in 1574. Robert Parsons' job at the Chapel Royal went to William Byrd when he drowned in a boating accident in the river Trent near Newark in 1572.

These fine musicians provide the hinterland for the four who both succeeded and surpassed them, summing up a style and an age. The second half of the sixteenth century belongs to four composers from four countries: Tomás Luis de Victoria, Orlande de Lassus, Giovanni Pierluigi da Palestrina and William Byrd.

The Later Sixteenth Century

Byrd cannot be considered in isolation from his colleague and teacher, Thomas Tallis.

Tallis lived through most of the sixteenth century. His achievement was to serve four monarchs who kept changing the rules of his trade, and to make masterful music for all of them. Plainsong-based works like the *Missa Puer Natus est nobis* (probably 1554) and the dense canons at different speeds in *Miserere nostri* (published 1575) root him in his medieval inheritance. Music for the two Marys, Queen and Virgin (like his motet *Gaude, gloriosa Dei mater* of possibly the mid 1550s), soars with fervent rapture. Miniature pieces for the new church like his psalm tunes for Archbishop Parker's psalter of 1567 are tiny, chiselled perfection. At the other end of the scale, the forty-voice *Spem in alium* of c.1570 surely shows a familiarity with the Continental taste for massive canonic pieces, like those by Ockeghem and Josquin, and possibly with later examples. But Tallis's control of harmony and counterpoint is on a different level from his possible models: an astonishing, inexplicable masterpiece. Perhaps most precious of all is the music he composed in late maturity, when he and his former choirboy William Byrd set about synthesising something entirely new from their precarious position as Catholic composers at the court of the Protestant (but passionately musical) Elizabeth I (while also making some money from the carefully secured royal monopoly on music printing). Among the older man's contributions to their joint ventures are two settings of the penitential *Salvator mundi* (both later appeared with English contrafacta texts uglily shoe-horned onto the notes): suave, singers' music, restrained and beautiful. When Tallis died in 1585 Byrd hymned him in music, European-style: 'Tallis is dead, and Music dies.'[27]

Alongside the shared requirements of the liturgy, one of the reasons why the great composers of the later Renaissance have much in common is that the style is highly technical. Much of its basic grammar could be taught. An account of 1552 describes how one composer showed suitably promising pupils 'the perfect and imperfect intervals and the different methods of inventing counterpoints against plainsong ... then he would teach them in a few words the rules of three-part and later of four-, five-, six-part, etc., writing, always providing them with examples to imitate'.[28] In 1597 the English composer Thomas Morley described his own course of instruction with a certain 'Master Bold' (a not very convincing pseudonym for William Byrd),[29] an experience he clearly found as enjoyable as it was thorough, no doubt based in turn on Byrd's own studies with Tallis.

Byrd was born in the early 1540s. He was almost certainly a choirboy at the Chapel Royal (his two older brothers sang at St Paul's), returning as a 'Gentleman of the Chapel' (adult singer) in 1572 after a period as organist at Lincoln cathedral, where he wrote some of the earliest music for the new services of Cranmer's Book of Common Prayer. He and Tallis were active (and successful, at least latterly) in their joint publication ventures, and became joint 'Organists of the Chapel', the first to use that title. Byrd remained a member of the Chapel Royal for the rest of his long life, though increasingly retreated from active involvement after the accession of James I in 1603. He spent his last decades composing mostly introspective Catholic music in a series of noble households away from London. He died in 1623.

Byrd stands slightly apart from his great contemporaries. Largely this was because, as a Catholic in a Protestant country, he did not serve the daily needs of the Roman liturgy: where Palestrina composed well over a hundred settings of the Mass, Byrd wrote just three, smuggled in single sheets into the redoubts of Catholicism in remote country houses, to be sung in strict secrecy, away from the prying eyes of Lord Burleigh's sniffers-out of sedition (although Byrd, his wife and household had their share of brushes with the law). But partly it was temperament: his music is deeply intellectual, teasing out theological and contrapuntal ingenuity, mining the spiritual dramas of the Christian soul in ways that the cooler Palestrina never did. His range is vast. He set searing elegies like '*Infelix ego*' ('Unhappy am I'), a meditation on Psalm 51 penned by Savonarola after being handed his sentence of death, and clearly intended by Byrd as a commentary on the repression of the Catholic faith in England.

Many texts with similar resonance drew superb music from his pen: *Civitas Sancti Tui* (published 1589) fashions a restrained, overlapping lament from repetitions of '*Jerusalem desolata est*' ('Jerusalem is destroyed'). The later music of the *Gradualia* collections of 1605 and 1607 forms a kind of Requiem for his art and his faith. There is a valedictory quality, too, to many of the texts in his last English collection of 1611 (described by the composer as his 'final farewell').[30] Perhaps we can claim Byrd as the most emotionally varied and wide-ranging of the four late masters.

Tomás Luis de Victoria was born into a well-placed family in Ávila in central Spain in 1548. By 1565 he was in Rome (where he must certainly have known Palestrina), holding a series of posts as a singer and organist. In 1573 he became maestro di cappella at the Jesuit college there (where he had studied), and was ordained in 1575 (by the last surviving English Catholic bishop). He joined the Congregazione dei Preti dell'Oratorio, a new community of lay priests in Rome led by Philip Neri. Between 1578 and 1585 he served as a chaplain and published five sumptuous volumes, each covering a different aspect of music for the liturgy. The dedication of the 1583 volume expressed a wish to return to Spain, granted by Philip II in the form of a post as chaplain to his sister at her convent in Madrid, which had a good choir of priests and boys and where he was employed variously as cleric, maestro and organist. The early 1590s found him back in Rome to oversee publication and performance of his works. His last years were spent in Madrid, issuing a collection of large-scale works in 1600, some of them polychoral in the fashionable new Venetian manner. He died in 1611.

Priest, Jesuit, friend of saints: Victoria was the most professionally religious of this group of musicians (a dual role much less common than in the earlier medieval monastic period). All used printing and the commercial instincts of the age to distribute their works, but Victoria achieved a particularly wide reach for his music, including in the Americas. He wrote (or at least, has left) far less music than either Palestrina or Lassus, and it is entirely limited to sacred Latin texts.

Spanish music often has a passionate, fiery quality lurking within it. It's there in Victoria's *'Vere Languores Nostros'* with its distinctly un-Palestrinian chromaticisms. There is drama, as in the curtain-raising chords at the beginning of *'O Quam Gloriosum'*, followed by the pealing rejoicing of the saints in glory at *'gaudent'*. There is also a lot of skilful, thoughtful liturgical music for regular use like the Magnificat and hymn settings, with alternate verses sung to plainsong, some of which are still used in choral worship today – a tribute to their lasting quality and professional practicality. He had little use for older techniques like canon. His lines can be quirky and unpredictable. Posterity has found him at his most interesting in his motets, particularly his penitential pieces, and in mournful moods like those conjured by his late-published Requiem of 1605.

The wanderings of our next composer can be captured in the varied versions of his name: he was Roland de Lassus in France, Orlando di Lasso in Italy, Orlandus Lassus in his Latin moods, and various other variants between.

Lassus is a wonderful composer. There is something intensely human in the way he speaks to us about faith, love and wine across the wide range of his output, in music beautifully fashioned for singers. Tracing his gently overlapping lines to the words *'vos fugam capietis'* in the Passiontide motet *Tristis est anima mea* is one of the best things the choral singer of this (or any) repertoire gets to do. His Masses can be conservative compared to some, but contain plenty of creative approaches to reworking secular models like Gombert's *Triste départ*, and to the new sounds of polychoral effects, as in the massive, terse sonorities of the *Missa Bell' Amfitrit' altera*. But there are also Italian madrigals which prefigure the mannerist theatricality of the later musica reservata style, like the ending of *Che più d'un giorno*, which settles onto a minor chord on the word *'moria'* ('dies'), then has the tenor slide up an anguished semitone to make the strange

The technique of the parody mass. A passage a) from the chanson 'La Guerre' by the French composer Clément Jannequin, one of many songs which take gleeful delight in the vocal imitation of the sounds of real life, in this case a battle. b) is part of the Kyrie of the late sixteenth-century Spanish composer Tomás Luis de Victoria's Missa Pro Victoria, *in which he borrows several distinct musical ideas from Jannequin's chanson and recasts them with new words and much enlarged vocal forces: music transfigured for a new purpose.*

change from minor to major chord – and then does it again. *Madonna sa l'amor* plays with the word *'lasso'* ('then'), not just because it's his name, but because the solmisation syllables 'la–sol' produce the two-note musical phrase A–G. There are French chansons and German lieder, secular and sacred. His range of models and styles, and the cross-pollination between them, is vast.

His life covers familiar territory, professionally and geographically. Lassus was born around 1530 in Mons (Binchois's birthplace, and near to where Josquin had died a decade of so earlier). At the age of twelve he entered the service of Ferrante Gonzaga at Mantua, and there is a persistent but unverified story that he was abducted several times for the beauty of his voice – talent-scouting by courtly choirmasters was a well-established practice all across Europe at this time. Employment in several leading Italian cities (including Rome) led him back north in the mid 1550s, when he began publishing his music. In 1556 he joined the cosmopolitan musical establishment at the court of Duke Albrecht V of Bavaria in Munich, before becoming leader of the duke's chapel in 1563, a position he held to his death, combining it with travelling, composing, publishing, meeting many well-placed colleagues, including both Andrea and Giovanni Gabrieli, but also acting, writing and teaching the next generation of German contrapuntalists.

Lassus was honoured in his lifetime. A series of letters from the 1570s show him on easy terms with the music-loving Duke Wilhelm, quite different from the usual stiff sycophancy of such relationships. He also jokes around in a variety of languages, signing himself 'Orlando Lasso col cor non basso', 'Orlandissimo lassissimo, amorevolissimo', 'secretaire publique, Orlando magnifique', gently ribbing fellow composers like Heinrich Isaac and Jacques Arcadelt, and rhyming 'falsibordoni' with 'macaroni'.[31] Among his pupils were the influential Johann Eccard and one of his Munich choirboys, Leonhard Lechner, who later became a Protestant. Lassus died in June 1594, just a few weeks after Palestrina. In a practice that became increasingly common into the seventeenth century, he was succeeded in Munich by both of his sons in turn, and, much later, by a grandson. The sons helped cement Lassus's already considerable reputation by publishing the justly named *Magnum opus musicum* in 1604, containing most of his over 500 motets, in one of the first conscious attempts to assemble a complete and authoritative edition of a composer's work.

The life and music of Giovanni Pierluigi da Palestrina sum up the musical Renaissance. He brings full circle the theme of a style and manner forged in northern Europe that increasingly drew its greatest exponents towards its spiritual centre in Rome.

At the same time, he exemplifies a paradox. Although Palestrina polished and perfected what justly became known as the 'Roman style', he did so alone. There are no other significant Roman (or even Italian) composers of the late sixteenth century. His 'school' consisted entirely of visitors from elsewhere.

Like some other composers of the time, Palestrina is known to posterity after the town he (almost certainly) came from. Palestrina is a pleasant, historic city sitting among the sandy hills and fragrant pines about twenty-five miles east of Rome. Giovanni Pierluigi da Palestrina was steeped in the rich Roman tradition of well-trained and well-funded choirs throughout his life.

Born around 1525, he probably sang as a boy at the church of Santa Maria Maggiore in Rome, where his choirmasters may well have been French. This was followed by a job as organist back in Palestrina cathedral. He married in 1547, fathered three sons, and in 1551 followed the former bishop of Palestrina (now Pope Julius III) back to Rome as maestro of the Cappella Giulia (the private papal choir), where his first book of Masses was published in 1544. In 1555 he joined the more public Cappella Sistina, serving the short-lived Pope Marcellus, was sacked by the third pope of that year, Paul IV, because he was married, then quickly got Lassus's old job as maestro at St John Lateran. In 1560 he left in a row over funding, taking his son Rodolfo with him, rejoined Santa Maria Maggiore and worked also for Cardinal d'Este at his beautiful Roman villa. His reputation spread through the 1560s – although negotiations to get him appointed as imperial choirmaster in Vienna fell through because his terms were too high (the job went to de Monte). In 1571 he became choirmaster back at the Cappella Giulia, a post he held until his death. Between 1572 and 1581, the plague killed his wife, his brother and two of his sons. Perhaps unsurprisingly, he considered the priesthood, but instead married the wealthy widow of a fur merchant, who helped him complete his ambitious series of beautifully produced publications. He died in 1594, never, it seems, having left the immediate environs of Rome.

Palestrina is one of the two or three composers whose music is so consistent, so assured, and so perfectly matched to his times that he has become, and remains, a textbook of style and technique as well as a limitless resource of beautiful, practical music for worship. Allowing for an inevitable (though limited) period of obsolescence and neglect, every later composer studied him; they still do.

Palestrina's relationship with the intellectual and doctrinal currents of the Counter-Reformation are intriguing, and not entirely clear. Evidence of his having simplified his style in response to the requirements of the Council of Trent is inconclusive: his approach to word-setting and dissonance was naturally smooth and ultrarefined, but that was surely a reflection of his own nature as much as ecclesiastical fiat. The abstract beauties of the Mass, like the ineffable simplicity of the second Agnus Dei of the *Missa brevis*, suited him better than the grubbier emotions so often on display in Byrd and Victoria.

As the sixteenth century ticked over into the seventeenth a few short years after his death, Palestrina's style quickly became the *stile antico*: fixed, peered at, ossified, pinned inside a glass case to be drawn on when a composer wants something old, as indeed they did right through to the deliberately archaic church music of the nineteenth-century Oxford and Cecilian movements, where it is served sweetened with Victorian sentimentality.

Fortuna was turning her wheel once again.

5

REFORMATION

The principal thinker and agitator of the Protestant Reformation was also a musician. The ideals and character of Martin Luther resonated through the music of large parts of northern Europe throughout the late Renaissance and long after. They still do.

Crucially, the musical echoes of those ideas are heard not just, or even principally, in sacred music for church choirs, but in music for the home, workplace and schoolroom, too. Luther's contemporary John Calvin exhorted 'all men and women and little children' to sing psalms 'as a means of associating themselves with the company of angels', and to do so 'even in the houses and in the fields'.[1] This was a Reformation for everyone.

The Reformation was a revolution. Like all revolutions it had its big set-piece events, commemorated in statues, town squares and famous dates. But, again like all such movements, it was also a process – slow, partial and incomplete, with plenty of people wanting it to go faster and further, others trying to hold it back, some ignoring it through habit, inertia or lack of comprehension, many just muddling through. Music echoes all of this.

The Reformation took on local characteristics from the social and political traditions of its main geographical centres. Luther's *Formula Missae et Communionis* of 1523 kept the Mass in Latin, largely similar to the Catholic rite. Only later did he move to a liturgy in German. This had parallels in England, where Henry VIII maintained Catholic styles of worship even after his break with Rome in 1534.

Alongside theology and ecclesiastical politics, the eternal debate about musical elaboration fed into the forces acting on musical development. The Dutch reformer Erasmus (himself a former choirboy) complained after a visit to Cambridge that 'modern church music is so constructed that the congregation cannot hear one distinct word. The choristers themselves do not understand what they are singing.'[2]

Henry VIII's chief minister Thomas Wolsey told monasteries to admit no 'lascivious melody' to 'seduce the ears'.[3] The antidote to these evils was clarity. Archbishop Thomas Cranmer famously told the king in 1544 that he had tried making simple music for the liturgy with 'for every syllable a note, so that it may be sung distinctly and devoutly'.[4] Luther said, 'Next to the Word of God, the noble art of music is the greatest treasure in the world.'[5] The order of priority is clear: words first, music second.

To give their ideals musical form, Luther and Cranmer both happily raided the familiar repertoire of tunes from the old Catholic services (and elsewhere) for their new congregational hymns and canticles. The trick was to fit new words, or translations, to melodies which the parishioner already knew. Practicality, as always for the Protestant, was key.

But Luther was no Puritan. He was a passionate admirer of musical sophistication in its proper place. Josquin was a particular favourite. Polyphony, he said, reveals 'the great and perfect wisdom of God in music'; and 'we marvel when we hear music in which one voice sings a simple melody, while three, four, or five other voices play and trip lustily around the voice that sings its simple melody and adorn this simple melody wonderfully with artistic musical effects, thus reminding us of a heavenly dance'.[6] Elizabeth I of England similarly prized both 'a modest distinct song' and 'the best sort of melody' for 'such as delight in music' (in which category she clearly included herself).[7] In this duality lies much of the rich and sometimes contradictory progress of musical art through the Protestant Reformation. The Protestant heartlands produced much fine art music alongside simple hymns and psalms, often sounding very similar to their Catholic cousins.

Like many other plain-speaking musico-theologians of the time, Luther signed off with a swipe at those who disagreed with him:

> A person who gives this some thought and yet does not regard music as a marvellous creation of God, must be a clodhopper indeed and does not deserve to be called a human being; he should be permitted to hear nothing but the braying of asses and the grunting of hogs.[8]

Lutheran chorales, or hymns, fall into four broad categories:

translations of established Catholic liturgical items, with or without their original tunes (*'Veni Redemptor Gentium'* becomes *'Nun komm, der Heiden Heiland'*); translations of pre-Reformation religious songs (*'Puer natus in Bethlehem'* becomes *'Ein kind geborn zu Bethlehem'*, while the evergreen *'In dulci jubilo'* alternates lines in Latin and German); new texts to old melodies, known as contrafacta (the secular song *'Aus fremsden landen'* becomes a children's song, *'Vom Himmel hoch'*); and, most importantly, brand-new works such as Luther's own *'Ein feste Burg'*. England had its equivalents, particularly translations of established liturgical items and new texts for old melodies; but by far the most important development in England was psalm-singing. Metrical translations were enormously popular, mostly in a simple rhyme and metre scheme known, appropriately, as 'Common Metre': any psalm could be sung to any tune in the same metre.

Psalm books circulated in their many thousands, perhaps millions, propelled by the artisans and entrepreneurs of the new science of printing, like John Day in London. Printing supported the wide dissemination of other kinds of music books, too. *Piae Cantiones* is a school songbook printed in 1582 in Turku, Finland. Old-fashioned Catholic items like *'Ave Maris Stella'* sit alongside a Latin/Swedish version of *'In dulci jubilo'*. There is a version of a song which began life back in the thirteenth century in *Carmina Burana* as a celebration of what maidens and priests get up to in springtime, here with a rather more modest text about trees and flowers, infinitely more suitable for the young scholars of Turku's cathedral school. The tune of this song, along with many others in the collection, resurfaced many centuries later with yet another set of words, 'Good King Wenceslas'. Other items remain in use today much as they appear in the *Piae Cantiones*, including the irresistibly rhythmic Christmas songs *'Personent hodie'* and *'Gaudete, Christus est natus'*. The book exemplifies both the rich Scandinavian tradition of singing, particularly among young people, which is rooted in Lutheran practice and is still emphatically flourishing today, and the ability of moderate Protestantism to absorb and repurpose the best of its inheritance, Catholic, secular and frankly pagan.

Composers in the Lutheran heartlands continued to provide music for skilled choirs. Johann Walther's *Geystliche Gesangk Buchleyn* of 1524 contains five Latin motets and thirty-eight German lieder in three, four or five parts. Luther wrote the foreword, as he did for his friend Georg Rhau's *Symphoniae Jucundae* of 1538. Much earlier, in 1519, Rhau composed a Mass in no fewer than twelve parts to introduce the famous Leipzig debate between Luther and Eck. Ludwig Senfl artfully wove several chorale melodies together in his *Christ ist erstanden* (published in 1544, the year after Senfl's death). Typically, Rhau also turned his hand to simpler fare in a German songbook '*für die gemeinen Schülen*' ('for the "common" schools'). English composers were similarly adaptable.

German composers of the later Reformation continued to build on the examples of predecessors like Heinrich Isaac to adorn their new church with music which, in sound and technique, often differs little from its Catholic counterpart. Among composers of the later sixteenth century, Johannes Eccard, who was a student of Lassus, combined contrapuntal mastery with a true reformed religious spirit. Perhaps most important of all, Hans Leo Hassler studied and worked alongside the Gabrielis, uncle and nephew, in Venice, bringing the Venetian style back across the Alps, in a key first step towards the Italian-influenced German Baroque. As a Protestant employed by Catholic courts, Hassler trod the opposite line to that of his older contemporary William Byrd in England.

Somewhere among these musicians walked Veit Bach, a cittern-playing baker who fled to Germany from Hungary because he was a Lutheran. The hinterland of the German musical Reformation rings with pre-echoes of the world of his great-great-grandson Johann Sebastian: Luther and J. S. Bach attended the same Latin school in Eisenach two hundred years apart; Luther's writings were on Bach's shelves; Bach got Rhau's job as cantor of Leipzig's Thomasschule; Luther's chorales run through Bach's musical output like a strand of DNA.

Protestant Reformations sounded different in different parts of Europe. The other key centre was Switzerland, in particular the lakeside city of Geneva. Its cobbled, sloping streets and squares bred an austere form of Protestantism under the leadership of a Frenchman, Jean (or John) Calvin. Calvin was no Luther. To him, music was a dangerous temptress with the power 'to arouse and inflame the hearts of men' with its 'deadly and Satanic poison'.[9] The only acceptable music was psalms, in French, to single-lined, metrical tunes.

The principal composer of the Genevan psalters was Louis Bourgeois, who shared Luther's instinct for the appeal of a sturdy, well-shaped tune, 'so that a whole Christian congregation may sing along', as the preface to a psalter of 1586 put it.[10] Bourgeois did his job well (and, in passing, seems to have invented the idea of hanging up hymn numbers on the wall of the church on a slate or board: the practical Protestant at work once again).

The progress of one of Bourgeois' tunes shows how the simple but revolutionary idea of singing to God yourself, in your own language, rather than listening to a trained initiate do it for you in a language he understands but you don't, spread around Europe, adapting to local needs as it went. Protestant congregations travelled in response to changing levels of official toleration, or the reverse – French Huguenots in London under Edward VI, English Protestants in Geneva under Mary I, Calvinists in Scotland, Puritans (later) in America. Their music travelled with them. Bourgeois published his setting of Psalm 134, '*Or sus, serviteurs du Seigneur*', in the *Genevan Psalter* of 1551. Less than a decade later, an English writer noted with excitement the advent of congregational singing, accompanied on the organ, at the very dawn of Elizabeth I's reign: 'after the sermon done they songe all, old and yong, a salme in myter, a the tune of Genevay ways'.[11] Later, Bourgeois' tune appeared in many English psalm books, often in four-part harmony with the tune in the tenor, to a variety of English psalm paraphrases, as for example in the volume *All the French Psalm Tunes with English Words* of 1632 where it is sung to 'Ye Servants of the Lord of Might'. Later still the tune migrated to the top part, allied to yet more words, this time a version of an entirely different psalm, number 100, as 'All People That on Earth Do Dwell', in which form it has remained in use ever since. By the time it was thundered out at the coronation of Queen Elizabeth II in 1953, complete with Ralph Vaughan Williams's fanfares, Bourgeois' modest melody had come a long way from Calvinist Switzerland.

The defining feature of the English musical Reformation was that frequent changes of monarch in the mid sixteenth century brought numerous changes of official doctrine. Musicians kept having to adapt, and did so skilfully. It was Elizabeth I's typically astute political and religious settlement, as much as her own love of what she called 'the laudable science of music', which allowed England to develop its own distinctive version of the new musical order.[12] It produced perhaps England's finest musical hour.

Like all Protestants, English musicians developed art music for

A tune travelling through time. a) One of many melodies published by the French Calvinist hymn-writer Louis Bourgeois in the mid sixteenth century. b) In 1635 the tune turned up in the tenor in a four-part harmonisation in the Scottish Psalter, with words from an English metrical psalm.

choirs alongside offerings for ordinary people. Simplified forms of notation, allowing those not trained in mensural notation to sing, had been cultivated in England as far back as the mid fifteenth century, a principle brilliantly applied in 1550 to the words of the new English Book of Common Prayer by Calvinist convert John Merbecke. At much the same time, exquisite choral miniatures like Thomas Tallis's 'If Ye Love Me' (which first saw the light of day in the Wanley Manuscripts part books of around 1548–50 and was thus certainly composed under Edward VI's reforms) emerged from John Day's printing press (in his collection *Certaine Notes Set Forthe in Three and Foure Partes*, issued in 1565). Tallis and his friend, pupil, collaborator and colleague William Byrd helped advance new forms to meet new needs: settings of the English texts of the Book of Common Prayer, and new things like the consort song and verse anthem, in which passages for solo voice alternate with music for choir. The earlier technical reliance on equal, multi-voiced counterpoint is retained in both chorus and accompaniment. Large-scale 'great' service settings, including Byrd's, aped the grandeur of an earlier age. Their place of work, the monarch's Chapel Royal, provided the testing ground and model for all musical and liturgical innovations, as well as the best choir. The English music of Tallis and Byrd is skilful and varied: Catholics singing the Lord's song in a strange, Protestant land.

Politics, geography and history kept England in its own, isolated version of the Renaissance for rather longer than its European neighbours. The civil war and interregnum of the mid seventeenth century cast their baleful frosts: church music was banned and theatres closed. William Child marked his beautiful but backward-looking motet 'O Lord God, the Heathen are Come into Thine Inheritance' 'for the abolition of the Book of Common Prayer 1645'. Thomas Tomkins composed his 'Sad Pavan for These Distracted Times' in his Welsh fastness, written in response to the execution of Charles I in 1649. But unpropitious circumstances allowed some peculiarly English forms to survive, even to flourish, including old-fashioned things like viol fantasias by men like John Jenkins and William Lawes, sadly scraped in isolated musical households out in the safe, flat, dreary depths of the Midlands countryside.

Secular and Instrumental Music

The period witnessed the further emancipation of music from largely clerical use to the laity. Instrumental and secular music is neither Protestant nor Catholic, English nor European, nor exclusively for church or home. But, in style and performance context, it overlapped and coincided with all of these.

A well-worked piece of Renaissance polyphony could be sung, played, or both, and the composer often didn't specify which. When a composer started adding the instruction '*da sonar*' ('to play') or '*da cantar*' ('to sing') to a composition, it was a recognition of the fact that saying which was which was new. There are snatches of polyphony by Tallis which exist in versions with English words, Latin words and no words at all. Terminology, as always, followed usage in a slightly haphazard way. the late Renaissance 'canzona' is a piece for instrumental ensemble, even though the word is the Italian version of the French word for 'song'. The masters of the genre at the turn of the seventeenth century, Girolamo Frescobaldi and Giovanni Gabrieli, called their pieces '*canzoni da sonare*' (literally, 'songs to play').

The Renaissance was a period of innovation and creativity in instrument-making of all kinds. In church, the bellows organ comprehensively ousted the water-powered medieval hydraulis. The father of the sixteenth-century polymath Benvenuto Cellini was a craftsman who 'fashioned wonderful organs with pipes of wood, spinets the fairest and most excellent which then could be seen, viols and lutes and harps of the most beautiful and perfect construction', as his son recorded proudly.[13] Cellini senior was also a member of the Florence town band (though failed to pass on his enthusiasm to his son, who had an 'inexpressible dislike' for music). Bands of all kinds made music at all levels of society, depicted in countless paintings and images of the period. In Lutheran Germany musicians played from the city walls and galleries of the town hall, hinterland of the many-branched Bach family. The Low Countries developed a particular fondness for dance-type ensemble pieces like the bransles arranged and published by Tielman Susato in the 1550s. Battle pieces like Susato's *'Pavane la bataille'* were popular: their cheerful imitations of martial excursions and alarums worked just as well for voices. The French publisher Attaingnant produced many such pieces by composers like Claude le Jeune, Claudin de Sermisy and Clément Jannequin. *Orchésographie* of 1588, by the French cleric Thoinot Arbeau, was a dancing manual, complete with skilful woodcuts of a young man named Capriol and his sweetheart balefully practising their courante to the instruction of Maître Arbeau. A cheery English subset of this type of music were the Cries of London, musical compilations of the calls of street vendors and stall holders, assembled and arranged by composers including Orlando Gibbons.

Instrumental chamber music, often made by families, suited the quiet, domesticated viol consort (kept in a large chest) perfectly. Outdoor and ceremonial music was left to the more robust raspings of the sackbut, a kind of small-bore trombone, and the cornett (known in Germany as a 'zink'), a curved wooden instrument with a mouthpiece like a modern trumpet. A 'broken' consort of different kinds of instrument could blend exquisitely with voices: the English nobleman William Leighton's penitential 'Tears or Lamentations of a Sorrowful Soul' of 1614 accompanies its mournful singer with plucked, bowed and keyed strings.

Instruments accompanied music for the grander forms of worship, too. Late in the sixteenth century the Duke of Würtemmburg's secretary wrote home with an account of a chapel service at Windsor:

> His Highness listened for more than an hour to the beautiful music, the usual ceremonies, and the English sermon. The music, and especially the organ, was exquisite. At times could be heard cornetts, then flutes, then recorders and other

instruments. And there was a little boy who sang so sweetly, and lent such charm to the music with his little tongue, that it was really wonderful to listen to him. Their ceremonies indeed are very similar to those of the papists ...[14]

So much for the Reformation.

The Renaissance continued the process of turning music for solo keyboard into a genuinely idiomatic vehicle for thematic development and virtuosic display. In the 1530s the French publisher Attaingnant issued florid keyboard elaborations of motets and other sacred choral items for organists to use during the liturgy, no doubt catching up with established practice. Other sacred improvisations to emerge into written-out form included the toccata (essentially a flurry of runs, scales and trills added by German organists to plain chords on the page, often alternating blocks of chordal and florid music). One of the most skilful and rewarding books of organ tablature is the *Obras de música para tecla, arpa y vihuela* by the blind Spanish composer Antonio de Cabezón, published in 1578 with a colossal print run of 1,200 copies. Late Renaissance English composers like Byrd, Gibbons, John Bull and Giles Farnaby used dance-based character pieces ('Doctor Bull's My Selfe – A Jigge') and new forms like variations to spin blizzards of notes from the rattling keys of the harpsichord or the quieter sounds of the virginal or spinet. This is music for the home and for teaching and study (particularly of rich young ladies), a lucrative sideline for the well-placed composer.

Lute music was in some ways a subset of music for keyboard: many pieces exist in versions for both. The Venetian publisher Petrucci pioneered both the repertoire and notation of dance-based lute pieces like the passemezzo. The lute and its many variants were the perfect vehicle for the introspective musings of the educated Renaissance mind ('My Lady Carey's Dump'; 'The Queenes Goodnight') as well as more cheerful moments ('Captain Humes Musicall Humours'; 'Whoope, Doe Me No Harm, Good Man'). The characteristic Spanish instrument was the vihuela, a small six-stringed guitar. Spanish string music of the period reveals fascinating Arabic influences.

Secular song, as always, was a public creature, existing in many different forms, passed around by word of mouth, often without being written down at all. In England, the innumerable ballad sheets and penny broadsides allied familiar tunes like 'Greensleeves' to all sorts of texts about the latest plot, murder or execution, celebrity or favourite saint.

Music was a key element of Renaissance theatre, too. The Italian commedia dell'arte dropped madrigals into its fast-paced plots to add colour and character, and one of its standard characters, the smooth-tongued servant Brighella, was often seen with a guitar. Lassus played the part of Magnifico in a commedia at a courtly wedding in 1568.

English theatre, unlike its Italian counterpart, did not feature women on stage. Female roles were taken by boys and young men. The boys could become real stars: when the actor Salomon Pavy died at the age of thirteen in 1602, Ben Jonson recorded that he had been 'the stage's jewel' for three years.[15] Pavy was a child of Elizabeth I's Chapel Royal: in an intriguing sideline from their main task, top choirs including those at St Paul's cathedral and St George's chapel, Windsor, maintained fully fledged theatrical troupes formed from their choirboys, run by professional choirmasters like William Hunnis, Richard Edwardes and Nathaniel Giles. The 'dolefull and straunge noyse of violles' added atmosphere to a dumbshow played at Gray's Inn in 1566,[16] and well-known folk tunes were added to shows like *The Commodye of Pacient and Meeke Grissill*, ancestor of the riotously popular ballad operas. Wordsmiths like William Shakespeare and Ben Jonson worked closely with composers like Thomas Morley and Robert Johnson at Blackfriars and the Globe.

France, as ever, favoured the ballet in its theatrical entertainments. Juan del Encina, founder of Spanish drama in the early sixteenth century, was himself a composer: at the height of the Spanish Renaissance Miguel de Cervantes, best known for his novel *Don Quixote* (published in 1605 and 1615), filled his writings with music, as, for example, when a solemn procession of Moors is greeted by a 'trompeta bastarda' in his 1615 play *Los baños de Argel*,[17] or a song in another play finished that year, *Pedro de Urdemalas*, is introduced by 'all kinds of music and bagpipes from Zamora'.[18]

In Germany the art of civic, secular song reached a distinctive phase in the fourteenth to the sixteenth centuries in the singing guilds of tradespeople and artisans known as the Meistersinger. Strict rules governed the writing and singing of both words and music, examined in public contests in church and town hall, rewarded with wreaths, crowns and progress through the various categories of membership of the guild. The songs aspired to many of the same ideals as those of the French troubadours two centuries before. The most celebrated singer in the most garlanded guild was Hans Sachs of Nuremberg. Sachs has left us a large body of songs – fairly plain on paper, testament to the discipline inherent in the idea (though the Meistersinger allowed themselves flights of fancy in the names of their tunes: '*Gestreiftsafranblumleinweis*' ('little striped saffron flower melody'); '*Vielfrassweis*' ('melody of much food')).[19]

The Madrigal

Key musical form at the end of the Renaissance, and seed bed of the Baroque, was the madrigal, another marker of the liberation of music for use by the educated laity at home.

Countries and regions had their own version of this type of secular part song. In the early sixteenth century Franco-Flemish composers dominated, as they did sacred music. Josquin couldn't resist a good canon even when he was telling us that '*Faute d'argent, c'est douleur nompareille*' ('lack of money is the worst kind of misery'). Important pioneers who spent time in Italy and wrote secular vocal pieces in both Italian and French included Adrian Willaert, Cipriano da Rore, Philippe Verdelot and Jacques Arcadelt. Chief among the native Italians was Costanzo Festa. In Germany, a *Liederbuch* or songbook might well contain imports from northern and southern Europe as well as local offerings, sacred and secular. Heinrich Isaac was a key figure around the turn of the sixteenth century, as he was in sacred music, writing chansons and frotolle in French and Italian as well as German lieder, including his celebrated polyphonic song '*Innsbruck, ich muss dich lassen*' ('Innsbruck, I Must Leave You'). The Italian frottola fitted words to the top and bottom parts, meaning that the inner parts were not conceived with the words as their framework – a fundamental difference from the later madrigal. The frottola was also a form restricted to northern Italy, its proponents relying on the patronage of aristocratic families like the d'Este family in Ferrara, Modena and Reggio Emilia, limiting its geographical reach.

Later master madrigalists included north Europeans Orlande de Lassus and Giaches de Wert, and Frenchmen Claude le Jeune and Philippe de Monte. Themes echo across Europe: '*Pleurez, mes yeux,*' sang the lovesick Frenchman Dominique Phinot in 1548; 'Weep, O mine eyes,' echoed the English composer John Bennet half a century later. The madrigal revels in simple, naïf word painting. Form is sectional, emotions vivid but static. Palestrina wrote madrigals, but claimed on more than one occasion to have 'blushed and grieved' at using his art for such worldly purposes.[20] Professionally, this may have been partly an attempt not to blot his copy-book with his ecclesiastical employers; but artistically he was right; his emotionally restrained art is much better suited to his smooth style of sacred music.

Musica Transalpina, a collection by all the leading Italians, was published in London in 1588. English composers responded enthusiastically. Thomas Weelkes' 'Thule, the Period of Cosmography' is a six-voice travelogue taking the listener to Greenland's 'frozen climes' and the 'sulfurious fire' of 'Trinacrian Aetna's flames', all compared to the meteorological vagaries of the poet's own heart. Orlando Gibbons's 'The Silver Swan' is a perfect, lovesick miniature. The older English tradition of roustabout 'three-men's' (or 'freemen's') songs, mentioned by Shakespeare, is kept alive in Weelkes' 'Strike It Up, Tabor', among many others, written for two tenors and a bass, lute in one hand, pint in the other. *The Triumphs of Oriana* is a huge collection of twenty-five madrigals by twenty-three composers, published by Thomas Morley in 1601 in honour of the ageing Queen Elizabeth I. The texts all end with a salutation greeting the queen by one of her nicknames: 'Long Live Fair Oriana'.

The madrigal was a literary form first, fashioned around the rhetoric and rhyme schemes of old writers like Petrarch and new poets like Torquato Tasso in Italy and the Frenchman Pierre de Ronsard. 'The notes are the body of the music, but the words are the soul,' said the composer Marc'Antonio Mazzone in the introduction to his *First Book of Madrigals* of 1569. As the century moved towards its end, composers in all parts of Europe moved increasingly away from relying on literary form and rhyme scheme to create musical structure, in favour of a direct interpretation of the expressive potential of the text. The mannerist style known as 'musica reservata' pushed word painting and chromaticism to extreme. Carlo Gesualdo, prince of Venosa, is perhaps as famous for his part in the murder of his wife and her lover as for his bizarre, but somehow always logical, melodies and harmonies, sacred and secular. It is surely not wrong to hear torment and guilt in the strange, twisted music of late madrigals such as *'Moro, lasso, al mio duolo'* and penitential sacred works like the *Tenebrae responsoria*. Less extremely, Luca Marenzio serenaded his 'pretty, light-footed nymph' and asked his faithless lover 'Cruel one, why do you flee?' in expressively shifting harmonies and vocal lines interweaving in stepwise motion over a single chord. Marenzio died in 1599. His successor as Italy's leading madrigalist, Claudio Monteverdi, took the form on a rich stylistic and emotional journey in his eight books of madrigals. Book Five (published in 1605) marks the decisive change from the purely descriptive to music that is personally and emotionally involved: old-style 'fa la la' replaced by heart-felt 'Ohimè' and 'Ahi'.

One more secular form carried the well-bred love of words, women, melody and melancholy in delicious directions, particularly in early seventeenth-century England: the lute song. John Dowland lamented 'Now, O Now I Needs Must Part' in a magically mournful major key, complete with his characteristic touches of syncopation and ornamented cadence figures; Thomas Campion (who wrote his own words) hymned his god like a lover in 'Never Weather-beaten Sail', with its rapt repetitions of 'O come quickly, glorious Lord'. One of the finest of these songs is the anonymous 'Miserere, My Maker', with its plangent, almost Baroque, harmonies. These are among the most artful songs of any style or age. English lutenists had the habit of travelling abroad for work and study – Dowland to Denmark, Andrew Borrell to Stuttgart, Nicholas Lanier to Italy.

The Intermedi

Towards the end of the sixteenth century chattery groups of literati, known as academies, took to gathering in centres of art and thought such as Florence to talk, make music and plan the future. During the same period, madrigals and other items were added to stagey court spectaculars on mythical themes known as 'intermedi', written to go between the parts of a straight play, often glorifying the local noble family. The most celebrated were the Florentine intermedi of 1589 (for which 286 costumes were specially made), lavishly described in illustrated 'festival books', hungrily read all round Europe.

The humble madrigal, like the Renaissance itself, was turning into something else.

Part Four

BAROQUE (1600–1759)

INTRODUCTION

In the words of the musicologist Tim Carter, the later sixteenth and early seventeenth centuries saw the 'transformation of ... style under the pressure of new aesthetic and functional demands made upon music, and of shifting social, political and cultural circumstances as Italy moved into the period of the Counter-Reformation, and the arts moved through Mannerism into the Baroque'.[1]

School and Home

Education continued to evolve: many composers both studied and taught at parish '*schulen*' in Germany or chapel and choir schools in England (though few went as far as Georg Philipp Telemann's schoolteacher J. C. Losius, who got his young pupil to set the geography syllabus to music). Charity and philanthropy played their part: Antonio Vivaldi presided over a large and celebrated group of young female orphans at the Ospedale della Pietà in Venice, and the politician and writer Horace Walpole admired the music-making at the Magdalen Hospital for Penitent Prostitutes in London. The six Scuole Grandi of Venice organised (and paid for) the artistic and charitable life of the parish.

Music was made in a social and domestic context, too, for study, prayer, or just plain fun. Samuel Pepys described a typical Sunday afternoon in 1664:

> my wife and I above, and then the boy and I to singing of psalms, and then came in Mr Hill and he sung with us a while; and he being gone, the boy and I again to singing of Mr Porter's motetts ... Mr Hill came to tell me that he had got a gentlewoman for my wife, one Mrs Ferrabosco, that sings most admirably.[2]

Pepys enjoyed taking his theorbo (a large member of the lute family) to the pub for a sing-song, too. Henry Purcell wrote rounds and catches for such convivial occasions (some of them extremely rude). J. S. Bach told a friend in 1730 that his family (including a boy of six) 'are all born musicians, and I can assure you that I can already form an ensemble both *vocaliter* and *instrumentaliter* within my family, especially since my present wife sings a good, clear soprano, and my eldest daughter, too, joins in not badly'.[3] It's a touching image, no doubt replicated in educated households across Europe (though probably not to the same standards as *chez* Bach).

Employment, Patronage, Politics

Despite increasing opportunities for entrepreneurship in the opera house and elsewhere, the Baroque composer still needed a job. For most, this still meant a position of middling rank in a hierarchical establishment run by the church, civic authorities, some noble or royal court, or some combination of all three.

Working for aristocratic patrons meant plenty of music for royal birthdays, funerals and trips to the races, with dedications stuffed with the usual flowery guff: 'May it please Your Majesty, I had not assum'd the confidence of laying ye following Compositions at your Sacred feet …';[4] 'may Your Majesty deign to dignify the present modest labour with a gracious acceptance …';[5] 'of all my works it is the one I deem the least happy since it has not yet had the advantage of appearing before Your Majesty …'[6] (from the dedications of three fine pieces of music to, respectively, Charles II of England, Frederick the Great of Prussia and Louis XIV of France). Court politics affected musical opportunities, from groups of singers favoured by rival factions being 'thrown together, like so many feather'd Warriors, for a Battle-royal in a Cock-pit', as the English actor manager Colley Cibber put it,[7] to the joint dukes with different tastes at Bach's place of work in Weimar placing contradictory demands on their talented young organist, and Louis XIV's choice of mistress diluting his enthusiasm for dancing.

Politics showed up in the music, too, through an allegorical choice of opera plot, an ode or anthem marking the failure of some conspiracy against the royal person (very much a feature of the English composer's repertoire since the days of the Gunpowder Plot and before), or a popular tune by Purcell being press-ganged into service as a campaigning song about a contested election for Lord Mayor of London:

> Now, now, the work's done and the Parliament's set
> Are sent back again like fools as they met[8]

The courtier Lord Hervey made clear how rival opera companies became associated with rival court factions in 1730s London:

> The King and Queen ... were both Handelians, and sat freezing constantly at his empty Haymarket Opera, whilst the Prince with all the chief of the nobility went as constantly to that of Lincoln's Inn Fields ... An anti-Handelist was looked upon as an anti-courtier, and voting against the Court in Parliament was hardly a less remissible or venial sin than speaking against Handel or going to the Lincoln's Inn Fields Opera.[9]

Such rivalries could easily encompass other proxies, too: Protestant against Catholic, native against foreigner, Tory against Whig.

Political and social organisation varied: in England, France and Spain the monarchy was essentially the only game in town for the ambitious musician, while Germany and Italy maintained a patchwork of smaller city states and courts, each with its own tastes and resources. Purcell was composing for the king at age seventeen; Telemann was writing what he called 'sausage-symphonies' for the local town band.[10]

Many courts were lax about pay: Monteverdi was always moaning about money; in Saxony Heinrich Schütz petitioned his Elector for over two years' unpaid salary in 1630; and royal household musicians in London in 1666 were '4¾ years in arrear'.[11] Conversely, a genuinely musical patron could be a real driver of musical creativity. In Handel's London Frederick, Prince of Wales, was an avid performer. So was his flute-playing namesake Frederick the Great of Prussia, who whistled much fine music into existence at his enlightened, Frenchified court at the palace of Sans Souci outside Berlin. Women could play an equally influential role, if they were rich: music at the court of Wolfenbüttel in the middle of the seventeenth century was ordered and directed by the duchess, Sophia Elisabeth of Brunswick-Lüneberg, who was a student of Schütz and a considerable composer in her own right. In the eighteenth century, her example was amply continued by Princess Wilhelmine of Prussia, Margravine of Brandenburg-Bayreuth, representative of several royal and noble families and an accomplished composer of works including the stylish opera *Argenore* of 1740.

Music suffered when political structures broke down: most obviously through war, including the overlapping tragedies of the Thirty Years' War and English Civil War during this period, but also from boring things like a lack of money or the accession of an unmusical prince (Bach and Purcell both knew people like that), or nascent democratic forces like public censorship of theatres.

At the same time, the later Baroque saw composers begin to move out from the demands and restrictions of employment to something approaching a freelance career. The able and affable Telemann put considerable effort into democratising access to music of all kinds through the public concerts of his Collegium Musicum in Leipzig in the first decade of the eighteenth century (a role later taken on by his friend Bach). In the same decade the young Handel competed with the popular Reinhard Keiser for the attention (and wallets) of Hamburg's Italophile and opera-loving public. Another operatic entrepreneur, Jean-Baptiste Lully, apparently made 10,000 francs from just the opening night of his *Armide* in Paris in 1686. In London, Handel, the ultimate self-made man and canny operator, successfully traded South Sea Company stock as it fluctuated alongside shares in the Royal Academy of Music, wittily parodied by Richard Steele in 1720: 'At the rehearsal on Friday last, Signor NIHILINI BENEDETTI rose half a Note above his Pitch formerly known. Opera stock from 83 and half, when he began; at 90 when he ended.'[12]

Sources: Printing and Manuscript

Entrepreneurship extended to printing, too. Monteverdi sent his music north to Antwerp to secure the services of a good publisher. Handel found an astute partner in the Walsh family firm (printing, like composing, often ran in families), who issued collections of individual arias and movements, often rearranged from the original, as well as an ambitious series of operas on subscription. Generally, composers ventured into print selectively, concentrating on smaller-scale items for the domestic market like keyboard or chamber pieces. Pirate editions were a problem – Handel published his keyboard

Suites in 1720 because 'Surrepticious and incorrect Copies of them had got Abroad',[13] and Telemann had the same problem in Paris. So were lax standards. Bach's first biographer, Johann Nikolaus Forkel, was merciless with shoddy publishers who allowed 'errors which a musical schoolboy would hardly let stand' into their editions.[14]

Most music remained in manuscript, which at this period still meant ruling the five straight(-ish) stave lines by hand with a special five-nibbed pen (an example sits crouched in a glass case in the Bach-Museum in Leipzig like an inky spider). Composers marshalled an entourage of copyists and amanuenses, often members of their own family, to help with the daily task of preparing performing materials. This was, in turn, a time-honoured and highly effective way for young students to thoroughly get to know the inner workings of a score. Some manuscripts were preserved in carefully compiled collections put together by people like Purcell's friend John Gostling; others were gathered like the 'Sebastianoren' given by C. P. E. Bach to his friend Forkel.[15] Many were lost, sold, thrown away, or simply vanished.

As in all ages, technology moved on. Copperplate engraving thoroughly superseded movable type from around the turn of the eighteenth century. Instruments, too, grew in stature. Dutch and north German organs by builders like the Silbermanns were bigger than elsewhere in Europe, with a wide range of stops and a full-compass pedal board, leading directly to the creation of a large and impressive body of work which forms the bedrock and foundation of the organist's repertoire (and much else) to this day. The piano tinkled into drawing rooms, ready to replace the harpsichord and spinet.

'Academy' and 'Cantata': Words

Words, like notes, move through time. In order to understand what the musicians of this period are saying to us, we must give some attention to what they mean when they use words like academy, concert, cantata and opera: in all cases, not quite what we mean today.

An academy could be a club or a society, dedicated to study and intellectual pursuit. In London and Paris the Royal Academy of Music was an opera company, supported by patronage and subscription. In Leipzig Lorenz Mizler's Corresponding Society of the Musical Sciences aimed to 'make of music a scientific or scholarly pursuit …

based on reading good books, listening to good music, [and] perusal of many scores by good masters' – not a problem when Bach, Handel and Telemann are on your membership list.[16] In Italy, an *'accademia'* could be a performance, or concert.

The dedicated concert room was something of a novelty. There was just one in Purcell's London in 1683, the 'Musick Meeting in York Buildings',[17] which was 'adorn'd with painting [and had] ... 4 Rows of Seats round the Room, stuff'd and cover'd with green Bayes, and rail'd in with Iron'.[18] Many performances took place in a grand house or a public space like an inn or guildhall. Handel's *Messiah* was first heard in 1742 in Neale's 'New Musick-Hall in Fishamble Street', near the river Liffey in Dublin. In Paris, *Le Concert Spirituel* was a long-running series of concerts held in a gilded room in the Tuileries from 1725. The German composer Dietrich Buxtehude's *Abendmusik* was a kind of sacred recital: choral music sung in his church in Lübeck after the main Sunday service, mentioned in seventeenth-century travel guides as unique in Europe. Many concert venues were crowded and cramped: the ladies and gentlemen of Dublin were requested to attend the early performances of *Messiah* without (respectively) hoops and swords, which 'will greatly encrease the Charity, by making Room for more company'.[19] Thomas Britton launched a concert series in a loft above a converted stables in Clerkenwell in 1678, where, according to one account, the audience would 'stew in Summer-Time like sweaty Dancers at a Buttock-Ball, or like Seamens Wives in a Gravesend Tilt-Boat'.[20] It somehow brings this great music alive to think that its first audiences may have looked (and smelt) more like the crowd at a modern gig or football match than earnest early music types politely clutching their programmes.

Chamber and instrumental music fashioned new forms and new words to describe them. Terms like sonata, toccata, symphony, ricercare and others moved through the Baroque, taking on more (or less) precise shades of meaning and local subsets as they went. A canzona (which could interchangeably be called a sinfonia or a sonata) might use echo effects between small and large groups of instruments, a clear pre-echo of the absolutely central Baroque principle of the concerto. A sonata (in its church or chamber, as opposed to ensemble, form) featured one or more solo instruments with a continuo bass. The continuo required two players, so that a *Sonata a due* has two musical lines but needed three performers. The *Sonata a tre* (for four players) took on a particularly rich life as the trio sonata: the texture of two equal treble lines and a bass is everywhere in the Baroque. The violin emerged as a solo instrument in a way that its older, quieter and more collegial cousin the viol never could. It found its soulmate in the concerto.

The Italian cantata was a secular vocal piece: Handel wrote a number during his youthful stay in Italy. The German sacred cantata was a relatively new creature when Bach inherited and nurtured it (though Bach typically didn't use the word, calling his works 'church piece' or simply 'piece'). Its principal feature is the use of different types of text: vivid, personalised madrigalian poetry by writers like Bach's collaborators Salomon Franck and the pseudonymous Picander for the solo recitative and arias, paraphrased biblical or psalm texts for the choruses, strophic Lutheran hymns for the chorales. English composers didn't write cantatas: the closest equivalent to the Continental multi-movement form is the glorious Restoration symphony anthem, consciously aping what one writer rather regretfully called 'the French fantastical light way'.[21]

The oratorio was an uncomfortable hybrid, parented by frilly Roman oratorians and the hirsute saints and virgins of chilly northern mystery plays, deliberately fashioned to fill the gap when the opera was closed in Lent by composers thinking up new ways of tapping into the lucrative public appetite for music without offending the clergy (or, at least, getting away with it). As always, the results generated plenty of opposition: one writer recorded 'an old widow of the nobility' greeting a performance of a concerted Passion setting in Germany in 1732 with the cry, 'God save us, my children! It's just as if we were at an Opera Comedy.'[22] 'An Oratorio either is an Act of Religion, or it is not: if it is one I ask if the Playhouse is a fit Temple to perform it, or a Company of Players fit Ministers of God's Word,' thundered a letter writer in the London *Universal Spectator* at Handel,[23] who had earlier responded to a similar accusation by stating publicly that his oratorio *Esther* would be 'fitted up in a decent manner', with 'no Action on the Stage'.[24]

Opera in Context

The pre-eminent art form of the musical Baroque was a flamboyant amalgam of all sorts of arts: opera. Monteverdi quickly turned the new art form into the first, and still among the greatest, examples of opera as drama: psychologically truthful, dramatically fluid, varied and vivid in the theatre.

The following 150 years of operatic history can be characterised as the march of the Italian manner through Europe and the varying degrees of resistance and assimilation it encountered on the way. As early as 1633 Schütz wrote that 'during my recent journey to Italy I engaged myself in a singular manner of composition, namely how a comedy of diverse voices can be translated into declamatory style and be brought to the stage and enacted in song – things that to the best of my knowledge ... are still completely unknown in Germany'.[25] France developed its own deliberately anti-Italianate operatic traditions, taking in the eternal Gallic love affair with the ballet alongside the main job of puffing up the king, led (ironically) by an Italian-born musician with an equal flair for the footlights and backstairs palace intrigues, Jean-Baptiste Lully. England (as usual) did things a bit differently: dramatic opera dropped musical numbers into the show as a kind of add-on, irrespective of the story, much as straight plays had always done. (In one notable example, a character in Colley Cibber's *Love's Last Shift* of 1696 accosts a group of passing players with the words, 'Here Gentlemen, place yourselves upon this spot and pray oblige me with a Trumpet Sonata.')[26]

Today's word opera encompasses all sorts of subspecies, from semi-opera (a term used by Henry Purcell) to serenata (which, rather pleasingly, means 'to be played under a serene sky'). Court opera was grander and more stylised than popular pieces for the public opera houses, helping to lead in time to a distinct division into two types, 'seria' and 'buffa'. A 'pasticcio' (or 'pastry') was a show put together from bits of several different operas, a bit like a Broadway review or a modern juke-box musical. Composers would happily write new numbers for a revival of someone else's opera, to change the story or suit a local singer. Not infrequently, more than one language would be heard in the same show. Dance, pyrotechnics, moving sets, echo effects and flying machines all added noise and colour (and sometimes physical danger) to what Cibber called 'that Succession of monstrous Medlies that have so long infested the Stage ... these Poetical Drams, these Gin-shops of the Stage, that intoxicate its Auditors and dishonour their Understanding'.[27]

Women sang on stage for the first time during this period (and, less often and even more controversially, in church). The best actor singers became hugely popular and hugely rich. But they worked hard for it: Handel had several operas in repertory at one time, swapping from one to another as the box office demanded. There were no understudies. Among the most celebrated of the superstar singers in Italy were the castrati, strange creatures with long limbs and clear, high voices, both the result of enforced castration as boys interrupting normal hormonal development. Italian church choirs used castrati, too. Fortunately the grim practice never seems to have spread beyond Italy.

In most countries, a more earthy and popular type of music theatre flourished alongside the highbrow like a primrose in a cowpat: sung in the vernacular; featuring tunes the audience already knew, like folk songs and street ballads; telling rude tales of regular people rather than elevated allegories and mythological moralities. Pantomime took its first bow. In the hands of composers who knew how to have fun, proper opera would learn to embrace all of this as the eighteenth century went on.

The world of the Baroque composer, however, was an increasingly international one. Some composers travelled a great deal, like the German composer Johann Jakob Froberger and, several decades later, his compatriot Handel. Others didn't, notably Purcell and Bach. Sometimes they would meet: contests of performance and improvisation staged between rival visiting virtuosi were a popular spectator sport among the musically literate elite. Style was a subject of debate, often conducted in pamphlets and public letters. It, too, was international, travelling and interbreeding as composers and performers did themselves: the courante turns up in all corners of musical Europe. Often, a whiff of patriotic nationalism would puff up one style over another.

Technique and Form

Technically, one of the defining weapons in the Baroque composer's armoury was the basso continuo: an independent bass line, supporting harmonies played by a chord instrument. Numbers and other symbols like sharps and flats were written above or below the continuo bass line, telling the keyboard or lute player what chord to play and how to distribute dissonance logically and correctly in inner parts, known as 'figured bass'. This allowed the solo on top to expand into something genuinely idiomatic for instrument or voice. The principle of the independent continuo bass line, with chord instrument, is fundamental, in every sense of that word, to Baroque music; some writers have called the period the era of the general bass.

This innovation also pushed music towards a definite system of harmony based around certain chords and their relationships (different from the old system of modes): keys. The Baroque, like its parent ages, loved learned treatises about temperament, tuning and how to modulate from any key to any other.

In terms of form, the ritornello ('little return') principle is key. An opening passage for the full ensemble (the 'orchestra') is followed by an alternation of new music for smaller forces and repeats of bits of the opening music in various keys (the ritornello). Vivaldi polished this simple recipe into a paradigm of formal perfection and soloistic variety; Bach took it to whole new universes of invention.

On the opera stage the ritornello principle gives us the da capo (literally, 'from the head', or 'from the top') aria, with its distinctive motto opening taken up by the singer before launching into the alternating ritornello/episode pattern, usually with a contrasting middle section before the opening is repeated (the da capo). The form became the defining feature of the hugely popular 'opera seria', perfect for fixing a particular emotion outside of time and action. There must be tens, maybe hundreds, of thousands of Baroque da capo arias. Arias are for reflection; the action is carried by the recitative, for solo voice and a continuo group of bass and chord instruments, the words delivered in a plain, free speech rhythm.

Counterpoint remained a god. The key skill was 'invention': combining a theme with itself and various counter-themes in a variety of skilful and rewarding ways in order to tease out its musical possibilities over the course of a piece. Its purest and highest expression comes in the suite of principles known collectively as fugue: not by any means just in pieces called fugues, but bound into every aspect of the composer's art. Bach's resourcefulness and range with the tools of fugue were simply infinite.

Music was made for the now. Even the best composers of this period could expect to be largely forgotten after their death as tastes turned. Publishing helped preserve much music, but only pieces which stood a chance of making money. Most music remained in

Part Four: Introduction

manuscript. Typically, we know lots about the professional dealings of these composers (mixed, as always); less about them as thinkers, artists and people. A melancholy example is the tradition handed down in the Couperin family of a lengthy correspondence between François Couperin ('le Grand') and J. S. Bach. The letters were used as lids for jam pots by some nineteenth-century Couperins. We can only hope they enjoyed their jam.

Fugue: one of the fundamental compositional principles of the Baroque. In this extract (the opening of Fugue 11 in F Major from Book I of The Well-Tempered Clavier *by J. S. Bach), the subject is marked A1; the answer (transposed version of the subject) is marked A2; and the countersubject is marked B. Bars 13–17 are an episode, building a harmonic sequence over the countersubject, B, followed by a middle entry beginning on the last beat of bar 17 and using both subject and answer, A1 and A2. At the last beat of bar 21 the music from the last beat of bar 4 is presented again, but with the two parts flipped so they are now the other way up, known as inversion. These techniques run through the art of J. S. Bach and the musical Baroque.*

6

VESPERS AND VIVALDI: THE CATHOLIC SOUTH

In April 1617, workmen digging gingerly in the damp foundations of St Mark's basilica, Venice, found a casket containing relics. One was declared to be a piece of the True Cross.

The bloodied splinter was honoured with a lavish ceremony: 'the Passion of Our Lord with most exquisite music', then a costumed procession round the piazza featuring 'four singers who sang the Litany of the Saints, and after the relics and immediately before the Doge there was the whole body of musicians with their maestro di cappella', then, back in St Mark's 'singing from the theatre [a raised platform] by a boy clad as an angel'.[1]

The maestro marshalling the musical magnificence that day was Claudio Monteverdi.

An even splashier musical spectacular was the annual 'watery Cavaleata', when the Doge went 'with all the Signory to marry the sea on Ascension Day' in a ship described by an English traveller as 'the richest gallie of all the world'.[2] Monteverdi wearily told a friend, 'I will be required to have ready a concerted Mass and motets for the whole day … after which I shall have to put in order a certain cantata.'[3]

This is the Baroque as display; an immersive, theatrical, all-embracing assault on the senses.

Prima and Seconda Pratica

Technically, the music on show in 1617 had a number of striking new aspects. The theorist Angelo Berardi categorised its innovations like this: 'the old masters [of the Renaissance] had only one style and one practice, the moderns have three styles, church, chamber and theatre style, and two practices, the first and the second'.[4]

This idea of a first and second practice, or old and new style (the 'prima' and 'seconda pratica', or 'stile antico' and 'nuovo') is key. It's a rare example in musical history of practice following theory – the new style arose out of a conscious critique of the old.

The theory was developed at the end of the sixteenth century in Florence by groups of aristocrats, led by Counts Bardi and Corsi, who called themselves the Camerata. They claimed to be reinventing the musical and rhetorical ideals of ancient Greece through their *'spezie d'harmonie ... quantunque Atheneo'*, as Vincenzo Galilei put it in his *Dialogo della musica antica e della moderna* of 1581.[5] The aim was to express genuine and shifting emotion over an entire passage of text (unlike the sectional and emotionally static Renaissance madrigal). The new musical weapon was recitative: text sung in a naturalistic, almost speech-like way, over harmonies provided by a continuo group. The invention of recitative might not sound like the most exciting moment in the annals of human artistic endeavour, but its possibilities changed music fundamentally.

The main problem with 'monodic' (single-lined) recitative was that it could quickly get boring (literally, monotonous). Composers built variety of form on the new musical foundations: rhythmically free writing alternating with song-like passages (an early version of what later became the formal pairing of recitative and aria); dance patterns in songs (like Monteverdi's favourite quick-fire alternation of two groups of three rhythmic units with three groups of two, as in Orfeo's 'Vi Ricorda o bosch'ombrosi' in *L'Orfeo* (1607)); repeating patterns in the bass (a key resource throughout the Baroque for composers as diverse as Monteverdi, Purcell, Couperin, Pachelbel and Bach); brief hints of imitation between treble and bass; strophic and verse-based forms to structure a musical argument, like Penelope's repeated appeals to her lost husband in Monteverdi's melancholy Mediterranean masterpiece *Il ritorno d'Ulisse in Patria* of 1639–40. There are clear links here into the later ritornello principle. To all of this singers added a layer of fancy vocal icing called gorgia, a carefully categorised system of ornaments and embellishments. French and English singers called these elaborations *broderies* and graces. Harmonies, built over the continuo bass, could begin to include expressive dissonances unknown to the Renaissance.

These are some of the features of the seconda pratica or stile nuovo. Berardi tells us that the two 'practices', old and new, were presented in three different contexts: church, chamber and theatre.

Church music maintained aspects of both practices, sometimes in the same piece (for example, Monteverdi's late Mass for Four Voices of 1650). Conservative Rome liked the old-fashioned style, while republican Venice preferred the opportunities for show in big antiphons and other music for Vespers, often featuring the 'concertato' style, in which contrasting groups of instruments or voices alternate the same musical material over the basso continuo, like an echo. Some composers stand like signposts representing the geographical spread of style: Lodovico Viadana the old north Italy, Alessandro Grandi the new Venice, Felice Anerio reactionary Rome, his younger brother Giovanni the more progressive side of Roman musical thought, particularly oratorio. Architecture played a part: St Mark's provided the perfect stage set for the '*cori spezzati*', the separated choirs (of instruments as well as voices), used to rich and spacious effect (though certainly not invented) by Giovanni Gabrieli. In 1608 the English traveller Thomas Coryat attended a sacred musical ceremony in the Scuola Grande di San Rocco: 'This feast consisted principally of Musicke, which was both vocall and instrumental, so good, so delectable, so rare, so superexcellent, that it did even ravish and stupefie all those strangers that never heard the like.'[6] The Scuola Grande di San Rocco's marbled halls still provide a cavernous canvas for the ecstasies and agonies of Tintoretto at his most overwhelming, his sanguinary saints peering across the piazza at the hangar-like church next door, evocative venue of the ravishment of Coryat. He'd certainly heard nothing like it back in England.

Opera: Beginnings

Opera is a multimedia form. The librettist (or poet) was as big a draw as the composer (perhaps even more so), and a popular libretto like Giovanni Battista Guarini's *Il pastor fido* of 1590 could inspire many musical settings over decades, even centuries. Guarini's idealised fol-de-rol on the not terribly successful love lives of shepherds and their impregnable nymphs is an example of the influence of one of opera's key antecedents, the pastoral drama. Another influence was French-style ballet, introduced to Italy from a visit to Paris by Ottavio Rinuccini, the very first opera librettist. As with church music, Rome had its own traditions distinct from the northern cities – saints and sacred subjects featured on stage, together with comic characters from the commedia dell'arte in a remarkably accurate pre-echo of the gossipy servants and scallywags of opera buffa.

The most important precursor of opera was the intermedio, glitzy musical interludes originally performed between the acts of a spoken play: 'intermedio', or 'intermezzo', means something like 'between the halves' or 'in the middle'. What they didn't do was tell a story. The key innovation of opera was that it took the musical and theatrical elements of the intermedio (madrigals, monody, songs, dances, instrumental pieces) and married them to the narrative possibilities of a spoken play. Music could be made to carry the action, both physical and psychological. For a composer of genuine psychological insight and real theatrical flair, this was the moment. Opera as drama was born.

The First Opera Composers

In the prologue of the first great opera, Monteverdi's *L'Orfeo* of 1607, the singer declares '*Io la musica son*' ('I am Music'). The composers who brought the new musical world to life in the years leading up to Monteverdi's masterpiece were a talented and colourful group.

Giulio Caccini was a member of the Florentine Camerata and an influential singer, teacher, composer (or co-composer) of three operas (two called *Euridice*) and, most importantly, of monodic songs. His preface to *Le nuove musiche* of 1602 is a lengthy and detailed treatise on the technical and artistic features of the new singing style, known as bel canto, including practical things like how to avoid singing flat, which is the best instrument for accompanying a singer (the archlute), how to choose a key so as to avoid the feeble sound of falsetto, and how to absorb 'all the delicacies of this art'.[7] He repeatedly makes clear that his words of wisdom are for men and women equally, and praises the singing of his female family members. Notably, he gives detailed instructions about how to interpret the still-new system of figured bass. This is a repertoire which has only emerged in the last thirty years of the twentieth century, revealing the links between Caccini and other early opera composers, and the innovations of the 'stile rappresentativo', where the singer often *was* the character rather than describing mythical characters or places.

Caccini's daughter Francesca was, like her father, a celebrated

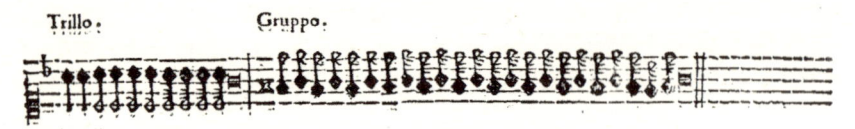

Examples of vocal ornamentation from Giulio Caccini's Le nuove musiche *(1602).*

singer and composer. Her substantial *Primo libro delle musiche* of 1618 contains some of the most exquisite and skilful song-writing of the period (including one ravishing little canzonetta with accompaniment for the ever-popular Spanish guitar). This is real singer's music. Her comedy ballet of 1625, *La Liberazione di Ruggiero*, is another opera on a much-used theme, in this case the magic island of the sorceress Alcina.

In addition to his musical accomplishments, her papa Giulio showed all the slippery skills of the backstairs schemer in the best sharpened stiletto tradition of Medici Florence. He leaked news of an illicit affair being carried on by a high-ranking married Medici lady, leading to her being murdered by her husband. He knocked the early oratorio composer Emilio de' Cavalieri off his perch as maestro at a big royal wedding in 1600. His rivalry with Jacopo Peri led him to rush his own version of *Euridice* into print before Peri's, and order his singers to have nothing to do with the rival show across town.

Peri has the distinction of having composed both the first and the first surviving opera. *Dafne* of 1598 (of which the music is now lost) used a libretto by fellow Florentine Ottavio Rinuccini (also set in a revised version three decades later by Heinrich Schütz, a setting which is also now lost). Peri's *Euridice* of 1600 survives in a typically handsome printed edition. His preface hymns the accomplishments both of his dedicatee Maria de' Medici and the ancient Greeks (in that order), and acknowledges the contribution of his contemporaries including (perhaps through gritted teeth) his rival Caccini. The music (some by other hands) is almost entirely monody – on paper, dry stuff to modern tastes. It needs its local circumstances of rich orchestration, vocal embellishment and lavish staging to come alive. Peri's gravestone describes him as '*Creatore del melodrama*', an appropriate (though anachronistic) portmanteau of the Greek words for 'song' and 'action'.[8]

Composers for Church and Chamber

Among church composers of the early Baroque, Lodovico Grossi da Viadana stands out for his (fairly minimal) use of figures to the bass line of his substantial collection of old-fashioned motet-style pieces, the *Cento Concerti Ecclesiastici* of 1602, an important staging post between the older 'organ score' and basso seguente of composers like Adriano Banchieri, which simply doubled and supported the voice parts, and a genuinely independent keyboard accompaniment. Alessandro Grandi in Venice and Ottavio Durante in Rome pioneered the introduction of the monodic solo singing style into church, complete with didactic essays explaining how, when and why to use expressive vocal effects like a crescendo *à la* Caccini.

The best keyboard composer of the early Italian Baroque was Girolamo Frescobaldi. This was an age when composers could begin to hold a reputation principally, or even solely, as keyboard virtuosi – Johann Jakob Froberger in Germany, Jan Pieterszoon Sweelinck in the Low Countries, John Bull in England (until he fled the country, pursued by debts and accusations of adultery). Frescobaldi was a true pioneer, combining deliciously experimental chromatic harmony with all sorts of formal innovations and a contrapuntal rigour which later led Bach to copy out the 100-plus pages of his *Fiori musicali* of 1635 in its entirety. Bach clearly recognised a kindred spirit, despite the distance of a hundred years and a very different religious denomination. Like Bach, Frescobaldi set out to adorn a given tune, used as a cantus firmus, for liturgical purposes. There are some strikingly proto-Bachian contrapuntal tricks in the *Fiori*, like the little fugue, complete with inverted subject and regular countersubject, wrapped around the plainsong melody of the 'Kyrie della Madonna'. The published *Fiori* is in full score, on four staves (because movable type, unlike manuscript, couldn't do stems-up and stems-down notes on the same stave), presenting the sort of sight-reader's brain bender which Bach ate for breakfast. At one point the player is instructed to make a five-part piece by playing the four written parts on the keyboard and singing a fifth part: the performer is given a snatch of melody and told to work out for himself where it fits, with the laconic note from the composer '*Intendami chi puo che m'intend' io*' ('Understand me if you can, so that I can understand myself'). Bach would have loved that.

The most important early Baroque composer before Monteverdi

was a Venetian who died a year before Monteverdi arrived in the city: Giovanni Gabrieli.

Born in the mid 1550s, Gabrieli was musically and personally close to his uncle Andrea, who may well have had a hand in his upbringing (many musicians of the age were raised by a musical relative from among their wider family). He travelled to Munich in his twenties to study with Lassus, a crucial influence. Back in Venice he held senior posts at the two grandest and most important musical establishments, St Mark's and the Scuola Grande di San Rocco, until illness began to limit his activities from around 1606. He died in 1612.

Gabrieli created some of the iconic noises of the first phase of the Baroque: big chordal blocks of sound echoing between groups of singers and players placed in various parts of some theatrical Venetian interior; small groups contrasting with larger, like a concerto; high-pitched groups alternating with low; single chords embellished with runs and scales, taking an almost tactile pleasure in the new freedom of functional harmony and the sheer joy of pure sound. He pioneered the use of dynamics, most famously in his *Sonata pian' e forte* of 1597, one of the first pieces to call for specific brass instruments. Our amazed English traveller Thomas Coryat recorded:

> for mine owne part I can say this, that I was for the time even rapt up with St Paul into the third heaven. Sometimes there sung sixteene or twenty men together, having their master or moderator to keepe them in order; and when they sung, the instrumentall musitians [sic] played also. Sometimes sixteene played together upon their instruments, ten Sagbuts, foure Cornets, and two Violdegambaes of an extraordinary greatness ... Those that played upon the treble viols, sung and played together, and sometimes two singular fellowes played together upon Theorboes, to which they sung also, who yielded admirable sweet musicke ...[9]

Coryat found the lute songs too quiet – an indication of the wide dynamic range on offer. The distance travelled from the smooth consistency of a Mass by Palestrina, barely a decade dead, could hardly be greater: Gabrieli's *In ecclesiis* of 1615 is a sonorous example.

Giovanni Gabrieli sits on the middle branches of a stylistic family tree leading from the big multi-choir pieces of his teacher Lassus and his uncle Andrea to his eventual successor Monteverdi and his pupils Hassler and, perhaps above all, Schütz. On his deathbed Gabrieli bequeathed Schütz his ring, handing his inheritance across the ages and across Europe.

Monteverdi

Claudio Monteverdi was (like many in this book) the son of a medical family. He was born in Cremona in 1567, and received his early training from the Palestrina disciple Marc'Antonio Ingegneri at the cathedral there. In the early 1590s he secured a prestigious court appointment in nearby Mantua, ruled with the required mixture of splendour, intrigue and immorality by the Gonzagas. He travelled with Duke Vincenzo, including on active military campaigns, getting as far north as Flanders in 1599. That year he married a singer (like many Baroque composers). In 1601 he became maestro in Mantua, having been overlooked in 1596, consolidating his reputation with a series of published collections of madrigals. Opera followed, including the imperishable *L'Orfeo* in 1607. That same year his wife Claudia died, leaving her husband with two young children – Monteverdi's letters of this period are full of the anguish, anger and desperate negotiations with in-laws and employers which such sad circumstances throw up in any age.

Musical history is marked with moments when a self-anointed new style goes head to head with an established, more conservative way of thinking. The result is usually a flurry of what Shakespeare called at the time 'words, words, mere words'.[10]

In 1600 Giovanni Artusi published *L'Artusi overo delle imperfettioni della moderna musica*, directly criticising Monteverdi. The debate swirled in the public presses. Contributors wrote under pen names like 'l'Ottuso Academico' ('The Obscure Academic') or anagrammatic pseudonyms like 'Alemanno Benelli' (Annibale Mellone). Giulio Cesare Monteverdi defended his brother with his spirited (if slightly incoherent) *Dichiaratione*. Monteverdi himself promised (but never delivered) a written rebuttal of Artusi and apologia for the stile nuovo. If anything, the controversy increased Monteverdi's standing (and sales). The most significant legacy of this learned little spat was that it clarified in words what was already obvious from the music: the two styles were different, and the new could not be explained in the terms of the old. As for Orfeo, there was no looking back.

L'Orfeo springs from the madrigal tradition. Monteverdi's dramatic innovations continued. The year 1608 saw a new opera for a high-end royal wedding, *Arianna*, featuring the almost obligatory 'wild rocky place in the midst of the waves'. The 4,000 people packed into the Mantuan court theatre to witness it heard

> the harmony of the instruments disposed behind the scene which always accompanied the voices, and as the mood of the music changed, so was the sound of the instruments varied; and seeing that it was acted both by men and women who were all excellent in the art of singing, every part succeeded more than wondrously, [and] in the lament which Ariadne sings on the rock when she has been abandoned by Theseus, which was acted with so much emotion and in so piteous a way that no one hearing it was left unmoved ...[11]

Of the music, only this lament survives in a later arrangement, a fine example of the expressive and dramatic capabilities of the new style.

In 1610 Monteverdi issued a collection which clearly indicated the parallel existence of the two practices, old and new, in church music. It included a Mass in the old-fashioned Roman style, alongside the glorious *Vespro della beata Vergine* (*Vespers for the Blessed Virgin*), joyously showing off every trick of the new, from grand chorus to seductive solo and back again. In 1613 he was head-hunted for the most prestigious job of all, continuing his shuffle east along the river Po and up the socio-musical scale to become, after staging a lavish demonstration of his abilities by way of an audition, maestro di cappella at St Mark's, Venice.

Like some other restless, creative minds, change and challenge seem to have invigorated Monteverdi (despite being robbed at knife point on the journey to Venice). He reorganised the substantial musical forces available to him, brought in Grandi as his deputy, kept up his professional contacts with Mantua and elsewhere, delivered a hugely demanding programme of services and ceremonies, sang, played, directed (alongside, among others, his brother and son) and composed. A fastidious and not terribly fast worker, he wrote letters full of fascinating tussles with librettists about aspects of the musical dramatist's art, and defensive negotiations with performers and commissioners about deadlines missed or delayed. Several projects remained uncompleted. Others are lost.

Venice remained unique, geographically and politically as well as architecturally. The outside world blew in like an unwelcome *sirocco* in 1630, when the distant effects of the Thirty Years' War finally crossed the lagoon, bringing the ubiquitous plague. A little later La Serenissima, diminished but not defeated, permitted its ageing maestro one final flourish. In 1637 the first public opera house opened. The following year a pair of talented opera composers, Francesco Manelli and Benedetto Ferrari, arrived from increasingly war-threatened Rome. The 70-year-old Monteverdi snapped them up for his St Mark's choir, but the real significance of this operatic revival was Monteverdi's own astonishing late flowering as an opera composer, in the form of two richly mature musical dramas, *Il ritorno d'Ulisse in Patria* (1640) and *L'incoronazione di Poppea* (1643). Another late opera has not survived.

In 1643 Monteverdi visited his former homes, the cities of Mantua and Cremona. He returned to Venice in the autumn, and died in November. He lies buried in a peaceful corner of the cavernous church of the Frari, resting place of many notable Venetians. On a visit to Venice in August 2018, I found his grave marked with a handful of carnations, as if Orfeo and his companions had just dropped in on their way back from their '*Care selve e piagge amate*' ('sweet forests and beloved meadows') to keep the grave of their maker '*sempre fiorita*' ('always adorned with flowers').[12]

Monteverdi is the best modern composer in this book. His madrigals, like Beethoven's string quartets, chart the progress of an entire creative career, taking an existing musical form to places a million miles from where it started, from cheery three-part canzonettas (some written for the celebrated three aristocratic singing ladies of Ferrara), through the abrupt change of emotional gear in the fifth book (1605), the revolutionary introduction of a separate instrumental continuo bass in the seventh book in 1619, to solo madrigals and the instrumentally accompanied concitato style, like mini operas. Like his contemporary Shakespeare at the other end of Europe, Monteverdi mined the human heart most deeply on stage. Words, form, style and technique combine so completely that they become one. For all the mercurial shifts of mood, it is the deeper emotions which dominate: the constancy of the love between Penelope and her hairy husband Ulysses; the unbeatable final duet of Nero and Poppea, a pair of thoroughly dislikeable lovers (Monteverdi may not actually have written this ravishing piece, which doesn't matter a bit: style and idea can flow through more than one musical mind and pair of hands, like the studio of a Renaissance painter). He was the most substantial of the first composers for the solo voice.

Like all Baroque composers, he was quickly forgotten after his death. His unique musical voice disappeared underground for almost 400 years before returning to the surface in the twentieth century, like Orfeo, lyre in hand, muse safely in tow.

The Late Seventeenth and Early Eighteenth Centuries: Opera and Oratorio

In the next phase of the Baroque, melodic writing for both voices and instruments took on a more lyrical character, exploring the possibilities of bel canto. In dramatic pieces, 'secco' ('dry') recitative (which carries the action) separated increasingly distinctly from aria (when people reflect on those actions). Keys and cadences became more functional, allowing for ubiquitous gestures like the melodic interval of the falling fourth to end a recit and affective harmonic alterations like the so-called 'Neapolitan' chord, which flattens the second degree of the scale. The slight arbitrariness of some earlier proto-tonal harmony took on a new symmetry and confidence. All of this can be seen blooming like the azaleas in the Piazza di Spagna in the tuneful music of mid-seventeenth-century Italians like Luigi Rossi, whose operas reached the heights of European fame, and Giacomo Carissimi, pioneer of the chamber cantata (amorous and humorous) and, most significantly, oratorio.

A fastidious north European lexicographer hinted at the ambiguity inherent in oratorio when he described it as 'a sort of spiritual opera … greatly used at Rome'.[13] Oratorios could be in either Latin or Italian, as if even they didn't quite know where they belonged – Carissimi's are all in Latin, featuring pictorial and expressive choruses alongside narrative monodic recitatives in pieces like *Jephte* (c.1648) and *Diluvium universale* (c.1650), colourful Old Testament stories which have appealed to composers of all styles and ages. A distinguishing feature of the Roman oratorio was the 'testo', or narrator, descendant of the old plainsong Passion narratives with brief 'turba' ('crowd') choruses. Sometimes the testo role could be taken by a small polyphonic group of singers.

The masked opera-goers of Venice continued to enjoy the liberation from the old courtly formalities offered by the public theatres after 1637. Like everything else in Venice, these were organisationally and geographically linked to their local parish and piazza (which is why many of the theatres carried the name of their local saint). The democratisation of the form clearly links into the theatrical themes and manner of later innovators like Carlo Goldoni and Lorenzo da Ponte, Venetians both (the more uptown Pietro Metastasio, by contrast, was a Roman).

The generation of opera composers who provide the chronological link between Monteverdi's Venice and that of Vivaldi include Antonio Cesti; Monteverdi's successor-but-one at St Mark's, Francesco Cavalli; and the man who missed out on succeeding Cavalli by one vote but got the job the next time round (thus becoming Cavalli's successor-but-one and Monteverdi's successor-but-three), Giovanni Legrenzi.

Cavalli wrote over forty operas between the late 1630s and the early 1670s, a unique record of changing times. He was a key figure in the evolution of the bel canto singing style. One modern writer has said that Cavalli 'all but invented the operatic aria'.[14] The lullaby in his *Ercole amante* of 1662 concentrates dramatic effect through the careful use of instrumental sound and early moves towards the da capo form, a central feature of the later repertoire; *Giasone* of 1649 sees him summoning the Furies alongside the full range of 'midnight assignations, misunderstood messages, stuttering servants, wisecracking subalterns, and a fair amount of sex',[15] and a lament with a creeping chromatic repeating bass figure known as a passacaglia or chaconne, which, with many other similar examples, provides a clear prototype for the immortal termination of Purcell's Dido, a few short decades in the future. Cavalli was Monteverdi's most important pupil and successor.

Many of Cavalli's later and most innovative operas were produced in Paris. Cesti, too, provides evidence of the international reach of the Italian model: his *Il pomo d'oro* was written for a noble wedding in Vienna in 1668, one of the most famously lavish productions in the gilded tradition of courtly splendour. His reputation also reached as far as London – Samuel Pepys (who had mixed feelings about Italian music) owned copies of some of his songs.

Some features familiar from the later world of Handel take their bow in these mid-century operas: 'ombra' ('shade') scenes summoning the soul of a lover or prophet, or depicting characters drifting drunkenly off to sleep by moonlight, usually to the sound of bassoons; arias with trumpet obligato for bellicose characters bent on revenge. Comedy began to feature in the previously serious world of opera following the arrival of a travelling troupe in Venice at carnival in 1637: even Monteverdi dabbled in comedy with *La finta pazza* (*The Fake Madwoman*), apparently unfinished, never performed, and now lost. A 1641 setting of the same libretto by Francesco Sacrati was a significant success. Among the innovations of operatic comedy, stammering patter songs, parodies and brief ensemble finales point the way to a future of Mozartian grace and fun.

The librettist of *La finta pazza* was Giulio Strozzi, a member of a notable Venetian family. Strozzi was illegitimate, adopted by his (probably biological) father. He in turn adopted his housekeeper's (and, most likely, his) daughter, Barbara. Barbara Strozzi grew up to be a talented, successful and prolific singer and composer, studying with Cavalli and publishing many volumes, unusually consisting almost entirely of secular music, much of it to texts by her father. Her music is beautifully vocal and enchantingly lyrical.

Her personal history is a testament not just to the prevailing democratic and dilettante spirit of Venice, but also to the role of music at this period as a passport into good society from sometimes unconventional beginnings: in different periods of the Baroque, Jean-Baptiste Lully, Samuel Pepys' houseboy Tom Edwards and Vivaldi's orphans at Venice's Ospedale della Pietà, as well as countless choirboys press-ganged from the provinces into service at various cathedrals and chapels royal, got an education and access to a place about halfway up society's top table directly as a result of their musical talent.

Cloister and Violin

Another place where a female composer could flourish (at least in Catholic countries) was in the cloister. There were several notable examples in seventeenth-century Italy. Chiara Margarita Cozzolani made skilful use of the full range of solo and choral sonorities in her stylish, accomplished sacred music. Her slightly younger contemporary (and near neighbour) Isabella Leonarda was a member of the convent of Sant'Orsola in Novara, near Milan, from the age of sixteen until her death in 1704, sixty-eight years later. She composed throughout her life: fine sacred music showing a thoroughly trained technique and expressive individual voice, and a remarkable series of instrumental works sharing many of the harmonic and contrapuntal characteristics of her much younger contemporary Arcangelo Corelli. She did not, perhaps, approach his perfection of melody, but outdid him in ambitious, multi-movement structures like her ten-section, 160-bar *Sonata da chiesa* no. 10, which has two interlocking refrains, one played three times and consisting of nothing but an F major chord, with violin figurations over the top. Almost all of what she calls '*questa mia Musicale Operetta*' bears a double dedication – to some well-placed noble or prelate, and to the Virgin Mary.[16]

In the age of the emerging mid-Baroque bel canto style it wasn't just singers who cultivated beautiful sound combined with an element of virtuosic display. Those virtues were enthusiastically borrowed by the most important instrument of the period: the violin. Certain cities played key roles: Cremona, home to the celebrated instrument-making Amati, Guarneri and Stradivari families; and Bologna, Modena and Venice, all of which hosted groups of composers, each city having its own local take on emerging forms and styles.

The 'sonata da chiesa', played as part of the liturgy with organ continuo, settled into a four-movement pattern, its sound gracefully matched to the spacious acoustics and airy interiors of the local *duomo*. The 'sonata da camera' could be looser in form, evolving alongside its sister the dance suite with its characteristic pairs of movements alternating speeds and time signatures: allemande and courante, sarabande and gigue. The gods of counterpoint remained objects of veneration: Tomaso Vitali (Bologna and Modena) regally informed the readers of his 1689 treatise *Artificii musicali* that 'he who cannot handle the most arcane contrapuntal arts in any way he chooses does not deserve the name of musician'. Giovanni Legrenzi (Bergamo, Ferrara and Venice) strikingly pre-echoed Bach in his distinctly modern use of tonic and dominant key areas and contrasting subject and countersubject, though not yet developed over long spans with Bach's limitless invention. (Bach studied, copied and arranged much Italian string music of this period: the influence is clear in his own concertos and in elements like fugue subjects based on repeated notes or string-crossing figures, like bow-strokes.)

Rome: Patrons and Protégés

It wasn't just Italy's sun-dappled cities which played a distinctive role in the development of the Baroque style. So did her aristocratic patrons. As so often, they were a characterful crew. Rome at this period found itself playing host to a succession of royals without a realm, some by choice, others less so (like the former James II of England and his factious family). Roman resident Queen Christina of Sweden was, in her later years, 'extream fat ... very masculine ... [with] ... a double Chin strew'd with some long Hairs of Beard ...'[17] She was also accomplished, opinionated, and a passionate supporter of the arts, particularly music and the theatre. One of her principal successors in the role of patron was Pietro Ottoboni, created cardinal in 1689 when his great-uncle became pope (as *cardinal nepote* or 'cardinal nephew', a well-established practice from which we get the English word 'nepotism'). The affable Ottoboni seems to have overseen every note of top-drawer music-making in turn-of-the-century Rome, while also finding time to father up to seventy illegitimate children (according to Montesquieu). He was not the only worldly cleric to play a key role in musical history (some good, some bad), in an age when a prelate could be little more than a prince with a prayer book.

One of Christina's most dazzling and dangerous talents was Alessandro Stradella. A pioneer of the emerging 'concerto grosso' form, Stradella was an embezzler and adulterer, attacked and left for dead by hired assassins as he left the convent in Turin where he had just married the ex-mistress of his ex-boss, a powerful Venetian nobleman. He survived, but met his fate in 1682 in the Piazza Banchi in Genoa, the victim of the glinting blade of another hired assassin and another jealous aristocrat. The wide influence of his many operas, cantatas, serenatas and instrumental music was rather overshadowed in the next generation by Vivaldi and Corelli, though some of his music was borrowed by Handel for *Israel in Egypt*. His life story was, appropriately, itself used as the basis for several operas through the nineteenth century.

Corelli and His Influence

Easily the most influential of Christina and Ottoboni's protégés was Arcangelo Corelli. His given name is appropriate – his music hovers like angel wings over the whole of the later Baroque.

Vespers and Vivaldi: The Catholic South 127

Born in provincial Fusignano in 1653, Corelli received his early musical training and experience in the nearby centre of all things violinistic, Bologna (the details remain sketchy). By his early twenties he was in Rome, where he was often referred to as 'Il Bolognese'. He found an honoured and lucrative niche among the cardinals and queens of musical Rome, and died rich and loved in 1713.

Remarkably for a prolific age, Corelli published just six collections of twelve pieces each (composers of the late Baroque liked grouping their pieces in sixes – Bach did it a lot). All Corelli's surviving music is instrumental, despite his immersion in oratorio and other forms as a violinist on the payroll of Cardinal Ottoboni and regular participant in his celebrated Monday concerts and Lenten oratorios at the Palazzo della Cancelleria (where Corelli lived in some style throughout his long residence in Rome). He concentrated almost exclusively on the trio sonata grouping of two violins and a basso continuo group of cello and keyboard: this unit forms the 'concertino', or solo group, in his concerti grossi, published much later than the sonatas but probably, like them, written before 1700.

Corelli's writing for the violin is characterised by purity, clarity and idiomatic figuration, not virtuosic display or elaborate ornamentation. So was his playing: the violinist and composer Francesco Geminiani commented to his contemporary Domenico Scarlatti on the 'nice management of his band, the uncommon accuracy of whose performance gave the concertos an amazing effect ... for Corelli regarded it as essential to the ensemble of a band, that their bows should all move exactly together, all up, or all down, so that at his rehearsals, which constantly preceded every public performance of one of his concertos, he would immediately stop the band if he discovered one irregular bow'.[18] His music sits at the moment at which the old order of modes finally emerged fully formed into the elegant new world of keys and perfect cadences. He often used fugal openings for his movements, sometimes not fully worked through as later composers would do (not unlike his older contemporary Buxtehude far away on the chilly northern fringes of Europe, though in a very different musical context): fugato rather than fugue. He loved sequential passages, particularly the mellifluous chains of suspensions over a chugging bass, imitated countless times, and aptly described by Francesco Gasparini as 'bindings and Dissonances so well regulated and resolved and so well interwoven with variety of

Themes, that it can well be said that he has discovered the perfection of ravishing Harmony'.[19] The eighteenth-century music historian Charles Burney discerned a certain limitation: 'Corelli's continual recourse to certain favourite passages betrays a want of *resource* ... All the varieties of Corelli's harmony, modulation and melody might perhaps be comprised in a narrow compass'[20] – which (entirely forgivably) misses the point that this very concentration of manner and idea is exactly Corelli's strength and achievement. His music achieves polished perfection on a small scale.

Very many composers benefited from Corelli's influence and example. One was a confident and talented young visitor from the across the Alps who sat alongside him in the second violins of Ottoboni's orchestra (and apparently once showed him how to reach a high A on his E string): George Frideric Handel.

Handel's Italian whirlwind of 1706–10, begun when he was just twenty-one, heralds the dawn of the fully mature Baroque. He went everywhere, from Venice to Naples via Rome and all points musical in between. He met everyone: patrons who paid him; singers who worked with him; composers whose music he liberally raided for his own later works. He went head to head with his exact contemporary Domenico Scarlatti in one of those public trials of improvisation and execution that were so popular with the musical elite of the time: an honourable draw, according to Handel's biographer John Mainwaring. He absorbed everything around him into his own copious compositional output: elegant Italian cantatas; dazzling (and difficult) psalm settings; a serenata about Acis and Galatea; an oratorio about Jesus Christ; and opera, including the successful *Agrippina* for Venice in 1709, whose audience cried out *'Viva il Caro Sassone!'* ('Long Live the Beloved Saxon!') even though he wasn't from Saxony (the source, again, is the not always reliable Mainwaring; but the story fits with the familiar noisy enthusiasm of audiences at the Italian opera where 'one hears nothing but a Thousand *Benissimo's* together').[21]

Musical style was becoming internationalised once again.

The Mid Eighteenth Century

Technically, the maturing of the system of tonality ('keys') allowed composers to project an intellectually satisfying tonal plan, or key structure, on to a contrapuntal texture, so that a fugue by Bach, for example, could pursue both the working-out of its theme and a carefully organised move away from and back to a home key in a fully integrated way. Much thought was given to ideal systems of tuning, or temperament: by the time Bach used the term 'well-tempered' in reference to works for the keyboard, or 'clavier', in the second decade of the eighteenth century it probably meant a system where the semitones were nearly, but not completely, alike. (This may be one reason why particular keys have definite musical and structural characteristics in his music.) The concerto principle embedded the idea of a ritornello alternating with more freely composed episodes using sequences like the ubiquitous 'cycle of fifths' (a pattern of chords built on a bass line moving down by the interval of a fifth in a regular rhythm), one of the most recognisable building blocks of the later Baroque style. Vocal writing became increasingly instrumental, a sort of reverse osmosis from the mid-Baroque bel canto period.

Opera: Seria and Buffa

To its audience, opera seria was more the child of its literary parent than its musical one. The poets of opera seria were the aristocrats of the page, wandering learnedly in the groves of Classical legend and ancient history. Principal among them were Apostolo Zeno and Pietro Metastasio. In their hands opera seria assumed a heroic, Classic dignity after the example of Racine. A celebrated libretto would be set many times, usually adapted in some way (English audiences sometimes heard shortened recitatives to make it easier for them to follow the translation in the printed word book which they'd purchased with their ticket). Often a libretto would be performed as individual musical items lifted from different operas by different composers.

Opera seria quickly became an international style with local features. In Naples, style and fashion was led by the da capo king Alessandro Scarlatti before he headed to Rome. From Rome he sent his young son Domenico ('an eagle whose wings have grown')[22] north to spread those wings in Florence and Venice, where he would have heard a small part of the extravagant operatic output of Vivaldi, Albinoni, and Antonio Lotti, who in turn carried the gospel of opera seria to Dresden, just as the Italianised Germans Johann Adolf Hasse and George Frideric Handel did to Hamburg and London. These operas opened with a sectional overture (or 'sinfonia') to gather the chatterati in from the lobbies and squares, and ended with a chorus of almost vanishing brevity, leaving room for a whole banquet of da capo arias in between, carefully distributed more or less equally in between the various principal singers. Recitatives with accompaniment for orchestra, rather than just continuo, became increasingly popular for their opportunities for acting: a striking example is Leonardo Vinci's 1726 setting of Metastasio's much-set *Didone abbandonata*, which actually ends with a recitative. Handel put this piece on in London (suitably altered by himself), and clearly relished the possibilities of accompanied recitative to convey changing mood and shifting psychological insight in his own works.

Opera buffa was about real, ordinary people, with a strong dash of the stock figures of the commedia dell'arte mixed in: the wisecracking manservant and the scheming chambermaid; the doddery old doctor and the maudlin matron. Their music is fast, funny, full of stuttering patter songs and quick-fire ensembles. Vinci's *Li zite 'ngalera* of 1722 is written in Neapolitan dialect. Pergolesi's *La serva padrona* of 1733 was conceived as an intermezzo for the interval of his own opera seria *Il prigioner superbo*. The familiar plot twists are all here: disguise, mistaken identity, fake marriage contracts, complications connected with class, status, money and sex, as well as, of course, a happy ending, usually involving the chance discovery of some important fact. All of this echoes happily through the century into the buffa universe of Salieri, Mozart, Paisiello (who composed his own version of *La serva padrona* in 1769) and Rossini.

The upmarket Venetian lawyer and composer Benedetto Marcello wickedly captured operatic mores in his *Il teatro alla moda* of 1720, in which he offered wittily satirical advice to everyone involved in making an opera, from scene-painters to 6-year-old page boys: modern librettists 'don't need to read the ancient poets because, after all, they never read you'; composers don't need to know the rules of good composition as long as they write 'un ben *lungo Passaggio v. g. Paaaa ... Impeee ... Coooo ... & c ...*'; he tells the conductor how to deal with a soprano who complains that the prima donna has a bigger part than she does (give her a cadenza to shut her up); and what an impresario can expect when a girl is brought along to audition by her mother, who won't stop talking in Venetian dialect ('*Ch'i compatissin mo Sgnouri, perch' in sta Nott' la Ragazza la n'hà mai psù durmir una gozza* ...' – she's feeling tired, poor dear), and will always knock ten years off her daughter's age: the Mrs Worthington of the Lido.

Vivaldi and the Concerto

The concerto was brought to its paradigm by a red-headed priest who couldn't celebrate Mass because of his asthma (not a happy complaint in clammy Venice): Antonio Vivaldi. Vivaldi's work built on the innovations of a series of important regional antecedents, notably Corelli in Rome and Giuseppe Torelli in Bologna. Torelli helped establish the standard three-movement fast–slow–fast form, set up the distinctive rivalry of equals between solo and tutti, and the distinction between the orchestral concerto grosso and the solo concerto. Further afield, the much-travelled German composer and organist Georg Muffat did much to increase the internationalisation of the new string style, professionalising things like bowing marks. In Vivaldi's own generation, Benedetto Marcello and Tomaso Albinoni pioneered the writing of concertos for solo wind instruments, notable the oboe. Francesco Geminiani travelled and taught widely, finding an unexpected outpost of Italy among the genteel coal merchants of Newcastle-upon-Tyne through the concertos and sonatas of his pupil, the English organist, concert promoter and Italophile composer Charles Avison. Treatises chart the still-new idea of idiomatic music for particular instruments, codifying and explaining things like ornamentation and the use of up bow and down bow signs: the rule of the down bow lies behind Baroque playing of today.

German composers employed the concerto form according to their own needs and inclinations: Handel in his Twelve Grand Concertos, Opus 6, first published in 1739, and, later, the organ concertos he composed for himself to play in the intervals of oratorios; Telemann (like Vivaldi) in works for pretty much every possible solo instrument and combination; Bach (as always) taking the Italian model as the springboard for his own infinite invention. The German violinist and composer Johann Georg Pisendel led a talented group of Saxon players and composers with impeccable Italian taste. The final flourish of the Baroque concerto was an injection of infernal virtuosity under the flashing fingers of Pietro Locatelli and the proto-Classical elegance of Giuseppe Tartini: the sound and manner of the later galant style lurk within, waiting to be born.

A page from Francesco Geminiani's The Art of Playing on the Violin *(1751).*

Vivaldi is best known today for his almost 500 concertos, a little under half of them for violin. Their sound world is unmistakable: tight, well-argued ideas in the fast movements; beautiful, lyrical legato writing known as cantilena (literally, 'lullabies') in the slow; a limitless resort to his ever-cheerful cycle of fifths in the episodes; a clear if undemanding sense of form and key structure. Many of the solo parts immortalise the talents of the generations of Chiarettas and Anna Marias who passed under his professional care as music scholars at the Ospedale della Pietà for female orphans, a short walk down the Riva degli Schiavoni from Monteverdi's stamping ground of a hundred years before. Charles de Brosses was not alone in pointing out the extramusical attractions of Sunday service at the Pietà: 'They sing like angels ... there is no instrument so large as to frighten them ... there is nothing so agreeable as to see a young and pretty nun, in white robes with a bouquet of pomegranate flowers behind her ear, conduct the orchestra.'[23] Like everything else in Venice, the Ospedale was linked with its coolly painted chapel (later the parish church) peering palely across the bustling waterfront at its reflection, San Giorgio Maggiore. Vivaldi wrote a lot of church music: for the Pietà, where all the voice parts were taken by the girls, including 'Paulina dal tenor' and 'Anneta dal Basso'; and for public places like St Mark's, where all the parts were sung by adult men, including castrati. It brims with tuneful, operatic solos, skilful orchestration and some perhaps surprisingly plangent harmonies (the expressive 'Et in terra pax' from his famous 1715 setting of *Gloria in excelsis Deo*, RV 589, and indeed the equivalent movement from his other extant setting, RV 588, composed at around the same time, moves through the keys like a page from a treatise). It is no disrespect to point out that as a contrapuntalist he was no Bach: he didn't need to be.

Vivaldi and Opera

The vast majority of the vast number of Baroque operas have not found an audience beyond the clatter and chatter of their first season crowds at London's Covent Garden or Haymarket theatres, the Goose Market in Hamburg or the Teatro San Bartolomeo in Naples: there are just too many of them. Vivaldi wrote (or had a hand in) over forty operas, including one written in just five days for Carnival 1719. He enjoyed a starry, if fluctuating, reputation as an opera composer: a visitor in 1715 admired Vivaldi's violin solo more than the opera it featured in at the Teatro Sant'Angelo (some of which, at least, was probably by Vivaldi), and even his friend, the playwright Carlo Goldoni, later described him as 'an excellent violin player and mediocre composer'.[24] But his operas are full of expressive and thrillingly virtuosic vocal writing, like the 'Weeping Nightingales' aria in *La Candace* (written for Carnival 1720) or *'Agitata de due venti'* from *Griselda* (1735): the divas of Vivaldi's day earned the cries of *'Ah cara! mi Butto, mi Butto'* ('Dearest, I throw myself at your feet') from the boxes.[25]

Vivaldi had a close personal relationship with the contralto Anna Girò, whom Goldoni described as *'bella e graziosa'* and, though weak of voice, a good actress.[26] Naturally, as a priest Vivaldi had to bat away accusations that his relationship with Anna (who, along with her sister, appears to have lived with him) was anything more than entirely professional.

Like all successful careers, Vivaldi's represents the happy coincidence of circumstance and talent. Venice suited him. Music poured from him to populate its printing houses, choir galleries, orchestras, opera stage and schoolrooms. His influence was considerable: Handel borrowed from him; Bach arranged him; everybody imitated him. He published widely, often through the celebrated Dutch firm of Estienne Roger: collections like *L'estro armonico* of 1711 carried his reputation far. At the same time, he played to his market with Handelian wile, telling an English visitor in 1733 that he had 'resolved not to publish any more concertos, because he says it prevents his selling his compositions in MSS which he thinks will turn more to account'.[27] He travelled, sniffing out high-end patronage (and boosting his marketability back home) with the best. He met his end on a visit to Vienna in 1741, and was buried, like Mozart exactly half a century later, with the minimum of expense in a now-vanished municipal graveyard.

The wheezy red-haired priest deserves his enduring if slightly lop-sided popularity. Vivaldi was not perhaps the most intellectual of composers, but he was certainly among the most stylish, fecund and melodious of the great masters of the Baroque.

Domenico Scarlatti

Our Grand Tour through the Italian Baroque ends with one of the most remarkable and, in many ways, one of the strangest stories in this book.

Domenico Scarlatti was born in 1685, the son of a celebrated, able, supportive but dominant father, the opera composer Alessandro Scarlatti. To begin with, young Mimo, as he was known, pursued a successful, if conventional career trailing on his famous father's coat-tails. As a young man in Rome he joined the Arcadian music parties staged by the principal priests and patrons at their palaces, which they referred to as huts, where they dressed up as shepherds, gave each other nicknames and sat around on the grass improvising Elysian canzonettas. In 1709 the younger Scarlatti succeeded his father as maestro di cappella to the latest realmless Roman royal, the quarrelsome Maria Casimira of Poland – a sort of B-list Christina of Sweden – for whom he wrote operas for the theatre in her palace on the Piazza della Trinità dei Monti. From around 1715 he was on the payroll of the Cappella Giulia, the papal choir at the Vatican. He began his career there with a cantata for Christmas Eve (the ceremony for which Corelli had very probably written his beautiful *Christmas Concerto* a couple of decades earlier) and wrote liturgical music in both the old mock-Palestrina prima pratica style and the highly expressive new manner, including a fine ten-part *Stabat Mater*.

The year 1714 saw a new job with the Portuguese ambassador, and by the end of the decade Scarlatti was in Lisbon in the service of the splendid (and solvent) royal court, one of the 'New and Excellent Musicians which His Majesty … had brought from Rome', as the *Gazeta de Lisboa* reported in 1722.[28] One of his duties was acting as tutor to the Princess Maria Barbara, later praised by the celebrated contrapuntal pedagogue Padre Martini (no mean critic) for her 'intimate knowledge of music and its profoundest artifices'[29] (though the British ambassador was less impressed, saying she had a 'large mouth, thick lips, high cheek bones and small eyes').[30] It was an important relationship: in her will Maria Barbara bequeathed a ring and two thousand doubloons to 'dn. Domingo Escarlati, my music-master, who has followed me with great diligence and loyalty' (though in fact she briefly outlived him).[31]

So far, so conventional. Scarlatti's modern biographer and interpreter Ralph Kirkpatrick dates the ending of a sort of second adult adolescence and the onset of full artistic maturity to the death of his father in October 1725.

In 1728, at the age of forty-three, he married 16-year-old Maria Catalina Gentili. The following year brought another wedding of lasting significance: the Portuguese royal family allied itself to its gloomy Spanish neighbour twice over when Maria Barbara of Portugal married Crown Prince Fernando of Spain and Crown Prince José of Portugal married the Spanish Infanta in a grand double wedding. Much symbolism accompanied the simultaneous shufflings across the border in a specially built pavilion over the river Caya, reached by the ponderous royal retinues in deep snow, marked with 'a fine Consort of Music perform'd by the Musicians of both the Kings' Chapels'.[32]

Scarlatti and his new wife followed Maria Barbara and her new husband to Spain and into the weird world of her new father-in-law, King Felipe V. Music was her principal solace. She needed one.

Felipe suffered cruelly from what the eighteenth century described as melancholy. He slept all day, dined at three in the morning, would not allow his hair to be cut or his clothes changed, and connected with his court only through his confessor and his queen, Isabel Farnese, who (fortunately for Spain) was a loyal, capable, determined and patient surrogate. In 1737 the British ambassador Sir William Cox reported that 'The queen is endeavouring to look out for diversion for the King, who has a natural aversion for music.'[33] Despite his aversion, the queen sought 'diversion' by engaging the services of the celebrated castrato Carlo Broschi, known universally as Farinelli, who had captivated audiences from Venice to Vienna and from London to Versailles, to sing to the bed-ridden king from an adjoining room. And 'from that moment,' says Sir William, 'his disorder took a favourable turn'.[34] Farinelli was put on a substantial pension to give up singing in public, run the royal opera company by day and sing to the king by night – which he did for ten years, apparently performing the same four arias every night. In his day job he brought the opera to perhaps the highest pitch of magnificence of any eighteenth-century outfit, calling on contacts from a lifetime on the starriest stages of Europe, and corresponding regularly with Metastasio about aspects of their art. He supervised other musical events, including a celebrated series of concerts on boats. He was first in Maria Barbara's favour, and, as Burney remarked, incapable of inspiring jealousy among his peers.

Scarlatti's routine involved travelling with the court round its annual circuit of palaces and estates, soaking up those distinctively morbid and fiery Spanish moods from Moorish ceilings and Mediterranean mountains as he went. Like most of the court, he set up home in Madrid, where he and Maria brought up their growing family. In 1738 he was admitted to a Portuguese order of knighthood. In February 1739 he published his *Essercizi per Gravicembalo*, handsomely engraved in London, with the usual gushing dedication to the king of Portugal and a much shorter and more revealing note to the 'Reader, Whether you be Dilettante or Professor, in these compositions do not expect any profound Learning, but rather an ingenious Jesting with Art ... Perhaps they will be agreeable to you ... Show yourself then more human than critical, and thereby increase your own Delight.'[35] Now aged well into his fifties, the whimsical, mercurial, endlessly inventive and entirely individual Scarlatti of the sonatas began to appear.

Scarlatti's wife Maria died in 1739, and some time between 1740 and 1742 he married for a second time, creating a bilingual, tri-generational household. Parallels with the contemporaneous Bachs diverge in one notable and perhaps surprising respect: none of Scarlatti's nine children became musicians. Was there perhaps a residue of not wishing to revisit the pressure imposed on him by his own father?

In 1746 poor, troubled Felipe V died. Fernando and Maria Barbara become king and queen, presiding over a court full of music, skilfully steered by Farinelli (though sadly Fernando did not escape the hereditary shadow of his father's afflictions). The year 1755 brought news of the catastrophic earthquake in Lisbon, which destroyed much of Portugal's proud musical heritage and sent many of her musicians into Spain. Scarlatti himself died in 1757, leaving his family seemingly well provided for (despite Burney telling us that Farinelli told him that Scarlatti had been 'addicted to play [gambling]').[36]

Apart from a few more or less predictable early pieces, all of Scarlatti's keyboard works come after the *Essercizi* of 1739. The vast majority, and the most fully mature, date from the last few years of his life, his late sixties and early seventies. They are among the most extraordinary and individual achievements in all music. They represent a synthesis of every aspect of his character and long life, from the piping of Neapolitan shepherd boys and the bravura of an operatic prima donna to the morbid piety and nasal chanting of Spanish clerics and choristers. Andalusian scales feature. Dance styles, particularly the rhythms of the seguidilla bolero, permeate many of the sonatas. They mine the depths of keyboard technique, including much hand-crossing and rapidly repeated notes. Harmony and dissonance are treated with extraordinary boldness. There is an endless melodic inventiveness which belongs to both the Baroque and the Classical, and to neither. The form itself is unique: there is simply no such thing as the single-movement keyboard sonata before or after Scarlatti (though there are stylistic parallels in the cosmopolitan but transitional works of his short-lived contemporary and pupil, the Portuguese Carlos Seixas).

After his death Scarlatti's reputation fared a little better than those of some of his peers, perhaps because keyboard music was easy to print and distribute. He found some notable admirers in England, including the eccentric Irish organist Thomas Roseingrave, the Newcastle-based composer Charles Avison, and the wealthy patron and collector Lord Fitzwilliam. He is often spoken of today alongside Bach and Handel as part of the great triumvirate born in 1685, but he is less familiar than either of them, and in some ways he doesn't really belong in their company. For most of his life he was, in truth, a rather ordinary Baroque composer. His unique contribution came in the astonishing late outpouring of keyboard music. Like Haydn a little later, he found his own way between two musical worlds by daily devotion to his art in aristocratic solitude, away from the demands and distractions of what anybody else did or thought.

The Spanish Baroque

Scarlatti and Farinelli stand emblematic of the Italian dominance of the Iberian Baroque. But, as elsewhere in Europe, native talents gave the imported example of their Mediterranean neighbour a distinctive accent.

The zarzuela is a sort of theatrical tapas, which mixes spoken scenes with operatic and popular music and dance. Juan Hidalgo de Polanca's *El Laurel de Apolo*, performed at the Prado in Madrid in 1657, takes Classical myth as its starting point, Italian-style. Sebastián Durón carried the banner into the eighteenth century until he backed the wrong monarch in the War of Spanish Succession, when his status as leading composer for church and stage (and his job at court) went to Antonio de Literes, whose stage works include his 1708 take on the love lives of a familiar pair of rustics, known in Spanish as *Azis y Galatea*.

Meanwhile, Joan Cererols wrote old-fashioned church music in the jagged fastness of the monastery of Montserrat, near Barcelona. Montserrat maintains its fine musical tradition to this day in the daily throaty chanting of its choir. Among many other musicians schooled within its walls was a former choirboy who became the most important Spanish composer of the eighteenth century, Padre Antonio Soler. Soler bridges several divides. His keyboard sonatas are flashy, unpredictable and transitional, clearly aligned with the more experimental side of Scarlatti (who may well have been his teacher) and foreigners like C. P. E. Bach. He wrote chamber music for strings, at the same time as Haydn was doing so in distant Austria-Hungary. His brilliant concertos for two organs were written for himself and his gifted royal pupil, the Infante Don Gabriel de Borbón, possibly to play on the two organs in the chapel of the Escorial where he worked (though some modern performers have found the instruments too far apart). He published a long and hugely detailed theoretical treatise called *Llave de la Modulación* (*Key to Modulation*) in 1762, full of mathematical detail about the relationships of intervals and practical advice about how to get from one key to any other (his own Sonata No. 90 in F Sharp Major does pretty much exactly that). Perhaps most fun, and most unexpected from a serious-minded monk, are his Christmas villancicos.

The villancico was a popular Iberian musical and poetic form, with words in the vernacular and music derived from traditional song and dance types, from the late Medieval through to the Classical period. Soler developed the villancico from its basic Renaissance stanza-and-refrain poetic model into something approaching a mini cantata. He then filled it with graceful, Rococo-style solo vocal writing, like a pre-echo of Mozart, and gleefully dramatic episodes like a storm at sea and a splendid depiction of a put-upon choirmaster whose Christmas offering would not be ready because the choirboys kept misbehaving in rehearsal, all vividly captured in music.

At its best, Spanish art music embraces the distinctive sounds of its folk heritage: stamping dance rhythms and the echo of instruments like Pyrenean bagpipes and, of course, the guitar and its ancestor the vihuela. Its organs snarl and spit. Spain's strong regional and linguistic identities remain in forms like the tonadilla, a type of satirical musical skit, and the sainete ('farce' or 'titbit' – a short comic opera designed to be played between the acts of a more serious entertainment, like its cousin the intermezzo).

A fabulous synthesis of all these influences emerged in the New World (particularly, though not exclusively, in Mexico), in the wonderfully colourful sacred music of Juan Gutiérrez de Padilla, Ignacio de Jerusalem and Manuel de Zumaya, who freely mixed the stile nuovo and antico with percussive Mexican rhythms and language, daubing the proud face of the European Baroque with a dash of Latin fire like the florid facades of the churches overlooking the squares in Puebla and Oaxaca.

7

VIOLINS AND VERSAILLES: FRANCE

'Song is a collection of sounds arranged according to rules set down by musicians, through which the passions of the soul are expressed.'[1]

So wrote the French polymath Marin Mersenne in his treatise *Harmonie universelle* of 1636. The achingly nuanced debate running through the French Baroque was exactly how those sounds should be arranged to express the passions, and whether the rules should follow the fashionable Italian example. The answer was often a formidable 'Non'.

In France, as in England, the first phase of the Italian Baroque found little echo. Another parallel with England (though in very different circumstances) was that political upheaval in the mid seventeenth century left the monarchy, rather unexpectedly, dominant and centralised, and thus able to indulge in (and pay for) art on a grand scale.

The principal art of the absolutist French court was the art of living. Philosophically, this was linked to the emerging Enlightenment idea of the self. The playwright Pierre Corneille wrote:

Je suis maître de moi, comme de l'univers.
Je le suis, je veux l'être[2]

[I am master of myself, as of the universe.
I am that which I desire to be]

High society became a sort of permanent game of open-air chess, designed to contain and circumscribe the passions within manicured walkways and elegant codes of behaviour. Art, nature and religion fitted into this system. The English traveller Thomas Coryat noted an early example of music and nature tamed and harmonised in the gardens of the Tuileries, where 'there is an exceeding fine Eccho. For I heard a certaine French man who sung very melodiously with curious quavers, sing with such admirable art, that upon the resounding of the Eccho there seemed three to sound together'.[3] The dramatists of the era explored the tension between high ideals and what real people actually did: Corneille and Racine as tragedy, Molière as farce. These two approaches found their analogues in, respectively, opera seria and opera buffa: it is no coincidence that many of Lully and Molière's comedies centre around a clash between the code and individual will: *Le Mariage forcé* (Marriage Compelled), *Le Bourgeois gentilhomme* (*The Bourgeois Gentleman*).

Of course, there was a strong element of fakery in the ultra-mannered *'galanterie'* of the nobs and fops satirised by Molière in 1659 as *Les Précieuses ridicules*, worrying about the shade of their pomade and whether a pet goose goes with their outfit. One courtier published a *Grand Dictionnaire des Prétieuses* in 1660. The satirist Jean de La Bruyère described the court's claims to accomplishment: 'they call themselves connoisseurs of music ... but have not two thumb's-breadths of profundity: if you push them, you will find nothing but *tuf* [a word which neither permits nor needs translation]'.[4]

Stylisation is everywhere in the French Baroque, from its ongoing love affair with the ballet to a whole universe of mannered little instrumental pieces depicting everything from the current passions and tastes to landscapes, grottoes, food and the weather (though not everyone went as far as Marin Marais in describing a bladder stone operation in a gamba sonata).

All of this revolved around the king, like the world round the sun. The multi-authored *Ballet Royal de la Nuit* of 1653 provided the name *Le Roi Soleil*, harnessing dance and music to political power. Louis XIV's tastes, and those of his ministers and mistresses, formed the musical law. For the high-end musician, this did not necessarily mean direct employment at court, as in England (though it might, for example, be as a member of the celebrated Vingt-quatre Violons du Roi or the Chapelle Royale), but it did require acquisition of the various patents, pensions and *privilèges du Roi* which permitted the publication of music, hiring of orchestras, purchase of sets and costumes and staging of shows (and paying a proportion of the proceeds back to the king in tax). These were the slippery arts by which the composer courtier Lully and the playwright Molière (like Shakespeare, a professional actor manager) prospered: both were very good at it.

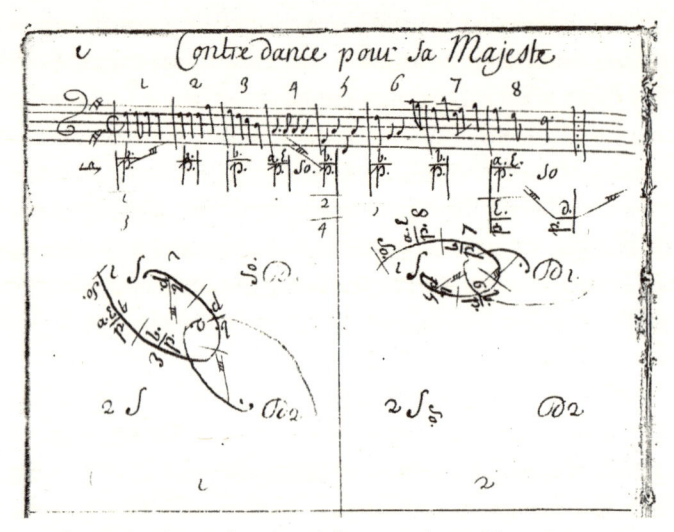

Choreographer's shorthand for steps danced by Louis XIV.

Like everywhere else in Europe, France had its self-conscious debates about the *Parallèle des anciens et des modernes*, as the fairy tale writer Charles Perrault called it:⁵ the chorus of the *tragédie lyrique* inherited its role as commentator from the ancient Greeks, just like Italian monody. An admiring but defensive attitude to Italian music was a constant, too: 'their Majesties love Italian music and verse more than French,' claimed Louis XIV's first First Minister Mazarin, an Italian (like Lully), who brought star opera composers Rossi and Cavalli to Paris.⁶ Later, in around 1688, François Couperin decided to burnish his credentials by publishing some fashionably Italianate trio sonatas. Like everyone else, he was 'charmed by those of signor Corelli', and in order to maximise the marketability of his new pieces he rearranged the letters of his surname into an Italianised anagram (but regrettably doesn't tell us how: Puceroni? Repucino?), earning 'great applause' under his *'nom italianisé'*.⁷ Companies of Italian players were well known in France, injecting the characters and manner of the commedia dell'arte firmly into the French comedy tradition. The writer Jean-Laurent Le Cerf de la Viéville consciously accentuated the deliberate distancing of the two national traditions in his lengthy *Comparaison de la musique italienne et de la musique française* of 1704, unleashing one of those intellectual tussles about musical style which the musically educated Baroque so much enjoyed.

The greater seriousness of Louis XIV's later years contributed to a shift of musical gravity from the court to the cosmopolitan life of Paris and its public opera houses: the aristocrat Madame de Sévigné described Lully's *Atys* of 1676 as 'the opera of the king', while *Phaëton*, performed in the public theatre in 1683, was 'the opera of the people'.[8] The great names of the French late Baroque, Jean-Philippe Rameau and Louis Marchand, lived in a more public world of salons, concerts and pamphlets, rather than the clipped absurdities of Versailles. The Paris of Gluck, J. C. Bach and the young Mozart is beginning to come into sight.

Lully

Jean-Baptiste Lully was born Giovanni Battista Lulli in Florence in 1632, the son of a miller (he later claimed that his father was a *gentilhomme Florentin*, which was a lie). His route to France was typical of his unconventional and opportunistic career: aged around twelve he was entertaining a crowd in the street by playing the violin dressed as Harlequin when he was spotted by a visiting French nobleman who was looking for a houseboy to help his rich niece learn Italian. Thus, a couple of years later, young Lulli entered the service of Mademoiselle de Montpensier, one of the greatest heiresses in history. His musical talent and natural showmanship flourished under her protection until *la grande Mademoiselle* found herself on the wrong side of the insurrection known as the Fronde in the early 1650s: Lulli, typically, came up smelling of roses as royal composer, indispensable favourite of the young Louis XIV and director of the king's personal band Les Petits Violons (whom he drilled with parade-ground precision, like Corelli in Rome, in contrast to what he saw as the flabby and over-elaborate ornamentations of the famous Vingt-quatre Violons du Roi). In the early 1660s, with the king's majority, he became Surintendant de la musique de la chambre du roi, took part in operas by visiting star composer Cavalli, married the daughter of the well-placed court singer Michel Lambert, and became a French citizen, formally adopting the French version of his name.

He also began a fruitful collaboration with the popular and successful actor manager Jean-Baptiste Poquelin, known as Molière (leading to Madame de Sévigné's nickname for them, *'les deux Baptistes'*). Their collaborations included the unmistakably French genre known as the comédie ballet, in which both Baptistes would often appear. As with the later opéra comique, *comédie* refers to a play acted by troupes known as *comédiens*, with musical numbers and spoken text rather than anything exclusively funny or comic: plays with *pliés*, plenty of dancing by a large troupe of entirely superfluous cooks and fiddlers in interludes between the scenes, with sometimes a more or less tenuous link to the actual plot (like the foppish dancing master in *Le Bourgeois gentilhomme* (1670)).

Like its earlier Italian cousin, the French tradition of music for the stage drew on a mixture of earlier influences: *al fresco* entertainments; the huge but rather bloodless repertoire of songs known as *airs de cour*; and the *ballet de cour*, a grand show containing choruses and recits as well as dances, often the work of more than one composer. The Lully/Molière shows are full of wit, grace and a distinctively French vocal style, much less clearly delineated by mood and formal divisions like recit and aria than their Italian bel canto cousins, partly as a result of the less heavily stressed nature of the French language. Mersenne explained the difference with Gallic suavity: 'the accents of passion are often lacking in French song because our music charms the ear without exciting the passions'.[9] Vocal ornaments were known as broderies ('embroidery'): less acrobatic than the Italian gorgia.

Not untypically, the ambitious and scheming Lully stage-managed a falling-out with Molière (who turned instead to the church composer Marc-Antoine Charpentier for his 1673 play *Le Malade imaginaire*). Opera took over, and Lully made sure he was centre stage by securing an exclusive *privilège du roi* in 1672 which ousted Pierre Perrin from the Académie d'Opéra and replaced it with the Académie Royale de Musique. Another casualty of the final rout of the Mazarin-inspired Italian faction was Robert Cambert (who in 1671 wrote the first opera to a French libretto, the enormously successful *Pomone*), who flounced off to the Frenchified court of Charles II in England, where he met his end in unexplained circumstances in 1677.

The second great phase of Lully's career as a stage composer effectively created French opera, in the serious, Classical form derived from Racine and Corneille known as tragédie lyrique, in collaboration with the poet Philippe Quinault.

French opera has a number of distinctive features, some shared with (or imitated by) other national styles. Stage machines grumbled gloriously, once bringing the entire royal family down from the heavens and back up again. Lully played a key role in the development of the overture, codifying it into a grand, slow opening section in dotted rhythms, followed by a fast fugue, often in triple time, characteristics of what later became known as the 'French overture'. There are magic scenes, pastoral episodes, a strictly limited use of the emerging principles of da capo and motto aria, and choruses more on the scale of the oratorios of Carissimi than the operas of Cesti, Cavalli and Rossi. Orchestration uses the fat sound of five-part strings (typically one violin line, three viola parts and a bass line played by cello and 'contrebasse', or double bass). One of Lully's most impressive trademarks is the great, rolling chaconne, with its repeated melodic figure in the bass: longer but less harmonically adventurous than those of his young English admirer Henry Purcell. The music, like its composer, often dances: French audiences always demanded ballet with their operas.

Évrard Titon du Tillet described Lully as *'Prince des Musiciens François ... l'inventeur de cette belle et grand Musique Françoise'*.[10] He also played the necessary power games with ruthless self-interest, and sometimes in a deeply unattractive way: a liaison with a young page boy called Brunet ended with the poor lad being incarcerated in a prison reserved for wives, children, foreigners and priests.[11] The writer Jean de La Fontaine compared Lully to a wolf: 'You don't yet know this Florentine;/ He's depraved, a lout/ who devours everything.'[12]

Other, more conscientious modern writers have pointed out that all this slagging-off was pretty standard, and that in his complex and Machiavellian dealings with Molière and others Lully was only doing what everybody else did, and indeed what the court required. He was certainly very good at it, owning (and building) several large houses in Paris, including the palatial Hôtel de Lully, still standing on the rue Sainte-Anne. Not bad for an orphaned Florentine fiddler.

His death remains one of the most famous in musical history. In 1686 Louis XIV was operated on for an anal fistula. To mark the king's recovery, Lully staged a performance of his ceremonial Te Deum at the society church of Saint-Honoré in January 1687. He conducted by beating time on the floor with a long, heavy baton, and inadvertently struck his own foot. The wound became infected. Doctors advised amputation, but Lully refused, allegedly because it would bring an end to his dancing days. Gangrene set in. Lully arranged his affairs, died in March, and was buried at the Madeleine with the sort of pomp and attention that had attended all the stages and ceremonies of his

146 *Five Straight Lines*

a) Argenore (1740) by Wilhelmine of Bayreuth

Martesia (soprano): Un cer-to freddo o-ro-re tut-to mi ge-la il sangue

b) Isis (1677) by Jean-Baptiste Lully

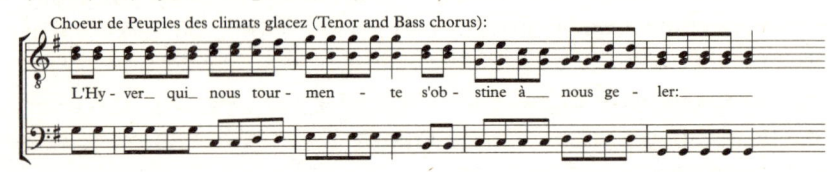

Choeur de Peuples des climats glacez (Tenor and Bass chorus): L'Hy-ver qui nous tour-men-te s'ob-stine à nous ge-ler:

c) King Arthur (1691) by Henry Purcell

Cold Genius (bass): What power art thou, who from be-low Hast made me rise, un-wil-ling-ly and slow From beds of e-ver-last-ing snow!

Musical gestures shared across the Baroque: shivering strings and trembling voices conjure up the cold in music by a German composer writing in Italian, an Italian-born composer based in France, and an English composer.

life as one of Louis' leading and most valued courtiers. His widow inherited a colossal fortune, and all three of his sons went on to hold his old job as '*Surintendant*' of the royal music.

Many leading figures of the musical Baroque were famous in their own day for something other than composition, at least to begin with: Bach and Vivaldi as performers, Rameau as a theorist. Lully's early fame was on stage. We should picture him acting alongside Molière as one half of '*les deux Baptistes*': as the young trickster Cléonte in *Le Bourgeois gentilhomme*; pretending to make Molière a gentleman while disguised as the Turkish Mamamouchi; or as one of a pair of Italian doctors attempting to give the playwright (as Monsieur Pourceaugnac) a purge. We should try to see him dancing a minuet with *Le Roi Soleil* at the end of a long and stately *ballet de cour*, a formalised display of status and power, ignoring the jealous flutterings of fans from the mistresses and monsignors ranged around the walls of the Galerie des Glaces.

Today, Lully's operas can test our ability to accept the stylisations of a previous age. But there is grace and beauty here in abundance. English ears can find themselves struck by the extent and depth of his influence on Henry Purcell, no doubt transmitted partly by Channel-hoppers from both shores like the ill-fated Robert Cambert and the Paris-educated Englishman Pelham Humfrey, Purcell's teacher – some bars sound like a direct copy from one composer to the other. Maybe, in the end, Purcell's ground basses are more flexible, his harmony richer and more expressive. But it wouldn't have happened without the vivid, theatrical, fascinating and dangerous example of Lully.

Church Music and Charpentier

Other forms played a definite second fiddle to the all-conquering opera during the French Baroque. But church music managed a distinctive contribution, often with a notable dash of the theatrical.

Its baroqueries were of course played out against the template of the Catholic liturgy, described by our friend Thomas Coryat on a visit to Notre Dame in Paris:

> No sooner did I enter into the Church, but a great company of Clergy men came forth singing ... Also in the same traine there were many couples of little singing choristers, many of

them not above eight or nine years old, and few above a dozen; which prety innocent punies were so egregiously deformed ... For they had not a quarter so much haire left upon their heads as they brought with them into the world, out of their mothers wombs ...

This was an authentically pre-Reformation sight of priests and tonsured choirboys singing plainsong (and lots of it), and our sturdy Englishman was unimpressed: 'very long and tedious devotion ... almost two hours in these pompous (I will not say theatricall) shewes'. Although he enjoyed the 'much excellent singing', he concluded by noting that the ceremonies were 'the first that ever I saw of that kinde, and I hartily wish they may be the last'.[13] (They weren't.)

Marc-Antoine Charpentier studied with Carissimi in Rome, and wrote frankly Italianate music in his long and productive service with the de Guise family and at the Chapelle Royale (though like Purcell he preferred vernacular terms to Italian: *Messe*, *airs sérieux* and *canticum* instead of *Missa*, *cantata* and *oratorio*, where possible). The influence of Carissimi is everywhere in oratorios like *David et Jonathas* (1688), with its substantial choruses, short and varied movements, 'ombra' scenes that are both spooky (with muted violins) and comical (characters drinking and dancing too much and needing to sleep it off) and flexible vocal writing. He loved the charming French habit of using Christmas folk tunes, called Noëls, in his church music – a habit much indulged by eighteenth-century organ composers like Louis-Claude Daquin and Nicolas Gigault. Charpentier's best-known essay in the form is the *Messe de minuit pour Noël* (c.1690), whose solos, duets, choruses and instrumental interludes are headed with the names of the descriptive little Christmas tunes on which they are based: '*Joseph est bien marié*', '*Or nous dites, Marie*', '*Où s'en vont ces gais bergers*'. This Mass uses the characteristically French voice type known as a 'dessus', a high treble or soprano: Marguerite-Louise Couperin was an admired exponent, singing the many solos written for her by her cousin François '*avec une grande légèreté de voix et un goût merveilleux*' ('with a fine lightness of voice and exquisite taste').[14] Another highly distinctive French voice type was the high tenor, or 'haute-contre': not a falsetto, but a light head voice. Leading composer Michel Richard Delalande took the Noëls out of church and repotted them in suites to accompany the king at any and every point of his day: *Musique pour les soupers de Roi, Simphonies des Noëls, Concert des trompettes pour les festes sur le Canal de Versailles*, and a virtually infinite supply of ballets and bourrées for the king to dance to.

Other distinctively French church forms included the pompous grands motets and, more intimately, the *Leçons de ténèbres*, settings for one or two solo voices, usually soprano, of the texts from the Lamentations of Jeremiah, to be sung during Holy Week. Couperin and Charpentier both made beautiful music from the prophet's penitential pining, perfectly matched to the high, clear voices of the black-clad 'Dames Religieuses de Lxx [Longchamp]', as Couperin called them, echoing up into the invisible vault of Sainte-Chapelle or Versailles. With characteristic practicality, Couperin informs his subscribers that he used the high dessus clef for the solo items in his *Leçons*, but that 'most accompanists today know how to transpose'.[15]

Charpentier took a perhaps rather unexpected step onto the theatrical boards after Lully's falling-out with Molière. His manuscript score for Molière's last comédie ballet, *Le Malade imaginaire*, is covered with the kind of hands-on alterations and theatrical flourishes familiar to theatre composers of all ages: a repeat bar is roughly scribbled out, a hastily written three-bar link squeezed onto handwritten staves in a blank space on the page, the violins are told to wait until one character is seen ready to sing under his mistress's window, then to play until another character hits him, which is their cue to stop. We can almost hear Molière barking out orders to his musicians from the wings. Charpentier responded admirably.

The musical meeting of Molière's two *maîtres* tells us something interestingly ambiguous about the imperfect internationalisation of style in the mid Baroque (as well as about the feisty characters involved): Lully, the Italian, stands champion of the French style against Charpentier, the Frenchman trained in Italy, as promoter of all things Italian. It was the next generation, and other countries, that brought all those influences fully together.

Instrumental Music

Among instrumental music of the French Baroque, Marin Marais painted drifting canvases of courtly life from the frankly old-fashioned sounds of the viol, in music of great insight and originality. The lute, instrument of the nobility, shared characteristics with keyboard music, including little ornaments called tremblements or agréments, and the mock-contrapuntal broken chord style known as the style brisé, originally used as a way of compensating for the lute's lack of sustaining power, but which developed its own grammar and gestures at the keyboard. Jean-Henri d'Anglebert provided a typically didactic guide to how to play ornaments, and expanded keyboard style by arranging orchestral numbers by Lully for harpsichord (rather as Liszt was later to do for the Romantic piano).

French composers added titles to their collections of keyboard pieces. 'Prélude' was a kind of generic catch-all. The 'tombeau' was a musical memorial. François Couperin's *Concerts* include two wonderful examples, *L'Apothéose de Lully* of 1725 and *L'Apothéose de Corelli* of 1726. In a typically learned gesture to his educated and enlightened player, Couperin borrows the different national customs in the use of clefs to symbolise the 'Parnassus' of European unity in his music: the French violin clef for Lully and the Italian G clef for Corelli. Couperin sought a similar stylised synthesis of style in the sections (called 'ordres' and 'concerts') of the suites he titled *Les Nations* and *Les Goûts réunis* (*The Tastes Reunited*).

The instrumental suite of dance-based movements moved around Europe. It was nudged in the direction of a semi-coherent pattern of paired dances by the much-travelled German keyboard composer Johann Jakob Froberger. One of its features was a slow movement played twice, the second time with florid written-out ornaments. This pairing finds it fullest form in the keyboard suites of Bach, where a sarabande (typically) is followed by its 'double', or ornamented version.

The dance suite entered the orchestral repertoire as a multi-movement work, often opening with a 'French' overture, whose dotted-note opening is a key feature of the *lingua franca* of the fused Baroque. Bach wrote four brilliant, dashing orchestral suites (which he called 'Ouvertures'); Handel's *Water Music* and *Fireworks Music* and Telemann's *Tafelmusik* are suites which encompass a whole range of musical styles, including hornpipes. Bach's Brandenburg Concerto No. 1 unexpectedly but effectively bolts a mini dance suite onto the end of the usual three-movement concerto form. French composers didn't really do concertos (too Italian), with the elegant exception of Jean-Marie Leclair, who fused Italian and French violin schools into a unique synthesis of his own. French orchestras and playing style were famous: at the very beginning of the eighteenth century the schoolboy Bach 'had the opportunity to go and listen to a then famous band kept by the Duke of Celle, consisting for the most part of Frenchmen; thus he acquired a thorough grounding in the French taste, which in those regions, was at the time something quite new'.[16] French organs, smaller than German instruments, produced a distinctive repertoire in the hands of a composer like Nicolas de Grigny.

Later French instrumental composers included 'one of the greatest organ players in Europe' (according to Burney), Louis Marchand.[17] Stories paint him as a prickly and jealous character as well as a talented composer: he fell out with Couperin, possibly over a woman; most famously, he was engaged to go head to head with Bach in a notable instance of the ever-popular public contests of performance and improvisation, but funked it by fleeing town on the dawn coach. Such stories must certainly be approached with caution, as the teller may well be a partisan of one participant or the other, but there's no doubt that eighteenth-century musical life specialised in big and often eccentric characters. Jean-Féry Rebel composed, among a great deal else, *Les Caractères de la danse* (c.1715), a highly original theatrical conception conducted by Handel in London, and the 1737 orchestral suite *Les Élémens*, whose opening movement depicts the creation of the world out of chaos in weirdly modernistic sounds pre-echoing Haydn's *Creation* and even some of the experiments of the twentieth-century avant-garde. It sounds a little mad: like many restless innovators, Rebel did not fully succeed in cohering his ambition into complete stylistic integrity. In 1695 he wrote *Le Tombeau de Monsieur de Lully* for his admired master: reverently laying to rest one phase of musical style without quite having the ability and strength of musical personality to usher in the next.

The prodigiously gifted Élisabeth Jacquet de La Guerre composed in a wide range of genres: sacred and secular cantatas, opera, the innovative 1707 set of *Pièces de Clavecin qui peuvent se Joüer sur le Viollon*, and keyboard suites with movements using a kind of unmeasured notation – clever, beautiful, accomplished music from a composer ranked second only to Lully by the well-informed commentator Titon du Tillet.

Unmeasured notation in a prelude (published 1687) for keyboard by Élisabeth Jacquet de La Guerre.

Les Couperins

The name Couperin dominates the French Baroque almost as much as the name Bach does the German. To take just one indicator: of the eight men to hold the post of organist at the church of Saint-Gervais in Paris between 1653 and 1829, seven were Couperins (and the eighth was the estimable Delalande, who was only standing in until the next Couperin was old enough to hop up onto the organ bench).

Louis Couperin established the family's musical fortunes in Paris in the 1650s as performer and composer for organ and harpsichord. First among this family of equals was Louis' nephew François, born in 1668, known as 'le Grand'. An agreeable and urbane character, he held a variety of posts in the increasingly devout later court of Louis XIV and his successor. He wrote church music to soothe the king's melancholy in the chapel at Versailles and chamber music for the *concerts du Dimanche*. Never the healthiest of the great composers, he observed wearily in 1730 that *'ma santé diminue de jour en jour'* ('my health fades by the day'), and expressed a grave hope that his family would find in his later works something to cause them to regret his passing ('if regrets serve any purpose when this life is over'), telling them that he had at least tried to earn that *'immortalité chimerique'* ('illusory immortality') to which almost all men aspire.[18] He died in his handsome house on the rue Neuve des Bons Enfants in 1733.

His daughter succeeded him as Ordinaire de la Musique at court, his cousin Nicolas as organist of Saint-Gervais. Another Nicolas, a nephew, was tasked with preserving much of his church and concert music, but failed to do so.

Chief among what remains of Couperin's works are the four books of short pieces for solo harpsichord, arranged in sets he called '*ordres*'. Their titles hint at the way they record and reflect the world around him: *Le Tic-Toc-Choc* (a clock), *Les Culbutes Jxcxbxnxs* (a not very well-disguised reference to an exiled troupe of English tumblers), *La Couperin* (a member of his family, or perhaps himself). Their names and notes evoke not just the sounds, but the manner and temper of his times: *Les Plaisirs de Saint-Germain-en-Laye*, *Les Folies Françoises*, a movement called *Je-ne-says-quoi*. Their harmony can be rich and impressionistic, dissonance (including advanced chords such as the eleventh and thirteenth) treated with almost vocal expressiveness, melodies witty and charming, contrapuntal skill lightly worn. In 1716 he published *L'Art de toucher le clavecin*, the most important resource for the understanding of eighteenth-century keyboard technique before C. P. E. Bach ('sit nine inches from the keyboard'; 'put a mirror on the music-desk to stop yourself pulling faces'; 'if your wrist is too high when playing, tie *une petite baguette-pliante* [a little bendy stick] to the top of it').

The keyboard works are, in the words of one his modern biographers, 'Couperin's memoirs ... all these reflections of a world which to Couperin was immediate and actual, are universalized in the pure musicality of his technique. A world of life has become a world of art.'[19] It is a distant world to us. He conjures up in sound the minority culture of a dwindling and disappearing milieu, sensitive, foolish and doomed. Perhaps his art is all the more compelling for that sense of something foreign and forgotten, just out of reach.

Rameau

Jean-Philippe Rameau was born in Dijon in September 1683, about eighteen months before Bach and Handel. He deserves to be considered in their company as one of the most original and unusual thinkers and composers in all music, despite only turning to his principal field of achievement, opera, after the age of fifty.

Rameau was a thoughtful and private man. His early career was spent as a cathedral organist in various French cities, with visits to both Milan and Paris, but he spoke little of these years, even to his wife. An anecdote reported much later suggests that he found small-town life irksome, and went so far as to deliberately play badly in order to persuade his then employer, the cathedral chapter of Clermont-Ferrand, to let him leave: 'He pulled out all the most displeasing stops and added to this all possible discords ... a choirboy had to be sent up to him ... Rameau left the keyboard and went out of the church.'[20] The chapter agreed to let him go, after which he played perfectly to make them realise how much they would miss him (coincidentally, the young Bach pulled a similar trick in Arnstadt at about the same time). Church music seems not to have interested him much.

Around his fortieth birthday he moved to Paris for good, married a singer (like so many Baroque composers) and in 1722 published his *Traité de l'harmonie*, followed in 1726 by the *Nouveau Système de musique théorique*. These are lengthy, detailed and immensely thorough works, addressing what he calls *'les veritables principes'* of music with scientific rigour (and the usual appeal to the example of *'les Anciens'*). They are key (to use an appropriate word) to the emerging codification of the system of tonality, and particularly to the idea of a fundamental bass underpinning harmonic movement – something Rameau seems to have been considering for some years.

The year 1724 saw the appearance of his first book of *Pièces de clavecin*, with another fastidious essay about fingering and ornamentation, whimsical titles like *Les Cyclopes*, cheery evocations of chirping birds and swirls of dust in the wind, and much imaginative use of the two manuals. The *Pièces de clavecin en concert* of 1741 add two obligato instruments to make genuinely Rococo chamber music, a million miles from Corelli and more than halfway to Haydn. Rameau claimed in his preface that the pieces can be played on keyboard alone without loss, but they can't: as if to disprove his own point he gave two versions of *La Livri*, one for solo keyboard in which the three instrumental lines are carefully presented in a contrapuntal texture, the other for the full ensemble with the clavecin taking an entirely different, florid, fully written-out role, almost like a piano trio by Mozart.

Rameau was clearly thinking hard about the ideals demanded of the opera composer long before he became one. The *Traité* of 1722 sets out the duties of the *'musicien dramatique'*. A rare surviving letter of 1727 tells us that he considered it desirable that there should be found for the stage a musician who has studied nature before painting her and who, through his learning, knows how to choose the colours and shades which his mind and his taste make him feel to be related to the required expressions.

I cannot deny that I am a musician; but at least I have more than others the knowledge of colours and shades ...[21]

Tellingly, he tells his reader that the opera composer needs skills in addition to, or even in spite of, being a musician. It is a remarkably clear analysis of what he went on to achieve on stage, and a fascinating pre-echo of the later approach and preoccupations of Weber and Wagner.

Rameau's first opera, *Hippolyte et Aricie*, premiered to great acclaim at the Académie Royale in October 1733, just a few days after the composer's fiftieth birthday. The succession of stage works which quickly followed are amply filled with striking examples of his unerring instinct for matching colours to expressions: an amazing dream sequence in *Dardanu*, first performed in 1739, features hushed echoes from the chorus and a terrific sea monster; a thunderstorm in *Hippolyte* uses hairpin dynamic markings; his favourite (and much-criticised) diminished seventh chord underpins Hippolyte's despairing cry of '*mort*'. Recits change time signature from bar to bar, and flow freely into the airs, in a key difference from Italian practice. (Carlo Goldoni, used to the Italian style, sat through an entire act of a French opera waiting patiently for an aria to begin. When told he had in fact heard six, he exclaimed, 'The instruments never ceased accompanying the voices ... I took the whole for recitative.')[22]

Rameau was a master of the stage as well as a brilliant tunesmith. His first attempt at comic opera, *Platée* (1745), which revolves around an ugly water nymph who thinks Jupiter is in love with her, is very funny. His orchestration, as in the hushed bassoon ushering in Telaire's lament '*Triste*' in *Castor et Pollux* (1737) and the many brilliantly theatrical evocations of nature in rushing strings, is beautifully considered. Orchestral sound can dominate voices and carry the emotional weight of a scene: the composer, writer and philosopher Jean-Jacques Rousseau remarked perceptively that Rameau used the voice as 'the accompaniment to the accompaniment'.[23] Harmony can match psychological imperative with wild, but always logical abandon, as in the famous 'Trio des Parques' from *Hippolyte*, whose extraordinary enharmonic changes at the words '*où cours tu, malheureux?*' were apparently too much for the poor singers at the premiere, and understandably so. Not for the first (or last) time in France, his innovations unleashed a paper war, between the Ramistes (sometimes called Rameauneurs) and the loyal Lullistes. The year 1745 was a key one for Rameau. Successful and established, he secured a position at the court of Louis XV and concentrated increasingly on lighter forms like pastorale and ballet. He died in 1764, just before his eighty-first birthday.

The colouristic landscapes of Rameau complete the story of Baroque opera in France, begun with the Italian imports to the middle of the seventeenth century, continued with the victorious establishment of a uniquely French style by Lully. The Franco-Italian style war would ignite again in the new operatic world of buffa and intermède in the 1750s, towards the end of Rameau's long life. Like all other operatic nations, France allowed itself a more light-hearted, earthier form of popular music theatre, too: parodies of pieces by Lully; the 'burlesque' tradition evoked by Couperin le Grand in some of his keyboard pieces; folk song style in the lyrical airs of André Campra and Rousseau's *Le Devin du village* of 1752, with its clear echoes of its English cousin, John Gay's riotously popular *The Beggar's Opera*, first performed in London in 1728. All this has more than a walk-on part in the next scene of operatic history.

8

PURCELL, HANDEL, BACH AND THE BACHS: BAROQUE MUSIC IN PROTESTANT NORTHERN EUROPE

Not Italy, the Mother of each Art
Did e'er a Juster, Happier son impart[1]

This appreciative puff of Henry Purcell, written right in the middle of the Baroque in 1693, follows the trajectory of the musical arts moving north through Europe from Italy.

It was a well-established idea. Earlier in the century the English composers Walter Porter and Nicholas Lanier worked with Monteverdi in Venice and brought the fruits of their labours home with them. Their compatriot John Cooper Italianised his name to Giovanni Coperario. Hans Leo Hassler brought a sprinkle of Italian sunshine back to Germany from his work with the Gabrielis, uncle and nephew, in Venice; his compatriot Heinrich Schütz studied with both Giovanni Gabrieli and Monteverdi, proudly describing his *Symphoniae Sacrae* of 1647 as being in the 'modern Italian manner'.[2] Johann Jakob Froberger studied with Frescobaldi in Rome. Buxtehude wrote choral concertos, derived in part from the Venetian model of choirs echoing each other across St Mark's.

In the middle Baroque the colours of Italian music continued to swirl through northern European culture like the flavoured stripes in a Neapolitan *gelato*. Purcell said in 1690 that English music was 'now learning *Italian*, which is its best Master, and studying a little of the *French* Air, to give it more Gayety and Fashion'.[3] Earlier, he described his miraculous *Twelve Sonatas of Three Parts* of 1683 as 'a just imitation of the most fam'd Italian Masters' (meaning Corelli, among others), and went on to give his subscribers a helpful glossary of Italian musical terms.[4]

Performers and performance style flew the Italian flag, too, particularly singers. Samuel Pepys heard 'some Italian Musicque' in 1667: 'the composition most excellent. The words I did not understand.'[5] In 1685 his fellow diarist John Evelyn recorded a visitor 'newly come from Rome, his singing voice was after the Venetian Recitative, as masterly as could be, & with an excellent voice both treble and bass'.[6] Native vocalists hungrily aped the imported manner. Opera increased the supply of these southern songsters into Hamburg, Dresden, London and other centres as the seventeenth century trilled into the eighteenth. As always, not everyone approved. The English actor manager Colley Cibber thought that 'the Opera is not a Plant of our Native Growth, nor what our plainer Appetites are fond of', and lamented that 'our *English* Musick had been so discountenanced since the Taste of *Italian* Operas prevail'd', vividly comparing and contrasting the talents of exotic visitors like the castrati Farinelli and Valentini with home-grown singers like Mrs Tofts.[7] Cibber was proved right about the limits of the appeal of all things Italian to English audiences: even the great Farinelli and imported composers like Nicola Porpora couldn't save the Opera of the Nobility, set up in 1733 by a group of aristocrats to rival Handel's patron and employer, the Royal Academy of Music.

This incomplete integration of international influences continued in the work of the great names of the first half of the eighteenth century. The young Bach studied, copied and arranged the music of Frescobaldi, Albinoni and Vivaldi (readily available in northern Europe); Handel's early travels in Italy from 1706 lit a firework under his natural, fizzing creativity; Francesco Geminiani carried his own take on the gospel of the archangel Corelli to London, Paris and Dublin, where it rooted and spread through his writing and teaching. Telemann added German recitatives to Italian operas by his friend Handel for the Goose Market Opera in Hamburg. One of Handel's London singers had to have the words of a psalm text written out in an Italianised phonetic transliteration because she couldn't read the archaic Prayer Book English: 'my heart is inditing of a good matter' became 'Mai hart is indeitin' of e gut matter'.[8] The double-dotted French overture and the French names for the movements of a dance suite turned up all over Europe: even in Germany the 'German' dance was called an allemande (which is French for 'German'). Bach didn't call his French Suites French (though they are, a bit), nor his English

Suites English (though they aren't): both names were added later, for different reasons, not all to do with style. Handel's imported diva Élisabeth Duparc was known to English audiences as 'la Francesina', which means 'the little Frenchwoman' in Italian. Melting pots don't always melt everything together completely evenly, and nor should they.

Religious music in the northern Baroque centred, naturally, around the needs and ideals of the reformed, Protestant churches. This certainly didn't just mean music in church. Devotional and moralising songs in the singer's own language and an approachable style, for use in the home and schoolroom, were a key component of the musical Reformation and Enlightenment: Heinrich Schütz's *Becker Psalter* of 1627 is a collection of simple psalm settings 'for the morning and evening devotions of the choirboys in my charge'.[9] German Pietists added devotional poetry to the composer's library of sacred texts earlier than did English Methodists. In Amsterdam, Jan Pieterszoon Sweelinck composed and improvised keyboard pieces on Genevan psalm tunes, showing the way to the mighty glories of the north European Baroque organ school. No hint of Mediterranean warmth penetrated this chilly corner of northern Calvinism. Art music for church reached its apotheosis in the mid-eighteenth-century German sacred cantata.

Germany: Heinrich Schütz and His Younger Contemporaries

Heinrich Schütz was born a hundred years before Bach, in 1585. He was the greatest German composer of the seventeenth century. His long life and large output linked the musical neologisms of the very beginnings of the Baroque through into the Lutheran soundworld of Buxtehude and Bach. His work grew with the century, from early studies in Italy with both Gabrieli and Monteverdi, through Italian madrigals and simple psalms to spacious choral symphonies, a fine German Requiem, and elaborate, dramatic sacred works like *Saul, Saul, was verfolgst du mich?* (1632), where the voice of God echoes up from the deeps like the infernal ferryman Caronte in Monteverdi's *L'Orfeo*. He wrote the very first German opera, *Dafne*, as early as 1627 (sadly, the music does not survive). He published regularly, and negotiated the requirements of reputation and employment skilfully. Like Bach and Telemann, he suffered the loss of a beloved wife; unlike them, he did not marry again. His legacy is rich and varied, sometimes wringing some surprising harmonies from the great sonic blocks of the first phase of the German Baroque.

One of the reasons a musical style achieves coherence in time and place is that composers often knew and worked with each other. In 1619 Schütz played the organ for the Margrave of Brandenburg-Bayreuth with two fellow composers: Michael Praetorius, pioneer of chorale-based compositions, and Samuel Scheidt, pupil of Sweelinck and first flower of the north German organ school. The internationalisation of keyboard style was continued by Froberger, developer of the dance suite. Heinrich Biber employed a range of unusual tunings, cross-stringings and bowing techniques as religious symbolism in his unique *Rosary Sonatas* for violin, probably written around 1676.

The Baroque north German organ school is one of the great buttresses of Western music. It rests on a holy trinity of foundation stones: chorale melodies and the liturgy; the art of counterpoint; and improvisation. Among its late seventeenth-century architects were the short-lived Nicolaus Bruhns, the long-lived Johann Adam Reincken, who heard and admired the young Bach, the influential Johann Pachelbel, and the most important German composer of the late seventeenth century, Dietrich Buxtehude.

Born in Denmark in 1637, Dietrich Buxtehude presided benignly from the loft of his magnificent organ in the Marienkirche, Lübeck, until his death in 1707. The teenaged Handel visited him there in 1703 with his friend, the mischievous Johann Mattheson. So, a few years later, did Bach, getting into trouble with his employers back home in Arnstadt for staying away too long. Buxtehude's music is sturdy and robust: sacred choral music employing different types of text, sectional organ pieces alternating florid, improvisatory passages (including for the feet) with short, strong-boned fugues; all clearly pointing the way forwards to the vaster canvases of Bach.

England

English music at the beginning of the seventeenth century built more on its Elizabethan heritage than on the modernism of the *seconda pratica*. There are some distant echoes of Venetian splendour: the grand, Monteverdi-flavoured 'Amen' at the end of Thomas Tomkins's *Seventh Service* or Edmund Hooper's massive 'O God of Gods', surely performed with a big 'broken' consort of wind and string instruments, Venetian-style; the English exile Richard Dering included a continuo bass in some of his madrigals, like middle-period Monteverdi; later, the beautiful subtlety of Henry Purcell's setting of the English language surely owes much to the example of earlier composers like Orlando Gibbons, music he sang as a boy under the direction of Gibbons's brilliant but drunken son Christopher.

Court masques by poets like Ben Jonson, with sets by wizards in woodwork like the architect Inigo Jones and lots of music by court composers (mostly now lost), drew on the lavish descriptions of the Florentine intermedi (though the English version was always a free-standing item rather than an *entr'acte*). The notoriously louche early Stuart court didn't always manage the basics: in one allegorical spectacular of 1606, the Queen of Sheba tripped over the steps and dropped her gifts in the King of Denmark's lap; the king then got up to dance but fell down drunk; 'Hope did assay to speak, but wine rendered her endeavours so feeble that she withdrew', then Faith 'left the court in a staggering condition' to join her sister, 'both sick and spewing in the lower hall'; and while 'the show went forward ... most of the presenters went backward, or fell down; wine did so occupy their upper chambers'.[10] Milton's pastoral *Comus* of 1637, with music by Henry Lawes, fared better. The poem was later set by Thomas Arne, achieving considerable popularity.

The English Civil War affected musicians directly. Some, like Matthew Locke, went abroad. Chapel Royal singer Henry Cooke joined up on the Royalist side, later being known to Pepys and everybody else as 'Captain Cooke'. William Lawes died in action at the battle of Rowton Heath in September 1645.

One green shoot did emerge through the Puritan gloom of Cromwell's Commonwealth. *The Siege of Rhodes* is the first English opera, a joint effort by no fewer than five composers to a text by William Davenant. It was staged in 1656 by special licence from Cromwell's government in a small theatre attached to a private house: 'The siege of Rhodes made a representation by the art of prospective in scenes, and the story sung in recitative musick ...' The music, like so much of the period, is lost. But the surviving sketches for the stage sets clearly show the romantic appeal and theatrical potential of the exotic, foreign location, not lost on the next generation of makers of opera.

Soon after the restoration of the monarchy in 1660 Samuel Pepys attended morning service at the newly reopened Chapel Royal in Whitehall, where he heard, much to his amazement and delight, 'a most excellent anthem (with Symphony's between) sung by Captain Cooke'.[11] The court and its music, complete with expensive new string band consciously modelled on the French Vingt-quatre Violons du Roi, became a kind of stage set, ready to be filled with musical wonders. It was Cooke's job to reassemble the Chapel Royal choir. He gathered a starry group of musicians around him, including members of the Purcell, Gibbons and Lawes dynasties. Several, like him, had been Chapel singers before the Civil War. His new generation of singing boys was, if anything, even more impressive than the adults: John Blow, Pelham Humfrey (who studied in France), Michael Wise and, a little later, brothers Henry and Daniel Purcell.

Henry Purcell and His World

Henry Purcell was born in 1659, just before the Restoration, and died in 1695. He produced a body of work of astonishing variety, quantity, inventiveness and range in a working life of probably slightly less than twenty years. By far the greater part of it grew out of the practical needs of the musical universe in which he lived and breathed: sparkly symphony anthems while the court liked (and could afford) them; songs and chamber music to publish and sell to the domestic market; sacred songs for singing at home; extremely unsacred songs for singing in the pub; odes to welcome royal personages home from their various trips around Europe or to the race track; masses of wonderfully vivid theatre music which never quite tipped over into full-scale opera; big pieces for coronations and small pieces for evensong. There is music where the composer seems to be conversing with his own muse, like the wonderful but frankly rather odd *Fantazias* (Purcell's own typically idiosyncratic spelling) for viols of 1680. He blended old-style counterpoint with the most plangent, modern harmony in a way which perhaps only Monteverdi has matched before or since. He was as good a contrapuntalist as anyone bar Bach. His harmonies can be so unusual and expressive that much later musicians like Elgar assumed they were mistakes and 'corrected' them.[12] His dance music really dances, like Lully's. His theatre music can show the same sheer good-humoured, grown-up fun as Mozart's, full of gloriously theatrical touches like off-stage echoes in *King Arthur* (1691) and the rapid alternations of mood and manner in the brilliant, poignant *Dido and Aeneas*, first performed at a girls' school in Chelsea in 1689. He could make harmonic rhythm and melodic line float and wander over a repeated bass line with beguiling flexibility and perfect skill.

Perhaps Purcell's most profound contribution was his development, almost creation, of the art of setting the English language to music. His friend and publisher Henry Playford wrote the preface to the volume *Orpheus Britannicus*, issued in 1698, three years after Purcell's death: 'The Author's extraordinary Talent in all sorts of Musick is sufficiently known, but he was especially admir'd for the Vocal, having a peculiar Genius to express the energy of English Words.' Professionally, his training and employment chart a highly successful and intensely practical career, much of it alongside his friend John Blow: Child of the Chapel, a court post in which he helped his godfather fix and maintain the royal musical instruments; organist of the Chapel Royal (still based at Whitehall Palace until it burned down not long after Purcell's death) and of Westminster Abbey. Geographically, he spent his whole life in the compact and close-knit neighbourhood around Whitehall and Westminster, neighbour to the many sociable, talented, gregarious, inquiring, creative intellects of Restoration London, a world described in all its colourful variety by his uncle Thomas's friend and partner in domestic music-making, Samuel Pepys.

A couple of examples will have to stand representative of all his constellation of wonders. 'My Beloved Spake', probably composed in the mid 1670s when Purcell was aged around seventeen, is a 'verse' anthem, alternating passages for string orchestra with music for one or more solo voices (the 'verses'), and brief bursts for the full choir. From this time-honoured template Purcell fashioned a kaleidoscope of texture, tempo and tonality gleefully chucked around the spaces and galleries of the Whitehall Palace chapel. The solo writing caresses the almost tactile English words: the 'tender grape', the 'green figs'; 'Rise, my love, and come away'. The 'voice of the turtle' is heard in a Schubertian twist of harmony followed by the most outrageous false relation ever written. This is a young man's song, bursting with life, love and potential. There's not much God in here.

The masque-like *Fairy Queen* of 1692 is on a bigger scale than its better-known operatic baby brother, the semi-opera *Dido and Aeneas* (featuring another operatic hero beached on the bosky fringes of the Mediterranean). *The Fairy Queen* is based on a typically irreverent rewrite of *A Midsummer Night's Dream*, in which he throws in a stammering drunk, a countertenor in drag, dancing monkeys, a Chinese dance, magic, trumpets, muted violins (for the first time in England), strophic songs of ravishing simplicity, elaborate stage effects and children dressed as fairies. Innovations include the ambitiously structured 'Masque of the Four Seasons', its sections linked by a repeating refrain.

Elements of *The Fairy Queen* are modelled on music by Lully. However, the composer whose work shows up most often and obviously in Purcell's output is his friend and slightly older contemporary John Blow. It was clearly a close and symbiotic relationship. The two men shared everything – jobs, friends and, in particular, musical ideas, techniques and innovations. Often they can be seen sparking off one another. They may even have written music jointly (as Blow did in 1664 with Pelham Humfrey and William Turner in the 'Club Anthem', written in their mid-teens).

Like some others in this story, the composers around Purcell inevitably shine less brightly in the historical skies by comparison with their starry colleague. But Blow was an ambitious, inventive and skilful composer, much honoured in his day. So, too, were the short-lived Francophile Pelham Humfrey and the older Matthew Locke (whose Catholicism put certain limits on both his working life and his output). Purcell wrote an eloquent elegy on the death of Locke in 1677. Eighteen years later, Blow performed the same service for Purcell when he fell unexpected victim to a sudden and unexplained illness in November 1695, dying in his mid-thirties, like his brother in youthful brilliance, Mozart, a century later.

English music around the turn of the eighteenth century has a transitional feel to it. There is a sense of waiting for something to happen. This is partly because we know what happened next; partly because the tastes (and wallets) of the later Stuart monarchs were not as extravagant as their forebears'; partly because the generation of native talent following Purcell, led by William Croft, was worthy but unspectacular. Meanwhile, foreign musicians at court became a nervous nexus for religious and political differences: the Italian Giovanni Battista Draghi at the Queen's Catholic chapel, the

Frenchman Robert Cambert and the Catalan-born Louis Grabu fluttering around the king and the public theatres.

Handel arrived in London less than twenty years after Purcell's death. There are many links, personal and musical, between the two.

Eighteenth-century Germany: Telemann, and Opera before Handel

Georg Philipp Telemann was born a few short years before Bach and Handel, in 1681, and outlived them both, dying in 1767.

Listeners today probably don't think of Telemann as an opera composer (if they think of him at all). But *Der Geduldige Socrates* of 1721 mixes a vivacious variety of vocal ensemble writing into the prevailing style and a plot about ancient Athenian bigamy; *Pimpinone* of 1725 is a *Lustiges Zwischenspiel* (comic intermezzo), a riotous slice of classic opera buffa about a scheming young chambermaid and a gullible old bachelor, designed to be dropped in between the acts of Handel's far more serious *Tamerlano*; *Pastorelle en musique* (written probably between 1712–21) is a bilingual wedding serenata in German and French, an Arcadian idyll based on Molière (featuring a character called Knirfx). As a young (and reluctant) law student at the very beginning of the eighteenth century, Telemann ran Leipzig's (slightly amateurish) Opernhaus auf dem Brühl; later he took over from Reinhard Keiser at the (rather less amateurish) Oper am Gänsemarkt (Goose Market Opera) in Hamburg. He travelled widely, dominating civic musical life wherever he hung his professional hat (sometimes to the annoyance of established older colleagues like Johann Kuhnau in Leipzig). His private life was decidedly mixed: his first wife died young, while his second, having borne him nine children, took up gambling and eventually ran away from both her husband and her debts. He was affable and gregarious: godfather to J. S. Bach's second son Carl Philipp Emanuel, who succeeded him as cantor at the Latin school in Hamburg, he was also a lifelong correspondent with Handel, about everything from the abilities of the latest soprano to gardening. He was celebrated and successful, and was first choice to succeed Kuhnau in the prestigious post of cantor at the Thomasschule in his old student haunt, Leipzig, turning it down when he secured a pay rise in Hamburg (a well-established negotiating tactic: the job eventually went to the third choice candidate, Bach). He was a constantly inventive composer, writing concertos for all sorts of instruments and pushing at the scale and range of the form. He liked whimsical titles like *Methodical Sonata* and *Tafelmusik* (*Table Music*). His output was colossal, even by the prolific standards of the age. This doesn't necessarily help us with the task of assessing his work as a whole: there is no one standout work. He wasn't a Bach or a Handel, but nor did he write '*Fabrikwaare*' ('factory products'), as one nineteenth-century critic unkindly claimed.[13] Like John Blow in England, Telemann has been historically thoroughly overshadowed by his contemporaries. That was not how he was seen at the time, and not what he deserves.

As in most of the rest of Europe, German opera was stylistically an outpost of Italy. Around the turn of the eighteenth century the hard-working Reinhard Keiser wrote lively, popular opera seria, sometimes bilingually in Italian and German to accommodate his cosmopolitan casts. Keiser helped turn opera into a public, rather than courtly, art form. He composed more than a hundred operas; Mattheson considered him 'the greatest opera composer in the world'.[14] In the next generation, Johann Adolf Hasse, who was friend and colleague of the epoch-defining librettist Metastasio and husband of Handel's star soprano Faustina Bordoni (who apparently wouldn't let him write opera buffa because it didn't suit her voice), was considered by Burney 'superior to all other lyric composers'.[15] But there's much more to Hasse than his lyricism: Act II of *Cleofide* (1731) begins with a jaunty march, then a busy recit driving characterisation and action forward, giving way to a ravishing, inward-looking duet, '*Sommi Dei, se giusti fiete*', which breaks off mid-phrase, after just a few seconds, interrupted by a bellicose aria with whip-like multiple-stopping in the orchestral violins, manipulating form and texture to match mood and plot, as Handel did.

Handel and His World

Sometimes style and circumstance come together in a way which a particular individual stands perfectly poised by taste, talent, training and temperament to exploit and complete.

Handel was born in Halle on 23 February 1685, about a month before and ninety miles away from Bach. As a youth he was thoroughly trained in the German traditions of counterpoint and keyboard, then worked in organ loft and opera house in Halle and Hamburg before travelling to Italy in 1706, where he met everyone and heard everything. He briefly held a post back in Germany as Kapellmeister to the Elector of Saxony (later George I of England), before settling for good from 1712 in London, where he found supportive patrons, lively theatres, competing opera companies, a well-trained Chapel Royal with a proud performing tradition, a mature market in international singing talent, plenty of loyal friends (and some rivals), a musical (if fractious) royal family, and a ready and appreciative (though fickle) audience for his ambitions in opera and, later, oratorio. He died on Easter Eve, 1759. His *Messiah*, composed in 1741, was the last music he heard, in the Foundling Hospital chapel a few days earlier. He was buried in Westminster Abbey, where his monument still stands.

Handel played the worldly game well. He had generous pensions from the English court as composer to the Chapel Royal and teacher of the musical and supportive princesses. For the large and well-established public market, he would write with white-hot intensity during the 'off' season (three operas in one particular year, 1724, including his masterpiece *Giulio Cesare*), managing every aspect when the season opened, directing from the keyboard like 'a necromancer in the midst of his own enchantments', in the brilliant phrase of his great friend and supporter, Mary Pendarves.[16]

These were the external circumstances that made Handel what he was. From within came a deep, almost limitless humanity, an innate insight into the psychological possibilities of drama, a natural feel for melody and the human voice, technical skill learnt over long years of effort, a gregarious and larger-than-life personality (with, at the same time, a need for privacy), a refined and educated artistic taste, a great gift for friendship, and the successful composer's indispensable addiction to high standards and hard work.

Handel's art evolved continuously. Sometimes his choices were driven by practicalities: the size of the band at Cannons, the Middlesex home of one of his aristocratic patrons; or the very public debates about the propriety of singing sacred words on stage, a key factor in the fashioning of the sacred oratorio in English (debates which Handel, typically, either turned to creative account or simply ignored). Mostly, though, his innovations come from his ability to use form and technique to peer into the minds of his characters.

Examples abound: the extraordinary orchestration of the magic opera *Rinaldo* (1711), bringing the dramatist Aaron Hill's phantasmagorical scenario to vivid life; the mad scene in *Orlando* (1733), written in 5/8 time (for the first time in music, ever); a da capo aria cut off in the middle and in the wrong key in *Messiah* so the chorus can go crashing head-first into the breaking of bonds and casting away of yokes; bizarrely modern melodic writing like the opening of the first aria in *Belshazzar* (1744). Supreme are the great dramatic character studies spread over carefully paced canvases in the oratorios: the fateful last act of *Saul* (1739); 'a father's woe' expressed in a recit whose very grammar collapses in grief in *Jephtha* (1751); the resignation of the doomed Christians in *Theodora* (1750). These are operas in all but name, complete with stage directions, all the more immediate for being sung in English. *Messiah* is an intense, inward-looking psychodrama, not telling a story but reflecting on themes of life and death, light and darkness. *Esther*, arguably the first English oratorio, exists in various incarnations following its appearance in 1718; each is unique. So, too, is *Semele*: its original audience at the Royal Opera House in February 1744 expected a seemly Lenten oratorio, but instead got a secular tale of seduction and sex. Every piece is different.

A key part of Handel's method was borrowing music from other works, his own and other people's, and, as was established Baroque practice, reworking it for a new context. It wasn't plagiarism: you weren't allowed to simply copy someone else's piece and pass it off as your own – Handel's arrogant operatic rival Giovanni Bononcini tried that trick and suffered a gruesomely spectacular fall from grace as a result.

Handel borrowed more than most. Usually he was very good at it, showing that composition can be a recreative as much as a creative act. Some instances are straightforward: when the 1732 version of *Esther* required a celebration, Handel simply dropped a couple of his own coronation anthems into the story, with some of the words changed. Usually his rewriting involved more fundamental changes, to texture, words, structure, orchestration and other features. Just occasionally his use of music from another source produced a stylistic gear change: the chorus 'And I will exalt him' in the last part of *Israel in Egypt* (1739) (a work liberally stuffed with other men's music) is based on a late Renaissance style ricercar by Gabrieli, creating a slightly uncomfortable lurch back into the prima pratica, a bit like Monteverdi trying out the two styles alongside each other a hundred years before.

There are many aspects to Handel's mercurial genius, some of them puzzling. His relationship with the English language was never entirely straightforward. In 1732 the theatre manager and dramatist Aaron Hill was encouraging him to explore the potential of stage drama in the vernacular: 'My meaning is, that you would be resolute enough to deliver us from our Italian bondage; and demonstrate that English is soft enough for Opera; when compos'd by poets who know how to distinguish the sweetness of our tongue from the strength of it.'[17] Later, in 1745, aged nearly sixty, Handel acknowledged how important this idea had been to him:

> As I perceived, that joining good Sense and significant Words to Musick, was the best Method of recommending this to an English Audience; I have directed my Studies that way; and endeavour'd to shew, that the English Language, which is so expressive of the sublimest Sentiments is the best adapted of any to the full and solemn kind of Musick.[18]

But his spelling, word stresses and (apparently) spoken accent retained an idiosyncratically Teutonic tinge (in the manuscript of *Messiah* he consistently mis-spelled 'strength' as 'strenght' and 'dead' as 'death').

Like many composers for the stage, Handel was at the mercy of the variable quality of his 'poets', even though he could badger them mercilessly to get what he wanted (and sometimes vice versa). His prickly but brilliant friend Charles Jennens (*Saul*, *Belshazzar*, *Messiah*) was his best librettist. Others, like James Miller (*Joseph and His Brethren* (1743)), didn't always allow sense to escape through their eighteenth-century circumlocutions (though Miller is not as bad as is sometimes claimed).

On his private life, Handel has slammed up the historical shutters as firmly as those behind the sturdy sash windows of his house in Brook Street, Mayfair, on a foggy day in London. The man who wrote about the lives, loves and losses of men, women, fathers and daughters with Mozartian grace and sympathy, has left no evidence (apart from a few brief and inconclusive reports) of any romantic involvements of his own. The most personal of his few surviving letters are those to his brother-in-law about the affairs of his family in Germany; to Telemann he writes about music and gardening. His religion appears conventional, though sincere. There are many anecdotes (including one about a duel with Mattheson over continuo duties in Hamburg when Mattheson headed off unexpectedly to the gaming tables – an encounter which, according to Mattheson, ended when his blade struck a brass button on Handel's coat, thereby saving his life). No doubt the details of such stories have been embellished over time like the ornaments in a da capo.

History hasn't always helped Handel. Apart from murdering *Messiah* through over-orchestration, it largely ignored him for the best part of two centuries. The operas lurked in libraries, an impenetrable heap of da capo arias and stupid plots, long, boring and all the same. Taste and performing style simply moved on, as indeed he would fully have expected it to, and either left Handel behind or tried to pretend he was something he never was or could ever be – a sort of primitive Elgar (but not as good).

Today we can begin to try to see Handel in the round. He stands revealed as one of the great poets of the human heart.

Even more than in the age of Purcell, the rest of the English Baroque winks at us wanly from under Handel's shadow like a candle in sunshine. But it casts some notable glimmers.

Popular opera packed in the punters with John Frederick Lampe's *The Dragon of Wantley* of 1737 and John Gay's *The Beggar's Opera* of 1728, hugely successful mixtures of irreverent satire and good tunes. Promoters like John Rich put on zany dumbshows full of slapstick, magic tricks and music which they called pantomimes, a riotously English take on Continental originals like Pierrot and Harlequin, whose descendants are still easily identifiable in the end-of-the-pier high jinks of our own Christmas season. At the high end, Giovanni Bononcini, a stylish exponent of all the prevailing Italian styles who set himself up as a rival to Handel (and lost), played the part of the resident difficult foreigner. There was some fine local talent: Maurice Greene, organist of St Paul's and Handel's drinking companion; Greene's close associate William Boyce, composer of some splendid ceremonial church music and elegant Rococo symphonies and co-editor with Greene of an important collection of *Cathedral Music* (1760); and Charles Avison, presiding presence in fashionable Newcastle-upon-Tyne and composer of the best English eighteenth-century concertos and trio sonatas in a style skilfully absorbed from his teacher, the much-travelled Francesco Geminiani.

Bach (Johann Sebastian)

Writers have noted the points of similarity between the lives of George Frideric Handel and Johann Sebastian Bach from the beginning: they were born geographically and chronologically close together; they had friends and colleagues in common (notably Mattheson and Telemann); they knew and admired each other's work but never met (though they tried more than once); in a sad coincidence they both lost their sight in old age and were 'treated' by the same travelling English quack, with the same painful and predictable lack of success.

But the differences are more instructive than the similarities.

On a personal level, Bach lived a happy, busy family life in a series of the kind of small-town employments he was born into, while Handel travelled alone through the triumphs and uncertainties of chasing the bubble reputation across the starriest stages and biggest cities of Europe.

As composers, they both showed the ability of genius to use local circumstance to allow it to become, and to be, itself to the fullest possible degree.

Johann Sebastian Bach was born in March 1685 into a large family of working musicians. Orphaned aged not quite ten, he received a thorough and practical education in the home of an older brother and at the kind of well-run boys' schools in which Lutheran Germany specialised. From his late teens he held an unbroken succession of the kind of musical jobs which his father, uncles, cousins and brothers had made their own for centuries: as cantors, Kapellmeisters, organists, bandsmen and teachers in a series of small and medium-sized courts and towns around the pleasantly wooded region of Thuringia where he was born.

His principal places of work included Weimar, where he played an organ placed high in a fourth tier of galleries in the now-vanished chapel of a court run in a rather odd arrangement by two joint dukes, one of whom briefly imprisoned Bach when he asked to leave in 1717; Cöthen, seat of 'a gracious prince who both loved and understood music', who maintained a fine house band but had no use for church music in his Calvinist establishment;[19] last and longest, from 1723, as cantor at the Thomasschule in the busy provincial centre of Leipzig, former stamping ground of his friend Telemann, where he wrote and performed music for the regular services in the city's main churches, taught (and lived) in the school, and made music for civic occasions and, later, for public concerts like the series held at Zimmerman's coffee house. He could be a difficult and demanding employee, regularly berating his bosses about what he saw as their failure to meet his optimal required conditions for music (and also moaning about money), while at the same time receiving a series of exasperated reprimands for neglecting the bits of his job that didn't interest him: '[he] did not conduct himself as he should ... sent a choir student to the country; went away without obtaining leave ... he did not hold the singing class ... he shows little inclination to work ... there were other complaints in addition ... not only did the Cantor do nothing, but he was not even willing to give an explanation of the fact'. One Leipzig town councillor called him 'incorrigible'.[20]

Bach married twice and fathered twenty children, of whom half lived to adulthood, three going on to very significant musical careers of their own. Like the two other great masters in this chapter, Purcell and Handel, Bach reveals only glimpses of his inner self to posterity. His library speaks of a well-read and sincere Lutheran. Accounts by his son Carl Philipp Emanuel and by Johann Elias, a cousin who lived with the Bachs as a sort of extra musical pair of hands, suggest a busy, noisy, family home, full of food, affection, music and flowers: Bach often worked at night, presumably after his quiverful of children had done their practice, said their prayers and gone to bed. Other aspects of his nature can be inferred: in the slightly coy words of one of his best modern biographers, 'a man who ... fathered twenty children cannot have been indifferent to sensual pleasures'.[21] He never travelled outside Germany, and all of his places of employment were within little more than a hundred miles of his birthplace.

To some extent, his work followed his thorough immersion in his inheritance and the progress of his employment: the mighty *Passacaglia and Fugue in C Minor*, written while he was in his twenties, is emblematic of much organ music from early in his career; his early keyboard music used Buxtehude-like zig-zag motives and includes florid harpsichord toccatas like those of Buxtehude and Böhm; the *Brandenburg Concertos*, written in 1721 when he was Kapellmeister at Cöthen, rolled out the basic principles of ritornello to include the wild hunting horns of no. 1 and the mammoth harpsichord cadenza of no. 5 (the first real keyboard concerto, written to show off a new instrument recently procured by Bach for his prince); cantatas like

Ein feste Burg ist unser Gott, reworked soon after he arrived in Leipzig in 1723 from an original version composed for Weimar, wrapping Luther's faith-defining hymn as a canon above and below a whole series of fugues; concertos and secular cantatas for the later Leipzig coffee-house concerts. The cycles of liturgical cantatas, one complete year-long set sadly lost, are a vast repertoire. The Passion setting is another form he inherited from countless examples by other composers, the tenor narrator binding his listeners into the drama, ushering in the bloodthirsty crowds, the great rolling choruses and lullabies which begin and end the works, and the corporate, inward-looking chorales. Despite his huge output of vocal music, Bach wrote less sympathetically for the voice than Monteverdi, Purcell or Handel.

His pursuit of the gods of counterpoint was a sort of permanent personal pilgrimage, teasing out the innate possibilities of a theme (or 'inventio', as Bach's age called it), so that subject and countersubject 'converse together, like two persons of the same rank and equally well informed', in the admirable analysis of his first biographer, Johann Nikolaus Forkel.[22] Late in life Bach wrote a series of works where he seems to disappear inside his own brain, mining the cosmic possibilities of counterpoint in music where the concepts of intellectual exercise, study, performance and listening seem to blur into each other and become one: *The Musical Offering*, *Goldberg Variations*, *The Art of Fugue* and other works.

In 1750 Bach's second son inscribed a laconic note on his father's manuscript of *The Art of Fugue*: 'While working on this fugue, in which the name BACH appears in the countersubject, the author died.'[23] The music peters out, poignantly, mid-bar.

His music remains one of the defining achievements of the human spirit. He was no stylistic innovator, and he knew it. Even in his lifetime he was known as 'Old Bach' (even, according to rumour, 'Old Wig' to his own family), and was criticised for his backward-looking style.[24] Like Monteverdi, he found himself the unwilling focus of a public spat about style, with the difference that Bach stood representative of the old, not the new. His unique genius was to take his inheritance of form, manner, musical material, liturgical tradition and technique, and polish, refine, extend, reinvent and redefine the reach and range of their possibilities, constantly, in every piece. As Forkel rightly says, 'no bar (I might even say, no part of a bar) is like another'.[25]

Johann Sebastian Bach's influence and example resonate through the rest of this book and the whole of musical history. Even when public taste thought it had forgotten him, working composers never did. The standing and reputation of 'a man who contributed quite exceptionally to the honour of music, of his fatherland, and of his family', in the words of his obituary of 1750, helped nudge the tectonic plates of musical time into a new, Teutonic formation.[26]

The next age would be a German one.

The connections and disconnections between the three great contemporaries, Bach, Handel and Scarlatti, are instructive. Bach summed up the Baroque in an achievement of colossal reach and variety, essentially looking back for his inheritance and immediately around him for his audience. His reward was to be admired but mostly unplayed for many decades after his death. Handel synthesised his cosmopolitan credentials into something new and uniquely human. His legacy was to be selectively revered, in the form of two or three big pieces which succeeding generations murdered by over-orchestration, and a few bleeding chunks amputated from the operas – part of a fixation on a fake version of the old which effectively throttled at birth indigenous English musical creativity for the next hundred years. Scarlatti looked to the future by focusing in on one small musical object, the keyboard sonata. He showed one way forward to a new age.

The word Baroque was originally a term of disapproval, carrying hints of something dense, ornate and overblown. As Bach's legacy moved into the hands of his sons, the tide of taste was moving definitively towards something cleaner and more enlightened: the Classical.

Part Five

CLASSICISM (1740–90)

INTRODUCTION

Shortly after J. S. Bach's death in 1750, a well-informed writer noted the presence of the 'old, dark burrowings' alongside 'the brighter taste and more beautiful expression of our newer music' in his work.[1] It's a restatement of the debate stirred up by the polemicists Johann Adolph Scheibe and Johann Abraham Birnbaum about Bach's merits as a composer in the late 1730s: the old contrapuntal manner was 'turgid', 'confused', the 'natural elements' darkened by 'an excess of art'.[2] Composers and thinkers of the new age of the Enlightenment were, in the vivid if rather brutal words of one modern scholar of the era, 'clearing away the rubbish'.[3] Music grew up quickly, from the preening galant to the first stirrings of romantic yearning, with the beautiful thing we call 'classicism' poised somewhere between. Right at the end of its charmed but short life, Haydn summed it up perfectly when he set the words of Genesis to nothing more dense and intellectual than a chord of C major: 'Let there be light: and there was light.'

Music in Context, Social and Aesthetic

The more tolerant spirit of the times allowed a rounded, varied cast of characters to walk onto the opera stage. Aristocrats could be portrayed as fallible, servants human and self-aware. Scary alien types like Mozart's Turkish Pasha in *Die Entführung aus dem Serail* (*The Abduction from the Seraglio*) (1782) or the Masonic-influenced High Priest in *Die Zauberflöte* (*The Magic Flute*) (1791) could reveal themselves as enlightened figures of wisdom. Church music, meanwhile, became little more than a tuneful subset of opera: the Viennese church style hardly functioned as a vehicle for teasing out knotty points of theology, as Bach and Byrd had done in their music. Ideas had moved elsewhere.

A crucial development was the transfer of the ability of music to imitate human emotion to the purely instrumental sphere. In 1747 the Frenchman Charles Batteux wrote that 'music without words is still music', adding, 'Music speaks to me through Tones: the language is natural to me: if I do not understand it, then Art has corrupted Nature rather than adding a perfection to it.'[4] Music has meaning, and the role of art is to communicate that meaning to a listener who possesses both understanding and taste. That is what the forms and melodies of the Classical style are there to do.

The learned arts of counterpoint were still an object of veneration, but good taste required them to be displayed with discretion. This wasn't a new idea: in 1737 Jean-Philippe Rameau boasted that 'it is not obvious that I make a great display of learning in my compositions, where I seek to hide art by very art; for I consider only people of taste and not at all the learned, since there are many of the former and hardly any of the latter'.[5]

The key for the Classical composer was to have both. Haydn famously told Mozart's father Leopold (or, at least, Leopold told his daughter that Haydn had told him) that 'Before God and as an honest man I tell you that your son is the greatest composer known to me either in person or by name. He has taste, and, furthermore, the most profound knowledge of composition.'[6] Haydn's choice of words is telling: he praises Mozart junior's *'geschmack'*, meaning good taste or sensibility, and *'die grösste Compositionswissenschaft'*, a phrase which has more than a hint of science and technique in it as well as simply knowledge. It's an important distinction: the two qualities are distinct but complementary; necessary but different. Mozart's early biographer Franz Niemetschek made a similar point, praising his *'Kunst des Satzes'* (literally, 'art of the sentence', or formal and technical skill) alongside the 'grace and charm' of his art.[7]

This assimilation of old techniques into a new style is key: Haydn, Mozart and Beethoven knew and loved the music of Bach and Handel, even as their audiences were increasingly declining to listen to it. There is a wonderful story of Mozart joyously reading an eight-part Bach motet just from the individual voice parts spread all round on him on the floor and chair backs in the song room of the Thomaskirche in Leipzig, and crying out, 'Now, there is something one can learn from!'[8] Elsewhere he talks of improvising fugues 'from my head',[9] and even of working out a prelude to go with one of them while engaged in the physical act of writing the fugue down (though, as so often with the lovably human Mozart, his motivation was not simply a celestial communion with the higher arts, but also an attempt to impress his pretty young wife Constanze, who apparently liked that sort of thing).

As with the Baroque period, opera provides the best road map of the evolution of musical aesthetics. The slightly mongrel quality of the mix of international influences continued. In one of those shaking-hands-across-the-ages moments, Johann Adolf Hasse, German high priest of Baroque Italian opera seria, met the young Mozart in Vienna. For the adult Mozart, the phrase 'German opera' could be a shorthand for the buffa-inspired Singspiel style of the popular theatrical troupes, by contrast with the grander Metastasian opera seria, sung in Italian. The much-travelled Irish tenor Michael Kelly captured the linguistic and musical hotch-potch of operatic fare in his description of the London season of 1791:[10] two well-known Italian pieces translated into English with the original music by Martini and Salieri arranged and augmented by the Englishman Stephen Storace; a 'serious opera' and a 'comic opera' given together in the Oxford Street Pantheon by a cast of mostly Italians; and two home-grown comedies, *The Country Girl* and *No Song, No Supper*, which turned out to be the last shows given at the old Drury Lane theatre before it closed, earning a touching obituary in the newspapers: 'Died, on Saturday night, of a gradual decay, old Madame Drury, who lived in six reigns, and saw many generations pass in review before her.'[11]

Audiences certainly didn't go to the opera just to see the show. According to the diplomat and theatre-lover Giacomo Durazzo in 1756:

> The theatre boxes are, so to speak, rooms for receiving company; gentlemen go from box to box to pay court to the ladies, and the ladies visit with one another ... people play cards in the boxes, eat their evening meal, and ... one can hardly hear the orchestra ... [but] the star singer performing a big aria will be able to instil silence.[12]

A couple of decades later William Beckford agreed: 'Every lady's box is the scene of tea, cards, cavaliers, servants, lap-dogs, abbés, scandal, and assignations ... all is noise, hubbub, and confusion, in an Italian audience.'[13] The Italian adventurer Giacomo Casanova found Parisian opera-goers a little better behaved: 'I was delighted at the

French opera, with the rapidity of the scene changes which are done like lightning, at the signal of a whistle – a thing entirely unknown in Italy ... I admired also the silence of the audience, a thing truly wonderful to an Italian.' Occasionally, he even commented on the music: André Campra's comic opera *Les fêtes vénitiennes* (1710) began with 'a symphony, very fine in its way and executed by an excellent orchestra' (though the set showed St Mark's Square the wrong way round, which made him laugh), and on another occasion he 'admired the start given to the orchestra by the baton of the leader, but he disgusted me with the movements of his sceptre right and left, as if he thought that he could give life to all the instruments by the mere motion of his arm'. Casanova made an interesting observation about Campra's recitative:

> The music, very fine although in the ancient style, at first amused me on account of its novelty, but it soon wearied me. The melopaeia fatigued me by its constant and tedious monotony ... That melopaeia of the French replaces ... our recitative which they dislike, but which they would admire if they understood Italian.[14]

While tagging along on one of Louis XV's hunting trips to Fontainebleau (full-scale opera company in tow, naturally) he found himself discussing the relative merits of French and Italian recitative with a noble stranger who turned out to be Cardinal Richelieu (before the two men fell to discussing the relative merits of the actresses' legs). He found the tendency of French opera singers to 'scream' slightly alarming, too.

Comic opera evolved more creatively than its serious sister. Successful shows like the 1752 Paris production of Pergolesi's (already nearly two-decades-old) *La serva padrona*, and Niccolò Piccinni's *La buona figliuola* of 1760 stirred up fruitful debates about style and helped embed some of the features of the comic manner in popular taste: simple, direct musical language portraying real emotions of ordinary people, lots of action, not much reflection, and plenty of jokes. Performers were often actors who could sing a bit, rather than the strutting superstars of seria. There were no castrati, and the bass voice – rarely a feature of the seria style – allowed for well-balanced ensembles and the evolution of the gruff, pattering comedy bass, one of the genre's most distinctive representatives. Types appear: march tunes for military characters (like Carl Ditters von Dittersdorf's Captain Sturmwald with his wooden leg in *Doktor und Apotheker* (*Doctor and Apothecary*) (1786)); the weeping maiden in a lilting, minor key 6/8 and extreme vocal virtuosity parodied from opera seria as a sign of something mechanical and unnatural (both found in *La buona figliuola*). All national traditions had their own version of what later became light opera, often mixing familiar things like folk tunes and popular songs with spoken dialogue rather than the high-flown recitative: French opéra comique, German Singspiel, Spanish tonadilla and English ballad opera.

Opera seria, though still widely performed and esteemed, rather lost is recreative edge. Its style, like its plots, seemed stuck in the past. Lavish court theatricals declined with the absolutist monarchies which supported them. Reformers closed in on its static and unlifelike absurdities. The ubiquitous da capo aria, with its lengthy, emotionally frozen repeat, gave way to something more fluid and forward-moving: the dal segno, then the sectional-type aria, almost a mini scena in itself. Rigidity gave way to reality: as the French writer Jean-Georges Noverre put it, 'la symétrie doit faire place à la nature'.[15] The Scotsman John Brown gave an admirably clear account of all the different types of vocal music he heard on his Italian travels in the 1780s: recitative for the 'simple narration of facts' and 'the transition from one emotion to another'; the 'pathetic part' in arias which he categorised skilfully and perceptively, including 'aria di portamento' ('chiefly composed of long notes ... or the beauty of sound itself ... held, by the Italians, to be one of the chief sources of the pleasure we derive from music') and 'aria di bravura' ('composed chiefly, indeed too often, *merely* to indulge the singer in the display of certain powers of execution').[16]

Other theatrical forms played a smaller, but significant, role. Jean-Jacques Rousseau in *Pygmalion* (1770) and Georg Benda in *Ariadne auf Naxos* (1775) experimented with text spoken against background instrumental music, known as 'melodrama' (or 'monodrama' or 'duodrama', depending on the number of performers). Mozart was an enthusiast: 'there is no singing but only Recitation – and the Musique functions like an obligato Recitative – now and then the words are recited with the Musique and then the effect is most magnificent'.[17] School opera was a charming subset of the intermezzo – Mozart wrote two: one in Latin (naturally) for choirboys (who were all older than his then eleven years); and a little amatory pastoral featuring the aria 'Diggi, daggi, shurry, murry'.

The pasticcio was alive and cooking: Durazzo remarked in 1756 how singers 'bring arias with them from other operas which they have sung to great acclaim, and force the composer to insert them, come Hell or high water, into their roles'.[18] So was the habit of composers writing extra bits for someone else's opera: when Mozart was asked to write his own ballet interlude for *Idomeneo* in 1780 he remarked, tellingly, 'I actually like it better this way, for the music will all be from *one* composer.'[19] The overture settled into a single movement, often fast and witty, sometimes with a slow introduction. The old-style overture of opera seria, with its contrasting sections, found its immediate successor in the multi-movement Classical symphony.

Another source of bubbling chatter was the competing roles of words and music. Antonio Salieri's glittering one-act opera *Prima la musica e poi le parole*, in which singers, composers and poets tussle over the primacy of different styles, was first performed at one end of the orangery of Schönbrunn Palace in Vienna on 7 February 1786. At the other end, on the same night, Mozart's Singspiel *Der Schauspieldirektor* was given its premiere: more bickering divas, this time in German. Like all successful stage composers, Mozart was clear that a good opera needed good words, saying of a colleague: 'Holzbauer's music is very beautiful. The poetry doesn't deserve such music.'[20] Librettists and translators felt free to change even a well-known text: Paisiello's *Il barbiere di Siviglia* has a different text from Rossini's, even though both are based on the same play. Its author, Beaumarchais, had views on when operatic music helped the drama and when it didn't: '*Notre Opéra pue de musique*' ('Our opera stinks of music'); 'The fault of our grand operas is too much music in the music ... Whenever the actor sings, the action stops, and whenever the action stops the interest drops.'[21] This classic statement of the new thinking is from the preface of a libretto intended for the composer Christoph Willibald Gluck, whose interest in reform he shared. Another leading light of the reform movement, Ranieri de Calzabigi, neatly noted the interface between text and music when he described spoken declamation as 'an imperfect kind of music' and music as 'a clever kind of declamation'.[22] The French composer André Grétry experimented with reproducing verbal inflections in music, once writing down the

Part Five: Introduction

way an affected friend said, *'Bonjour, monsieur'* in musical notes.[23] In 1787 Casanova wrote a novel about a tribe who speak only in pitched vowel sounds – a speculation on the autonomy of musical meaning from verbal sense and a remarkably modern idea.[24]

The most important development in opera at this time was the evolution of the ensemble. In the old style, Handel, among others, wrote some wonderful ensembles where the characters convey different, and often very subtle, emotions (notably the gorgeously tragic quartet in *Jephtha*); but those emotions don't change. A key feature of Goldoni's new creature, the dramma giocoso (literally, 'drama with jokes'), was the detailed, varied, witty, quick-fire ensemble used to end an act. Emotion, and action, could change, react and develop like sunlight flickering over a landscape. Characters could variously speak to (and be heard by) everyone, to some people on stage but not others, or just to themselves (and the audience). The dramatic possibilities were teased out with riotous enjoyment by the sparkling pioneers of the high buffa style: Paisiello, Salieri, Galuppi and others. Out of this came greater subtleties, like characters being only partly aware of their own motivation and emotional state. Emerging musical form helped give substance to these shifting conversations between mood and manner.

The seeds and building blocks of the mature works of Mozart can be seen emerging through all these developments, surely the most perfect example in all music of a mind perfectly poised to gather up everything around it into something fleeting, complete, precious and unique.

The Composer in Society

Socially, even the best composers of this time could still be hemmed in by their employment status. Mozart told his father that his hated boss, Archbishop Colloredo (a true Enlightenment churchman, for all Mozart's animus), 'treats me like a street urchin',[25] and was both amused and offended by his place at table – 'at least I have the honour of sitting above the cooks'.[26] When Haydn entered the service of the noble Esterházy family in 1761 he was contractually 'subordinate to and dependent on' the elderly Kapellmeister Werner;[27] by the time of Prince Nikolaus's death in 1790 he was 'Kapellmeister of Prince Esterházy' in his own right, free to pursue his own hard-earned reputation away from the princely palace. Mozart, after the break with Colloredo, threw himself on the mercies of a general aristocratic and middle-class public in Vienna. Haydn did the same but with more success in London, where it had long been easier, partly because he had a first-rate agent, partly because such a public – particularly the middle-class element – was much larger in London than in Vienna. In London the move towards reliance on the public had happened earlier in the eighteenth century; in Vienna it was considered almost a revolutionary thing to do. In this respect Mozart presented himself above all as a keyboard virtuoso, hence the preponderance of keyboard concertos, especially in 1784–6 (he composed no operas in these years). By the end of the eighteenth century the dedications of Beethoven's works replaced the standard sycophancy of just fifty years earlier with the names of his friends and admirers – there are titled persons among them, and some notable ones; but they are here because they were musicians (and/or women he admired), not because they were noble.

Technology and Education

As in all ages, technological innovation fed creatively into musical development, particularly the increased power and variety of the piano, and the emergence of the modern violin bow, allowing the full, rounded, cantabile sound which remained the ideal through the nineteenth century. Orchestral writing settled around the layered use of different groups of instruments, and the abilities (and availabilities) of players. Natural horns, with changeable crooks to transpose into different keys, made a particularly distinctive contribution to the orchestral sound, with their limited scale and hunting-style mouthpieces creating the characteristic fanfare-type patterns and long pedal notes, loud and soft. Horn players travelled in pairs: Mozart made brilliantly practical use of two pairs of horns in his late operas in order to shift mood and key quickly. The solos in his horn concertos require a quite different technique to his orchestral parts – they, like much of his solo music, are an eternal tribute to a talented collaborator, in this case his childhood friend Joseph Leutgeb.

Musical education moved out of the shadow of charitable philanthropy or the church: the French composer François-Joseph Gossec established the École royale de chant in 1784, followed by the first genuinely independent and meritocratic Conservatoire national de musique in 1795 (which may be why English-speaking countries still use the French word *conservatoire* for specialist, high-level music schools).

This nascent democratisation contributed to new kinds of musical events, in new kinds of places, with new musical forms to go in them: the symphony, the Classical sonata and chamber music. Much music was written for the home, and composers often appealed to both experts and regular music-lovers: Luigi Boccherini called them '*dilettanti e conoscitori*';[28] to C. P. E. Bach they were '*Kenner und Liebhaber*';[29] Scarlatti addressed his potential customer as 'Dilettante or Professor'.[30]

Social and Ceremonial Music

The musicologist Alfred Einstein nicely categorised the distinction between music for private and public use as 'social' and 'ceremonial': social was that made by an informal gathering of friends, while ceremonial was anything with an element of staging and an audience – opera, church service, concert or royal event.[31] The distinction shows up in the music: ceremonial pieces are bigger and more able to explore the full range of symphonic and contrapuntal invention; social pieces are content to rely on smaller ensembles and more immediate miniatures of form like variations, song forms and dance movements. That is a vast generalisation, of course, and there is plenty of overlap and crossover between the two: Haydn reworked the slow movement of his Piano Trio in F Sharp Major as the second movement of Symphony No. 102 (for a London concert at which a huge chandelier apparently fell from the ceiling, luckily missing the audience who had stormed the stage in enthusiastic delight); and there are suggestions that Mozart played at least one of his piano concertos in a pared-down chamber version. Both composers folded all the tricks and glories of the full symphonic and sonata style into every aspect of their later music from the mid 1780s, and in Haydn's hands the string quartet evolved from being an essentially domestic creature to a full-scale public concert work (or both).

Female performers, especially pianists, provided a large and lucrative market. Much of their fare fell into the less demanding *Liebhaber* category, but there were many notable exceptions, as in the music written by Mozart for Madame Jenamy, by Haydn for his English widow friend Rebecca Schroeter, and by Beethoven for several of his admired and admiring pupils. The duet for two players at one instrument became hugely popular, a fashion possibly instigated by the infant Mozarts. The opportunities for intimacy afforded by the form, complete with shared piano stool and discreetly designed hand-crossings, were not lost on maestros and maidens alike: a little later Wilhelm Friedrich Ernst Bach (son of J. C. F. and grandson of J. S.) went one further with a piece which requires a large male pianist, sitting in the middle, to play the top and bottom of the keyboard by putting his arms round two small females, one on either side. Other homely items in the chamber style included sonatas with the charming title 'conversations', a great many pieces in which a violin or flute part was described as the 'accompaniment' to the keyboard (and might even have been entirely optional), and canzonettas and prettified folk songs for ladies to play for delight and display. This is the music which filled the albums and mornings of so many of Jane Austen's sardonic heroines. Mozart wrote two duets for violin and viola as additions to a set by his admired but rather dissolute friend Michael Haydn (brother of Joseph).

Concerts helped nudge music in the newly bourgeois direction. These could be one-off subscription events, like those promoted by both Mozart and Beethoven in Vienna, or, increasingly from the 1760s, organised series staged by entrepreneurs like J. C. Bach and C. F. Abel in London. Their successor, Johann Peter Salomon, was the skilled and successful agent for Haydn's two London visits in the 1790s. Similar series flourished in many major cities. Management passed in time to boards and committees, modern-style. Some, like the long-running Concert Spirituel in Paris, lost their pull. Others took their place. Most saw the symphonies of Haydn gradually coming to dominate the programme lists as their popularity spread through publication and performances.

There were less formal concerts, too: serenades played outside, in town squares and other *al fresco* venues, including one of Mozart's under his own window, to his delighted surprise. Charitable concerts for widows, orphans, sufferers from venereal disease and other deserving causes garnered much philanthropic patronage. Charities for the impoverished relicts of musicians were a pleasing subset (though sadly didn't save poor, forgotten Anna Magdalena Bach from dying in poverty on the streets of Leipzig in 1760). Many concerts were very long, and a bit of a programmatical hotch-potch by today's standards: on one occasion Mozart gave the first three movements of his 'Haffner' Symphony, then an aria from *Idomeneo*, a piano concerto, a vocal scena, the 'Posthorn' serenade for winds, another piano concerto (with a new finale), a scene from *Lucio Silla*, a fugue ('because the Emperor was present'),[32] two sets of improvised variations on tunes from currently popular operas (one of which was repeated), a concert aria, and then, finally, the last movement of the symphony which began the concert. It seems that the inscription over the stage of one of the most emblematic of all the public concert halls, the Leipzig Gewandhaus, was taken as gospel: *'res severa verum gaudium'* ('real joy is a serious thing').

National and International

Art music became truly international. While earlier writers talked up national characteristics, by 1772 the cosmopolitan Gluck was aiming to 'do away with the ridiculous national differences in music'.[33] The French-speaking Frederick the Great attracted musicians from all over Europe to his cultured court in Berlin. Mozart, though conventionally patriotic (at least when not at home), could cry, 'If Germany, my beloved fatherland, of which I am proud, as you know, will not have me, then, in God's name, let France or England become richer by another talented German' ('another' meaning, perhaps, in addition to his friend J. C. Bach, then enjoying success as a composer and promoter in London).[34] A popular new symphony could quickly be heard all over the civilised world, including, for the first time, in America. German publishing houses like Simrock and Peters began to rival the established centres in Italy and northern Europe. National influences certainly didn't disappear from the mature Classical style – Mozart's Donna Anna in *Don Giovanni* (1787) is a genuine figure of Italian opera seria, and the fugues in Haydn's Masses would pass muster with the dustiest of Lutheran Kapellmeisters – but they were assimilated into a coherent and inclusive whole.

Writers on Music

The eighteenth century was the first great age of writing about music. There had been learned technical treatises, many of them highly detailed and complex, since medieval times and indeed long before. Now, writers began to describe music and musicians, concerts and context, in enlightened, historically well-informed and perceptive prose. Diderot and d'Alembert's *Encyclopédie ou Dictionnaire raisonné des sciences, des arts et des métiers* of 1751–2 included entries on music written by, among others, Rousseau (who told his readers that fugues more often make 'noise' than graceful melodies).[35] The early 1750s saw the rapid appearance of crucially important books on playing style and technique: for keyboard (Friedrich Wilhelm Marpurg and C. P. E. Bach), flute (Johann Joachim Quantz), violin (Leopold Mozart) and others. Stylish chroniclers like Casanova and the librettist Lorenzo da Ponte included erudite accounts of musical life in their memoirs alongside their other, in Casanova's case better-known, activities. Johann Joseph Fux codified the Palestrina style into a teaching method (still in use) in his *Gradus ad Parnassum* of 1725, beginning the habit of theorists describing a musical style after it had reached completion and become obsolete, as Carl Czerny was to do with so-called 'sonata form' in the 1840s. The witty and engaging Johann Mattheson asked his many musical friends to supply autobiographical notes for his wide-ranging and creatively unreliable articles: many did so. In England, Charles Avison wrote wisely and forcefully about musical meaning and the influence of the Italians, and John Mainwaring's *Memoirs of the Life of the Late George Frederic Handel* of 1760 was the first book-length biography of a composer (though sadly slapdash in terms of accuracy). Higher standards of scholarship took hold later in the century, in works like Giovanni Battista Martini's *La storia della musica*, the last volume of which was published in 1781, Johann Nikolaus Forkel's groundbreaking biography (and editions) of Bach, and in England Sir John Hawkins' *A General History of the Science and Practice of Music* of 1776 and, above all, the insightful, inquiring, informed and informative writings of the musical and much-travelled Charles Burney. These works, together with innumerable letters and journals of the leisured and literate on the Grand Tour, are our insight into the musical hinterland of Haydn and Mozart.

This new imperative of pinning reputations firmly inside the historical display case the moment the compositional wings had stopped flapping raises the question of who composers were writing for. Up to this point it had been understood, and to a large extent accepted, that each generation made its own style in preference to the last. As the English poet John Clare was to put it a few decades later, 'neglect is the only touchstone by which true genius is proved'.[36] Haydn and Mozart were the first generation for whom this was no longer true. At the same time, and as part of the same process, opinion began to value, and thus fix and preserve, older music. In 1776 a group of London aristocrats founded the Concerts of Antient Music: in a sure sign of just how neophiliac the general public taste was, 'Antient' was taken to mean anything over twenty years old. A little later, the annual Handel Festivals promoted his music in vastly swollen performances of *Messiah* and *Israel in Egypt*, effectively throttling English compositional creativity at birth for the next hundred years, as Burney pointed out with typical astuteness, in a misplaced veneration of a fake version of the old. The 'canon' of 'great works' was beginning to form, as an idea and as a corpus of works underpinning the repertoire. In the words of the modern pianist and writer Charles Rosen, 'We do not have to call upon any historical sympathy to appreciate the work of Mozart and Beethoven, and the late works of Haydn: they are still in the blood of most musicians today.'[37] They represent the first generation of whom that is true.

Styles, Types and Periods

Words describe the form, style and technique of the period with the usual mixture of accuracy and fluidity. The 'galant homme' was a figure of fashion, fond of simple, almost sentimental emotion, evoked in works of art of all kinds. The galant style in music, popular from around 1720–70, emphasised tunes, in short, singable phrases, with pleasing harmonies, elegantly exemplified in the violin sonatas of Giuseppe Tartini. This wasn't the most intellectual of phases of musical development, and produced no great masterworks, but in the hands of a conscientious and more than competent early Classicist like J. C. Bach it provided an important transition.

Rococo is a sort of hyper-Baroque without the counterpoint: courtly, embellished, stylised, aristocratic. Its signatures were keyboard pieces with whimsical titles, much ornamentation, and dance forms apotheosised into instrumental musettes and minuets.

The German *Empfindsamer Stil* ('sensitive style') concentrated on subtle emotions and nuanced shading. The many manuals of playing technique told students not just how to play, but how to feel: Leopold

Mozart opposed the addition of 'foolish frills',[38] and C. P. E. Bach told his readers to 'play from the soul, not like a trained animal'.[39] Burney describes Bach playing 'like one inspired. His eyes were fixed, his under lip fell, and drops of effervescence distilled from his countenance,'[40] which sounds closer in mood to the later manner of Liszt than to the controlled performances of his father; it also resonates with the sometimes emotionally ill-disciplined feel of some of his music. A key development was the move away from the Baroque idea that a single piece of music conveyed one emotion, or affekt, to the exploration and discussion of contrasting areas of feeling encapsulated within the principles and structures of the mature Classical manner.

One of the fascinating things about the Classical style in music is that it contained within it both the seeds from which it originated and the forces which pushed it over into something new, alongside each other. *Sturm und Drang* (conventionally translated into English as *Storm and Stress*, though the word *Drang* also contains elements of 'urging' and 'impulse') was the title of a play of 1776 by Friedrich Maximilian Klinger, and the phrase came to be associated with an artistic movement emphasising individual freedom and extremes of emotion. In music the term belongs to restless syncopations, rapid scales, sudden changes of texture and dynamic, and minor keys. Like all such terms, it resists attempts to fix it too precisely in time and place, but its rumblings can be heard in the opening of Mozart's dramatic D Minor Piano Concerto and expressive C Minor Fantasia, both dating from 1785. In the same decade C. F. D. Schubart, a figure of extremes but a talented musician and deep thinker, used a lengthy period of incarceration in Hohenasperg castle (following an intemperate attack on the Jesuits) to produce a wide-ranging work on musical aesthetics, capturing many of the ideas of his time and place in his florid but clear prose: the musical genius needs 'extremely tender feeling in the heart, sympathising with everything', because 'the heart is, as it were, the soundboard of the great composer'; 'if this is no good, he will never be able to do anything great'.[41] The floppy-haired Romantic genius can be glimpsed in the not too distant future, heading determinedly for his mountain top.

Form and Technique

Formal and technical changes were both cause and consequence of changes in style. The loss of the basso continuo allowed musical lines to function as equals in a texture (as, paradoxically, they had done in the music of the Renaissance, before the era of the general bass), leading to the colloquy of partners which is the string quartet. Melody became increasingly defined in terms of harmonic direction rather than contrapuntal possibility, leading to an increased reliance on homophony in the work of symphonists such as Johann and Carl Stamitz and Christian Cannabich associated with the fine orchestra at Mannheim in south-west Germany in the third quarter of the century. There is a slightly chaotic feel to the music of this period, with a rather random resort to effects like the famous Mannheim orchestral crescendo and rapid upward dash known as the 'Mannheim rocket', sudden silences or changes of dynamic, and an underlying tension between elements like phrase length and harmonic movement. The Mannheim composers, frankly, weren't good enough to synthesise all this as successfully as the high styles which came before and after: nor, in their different ways, were the three Bach sons, W. F., C. P. E. and J. C. The less mature works of Haydn and Mozart are not immune from these perils of a transitional style, which only serves to make the scale and coherence of their later achievement, together with the early works of Beethoven, all the more impressive. In the words of Charles Rosen, 'from 1780 onward we have only to sit back and watch two friends and their disciple sweep almost every kind of music, from the bagatelle to the mass, into their orbit'.[42]

The Classical style needed a new grammar of phrase, key and form. This came to be captured under the terms symphonic principle and sonata form. Of course, the ideas enfolded in these terms were, and are, fluid and dynamic: the basis of the Classical style is a feeling for balance, contrast and symmetry, not a set of rules.

The system of tonality, or writing in keys, reached a pleasing phase which allowed composers to exploit the gravitational pull of the hierarchy of chords based on the different notes of a major or minor scale. The structural importance of establishing key is exemplified by the ubiquitous presence of the repeated, arpeggiated broken chord figure, wholly absent from music before or after, known as the 'Alberti bass', after an otherwise unremarkable composer who used (but certainly didn't invent) the device.

Five Straight Lines

The complete first movement of the Sonatina in F Major, Opus 168 No. 1, by Anton Diabelli (published in Vienna in 1839). This little piece is often described as an example of sonata form in miniature. Bars 1–5 present a first subject in the tonic, F major. The music then modulates to the dominant, C major, for a new idea, or second subject, at bar 8. Bar 13 begins a discussion, or development, of these ideas in new keys, leading to a return (recapitulation) of the first subject in the tonic (bar 26), then an altered version of the linking passage to present the second subject again, but this time in the tonic (bar 33). A very brief closing passage, or coda, reaffirms the home key (bars 37–9).

The word 'sonata', like the word 'classical', has different meanings at different levels. In its guise as the descriptor of so-called sonata form, its principles include the setting-up of contrasting areas of feeling and key, some sort of discussion or elaboration of the contrasts, and a return to the mood and key of the opening. All attempts to fix this further into textbook patterns of first and second subject, development, recapitulation and coda inevitably fall at the first fence of the infinite number of exceptions to the rule. The best approach is to apply what evolutionary biologists call 'reverse engineering' – that is, don't ask what, ask why?

Sonata form is made of many things held in balance. One is phrasing. A little two-bar phrase which leads somewhere can be 'answered' with another which leads back, making a four-bar phrase. Or not – the composer can set up that expectation, and then do something else. Another is key: the music establishes its home key, moves away from it, sets up an expectation of heading back towards a cadence in the home key, and uses theme and phrase to lead us back home. Or not. A third thing is theme: two give an obvious opportunity for contrast, but sonatas can quite happily work with one, looked at from different directions, or with more than two, or with one or more made up of several complementary units. A first theme might be loud and brash, a second melodic and graceful. Or not. Another feature is the art of teasing out the inner potential of musical ideas, known as development. The composer and flautist Johann Joachim Quantz described a transitional phase of this concept: 'the best ideas ... must be dismembered and intermingled ... light and shadow must be maintained at all times ... '[43] Composers often did this in the links between themes and in the closing coda passages of the first and last paragraphs of a movement, as much as (or more than) in the development section in the middle (which might well begin with one of the main themes stated in a new key, giving it an element of recapitulation). A final element to mention (among many not mentioned) is counterpoint. The Classical age had to forget Bach and Handel and then rediscover them. The influence of this revelatory rediscovery is clearly discernible in the music of both Haydn and Mozart from the 1780s.

Sonata is a suite of principles, employing more or less consciously discernible internal correspondences to create the sense of unity valued in Western art since Aristotle. Crucially, music's unique status as an art which exists in time rather than space allows that unity to be implied before being granted: in Rosen's perfect phrase, 'symmetry withheld'.[44]

The symphonic principle extends this idea of discussing and manipulating a musical thought over time, so that the same tune looks different when viewed from the end of a movement from how it did at the beginning. This stands in opposition to the Baroque concept of a ritornello and its tightly organised themes being chopped up and re-presented across a movement, but staying basically the same.

The symphony grew out of the need for free-standing instrumental works to feed the new habit of concert-going, and it found a ready-made model in the opera overture or sinfonia, especially the Neapolitan variety: three movements, fast–slow–fast, with the musical weight concentrated in the first. A 'sinfonia del Sigr. Bach' (meaning Johann Christian) on a concert programme, for example, might well be lifted without comment or acknowledgement from an opera. England (for once) was ahead of the game and produced some of the very first symphonies in the well-trained hands of William Boyce. Each of the eight 'Symphonys' in his 1760 publication began life as the overture to something else: No. 1 in B Flat Major originally kicked off an ode for the king's birthday, and ends with a hunting finale, Mozart-style. It was written in 1756, the year Mozart was born, which seems appropriate.

Many other subsets of form enfolded the feeling of balance and return inherent in the sonata principle: sonata rondo, variations, rounded binary, minuet (or scherzo) and trio, the new, nervy, one-movement opera overture, and aria-like slow movements where the balance between theme and transition could produce an endless outpouring of song. Are there any more perfect moments in all music than the return of the main tune in the slow movements of Mozart's Clarinet Concerto or Piano Concerto No. 21 – simplicity distilled? In its pomp, the sonata principle could snap up any and every compositional trick into its sense of musical forces magnetically opposed and reconciled: the finale of Mozart's String Quartet No. 14 opens with a fugue (on one of his favourite rising four semibreve themes), which gives way to a second subject which is itself another fugue based on the second countersubject of the first; after batting other ideas around for a bit the music recapitulates by presenting a new fugue made of both themes joined together. The result is a joyful display of wit, charm and infinite skill lightly worn. What form is it in? The awestruck answer has to be: several, and at the same time something completely without model or precedent – surely a key component of genius.

Viewing the Classical period as a whole raises the question of the extent to which these formal principles appear on the opera stage. For example, in the very first number of *Le nozze di Figaro* (*The Marriage of Figaro*) (1786), Figaro is measuring out the bed to a jaunty, workmanlike tune. His bride Susanna asks him to admire her new hat, to a different tune with a different character. After the kind of you're-ignoring-me-dear discussion familiar to any couple, he takes up the second melody (and admires her hat). Writers like Adolf Bernhard Marx characterised contrasting sonata themes in terms of 'masculine' and 'feminine' from the start.[45] In the end, the form is infinitely more rich and subtle than that, and each contains elements of both, as indeed does a human personality and a human relationship. But the underlying feeling for form is unmistakably there in the background. Rolled out over a vastly bigger canvas, this alignment of human insight and musical form is what makes Mozart's operas, and in particular his ensemble finales, among the crowning glories of human achievement (and enormous fun).

The concerto borrowed many of the instincts of the symphony, the first movement often bracketed, Baroque-style, with an orchestral ritornello either side of the main business of the alternation of solo and tutti. The keyboard was a latecomer to the list of favoured solo instruments, and many concertos were written for the composer to play (or for a particular colleague such as Mozart's clarinettist Anton Stadler, who must have been a fine player and valued friend to inspire music like this). The bewildering variety of form on display in the mature Classical concerto includes a strong element of aria types – for, in some ways, the concerto soloist inherited the glitzy role of the vocal diva, as exemplified by the presence of the improvised cadenza and the fact that concerto and aria often occupied a similar position in a concert.

For the domestic market, pieces for the newly popular combination of two violins, viola (or 'violetta') and cello spun out of the presses of Paris and London in astonishing quantities in the couple of decades after 1760. Early examples, such as those of Luigi Boccherini, were advertised as 'symphonies' for more than one player to a part, 'or quartets' (in much smaller letters). The balance of musical power between the four players evolved: Boccherini liked to give high-pitched melodies to his own instrument, the cello, and use the viola as the bass instrument; middle-period Haydn gives most of the work to the first violin; the true colloquy of equals only appears with the mature Classical manner. The works of Haydn carry the quartet through this entire evolution, matching his own journey from provincial employee churning out fodder for the household in which he was currently employed to international star of the concert scene. The string quartet arose out of one of those happy coincidences in music history between what composers needed to do and what ordinary music-lovers wanted to hear (and play). In the family of social music, perhaps only the piano sonata took quite such a lengthy musical journey of discovery.

9

'BACH IS THE FATHER, WE ARE THE CHILDREN': ENLIGHTENMENT AND THE BIRTH OF THE CLASSICAL AGE[1]

This chapter about late eighteenth-century music could worthily be subtitled 'Everybody Who wasn't Haydn or Mozart'. Chief among that numerous tribe are the latest Bachs.

The Sons of J. S. Bach

When you read the name Bach in an eighteenth-century document, you have to stop and check where you are. We are thoroughly trained to use the unassuming little German word for 'brook' to mean the great Johann Sebastian. To a Berliner in the 1760s the name on its own meant his second son, Carl Philipp Emanuel. A slightly later music-lover in Milan, London or Paris would have been referring to C. P. E.'s much younger half-brother, Johann Christian.

In April 1782 Mozart wrote to his father from Vienna:

> Every Sunday at 12 noon I go to visit Baron von Suiten [his patron Gottfried van Swieten] – and there we play nothing but Händl and Bach – I am just putting together a collection of Bach fugues – that is Sebastian as well as Emanuel and Friedeman Bach ... You probably already know that the English Bach died? What a loss to the world of music![2]

It is telling that Mozart had to specify that he meant 'Sebastian [sic]' as well as the two eldest (but still living) sons.

Wilhelm Friedemann was the oldest Bach son, lavishly educated by his father, a fine keyboard player and recipient of much of Johann

Sebastian's greatest (and most difficult) clavier and organ music. His career in musical Leipzig, Dresden, Halle and Berlin was mixed, like his music: an uncomfortable combination of trying to carry the old ways of composing and making a living into the new world, and a dash of his father's impatience in dealing with unhelpful employers, without perhaps the doggedness and raw talent to get away with it. Works like his Piano Sonata in D Major of 1745 alternate a nervy charm with passages which look like something from a suite by his father. His legacy includes passing some of his father's manuscripts to one of his few pupils, Mendelssohn's great-aunt Sarah Levy (a key step towards the Bach renaissance of the early nineteenth century) and letting others head to Oklahoma with his daughter, where they were lost.

The next surviving son, Carl Philipp Emanuel, served at the court of Frederick the Great as an admired keyboard virtuoso before succeeding his godfather Telemann as Kapellmeister in Hamburg in 1768. Like his older brother he brought the thorough training received from his father to bear on the new *Empfindsamer Stil*, though with different, more personal, unusual and not entirely convincing results. Burney, writing in 1771, showed his customary uncanny ability to see musical style as if from outside the limits of his own time:

> There are several traits in the characters of the younger Scarlatti [i.e. Domenico] and Emanuel Bach, which bear a strong resemblance. Both were sons of great and popular composers, regarded as standards of perfection by all their contemporaries, except their own children, who dared to explore new ways to fame. Domenico Scarlatti, half a century ago, hazarded taste and effect, at which other musicians have but just arrived, and to which the public ear is but lately reconciled; Emanuel Bach, in like manner, seems to have outstript his age.[3]

Burney's historical antennae had slightly slipped here: Scarlatti's most hazardous experiments in taste were a lot less than half a century old; and there were plenty of people besides his own sons who came to regard 'Old Bach' as stylistically obsolete. But Burney's critical analysis is spot on. C. P. E. Bach's music treads various paths. His Magnificat pays homage to his father as clearly as his keyboard sonatas echo and extend the edgy world of Scarlatti. His unsettled and unsettling symphonies feed into the moody experimentation of early Mozart and middle Haydn. His remarkable 1769 oratorio *Die Israeliten in der Wüste* (*The Israelites in the Wilderness*) points the way between Handel and the Mendelssohn of *Elijah*. Emanuel remains a talented figure and precursor of Romanticism, whose talents never quite found an accepted style within which to cohere. That wasn't his fault. In some ways, the age outstript him.

Johann Christian, son of Johann Sebastian and his second wife Anna Magdalena, was fifteen when his father died. As was the case for his father (and many others), his musical education passed to a relative, in his case his half-brother Carl Philipp Emanuel, twenty-one years his senior. There is a beautiful portrait of Christian by the English society painter Thomas Gainsborough, giving him an amused, intelligent, quizzical, affable air: very London, very eighteenth century. This Bach worked first in Italy, with the contrapuntal pedagogue Padre Martini and as organist of the monster cathedral in Milan (becoming a Catholic in the process, which may have raised a few powdered eyebrows among the cantors and Kapellmeisters of his father's generation), then, from 1762, in London, as a composer of opera, symphonies and concertos (including one based on 'God Save the King' in a nod to his royal patrons), and promoter of a hugely successful concert series with his fellow symphonist Carl Friedrich Abel. His suave, tuneful music sounds like a dress rehearsal for Mozart: delightful, but not quite there yet. The two composers coincided twice: first when Mozart was eight and in London with his father; then, fourteen years later in Paris, when Mozart told Leopold that Bach was 'an Honourable man and fair to everyone; I love him, as you know, with all my heart – I have the highest respect for him'.[4] Mozart arranged sonata movements by Bach as some of his earliest essays in the keyboard concerto. He was, perhaps, along with Haydn, the only composer of whom Mozart never said a critical word. Sadly, as for some other leading members of his family, changing times did not protect his popularity and finances into old age, although Queen Charlotte, wife of George III, provided a pension for his widow (as, alas, nobody had satisfactorily done for his mother). He is buried tucked away around the corner from St Pancras station (while every piazza in Italy seems to have a flowing bronze statue of its local Baroque celebrity – Geminiani in Lucca, Galuppi in Burano – England tends to remember its musicians beneath grimy parish gravestones and behind blue plaques in lace-curtained suburban streets in Chelsea).

The Symphony: Progress and Practitioners

The new symphony was a cosmopolitan creature. The Milanese composer Giovanni Battista Sammartini was the son of a Frenchman called Saint-Martin. His seventy-plus symphonies, which move carefully between all the main phases of style, including a suave kind of melody which Rousseau called the 'Sammartini Andante',[5] provide a fascinating stage in the journey between the Baroque method of combining themes in a counterpoint and the Classical instinct for discussing them in a development. His music, unlike its creator, travelled widely throughout Europe. His starriest student was the internationalist Christoph Willibald Gluck. His brother worked for the Prince of Wales (and was, like him, a fine oboist who doubled on other wind instruments – a common practice, which explains why some symphonies of the period have a pair of oboes in one movement and a pair of flutes in the next). Another significant symphonist, the Bohemian Josef Mysliveček, is said to have described Sammartini as 'the father of Haydn's style',[6] though Haydn denied it, calling Sammartini a 'scribbler'.[7]

The Bohemian connection shows up again in the figure of Johann Stamitz, leading light (with the flautist Johann Joachim Quantz and violinist Christian Cannabich, among others) of the fine orchestra assembled by the Elector Carl Theodor at Mannheim, his jealous stab at a German Versailles. Burney famously said that 'there are more solo players, and good composers in this, than perhaps in any other orchestra in Europe; it is an army of generals', and vividly praised its startling effects.[8] As did C. F. D. Schubart: 'No orchestra in the world ever excelled the Mannheim. Its forte is a thunderclap, its crescendo a cataract, its diminuendo a crystal stream babbling away into the distance, its piano a breath of spring.'[9] Mozart met Cannabich on several occasions travelling around Europe, including during a lengthy stay in Mannheim from late 1777, and regarded him and his family with affection and respect. (This is partly because he had two musical daughters, the elder of whom shared Mozart's taste in smutty humour: 'I did some rhyming in the presence and company of Canabich, his wife and daughter ... nothing but crude stuff, such as Muck, shitting and ass licking ... I would not have behaved so godlessly if our ringleader, known as Lisel, namely Elisabetha Cannabich, had not inspired and incited me.') Musically, Mozart's critical eye was as sharp as ever, even with a valued friend more than twice his age:

'Cannabich is now a much better composer than when we met him in Paris.' He didn't think much of 14-year-old Rosa Cannabich's piano technique, either.[10]

Opera: Singers and Librettists

The eighteenth century was an age of big characters. Singers were among the biggest. At the expensive end, castrati continued to fascinate and appal: 'it looks for all the world like a man, though they say it is not,' says a character in Tobias Smollett's 1771 novel *The Expedition of Humphry Clinker*; 'it warbled so divinely that while I listened I really thought myself in paradise'.[11] Casanova called the celebrated Guadagni 'a man only in appearance', though 'handsome' and 'a thorough musician',[12] and describes several dodgy encounters between male singers whose female persona proved perhaps rather more convincing than they'd intended and their inflamed admirers. In 1773, just before his eighteenth birthday, Mozart wrote one of his most celebrated soprano showstoppers, the motet *Exsultate, Jubilate*, for the Milanese castrato Venanzio Rauzzini, writing to his sister, '*Ich vor habe den primo eine homo motteten machen welche müssen morgen bey Theatinern den producirt wird*', a typically virtuoso bit of wordplay which translates as something like, 'I for the primo a homo motet to make had tomorrow that at the Theatines performed will be.'[13] Later, he would suggest an ingenious way around the lack of female singers in the Salzburg opera company:

> we still have the castrato! – and you know what kind of animal that is? – he can sing in the high register and would, therefore, be excellent in a woman's role ... we'll allow Herr Ceccarelli [the castrato] to change back and forth between his male and female roles ... and I will ... write several dozen operas in which the male lead and the female lead never encounter each other on stage, for in this way the castrato can play both ...[14]

We can only regret that Mozart never composed his cross-dressing lover-avoiding panto-opera. The reign of the castrati remains one of the oddest and, to us, most distant episodes in this story. The painful irony is that a practice which began with the ultra-puritanical distaste for women singing in church ended by creating a species of unique moral and sexual ambiguity (but also unique musical accomplishment).

At the other end of the scale, singers in light opera and vaudeville didn't really have to know how to sing at all. Casanova recounts how one of his conquests, a 16-year-old called Mimi, ran away from home (after having and abandoning his baby) and joined a travelling troupe at the local fair:

> 'I did not know,' I said to her, 'that you were a musician.' 'I am a musician about as much as all my companions, not one of whom knows a note of music. The girls at the opera are not much more clever, and in spite of that, with a good voice and some taste, one can sing delightfully.'[15]

Young Mimi is a rather extreme example of the tradition of actor singers like Handel's Kitty Clive and Susannah Cibber and Mozart's friends Emanuel Schikaneder and his niece Anna (who played one of the three boys in the premiere of *Die Zauberflöte*).

The act of writing an opera still began with a pre-existing libretto. The composer would then engage a poet or translator to 'adapt, or rather to hash up, the drama to his taste', as the Venetian playwright Carlo Goldoni said about his collaboration with Vivaldi. Very often, adaptations would serve to showcase the talents (or mask the deficiencies) of a particular singer: Vivaldi told Goldoni, 'You see here, for instance, after this tender scene, there is a cantabile aria; but as Miss Annina does not … does not … does not like this kind of aria [Goldoni added parenthetically "that is, she could not sing it"] … we need here an aria of action.'[16] Goldoni did as he was told, and got the job. In addition to his sparkling straight plays, Goldoni wrote many comic libretti, including in 1750 *Il mondo della luna*, set to music by at least six composers including Galuppi, Haydn and Paisiello, whose second act is set on the moon (or at least, one of the characters thinks it is), and *La finta semplice* of 1768, set to music by Mozart at the age of twelve. His maxim, as stated in the preface to a 1756 revival of *Statira* (c.1740), was: 'When I write for music, I think of myself last of all. I think of the actors, I think very much of the composer, I think of the pleasure of the audience in the theatre.' Goldoni's big-hearted buffa spirit and larger-than-life characters underpin the world of later eighteenth-century comic opera like a series of running gags.

Another wordsmith whose own life story reads like something dreamed up by Henry Fielding or William Hogarth, only more rackety, was Pierre-Augustin Caron de Beaumarchais. Watchmaker, revolutionary, bankrupt, serial litigant and thrice-married adulterer, his Figaro plays are perhaps the most important theatrical operatic source texts of the age, richly reflecting the range of his human sympathy and experience in their cast of grasping nobles and their compromised courtiers. Louis XVI needed the persuasion of Queen Marie Antoinette, among others, to finally let subversive stuff like this past the censors and onto the public stage. In translation, the witty and scabrous account of the love lives of Count Almaviva and his servant produced three of the best and most influential of all comic operas, versions of the first play of the trilogy, *Il barbiere di Siviglia*, by Paisiello and Rossini, and of the second, *Le nozze di Figaro*, by Mozart.

Mozart's 'hash-up' librettist for his version of *Figaro* was Lorenzo da Ponte. A Jewish-born Roman Catholic priest who fathered many children by an assortment of mistresses, da Ponte arrived in Dresden in 1781 from his native Venice thinking he had a job lined up as court poet (he didn't). He provided texts for many leading composers including Salieri, the Englishman Stephen Storace, and Vicente Martín y Soler (*Una Cosa Rara*, written, like *Figaro*, in 1786 and wickedly quoted by Mozart, along with *Figaro*, at the end of *Don Giovanni*). Around the time of Mozart's death in 1791 da Ponte set out for a new life in Paris, but was deflected by the turmoil of the French Revolution to London, where he set up as a writer and grocer until debt propelled him and his mistress to America, where he taught Italian, became a US citizen, founded an influential opera company in a theatre which burned down (twice), wrote his memoirs, and died at the age of nearly ninety in 1838.

Da Ponte's importance in this story is his innate instinct for Mozart's artistic needs. Mozart was a picky partner, telling his father that 'an Italian poet [probably da Ponte] recently brought me a libretto that I may well use if he is willing to whittle it down to suit my wishes'.[17] Mozart also had an unfortunate habit of assuming (rightly or wrongly) that his professional rivals were ganging up on him, jealously placing da Ponte in the supposed Salieri camp. Whatever the pricklinesses, da Ponte provided the verbal architecture of three of the greatest of all works of music theatre: *Le nozze di Figaro*, *Don Giovanni* and *Così fan Tutte* (1790). In his preface to *Figaro*, da Ponte revealingly pointed out that he did not simply make a translation of Beaumarchais but 'an imitation, or let us say an extract': five acts became four; several characters were omitted; and, above all, he fashioned the imperishable pile-up at the end of Act 2 where characters entering in ones and twos add their plot twists and emotional takes to an ensemble of increasing musical and psychological complexity. The end of the opera is equal in matching musical style and structure to subtle and complex emotion, focusing in on the ineffable simplicity of Almaviva's moment of self-awareness: '*Contessa, perdono*' ('Contessa, pardon me'). Da Ponte says that 'our excuse [for writing a piece which is rather long] will be the variety of development of this drama … to paint faithfully and in full colour the divers passions that are aroused, and … to offer a new type of spectacle'.[18] He gave vivid life to some of Mozart's most creative ideas: *Così*, unusually, is not an adaptation of an existing text but 'something altogether New', as Mozart conjectured in 1783, adding, 'New – is always better'; most strikingly, he realised Mozart's vision of an opera which would be 'very *Comical*; and, if possible, include *2 equally good female roles*; – one would have to be a Seria … '[19] – a revolutionary stirring of the generic pot which led to the spectacle of the self-regarding lovers and nobles of *Così* and *Don Giovanni* having their strings thoroughly pulled by their sassy servants from the buffa side of the tracks, and not realising it. It's a key moment in the evolution of the art of opera as drama.

Among Mozart's other wordsmiths, the cheerful Emanuel Schikaneder can be represented no better than by an anecdote Mozart told about the premiere of *Die Zauberflöte*, a story given an almost unbearable added poignancy and resonance by the fact that we know that the young composer, so full of fire and fun amidst a sea of troubles, was in the last weeks of his short, vivid life:

> when Papageno's aria with the Glockenspiel came on, at that moment I went backstage because today I had a kind of urge to play the Glockenspiel myself. – So I played this joke: just when Schikaneder came to a pause, I played an arpeggio – he was startled – looked into the scenery and saw me – the 2nd time he came to that spot, I didn't play – and this time he stopped as well and did not go on singing – I guessed what he was thinking and played another chord – at that he gave his Glockenspiel a slap and shouted '*Shut up!*' – everybody laughed. – I think through

this joke many in the audience became aware for the first time that Papageno doesn't play the Glockenspiel himself.[20]

One writer whose progress outraked all others, even in this most picaresque of centuries, was Giacomo Casanova. As an educated and widely travelled top-drawer chancer he met many leading theatrical figures and charted opera's main currents. He knew da Ponte, who apparently did not take up his offer to write some new text for *Don Giovanni* (even though aspects of Casanova's own life paralleled the dissolute Don's with rapacious accuracy). One writer compared him to Figaro. He wrote a melodrama for Dresden, which amused the king, Frederick Augustus II of Saxony. The lowest point of his wild career was when he had to scrape a living as an opera fiddler at the Teatro San Samuele in Venice, 'where I earned a crown a day ... I was considered a worthless fellow, but I did not care.'[21]

It's surely no accident that while the authors of opera buffa often behaved as badly as the people in their plays, the long-lived high priest of opera seria, the Abate Metastasio, lived a life of modesty, learning and high art. Born Pietro Trapassi at the very end of the seventeenth century, his name was Hellenised by an early supporter who nurtured his precocious gift for Classical rhetoric. As a young man in Rome he earned the acquaintance and admiration of every leading composer, including Scarlatti and Hasse, all of whom set his works to music many times. He became a genuine superstar of the seria circuit, and his name continued to draw crowds all across Europe: his *Adriano in Siria*, first performed in 1732, was set to music by no fewer than sixty composers. In 1730 he moved to Vienna as court poet. Casanova met him there in 1753. The two men had a fascinating exchange on artistic matters: Metastasio said he wrote slowly (he didn't, or certainly not always); his favourite among his own operas was *Attilio Regolo* of 1740; the two men poured scorn on the French for thinking that true poetry could be translated and for 'the very strange belief that it is possible to adapt poetry to music already composed' (although it is, of course, perfectly possible, as Handel proved); perhaps most interestingly of all, Metastasio told his visitor that 'he had never written an arietta without composing the music of it himself, but that as a general rule he never showed the music to anyone'[22] (though he and the singer and impresario Farinelli, whom he called his 'twin', exchanged compositions as part of their lengthy correspondence).

The Metastasian seria aria is, as in the Baroque, essentially static, designed to deliver a single emotion. His *Artaserse* (written in 1730 and set to music no fewer than ninety times) contains this brief aria text:

Pallido il sole / Torbido il cielo / Pena minaccia / Morte prepara / Tutto mi spira / Rimorso e orror
Ti mormi cinge / Di freddo gelo / Dolor mi rende / La vita amara / Io stesso fremo / Control mio cor

[Pale the sun; Cloudy the sky; Pena looms threateningly; Death stands ready; All buffets and blows at me; Horror and remorse
Murmurs surround you with cold frost; Pain makes my life bitter; I tremble – Be still, my heart]

The fluid rhyme scheme, gentle metre, short lines, singable vowels and counterpointing of clear but simple imagery binding soul and nature together (pale/cloudy, cold/bitter, life/death, heart/horror) are a gift to the composer of lyrical flair and dramatic instinct. It is beautifully done.

Some Notable Viennese

Casanova met Metastasio in his apartment at the Michaelerhaus in Vienna. This sturdy building provides one of those happy reminders that the history of high-end music often seems to take place in a large village called Europe, with legendary figures bumping into each other on the stairs, making friends and falling out just like ordinary people. Typically for the Austrian capital, the social standing of the residents of the grand edifice in the Michaelerplatz was reflected in how high up the building they lived. On the ground floor was the dowager princess Esterházy. In the middle was the Martines family, including Marianna, an accomplished pianist and singer whose imaginative Italianate compositions, including the large-scale oratorio *Isacco figura del redentore*, were widely performed and earned her prestigious membership of the Accademia Filarmonica di Bologna in 1773. Her regular librettist was the family friend and lodger Metastasio: Marianna and her sister cared for him until his death. Also tinkling away somewhere in the house was another skilled composer and influential teacher,

Nicola Porpora. Right at the top, in a leaky attic worthy of the first act of *La Bohème*, was an indigent ex-choirboy and country lad who was trying (not very successfully) to scrape a living from his wits and talents and a spot of valet work for the demanding Porpora: Joseph Haydn. These names would coincide again.

Final mention in this smartly dressed parade around the handsome squares of Vienna and the musical hinterland of the rapidly changing Classical style must go to one of the most important patrons in the entire history of music, Baron Gottfried van Swieten.

Mozart played and arranged the music of Bach and Handel for him, creating the large-scale orchestrations of *Messiah* and other works which remained standard for the whole of the nineteenth century, a key stage in his own development. Van Swieten's passion for Baroque music was highly unusual, almost eccentric, for his age and circle, and the young Beethoven was another who benefited profoundly from mining his collection at the regular Sunday salons in Vienna. Beethoven dedicated his Haydn-esque First Symphony to the baron, and van Swieten helped Haydn find and adapt the librettos for his two great, late oratorios, *The Creation* of 1800 and *The Seasons* of 1801. For the latter he employed a sort of odd reverse-translation method, where he would put the Scotsman James Thomson's pastoral English verse into rather clunky German, then translate the words back into English in the same metre as the German, creating a fully bilingual musical work (the first published edition added a third language, French). Unsurprisingly, style and meaning didn't always survive unbutchered; the Augustan Thomson's 'By Nature's swift and secret-working hand / The garden glows, and fills the liberal air / With lavish fragrance' came back into English (via German) as 'Look at the meadows, the grassland, / look at all the fields ... look at the fish'. But he added some authentically rustic touches, like a couple of German folk poems which seem to have taken the elderly Haydn back to his childhood in a country village, and took out un-Enlightenedly realistic elements like a traveller freezing to death in a snowstorm (Schubert's shivering Romanticism would not be so squeamish). He also made many musical suggestions in the margins and footnotes, some accepted by Haydn, such as the memorable low-scored accompaniment to the Genesis paraphrase 'Be fruitful all / And multiply'.

Aside from his musical patronage, the baron arranged Mozart's funeral and supported his young widow and two infant sons, and paid for the carriage which took Haydn on his second trip to London in 1794. Unlike some later musical nobles, he was a patron, never a friend. But we owe the stiff-backed baron much.

Gluck

Christoph Willibald Gluck was another van Swieten protégé.

Gluck was born in the gap between the age of Handel and the age of Haydn and Mozart, in 1714, in a village in a Bohemian bit of Bavaria. His pupil Salieri later set running a continuing debate about his native language: 'Gluck, whose native tongue was Czech, expressed himself in German only with effort, and still more so in French and Italian.'[23] This sense of Gluck as a composer without the usual bookends of period and place is key.

His childhood sounds a little like Haydn's: son of a forester, he was a country lad, brought up in the orbit of various courts and monasteries in a working artisan family with lots of music around. Teenage years in musically cosmopolitan Prague led him to Milan in his early twenties, where he studied with the symphonist Sammartini and composed his first operas (mostly settings of Metastasio, as expected). From the early 1740s he travelled, including to London, where he met Handel and saw the actor David Garrick, celebrated pioneer of a naturalistic style of performance. A rising reputation and a couple of commissions (one of which failed to please its librettist, the ubiquitous Metastasio) took him back to Vienna, followed by a year or so on tour with the famous Mingotti theatrical troupe (on which he picked up a venereal disease from a prima donna and gave a performance on the glass harmonica in Copenhagen). Links with another travelling troupe and more Metastasio (including *La clemenza di Tito* for Naples in 1752) placed him more firmly back in Vienna, where he married well and landed a secure and prestigious post as Kapellmeister. In 1756 he was made a Knight of the Golden Spur by the Pope, afterwards proudly calling himself 'Ritter' or 'Chevalier' Gluck (Casanova and the 13-year-old Mozart were other roughly contemporary recipients).

The 1750s were a period of stylistic transition for Gluck. So they were for music generally, and opera in particular. A wordy little row in France exemplified the divisions.

In August 1752 an Italian company gave a performance of

Pergolesi's intermezzo *La serva padrona* at the Académie Royale in Paris. Jean-Jacques Rousseau, always ready for an intellectual spat, championed the Italian style in his *Lettre sur la musique Françoise*, concluding 'the French have no music and are incapable of having any'.[24] Others defended the more formal style of Lully and Rameau, founded on the character of French declamation. The pithy and pointed pamphlet polemic became known as the *Querelle des Bouffons* (Quarrel of the Comedians) and gained as much of its heat from national *amour-propre* and Gallic relish of a good philosophical argument as from the music. One young lady called Rousseau's one-act opera *Le Devin du village* 'a charming work which will always please those who like what is natural', and admired 'the most perfect declamation' in an ariette by 'the celebrated Rameau' – which seems to put her in both camps.[25] The *querelle* puttered out. Its legacy seemed to be a recognition that the future lay with a synthesis of national styles, not their division.

The thoughtful Gluck appears to have been pondering operatic problems for some time. He wasn't the only one. Francesco Algarotti's *Essay on the Opera* of 1755 proposed a simplified form of opera seria, with emphasis on the drama rather than formality and spectacle. His thinking influenced important figures including composers Tommaso Traetta and Niccolò Jommelli, the theatrical director Count Giacomo Durazzo, the librettist Ranieri de Calzabigi, the innovative dancer actor Gaspari Angiolini and the castrato Gaetano Guadagni, champion of an unadorned vocal line and Gluck's first Orfeo. Vienna in the 1760s also benefited from an enlightened and cosmopolitan public censor, Joseph von Sonnenfels.

Gluck's first steps towards Algarotti's reforms were taken in the ballet *Don Juan* of 1761. The following year came *Orfeo ed Euridice*, an azione teatrale (a genre of short, moralising works of which *Orfeo* is in some ways untypical), with words by Calzabigi. Both men were nearing fifty: for them, as for Rameau, theatrical maturity came after long experience and experiment. The 1760s saw further cautious prods at the reform agenda, including a Turkish opéra comique and azioni teatrali on Metastasian texts, crowned by the tragedy *Alceste* in 1767. *Alceste* has a famous preface, signed by Gluck but certainly written jointly with Calzabigi, setting out their aim of avoiding 'abuses' such as 'a useless superfluity of ornaments', words sung 'four times over', 'sharp contrast between the aria and the recitative' and making an 'actor' (not, tellingly, a singer) stand around waiting for 'a tiresome ritornello'. Instead, they sought 'a beautiful simplicity' and 'a well-assorted contrast of light and shade'.[26]

Drama is all. The key features of the reformed style are clearly audible in the music: an overture which plunges straight into the mood and manner of the drama; accompanied recitative which flows seamlessly into and out of arioso style; little extension or repetition of words; an active and dramatically engaged chorus; plenty of musical and psychological colour in the orchestra; few scene changes; no sea monsters, subplots, flying sets, folding flaps or other stagey flim-flam; and, above all, music of a direct emotional simplicity. The word used in an earlier preface was *'vraisemblable'* – truth-seeming, convincing, real.[27] To take just two examples: in *Alceste* the sepulchral aria *'Ombre, larve, compagne di morte'* grows imperceptibly out of the preceding music without announcing itself with a discrete new theme; Orfeo's appeals to the Furies to allow him to enter the underworld are met with repeated cries of 'No!' which gradually soften beneath Orfeo's pleading, binding chorus and soloist together. Structure and style become part of the overall span of a carefully paced scene. Sonnenfels summed up the objectives of reform opera in an eyewitness account of 1761: 'Bernasconi played Alceste with a truth, feeling and sympathy that are marvelled at …'[28]

Gluck's Calzabigi operas declined in appeal in Vienna. Ever the internationalist, he turned his attentions to another musical centre, Paris. His emissary François le Blanc du Roullet prepared the ground in a thoroughly modern way, with a series of letters in the newspapers. Gluck's French operas, supported and promoted by his young pupil Marie Antoinette, now Dauphine of France, are among his masterpieces, including the dramatically and psychologically compelling *Iphigénie en Aulide* and the French version of *Orfée et Euridice*, both dating from 1774. They occasioned a flare-up of the Italian vs French debate of two decades earlier, with the difference that this time the row was deliberately engineered. The Italophiles recruited the successful composer Niccolò Piccinni to their corner, and even tried to engineer a head-to-head by getting both men to set the same libretto. But Gluck refused to play ball and suppressed the music he had already composed, leaving the field clear for Piccinni to do his not-very-convincing best at grafting Neapolitan gestures onto the French language. The year 1779 brought Gluck's fifth opera for the French stage, the logical culmination of the reform agenda, with many self-borrowings, *Iphigénie en Tauride*. Later the same year, the pastoral *Écho et Narcisse* was an unfashionable flop. Gluck headed home. His successor in Paris was his pupil Salieri, his protégé since 1767. The opera *Les Danaïdes* of 1784 was announced as a joint venture between pupil and patron: after its huge success Gluck generously informed the Paris papers that the music was, in fact, all Salieri's.

The row chuntered along behind him, as Burney reported with his usual perspicacity:

> Party runs as high among poets, musicians and their adherents, at Vienna as elsewhere. Metastasio and Hasse, may be said, to be at the head of one of the principal sects; and Calsabigi and Gluck of another. The first, regarding all innovations as quackery, adhere to the ancient form of the musical drama, in which the poet and musician claim equal attention from an audience; the bard in the recitatives and narrative parts; and the composer in the airs, duos and choruses. The second party depend more on theatrical effects, propriety of character, simplicity of diction, and of musical execution, than on, what they style flowery description, superfluous similes, sententious and cold morality, on one side, with tiresome symphonies, and long divisions, on the other.[29]

Mozart described several friendly encounters with Gluck at the opera and over dinner. In June 1781 he gave his father the news that Gluck had suffered a stroke, the first of several; he died in 1787. Jommelli's Requiem was sung at his memorial the following year, alongside his own *De Profundis*, for choir and an ensemble with three trombones but no violins, written just before he died, directed by his friend and student Salieri.

Gluck remains an original, and something of an enigma. Burney reported Handel as saying 'he knows no more of contrapunto as mein cook'.[30] Mozart and his father exchanged views about Gluck in their letters: Mozart's critical generosity may have been tempered by the fact that when he eventually succeeded to Gluck's job as imperial and court chamber composer it was at less than half the salary. Gluck was friends with the influential early Romantic poet Friedrich Gottlieb Klopstock, and wrote lieder probing notions of death, for a singer to accompany himself at the piano, linking him forward to Schubert as well as back to Handel. His pursuit of a 'beautiful simplicity' left his legacy curiously unfulfilled in the Vienna of sonata form and the symphony.[31] The writer Friedrich Nicolai said in 1781: 'The *chevalier* Gluck is the most famous musician in Vienna. Although highly prized there, as elsewhere, he has, to my knowledge, not exerted any very marked influence on the city's musical taste.'[32] J. C. Bach cheerfully misunderstood his reforms by adding new arias to *Orfeo*, trampling on its dramatic unity as if he was dealing with an old-style pasticcio.

One of Gluck's signatures is the beautifully considered use of orchestral sound, always matched to a dramatic and psychological need, leading intriguingly from Rameau into the German Romantic operatic world of Mozart's *Die Zauberflöte*, Weber's woodman Max in *Der Freischütz* and the works of Richard Wagner. We will climb that family tree later, as no doubt the alert, impressionable young country boy Gluck did alongside his father in the shifting, rustling, whispering forest.

Some Other Musicians

For many other talents of the time, a walk-on part is less than they deserve but more than history has sometimes given them.

The operas of Jommelli, Paisiello and Piccinni are rarely seen today, but at their best burst with innovation and grace. Porpora's backward-looking opere serie hadn't saved the Opera of the Nobility in London back in the 1730s, but being Farinelli and Haydn's teacher is not a bad claim to fame. Boccherini took his childlike early Classical tunefulness to a successful career in Spain. Baldassare Galuppi's once-popular comedies came down to a later listener as 'cold music ... like a ghostly cricket'.[33] Dittersdorf, celebrated in his lifetime for his witty operas, also wrote a couple of gruffly lyrical solo works for double-bass, as well as playing quartets with Haydn, Mozart and Johann Baptist Vanhal. Michael Haydn, Joseph's younger brother, kept a touch of the rustic peasant (and a fondness for the bottle which he shared with his wife, mercilessly satirised by Mozart in one of his letters: 'Mad. Haydn is sickly – she has gone too far with her austere religious life').[34] England provided little innovation: the agreeable Thomas Attwood is better remembered as a student of Mozart (who genially told him, 'Attwood, you are an ass' in the margin of his workbook)[35] and a friend of Mendelssohn than for his own pleasing but insubstantial compositions – England in the late eighteenth century is perhaps more notable for developments outside the concert hall like hymn-singing, wonderfully nourished by Methodists and nonconformists of many kinds. By the end of the period France was in flames, ushering in one of those turbulent episodes when music had to do what it was told, not what it wanted.

As the eighteenth century made its troubled turn into the nineteenth, the Neapolitan opera composer Domenico Cimarosa backed the wrong side once too often in the military and political skirmishes around his native Naples, and ended up hiding from his enemies underneath the stage of his own theatre, until the stench of the decaying corpse of a dead colleague drove him out.

The world of Haydn and Mozart was turning into the Europe of Napoleon.

10

'LET THERE BE LIGHT': HAYDN, MOZART AND VIENNA[1]

Beginnings: Haydn

Joseph Haydn was born in 1732 in a small village in Lower Austria, the eldest of a large rural family. The tuneful country music which filled his childhood never left him. Talent and a pleasing voice took him first to the local provincial centre of Hainburg and then to St Stephen's cathedral in Vienna (described by Burney as looking like 'an old wardrobe') as a choirboy.[2] Here he encountered neglect and haphazard education, was teased by Empress Maria Theresa for singing like 'a crow' when his voice broke, expelled for cutting off another boy's pigtail, then scraped a living around Vienna on his fiddle and his wits. A typical Sunday saw the teenage Haydn playing the violin in one church at 8.00 a.m., the organ in a count's private chapel at 10.00 a.m. and singing in St Stephen's at 11.00 a.m., then spending an evening playing serenades in the streets with chums like the composer Carl Dittersdorf, sometimes being seen off by the riot squad, then back to his draughty garret to pore hungrily over the composition treatises of Fux, Mattheson and C. P. E. Bach (he later gave his well-thumbed copy of Fux's *Gradus ad Parnassum* to Mozart). It is perhaps not too fanciful to see the seeds of his entire aesthetic in that rich mix of early musical influences. Nicola Porpora gave him instruction, insults and work as a valet and accompanist when he was too idle to get out of his chair and do it himself. Haydn took pupils, and secured a commission for a Singspiel (successful but, alas, now lost), by improvising music to accompany swimming while the comic actor known as Bernardon lay across a chair, gasping and kicking his legs in the air.

The early 1760s saw several significant and lasting changes for

Haydn, now in his late twenties. Like Mozart he married his second choice of sister. He also landed a secure job, first as Kapellmeister to Count Morzin, then, from 1761, with the family he was to serve for the rest of his life, the Esterházys.

Haydn's output and influence can conveniently (though simplistically) be viewed by decade: early Masses and chamber music in the rackety 1750s; progressive maturity based on the Baroque and galant styles in the early Esterházy years to 1770; then mature modern mastery of the new forms of symphony and quartet in the *Sturm und Drang*-influenced decade before the advent of the young Mozart in Vienna in 1781. C. P. E. Bach was an admired influence and friend. Haydn was good-natured, easy-going, full of 'what the British call humour' (according to one of his contemporary biographers), and fully allowed 'the spirit of Austrian cheerfulness' to permeate pieces which 'tease the audience by wanton shifts from the seemingly serious to the highest levels of comedy'.[3] Like Mozart he was far from immune to the charms of a young woman, and flirted with that conventional mix of gallantry and explicit suggestiveness which was emphatically part of Austrian culture at the time but which has puzzled puritanical music-lovers of later ages, not least because his marriage, sadly, was joyless, childless and long. But he was also devout, well-behaved and disciplined by nature and upbringing – characteristics imbued in him by his God-fearing mother and never forgotten.

Beginnings: Mozart

Mozart was twenty-four years younger than Haydn. They didn't meet until Haydn was around fifty. Yet they can justly be considered contemporaries. This is partly because Haydn was a slow starter and a late developer, while Mozart was exactly the opposite (their respective first symphonies were written just five or six years apart, Haydn's at age twenty-seven, Mozart's at age nine). Partly it's because of one of those miracles of historical timing whereby style and manner reach full maturity at exactly the same moment as a musical mind that is perfectly poised to embrace and exploit them. Partly it's because Haydn lived a long time, and Mozart didn't. Sometimes they seem to have been working closely together, as in the respective sets of string quartets in the early 1780s, or their joint discovery of the music of Handel and Bach. More often they appear to have been operating in a kind of complementary symbiotic parallel, which allowed each of them to learn from and spark off the other, but at the same time permitted each to be, gloriously and uniquely, himself.

Mozart's childhood could not have been more different from Haydn's. Born in Salzburg to a professionally musical family, he never went to school. Instead, his father Leopold advanced the education and prospects of the precocious Wolfgang and his slightly older sister Maria Anna (known as 'Nannerl', perhaps to distinguish her from their mother, Anna Maria) by an endless series of lengthy and gruelling European tours, showing off their talents to kings and emperors, nursing them through repeated and serious illnesses, and neglecting his own job as Vice-Kapellmeister to the Prince-Archbishop of Salzburg. The longest trip took over three years, starting when Mozart was seven (though concert programmes could be creatively ambiguous about his actual age), and included Paris, The Hague and London, where they met J. C. Bach, an amiable and important influence. Three trips to Italy produced several early operas and a meeting with the contrapuntal pedagogue Padre Martini. In 1777 Leopold wrote: 'The greater the talents which children have received from God, the more they are bound to use them for the improvement of their own and their parents' circumstances.'[4] Alas, his son, now twenty-one, proved perennially hopeless at using his talents to improve his own or anybody else's circumstances, partly because of a childlike inability to manage his worldly affairs, partly because, unlike Haydn, he lacked the diplomatic skills necessary to secure and hold down a job (that is, he was no good at being told what to do). The words of the Elector of Bavaria took on a sad familiarity: 'But my dear child, there is no vacancy.'[5] That same fortune-seeking jaunt to Munich took in other musical centres, including Augsburg, where he met his young cousin (another Maria Anna), and Mannheim, where he heard the famous orchestra and struck up an acquaintance with the double bass player Fridolin Weber and his family, falling recklessly in love with his daughter, 17-year-old Aloysia, a talented singer. In Paris, on 3 July 1778, Mozart's mother died. In 1779 he took his second Salzburg job, as court organist (his first, as a 13-year-old third concertmaster and violinist, was unpaid). In 1780 he travelled to Munich where his opera seria *Idomeneo* was premiered in early 1781. The same year he was summoned to Vienna by his employer, Archbishop Colloredo of Salzburg, but broke with the archbishop in a furious exchange ('I hate the Archbishop to the point of madness').[6] Vienna would be his home for the remaining ten years of his life.

The people and stories around Mozart reflect him back to us. When the impatient Colloredo withheld Michael Haydn's salary because the composer was too ill (or possibly too hungover) to complete a commission, Mozart finished the piece himself and delivered it, with Haydn's name on it, without telling his friend. Families with teenage daughters were a constant: Wider, Cannabich, Weber. His affection could be more general than particular ('if I had to marry every lady with whom I've been joking around, I would easily have collected 200 wives by now,' he reported defensively to his disapproving father in response to stories which circulated back to Salzburg while he was lodging with the Webers in Vienna – rumours which turned out to be perfectly true).[7] He loved words, writing in an exuberant Babel of invention and smut, particularly to his sister and cousin, alongside laser-sharp critiques of fellow composers and musical politics. Like many creative types he liked getting up early to work, before the daily round of teaching and performing. His health was always fragile. He enjoyed conventional pastimes like dog-walking and target-shooting. His relationship with his father was one of the most significant, and saddest, in all music. By contrast, his mother remains an indistinct figure, relegated, like her daughter, to a less vivid role in the drama by character and convention.

Mozart: Character and Early Works

Mozart's works of this period reflect the eternal interface between what a composer has to do to keep his bread buttered and what he wants to do. Mozart's mind processed music all the time. He once said that he had 'gone for two weeks without writing a note … of course, I was writing, but not on paper'.[8] His creative development was constant and continuous, and firmly rooted in the day-to-day practicalities of being a working musician. Some jobs interested him more than others: he told his father that 'I can't stand' the flute,[9] but was this partly because he thought that Ferdinand de Jean, who commissioned two concertos, had underpaid him (he probably hadn't)? Does this typically unsatisfactory business arrangement show up in the music – charming, certainly, but definitely less engaged than, say, the later clarinet music? By contrast, the deliciously lyrical Flute and

Harp Concerto of 1778 has more substance, perhaps because it was commissioned by a musical Parisian count and his young daughter.

The teenage (and earlier) operas, seria and buffa, deserved the amazed plaudits of their first audiences; but an enforced operatic gap of five years before *Idomeneo* shows how far Mozart's dramatic reach had matured. *Idomeneo*, premiered in Munich in 1781, cost him much labour and artistically fascinating tussles with promoter, librettist and singers alike: his first Idamante was 'a pain in the arse', and the tenor, Raaff, 'stands around like a statue' and 'tends to go overboard with the Cantabile', though Mozart did value his affability and long-standing professional experience ('his grey hair demands some consideration').[10] Mozart is not as celebrated today as a seria composer as for his comic operatic creations. But *Idomeneo* is a bold and successful attempt to fashion a new kind of dynamic music drama from the conventions of opera seria, an effort thrillingly captured in his correspondence with his father. The work contains some wonderful vocal, orchestral and, particularly, choral effects (not least the magnificent storm sequence in Act 2, heavily influenced by Gluck), and a central character of Handelian depth, belying Mozart's twenty-four years. He was justly proud of this piece: it is the only opera for which a considerable correspondence survives, because Mozart was in Munich and his father in Salzburg; the work of a true, though not yet complete, man of the theatre.

The early symphonies were calling cards for his travels, reaching a first plateau of maturity in the C Major, G Minor and A Major symphonies of 1773/4, rich in melody and development. The later 1770s saw him creatively embrace what his father sniffily called the 'Mannheim mannerisms' of the famous orchestra there (perhaps because Leopold was suspicious of all things Mannheim, including the allure of the Weber sisters). Mozart, of course, treated the fashionable orchestral effects as a big joke: 'I made sure to include *le premier coup d'archet* [the distinctive opening bow stroke of the violins] ... what a fuss the oxen here [Paris] make of this trick! The devil take me if I can see any difference!'[11] His quartets, too, show a clear evolution from the early Salzburg 'divertimenti' (basically small symphonies for strings alone) to fully mature chamber music in the works for Milan of 1772, and the Viennese quartets of 1773, aping Haydn but not yet in a fully assimilated style. As with opera, a long break followed in his quartet writing – ten years.

The Mozart scholar Alfred Einstein nicely characterises aspects of the composer's early style as 'homemade Haydn'.[12] He also finds the Mozart of the mid 1770s 'confused by Haydn'.[13] There are links and differences in the decade when they knew and admired each other's work but had not yet met.

Links and Similarities: Style and the 1770s

Haydn was a religious man. Many of his pieces bear a devotional dedication. Mozart's greatest piece of church music, his Great Mass in C Minor of 1783, was written as a thank offering for getting Constanze to marry him. The Viennese church style has been consistently criticised, at the time and since, for being 'better fitted for a dance hall than a church', as one contemporary put it.[14] It's a constant refrain in the history of church music, and Haydn answered it with typical gracious humility (describing the composition of the Agnus Dei of Mass No. 4): 'I prayed to God … I experienced a sure joy so confident that as I wished to express the words of the prayer, I could not suppress my joy, but gave vent to my happy spirits, and wrote above the *miserere*, etc: Allegro.'[15] The flicker of the footlights is certainly there in both men's early Mass settings; but they are full of miniaturised delights, especially when performed with their original orchestration (often just two obligato violins with continuo cello and organ, the so-called 'Vienna church trio').

The year 1774 saw both men dip a compositional toe in the swirling waters of *Sturm und Drang*. Haydn's oratorio *Il ritorno di Tobia* ('monotonous', according to one biographer) contains choruses which are 'full of strength and vigour',[16] including '*Wenn auch in trüben Tagen*' (later reworked as the stand-alone anthem '*Insanae et vanae curae*'). Minor key scales and harsh dissonances rush about with expressive abandon. By coincidence, a swirling little phrase resurfaces in almost identical form at the end of the first movement of Mozart's G Minor symphony of the same year, as another exploration of the fractured lines and nervy gestures found in the service of what one modern writer calls 'the new goddess Restlessness'.[17]

For both composers, counterpoint meant seriousness. The old 'learned' style found its way into church music, naturally, but also, gradually, into chamber and symphonic compositions, particularly last movements like Haydn's '*Fuga a quattro soggetti*' to end the C Major

Quartet, No. 2 of the set of six composed in 1772. But the counterpoint of this period does not yet always fully assimilate the Bachian model into Classical form. Mozart points the way with the simple but brilliant two-part imitation between upper and lower voices in the first few bars of the A Major symphony – counterpoint as developmental tool, later a key resource of Beethoven (who does something very similar in his G Major piano concerto). Later, the last movement of Mozart's Piano Concerto No. 19 in F Major of 1784 links out of its first theme with a burst of fugue – what the modern scholar Cuthbert Girdlestone calls in another context 'a dialogue in imitation, a kind of irregular canon'.[18] The brilliant contrapuntal finales of the da Ponte operas and his 'Jupiter' Symphony of 1788 crown this aspect of his art.

The final comparison contrasts the two men on the operatic boards. Haydn is barely known as an opera composer today, but it was a key part of his exhausting schedule at the pleasure-loving Esterházy court. His surviving stage pieces (several were lost in a fire, some later reconstructed from memory) are quite good Haydn but less good opera. A piece like *La vera costanza* of 1779 clearly fulfils the brief for an agreeable diversion in the Esterháza theatre, but rarely aims higher than a nice tune and straightforward harmonies (Rosina's anguished monologue in Act 2 is the dramatic high point). His last opera, *L'anima del filosofo*, unperformed in his lifetime, makes some intriguing moves in the direction of Gluck-like neologisms. But in general he perhaps lacked that essential sympathy for the dramatic potential inherent in the contradictions of the human condition which Mozart possessed in abundance – perhaps Haydn was just too nice to write wholly successful opera. One contemporary thought Haydn would have been a good opera composer if he had travelled to Italy. His biographer Albert Dies disagrees, saying that it wasn't his way to ape foreign styles, and anyway he could hear Italian music in Vienna.[19] Dies is surely right. The last, typically self-effacing word in this particular comparison should go to Haydn himself. When asked to write an opera buffa for Prague in 1787, he refused, because 'the great Mozart can hardly have any rival'.[20]

Vienna: Meetings, Music, Miracles – The 1780s

None of the three great Viennese Classicists was from Vienna. Haydn visited on regular winter breaks from his duties at the magnificent but isolated Esterházy estates to the south. Mozart made Vienna his home as a refuge from the stifling atmosphere of provincial small-town Salzburg (and from his increasingly domineering father: 'have faith in me, I am not a fool any more').[21] As in all musical ages, both men were drawn by the rich cultural offering of the big city: 'Just to be in Vienna is entertainment enough,' said Mozart.[22] Vienna was full of music, morning and evening, amateur and professional, inside and out. Her staid squares and stolid *Schlösser* can claim the immortal credit of witnessing the meeting, and, over the course of the 1780s, the burgeoning of what Haydn's biographer called 'the noblest and most respectful friendship between the two men'.[23]

Mozart's last decade is one of the miracles of human creativity and achievement.

It began in the company of the Webers. In 1780 Aloysia rejected him for an actor. In August 1782 he married her sister, Constanze, at St Stephen's, the cathedral where Haydn used to shin up the scaffolding as a choirboy. Musical relations with the Weber sisters survived these various uncouplings, and Mozart wrote some of his most dazzling soprano solos for both women and another sister, Josefa. In 1782 Mozart became a regular at Baron van Swieten's musical gatherings, meeting many musical movers and shakers as well as the music of Handel and Bach. Works of that year include the brilliantly vivacious Singspiel *Die Entführung aus dem Serail* and the 'Haffner' Symphony. The following year he met the flamboyant Lorenzo da Ponte, and in 1784 he became a freemason (Haydn joined, too, though with less enthusiasm and, unlike Mozart, showed no discernible echoes of it in his music). These years also produced the great series of late piano concertos, lyrical show-pieces for Mozart to play himself. The year 1786 saw the publication of the six quartets dedicated to Haydn. The immortal trio of da Ponte operas began with *Le nozze di Figaro* at the Burgtheater in Vienna in May 1786. The Prague premiere in January the following year brought a sweet, though brief moment of genuine and triumphant success ('here they talk of nothing but – *Figaro* … it's all a great honour for me'),[24] and led to the commission for *Don Giovanni*, premiered there in October 1787. The same year brought two events of great significance: in March, Mozart met the 16-year-old Beethoven; in May, his father Leopold died in Salzburg. The year 1788 saw the Vienna premiere of *Don Giovanni* and the crowning of his symphonic career with Symphony No. 39 in E Flat Major, No. 40

in G Minor and his last symphony, the C Major 'Jupiter'. His domestic life was happy, but far from settled. In a close parallel with his own parents, Mozart had six children, of whom only two survived. Finances soon deteriorated after the *Figaro* flush: the family moved within Vienna often, and Mozart began borrowing money. The end of the 1780s saw the Mozart household filled with music, troubles and relentless optimism. There was to be more of all three.

Mozart's music of this period provides one of many occasions in this story when a whole universe of invention has to be represented by the merest glimpses.

Many of his piano performances were improvised on the spot. This includes some of the solo work in the form which Einstein characterises as his highest instrumental achievement, a unique synthesis of aria, concertante and symphonic ideals and 'a fusion resulting in a higher unity beyond which no progress was possible, because perfection is imperfectible': the piano concerto.[25] The form has a curious history. While concertos for other instruments were already an established feature of the Classical repertoire, the keyboard concerto evolved along with the instrument and its composers' needs as performer. C. P. E. and J. C. Bach followed their father's example in using the clavier as a concerto solo instrument, but, a few minor contemporaries aside, it was really only Mozart who explored the form in any depth before Beethoven and the Romantics. And what depth. These pieces are more aria than symphony, not just in the singing slow movements but in new tricks like the fleet-footed codas he used to end last movements, as in the Mannheim-flavoured Piano Concerto No. 20 in D Minor of 1785, with mood and manner manipulated through melody and form. Mozart the pianist is never far away: certain passages – not only his slow movements – are notated skeletally, requiring realisation and ornamentation from the player. Mozart the opera composer is always in the wings, too. So he is in the quartets: String Quartet No. 15 has the fickle restlessness of another creature of dark D minor, *Don Giovanni*, from the modal scales of the opening melody to the seductive simplicity of folk song in the finale and the passionate menuetto (with its charming trio in octaves, surely a nod to its dedicatee, Haydn, who used octave writing a lot in his own quartets). The two rich, late string quintets each has a symphonic counterpart in key and mood (G minor and C major respectively). These final symphonies mark the completion of the journey of the form from a curtain-raiser designed to stop the chatter and start the evening's entertainment, to a work with the weight to sit at its heart (Mozart sometimes split up the movements of a symphony to both begin and end a concert, like complementary bookends, as he did with his 'Haffner' Symphony at the famously long 'academy' of 29 March 1783 – individual movements might also be encored). Traces of his early association with the music of J. C. Bach remain, like the fanfare-style motto openings; and from Haydn he learnt much: for example, the slow introduction borrowed from examples such as the older man's 'Oxford' Symphony of 1789. All his own is the synthesis of these elements into something new: the crackling five-part invertible counterpoint in the finale of the 'Jupiter' is justly venerated; as remarkable is that Mozart integrates it effortlessly into a completely satisfying structure of seamless grace.

The key to all Mozart is his operas. The da Ponte pieces are beautiful, touching, funny, and consummate works of theatre. Buffa and seria blend as completely as high art and the simplest song (who could resist Giovanni's silver-tongued *'Là ci darem la mano'*? – not the innocent Zerlina, that's for sure). In Mozart's hands, the aria could become almost a mini opera in itself; for example, the Countess's two great scenes of troubled introspection in *Le nozze di Figaro*. There is no greater musical finale than Act 2 of *Figaro*. Form becomes character, and character drives plot.

Mozart's letters are full of opera. In a 1782 letter to his father, in which he outlined, with typically airy optimism, his fields of ambition, he said that it was opera 'to which I am drawn most of all'.[26] A year earlier a long letter described in fascinating detail how he worked words and music into shape for *Die Entführung*: 'I described to Stephani [the librettist] exactly what I needed ... Osmin's anger will be rendered comical by the use of Turkish music ... Bellmont's aria ... was written entirely for Adamberger's voice ... one can hear the whispering and sighing – which is expressed by the first violins with mutes and one flute playing unisono.' But there are limits: 'passions, violent or not, must never be expressed to the point of disgust, and Music must never offend the ear, even in the most horrendous situations, but must always be pleasing, in other words always remain Music.'[27] Here is the essence of Viennese Classicism: emotion organised and contained.

Like all successful opera composers, Mozart wrote for particular singers: 'I love it when an aria is so accurately measured for a singer's voice that it fits like a well-tailored dress.'[28] Early in their acquaintance he asked Aloysia Weber if she liked his new aria 'since I have composed it solely for you'.[29] The character of these singers surely shows up in their music: the brilliant young English soprano Nancy Storace had much in common, by history and temperament, with the sassy, sparky, put-upon but resourceful woman she first brought to life in the premiere of *Le nozze di Figaro*, the peerless Susanna. Anna Gottlieb was seventeen when she created the role of the dignified, loyal lover Pamina; just twelve when she played the first Barbarina, the young maid, which must affect our reading of these roles and their music. (Gottlieb died aged eighty-two in 1856, a few days after what would have been Mozart's hundredth birthday, surely the last surviving musician to have worked with Mozart.)

Haydn in the 1780s was still loyally serving up symphonies, operas and chamber music for the pleasure of the Esterházy court. Unlike him, his reputation travelled far. Three very different events of 1779 set the scene for the new decade: he made an important contact with the leading Viennese music publisher Artaria; a new contract with the Esterházy court omitted the prince's nominal ownership of Haydn's works; in March a violinist called Antonio Polzelli arrived to join the musical establishment, along with his 19-year-old wife Luigia, an indifferent soprano to whom Haydn gave many operatic roles and, it would seem, his heart. The year 1781 saw Haydn resume quartet composition with his Opus 33 quartets, described as being composed '*auf eine ganz neue, besondere Art*' ('in a quite new, special manner'), though it is not quite clear what stylistic neologisms this refers to, and might just be a bit of advertising puff.[30] There are also concertos and a Mass (his first for about seven years and last for another fourteen). In 1784, just as Mozart was hitting his operatic peak, Haydn composed and staged the last of his many Esterházy operas, *Armida*, though he went on arranging and conducting stage pieces by other composers (often simplifying arias and taking out the tricky bits for young Luigia). The mid 1780s were rich in symphonies, and towards the end of the decade Haydn returned in pomp and joke-filled majesty to the form which had earned him fame and of which he was still the unrivalled master, the string quartet.

That fame spread with his new freedom to publish. He exploited it skilfully and not always entirely honestly, sometimes offering more than one publisher exclusive rights to the same piece. Commissions arrived from Paris, Prussia, Naples and elsewhere. A letter from Boccherini in Spain led to the unique *The Seven Last Words of Our Saviour on the Cross* for the Good Friday service of 1786 in the Oratorio de la Santa Cueva in Cádiz: essentially, seven slow movements. Very few composers could have carried it off without a sense of sameness: Haydn did. Programmes at all the leading European concert societies saw his name move steadily up the list from a place about equal with the fashionable Mannheimers to total dominance. Although still living (and working hard) in the gilded retreats of the Esterházys at Eisenstadt and Esterháza (and declining all invitations to travel), his mind and music were increasingly elsewhere.

Personally, that meant Vienna. It is not entirely clear how often he visited, when he first met Mozart, or how regularly the two met. But both man and city clearly became dear to him. The flamboyant Irish tenor Michael Kelly (who succeeded in persuading Mozart that the character of Don Curzio should stutter in the ensembles in *Figaro*) describes the two men playing string quartets with fellow composers Dittersdorf and Vanhal – a nice story, and entirely credible in the context of Viennese musical life (though Kelly can be creative when it comes to facts).

Haydn's musical preoccupations at this period include the ever-present jokes ('like merry boys [who] ... romp about in innocent mischief,' he told Dies),[31] including minuets which deliberately confuse the listener's sense of where the first beat of the bar falls, or quartets which sound like the cellist has gone wrong (was this a private joke with a favoured chum? Haydn does it a lot). The finale of the 'Oxford' Symphony chucks its little scrap of tune around, continuously teased and tickled, like the fleeting kaleidoscope of moods across the face of a brilliant buffo actor.

Like its predecessor, the decade closed with events of significance on several levels. In 1789 he struck up a friendship with Marianne von Genzinger, wife of a leading Viennese doctor, who showed him the charms of a warm and sympathetic family home filled with a circle of like-minded friends, and engaged in a lengthy and revealing correspondence with the ageing composer, almost a quarter of a century her senior. In 1790 both Princess Maria and Prince Nikolaus Esterházy died. The new prince, Anton, had little taste for music and, in a familiar turn of fortune known to Bach, among others, dismissed most of the court musicians. He did, however, retain Haydn as titular Kapellmeister, on full salary but with no duties. Haydn was free. Aged nearly sixty, he moved to Vienna.

The 1790s: Mozart's Last Works, Haydn's Travels

So far, Haydn seems, like J. S. Bach before him, to have ventured no more than a hundred miles or so from his birthplace. An unexpected visit changed all that. Johann Peter Salomon was a German violinist and composer who succeeded J. C. Bach and C. F. Abel as the leading concert promoter in London. Haydn had been invited to follow his fame north before (the London papers had even erroneously announced his imminent arrival), but it was Salomon who took advantage of the news of Prince Nikolaus's death to turn up on Haydn's doorstep and announce, 'Get ready to travel. In a fortnight we go together to London.'[32] A leave-taking dinner with Mozart followed, recounted in a roundly romanticised reconstruction by Haydn's biographers ('tears welled from the eyes of both', recorded one); Mozart feared they were saying 'our last farewell in this life'.[33] His fears proved sadly prophetic, though not in the way they both assumed.

If Mozart's last decade was a miracle, his last five years were astonishing, and the last two beyond comprehension.

In 1790 the third da Ponte opera, *Così fan Tutte*, was premiered at the Burgtheater, and Mozart travelled (uninvited) to take part in the coronation of Leopold II as Holy Roman Emperor, a trip which, yet again, yielded little. In 1791 he composed a piano concerto, the Singspiel *Die Zauberflöte* for his old friend the comic actor and impresario Emanuel Schikaneder at the lowbrow suburban Theater auf der Wieden, the Clarinet Concerto, the Requiem, the opera seria *La Clemenza di Tito* and a motet, *Ave Verum Corpus*. Towards the end of the year his frail health overtook him, and he died after a short illness, still working on the unfinished Requiem, on 5 December 1791. He was buried, according to custom and expectation, in an unmarked grave.

Mozart's early death has curious parallels with Purcell's almost a century earlier: their age; the rapid and unexpected onset of illness (it was Constanze's health, not Mozart's, that had previously been the cause of alarm); the homely surroundings filled with music, friends and young children; the admired older colleague and teacher who had probably expected to go first living on into a new musical century; the young widow left to manage family, finances and musical legacy as best she could.

The quality of Mozart's invention in these last months defies understanding. The background of debt, worry and Constanze's constant confinements and serious illness leave no shadow on the rich mastery of these masterpieces (*La Clemenza di Tito* is, perhaps, the slight exception to the consistency of creative engagement – a superbly but quickly written response to a rather routine commission for a coronation opera). Nor do they on his irrepressible letters, constantly joking around with friends like his pupil Franz Sussmäyr and the choirmaster Anton Stoll:

Dearest Stoll! / Good old troll! / you sit in your hole / drunk as
    a mole ... I remain
your / true friend / Franz Sussmäyr / Shithead. / From the
    Outhouse, July 12.[34]

Friends come into focus in the music: Sussmäyr and Joseph Eybler, who completed the anonymous commission for the Requiem; Anton Stadler, the clarinettist who inspired some of the most beautiful music for his (or any other) instrument; Emanuel Schikaneder and his variegated troupe of singer-actors who conjured up *Die Zauberflöte*, an extraordinary musical melée of tumbling buffa overture, extravagant coloratura, rich masonic wind music, a frankly rather weird plot and, perhaps above all, songs of an unutterable simplicity sitting unblushingly alongside the greatest sophistication. Only the very greatest musical dramatists (Monteverdi, Purcell, Verdi) have dared risk the artistic exposure of such direct and simple utterance and succeeded. *Così* is perhaps the most consistently seria of the da Ponte operas, though with plenty of fun at the expense of the self-absorbed lovers at its centre, and witty references to fashionable fads like the medical treatment with magnets pioneered by an old Mozart family friend, Franz Anton Mesmer.

As well as his inexhaustible music, Mozart has left us another unique testament to the human spirit: his letters. His love of life tumbles out of them in an irrepressible mixture of real and made-up languages, bad spelling and worse handwriting, sometimes in rhyme, backwards, upside down, full of jokes, games and wordplay, penetrating, playful, poignant and precise. They are, of course, untranslatable: a recent rendering by Robert Spaethling successfully captures much of the spirit as well as the meaning by, for example, recreating Mozart's occasional rhyme schemes in Edward Lear-like English. Spaethling also (unlike some of his nervous predecessors) fully indulges Mozart's childlike taste for toilet humour (he once joyfully told his sister that every time a famous ballet dancer performed a leap he 'let out a little fart'),[35] particularly in the letters to his young cousin Maria Anna Thekla, known as 'Bäsle':

> Dearest cozz buzz! I have received reprieved your highly esteemed writing biting, and I have noted doted that my uncle garfuncle, my aunt slant, and you too, are all well mell ... I now wish you a good night, shit in your bed with all your might, sleep with peace on your mind, and try to kiss your own behind ... [I] stick my finger in my ass ... Now farewell, I kiss you 1 00000 times ... Miehnnam eht ^{ht}5 rebotco 7771.[36]

We no longer need to be shocked by this. It was part of the cultural hinterland. The eighteenth century was generally much less prudish than the Puritans before it or the Victorians after. Mozart even sometimes wrote like this to his own mother. It is noticeable that the crudest letters came at times of stress, no doubt partly as a release. Mozart's personality had many opposing and complementary facets: fart jokes and high art can, it seems, go quite happily together.

Most significantly, the letters chart the relationship with his father Leopold. The story is all the sadder for being so recognisably human: the father's pride in the talents and easy charm of his children; the realisation that they are growing away from him; the young man's need to assert himself and find his own way; the parent's fears that the son will fail to manage his affairs and fall in love with every pretty girl he meets, suitable or not (both perfectly true); the irreversible break; the father finally facing the future as a middling composer in a dead-end job in a small city, *sans* wife, *sans* fame, *sans* family. The emotion in these letters can be palpable: Mozart tenderly and tactfully wrote home from Paris asking a friend to tell Leopold that his wife was gravely ill and prepare him for bad news, when in fact Maria Anna had died some hours earlier: Leopold later implicitly blamed Mozart for his mother's death, an unforgivable accusation born of impotent grief. Mozart clearly loved and respected his father deeply, but needed to make his own way; Leopold manifestly wanted to do the right thing for his wondrous, vulnerable child, but just didn't know how. Both, at times, reacted badly.

Haydn heard of Mozart's death in London. He made two trips there, in 1791 and 1794. Both were well-organised, productive and successful, involving enticing commissions which inspired a remarkable late symphonic flowering, concerts, friendships, a visit with Burney to Oxford to receive an honorary degree (where he found the requirement to walk around in full academic fig for three days both uncomfortable and amusing, but treated the audience in the Sheldonian Theatre to a little curtsey, which apparently earned more applause than the soprano soloist), a close encounter with a tiger at the Tower of London and with Beethoven in Bonn on the way home. His amorous attentions were focused on Rebecca Schroeter, a widow and capable pianist. Another friend was Anne Hunter, wife of a well-known doctor, who provided him with English song texts. He was welcomed at court and in society: 'I could have an invitation every day; but first I must consider my health, and second my work.'[37] He attended the famous large-scale Handel commemorations at Westminster Abbey. A rival concert promoter tried to puncture his popularity by recruiting his pupil Ignaz Pleyel, but, according to Haydn, instead of the predicted 'bloody harmonious war between master and pupil ... Pleyel behaved so modestly towards me [that] ... we shall share our laurels equally'.[38] He heard serenades in the Vauxhall Pleasure Gardens, 4,000 charity children singing at St Paul's cathedral ('full of devotion and innocent'); he watched 'English dancing' in a room 'like a subterranean cave',[39] inspected Herschel's telescope, flirted with the Queen and made a lot of money ('only in England can one do this').[40] The principal works of the period are the twelve 'London' symphonies. Arranging British folk songs provided a surprising, and lucrative, new field. An opera based on the familiar story of Orpheus and Eurydice was commissioned and completed, but never performed.

Haydn's Last Years

Many Londoners, including the royal family, tried to tempt Haydn to stay. But it was news of another change in the family which still employed him that provided the impetus, or perhaps the excuse, to head home. In 1794 the middlingly musical Prince Anton Esterházy died, less than four years after his father. His successor, another Nikolaus, required Haydn to resume his duties as Kapellmeister, this time based in Vienna.

The job was less onerous than before, and left him with plenty of time for other work. Haydn's seventh decade produced the late quartets, no further symphonies, six great Mass settings, the 'Emperor's Hymn', and two immortal oratorios. Haydn himself found the archangels of *The Creation* more deserving of his inspiration than the frogs and tipsy peasants of *The Seasons*, which is looser in construction though full of character. Both draw richly on Haydn's English experiences, explicitly on his hearing the music of Handel in Westminster Abbey. While *The Seasons* is less widely performed, *The Creation* has never lost its immediate popularity. Haydn set out to fulfil van Swieten's request for a work 'in the manner and spirit of Handel':[41] choirs to this day can testify to his complete success.

Haydn (and his parrot, brought from England) passed the closing years of his life in a solitary, neat and modest cottage in a quiet Viennese suburb, sharing recollections of his long life with his patient and attentive biographers when health and memory allowed. In March 1808 he was carried into the great hall of the university in Vienna to hear Salieri conduct *The Creation*, and was much moved by the reverence of performers and audience alike. In May 1809 Napoleon's troops bombarded and besieged Vienna (across town Beethoven cowered in a basement, pillows clutched to his ears in a tragic attempt to preserve what remained of his hearing). The city captured, Napoleon ordered a guard of honour to be placed outside Haydn's house. A captain in the French army, who recorded his name in Haydn's visitors' book as Clement Sulemy, asked to be allowed to pay his respects to the famous composer. Haydn, though bed-ridden, admitted him graciously. The officer nervously revealed that he knew Haydn's oratorios well and, from an adjoining room, sang him the opening tenor aria from *The Creation* (or possibly the difficult equivalent from *The Seasons* – accounts disagree). Like Handel almost exactly half a century earlier, the last musical sounds Haydn heard were from his own great oratorio of praise. Haydn died, prayerfully and calmly, on 31 May 1809.

Today, Haydn is not as good box office as Mozart. That is partly because his characteristic gestures are often subtle and understated, easily missed beneath an outwardly pretty surface. Partly it's because he just wrote so much – one perceptive modern programmer has said that if Haydn had written twenty symphonies rather than 104 we'd hear all of them all of the time. Partly it's because there are no big characters or standout work (with the possible exception of *The Creation*): he has left us no Leporello, Osmin or Queen of the Night. After his death he was historically stuffed and put on display as 'the father of the symphony': revered, but played only selectively. The process of rescuing him from that retrospective taxidermical sanctification, and seeing him for what he really is, continues.

The Classical style is like a rainbow. It needed both the brittle sunshine of the galant and the gathering rainclouds of Romanticism to hold its complex, fragile, incandescent beauty briefly in place.

At Haydn's memorial service in June 1809, Mozart's Requiem was conducted by Salieri. The conjunction of those three great names, in life, death and music, stands as an apt image of the turning of the musical spheres. Within four short years many of the giants of the next era would be born: Chopin, Mendelssohn, Schumann, Liszt, Verdi, Wagner.

The gods were preparing to cross the rainbow bridge into a new kingdom.

Part Six

THE ROMANTIC CENTURY (1770–1914)

INTRODUCTION

Aesthetics, Philosophy, Literature, Nature and the Sacred

The Victorian critic Walter Pater characterised Romanticism as 'the addition of strangeness to beauty'.[1] By the end of the Romantic century some of the areas of experience newly opened to view were very strange indeed.

Philosophers codified its currents and debates. Immanuel Kant thought that 'beauty has nothing to do with being moved' and that genius 'provides art with rules'.[2] Johann Gottfried Herder took a different view: 'Who counts and calculates when he experiences music's deepest and life-giving joys?'[3] Friedrich von Schlegel carried the concept of communicating idea and emotion into non-verbal music: 'philosophical speculation is not at all foreign to the spirit of pure instrumental music. Must not purely instrumental music create its own text?'[4]

Literature became a key resource. The folk tales of, among others, the Brothers Grimm, Hans Christian Andersen, Walter Scott and Robert Burns, the German collection known as *Des Knaben Wunderhorn*, the Finnish *Kalevala*, the tales of King Arthur and the Nibelung legends provide a running thread. Scholars and writers like William Chappell and John Clare in England began the methodical study of folk art. Writers like Klopstock, Jean Paul and E. T. A. Hoffmann put Romanticism on the page: Hoffmann wrote music, wrote about music, and had music thrust upon him (by Jacques Offenbach in the opéra fantastique *Les contes d'Hoffmann (The Tales of Hoffmann)*); and even awarded himself a new middle name, Amadeus, in honour of his hero Mozart.

Shakespeare and Goethe presided as joint literary deities, creators of brooding, troubled, tragic heroes and lovers. Shakespeare crossed Europe in translation, his occasional hints of dangerous revolutionary republicanism excised from his plots by the censors. Goethe's moody young anti-hero Werther sums up William Wordsworth's 'spontaneous overflow of powerful feelings'[5] on hearing his beloved Lotte play the piano: her lips 'open in thirst to drink the sweet notes welling up from the instrument ... where the ghosts of heaven play',[6] a striking contrast to Mozart's 'well-tailored' tinklings.[7] Beethoven found Klopstock 'so restless; and he always begins too far away, from on high down; always *maestoso*, D flat major! ... But Goethe – he lives and wants us all to live with him. That is the reason he can be set to music.'[8] Goethe himself preferred well-behaved composers who preserved his versification and ballad style (like Johann Friedrich Reichardt's slightly ploddy 1794 setting of the famous *Erlkönig* – 'unparalleled by anything I know of their kind') to wilder interpreters like Schubert.[9]

By the middle of the century, daringly modern writers like Gustave Flaubert could use music as the image and trigger for the repressed longings of his bored heroine Emma Bovary: stuck with her dull husband, 'She gave up music. Why play? Who'd listen to her? Since she'd never be able to play at a concert, on an Erard piano, wearing a short-sleeved velvet dress'; melodies wheezing from a barrel organ come to her as 'tunes that were being played in other places ... echoes of the world filtering through to Emma'; eventually, and disastrously, it is a performance of Gaetano Donizetti's *Lucia di Lammermoor* which tempts her first steps into emotional freedom, crying out silently 'from the back of a box, behind the golden trelliswork ... "Take me away! Carry me with you! Let us go! Thine, thine! All my ardour and all my dreams!"'[10]

Eighteenth-century composers' thoughts about music have reached us mainly through their letters. This continued into the nineteenth century, for example, in the long, emotionally guarded correspondence between Johannes Brahms and Clara Schumann and the copious self-justifying outpourings of Richard Wagner. But many nineteenth-century composers also dabbled in journalism. Some were very good at it: Robert Schumann was moving and insightful, Hector Berlioz could be both extremely funny (he describes a viola player who 'puts on a fairly brave show for the first hour' of 'a vast oratorio' and then falls soundly asleep)[11] and deeply romantic (he tells of an ardent young man 'going to hear *La Vestale* ... Even if he were to die after this overwhelming joy, had he any right to complain?' – in the event he did both).[12]

Nature challenged conventional religion in importance, part of a view of creation as an organic whole shared by painters, thinkers, writers and scientists. Beethoven wrote: 'You will ask where my ideas come from ... It seems to me that I could wrest them from Nature herself with my own hands, as I go walking in the woods.'[13] Forests, caves, seascapes and birdsong were no longer just decorative backdrops or pretty noises off, but fundamental to an exploration of man's place in the universe: a very different creative engagement with nature from that of an earlier composer like Gluck, who would have his harpsichord placed in a field with a bottle of champagne on top before settling down to compose: very Watteau.

Sacred music entered a transitional phase. In the words of the scholar Charles Rosen, 'the last defences' against the dominance of the Baroque style 'fell with the two Beethoven masses, ironically, at the last minute, just as a new interest in the Baroque was beginning to reach the public as well as the professional musician'.[14] Older things like the so-called church modes of plainsong and sixteenth-century polyphony became a library for a particular kind of gesture, but of limited interest in their own right. To Berlioz, the music of Palestrina was 'not complete music ... [because] ... we never transform our scores into logarithm tables or chess-boards'.[15] But the ancient Roman master continued to cast a fascination over composers of the nineteenth century, notably in the late quartets of Beethoven and through to the tuneful sacred polyphony of the high church Cecilian and Oxford movements later in the century: Palestrina with sweetener. Music in ordinary churches, meanwhile, continued in its rackety, ill-disciplined way, with writers across Europe noting wryly how an organist 'entertains us with the scrap of a song' in the middle of a psalm (England),[16] or 'plays a little dance tune out of an old Opéra ballet, which contrasts so grotesquely with the choir's time-honoured chant that you go out in disgust' (France).[17] The English (and the Welsh) lustily pursued one of their chief musical glories: hymn-singing. The sacred oratorio learnt to encompass the disciplined narrative tradition of Handel (Mendelssohn) and something vaster (Verdi, and even the pantheistic symphonic finales of Mahler).

Opera: Social Context

Opera is expensive.

At the beginning of the nineteenth century the key skill was still pleasing the aristocratic patron. In 1810 Carl Maria von Weber followed the advice of his teacher, the canny old operator Abbé Vogler, and flattered the affected Grand Duke of Hesse with the dedication of his opera *Abu Hassan*: 'I dressed up the rogue in neat red morocco, dedicated him to the Grand Duke and sent him over ... I hope he'll say, "*Musje, je tien bocop de ce*".'[18] It worked – the duke forked out forty gold pieces and bought 120 tickets for the first performance (which began, appropriately, with a Chorus of Creditors singing '*Geld! Geld! Geld!*' ('Money! Money! Money!')). Three decades later Berlioz wrestled with a new phenomenon, the *claques* – gangs of opera-goers paid to applaud certain singers and not others: 'The *claqueurs* in our theatres have become experts ... By means of the *claque*, managers make or mar at will what one still calls a success.'[19] Later still, old money was wooed into the opera by deliberately keeping new money out: Newland Archer, the languid hero of Edith Wharton's *The Age of Innocence*, goes one snowy evening in 1870s New York to 'the shabby red and gold boxes of the sociable old Academy. Conservatives cherished it for being small and inconvenient, and thus keeping out the "new people" whom New York was beginning to dread.' His enjoyment has little to do with the music: 'he was at heart a dilettante, and thinking over a pleasure to come often gave him a subtler satisfaction than its realisation'.[20] The actual opera is just one element of his immersive social and sensual experience, to be inhaled when the mood takes him, like his cigar. The opening of two opera houses symbolised, in different ways, the changing of all that: the Metropolitan Opera House in New York in 1883, and Wagner's Festspielhaus in Bayreuth in 1876.

With the democratisation of audiences, it was becoming increasingly important to please the critics as much as the iron-crossed old nobility. But critics wanted to be fashionably right, too. First-night jitters over the premiere of Weber's *Der Freischütz* in Berlin in 1821 were sharpened by the recent rival success of Gaspare Spontini's *Olympie*: Julius Benedict nervously noted among the assembling audience 'E. T. Hoffman ... Heinrich Heine, and a host of literary and musical aspirants, amongst them little Felix Mendelssohn, with his parents ...' Hoffmann tried to triangulate between the rival successes, raising a

Part Six: Introduction

glass at Jager's restaurant in Unter den Linden: 'To my favourite composer – after Spontini.'[21]

Centre of the operatic world was Paris. In the mid 1850s Verdi described its demands and expectations with his usual cantankerous bloody-mindedness: 'I am not a millionaire and I do not intend to spend the few thousand francs I can on publicity, a claque and suchlike dirty things. That seems to be necessary for success.'[22]

Berlioz captures the art form's personalities and frailties brilliantly: to the manager, 'well-written music ... is music which doesn't spoil anything in an opera'; in Paris, 'the Opéra [is] madly in love with mediocrity'; 'In London, the all-important thing for the manager of the opera-house is the poster'; conductors correct missed entries by whacking the prompt box with a violin bow (on one occasion causing the poor prompter to expire from shock with the word 'tack' wheezing from his lips); at rehearsals, 'everybody chats away very peacefully about politics, industry, railways, fashions, the stock exchange, dancing and philosophy until two o'clock', when it's time for lunch; a famous prima donna lets out 'such an ear-splitting high D that we thought she was in labour. The public stamps with joy.' Like Verdi, Berlioz reserves particular scorn for the habit of hacking around great masterpieces to suit popular taste: in England 'I saw a performance of Mozart's *Figaro* at the Queen's Theatre, but the opera was trombonized, ophicleided, in short copper-bottomed like a ship of the line', while 'the Paris Opéra felt bound to put on *Don Giovanni* and *The Magic Flute*; but it presented them mutilated, sullied, disfigured, transformed into vile pastiches by wretches whose names should be anathema', and publishers issued arias turned into 'a kind of drawing-room Gluck, complete with a pretty accompaniment for the piano'. Perhaps the most egregious example of such grotesque disfigurement was *Robin des Bois*, a French version of Weber's *Der Freischütz*, with additions by the critic, author and D-list composer Castil-Blaze, who thought it was 'very ungrateful of M. Weber to reproach the man who had popularized his music in France'.[23] (On occasion Berlioz dabbled in a spot of arranging and recomposition himself, partly because he needed the money, partly to prevent the job being done worse by someone else.)

Typically, serious thought and consistent artistic integrity underlie Berlioz's witticisms. He felt he could not succeed as a composer of opera unless I felt myself to be absolute master of a great theatre ... assured of the goodwill and obedience of all, from prima donna and first tenor, the chorus, orchestra, dancers and supers, down to the scene-painter, the machinists, and the stage manager. A lyrical theatre, as I see it, is before everything a vast musical instrument. I can play on it, but in order that I play it well it must be entrusted to me without reserve. This is just what will never happen.[24]

It did happen; but in the hands of his great successor as the visionary maverick of music drama, the iron-willed Richard Wagner.

Politics and the Composer in Society

All musical eras reflect their politics.

Revolutionary France produced popular singing festivals capturing national sentiment. Napoleon compelled Paris-based composers like Paisiello, Cherubini and Méhul to ditch their former associations and compete with each other for the emperor's ear. Court *'fêtes'* (festivities) and concerts were set up to amuse the ladies, as in the days of the most patronising potentates of the previous century.

The artistic legacy of the upheavals in France was complex. Musical historian Giorgio Pestelli says that 'the French Revolution was foreign to the Romantic movement ... it worshipped Reason and rejected fantasies'.[25] Established church music disappeared along with the deep roots of the machinery of the state in the structures and commandments of Catholicism, and has never really come back. Beethoven captured something of the stirring, naïf flavour of revolutionary marching songs in things like the simplistic C major fanfares at the end of his Fifth Symphony, suffered under Napoleon's bombs in Vienna, and avoided political difficulties himself because, according to his early biographer Alexander Wheelock Thayer, 'the police paid no attention to his utterances, either because they looked upon him as a harmless fantastic or had an overwhelming respect for his artistic genius'.[26] About revolutionary rumblings in Austria, Beethoven wrote: 'it is said that a revolution was about to break out – But I believe that so long as an Austrian can get his brown ale and his little sausages, he is not likely to revolt.'[27]

As always, music played its less formal part in cultural history, too:

in *War and Peace* Tolstoy gives us young Vincent Bosse, a drummer boy in Napoleon's Grande Armée, captured by the Russians and co-opted into their band (with a ration of mutton and vodka to warm his fingers) during the doomed advance on Moscow; in *Vanity Fair* Thackeray vividly describes Wellington's 'brilliant train of camp-followers ... dancing and feasting, as it were, up to the very brink of battle' in Brussels in 1815, their revels interrupted by 'a bugle from the Place of Arms ... the drums of the infantry, and the shrill pipes of the Scotch',[28] summoning the red-coated regiments to Waterloo and glory.

Turmoil engulfed European politics, and its music, at the century's midpoint in 1848. Wagner manned the barricades in Dresden in 1849. His muse, the remarkable singer actor Wilhelmine Schröder-Devrient, actually went to prison. Louis-Napoléon's seizure of power in 1851 appalled him: 'it seemed to me that the world was really coming to an end. When the success of the coup d'état was confirmed ... I turned my back on this incomprehensible world.'[29]

One result of the revolutions across Europe of 1848 was the eventual end of the patchwork of small, poor pocket principalities (where, in the words of Mark Twain, 'people had to sleep with their knees pulled up because they couldn't stretch out without a passport'),[30] which had played such an important role in musical patronage and employment. Their successors, big, hungry, new creatures called Germany and Italy, needed a sense of self and a viable history: Wagner and Verdi waited in the wings, ready to respond.

In the collection of writings published in 1852 as *Les soirées de l'orchestre* (*Evenings with the Orchestra*), Berlioz tells how the first violinist Corsino gets to his feet at a post-performance dinner and proposes a toast 'To music ... It has lived through the Terror, the Directory and the Consulate ... it has formed its court from all the queens whom it has dethroned'. A fellow diner, the conductor, is less sanguine in reply:

> '[D]id the last storm not ravage and exhaust it cruelly? Are music's wounds already healed, and will it not bear terrible scars for years to come? ... Look how we were treated during the last European upheaval [1848] ... What are our orchestras compared to those fearsome hosts, kindled by fire and brimstone, who are the performers of the storm, conducted by the

tireless Kapellmeister whose bow is a sickle, and whose name is Death?'[31]

Berlioz's republican sympathies faltered on his 'repugnance for the multitude, the mob',[32] and he dreamed up an imaginary society which he called Euphonia – dedicated to high musical standards but organised like a military dictatorship.

Thus do ideas pass from innocence to experience.

Nationalism

National and cultural identity in music evolved alongside ideas of nationhood. Distant cultures remained something exotic and foreign – Berlioz was baffled and appalled by the drones, modes and scrapings of traditional Chinese music which he heard on one of his visits to London around 1850 ('agonising', he called it).[33] The model of Romantic *chinoiserie* remains *The Mikado*, or even *Turandot* – with parodied Oriental-sounding parallel fourths and pentatonicism slapped on like face paint, successors to Mozart's Turkish cymbals and triangles. Jewishness provides a running thread, from the contributions of converts to Christianity like Mendelssohn, Moscheles and Mahler to Wagner's sinister 1850 essay '*Das Judenthum in der Musik*'. Perhaps most significant of all was the tenacious idea of the innate superiority of Germanness in art, already familiar to Mozart and Haydn and central to Wagner's view of music and history. Nationalism also produced some colourful results later in the century, especially in the Slavic countries: nationalism in music prospered when nationhood was an achievement, not a birthright.

The handsome Austrian capital Vienna provided far more than just the stage set for the best music of the late eighteenth and early nineteenth centuries. Its stolid squares and streets, its parks, apartments and palaces housed the varied and voracious social and cultural milieu which would gather in a hotel ballroom to hear Mozart play a piano concerto, file into the great hall of the university for Haydn's *Creation*, be seen at the opera at the Burgtheater or not seen at the less highbrow Freihaus Theater, or slip soberly on a Sunday into the cavernous gloom of St Stephen's cathedral for a tuneful Viennese Mass. Big buildings with whimsical names like Zum Auge Gottes ('At the Eye of God' – Mozart's lodgings with the Webers) held hidden rooms round courtyards and up stairs where Schubert's shifting group of friends would meet to hear his latest songs. Perhaps most importantly of all, nature flows into the city's heart in the elegant form of the river Danube (beautiful, if not always blue), with its channels and tributaries, and the city's woods, parks and fields extending out from the centre to easily accessible villages round about where Schubert and Beethoven (and, later, Mahler) would retreat for refreshment and recreation. Haydn's house at Gumpendorf nestled in a leafy enclave less than a couple of miles from St Stephen's. Beethoven forged and fashioned much of his mature music on his daily tramps round the green spaces and wide walls of the city, sketchbook in hand. Many fine and familiar pieces of music are really tales from the Vienna woods.

The nineteenth century became a (perhaps *the*) German century. Walking around Leipzig today can feel a bit like stumbling into a musical time warp: peered at by Bach and Mendelssohn from their plinths, passing the front doors of the stroppy youth Wagner, the tongue-tied Schumann and his in-laws, the house where Mahler wrote his first symphony, or reading a play bill for Mendelssohn's orchestra. Hamburg has its KomponistenQuartier, where its famous musical sons, from Telemann and C. P. E. Bach to Mahler and Brahms, are lined up in a row of museums as if on a library shelf. Heidelberg carries echoes of its role as 'one of the capital cities of Romanticism', where in 1805–8 Clemens Brentano and Achim von Arnim assembled the influential collection of folk poems *Des Knaben Wunderhorn* and 'practically founded the German Romantic delight in the Rhine'.[34]

Elsewhere, Italy lost its pre-eminence in everything except opera-singing ('concerts and festivals … are quite unknown here … as for religious music, it is just as much in abeyance,' wrote Berlioz).[35] Nineteenth-century England will forever be remembered as '*das Land ohne Musik*' ('the land without music'), in the caustic characterisation of the German journalist Oscar Schmitz in 1904: a fair if ungenerous comment on her native compositional talent (at least until Elgar), if not her vibrant concert life.[36]

Making a Living: Conductors, Teachers, Composers and Performers

Employment for musicians continued to evolve. The time-honoured German Kapellmeister system declined along with the princely courts it served. Its successor was the conductorship of the town orchestra or opera house (complete with its fair share of hack work rewriting other people's operas for the local diva), still preserved in the use of the word Kapelle in the title of several German orchestras. The importance of the courtly Kapelle in nurturing native talent perhaps partly explains the relative lack of such talent in England, where only the provincial church organist might be 'worthy to compare with many a noted Kapellmeister in a country which offers more plentiful conditions of musical celebrity', as George Eliot put it.[37]

A job provides security in return for duties and restrictions. Freelance life grants freedom but no security. Among nineteenth-century composers, ambitious self-promoters like Niccolò Paganini and Giacomo Meyerbeer were colossally successful. By contrast, Edward Elgar moaned around the time of his marriage in the 1880s that 'my prospects are about as hopeless as ever ... I have no money, not a cent'.[38] Berlioz noted acidly that 'the important thing ... is not to produce a few good works, but numerous second-rate works, which will bring swift success and returns'[39] – although, fortunately, neither Elgar nor Berlioz succumbed to that temptation. It's a conundrum musicians have yet to fully solve.

The Romantic century promoted, even if did not actually invent, the idea of the itinerant freelance composer/performer, creating the almost superhuman demands placed on long-haired, long-fingered superstars of the salon circuit like Chopin and Liszt, Paganini and Rubinstein. Musicians of this type contributed to the evolution of social aspects of music-making. Well into the twentieth century T. S. Eliot could describe a society lady going to hear 'the latest Pole/Transmit the Preludes, through his hair and finger-tips' – but 'only among friends'.[40] The element of improvisation in concert needs to be kept in mind, evolving from the technical, highly skilled display of extempore fugues and variations practised by Bach and Mozart to Chopin playing his own compositions quite differently from one rendition to the next, embellishing and emphasising aspects in some ways more like a modern jazz singer than an obedient classicist.

Singing and acting moved with the times, too. Like many artistic activities, it often ran in families. The eighteenth-century Arne, Cibber, Linley and Storace families were succeeded by the extravagant and talented Devrients, a key influence on the (very different) achievements of Mendelssohn and Wagner. Wagner said that

Wilhelmine Schröder-Devrient 'taught me the nature of Mimetic art-truthfulness',[41] and in 1845 cast her alongside his young step-niece Johanna in *Tannhäuser*. The histrionic singing/acting style is reflected in the popularity of lengthy, narrative, piano-accompanied ballads, particularly the settings of Carl Loewe. Wagner would often accompany young Johanna in Loewe's *Edward* of 1818, a spooky tale in which Edward tells his mother he has killed his hawk and his horse before confessing he has in fact slain his own father (more dysfunctional family tropes feeding into the Wagner world view), and is condemned to wander the seas in a sort of cross between *The Ancient Mariner* and *The Flying Dutchman*. Weber took the style one step further by improvising while Duke Friedrich of Prussia sat next to him on the piano stool, dreaming up imaginary scenes, like a sort of prototype silent movie pianist. Schumann did the same to recitations of Shelley. The sudden, shivering German sixth chords of the 'dark and stormy night' have their origins here.

Technological Innovations: Instruments

Instruments, like the orchestras they played in, got bigger and louder. New instruments named after their inventors included the saxophone and the Wagner tuba. Outside the formality of the concert hall, military parades and parish church bands featured a rich menagerie of squawks and cluckings, from the ophicleide to the serpent. In grander churches the organ grew from the essentially pre-Bachian instrument, lacking even a full-compass pedal board, played by organists like Thomas Attwood of St Paul's at the turn of the century, to the grand creations of the French organ-builder Aristide Cavaillé-Coll, which could (and did) play whole symphonies. Big French churches often had two organs, one in the nave, the other in the choir.

The key musical technology was the piano. Several early makers were also composers, performers and teachers, notably the Paris-based manufacturers Friedrich Kalkbrenner and Camille Pleyel (whose wife Marie was one of many famous female pianists of the period). In the 1820s and 1830s Broadwood in London and Graf in Vienna joined Pleyel in feeding the sudden and immense popularity of the piano, requiring greater physicality from the player's shoulders and back to work their bigger, heavier instruments (not appreciated by Chopin, whose 'exquisite delicacy of touch' was admired as a 19-year-old in

Vienna).⁴² Berlioz wittily parodied the conscientious efforts of the fine maker Sébastian Érard to 'run in' a new instrument by offering it for use in a competition where Mendelssohn's Piano Concerto in G Minor would be played thirty-one times: by the end, the piano was so well run in it played the concerto all by itself. Leading German firms Bechstein and Blüthner and the American firm Steinway were all founded in 1853. In 1859 Henry Steinway patented a new system of cross-stringing his big grand piano, producing unprecedented power and resonance, particularly in the bass. By the 1870s he had a substantial factory in Manhattan and a prominent place at trade fairs and expos, aided by a little light New York-style bribery. Many still regard the Steinway as the *ne plus ultra* of piano-making.

Composers and publishers joined manufacturers in nurturing and exploiting the new piano fad, some more fastidiously than others. In England, European immigrants Muzio Clementi and his pupil Johann Baptist Cramer added orchestral and other colours to the Classical piano piece. In Europe, Mozart's much-loved pupil Johann Nepomuk Hummel published a wildly popular manual of piano technique in 1828, codifying things like fingering and ornamentation. Hummel taught Carl Czerny, theorist of sonata form, editor of Bach's 'piano music', friend of Beethoven and kind supporter of Beethoven's troubled nephew Karl. Jan Ladislav Dussek was one of the first pianist composers to make a living touring Europe as a travelling virtuoso. The Irishman John Field met and impressed all the right people in London and Vienna before settling successfully in Russia, composing an entirely new kind of wandering, legato melody over dreamily pedalled harmonies which earned him a mention in *War and Peace*. He also clearly influenced Chopin and thoroughly impressed Liszt (who wrote of Field's 'half-formed sighs floating through the air, softly lamenting and dissolved in delicious melancholy').⁴³ The long-fingered Weber pioneered important pianistic tricks of the trade like scales in thirds and arpeggiated leaps. The influential Ferdinand Hiller played Bach with Liszt, conducted with Mendelssohn, was the dedicatee of Schumann's only piano concerto and assistant at the Dresden staging of Wagner's *Tannhäuser*.

Other piano composers, including Daniel Steibelt, Louis Gottschalk and Sigismond Thalberg, overused effects like tremolo, the 'thumb melody' and the pianistic storm scene. Hans von Bülow played his part in forging the myth of the performer as monster, placing two pianos on stage, nose to tail, so he could decide as he strode onto the platform whether the audience was going to see his face or his back as he treated them to marathons such as the last five Beethoven sonatas in a single concert. The brilliant French virtuoso and friend of Chopin and Liszt, Charles-Valentin Alkan, wrote dense and difficult music complete with clusters, complex chromaticisms, strange markings ('satanique') and formidable technical challenges for both performer and listener. He took a twenty-year career break after the death of Chopin, and left little direct influence except on fellow mavericks like Busoni, Scriabin and Sorabji. Nineteenth-century pianism begins and ends with the man who invented the all-solo piano concert and the word we use for it, 'recital'; the finest pianist of the age, perhaps ever, Franz Liszt.

A notable occasional subset of piano composition was the set of variations by lots of different composers. In 1823 the affable Italian Anton Diabelli published no fewer than eighty-three variations on a jaunty waltz of his own, by a total of fifty-one composers, including Czerny, Schubert, Moscheles, Hummel, Kalkbrenner, Beethoven's pupil Archduke Rudolph, Mozart's son Franz Xaver, and Franz Liszt, who was only seven when the original invitation was issued and was probably included a little later (at the ripe old age of eleven) on the initiative of his teacher Czerny. The variations appear in alphabetical order of the composer's surname, which may or may not be a good way to achieve musical coherence over such a long span. Beethoven did not contribute, but instead wrote thirty-three variations of his own: his last piano work. Another notable multi-composer piano piece, *Hexameron*, was written in 1837 for a benefit concert in a Parisian salon.

Technology: Photographs

Another emerging technology which has had a lasting impact on how we see this era was photography. Chopin is perhaps the first major composer who gazes at us, dapper and brooding, from his distant historical berth before the midpoint of the nineteenth century. Photographs convey character, and fashion: Berlioz's hair, Brahms's beard, Elgar's moustache – all reveal (or maybe conceal) something. The elusive Alkan appears in two photographs, one from the back, which seems somehow fitting. In another image, Verdi wears an old-fashioned button-up black coat, while his younger librettist Arrigo Boito sports a natty three-piece suit in a loud check, complete with tie pin and cigar. He looks like Mr Toad. This photograph seems to show one musical century fading into the past as another ticks into view.

Opera vs Symphony: Old Music, Light Music

Very broadly, nineteenth-century composers either wrote symphonies or operas.

The symphony suited those who instinctively felt that Schlegel's 'philosophical speculation' in music was an abstract process, best teased out in an intellectual dialectic of form and content. That dialectic found its most supple and creative medium in forms inherited from Classical practice, which came to be known as sonata form and the symphonic principle.

Opera, by contrast, served those whose instincts made music a human creature, suitable for probing and describing human motivation and action on stage. Like its symphonic cousin, operatic composition evolved to include both re-creations of Classical formalities like duets and ensembles, and a more fluid type of music drama not broken up into 'numbers', which came to be known as 'through-composed'.

The century continued its curious relationship with the musical past, which was both revered and thoroughly reinvented in Victorian costume, like the architectural fantasies of Gilbert Scott, Viollet-le-Duc or King Ludwig of Bavaria. London heard Handel's *Messiah* with 5,000 performers: Verdi found it 'an immense humbug',[44] while Dickens commented that 'people who complain that they cannot hear the solos, are probably too stingy to pay for the best seats'.[45]

All eras have their lighter music, too: in the nineteenth century it could be found in the music hall and the Moulin Rouge, the parlour song and the operetta. London, in particular, rang with street music of all kinds, from the cries of barrow boys and gypsies selling lavender to theatre fiddlers earning a few bob with a spot of busking, Scots pipers and 'bogus Abyssinians' (according to a French visitor in the 1850s).[46] The operettas of Gilbert and Sullivan in England, Strauss and Lehár in Austria and Offenbach in France were to a large extent tuneful and affectionate parodies of their weightier cousins.

Early Romanticism. An extract from Der Neugierige (The Curious One), *no. 6 of the song cycle* Die schöne Müllerin, *composed by Franz Schubert in c.1823. The poet Wilhelm Müller depicts his ardent lover communing with Nature: the little words 'Yes' and 'No' become 'the whole world for me. O my beloved brooklet, how strange you are!' Schubert captures his yearning by settling into G major (bar 41–2), sliding into B major (bar 42–3), only for major to turn to minor (bar 45) with all the exquisitely painful capriciousness of the distant beloved's moods.*

11

I, GENIUS: WEBER, BEETHOVEN, SCHUBERT AND THEIR WORLD

Weber

We enter the nineteenth century in the company of an odd-looking man with a limp and a cough, a true original of huge influence and a key figure in the emerging story of musical Romanticism, who managed, unlike so many of his great near-contemporaries, to make it to the age of forty (but only just): Carl Maria von Weber.

Weber's life reads like a picaresque novel of the period. Born in 1786, he was first cousin to Mozart's wife Constanze and her singing sisters. His father was a feckless but affectionate former Kapellmeister and travelling actor, who awarded the family the fictitious honorific 'von', and once turned up at his son's lodgings in Stuttgart with a double bass strapped to the top of his carriage and helped himself to 800 gulden. Carl's early travels included a period studying with the 'shrewd old charlatan' the Abbé Vogler in Vienna, where he imbibed technical facility, Romanticism, folk song, and the pleasures of evenings in the tavern with a guitar and a pretty girl.[1] Further travels took in a hands-on operatic apprenticeship in Breslau (which encompassed rows with rivals and an affair with a prima donna), cut short when he absent-mindedly drank engraver's acid from a wine bottle (ending his singing voice and almost his life), and service with a series of decaying European royals such as Friedrich of Württemberg (who was so fat he had a semi-circle carved out of his dining table so he could sit down). He encountered exposure to ideas, alcohol and friendships with composers like Franz Danzi and Gottfried Weber (no relation) and the singer actor (also his lover) Gretchen Lang. Debts piled up and pursued him round Europe. Expelled from Stuttgart in 1810 for allegedly stealing a pair of silver candlesticks, he went to

Mannheim and Heidelberg, where he orchestrated an outdoor serenade with students at the famous university which turned into a riot and had to be quelled by the police. In Darmstadt he renewed his studies with Vogler, alongside friends and fellow composers Gottfried Weber, Johann Gänsbacher and a wealthy, precocious teenager called Jacob Beer, later to be known as Giacomo Meyerbeer. Vogler rated his pupils: 'Gottfried knows the most, Meyer does the most, Carl Maria has the most ability and Johann hits the mark most frequently.'[2] The friends wandered the countryside hearing folk songs which turned up in some of Carl Maria's later pieces like 1819's *Aufforderung zum Tanze (Invitation to the Dance)* (according to the composer's son Max Maria). At Stift Neuberg Carl Maria and his friend Alexander von Dusch bought a book of ghost stories and sat up all night pondering the operatic possibilities of the opening tale, *Der Freischütz*.

The second decade of the century brought success in publication, a semi-autobiographical novel about a composer called Felix, and an opera featuring a singer/actor/mime artiste called Caroline Brandt whose premiere was delayed by the rival appeal of a lady hot air balloonist (Mozart had been similarly inconvenienced two decades earlier). In 1813 Weber was appointed director of the Opera in Prague, working tirelessly to restore standards and corresponding with Gänsbacher about the competing charms of two girls they called 'F Major' and 'D Minor'. He visited Vienna, learnt Czech in order to eavesdrop on his grumbling servants, gave badly received piano recitals, fell dangerously ill with incipient tuberculosis, and moved in with an actress, her husband and five children until she played them both off against a rich banker. The year 1814 saw him become secretly and stormily engaged to his 'D Minor', Caroline. He travelled, his fame and physical frailty both increasing, reaching Munich on the day of the battle of Waterloo in July 1815.

In 1816 he quit his arduous duties in Prague and, after some time in Berlin, took up the prestigious position of Royal Saxon Kapellmeister and Opera Director in the city which was to remain his principal base for the rest of his short life, Dresden. Dresden's musical life had slipped sadly backwards towards provincial bitchiness since the glory days of C. P. E. Bach and Frederick the Great, but it allowed Carl Maria and D Minor to marry, setting up a lively home full of music, visitors, children and animals (including a monkey he brought back from a visit to the king of Denmark) in a pleasantly rural suburb, close to his beloved nature. A talented teenager from Stuttgart, Julius Benedict, became a pupil and sort of supernumerary family member (as Hummel had been to the Mozarts). Music flowed. The year 1821 saw the premiere in Berlin of his opera *Der Freischütz*. (The title, taken from the folkloric source, is sometimes rendered in English as *The Marksman*, but a more literal translation would be something like *The Free Shooter* or *The Free Shot*.) Not all critics appreciated its novel orchestration, magical plot and vivid supernatural effects, and some tried to talk up the expected partisan rivalry with the current celebrity opera composer, Spontini. But *Der Freischütz* was a huge success. There were thirty different productions by the end of the following year, three at once in London in 1824. Lorenzo da Ponte staged it in New York in 1825. One English nobleman became so tired of its popularity that he advertised for an employee on condition that the applicant could not whistle the airs from *Der Freischütz*.

Weber never lost his youthful wanderlust. His later years included feted visits to London, where he eventually succumbed to the ravages of tuberculosis in 1826. In 1844 Wagner, Meyerbeer and others arranged the reinterment of his body in Dresden.

Weber's alter ego Felix, in his unfinished novel *Tonkünstlers Leben*, made the true Romantic's link between nature and art with Wordsworthian explicitness:

> The contemplation of a landscape is to me the performance of a piece of music ... strange as it may seem, the landscape affects me in the dimension of Time ... If I see a view steadily in the distance, the picture always conjures up a parallel musical image in the sympathetic world of my imagination ... [But] when Nature is gradually unrolled before my eyes, how the funeral marches and rondos and furiosos and pastorales somersault after each other![3]

Like many composers of the period, he wrote wisely and widely about music and musicians. As a conductor, he demanded high standards and plenty of rehearsal. He experimented with the layout of the orchestra and pioneered the use of sectional rehearsals. His approach to staging an opera began with the text, which he would read aloud to the cast at the first *Leseprobe*, or reading rehearsal, vividly bringing character and drama alive (in a fascinating echo of the habits of two other artists whose modus, method and mindset were firmly rooted in the theatrical, Wagner and Dickens). He was a fine pianist, with big hands and especially long thumbs.

Among his varied compositional genres, his songs are charming but less serious than Schubert's (though in a nice link, the poet Wilhelm Müller dedicated his collections *Die schöne Müllerin* and *Winterreise*, later immortally set by Schubert, to 'Carl Maria von Weber, master of German song, as token of friendship and admiration'). His piano music ('a strange mixture of naivety, chivalry and sheer tomfoolery', according to the pianist and writer Alfred Brendel)[4] set the scene for the pictorial Romantic fantasy piece: his *Invitation to the Dance*, later orchestrated, virtually invented the idea of the Romantic concert waltz – a potent presence right through the nineteenth century and beyond. He pioneered many aspects of piano technique, such as playing two different kinds of articulation with one hand at the same time in order to bring out a tune, like a later big-fingered virtuoso, Sergei Rachmaninoff. His piano concertos, like Beethoven's, eschew the flashy indiscipline of the improvised cadenza (though they still have plenty of flash). Like Brahms and Mozart he fell in love with the clarinet; where his cousin-in-law Mozart turned the instrument into a sweet-toned operatic heroine, and Brahms made it a soulful contralto, Weber treated it like a ballerina.

In some respects, Weber was a Classicist in Romantic costume. He perhaps described this dual aspect best himself: '[I] can defend my own music from a logical and technical point of view, and produce in every piece a definite effect.'[5] His influence was long-lasting: Mahler orchestrated him, Hindemith composed variations on a theme of his, Stravinsky admired him, Debussy (who shared his fondness for an occasional Spanish rhythm or touch of Oriental colour, though neither of them knew much about either Spain or the East) called him a 'magician'.[6] His immediate, acknowledged successors, in many and varied ways, were Berlioz and Wagner. If that lineage makes him sound like a colourful, original, hugely influential and in some respects transitional figure, then it's a fair assessment.

Beethoven

Weber found the later works of his older contemporary Beethoven both 'incredibly inventive' and 'chaotic'.[7] He wasn't alone.

Ludwig van Beethoven was born in December 1770 in Bonn (though he was under the impression that it was two years later for most of his life). His family originated in the Low Countries (hence 'van' rather than the German 'von' – the etymology of the name hints at possible antecedents among beetroot farmers). His grandfather Ludwig served as a respected and successful court musician, and latterly Kapellmeister to the Elector in Bonn, supplementing his income as a wine merchant. Unfortunately, both his wife and son, the composer's grandmother and father, found the alcoholic aspect of their inheritance more congenial than the musical: Johann Beethoven, a court tenor, was a proud, abusive drunk; his wife Maria was affectionate but unable to cope. Music mixed with domestic turmoil formed part of Beethoven's story from the start.

His musical upbringing was immersive but disorderly. Paraded by his father Mozart-like at court concerts as 'a little boy of six' (when he was actually seven), he 'studied' with a series of monks (one of whom, he thought, 'ought to stay in his monastery and tell his beads').[8] In 1779 the gifted organist Christian Gottlob Neefe provided him with a disciplined training in counterpoint, figured bass and the music of Bach. In 1783 Carl Friedrich Cramer's *Magazin der Musik* praised Neefe's pupil 'Louis van Beethoven ... a boy of eleven years and of most promising talent'[9] (he was actually twelve), and referred to the first published composition of 'this youthful genius', a set of piano variations.[10] Aged fourteen, he was told off for his outlandish piano harmonies during a Holy Week chapel service (and 'graciously reprimanded' by the Elector, Max Franz).[11] As he turned sixteen he made a brief trip to Vienna, including making his only (rather inconclusive) meeting with Mozart, cut short by news of his mother's illness.

Maria Magdalena Beethoven died in July 1787. Beethoven's father descended deeper into dissipation. In November 1789, aged eighteen, Beethoven became the effective head of the family. When Johann finally died in December 1792, the Elector wrote that 'the revenues from the liquor excise have suffered a loss'.[12]

In late 1792, with the revolutionary forces rumbling out of France threatening Bonn and all Europe, the 21-year-old Beethoven left for Vienna. In a farewell album his friend Eleonore von Breuning told him that 'Friendship, like good, grows like the evening shadow, until the sun sets'.[13] Count Ferdinand von Waldstein, his first great patron, wrote, 'You are going to Vienna in fulfilment of your long-frustrated wishes ... you shall receive Mozart's spirit from Haydn's hands', signing himself 'Your true friend, Waldstein'.[14] Beethoven never saw Bonn, or the Rhine, again.

He began his sojourn in the big city by setting himself to study. His first teacher, naturally, was Haydn. His early biographer Thayer puts it neatly: 'this small, thin, dark-complexioned, pockmarked, dark-eyed, bewigged young musician of 22 years had quietly journeyed to the capital to pursue the study of his art with a small, thin, dark-complexioned, pockmarked, black-eyed and bewigged veteran composer'.[15] The pairing was not a success: Haydn thought the young man needed a course in the basics; the young man did not. Beethoven's friend and pupil Ferdinand Ries tells us that when Haydn asked for the description 'pupil of Haydn' to be added to Beethoven's compositions, Beethoven refused, because 'though he had had some instruction from Haydn he had never learned anything from him'[16] (which is manifestly untrue, as works like the six string quartets of Opus 18 and First Symphony (both published in 1801) amply demonstrate, even if that instruction came through absorption and imitation rather than in formal lessons). He studied counterpoint with the celebrated theorist and teacher Johann Georg Albrechtsberger, and vocal writing with the generous and ubiquitous Salieri. Czerny records that Salieri criticised a song of Beethoven's for faulty word setting, but told him the next day, 'I can't get your melody out of my head.' 'Then, Herr von Salieri,' replied Beethoven, 'it cannot have been so utterly bad.'[17]

Vienna also offered Beethoven the opportunity to meet many music-loving nobility, including Princes Lichnowsky and Lobkowitz, the Kinskys, Erdödys and Esterházys, whose various household ensembles included important contacts like the violinist and quartet leader Ignaz Schuppanzigh and his colleagues Vanhal, Karl Holz and the cello-playing father and son Antonín and Nikolaus Kraft. March 1795 saw Beethoven perform for the first time to a Viennese public which so far knew him only by repute. At the first of two benefit concerts for the widows of musicians, at the Burgtheater on 29 March, he performed a new piano concerto (his friend Wegeler relates that he transposed the piano part up a semitone because the wind and piano weren't in tune, which may or may not be entirely accurate). At the second concert on 30 March, Beethoven improvised. The very next day he played in public again, as soloist in a piano concerto by Mozart given between the acts of a performance of *La Clemenza di*

Tito arranged by Mozart's widow Constanze. Alas, there is no record of which piece he played at this notable event, but it may have been that most Beethovenian of all Mozart's concertos, No. 20 in D Minor, a work he admired and for which he wrote cadenzas. He travelled to Prague, earned an increasing reputation as a pianist and composer, and met singers, composers and supporters, including Czerny, Mozart's protégé Hummel, and the baritone Johann Michael Vogl.

The dedications of the piano sonatas tell the story of his progress well. The first three, Classical in form if not always in mood, are dedicated to Haydn. Thereafter, apart from some smaller-scale pieces, all the sonatas of the period are dedicated to an individual, mostly a noble, usually a lady: Countess Giulietta Guicciardi; her cousin Therese von Brunswick; and many a Gräfin and Baronin, Babette and von Braun. Among the men, Count Ferdinand von Waldstein, friend and supporter from Beethoven's Bonn days, is immortalised in the dedication of the great Sonata No. 21 in C Major of 1803, and the indispensable Prince Karl Lichnowsky its earlier, darker cousin, No. 8, the (mostly) C minor Grande Sonata Pathétique of 1798. Later, the most potent noble of all, the Archduke Rudolph, gets the most powerful sonata of all (by Beethoven or anyone else), the colossal Grosse Sonate für das Hammerklavier, Sonata No. 29, of 1818.

On 1 June 1801 Beethoven wrote to Carl Amenda:

> my noblest faculty, my hearing, has greatly deteriorated. When you were still with me I felt the symptoms but kept silent; now it is continually growing worse ... I beg of you to keep the matter of my deafness a profound secret to *be confided to nobody no matter who it is*.[18]

He paid tribute to Lichnowsky, who had settled an annual annuity of 600 florins on him. Alas, his hopes of a cure were doomed. The many treatments he endured benefited nobody except the makers of powders, potions, plasters and pills and the proprietors of expensive spa town hotels.

Two documents draw together several important strands in Beethoven's story.

In October 1802 he wrote a lengthy letter during a stay in the secluded village of Heiligenstadt, just outside Vienna. It is addressed to his brothers, Karl and Johann. The letter is partly a legal document, bequeathing 'my small fortune (if such it may be called)' to them. Far more importantly, it is an intensely moving record of the isolation occasioned by his deafness ('born with an ardent and lively temperament ... I was compelled ... to live in loneliness ... Forced already in my 28th year to become a philosopher, O it is not easy, less easy for the artist than anyone else'). Sadly, he recounts walking in the country with a companion who alerts him to a shepherd piping happily on a flute fashioned from a twig, 'and I heard nothing' (Ferdinand Ries confirms the veracity of this melancholy anecdote). His consolation was in virtue, art, and the love of his friends, 'particularly Prince Lichnowsky'. He looked death in the face, eschewed the easy solution of suicide, and signed off, 'Farewell and do not wholly forget me when I am dead ... Ludwig van Beethoven.'[19] The letter was never sent, stayed with him through several changes of residence, and was found in his desk after his death a quarter of a century later.

The second document dates from a decade later, July 1812. It is a love letter, written in three sittings between 6 and 7 July, each dated, although without giving a year or a location:

> My angel, my all ... I can live only wholly with you or not at all ... your love makes me at once the happiest and the unhappiest of men – at my age I need a steady, quiet life – can that be under our conditions?

The third section opens by addressing the object of his adoration by the name by which she lives eternally, though unknown: 'my thoughts go out to you, my Immortal Beloved'. The search for the identity of Beethoven's Immortal Beloved (his *Unsterbliche Geliebte*') began the moment this document was discovered, like the Heiligenstadt Testament, unsent, among his papers after his death.[20]

But the missing details, whether deliberate or the result of his habitual lofty absent-mindedness, are key to the significance of both documents. The Heiligenstadt letter is a testament to human virtue and resilience. The letter of ten years later is an interrogation of the life force that is human love. They are abstract as much as actual. Beethoven is talking to himself, as an artist and as a man. His words should not, perhaps cannot, be circumscribed and limited by trying to find a normal, ordinary individual to stand as their object. He deals in the cosmic, the universal, the ideal. So does his music.

The year 1805 brought the public premiere of his Third Symphony, the 'Eroica' (his patron Prince Joseph Franz von Lobkowitz had already performed it privately a number of times). Beethoven's bravura assault on his technical inheritance was well underway: Ferdinand Ries 'came pretty close to receiving a box on the ear' from Beethoven for thinking that the daring overlapping of the preparatory dominant seventh chord with the return of the first movement's main theme in the tonic sounds as if the horn player has made a mistake (he's right – it does).[21] By now, Beethoven had earned acknowledgement as the true successor of Haydn and Mozart. But admiration was mixed with puzzlement. One thoughtful reviewer said that some listeners believed this symphony exemplified 'the true style for high-class music', while others heard 'an untamed striving for singularity which had failed'. All found it 'too heavy, too long', full of 'strange modulations and violent transitions'. Sadly, our critic admonishes Beethoven for not turning to nod in acknowledgement of the applause: perhaps he simply hadn't heard it. Fascinatingly, the review suggests that if Beethoven's music 'does not please now, it is because the public is not cultured enough, artistically, to grasp all these lofty beauties; after a few thousand years have passed it will not fail of its effect'[22] – in perhaps the first appearance of the singular idea that Beethoven's works 'are not for you but for a later age!'[23] as he himself said about the Razumovsky Quartets of 1806. The Classical model of the composer fitting his art into a predetermined form and context was gone.

The Third Symphony reflects outer pressures, too. In the year of its premiere, 1803, Napoleon's troops made their first entry into Vienna. Society fled. Beethoven had originally dedicated the symphony to Napoleon, but when he declared himself emperor in late 1804 Beethoven, so Ries tells us, broke into a rage and exclaimed, 'So he is no more than a common mortal! Now, too, he will tread under foot all the rights of Man, indulge only his ambition; now he will think himself superior to all men, become a tyrant!' Beethoven went to the table, seized the top of the title page, tore it in half and threw it on the floor.[24]

Again, Beethoven's ideas and ideals were beyond association with any 'common mortal'.

Other creative relationships included with the travelling Polish-Barbadian violin virtuoso George Polgreen Bridgetower ('lunatic mulatto composer', in the original, jocular dedication of the 'Kreutzer' Violin Sonata of 1804) and, intriguingly, with Mozart's high-spirited theatrical collaborator, Emanuel Schikaneder, who gave Beethoven a generous commission which eventually led to his only opera, *Fidelio*. Thayer gives him an entirely apt curtain call: 'Schikaneder – that strange compound of wit and absurdity; of poetic instinct and grotesque humour; of shrewd and profitable enterprise and lavish prodigality; who lived like a prince and died like a pauper – has connected his name honourably with both Mozart and Beethoven.'[25]

A productive period led to the astonishing all-Beethoven, all-premiere concert of 22 December 1808: the Fifth and Sixth Symphonies, the Piano Concerto No. 4 in G Major, the remarkable *Choral Fantasia* (billed as a 'Fantasia for the Pianoforte which ends with the gradual entrance of the entire orchestra and the introduction of choruses as a finale'), and several other works.[26] He read, squabbled with his brothers, received a job offer from Napoleon's brother Jérôme, and memorialised important relationships with the talented young Archduke Rudolph and the Russian Count Razumovsky in music.

The period around 1810–12 marked a change in Beethoven. His creative output fell away markedly. His hearing, and his general health, deteriorated alarmingly. As for many other composers, a fallow period was followed by an intense burst of activity: the Seventh and Eighth Symphonies and Violin Sonata No. 10 in G Major (for Rudolph and the violinist Pierre Rode) in 1812, the bombastic but hugely popular *Wellington's Victory* (marking Napoleon's defeat at Vitoria and originally conceived for a kind of mechanical orchestra called a panharmonicon) in 1813, and the following year the substantial and successful revision of *Fidelio*, the work on which he probably lavished a lengthier labour of love than any other.

The year 1815 brought for Beethoven a personal event of lasting significance. On 15 November his brother Karl died. Earlier, Beethoven had petitioned for guardianship of Karl's son, also Karl, then aged nine. The boy's mother was a troubled, difficult and unstable woman (Beethoven referred to her as the 'Queen of Night'), and a long series of legal and emotional tussles ensued. For Karl, shunted between boarding schools, his unsatisfactory mother and the chaotic home and smothering affection of his deaf, domineering uncle, matters reached a crisis at the age of nineteen, when he abandoned his university studies and announced his wish to join the army. Beethoven was furious. In despair, Karl purchased a pair of pistols, clambered up the Rauhenstein ruins in Baden, and attempted to shoot himself. He caused only a graze to his temple. He later told the police, '[M]y uncle has tormented me too much ... I became worse because my uncle wanted me to be better.'[27] (In a comforting footnote, Karl was with Beethoven through much of his final illness, became his heir, and went on to serve successfully in the military, marry happily and raise his own family. Photographs show his fringe worn long to hide his scar.)

Professionally, the Karl years saw much correspondence between Beethoven and friends and promoters in England, including two men who visited him in Vienna, Cipriani Potter and Sir George Smart (England's top musicians of this period are often best remembered for their friendships with their towering European contemporaries, like 'a candle in sunshine', as their compatriot William Blake put it).[28] The manufacturer John Broadwood & Sons sent Beethoven a piano, much prized and later owned by Liszt. A plan to visit England got no further than letters. The ravaged old lion (though still only fifty) met younger stars like Weber, Marschner, Rossini and the boy Liszt (though probably not Schubert), encounters often recorded in the composer's conversation books in puzzled accounts of conversations conducted in a mixture of shouting and scribbling in a variety of languages, compounded by Beethoven's habitual lack of social graces and the sort of unreliable mythologising which always surrounds a celebrity.

Musically, the turn of the 1820s brought the last in the great sequence of piano sonatas. In February 1824 thirty of Beethoven's friends (princes, patrons, performers and publishers, corralled by the admirable Lichnowsky) wrote him a florid letter eulogising him as part of the 'sacred triad' with Haydn and Mozart, and asking about 'the latest masterworks of your hand ... in which you have immortalised the emotions of a soul, penetrated and transfigured by the power of faith and superterrestrial light. We know that a new flower glows in the garland of your glorious, still unequalled symphonies.'[29]

It worked. Beethoven's isolated despondency lifted, and he threw himself into the complex negotiations for a 'Grand Musical Concert', which took place on 7 May 1824. The works heard on that auspicious evening were the overture *The Consecration of the House*, parts of the Mass in D Major (the *Missa solemnis* – already performed complete in

St Petersburg the previous month), and the work which had occupied him, Wagner-like, for over twenty years, the Ninth Symphony.

His labours were not quite over. Between 1825 and around September 1826 Beethoven wrote some of the most intensely and searchingly inward-looking works in all music, reimagining form, technique and tonality to reach into his memory and his own soul: the late string quartets, Nos. 12–16, and the *Grosse Fuge* (originally the finale to String Quartet No. 13 in B Flat Major).

Illness overtook him in the winter of 1826–7. Visitors to his sick room included Schubert, Hummel and the newest representative of his loyal friends from childhood, the von Breunings, a cheerful and attentive boy called Gerhard, whom Beethoven nicknamed Trouser-Button from his habit of hanging onto his father Stephan's breeches.

Beethoven died on 26 March 1827, aged fifty-six.

Physically, Beethoven was short, powerfully built, and untidy. Weber describes a 'square Cyclopean figure … in a shabby coat with torn sleeves'.[30] Like Mozart, Haydn and Gluck, he carried the facial pits and pockmarks of smallpox – a feature always omitted by convention in portraits. His living quarters were fabulously messy, littered with broken instruments, half-finished manuscripts and half-eaten food. He could quite easily simply forget to eat. Relations with put-upon domestic servants were, unsurprisingly, a kind of permanent war. He once confessed, 'My household greatly resembles a shipwreck.'[31]

He read widely, and had some words, allegedly from an ancient statue of Isis and popular among early Romantic thinkers as a metaphor of revealed truth, framed on his desk:

I am that which is.
I am all that is, that was, and that shall be.
No mortal man hath lifted my veil.
He is alone by Himself, and to Him alone do all things owe
    their being.

He copied mystical Eastern texts referring to God as 'Sun, Ether, Brahm'. He was a committed letter-writer, often adding snatches of music to his missives, some of them quite lengthy. Close male friends like Nicolaus Zmeskall were given bantering military nicknames: 'The Adjutant'; 'The Generalissimo'. The violinist Ignaz

Schuppanzigh, who was rather fat, was 'My Lord Falstaff'. A grim version of Mozartian wit occasionally appears: when his brother wrote signing himself 'Johann Beethoven, Landowner' he got a reply from 'Ludwig van Beethoven, Brainowner.'[32] In business dealings he was demanding but astute, and remained comfortably off through publication, commissions, performances and support from patrons.

The piano, emblem of emerging musical modernity, was central to his musical modus. As a youth he was praised for his sight-reading and his mastery of Bach. When asked to improvise, he would often feign reluctance, sometimes slapping the keys with the palm of his hand, presumably a showy way of buying time to gather his thoughts before settling down to display. Challenged to one of the popular contests of pianistic skill with the flashy Daniel Steibelt, he apparently dismissively turned one of Steibelt's compositions upside down on the music desk and improvised on the resulting inverted melody. He wrote well for instruments, and expanded the sonic range of the orchestra (as he did of everything else), though without that sense of the sensual appeal of sound and colour which characterises theatrical composers like Weber and Berlioz.

Like some other great composers who treated music more as an abstract than a physical art, his writing for the voice can be unsympathetic and challenging. Caroline Unger, contralto soloist in the marathon concert featuring the *Missa solemnis* and the Ninth Symphony, called him a 'tyrant over all the vocal organs'[33] – something to which anyone who has sung the Ninth will answer 'Amen' (probably rather hoarsely). Unger and others asked Beethoven to rewrite some of the highest passages, but he refused: Thayer reports that some singers left them out anyway and the deaf composer simply didn't notice (although, according to one famous anecdote, Unger apparently turned the composer round to face the audience and witness the tumultuous, but to him completely inaudible, ovation).[34]

He composed with the characteristics of particular players in mind, not always appreciatively, writing about the violinist Rode, '[W]e like quick, full-toned passages in our *Finales*, which do not suit R., and this rather cramps me.'[35] He moaned to the baritone Sebastian Meier 'all *pp.*'s, *cresc.*, *discresc.*, and all *f.*'s and *ff.*'s may as well be struck out of my Opera, for no attention whatever is paid to them'.[36] His conducting, especially as deafness overtook him, seems to have been more histrionic than accurate: a famous account originating with

Louis Spohr, who played the violin in the epic concert of December 1808, describes how Beethoven would 'indicate expression to the orchestra by all manner of singular bodily movements. At *piano* he crouched down lower and lower ... clean under the desk ... If a *crescendo* then entered he gradually rose again and at the entrance of the *forte* jumped into the air.' (In this account Beethoven managed to get 'ten or twelve measures ahead of the orchestra' because 'he could no longer hear the *piano* of his music', and only 'found his bearings when the long-expected *forte* came'.)[37]

His working methods included regular summer sojourns in the countryside. As he told one correspondent (a lady, naturally), '[W]hen you stray through the silent pine forests, do not forget that Beethoven often wrote poetry there, or, as it is termed, *composed*.'[38] His pupil Czerny says the running theme of the last movement of Piano Sonata No. 17 in D Minor was inspired by the beating hooves of a galloping horse. Ries describes going with Beethoven on a walk which lasted all day, during which 'he had been all the time humming and sometimes howling, always up and down, without singing any definite notes'.[39] He was also 'often at work at three or four things at the same time'.[40]

Among other composers, Beethoven revered Bach and Handel. He could be both kind and competitive with his contemporaries, like all artists taking from them what he needed. He regarded himself as 'an artist who continues to make progress',[41] and his manner and method evolved continuously, both within individual works and across his career as a whole.

Technically, this evolution encompassed the key idea of unity or relationship between themes in his music, identified as early as 1810 by the ever-perceptive E. T. A. Hoffmann in the Fifth Symphony:

The inner arrangement of the movements, their development, instrumentation, the manner in which they are ordered, all this works toward a single point: but most of all it is the intimate relationship among the themes which creates this unity.[42]

This process is aided by a reductive approach to theme, taking music back to its basic components: many of Beethoven's melodies are really just scales, from which he wrings unstoppable power, like Prometheus forging the world from fire and clay. Bass lines can work in contrary motion to upper tunes, providing another level of internal unity. Rhythm can become a theme in its own right as never before (or after, at least until Stravinsky): the first movements of the Fifth and Seventh Symphonies hammer out their motto rhythms in virtually every bar; the wonderful Allegretto of the Seventh does something similar and no less striking with a less aggressive rhythmic unit.

The critic Ernest Newman spoke for Beethoven's best analysts when he observed that

> his mind did not proceed from the particular to the whole, but began, in some curious way, with the whole and then worked back to the particular ... the long and painful search for the themes was simply an effort, not to find workable atoms out of which he could construct a musical edifice according to the conventions of symphonic form, but to reduce an already existing nebula, in which that edifice was implicit, to the atom, and then, by the orderly arrangement of these atoms, to make the implicit explicit.[43]

Tracing a particular work from the explosive turbulence of the sketchbooks through to the finished form reveals how that 'long and painful' process worked. Experiencing the completed whole becomes a journey to its eventual fulfilment, mysterious and complete.

Any overview of Beethoven's artistic journey must mention the conventional division of his life and work into three periods. By date, these refer roughly to his first decade in Vienna as an active, mature young professional (broadly, his twenties); then the period of worldly success and gathering deafness and spiritual isolation to 1812 (his thirties); finally, the remarkable last fifteen years of his life, when resignation and acceptance of his fate – unmarried, unhearing and alone – led him deeper into his own inner world. *'Muss es sein?'* ('Must it be?') asks the superscription over the slow introduction to the last movement of almost his very last work, the String Quartet No. 16 in F Major, followed by the Allegro, headed *'Es muss sein!'* ('It must be!')

Musically, the first period finds him filling the forms of his Viennese inheritance with his own ideas and manner; the second sees him expanding those forms by, for example, rolling sonata, rondo and variation forms further together and adding extra repeats to the Classical standard scherzo–trio–scherzo arrangement; in the last period he disassembles and dismantles forms and techniques and puts them back together to make new things – a piano sonata on hitherto unimagined proportions, a seven-movement string quartet, a symphony three or four times longer than anything Mozart ever wrote, which veers off into a long and discursive review of its entire thematic material before exploding into a finale with words, voices, and all of human experience.

Among the string quartets, three groups of works cover all three periods: Nos. 1–6, which together form Opus 18, fall in the first period, the Razumovsky Quartets (Opus 59) and Nos. 10 and 11 in the second, with the late quartets beginning with No. 12, Opus 127, in E Flat Major, in the last. The symphonies and piano sonatas chart a similar journey across the complete span of his working life and artistic development. Other works stand slightly outside that pattern: the seven great concertos (five for piano, one for violin, and the Triple Concerto for violin, cello and piano) all date from the opening decade of the nineteenth century (though show plenty of stylistic development from the charm and grace of the first two piano concertos to the splendour of the last, the mighty 'Emperor'); *Fidelio* is unique, having been revised and revisited over ten years from 1804 (gaining two titles and four overtures in the process). Beethoven would sometimes not scruple to take a step back from the main current of his artistic progress and indulge himself in a work of charm or modesty: the Eighth Symphony, composed in 1812 on the cusp of the last period, is, in the estimable words of his biographer Marion Scott, 'frankly a little darling'.[44] The tiny dimensions of the smaller piano pieces, including several sets of bagatelles, provide fascinating glimpses into Beethoven's various compositional preoccupations across his career, like shavings from a craftsman's workbench: the Bagatelle in F Major of 1802 slips coyly into D major and back, exploring key relationships by thirds like the mighty 'Waldstein' Sonata a year later. Some believe that deafness liberated Beethoven from the tyranny of the well-tempered scale. Prevented from playing or conducting, he perforce invented the idea of the composer who wasn't also, indeed primarily, a practising professional: the Romantic genius was born.

Is it possible to criticise Beethoven? Some have found the relentless pounding against fate a bit, well, relentless. In a classic example of an artist revealing more about himself than the subject of his comments, Benjamin Britten thought his music sounded like 'sacks of potatoes'.[45]

Beethoven's achievement transcends all this. It does not just belong to him. The challenge and example it set forms part of the inheritance of every serious composer and thinker about music to the present day.

And yet there is more to Beethoven even than that. His hard-won vision came partly through his own suffering, partly through his bearing witness to his times. That vision remains relevant. When the Berlin Wall came down in 1989 it was Beethoven's great symphony of brotherhood, with its setting of Schiller's 'Ode to Joy', which was performed to mark the reunification of his homeland. That same hymn was the only possible choice as the anthem of the edifice of peace arising out of the ashes of war, the European Union: *alle Menschen werden Brüder* ('all people will be united').

That vision has come under strain, not least through Nazi distortion of the Ninth Symphony. It still stands as a challenge and an ideal today. But it hasn't dwindled with the circumstances which produced it. It remains universal.

Schubert

In 1822 Beethoven was the dedicatee of a set of piano variations by a composer who signed himself *'seinem Verehrer und Bewunderer'* ('his worshipper and admirer'): Franz Schubert.[46] Whether Schubert was brave enough to offer his manuscript to Beethoven in person, or whether Beethoven received it if he did, remains unclear from several competing and contradictory accounts. It's the kind of a tantalising detail which hints at Schubert's sometimes shadowy presence in a sort of parallel musical Vienna, beneath the glance of the princes and the divas, separate from the celebrities because he wasn't Italian or good at the piano, often overlooked (perhaps literally – even by the diminutive standards of the great Viennese composers, the man affectionately known as 'Schwammerl', or 'Little Mushroom', was noticeably short), making music largely among friends. But to those friends, and to critics wise enough to notice, that music quickly earned him his rightful place as the completion and fulfilment of the quartet of Viennese musical 'princely spirits', as Lichnowsky called them,[47] finding a new direction in which to take their legacy, forging a uniquely lyrical version of Romanticism which opened up new vistas on the human heart, and, perhaps above all, fashioning some of the finest songs ever written.

The Little Mushroom's life story is easily told. He lived just thirty-one years, hardly travelled, neither married nor consorted with princes, and had no glittering career. He was barely a professional musician at all: the closest he came to regular employment was as tutor to the daughters of a branch of the ever-present Esterházy family, a job in truth more closely related to his background as a schoolteacher than to his rightful later standing as prince and giant of music in his own right.

Franz Peter Schubert was born in 1797, the youngest of four surviving children (all boys) of the twelve born to Franz Theodor, a devout and hard-working schoolteacher, and his wife Maria Elisabet. His upbringing was supportive, suburban and happy. Early instruction was within the family, and around the age of nine he took the time-honoured route of musical study with the local parish church organist, Michael Holzer, who had his profession's traditional twin fondnesses for good counterpoint and good wine and remarked of his young pupil: 'If I wished to instruct him in anything he already knew it. Consequently I gave him no actual tuition but merely conversed with him and watched him with silent astonishment.'[48]

In late 1808 young Franz became a choirboy at the Imperial Chapel and student at its well-resourced school (his examiners included Joseph Eybler, who had attended Mozart on his deathbed and had a hand in the completion of Mozart's Requiem, and the ever-present Salieri). He did well, was trusted to leave the school building for lessons with Salieri, and demonstrated a gift for male friendship which was such a feature of his later life (one friend, Joseph von Spaun, supplied him with manuscript paper because he was too poor to buy his own). The holidays brought together a family string quartet with his father and two of his brothers. In 1812 his mother (who is, like many musical matrons of the period, a shadowy historical presence) died, and so did his treble voice: like naughty choirboys throughout the ages he scribbled on his music 'Schubert, Franz, crowed for the last time, 26 July 1812'.[49] His father remarried, again happily. Franz left school, worked for his father as a class teacher, and began wearing the familiar spectacles. Music poured from him, including chamber pieces for the domestic fireside, and some of his finest songs. He met friends like the poets Franz von Schober and Johann Mayrhofer, among the first of the noble brotherhood of Schubertians – cultured, worldly young men who deserve our posthumous thanks (and envy) for their companionship and support of their short-sighted little friend. In May 1816 Schubert took lodgings with the first of a long series of congenial housemates, Josef Witteczek. The domestic musical evenings known as Schubertiade began.

As he moved into his twenties he moved house (including a spell with Schober's wealthy mother), flirted with independence from working for his father (now at a new school and with young children from his second marriage), assimilated the rage for Rossini (quickly subsumed into his own style), and continued to collect friends, among them the well-connected baritone Johann Michael Vogl.

July 1818 brought the flattering offer of a job as music teacher to the young daughters of Count Johann Esterházy at the family summer retreat of Zseliz, about 125 miles east of Vienna. The two princesses inspired several piano duets – music for two players at one piano was a medium he made particularly his own. Life was pleasant enough, but, like Haydn, he clearly missed the stimulation of the big city. 'At Zseliz I am obliged to rely entirely on myself,' he wrote to Schober, 'I have to be composer, author, audience and goodness knows what else ... I am alone with my beloved and have to hide her in my room, in my pianoforte and in my bosom. Although this often makes me sad, on the other hand it elevates me the more.'[50] When the Esterházys returned to Vienna in November 1818, Schubert went with them. He didn't return to full-time domestic employment, or schoolteaching, or indeed any kind of job, for the rest of the ten years of life left to him.

The year 1819 saw the first of several summer sojourns in the country, with Vogl. The joyously sunny *Trout Quintet* captures the unclouded happiness of the 'inconceivably lovely' countryside around Steyr.[51] Back in Vienna Schubert attempted to make his way in the popular and lucrative field of theatre, with some success, including a piece in which Vogl played both of a pair of twins. Schubert's operas and other theatrical pieces founder, like Haydn's, on the lack of Mozart's dramatic instincts. But they contain some lovely things, often extracted for concert use. In 1820 a public performance of *Erlkönig* brought resounding and far-reaching success, and friendships with the musical Fröhlich sisters and Franz Grillparzer, Austria's leading dramatist. Increasing renown was not matched by similar success with publishers, largely because, unlike many lesser composers, Schubert was not also celebrated as a virtuoso performer. A few songs were printed privately, a successful venture aided by some well-placed dedications ('the Patriarch has forked out 12 ducats,' he told Spaun).[52] Summer 1821 was the first of three spent happily at Atzenbrugg, captured in one of several evocative paintings of Schubert surrounded by friends in some handsome drawing-room, images full of life and character, the composer invariably at the piano, the still centre of vivacious activity.

In 1822 he met Weber, composed the two completed movements of the Symphony in B Minor and, sadly, began behaving in an uncharacteristically offhand manner to his friends. The failure to finish the symphony and the erratic behaviour may both, possibly, be connected with the onset late that year of the disease which eventually killed him, syphilis. In any event, his friendships began to come under strain.

Bedevilled with recurrent illness and some bad business deals, he moved briefly back in with his father. In 1823 he composed his first great song cycle, *Die schöne Müllerin*. His reputation grew steadily through performance and publication. In 1825 he sat for an agreeable watercolour portrait (Schubert was unusually well-served by the visual arts: a beautiful pencil sketch by Josef Teltscher of the composer with Anselm Hüttenbrenner and Johann Baptist Jenger reads like a study in friendship, easy and intelligent, one man gazing at us calmly, the other two looking away into the distance, a hand resting lightly on a shoulder, spectacles on nose, faces framed by curly hair and fashionable cravats). Summer visits to the country included Dornbach with Schober and Graz with Jenger. Reviews appeared, many, though not all, sympathetic. In 1827 he visited the dying Beethoven, their only meeting. In late March he was one of thirty-six torch-bearers at Beethoven's funeral.

Schubert's last year stands some comparisons with Mozart's. Benjamin Britten called it 'the richest and most productive eighteen months in our music history'.[53] He composed (or completed) the 'Great' C Major Symphony, the song cycle *Winterreise* and other songs including the *Schwanengesang* collection and *Der Hirt auf dem Felsen* (*The Shepherd on the Rock*), with its rippling, yodelling, clarinet obligato, the Mass in E Flat Major (dramatic and richly scored, but hardly religious in character – a friend once wrote Schubert a letter which included the words '*Credo in Unum Deum*' ('I believe in one God') with the aside 'You don't, as I very well know';[54] the '*Et Incarnatus est*' of this Mass is a song so charming the composer simply repeats it three times, letting the soloists show off their legato and Italianate Latin vowels), and the almost hour-long String Quintet in C Major, with its sonorous pair of cellos and slow movement frozen in time, borrowing the strange, suspended stillness of Beethoven's late string music. In March 1828 there was an all-Schubert concert, to a packed and partisan audience, successful but overshadowed in the public prints by the advent of the virtuoso violinist Niccolò Paganini. Illness, exhaustion and lack of funds kept him in Vienna apart from a short walking tour to Haydn's burial place at Eisenstadt. In September he moved in with his brother Ferdinand. On 19 November, tended to the last by Ferdinand and their young half-sister Josefa, he died. His friends gave him a musical funeral, laid him to rest three graves along from his idol Beethoven, and raised money from subscriptions and a benefit concert for a permanent memorial, with his bust in bronze by the renowned sculptor Joseph Dialer. It bears an epitaph by the dramatist Franz Grillparzer: 'Music here buried a rich possession, but even more beautiful hopes.'

The pianist Alfred Brendel addresses Schubert's technical inheritance neatly and accurately:

> I see it like this: with Mozart and Beethoven, we hardly ask ourselves what they are doing and why they are doing it. The musical architecture is its own justification: Mozart tends to build with finished parts, whereas Beethoven constructs and develops. Beethoven builds, even when he dreams, while Schubert dreams even when, exceptionally, he builds.[55]

In practice, this meant a new approach to sonata and symphonic structure, based on long-breathed melodies which did not (and did not need to) lend themselves to being deconstructed into 'parts' for building. Another fine pianist and thoughtful writer, Charles Rosen, says that 'Schubert works within the late and loosely organized post-classical style, in which the melodic flow is essentially more important than the dramatic structure'.[56] Interestingly, our two philosophers of the keyboard differ about how successful the Schubertian approach is: Rosen points out its 'deficiencies' and goes so far as to call the style 'degenerate';[57] Brendel believes that 'one can get lost in many Schubert movements, as in a thick forest, and we do it willingly'.[58]

Similar considerations apply to the symphonies. Robert Schumann (who as an 18-year-old wrote Schubert a letter but never sent it) praised the 'heavenly length' of the C Major Symphony of 1828 (the 'Great').[59] The historian Donald Jay Grout thinks this aspect 'would be less heavenly were it not for the beauty of Schubert's melodies', which are 'expanded ... almost to breaking-point'.[60] Brendel thinks Schubert's structures are 'hardly ever too long' (which perhaps recalls an exchange from a later work of nineteenth-century music theatre: 'What, never?' 'Well, hardly ever').[61]

Grout writes about the 'shimmering magic carpet of Schubertian modulations' in the slow movement of the B Minor Symphony of 1822 (the 'Unfinished').[62] That 'magic carpet' is woven from threads and favourite tricks like enharmonic shifts, sideways slips between keys a third apart, and ambiguous hoverings between major and minor. Is *'Ständchen'* ('Serenade') (D. 597) a song in D minor which ends in the major, or a song in D major which begins in the minor? Another late work, the wonderful string quintet, begins in C major (sort of), until the two cellos stop time on a unison G before embarking on a lyrical duet in E flat major. (And, as so often, these harmonic jewels are clothed in the most ravishing and carefully imagined instrumental and orchestral textures: the shivering opening of the B Minor Symphony is a perfect example.) All attempts to fix these subtle oppositions of areas of feeling into reductive definitions like happy/sad, life/death, light/dark (even gay/straight) fall when Schubert shows us, as he does with unfailing instinct, that the human personality is infinitely more fluid and interesting than that. His *Ständchen* is, like a human life, major and minor at the same time.

Schubert's art is essentially lyrical. The key to it lies in his songs. The greatest fifty or so of his more than 600 songs take the form beyond anything before or since. Their sheer variety is amazing: he deepened the reach of the Beethovenian idea of the 'cycle', or 'ring', of songs; individual songs can be simply strophic (*'Das Wandern'*), dramatic and ballad-like (*'Erlkönig'*), hymn-like (*'Litanei'*); they can set up a verse-like structure and then vary it (*'Du bist die Ruh'*); or borrow an almost recit-and-aria model to mark changes of mood (*'Der Neugierige'*). His piano parts support the vocal line with utmost simplicity (*'An die Musik'*), the visually and psychologically pictorial (*'Gretchen am Spinnrade'*) and the virtually impossible (*'Erlkönig'* again). There are songs with guitar, part songs of all kinds, and songs with an obligato instrument like a horn or clarinet, acting almost as a second singer. His predecessor in an art founded on vocal cantabile was Mozart. His successor in the subtlety and craft of the song cycle was Schumann.

The chiefs of this chapter died in consecutive years (though born in three different decades): Weber in 1826, Beethoven in 1827, Schubert in 1828. The next generation was beginning to emerge out of musical short trousers. It was to be a remarkable, though in most cases brief, maturity.

12

1812: OVERTURE

In September 1812, Napoleon's army faced the forces of Marshal Kutuzov across the battlefield of Borodino in the gathering Russian winter. The event, later commemorated in some of the most magnificent musical tub-thumpery of the entire nineteenth century, marked the beginning of the end of thirty era-defining years of French struggle, glory and terror.

At around the same time, far away in distant provincial Leipzig, a baker's daughter named Johanna Wagner was perhaps becoming dimly aware that she was expecting her ninth child.

In other outposts of musical Europe, a Hungarian court musician, Adam Liszt, was perhaps soothing his baby son Franz by playing some of the gentler melodies of his erstwhile friends and acquaintances, Haydn, Hummel and Beethoven. In Zwickau, did little Robert, just one year old and the youngest of the five Schumann children, clench a fist or avoid a gaze in ways which a modern child psychologist might read as hints of the cruel mental instability that would haunt him as an adult? In Poland, baby Emilia arrived to complete the cultured Franco-Polish Chopin family, already numbering two older sisters and a brother, Fryderyk, now aged two. In Berlin, the Mendelssohns led a prominent, prosperous life, in time a fertile intellectual and musical breeding ground for the precocious talents of 3-year-old Felix.

Not all of these young men went on to earn the title of Infant Prodigy (to borrow a term from another notable artist born that year, Charles Dickens). Some achieved greatness a little later in their careers. But their lives were destined to interact in all sorts of fascinating and revealing ways among the music stands and coffee shops of the large musical village called Europe.

As the post-Napoleonic era began to look around and test the air, the musical prospects were good.

Four Contemporaries: Youth

The interactions, coincidences, friendships and achievements of Mendelssohn, Chopin, Schumann and Liszt – born within three years of each other – chart an intriguing musical path through the events and manner of the first half of the nineteenth century.

Felix Mendelssohn, the eldest of the four, was born in February 1809 in Hamburg (in a curious parallel with Beethoven, in the same house as a notable violinist, Ferdinand David). Politics intervened early: in 1811, because the family bank had resisted Napoleon's blockade of the port, the Mendelssohns fled in disguise to Berlin, where they established a richly intellectual salon of artists and thinkers. Like Mozart, young Felix shared the musical limelight with a talented sister four years his senior, Fanny. An early teacher was Marie Bigot, pupil and friend of Beethoven. He travelled widely with his father, and, by the age of thirteen, he had met Goethe and Hummel. Chopin's family was displaced, too: his French father Nicolas distanced himself from his humble Paris background, finding sufficient security and status as a tutor and schoolteacher in his adopted Poland to marry and prosper, despite Russian domination following the fall of Napoleon after 1815, when his son was five. For the frail and sensitive Fryderyk, it was a provincial upbringing with a good education and a dash of aristocratic patronage, even as the old order came under increasing challenge. The same could be said for the youngest in this varied group, Franz Liszt, born in late 1811 in another outpost of eastern Europe, Hungary, where his father served the eternal Esterházys, first playing the cello in the orchestra at Eisenstadt, and then, from 1809, in the less exalted post of sheep inspector at one of their other estates, Raiding. Schumann's parentage showed another variant on changing economic times: his father August was bookseller and publisher in the small but handsome east German town of Zwickau. In a worrying pre-shadow of later tragedy, August suffered a 'nervous disorder' in the year of Robert's birth.[1] Portraits of the artists in childhood and youth convey a cultured, occasionally almost feminine, grace.

Maturity: The 1820s

For all four composers, their second decade, the 1820s, brought adolescence, travel, experience of wider European cultural life, varying degrees of parental resistance to the potential perils and pitfalls of professional musical life, and many meetings with music, musicians and each other. In 1819 Schumann, aged nine, heard a concert by a musician whose name and influence resonate through these pages, the Jewish-Bohemian pianist and composer Ignaz Moscheles. A year later little Liszt was in Vienna, taken up enthusiastically by the generous Czerny and the unsinkable Salieri. In April 1823, Beethoven was invited (via his conversation books) to hear the 11-year-old Liszt play. Liszt later recalled their meeting with tearfully reverent emotion, though biographers from Thayer on remain unconvinced whether Beethoven did actually attend the concert (conversely, Liszt denied meeting Schubert, whereas scholars believe he did). In late 1823 Liszt moved with his family to Paris, giving concerts in major German towns on the way, but was refused entry to the Paris Conservatoire by its director, Luigi Cherubini (who was himself of Italian origin), because he was foreign.

Mendelssohn also travelled extensively at this period, reaching Paris in 1825. Cherubini had a rather more benign influence on the career of young Felix, praising his piano quartet. This was the latest instalment of a remarkable early phase of composition which already included four concertos and the string symphonies, but nonetheless barely hints at the explosion of creativity which burst forth a year later with his miraculous Octet in E Flat Major for strings, surely the finest work ever penned by a 16-year-old. Chopin spent 1823–8 studying dutifully at his father's high school and the conservatory in Warsaw. He showed none of the worldly, precocious brilliance of Liszt the performer or Mendelssohn the composer, though the conservatory's director, József Elsner, deserves credit for a perceptive end of term report: 'Extraordinary ability. Musical genius.'[2] Liszt, meanwhile, was everywhere: London and Manchester in 1823, then all round France, England again to play to the king in 1824, Switzerland, France again, followed by a third hop across the Channel in 1827. In the midst of these travels Liszt and Mendelssohn met in Paris, shortly after Mendelssohn's sixteenth birthday. Chopin had no such cosmopolitan confidence even by the age of eighteen: on holiday in Berlin in 1828 he found himself in the same room as Mendelssohn and the star opera composer Spontini, but was too shy to speak to them. Schumann, too, led a provincial existence through which many of the themes and preoccupations of his short life began poking their heads: he did well at school; formed *Schülerverbindung* (secret schoolboy clubs); missed the chance to study with Weber through the older man's early death in 1826; suffered the loss of both his father and his invalid sister the same year; read, wrote and lost himself in 'literary fantasies in Jean Paul's manner';[3] and fell in love with schoolgirls and older married women, such as Agnes Carus, a singer and the wife of a doctor from Colditz. In 1828, like Telemann long before him, he obediently but reluctantly enrolled as a law student in Leipzig, where (also like Telemann) he found the lively musical scene far more to his taste than eating his legal dinners. Fear of insanity began to stalk his 'night raptures'.[4]

The decade approached its end with new steps and a degree of reaction. Liszt retrenched from his frenetic teenage touring, entering a period of retreat between 1827 and 1830, during which he considered becoming a priest. Chopin played successfully in Vienna in mid-1829. The same year, Mendelssohn (with the help of his friend Eduard Devrient, singer and scion of a notable theatrical family) led one of the defining concerts of musical history, the first performance of Bach's *St Matthew Passion* since the composer's death. Just a month later Mendelssohn made the first of what turned out to be many visits to England, playing Beethoven's 'Emperor' Concerto and his own youthful Double Concerto in A Flat Major for two pianos (with Moscheles), taking in Scotland, a visit to Sir Walter Scott at Abbotsford and the celebrated steamboat crossing to Staffa and Fingal's Cave, inspiration for one of his most characteristic early pieces, the *Hebrides Overture* of 1833. In August 1828 Schumann started lessons with a well-known Leipzig piano teacher, Friedrich Wieck, whose 9-year-old daughter Clara was already a skilled and highly trained pianist. When Schubert died in November he cried all night.

Schumann managed to solve the conundrum of whether to study law or music by the simple expedient of finding a musical law professor, Justus Thibaut at Heidelberg University, and persuading his mother to let him transfer there for a year. A happy and productive period ended with his return to Leipzig and a partly successful attempt to persuade Wieck to encourage his mother to let him abandon the law for music: Wieck thought he had the talent but doubted the steadiness of his character, a trope he was to return to. Schumann moved in with the Wiecks and promised to smoke, drink and spend less – all of which he apparently failed to do. His writings of the period award nicknames to friends and acquaintances (Clara is 'Zilia', a girl called

Christel is 'Charitas') and to fantasy characters. He gives himself two names: 'Florestan' the *improvisatore*, exuberant and outgoing; and the thoughtful, introspective, critical 'Eusebius'. The duality adds a rich vein of both humour and psychological complexity to his writings about music. Both appear in an enthusiastic article of September 1831 about a new musical idol, who was at exactly that moment arriving in Paris following a second, frustrating sojourn in Vienna: Frédéric – formerly Fryderyk – Chopin.

The 1830s: Politics

Politics cuts regularly through the five straight lines at this period. The July revolution in Paris in 1830 inspired Liszt out of his self-imposed retirement with a planned Revolutionary Symphony. The related, failed Polish revolt against Russian rule trapped Chopin and his friend Tytus Woyciechowski in Warsaw before they made it to Vienna, political pressures perhaps reflected in the new turbulence of Chopin's works of the period, such as his Ballade No. 1 in G Minor. When he eventually headed to Paris in 1831 (without Tytus), he had to lie on his passport about where he was going. He never saw Warsaw again.

Mendelssohn spent the year travelling south, via Weimar (where he paid a last visit to Goethe) and Venice to Florence, Rome and Naples, fluently finishing the works inspired by the previous year's Scottish jaunt, and starting a new Italian Symphony evoked by the warmer waters of the Mediterranean. He met Berlioz and Beethoven's pupil Dorothea von Ertmann, headed back north by way of Genoa, Milan and Switzerland, then spent the second winter of his two-year odyssey in Paris, where he and Chopin met. This time the younger man had no need for nerves. Schumann's recent article had captured Chopin's promise (even if Vienna had not): '*Hut ab, ihr Herrn, ein Genie!*' ('Hats off, gentlemen, a genius!')[5]

Three Italians

Like Mendelssohn, the narrative now steps briefly into the Italian sunshine to meet three *maestri* who made their mark across the capitals of Europe.

By the time Antonio Salieri died in 1825, his sparkling operatic achievements had already slipped into the forgettable past. But he was a big character. He knew, worked with and, in most cases, helped Gluck, Haydn, Mozart, Beethoven, Weber, Meyerbeer, Schubert and Liszt, among many others – not a bad address book. In Gluck and Liszt he met men born almost a whole century apart. He helped Haydn in old age and supported Mozart's widow and orphaned infant boys. He was able, industrious, generous and omnipresent. He is only now beginning to take his rightful place in the long view of musical history. He deserves it.

Two Italians of a later generation require a walk-on introduction now, because they keep popping up in the action like Figaro from the wings: Gioachino Rossini and Niccolò Paganini.

Rossini, still loved and celebrated for his operas, electrified the Italian style. His chattering bel canto had little obvious impact on the more serious-minded instrumentally based composers featured in this chapter, none of whom made any real headway in opera (though Liszt turned Rossini's music into tumultuous piano transcriptions and fantasies, as he did with everyone else); but he was a key part of the hinterland in which they moved. Liszt, Chopin and Mendelssohn all met him in Paris, in circles which included Cherubini, Paër, Hummel, Moscheles, Meyerbeer and *le tout Paris musical*. The closest Schumann came was hearing the influential singer actor Giuditta Pasta in Rossini's 1817 opera *La gazza ladra* at La Scala, Milan, on a vacation jaunt from his law studies in Heidelberg.

Shortly afterwards Schumann heard Paganini play in Frankfurt. He was fascinated by the 'magnetic chains' of sound flowing from Paganini's violin,[6] invested him in *Davidsbündler*, the imaginary literary club he founded in defence of contemporary music, painted him in music in *Carnaval* of 1834–5, and wrote other works inspired by his example. Liszt heard Paganini in Paris (at the Opéra and at the Rothschild salon), and feverishly set out to emulate his virtuosic charisma at the piano, succeeding brilliantly.

Paganini was a phenomenon, not a development. His main contribution to musical history was to show what his new invention, the wandering virtuoso superstar showman, could do. Berlioz thought that both Paganini and Liszt wrote music which only they could play. He was right about Paganini:

[W]hat he was unable to communicate to his successors was

the spark which gave life to these shattering feats of technique. The idea can be set on paper, the form sketched, but the feeling which the performance needs escapes all definition.[7]

But later generations have not wholly agreed with Berlioz that 'Liszt created it [his piano music around the time of the *Transcendental Studies*] for himself, and no one else in the world could flatter himself that he could approach being able to perform it'.[8] Brave pianists have found many (though not all) of the pianistic peaks of Liszt's artistic achievement worthy of the difficult and dangerous assault. They may well have been lower without the example of Paganini.

The 1830s: Travel

The four continued to intersect through the 1830s. Chopin, recently feted by Schumann, gave his first Paris concert in Pleyel's showroom in early 1832. Liszt and Mendelssohn were both there; Liszt praised his 'poetic sentiment' and 'happy innovation'.[9] Liszt's piano fantasies of the period included the *Konzertstück* for two pianos on Mendelssohn's (very un-Lisztian) *Lieder ohne Worte*. Others in the prevailing Parisian artistic circle were the novelists Victor Hugo and Amantine Aurore Dupin, known as George Sand, and, a little later, the painter Eugène Delacroix.

Chopin and Liszt were good friends and near neighbours. But there remained a distance, both professional and personal, between them. Chopin always resisted too much limelight, performing in public just a couple of times a year, preferring to compose in peace and pocket large fees teaching titled ladies. Artistic *hauteur* rubbed shoulders with a tinge of jealousy in his attitude to flashier populists like Thalberg and Liszt, neatly captured in an ambivalent remark in a letter of June 1833: 'at this moment Liszt is playing my études ... I should like to steal from him the way to play my own études' and he debated with himself whether to spend three years practising the piano.[10] Field and Kalkbrenner stood as ideals of taste and technique. His ambivalence extended to high society, which never interested him much: 'I sit with ambassadors, princes, ministers, and don't know how it happened, because I did not try for it.'[11] An English periodical made a nice analogy, calling him 'a species of musical Wordsworth, inasmuch as he scorns popularity and writes entirely up to his own standard of excellence'.¹² This slightly puzzled reception is captured by Berlioz in the imagined words of a society *'simia parisiensis'*, or Parisian she ape, who 'announced to her subjects that M. Chopin was a mere eccentric who played the piano tolerably well, but whose music was nothing but one long, highly ridiculous conundrum'.¹³ Liszt, meanwhile, collected countesses as assiduously as they cultivated him.

In May 1832 Friedrich Wieck returned to Leipzig from a gruelling European tour showing off the talents of his wunderkind Clara, now aged twelve. The domineering Friedrich joins a by now familiar species of parent, with the new complication that he and Clara's mother had separated, leaving her entirely under his meticulous control. Meanwhile her friend, admirer and family lodger, the 21-year-old Schumann, faced an end to any serious pianistic aspirations of his own because of trouble with his hand (ascribed, like all historico-musico-medical maladies, to a host of possible causes, from mercury poisoning caused by treatment for syphilis to a mechanical device used to isolate and strengthen individual digits). In November 1832 Robert and Clara appeared on the same concert bill at the Leipzig Gewandhaus, he represented by a single symphonic movement, she as composer of one piece and soloist in four others. Familiar notes sound in his story: a passionate but thwarted love affair (captured in the piano *Carnaval* suite of 1834–5 through some not very cryptic references spelled out in the names of the notes of the main four-note theme); more family sadness from the death of a brother, a sister-in-law, and the slow decline of his close friend, the fine piano composer Ludwig Schuncke, from consumption at the age of twenty-three; physical and mental illness precipitating an envisioned or actual suicide attempt from a high window, leading to a lifelong fear of upper storeys; the shivering dread of incipient insanity.

The years 1833–4 saw some musical meanderings with a leaning towards Leipzig. Mendelssohn (surely the hardest working of all the great composers) conducted his Italian Symphony in London and a whole series of Handel oratorios and operas by Mozart and others in Düsseldorf, as well as composing his own (notably Handelian) oratorio *St Paul* and dealing with the sort of administrative hassles which musicians shouldn't get saddled with but always do, leading to his departure from Düsseldorf in mid-1835 for a new post as conductor of the Gewandhaus orchestra in Leipzig, witnessing the August uprising in Berlin on the way. Chopin set off from Paris in May 1834 with Ferdinand Hiller for a lengthy trip which took in Düsseldorf, though he actually met up with Mendelssohn in Aachen. In Dresden he had his own doomed romance with the teenage daughter of some Polish friends, then headed in his turn to Leipzig. In October 1835 Mendelssohn introduced Chopin to Schumann, Clara and Moscheles, a notable gathering. Chopin said of Clara that she was 'the only woman in Germany who can play my music'.[14]

Mendelssohn's stewardship of his new orchestra was typically fastidious and ambitious, featuring much Mozart, Weber and Beethoven, and renewing his interest in Bach with a performance of the Concerto in D Minor for three claviers (in this case, three grand pianos), with Clara and another pianist, Louis Rakemann, in November 1835, and again with Liszt and Hiller in 1840. New music included works by visitors William Sterndale Bennett from England and Niels Gade from Denmark. In 1839 Mendelssohn gave the belated premiere of Schubert's 'Great' Symphony No. 9 in C Major, retrieved by Schumann from the composer's brother Ferdinand on an otherwise unsuccessful trip to Vienna in 1838. In 1837 Liszt beat Thalberg in a public pianistic duel in Paris, and Chopin paid a private visit to London with Pleyel.

Private Lives

As in all ages, these men's lives and careers reflect society's way of expressing its emotional life, as well as its intellectual and aesthetic ideas.

Clara Wieck's parents were divorced and her mother remarried. Both of Liszt's long-term partners were married to other people (and remained so). Later, his daughter Cosima left her first husband, the conductor Hans von Bülow, for Richard Wagner. Schumann and Liszt both went through tortuous legal processes in their attempts to marry, one successful, the other not.

Schumann's first fiancée, Ernestine von Fricken, was illegitimate (though he didn't know that at the time); so were Liszt's three children with Countess Marie d'Agoult.

Chopin's many letters to his old friend Tytus Woyciechowski are often unambiguously homoerotic: 'there are natural forces. Today you will dream that I embrace you! I must avenge myself for the terrible dream that you gave me last night';[15] 'My dearest life ... my little

Saul ... you don't know how much I love you, I can't show it to you in any way, and I have wished for so long that you could know. Ah, what would I not give, just to press your hand, you can't guess – half of my wretched life.'[16] This letter of 1830 is well beyond the conventional expressions of romantic warmth within male friendship at the time.

Liszt was contentedly consorting with countesses, experiencing what one biographer rather coyly calls 'his first mature liaison',[17] with the beautiful and sonorously named Adèle du Chelerd Comtesse de Laprunarède, Duchesse de Fleury, in 1831, before moving on to Marie in 1833.

In 1835 Schumann's admiration for Clara, nine years his junior, blossomed into their first kiss, two months and twelve days after her sixteenth birthday (her father's understandable disquiet increased by the probably justified suspicion that Robert had syphilis).

In 1836 Chopin was briefly engaged to Maria Wodzińska, vivacious sister of three schoolchums: he kept her letters in a packet inscribed '*Moja Biéda*' ('My Sorrow').

That same year, Mendelssohn, by some way the most conventional of the quartet, became engaged to Cécile Jeanrenaud, a member of the prosperous Souchay family.

Liszt's paramour, Marie d'Agoult, wrote novels under a man's name. So, too, did the unmissable Baroness Aurore Dudevant (née Dupin), who was brought up as a boy, dressed as a man, smoked cigars, had several lovers, left her husband the baron after bearing him two children, and was known to her circle and to posterity by her *nom de plume*, George Sand. Sand was introduced by Liszt to Chopin, eight years her junior, at the apartment he shared with Marie in the Hôtel de France in October 1836. It was not a promising initial meeting. 'Is she really a woman?' asked Chopin,[18] and Liszt observed that 'Chopin at first seemed to dread Mme Sand'.[19] One friend warned him darkly that 'the woman has the love of a vampire!'[20]

Mendelssohn, meanwhile, married.

His initial doubts overcome, Chopin took off with Sand for Majorca in autumn 1838 for the sake of her son Maurice's health, staying in a monastery in Valldemossa after they were kicked out of their villa because the landlord feared that Chopin had consumption. They were followed across the clear waters of the Mediterranean in January 1839 by the pianino he had ordered from Pleyel in Paris, replacing an unsatisfactory locally made instrument. Majorca was peaceful ('the silence is deeper than anywhere else,' said Sand),[21] but cold, backwards and damp. They drank goat's milk, laughed at the locals, gave Sand's children their lessons in the mornings, and wrote, Chopin dreaming up his *Preludes* on the bad local piano in a 'cell ... shaped like a tall coffin'.[22] In May 1839 the unlikely improvised family group moved on to Sand's handsome inherited house and estate in the tiny, rural commune of Nohant, in the middle of France, in what proved to be a happy and productive time for Chopin. Their friend and regular visitor, the painter Delacroix, recalled communal meals, walking, lounging, reading and playing billiards as, 'Sometimes, through the window which opens on the garden, a gust of music wafts up from Chopin at work. All this mingles with the songs of nightingales and the fragrance of roses.'[23] Sand moved quickly from lover to maternal figure to carer, calling her coughing composer 'my dear child' and 'Chip-Chip',[24] even, in moments of frustration, her 'beloved little corpse'.[25] In a clearly autobiographical novel published a few years later she describes her sickly Polish-named anti-hero as 'delicate both in body and mind ... with neither age nor sex ... a beautiful angel, with a face like a sorrowing woman'.[26] It was an unlikely ménage. But it worked for them, and for some of Chip-Chip's most beautiful, quietly revolutionary and modestly modernist music – at least for the time being.

Liszt and Marie's relationship was changing, too. Their third and last child, Daniel, was born in 1839. But the growing strain between two powerful personalities partly prompted Liszt to resume his hugely successful life as a travelling virtuoso, seeing Marie and the children only in the summers, before they finally separated in 1844.

In Leipzig, Friedrich Wieck and Schumann battled through the courts about whether the young composer could marry Clara. Eventually, despite his courtroom histrionics, Friedrich failed to satisfy the court that his prospective son-in-law was an unsuitable drunk, and Schumann wed his 'Zilia' in the parish church of Schönefeld, near Leipzig, on 12 September 1840, the day before her twenty-first birthday.

Between them, the four varied characters of this chapter had four and a half engagements, two marriages, several lovers, sixteen children and five unofficial step-children, categories which did not by any means always overlap in the conventional way.

Endings: The 1840s

Through the 1840s the musical careers featured in this chapter moved into what, for most, proved to be a final phase. Although barely entering their thirties, some found their creative powers falling away after the white heat of youthful achievement.

In 1840 Liszt was in Leipzig (where he first met Schumann, whom he did not much admire) for Mendelssohn's concert series, which went on to feature some notable new names of the next few years, including the Swedish soprano Jenny Lind, the 13-year-old violin prodigy Joseph Joachim and another wunderkind, the Russian pianist Anton Rubinstein, who also played to Chopin and Liszt in Paris in December 1840, aged just eleven.

In April 1841 Sand told a friend that 'little Chip-Chip is going to give a Grrrrrand concert ... he doesn't want posters, or programmes, or a large audience'.[27] (Unlike Liszt, who did.) The repertoire was his 'Majorcan programme', the *Preludes*: new, strangely reticent, and widely acclaimed. In an interesting observation (sustainable to a point), *La France musicale* compared Chopin to Schubert: 'One has done for the pianoforte what the other has done for the voice.'[28] These were good years for Chopin, his health, his career, his creative powers, his domestic life and public persona held in a precarious equilibrium. As his biographer Nicholas Temperley nicely observes, 'this period of pleasing the wealthy, teaching their daughters and retiring to Nohant for intervals of poetic seclusion was the one in which most of his greatest masterpieces were composed'.[29]

In Paris, Marie d'Agoult bitchily tried (and failed) to talk up a rivalry between Chopin and the more flamboyant Liszt, naturally falling out with Sand in the process. These were Liszt's *Glanzperiode* years, his 'age of glitter', when he earned honours from colleges and kings and 10,000 francs per concert, before staging a well-timed withdrawal from the pianistic circus (which he had invented) in his mid-thirties to devote himself to composing, conducting, giving large sums to causes like the Beethoven monument in Bonn, the Music Academy in Budapest and many others, and generously promoting and supporting many fellow composers including Berlioz and Wagner. This can all be seen as part of his unique place at the peak and centre of the Romantic century, part-man, part-myth.

Early married life was a productive period for Schumann in all the main musical genres: song, choral, chamber and piano music.

Clara persuaded him to confront the challenge of writing for orchestra: Mendelssohn premiered his first symphony, the joyous Spring Symphony, in early 1841, and the second five years later. Schumann also joined an impressive list of professors at yet another demanding project led by Mendelssohn, the new Leipzig conservatory.

All continued to travel. In 1844 Robert and Clara Schumann visited Russia, a cause of much nervous strain for Robert. England was a regular destination: Mendelssohn visited many times, notably for the triumphant premiere of his oratorio *Elijah* in Birmingham in 1846, and several calls on the young Queen Victoria and her musical consort, Mendelssohn's compatriot Prince Albert. The royal couple impressed him with their extempore performance of one of his choruses on the Buckingham Palace house organ, then asked Mendelssohn to play one of their favourite songs, *Italien*, only for him to confess embarrassedly that the song was actually written by his sister Fanny and he'd only put his name to it to get it published. Chopin, meanwhile, found London (and the cloying attentions of a young Scottish admirer, Jane Stirling) tedious: 'whatever is NOT boring here is NOT English,' he wailed.[30] England's musical reputation for large-scale enthusiastic dullness was clearly beginning to take its porridge-like hold.

Political ideas and events resonated through the 1840s. The decade opened with Chopin and Sand attending Berlioz's symphonic commemoration of the Paris uprising ten years before. Sand took an increasing interest in radical ideas; the ailing, increasingly withdrawn Chopin did not. In 1843 Beethoven's former pupil Bettina von Arnim (née Brentano) wrote a book advocating a republic: even Mendelssohn considered an opera set in the time of the German peasant revolt, to a libretto by his flamboyant friend Eduard Devrient. The year of revolutions, 1848, saw Chopin limping sickly towards London from the noise and ferment of Paris, fearing for his friends in France and Poland. The Schumanns were in Dresden, she alarmed, he excited and inspired out of a long convalescence from another period of mental torment into a torrent of composition and polemical articles. In early May 1849 they were dramatically caught up in political events, fleeing the shots, barricades and forced conscription of the Dresden uprising with their eldest child, 7-year-old Marie, leaving their younger children behind, finding refuge with a friend at Maxen, from where Clara (who was seven months pregnant) later walked back to Dresden at 3.00 a.m., finding the younger children at home in the care of an inattentive maid, but safely asleep. The insurrection over, the Schumanns found the streets 'swarming with Prussians'.[31] Liszt, based in Weimar, helped Wagner flee Germany after his own involvement with the Dresden revolt. Schumann, following a depressive reaction to the heightened emotions of early 1849, quickly wrote a series of republican 'barricade marches' (published under the safer title *Four Marches*).

The events of 1848/9 changed music, partly by creating a large middle class eager for a form of entertainment previously reserved for its social superiors, just as the railway shrank musical Europe for performers, publishers, promoters and pianos. As the writer Paul Kildea puts it, 'In France the salon had been the incubator of Chopin's music, but the concert hall would be its guardian.'[32]

The approaching midpoint of the century brought some endings and a few beginnings.

The Schumanns seriously considered moving from Dresden to Berlin, partly because of Clara's friendship with Mendelssohn's sister Fanny Hensel. But Fanny died unexpectedly following a stroke in May 1847. Felix composed his String Quartet No. 6 in F Minor as a 'Requiem for Fanny', but was dead himself from the same cause (sadly common in their immediate family) within six months. He was thirty-eight. Schumann, Moscheles and the Danish composer Niels Gade were among his pallbearers.

Chopin's strange affair with Sand collapsed in rows involving both of her children. A sad exchange of letters in July 1847 ended with her bidding him, 'Adieu, my friend. May you soon recover from all your ills … I shall thank God for this queer end to nine years of exclusive friendship. Let me hear now and then how you are.' After they met by chance the following year, she wrote: 'I shook his trembling, icy hand. I wanted to talk; he escaped. I suppose it was my turn to say he no longer loved me, but I spared him this suffering, and left all in the hands of Providence. I was never to see him again.'[33] Chopin's exhausting 1848 trip to London included his final public performance. He spent most of 1849 in Paris, talking to the attentive Delacroix, who faithfully recorded his reflections about Mozart, Meyerbeer, Beethoven, Berlioz and Sand, of whom he spoke without bitterness. He died in October, aged thirty-nine.

Among beginnings, in 1847 Liszt met the married Princess

Carolyne zu Sayn-Wittgenstein, another striking character whose fabulously wealthy father had given her cigars as a child, and spent the winter with her at her estate at Woronince, in the heart of the Ukraine. She would dominate the rest of his long and eventful life, though attempts to annul her marriage, involving both the Pope and the Tsar of Russia, never quite succeeded.

In 1850 Schumann finally made it on stage as an opera composer with *Genoveva*, conducting performances that were attended by many leading figures. It was only partially successful. The same year he took a job in Düsseldorf. All began happily, allied as usual with a productive period of composition. But relations soon foundered on Schumann's ineffectiveness as a conductor and rehearser. He suffered an apparent stroke in July 1853. Late 1853 brought two meetings of great significance: with the young violinist Joachim, for whom he wrote two works including his Violin Concerto in D Minor, and, on 30 September, with Joachim's new friend, the 20-year-old Johannes Brahms. The two men wrote a joint sonata for Joachim (with another composer) based on Joachim's motto, the Beethovenian '*Frei aber einsam*' ('Free But Alone'). Schumann captured the visionary promise of his young friend and disciple Brahms in an article called '*Neue Bahnen*' ('New Paths'), like Simeon murmuring his *Nunc dimittis* and passing on the torch.

In late 1853 the Schumanns toured northern Europe, meeting Brahms again. In early 1854 Schumann reported the return of 'painful aural symptoms' and hallucinatory visions of angels, demons, tigers and hyenas.[34] On 27 February he slipped unwatched from the house, ran to the Rhine bridge and threw himself into the tumbling waters. Rescued by fishermen, he was taken to a private asylum near Bonn. He lingered in and out of lucidity, writing sometimes to friends, and receiving visits from Joachim and Brahms. But not from Clara, who was only permitted to see him for the first time in almost two and a half years on 27 July 1856. He died two days later.

Character and Method

The methods and personalities of the composers in this chapter show some of the familiar characteristics of their trade, and some striking new features.

As performers, Mendelssohn was the complete professional,

Chopin the reluctant celebrity (he probably only gave around thirty public concerts in his life, and always preferred the old-style shared billing with other performers to the solo recital). Liszt was the rock star of the piano, while Schumann, with his damaged hand and ineffectiveness as a conductor, was not really a performer at all.

As creators, all except, perhaps, the industrious Mendelssohn had periods of intense compositional activity alternating with oases of stasis.

As people, the image of Mendelssohn as placid and agreeable was launched in the memoir written by his nephew Sebastian Hensel, but is qualified by recollections of friends like Eduard Devrient, who talked of an aloof manner giving rise to the nickname 'discontented Polish count',[35] and fits of excitement cured by long, deep sleep, which can perhaps be related to the seizures and strokes which killed him and several other members of his family. Mendelssohn was good at everything: conductor, rehearser, administrator, organist, pianist, painter, writer of lively letters and diaries; proud and devoted product of a remarkable and wide-ranging family who not only nurtured his talents but provided him with a prodigious and disciplined appetite for work.

For Schumann, mental discipline was harder to find. He addressed his demons through drink, smoking and (probably) sex (in which he is not alone in this book). The loyal company of friends helped, though sometimes he was so prostrated by mental suffering he could hardly speak or even walk: one severe breakdown made even the sound of music 'cut into my nerves as if with knives'.[36] Links between Schumann's external circumstances and his music can be imagined rather than always be seen clearly: the two collections of the charming, childlike *Album for the Young* of 1848 are near in time to the first birthday of one of his and Clara's children, the death at the same age of another, and the loss of his last surviving brother.

Musicians have always played the game of business with varying degrees of success. The indecisive Chopin could be surprisingly ruthless in matters of publication and editions, relying heavily on two of his Polish friends, Wojciech Grzymala and Julian Fontana, to shoulder the grunt work of copying and contracts. Liszt carried his habitual generosity to the point of deliberately not taking fees for teaching, and took up his performing career in 1840 partly in order to make good a promise to fund the proposed Beethoven monument in Bonn from his own pocket.

Attitudes to religion cover a range of viewpoints. Mendelssohn might have echoed the words of a near-contemporary who also converted from Judaism to Christianity in childhood, Benjamin Disraeli: 'I am the blank page between the Old Testament and the New.'[37] His Jewish origins left little trace, except perhaps in the enlightened world view he learnt from liberal Judaism (by contrast, Ignaz Moscheles attended and wrote music for the Jewish congregation in Vienna before himself converting to Christianity as an adult). Mendelssohn actually ran a cathedral choir in Berlin for a while, and shows a typically thorough assimilation of his assumed Protestant inheritance in his liturgical music, although the dramatic, narrative, personalised religious experience explored in his oratorios clearly interested him more. 'Hear My Prayer', a motet of imperishable charm and character, was written in 1845 for an English concert society rather than a church, using a text in English with a metrically matching German translation so the music can be sung in either language – a neat habit also used by Haydn in his late oratorios and Schubert in some of his song settings of Shakespeare.

Liszt's father had been dismissed from the Franciscan novitiate in his youth because of an 'inconstant and variable character'.[38] Perhaps this was a precursor of his son's deep, lasting but fluid relationship with the church: at several periods he contemplated the priesthood, and did take minor orders in 1865 on one such period of retreat following the deaths of two of his three children. There is a huge range of religious imagery captured in his piano music, from St Francis preaching to the birds to evocations of a *Miserere* by Palestrina and hymns round a Christmas tree. But it is the mystical, transcendental side of religious experience, rather than the liturgical or doctrinal, which appealed to him, captured in a title he used more than once, *Harmonies poétiques et religieuses*. (Also, though undoubtedly devout, he clearly had little trouble breaking things like the sacred vows of marriage, even if they were someone else's, not his.)

Our composers' use of old music is related in a way to their religious inheritance. All studied and admired the music of Palestrina. All except Chopin wrote Bach-derived organ works, including Schumann's fugue on Bach's musical cipher, B. A. C. H. The 18-year-old Chopin thought a Handel oratorio which he called '*Cz'icilienfest*' (presumably the *Ode for St Cecilia's Day*) 'came nearest to the idea I have formed of great music'[39] – though the passing influence left no trace and may reflect his limited exposure to such things to that point. Mendelssohn staged a typically wholesome series of 'Historical Concerts' in Leipzig in 1837, including works by Mozart and Haydn as well as by Handel and Bach (history was shorter then). As well as Mendelssohn's famous *St Matthew Passion* performances, Schumann put on Bach's *St John Passion* and parts of the *B Minor Mass* in his Düsseldorf years. Liszt consumed Scarlatti into his paraphrases, as he did so many others. Mendelssohn and Schumann wrote piano parts to Bach's unaccompanied string music, from which we should avert our historically informed eyes and admire their wish to bring that music back into the currency of their times. Both were also involved in creating a Bach memorial outside the Thomaskirche in Leipzig, dedicated in 1843 in the presence of the composer's grandson Wilhelm Friedrich Ernst Bach, whom Schumann described as 'a very agile old gentleman of 84 years with snow-white hair and expressive features'.[40]

The Music

If there is one word that captures these four friends' contribution to musical manners, it is 'lyricism'.

Chopin's *Preludes* reset the nature of melody. They caused considerable puzzlement when they were first heard: 'The Preludes are strange pieces,' wrote Schumann; 'they are sketches, beginnings ... ruins, eagle wings, a wild motley ... He is and remains the boldest and proudest poetic mind of the time.'[41] Liszt believed that 'They are not simply, as their title would suggest, pieces intended as an introduction to something further; they are poetic preludes ... which gently ease the soul into a golden dream world and then whisk it away to the highest realms of the ideal.'[42] Liszt's words are Romantic vagueness at its most florid. Sand was among many who went too far in the opposite direction, finding in the *Preludes* 'visions of long-departed monks' and other pictorial and literal images.[43] Some tried to give them titles. Such attempts to fix meaning always subtract more than they add. Ambiguity is all: the endless A flat/G sharp in the middle of the harmony of Prelude No. 15 pins the melody to something out of sight, present but hidden; No. 2 in A Minor isn't really in A minor at all – or, if it is, why do bars 12–14 contain chords with the notes C sharp, C double sharp and C natural all mixed together? Its opening sounds like Gershwin.

Mendelssohn's version of this unspecific lyricism is captured in the title he invented for his own species of short piano pieces, written between 1829 and 1845: *Lieder ohne Worte* (*Songs Without Words*). Unlike Chopin's *Preludes*, a few of them do have descriptive titles, although most do not. As with Chopin, some people tried to turn them into songs with words, prompting Mendelssohn's celebrated response: 'What the music I love expresses to me, is not thought too *indefinite* to put into words, but on the contrary, too *definite* [his italics].'[44]

Intriguingly, sketches show that the finished forms of the *Lieder ohne Worte* were often quite different from the initial ideas. This is linked to the habit of composing, to a greater or lesser extent, by improvising. Sand's description of Chopin humming to himself on country rambles recalls Ries' account of Beethoven, and was always followed by what Sand calls 'the most crushing labour I have ever witnessed ... a train of efforts, waverings, frustrated stabs at recapturing certain details of the theme that he had heard'. Significantly, she notes that 'what he had conceived as a unity he now over-analysed in his desire to get it down, and his chagrin at not being able to rediscover it whole and clear plunged him into a sort of despair'.[45] Joseph Filtsch likewise found the original improvisation 'immediate and complete', resulting in 'days of nervous strain' trying to write it down.[46] Grzymala thought the finished piece was often less daring than the first spark, and Delacroix debated with himself about the extent to which the process could be compared to a painter's or an architect's sketch. It all adds to the ambiguity of Chopin's creative persona: he was known to play his own pieces differently on different occasions, and allow conflicting versions to circulate. Add shifting ideas about things like rubato, and even whether the two hands should play at the same speed, the question is left hanging of the extent to which there is such a thing as a single, correct version of a piece, or even whether a particular piece of music can truthfully be said to exist at all. The exact relationship between the divine spark and the finished work was a theme which ran through the century, captured by a later composer, Arthur Sullivan, in a song written, poignantly, at his dying brother's bedside, where he discovered a beautiful chord, only to find that it 'trembled away into silence ... I have sought, but I seek it vainly'.[47] Perhaps it was never there in the first place.

Schumann's version of this process was to roll together snatches and patches written in his various bursts of heightened creativity, full of hints, feints, quotations, evocations, echoes and reworkings, into complete works in a kind of free form, like snapshots of his various ideas, friendships and preoccupations over time. In 1832 he assembled a set of piano pieces made up partly of some waltzes written the previous year, partly of reworkings of some polonaises for four hands dating from 1828, partly of new music, all of which he related to a party scene in a novel by Jean Paul and to which he gave the whimsical catch-all title *Papillons* (*Butterflies*). *Carnaval* is an exquisite example, capturing fleeting portraits of Liszt, Chopin, Clara, himself as both Eusebius and Florestan, Ernestine, Paganini, Harlequin and Columbine in a patchwork of quotations, like characters at a ball. The *Davidsbündler* are there, too, his imaginary League of David set up to defend modern music against the musical Philistines. Schumann becomes like a sort of musical Proust, creating whole worlds from a little electric shock of memory.

In this century of things getting bigger, many of the pieces mentioned here are miniatures. The shorter *Lieder ohne Worte* occupy a single page. Some of Chopin's preludes last just a few bars. The briefer sections of *Carnaval* are measured in seconds, most not more than two minutes. Liszt's shorter lyric pieces can be more musically rewarding than the Rococo fantasising of some of his longer and less disciplined pieces.

More formal structures like sonatas feature less often, with the composers taking a variety of approaches to their Beethovenian model. Interestingly, the piano sonatas of Schumann, Liszt and Chopin are all in minor keys (Mendelssohn's organ sonatas are a new creation – recital pieces rather than free-standing church voluntaries, often ending with big-boned Bachian fugues). Much more common are catch-all titles with often only a vague relation to musical form: preludes which don't prelude anything; intermezzi which are no longer 'inter' the 'mezzi' of something else; not-always-nocturnal nocturnes; mazurkas and polonaises that feel more Parisian than Polish; a whole host of fandangos, funeral marches, waltzes, plainsong hymns and hunting tunes rolled into sectional suite-like works with poetical names.

Liszt hinted at his Hungarian gypsy heritage, but with more art and less authenticity than later composers like Dvořák and Bartók. Mendelssohn also synthesised folk style and national accents into a whirling symphonic Italianate tarantella or a dreamy Venetian gondola song in thirds and 6/8. Among folk and literary sources, Felix and Fanny Mendelssohn and Schumann were all drawn to the Nibelung legends as potential operatic material, and Liszt and Clara Schumann were among many composers who netted Heine's *Lorelei*, a watery cousin of Wagner's Rhinemaidens, in song. Folklorists Hans Christian Andersen and the Brothers Grimm were contemporaries and occasional acquaintances. Shakespeare in his nineteenth-century costume continued to fascinate; for instance, Schumann, perhaps unsurprisingly, felt a musical affinity for the unstable Hamlet. Goethe, admired friend of Mendelssohn's youth, provided Romantic music with one of its most potent and popular characters, the universe-defying Faust. Schumann dabbled in the writings of the group of poets nearest in manner and biography to his own musical circle, Byron, Shelley and the English Romantics.

The musical fruits of this rich mix could hardly have been more different. Mendelssohn the Romantic Classicist was master of the swift, light, gossamer-like scherzo (the third movement of the Octet and the scherzo from the music to *A Midsummer Night's Dream*, for example). Chopin was the first and finest poet of the piano (he never wrote a single piece without it), while Liszt lived long enough to influence brave new worlds of harmony and form. Schumann's symphonies are beginning to escape from their reputation for doing lots of fine things which someone else always did just a little better: his best music lies in the aching tenderness of miniatures like those in his 1840 song cycle *Dichterliebe*, flitting between Florestan and Eusebius like clouds across the sun, with its wholly original use of long passages just for the piano, with right hand melodies deliberately placed just behind or ahead of the beat and accompanied by ambiguous chords which change, but not all at once and not always in step with the voice, creating delicious overlaps and strange, shimmering shifts of harmony. These beautiful things can be found throughout his music, like the half-beat harmonies of *Intermezzo*, the gently yearning melody of the opening of the *Humoreske*, and the strange subtleties which begin and end *Dichterliebe*.

Fanny Mendelssohn and Clara Schumann

The career of Fanny Mendelssohn sits neatly between those of Nannerl Mozart (who left no compositions, gave up performing when she reached marriageable age and was entirely subservient to her father) and slightly later (or longer-lived) composers like Louise Farrenc and Cécile Chaminade. Felix wrote that his sister had 'neither inclination nor vocation for authorship. She is too much all that a woman ought to be for this', and referred to household management as her 'first duties'.[48] Their father told her, 'Music will perhaps become his profession, while for *you* it can and must be only an ornament.'[49] The leading Berlin musician Carl Zelter told Goethe that 'she plays like a man' – praise indeed.[50] But her musical life was more than just a watered-down version of her brother's. She composed voluminously. Publishing under his name appears, at least partly, to have been designed to protect and help her (female novelists routinely used male pseudonyms), but on one occasion she ventured into print under her own name without, it seems, consulting Felix. She played often in Sunday salons at home in Berlin, but apparently just once in public, as soloist in her brother's first concerto. Most of her music is in smaller forms – songs and lyrical piano pieces. There are no symphonies or concertos. But a piece like her Piano Sonata in G Minor, written shortly after a visit to Berlin by the French composer Charles Gounod in early 1843 ('His presence was a very lively stimulus for me, for I played and discussed music a great deal with him,' wrote Fanny),[51] shows a thorough engagement with the sonata principles of Beethoven, a Schubertian freedom of key, a fine melodic sense and formidable pianism. Another sonata, the pictorial 'Easter' Sonata in A Major, depicting the death and resurrection of Christ, was only found in France in 1970, unhelpfully signed 'F. Mendelssohn', with predictable results (and rightfully reassigned to Fanny forty years later).

Clara Schumann also wrote a Piano Sonata in G Minor at around this time, initially as a gift to Robert shortly after their marriage: 'Accept with love, my good husband, and be patient with your Clara, at Christmas 1841.'[52] (Two further movements were added the following year.) There are parallels with her friend Fanny: both wrote mostly shorter pieces; Robert mischievously issued a published collection of *Twelve Rückert songs ... by Robert and Clara Schumann* in 1841 without saying which was whose. But Clara got much further than Fanny, both as a performer and as a composer. Her work was widely performed, by her and others. In her early career she stepped into bigger forms with the piano concerto of 1833–5 (in A minor, like her husband's, which she premiered in 1846 after he'd worked on it for eight years). Written when she was fourteen and conducted by the unstoppable Mendelssohn with the young composer at the piano, it is a fine piece with a demanding and brilliantly written piano part, some carefully crafted chamber-like textures, and imaginative touches like the movements running into each other without a break and a lyrical second movement Romanze for piano and solo cello and a dance-like finale (surely both later remembered by her friend Brahms in his own concertos).

Clara lived a long time, dying a year before Brahms, in 1896. She was acquainted with grief, outliving not just her husband by nearly forty years but also four of their eight children, bringing up two sets of grandchildren (with the help of her eldest daughter Marie), and seeing her eldest son Ludwig committed to a mental institution, in a deeply painful echo of his father's sufferings. ('I have not felt such pains since the misfortune with Robert ... I can find no words for grief such as this; it tears my heart,' she told her diary,[53] and remarked to Brahms, 'It is really a hard fate to have two such experiences in one's lifetime, but I have made up my mind to bear it as calmly as a mother can ... I have to go on living for the others.')[54] Images of her range from the conventionally posed sketches and watercolours of her youth, through pictures of her at the piano and with her children, to photographs of an old lady in black crepe, still handsome, with soulful, sorrowful eyes. Her correspondence with Brahms is a rich resource of the manners and music of the times, though tempered by the habits of 'two such intimate friends, who are accustomed in conversation to guess at each other's thoughts and to convey the burden of whole sentences by means of a single word', as the translator of the letters has it.[55] Above all, Clara's presence in Robert's music, and his in hers, allowed one of the most touching, fluid, truthful evocations of a loyal, loving relationship, often challenged but never failing, in all music. She is a big presence in nineteenth-century music, and a presiding genius of many of its most fruitful and rewarding aspects.

Late Liszt

In a sense, the two great survivors of this chapter exemplify the aesthetic divide with which we began: Clara Schumann the guardian of the restrained, Classical aesthetic picked up in musical form by her friend Brahms; Franz Liszt the standard-bearer of experiment and modernism.

The year 1848 began a highly productive decade or so for Liszt, now based in Weimar with his new companion, the Princess Carolyne. In 1850 he conducted the premiere of Wagner's *Lohengrin* during its composer's enforced exile in Switzerland following his involvement in the Dresden uprising of May 1849. Liszt came late to conducting, but he was clearly highly effective: other operas to pass under his baton included *Tannhäuser*, Schumann's *Genoveva*, *Benvenuto Cellini* by Berlioz and works by Bellini, Donizetti and Verdi, as well as the belated premiere of Schubert's *Alfonso und Estrella* in June 1854. Berlioz records him stopping one shaky performance in order to start again and get the notes right, while managing to give the impression he'd been asked to do so by the king, who was seated in the front row. In Weimar, a smooth start gave way to more unsettled times. Joachim left as leader of the orchestra in opposition to Liszt's innovations. His liaison with the still-married Carolyne and support for the refugee Wagner undermined his position. In 1858 he resigned following demonstrations at a performance which he conducted of Peter Cornelius's opera *The Barber of Baghdad*, viewed as the unacceptable face of modernism. The crisis was exacerbated by the death of his son Daniel in 1859 at the age of twenty. His daughters, meanwhile, married: Cosima to the martinet pianist and conductor Hans von Bülow, Blandine to Émile Ollivier, later prime minister of France.

In 1860 a letter protesting against the 'New German School' of Liszt and Wagner appeared in the Berlin *Echo*, signed by Brahms, Joachim and others. In 1861 Liszt and Carolyne moved to Rome, maintaining separate households and pursuing their lengthy and ultimately fruitless efforts to persuade the Pope to annul her marriage. In 1862 tragedy fell again with the death of his daughter Blandine at the age of twenty-six, provoking from her father some religiously inspired music and a further period of retreat, to a monastery where he took minor orders, and to a suite of rooms at the tranquil Villa d'Este, ancient home of cardinals, whose famous fountains he captured in the third of the piano suites *Années de pèlerinage* (*Years of Pilgrimage*), composed between 1867 and 1877.

In the late 1860s life settled into what Liszt called his '*vie trifurquée*',[56] triangulating between Rome, Weimar and his home capital city Budapest, visited by many emerging composers, including Albéniz, Borodin, Saint-Saëns, Smetana, Fauré and, in 1885, Claude Debussy. His sole surviving child, Cosima, began an affair with

Wagner, marrying him in 1870, causing a breach with her father which lasted into 1872. In 1882 Liszt was in Venice with the Wagners and had an apparent premonition of Wagner's death, captured in the strangely atonal piano piece *La lugubre gondola*: Wagner died in early 1883 and was carried by gondola to the Santa Lucia railway station, *en route* for Bayreuth.

In 1886, aged seventy-five, Liszt undertook a wide-ranging farewell tour, on which he was greeted with enthusiastic admiration at performances of his works in Paris, Budapest, London and elsewhere. He played the piano in public for the last time in Luxembourg, heard Wagner's *Parsifal* and *Tristan und Isolde* in Bayreuth, and died there in late July 1886. He had outlived Schumann, longest-lived of his three near-contemporaries in this chapter, by thirty years and two days. Carolyne, devastated by his death after forty years together, died the following year after completing the twenty-fourth and final volume of her dense critique of the state of the Catholic church.

Writing at the time of the Beethoven celebrations in Bonn, Berlioz said:

> One wonders how and why hostility can have existed against Liszt, that eminent musician whose unchallenged superiority is, moreover, German, whose fame is boundless, whose generosity is proverbial ... Some bore a grudge against Liszt because of his amazing talent and exceptional success, others because he is witty, others because he is generous, because he had written too fine a cantata ... because he has his own hair instead of a wig, because he speaks French too well, because he knows German too well, because he has too many friends and doubtless because he has too few enemies, etc. The motives of the opposition were many.[57]

As a composer, Liszt's modernisms are often said to include pioneering the principle of thematic transformation, and the rather wayward harmonic experiments of late pieces like *Nuages gris* (1881), the *Bagatelle sans tonalité* (1885) and *La lugubre gondola* (1883), exploring the possibilities of the augmented triad as a central harmonic unit, unconventional scales with a hint of folk elements like the Hungarian minor, and deliberate avoidance of cadence and resolution of dissonance.

This is all true. It's also not really the point.

Simply in terms of physical appearance, Liszt exemplifies the artistic chasm which his generation opened on its predecessors. Born into a world where (at least until recently) composers were short, wore wigs and played the harpsichord neatly, he was tall, elegant, wore his hair long and played what is essentially a modern grand piano not very neatly at all. Marie d'Agoult described his 'sea-green eyes', 'indecisive walk in which he seemed to glide' and 'unquiet appearance like that of a ghost about to return to the darkness'.[58] A later pupil said, 'His mouth turns up at the corners', giving him 'a sort of Jesuitical elegance and ease',[59] while another writer made a common comparison, calling him 'Mephistopheles disguised as an abbé'.[60] Liszt's recreative compositional method extended to his own playing: Joachim said it was wonderful to play through sonatas and other pieces with him, but only once, because after that he would fill the piano part with embellishments and additions of his own, restlessly reinventing the original, and the world, as he went. But he was consistent in his inconsistencies: part-gypsy, part-priest, part-demon, the first genuine superstar composer, punctiliously generous and sometimes self-effacing. His later experimental music, like Bach's, was written as much as a conversation with himself as for publication or popular plaudits. He was, perhaps, the first artist for whom the work was as much the life as the art: more Bowie than Beethoven. He was an original. Nobody else could do what he did, because, like his son-in-law Wagner, the only way to do it was to be him.

13

A TRADITION FULFILLED: SYMPHONY, SYMPHONISTS AND SONATA

The Symphony: Origins and Openings

The symphony as a free-standing concert work grew from the varied examples across eighteenth-century Europe of Stamitz and Cannabich, Mysliveček and Vanhal, Boyce, Boccherini, Sammartini, J. C. and C. P. E. Bach.

Through the late Classical and early Romantic periods, composers began to use the new form as a medium for an increasingly complex and profound discussion of theme and key. The symphony was becoming symphonic.

In 1789 Haydn began his Symphony No. 92 in G Major with a slow introduction. Its second phrase, beginning with a dominant seventh chord, reappears as the opening of the fast section which follows. In the first year of the new century Beethoven went a step further by beginning the Haydn-esque slow introduction to his First Symphony with a dominant seventh chord. Its little melodic tag made of a rising semitone becomes part of the first group of themes in the Allegro.

Openings: internal references and relationships at the start of Haydn's Symphony No. 92 (1789) and Beethoven's Haydn-esque First Symphony (1800).

Developments

One key tool for teasing out the implication of theme or themes of a piece is counterpoint: combining a melody or snatch of melody with another, or with itself, in order to explore and develop its character.

Mozart in his early Symphony No. 29 in A Major and Beethoven in his Fourth Piano Concerto both move on from the initial statements of their graceful opening themes by treating them as Bachian two-part inventions between treble and bass. Here, Mozart takes the melody which opens his movement and turns it into a conversation between the high and low registers of the orchestra:

Counterpoint. Mozart's A major symphony, K. 201 (1774), begins with a charming melody which then provides the material for a linking passage, echoed between the upper and lower voices of the orchestra.

Beethoven expanded every aspect of symphonic form. His late works roll together all the formal processes known to him – sonata, variations, fugue, cyclic form, scherzo and trio – into visionary new structures. The Ninth Symphony opens with the unsettled sound of open fifths: key withheld. The Piano Sonata No. 31 in A Flat Major treats its opening melody made of thirds and fourths to all sorts of transformations; the String Quartet No. 14 in C Sharp Minor has seven movements in six keys, starting with a strange fugue, a short third movement serving as introduction to a long set of variations at the midpoint. Texture begins to take its place as a structural determinant: a bizarrely avant-garde passage at the end of the fifth movement produces a weird, high effect by having the players play with the bow close to the bridge of their instruments.

The symphonies of Robert Schumann bridge the symphonic worlds of Beethoven, Mendelssohn and Brahms. Until fairly recently their reputation suffered by comparison, not helped by the composer's sometimes wayward markings; but they have benefited inestimably from being rescued from what one of his modern champions, the conductor Heinz Holliger, calls the 'very heavy "German potato soup" sound'[1] and restoration to the kind of orchestra used by Mendelssohn at their premieres. Schumann's willingness to make changes in response to well-meant but not always constructive criticisms is another complicating factor: Brahms found the early 1841 version of the Fourth Symphony 'bright and spontaneous' in comparison to the version Schumann wrote later, in the grip of depression. Another modern proselyte, the conductor Simon Rattle, states: 'Brahms was completely right.'[2] There are, as always with Schumann, angels and demons in this richly rewarding music.

Among other notable symphonists in the Mendelssohn/Schumann hinterland, the Danish composer Niels Gade used an orchestral piano in his Symphony No. 5 in D Major of 1852. The long-lived Louis Spohr eschewed Gade's formalism but allied a rather dull type of B-list Beethovenian melodic invention with a frankly eccentric approach to form and programme: a double orchestra for his Seventh Symphony's Mahlerian account of a human life; his Sixth reviewing the styles of, respectively, Bach, Mozart and Beethoven in a sort of cod history of music. Berlioz called Mendelssohn's friend Norbert Burgmüller an 'artist whose talent equals his modesty'.[3] Burgmüller's death at age twenty-six by drowning during an epileptic seizure was described by Schumann as the greatest blow to music since the death of Schubert. His work list is understandably short – just seventeen opus numbers – but covers a tantalising range of forms and moods, skilfully crafted. Ludwig Schuncke died even younger, aged just twenty-three: echoes of Schuncke's Piano Sonata in G Minor of 1832 can clearly be heard in the long-gestating A minor piano concerto of its dedicatee, his friend Robert Schumann. The third symphony of Louise Farrenc, composed in 1847, shows an accomplished loyalty to the model of Beethoven unusual not just because she was a woman but also because she was French – at a time when most of her composer compatriots were more interested in the allure of the Opéra. Only today is her music receiving the attention it deserves, free from the constraints which, despite the support of a musical family and friends like Joachim, she had to fight hard, and not always successfully, to overcome.

The Keyboard Sonata in the Early Romantic Period

'Sonata form' was first described and codified by writers in the second and third decades of the nineteenth century, including composers like Carl Czerny and theorists like Adolf Bernhard Marx. Earlier descriptive accounts of musical structure, like E. T. A. Hoffmann finding 'laughing children' and 'vast green woodlands' in the music of Haydn,[4] give way to a more rigorously analytical discussion of key and theme. Later writers moved on from the idea of sonata form as a template, seeing it instead as 'a feeling for proportion, direction and texture rather than a pattern', as Charles Rosen puts it.[5]

All composers, of sonata and symphony, struggled to assimilate the gigantic example of Beethoven in their attempts to move form forward. At the keyboard, Schubert and Chopin helped the sonata principle find a place in a world where the sonata itself was less central to compositional thought. Schubert's very last piano sonata, written in 1828, is in B flat major; though the 'magic carpet' of modulations is woven so wonderfully that it would almost be more accurate to say that it begins and ends in B flat major, but that's about it. The stately first theme is interrupted by a grumbling low trill, beginning a long passage teasing out the melody in G flat major, which then slip-slides into F sharp minor and then F major, which is the dominant of the home key, but approached so obliquely that it hardly sounds like it. The recapitulation performs the same wandering fantasy of key relationships, but with a step up a fourth after the first subject, so that the eventual tonic, B flat major, is approached via B minor: the principle reheard.

B minor was the starting point for Chopin's third and last piano sonata, written in 1844. After a vigorous opening, the beautiful second theme is in D major, its relative major: so far, so Czerny. But then part of this theme (not its opening) reappears in the middle of the development section in D flat major. When the recapitulation arrives, Chopin omits the first theme altogether, proceeding straight to the loveliness of the second, in B major.

Such innovations led thinkers, starting with Schumann, to question from the outset if their composers' more lyrical art made them less suited to the strictures of sonata form; or even whether they just weren't very good at it. This is not so much the wrong answer as the wrong question. They were doing something different. Schubert's sketches for the three late piano sonatas reveal that he expanded his conception of form during the composition process. Pianist Alfred Brendel, borrowing a famous comment of Schumann's, points out that 'the "heavenly lengths" of the sonatas were actually a later addition ... Schubert elaborated on his themes and expanded them ... allowing breathing space'.[6] Schubert hadn't damaged sonata form, or done it wrong; he had spread it out.

Cyclic Form

Thematic cross-referencing between movements has become known as the cyclic principle, or cyclic form. Like all such descriptors, it covers the general idea as much as any specific technical detail: analysis is often a question of judgement and interpretation as well as fact. Like many such ideas, trying to fix its emergence too precisely in time is hazardous. Examples date back into the Classical period and before.

The little-known symphonies of Étienne Méhul provide a fascinating link in the process by which, as one writer has it, '*Sturm und Drang* raised a mortgage which, in the musical field, could be fully paid off only by ... full romanticism'.[7] (The last movement of his second symphony sounds like a mixture of Mozart's in G minor and Beethoven's in C minor.) One modern musicologist adjudges Méhul's fourth and last symphony of 1810 to be the first to fully employ cyclical form[8] (though Berlioz found 'something house-wifely' and 'a trifle unimaginative' about his manner).[9] Schubert's 'Unfinished' Symphony of 1822 uses a little rhythmic pattern in the first movement's second theme, echoed in a melody which appears part-way through the second movement: the second can appear like a variation, or inversion, of the first (especially if conductors take the 3/8 of the second movement at the same speed as the 3/4 of the first, as many do). Linking elements in Schubert's other mature symphony, the 'Great' C Major Symphony of the late 1820s, include more amorphous things like all the movements referencing the relationship between C major and A major. Beethoven sometimes unified symphonic movements by use of a rhythm rather than (or as well as) a tune: the first and last movements of the Seventh Symphony generate unstoppable energy from short nuggets of rhythm. The Fifth Symphony gives each movement its own version of the famous opening 'short–short–short–long' motif: analysts argue over the extent to which these can genuinely be seen as variants of each other or simply as discrete themes with a similar shape.

A clear way to unify a symphonic structure is to join the movements together. Beethoven, as so often, pioneered the principle, for example, by linking the third and fourth movements of the Fifth Symphony. In 1811 he ended the second movement of his Fifth Piano Concerto by allowing the bassoons to settle on the note B, which then slides down a semitone to B flat, ushering in a transition back to the home key of the work as a whole, E flat major. Over three decades later, Mendelssohn ended the first movement of his Violin Concerto in E Minor by allowing exactly the same instrument, the bassoon, to settle on exactly the same note, B, which this time slides not down but up a semitone, to C, beginning a strangely chromatic transition into the key of the lyrical second movement. Between these two concertos, in 1841, Schumann followed the success of his First Symphony with a work which Clara described as 'a symphony … which is to consist of one movement, but with an Adagio and a finale'.[10] This continuous structure confused some of its first listeners, and was one of the elements substantially diluted by Schumann in the 1851 revision (earning this piece its habitual numbering as Symphony No. 4, even though it was originally written second: the nineteenth century is full of such traps for the compilers of chronological lists and catalogues). There are many other links and references across movements in this striking and unusual piece. The genuine one-movement symphony had to wait until much later for its finest exponents, but there are many models throughout the Romantic period and before, often in lengthy piano works with vague, catch-all titles like *Fantasy*.

Berlioz

Three years after Beethoven got his string players to use their bows in odd ways in his last quartet, Berlioz told them to turn them upside down and tap the strings with the wooden back. The symphony was about to get developed further than it ever knew it could go.

Initially persuaded to follow his father in a medical career, the young Hector Berlioz revolted against 'the fragments of limbs, the grinning heads and gaping skulls, the bloody quagmire underfoot and the atrocious smell' in the charnel house.[11]

His musical studies began privately with the composer Jean-François Le Sueur, and he enrolled at the Paris Conservatoire in 1826, when he was in his early twenties, immersing himself in the cultural life of the city. He relished the works of Gluck, praising his technical innovations ('One can only wonder at those unfortunate rules of harmony which Gluck broke so daringly'),[12] and the unadorned directness of his style ('Ugly women need sumptuous finery. Nakedness is only for goddesses').[13] He sang in a theatre chorus to earn money, and learnt English to read Shakespeare. Beethoven and Goethe completed the usual trinity of artistic deities. The Paris papers carried his first sallies into musical journalism, in defence of all things French against the march of the Italians. This marked the start of a lifelong and lucrative sideline: despite his bitter and regular grumbles about the lowly status of musical hack, he was a witty and perceptive critic. He obediently entered the prestigious composition competition the Prix de Rome four times, eventually succeeding in adapting his style to the examiners' requirements in 1830.

The young Berlioz fell in love often and easily. In his early twenties he experienced what one of his biographers calls 'an emotional derangement' from watching the celebrated Irish actress Harriet Smithson play Shakespeare, which acted as the creative impetus for the *Symphonie fantastique*.[14]

The *Symphonie fantastique* has five movements, telling a story, linked by a common theme known as the *idée fixe* (representing Harriet Smithson, the as-yet unobtainable object of his devotions) in an advanced and entirely personal version of cyclic form, ending with a dream sequence featuring a bone-rattling march to the scaffold. Written in 1830, just three years after the death of Beethoven but before the Classically formed symphonies of Schumann and the mature Mendelssohn, this work is closer in spirit to the tone poems of Richard Strauss, still sixty years and more in the unknowable future.

In 1830 Berlioz retrenched from his long-rebuffed passion for Harriet and became engaged to a young pianist, Marie Molke. Shortly afterwards he set off for two years' study in Rome. But Berlioz found Rome 'stupid and prosaic'[15] and disliked modish Italian music, though enjoyed the company of another visitor, the ever-friendly and supportive Mendelssohn. Worse, he heard that Marie had broken their engagement and was instead to marry the piano-maker Camille Pleyel. Jealously, Berlioz hatched a bizarre plot to murder them both and Marie's mother (whom he referred to as *'l'hippopotame'*) and, having purchased poisons, pistols and a disguise, set off for Paris. Fortunately, he thought better of this madcap scheme and returned to Rome, though left before the official end of his two-year term. Back in Paris his music attracted the admiring attention of many leading artistic figures. In 1834 Paganini asked him to compose a work to show off a newly acquired viola, but declined to perform the resulting 'symphony with viola obbligato', *Harold en Italie*, because 'there's not enough for me to do'.[16] Later, when Paganini heard the work played by someone else, he came on stage to kneel in homage at Berlioz's feet and (perhaps even more welcome) sent him a cheque for 20,000 francs.

Berlioz simply declined to observe conventional genre boundaries in his works. Listen to the 'dramatic symphony' *Roméo et Juliette* of 1839 expecting a symphony, as it says on the cover, and you will be baffled and bewildered. Listen instead to the love music, the Queen Mab scherzo, and the slow unfolding of the string fugue backed by the monkish chanting of the chorus on a single note and obsessively repeated snatch of text to depict Juliette's death, and you will discover one of the most sympathetic evocations of Shakespeare of the entire musical century. *La damnation de Faust* of 1846 is a 'dramatic legend', 'mixing illustration, symphonic meditation, narrative by soloists and active choral participation into a kind of concert opera'.[17]

Berlioz deployed his often huge orchestra with subtlety, imagination and restraint. In 1844 he collated his writings on the subject of orchestral writing into the *Traité de l'instrumentation*, one of the first textbooks which addressed orchestration as an art in its own right. His approach was rooted in the day-to-day practicalities of a working professional: reviewing the Beethoven festivities in Bonn in 1845, he picked apart a performance of the Ninth Symphony by listing by name the leading instrumentalists from across Europe who would have made a better fist of various passages, with plenty of technical detail about what Vivier might have brought to the horns and Dragonetti to the basses. Interestingly, Berlioz regarded his own lack of ability at the piano, the relic of an unmusical upbringing, as a benefit in composing because it 'saved me from the tyranny of keyboard habits, so dangerous to thought, and from the lure of conventional harmonies'.[18]

Harriet Smithson eventually succumbed to Berlioz's renewed attentions, and they married in 1833. Their son, Louis-Clément-Thomas, was born the following year. Initially happy, the marriage foundered as her career waned and his prospered, and Harriet sought solace in drink. Eventually, Berlioz turned to the company of a singer, Marie Recio, maintaining parallel households with Harriet and Marie from the early 1840s. Harriet suffered a series of strokes and died in 1854, supported by both her estranged husband and her son. Berlioz and Marie married, having lived together for some time, but she died suddenly in 1862 at the age of forty-eight. Berlioz remained devoted to her mother, who cared for him for the rest of his life. Louis became a captain in the merchant navy, and died of yellow fever in Havana in 1867. For Berlioz, a pair of autumnal romances included a lengthy and friendly correspondence with a widow in her late sixties with whom he had first fallen in love fifty years before when she was eighteen and he was twelve.

Frustrated by promoters abroad earning more from his works than he could at home, in the 1840s and 1850s Berlioz sought out opportunities to conduct and earn money on lengthy tours in London, Germany, Belgium and elsewhere. Reaction, as always, was a blend of rampant enthusiasm from sympathetic supporters mixed with bafflement at the innovative form and sheer length of his works. There were also practical difficulties in bringing them to an audience caused by the considerable demands of his unique vision. Demoralised, Berlioz wrote no more music. In the late 1860s, in failing health and mourning the loss of his wife, son and many friends and contemporaries, he undertook a successful but strength-sapping trip to Russia (Rimsky-Korsakov, sounding slightly hurt, ascribes 'the complete indifference of Berlioz to Russian musical life' to the visiting Frenchman's age and failing health, which allowed him to receive only the composer and promoter Mily Balakirev).[19]

Berlioz died in 1869, aged sixty-five, and was buried in Montmartre cemetery, near to where he and Harriet had lived in the early days of their marriage. His two wives were later laid to rest on either side of his grave.

The Dramatic Symphony, Tone Poem and Concert Overture

Mention of the *idée fixe* brings into play a key divide in the development of orchestral music in the later part of the nineteenth century. As conventional ideas of symphonic structure became part of music's past, composers recast its basic feel for contrast and progression in works which moved away from the formal discussion of different themes towards pieces which relied instead on the organic manipulation of a single musical idea or more amorphous things like orchestral texture.

Alongside this technical evolution grew the principle of wrapping a narrative, pictorial or philosophical thread into the musical argument. In the early years of the Romantic century this idea prompted composers to take the orchestral overture out of the opera house and recast it as a free-standing work for concert use. By the end of the century the ideas of narrative content and organic treatment of theme had combined to create the tone poem.

On the way, the approach went under a variety of different names and titles. Liszt called *Les Préludes* of 1848 a 'symphonic poem'. The work was composed as a sort of detached orchestral introduction to an existing set of choral songs, borrowing their mood without their text, captured in a prose introduction leading the listener into a series of 'poetic meditations': 'What else is our life but a series of Preludes to that unknown hymn … ?' The musical analogue for this peregrination is a single motif of three notes which goes through a series of metamorphoses in response to the mood of the moment.

The young Richard Strauss, under the tutelage of Hans von Bülow and the Liszt disciple Alexander Ritter, came to regard the sonata forms of his early Brahmsian pieces as 'a hollow shell'. His slogan became: 'New ideas must seek new forms.'[20] The series of orchestral poems written between 1886 and 1898 (with, typically, the curious addition of two later pieces both appropriating the name 'symphony', the *Symphonia Domestica* of 1903 and *Eine Alpensinfonie* of 1915) show those new forms emerging in brilliant orchestral colour. *Till Eulenspiegels lustige Streiche* (*Till Eulenspiegel's Merry Pranks*) of 1895 depicts the eponymous Till's '*lustige Streiche*' by treating three themes to a wild, frankly pictorial ride. *Also Sprach Zarathustra* (*Thus Spoke Zarathustra*) of 1896 charts not a story or a painting, but the philosophical ideas of Wagner's quondam acolyte and later nemesis, Friedrich Nietzsche. The famous opening sunrise provides a motif for the seven sections of the work, including a strange, slow fugue for a meditation 'On Science', using all twelve notes of the chromatic scale.

Like Strauss, the Finnish composer Jean Sibelius broadly wrote his tone poems in the closing years of the nineteenth century before turning elsewhere as the century turned (Strauss to opera, Sibelius to the symphony). Sibelius heard the premiere of Strauss's first tone poem, *Don Juan*, in Germany in 1889. Back in his home country, he drew richly on the *Kalevala*, a collection of Finnish and Karelian folklore assembled in the nineteenth century and a key contributor to the development of Finnish national identity in the long progress towards eventual independence from Russia in 1917. A review of the choral symphony *Kullervo* of 1892 reported, approvingly, 'Finnish music undoubtedly has its future in Mr Sibelius.'[21] Other nationalistic pieces included the *Karelia* music from 1893, several tone poems based on the hero Lemminkäinen, *Finlandia* of 1899, and others, full of his unmistakable sonic signatures: Brucknerian brass; whirling wind; harmony which moves slowly even when the notes move fast; and a sort of stubborn, Nordic lugubriousness. Two of his best-known incidental orchestral works are the *Valse triste* of 1903 and the *Andante festivo* (1922, orchestrated in 1938): only Sibelius could have regarded a valse as *triste* or an andante as *festivo*.

French composers largely eschewed the tone poem as they did the symphony. Oddly, they seemed to prefer evoking the sounds and moods of Spain: Emmanuel Chabrier in his *España* of 1883; Édouard Lalo in his *Symphonie Espagnole* of 1874 for violin and orchestra; while Bizet, Ravel and Debussy all conjured a dash of Iberian verve in their music, too. Meanwhile, Spanish composers captured their own inheritance in free form piano suites like *Iberia* of 1909 by a composer praised by Liszt, Isaac Albéniz, and Enrique Granados's *12 Danzas españolas* (1890) and *Goyescas* (1911).

Late-century Symphonists: Brahms and the Brahmsians

In the face of these new approaches to orchestral form, the more traditional symphony rather lost its creative way in the 1850s–1870s. But the flame was never quite extinguished. The Swiss composer Joachim Raff found an intriguing middle path in his Classically constructed symphonies with programmatic titles, sometimes said to stand between the tone poems of Liszt and descriptive pieces by Sibelius and Strauss.

Johannes Brahms was born in Hamburg in 1833, the middle of the three children of Johann Jakob Brahms, a successful jobbing musician (who, among other talents, played horn in the band of the local militia and double bass in the theatre) and Johanna, a seamstress seventeen years his senior. As well as studies with his father, Johannes learnt piano with Otto Cossel, who said of the 9-year-old Brahms that he 'could be such a good player, but he will never stop his endless composing',[22] and composition with Eduard Marxsen, who grounded him in the traditions of German counterpoint. Early adulthood brought wide experience as a piano recitalist and accompanist and encounters with leading figures including Liszt, Cornelius and Raff.

Violinist Joseph Joachim and composer Robert Schumann both met Brahms in 1853. Their reactions to the handsome young Hamburger were similar: 'Never in the course of my artist's life have I been more completely overwhelmed,' said Joachim,[23] while Schumann published an article in his Leipzig periodical *Die Neue Zeitschrift für Musik* marvelling at how the young man turned the piano into an 'orchestra of lamenting and jubilant voices'.[24] The article was titled '*Neuer Bahnen*' ('New Paths'). Brahms responded by telling Schumann that 'the public praise that you have deigned to bestow upon me will have so greatly increased the expectations of the musical world that I do not know how I shall manage to do even approximate justice to it' – an early indication of an intensely self-critical perfectionism which lasted his entire career, leading him to destroy many works.[25] (This was also in part an indication of changing ideas about what the artist, and the artwork, were for: Mozart and Haydn would surely have found the idea of spending time and professional skill writing a piece and then discarding it inexplicably quixotic.)

Brahms became the principal liaison between Schumann and his wife Clara when Schumann was incarcerated following his apparent suicide attempt in 1854, and Clara was prevented from seeing him. A deeply moving series of letters begins at this time, recounting his visits to Robert, accounts of the children's piano lessons, apologies for his handwriting, jokes, nicknames and plenty of music. Salutations evolve from 'Dear and Honoured Herr Brahms' and 'Most Honoured Lady' to 'My Most Beloved Friend' and 'My Dearly Beloved Clara'.[26] The correspondence lasted forty years.

The rest of the 1850s saw success and struggle intermingled: an undemanding old-fashioned court post in tiny Detmold, the slow and not always straightforward emergence of working relationships with publishers, a tortured amour and brief engagement to the talented soprano Agathe von Siebold ('I love you! ... but I am incapable of bearing fetters,' he proclaimed),[27] and long and agonisingly self-critical work on pieces including his first major orchestral piece, the Piano Concerto No. 1 in D Minor. This took five years to emerge from its beginnings as a two-piano work to its premiere in 1859, described by Brahms to Joachim as 'a brilliant and decisive – failure ... it forces one to concentrate one's thoughts and increases one's courage ... But the hissing was too much of a good thing.'[28]

In 1863 Brahms became conductor of the Singakademie in Vienna, the city which had increasingly become his home, programming early music by Gabrieli and others alongside works by Mendelssohn and Beethoven, and new pieces of his own. In 1865, prompted by the death of his mother, he began work on *Ein Deutsches Requiem* (*A German Requiem*). Other works of the prolific late 1860s and early 1870s included songs, chamber music and, in 1873, both the orchestral *Haydn Variations* (on a theme which, unbeknown to Brahms, was not actually by Haydn but which he had borrowed for a string quartet) and the instantly and everlastingly popular first set of *Hungarian Dances*. He became conductor of a leading Viennese orchestral concert society, professionalising its standards.

The international success of his First Symphony in C Minor in 1876 released Brahms into a long and productive period of large-scale work: three more symphonies, the Second Piano Concerto in B Flat Major and concert overtures, alongside smaller-scale works. He met, befriended and encouraged Antonín Dvořák. Later, enthusiastic supporters from the younger generation included Mahler and Strauss. In 1878 he grew a beard. His last years included a close, if perhaps surprising, friendship with the waltz composer Johann Strauss II. He enjoyed the company of a young singer, Alice Barbi, and (like Verdi) toyed with retiring from composition. Instead, two friendships, one just beginning, the other approaching the moment of its ending, inspired some of his last works: the *Vier ernste Gesänge* (*Four Serious Songs*) – settings, like his Requiem, of Lutheran biblical texts, prompted by the illness and death in May 1896 of his friend of half a century, Clara Schumann; and a number of works prominently featuring the clarinet, inspired by the playing of the principal clarinettist of the Meiningen orchestra, Richard Mühlfeld.

Brahms died in April 1897, aged sixty-three. The last music he wrote, found after his death, was a chorale prelude for organ on the Lutheran melody '*O Welt, ich muss dich lassen*' ('O World, I Must Leave Thee').

The parent and shadow of Brahms's symphonic world is, of course, Beethoven. Like Beethoven's Fifth, Brahms's First Symphony travels from C minor to a triumphant C major. The big tune in the last movement bears an obvious relation to the main theme of the finale of Beethoven's Ninth, like a sort of cyclic variation fifty years on. (When this was pointed out to Brahms, he replied, 'Any dunce can see that.').[29]

Arnold Schoenberg teased out some key points in Brahms's practice in his essay *Brahms the Progressive*, delivered as a lecture in 1933 and published in 1946. In Schoenberg's account, Brahms could deploy harmonic innovation with as much boldness as Wagner, and asymmetrical rhythmic and melodic construction with the freedom of Mozart (almost). Brahms, said Schoenberg, combined 'inspired composing' and 'intellectual gymnastics':[30] the last movement of the Fourth Symphony uses the same figure built from descending thirds which opened the first movement, as if by chance, design, intuition, or some mysterious combination of all three. The same notes, in the same key, begin the third of the *Four Serious Songs*, '*O Tod, wie bitter bist du!*': here, Brahms again reuses the opening idea, but this time in the major mode and with the interval of a third inverted to a sixth: death, and theme, transfigured. Schoenberg regards these 'subcutane beauties' as 'specimens of a perhaps unique artistic quality'.[31]

Stylistic Divide and the Controversy of 1860

In 1860 Brahms found himself embroiled in one of those public spats about musical style which have been a notable occasional feature of this story. In his buttoned-up way, Brahms had long been marinating the young man's usual impatience with the manner of his immediate seniors, in particular the evolving style of Liszt (who had, as always, been perfectly polite and encouraging). In 1859 Brahms told Joachim 'my fingers often itch to start a fight and to write something anti-Liszt', adding, 'but who am I? ... I don't know what to write.'[32]

Brahms would have been better advised to let his inhibition rule his ambition. He and Joachim began trying to put together a 'declaration' expressing their views. It would be signed by as many leading musical figures as possible. But attempting to draft a joint multi-author manifesto by letter had obvious pitfalls. Joachim sought the support of the *lieder* composer Robert Franz, intemperately telling him, 'We felt that we had been slack, if not actually cowardly, in not protesting long ago against those who in their vanity and arrogance regard everything great and sacred which the musical talent of our people has created up to now as mere fertilizer for the rank, miserable weeds growing from Liszt-like fantasias.'[33] Franz sensibly and sensitively demurred. When the declaration appeared in the *Berliner Musik-Zeitung Echo* on 6 May 1860, it carried just four names, of whom only Brahms's and Joachim's had any real prominence. The text is brief, carping at the pretensions of what it calls the New German School to have discovered 'the so-called Music of the Future'.[34] It is also unremittingly negative, offering no alternative direction. Worse, it had leaked, and a parody version had appeared in the *Neue Zeitschrift* two days earlier, claiming to emanate from a 'brotherly association for the advancement of monotonous and tiresome music', signed by 'J. Fiddler' (Joachim) and 'Hans Newpath' (Brahms, after Schumann's article of 1853).[35] Bülow, artistically sympathetic to both camps, summed up the reaction (or lack of it) in Berlin: 'The Declaration of the Hanoverians has made not the slightest sensation here. They have not even enough wit mixed with their malice to have done the thing in good style, and to have launched it at a well-chosen time.'[36] Brahms never again risked getting his fingers burned in the public prints. But he continued to mutter and moan sulkily in his letters, calling one 1869 Liszt premiere 'the new swindle by Liszt' and another in 1871 'monumentally boring, stupid and senseless'.[37]

By contrast, the other (very different) pillar of the New German School, Richard Wagner, attracted Brahms's consistent, though qualified, admiration. He owned a part of the manuscript of *Tannhäuser*, acquired (illicitly, it seems) through the composer Peter Cornelius. Brahms called parts of *Die Walküre* 'especially beautiful'; Siegfried has a 'fresh and breezy song'; *Die Meistersinger* 'provokes one to talk'; the Ride of the Valkyries is 'a taxing pleasure'.[38] Some of this is filtered through the prism of writing cautiously to the most adamantine of armoured anti-Wagnerians, Clara Schumann: but at least it shows genuine critical engagement, which is more than he offered poor Liszt. Wagner, of course, repaid Brahms by casting him into the special circle of hell reserved for reactionary symphonic scribblers.

And he demanded his score back. They were not the first or the last composers to take pot shots at each other: as usual, their broadsides tended to generate more heat than light.

The Brahmsians: France and England

Brahms's career stands as a sort of personal autumn of a kind of Romanticism, decking its late-flowering branches with a rich formality and restrained passion. In some ways, he acquired his artistic and emotional world view as the 20-year-old lauded by Schumann as 'a young blood, at whose cradle graces and heroes kept watch',[39] and stuck (or got stuck) with it through the long years of his loyal friendship with Clara. In his lengthening shadow flourished a disparate group loyal to the old ways, spread around the expanding musical world: Dvořák in the Czech regions and America; native-born American inheritors like John Knowles Paine in Boston; Camille Saint-Saëns in France; and in England a brace and a half of handsomely moustachioed knights, Sir Charles Villiers Stanford, Sir Edward Elgar and Sir Charles Hubert Hastings Parry.

Brahms's principal French outlier was Saint-Saëns, who (very un-Frenchly) wrote concertos as well as symphonies, often exploring a distinctive two-movement approach to traditional form, alongside some Lisztian symphonic poems (most famously the bone-rattling *Danse macabre* of 1874). Saint-Saëns lived long enough to be admired for his craftsmanship by Neoclassicists like Poulenc and dismissed as reactionary by Schoenbergian modernisers and his pupil Edgard Varèse, who told him, 'I have no desire to become an old powdered wig like you!'[40] (Saint-Saëns was also the first established composer to write a film score, *L'assassinat du duc de Guise*, in 1908.) He even wrote a poem accusing himself of being insufficiently decadent: 'My Muse dare not bite into these over-ripe fruits.'[41]

César Franck describes an individual arc through much of the nineteenth century. Pupil of Beethoven's friend Anton Reicha, he had to clamber over the Paris barricades in 1848 to get to his own wedding. He was a fine organist and finer pianist (his enormous hands, like some others of his century, led him to litter his pieces with superhuman stretches and leaps without a thought for lesser mortals), a sought-after teacher, a thoughtful and innovative composer and, in the words of Louis Vierne, 'a man of utmost humility, simplicity, reverence and industry'.⁴² His reputation rests on a small but varied group of works: a violin sonata (which may be the model for the sonata by Vinteuil in Proust, with its evocative '*petit phrase*'); the sacred song *Panis angelicus* of 1872 (which, like the sonata, features his favourite cantabile canon in A major); the late, elegiac *Trois Chorals* for organ, written only a few months before he died in 1890; the *Symphonic Variations* of 1885 for piano and orchestra; and his Symphony in D Minor of 1889, which fuses Bachian counterpoint with Wagnerian harmony and cyclic symphonic form in a way that was always bound to place him uncomfortably between musical traditionalists and progressives, symbolised rather awkwardly by his wife in the one camp and his pupils in the other.

A perhaps even more distinctive fusion of harmonic innovation and traditional form can be heard in the work of the short-lived and un-prolific Franck acolyte Ernest Chausson, cut sadly short by his death in a bicycle accident at the age of forty-four.

Across the grey heave of la Manche to the north, Irishman Charles Villiers Stanford championed new music by Brahms and others as conductor of the University Musical Society in Cambridge. Cambridge went on to welcome and honour many leading lights of European music (Tchaikovsky, Dvořák, Saint-Saëns, Boito and Bruch came to Cambridge, Brahms and Grieg were invited but didn't), a key step in England's long-delayed engagement with important trends elsewhere. Stanford's role in this process continued through his wide-ranging and influential work as a teacher at the Royal College of Music, though, inevitably, many of his pupils reacted against his Brahmsian credo just as, as a student in Leipzig, he had himself kicked against the 'desiccated' teaching of Carl Reinecke, who 'loathed Wagner ... [and] sneered at Brahms ...'.⁴³ (Traditional tribalism normally asked people to loathe one or the other, not both.)

The Brahmsian symphonies of Stanford and his (sometime) friend Parry were comprehensively overshadowed by the example of a man whose curious place in musical time is perceptively captured by the scholar Donald Mitchell: 'It is a strange but undeniable fact that a time-lag seems to operate, whereby English composers often come late – and fresh – to a language that elsewhere may already have grown tired. How else can one explain the astonishing feat of Elgar? ... [T]he romantic tradition of symphony dawned later in England than anywhere else. Through the redemptive power of Elgar's genius, it was lent, out of time, a new lease of life.'⁴⁴

Success came late to Elgar. His large-scale mature works date from the two decades between the *Enigma Variations* of 1899, when he was already in his mid-forties, and the Cello Concerto of 1919, written in the aftermath of the Great War and shortly before the death of his wife Alice.

Before came the long apprentice years, in which the composer emerged from a lowly provincial background in his beloved Worcestershire, his lack of formal study compensated for by odd jobs conducting the band of the local mental asylum and playing the organ in church, as well as his marriage to a woman eight years his senior and considerably his social superior. He was a Catholic at the heart of established Protestant society, flag-waver-in-chief of the Edwardian world view who went on to hear the thump and thud of Great War bombardments across the Channel from his home in rural Sussex, and, like so many, found himself socially and stylistically stranded in the brave new world of its aftermath.

Musically, Edward Elgar was, to borrow a phrase from Thomas Hardy, a 'time-torn man'.[45] His mature contribution to the great European tradition of Schumann and Brahms takes in familiar things like fugue and sonata in his sparkling string works, variation forms (most obviously in the *Enigma Variations* of 1899), a Brucknerian parade of themes in the Violin Concerto of 1910 and a Beethovenian recollection of previously heard tunes at the end of the Cello Concerto of 1919, careful use of motif in the three magisterial and challenging oratorios, and Straussian warmth and colour in a series of descriptive orchestral pieces, evoking scenes from London to Italy to Falstaff's forest in Shakespearean Windsor.

His two symphonies, written fairly close together between 1907 and 1911, mine the resource of old-fashioned structural principles for new ways of looking at theme and idea. The First Symphony makes striking use of revisiting its opening tune ('simple ... noble and elevating', according to its composer);[46] the second theme is in an unstable, ambiguous D minor, a dislocating wrench from the diatonic A flat major of the opening. Conductor Adrian Boult apparently claimed that this tonal variety was the result of a bet that he had with Elgar that couldn't write a piece in two keys at the same time: in the part-song 'There is Sweet Music' he did exactly that – the four upper voice parts have a key signature of four flats, the four lower ones one sharp, the alternating textures exploring the points of meeting between the two keys (sometimes in a shape-shifting 5/4 time), ending with a gentle rocking back and forth between the two triads, like a pre-echo of the opening of Britten's *A Midsummer Night's Dream*.

The Second Symphony presents a complex engagement with sonata form, rondo and fugue: its Beethovenian funeral march opens with a gently lop-sided seven-bar phrase, playing with drum rolls and harp chords sounding quietly on the wrong beats. The Third Symphony (left incomplete at the time of his death in 1934 but ably reconstructed many decades later by the composer Anthony Payne) hints intriguingly at a new sound world. Even the global smash hit *Pomp and Circumstance March* No. 1 of 1904 begins with music whose key centre is withheld, if not exactly absent, before the rattling D major march and the slow, inevitable, glorious unfolding of the 'Land of Hope and Glory' tune: Elgar stepping back into character. He was, perhaps, the last, best old-school orchestrator: not an innovator in the manner of Mahler, Strauss or Debussy, but just very good at it. Unlike the English generation which succeeded him, he had no use for folk song, though he did claim that the slow viola melody in the sparky *Introduction and Allegro* for strings of 1905 had been inspired by his hearing Welsh folk songs sung in the distance on holiday in Cardiganshire, catching their manner if not their actual notes (a story which contains yet more layers of disguise and partial revelation). It is a unique and personal vision, his generous melodiousness shielding something darker and more challenging within.

In 1923, old, widowed, famous and alone, Sir Edward Elgar took a shadowy journey to South America and up the Amazon by steamer. Sixty-six years later James Hamilton-Paterson reimagined this curious episode in his novel *Gerontius*. The title is borrowed from *The Dream of Gerontius*, the poem by Cardinal John Henry Newman memorably set to music by Elgar at the moment the nineteenth century ended, catching his Catholic sensibilities alongside Wagnerian gesture, generous tunefulness and Brucknerian brass. 'Gerontius' means 'old man'.

Benjamin Britten said of Elgar's First Symphony, following a Proms performance in 1935, 'only in Imperialistic England could such a work be tolerated'.[47] More wittily, and revealingly, in 1937 Britten characterised Elgar as 'a member of the Governing Board' of English music, while Ralph Vaughan Williams was 'of course the Headmaster', William Walton head prefect, and himself 'the promising young new boy'.[48]

Between them, governor and new boy bookend and define English music in the first two-thirds of the twentieth century.

The Bruckner Problem

Anton Bruckner's version of the life of a great composer was unlike anyone else's.

After a rehearsal of his Symphony No. 4 in E Flat Major, Bruckner reportedly gave the conductor Hans Richter a tip and told him to treat himself to a glass of beer.

Another conductor, Hans von Bülow, called Bruckner 'half genius, half simpleton'.[49] He was ambitious as a musician but humble as a man, making his living as an organist, both in the magnificent but provincial monastery of Sankt Florian in Upper Austria and later as a recitalist. He came late to the form which defines his achievement, the symphony, after the three great Masses of the 1860s, key works in his development. He studied, and later taught, in Vienna. He was consistent in his artistic aspirations, his faith, his integrity, his personality and his sense of humility, even inferiority, dating from his lowly origins as the eldest of eleven children of a poor village schoolmaster. He never set himself up as the equal of composers he revered, even when, late in life, he earned recognition, honours and the admiration of younger contemporaries such as Gustav Mahler.

Bruckner's art is a unique amalgam of his Catholic faith and German symphonic inheritance, especially Beethoven (in particular the Ninth Symphony) and Schubert, whose late G major string quartet is strikingly similar in technique to Bruckner's late style.

His reputation included criticism of an apparent lack of formal coherence by Brahms and his satellite Eduard Hanslick. His legacy is compounded by the politics surrounding his later editors: the first, Robert Haas, played a key role in fostering Bruckner's popularity with the Nazis, including with Hitler personally (though Bruckner's reputation suffered no lasting damage, because, unlike Wagner and Richard Strauss in their different ways, his own simple and devout world view left no opportunity to associate him personally with the uses to which his music had been put). In 1945 Haas was replaced by the more scholarly but less creative Leopold Nowak. The complex process of producing a complete and authoritative edition of Bruckner's work continues.

The eight completed symphonies (and an unfinished ninth) are in some ways like a variation on each other, part of a continuous process, like a row of hills rather than separate peaks. There are no compositional periods across his symphonies, as with Beethoven (at least from the full maturity of the Third Symphony). They have structural features in common: four movements, starting with a modified sonata with three groups of themes (respectively slow, song-like and contrapuntal, and rhythmic); a richly scored adagio in a version of rondo form; a fiery scherzo with a short ländler-like trio (these middle movements may be in the opposite order); and another modified sonata structure to end, closing with a reprise of earlier music and a grand hymn-like ending.

The phrase 'the Bruckner problem' was coined by the musicologist Deryck Cooke in 1975:

> The textual problem presented by the different versions of Bruckner's symphonies is one of the most vexatious in all musicology, and the person ultimately responsible was Bruckner himself. Had he only possessed the normal self-confidence of the great composer, he would have produced, like Beethoven or Dvořák, a single definitive score of each of his nine symphonies ... But it was not to be.[50]

From the premiere of his Second Symphony in 1873 friends began suggesting changes; Bruckner in his humility accepted their advice; 'and so began that sorry business of the composer's revising his symphonies under the influence of well-meaning colleagues who wanted to make them more easily accessible to the public'. Some even made changes themselves, and 'after that, Bruckner himself became afflicted with the revising mania', though making 'muted protests' against some of the more egregious changes getting into print, and scrupulously preserving his original manuscripts 'for future times'. Cooke summed up the residue: 'by 1903 [seven years after Bruckner's death] there were in existence no less than 25 different scores of the nine symphonies; moreover, the 10 published ones did not represent Bruckner's own intentions'.[51] Cooke's essay is titled 'The Bruckner Problem Simplified'. Alas, the result has been anything but.

Editors and conductors have thus been faced from the start with a complex trail working out which version represents the composer's first or best intentions, which revisions work, which have his authority and when. There is often no single definitive answer.

Choices made, what emerges is an utterly distinctive symphonic voice. The Seventh and Eighth Symphonies both open with expressive, chromatic melodies below quietly shimmering strings, giving way to song-like themes with Wagnerian harmonies, and a third theme featuring Bruckner's favourite octave doublings. Both works make much use of presenting their melodies in inversion and various kinds of contrapuntal combination – relics of his long working life as a church organist and intimate knowledge of the music of Bach. Slow movements are rich and expressive: the second movement of the Seventh was written around the news of the death of Richard Wagner in February 1883, and uses Wagner tubas for the first time in a symphony. The shape of its theme finds an echo in the second theme of the second movement of the Eighth Symphony of 1887, whose third movement presents a distinctive example of Bruckner's familiar alternation of triplet and duplet rhythmic groups, to strangely unsettled effect. Finales combine theme and mood to grand perorations. The shadow of Beethoven, particularly the eternal Ninth Symphony, hovers in the tremolo openings and muscular themes in octaves. These are long pieces: the shorter middle movements can provide a way into his wonderful sound world and unique capacity to wring expressive melody and striding rhythmic power from his material.

Richter, reportedly, never spent Bruckner's proffered *thaler* on beer, but wore it on his watch chain as a treasured talisman.

The Symphony, Nationalism and Folk Song: Dvořák

By the time Antonín Dvořák returned to Europe from America in 1895 he was so famous he had to take care not to announce his arrival.

The Czech region of Bohemia where he was born in 1841 was ruled at the time by the Austrian Empire. From his native soil Dvořák drew a lasting love of his homeland, deep religious sensibilities enriched by his experience as a church organist, and support from his older compatriot Bedřich Smetana. As an impoverished young would-be composer in Prague he scratched a living teaching and playing the viola, on one occasion under the baton of Richard Wagner. Like Mozart, he fell in love with a singer who rejected him, and married her sister.

Success from his mid-thirties led to visits to England, Russia and elsewhere. Brahms and the critic Eduard Hanslick were important supporters. His most significant overseas invitation came in 1892. Jeanette Thurber was a wealthy American philanthropist. Her new National Conservatory of Music in New York City offered places to women and Black students as well as to white men. Dvořák became its director in 1892, on the impressive salary of $15,000 per year. His directorial duties were relatively light, and he set himself the task of discovering and engaging with American music, just as he had with the idioms of his own native Czech regions. In this he was aided by his friendship with the celebrated baritone Harry Burleigh, a descendant of slaves and well-known singer of African-American spirituals, as well as through visits to Czech communities in the Midwest.

Public honours followed his return home in 1895. In 1897 he attended the funeral of his generous and loyal supporter Brahms. The same year his daughter Otilie married the composer and violinist Josef Suk, his successor as leading light and ambassador of Czech music.

Dvořák died in 1904. There are statues of him in both New York and Prague, a fitting tribute to perhaps the only composer to have founded the nationalistic art music of not one but two countries.

Symphonically, Dvořák blended the example of his friend and supporter Brahms with the creative use of folk song, often blurring the boundaries between real folk melodies collected and noted down in the woods and fields and original material which borrowed their character.

Dvořák's Sixth Symphony of 1880 displays his two good angels equally well: the first movement shows a clear debt to Brahms's Second in its key, melodic shapes and mood; but the third movement is a fabulously off-beat furiant, a Czech dance.

Many of his works record his devotion to the character and inheritance of his native land. In some the folk element is explicit, either in the melodies, as in the *Slavonic Dances* of 1878 and 1886, or in adapting folk ballads into narrative form, as in his symphonic poems and several of his operas. Often it is more veiled, recalling folk style in melodies like his *Humoresques* of 1884 and 'Songs My Mother Taught Me' of 1880, or works like the skilfully crafted 'American' String Quartet, No. 12 in F Major, written in 1893 among the Czech community in Spillville, Iowa, and featuring the song of American birds as well as folk-influenced melodies.

In common with his admired Schubert, Dvořák's best and

best-known symphonies are his Eighth and Ninth. The Eighth, written in 1889, is a sunny and uncomplicated work, moving from G minor to major through some deliciously lyrical tunes, a straightforward and undemanding use of cyclic and motivic elements, and a folksy G major trio to the waltz-like G minor third movement which features his characteristic shift to the submediant chord, and one of those chugging string accompaniment figures which instantly identify his style (the finale of the 'American' Quartet is another).

Dvořák's Ninth Symphony, 'From the New World', written in 1893 when he was director of the National Conservatory of Music of America, can be heard as a kind of founding document of a version of American vernacular. The pentatonic melodies also heard in the 'American' Quartet; the clear, tuneful idiom; the hymn-like slow movement; the breezy little flute melody over cantering strings in the middle section of the third movement; the distinctive bass figure at the very end – all these find later echoes in American music, as if her composers were somehow all panhandling in the same stream.

National Influences Elsewhere

Dvořák's older friend and patron Bedřich Smetana briefly manned the barricades on the Charles Bridge in Prague in 1848: his 1872 work *Má Vlast (My Homeland)* embraces Czech history and character in his generous melodiousness. It is dedicated to the city of Prague.

Smetana spent time in Scandinavia: a musical nationalist of very different heritage was the Norwegian Edvard Grieg. His antecedents were Scottish (the name was originally spelt Greig), and he brought Norwegian folk song to international prominence in works of charm and character like his many short piano works. Many other pieces are infused with spirit if not its actual melodies of folk song, for example, the sprightly *Holberg Suite* for strings of 1884 and his music for Ibsen's drama *Peer Gynt*, first performed in 1876. Where Grieg stands rather apart from Smetana is in his adherence to traditional symphonic and sonata structures: his celebrated Piano Concerto in A Minor of 1868 is obediently and brilliantly constructed on lines Schumann would have recognised, and the Piano Sonata in E Minor, written in 1865 when he was only twenty-two, follows a three-movement sonata–aria–rondo pattern which would scarcely have brought a blush to the cheek of Czerny half a century before.

The Symphony in Russia: The Five

Reviewing nationalism in the symphonic tradition involves continuing the long train journey north, to Russia. Imperial Russia had long been a distant but significant player in the European musical scene. J. S. Bach's boyhood friend Georg Erdmann moved to Danzig, then part of the Russian Empire: Bach asked about getting a job there himself. St Petersburg, the imperial capital from 1713 to 1917, was more easily accessible than Moscow: Domenico Cimarosa, Vicente Martín y Soler, John Field and François-Adrien Boieldieu were among many Western musicians to find favour working at court there. Robert and Clara Schumann made it to Moscow in 1844, where they met Mikhail Glinka; Berlioz performed in St Petersburg in the late 1860s. In the other direction, the Russian virtuoso pianist and composer Anton Rubinstein made his own mark on the European Mozart circuit as an itinerant child prodigy. Back in Russia, he and his pianist brother Nikolai founded the Russian Musical Society and, respectively, the conservatories in St Petersburg and Moscow. This was an important step – one society lady apparently commented, 'What! Music in Russian? That is an original idea', while Anton himself noted in his autobiography:

> it was surprising that the theory of Music was to be taught for the first time in the Russian language at our Conservatory ... Hitherto, if any one wished to study it, he was obliged to take lessons from a foreigner, or to go to Germany.[52]

The initiative certainly succeeded in raising standards and awareness of the main European schools. It also introduced a vein of academicism which was not always in tune with the instincts of Russian composers. The duality can be heard playing out in their attitude to symphonic and other concert works.

The key figure in the first half of the nineteenth century was Mikhail Glinka, whose folk-infused, formally conventional works gained wide recognition and set the example for the next generation. In the middle of the century a small and initially fluid group of composers coalesced around the example and leadership of Mily Balakirev. They were anointed by a critic in 1867 as the '*Moguchaya kuchka*' ('Mighty Bunch' or 'Handful') – and loosely referred to elsewhere as The Five: Balakirev, César Cui, Modest Mussorgsky, Alexander Borodin and Nikolai Rimsky-Korsakov.

Balakirev was, at least to begin with, the only professional musician in the group. He was a complex character and his leadership of musical life was marked by sometimes controversial artistic innovation, stubborn rows with patrons, employers and promoters, and a fertile friendship with Tchaikovsky arising from Tchaikovsky's defence of Balakirev following a hostile review. He also had a curiously obsessive old age following a nervous breakdown and retreat from musical prominence, marked by extreme religiosity, vegetarianism, petty anti-Semitism and the protection of small animals, characterised by Rimsky-Korsakov as 'this medley of Christian meekness, backbiting, fondness for beasts, misanthropy, artistic interests, and a triviality worthy of an old maid from a hospice'.[53] Stravinsky 'pitied Balakirev because he suffered from cruel fits of depression'.[54] Musically, Balakirev continued Glinka's work of finding a distinctively Russian approach to Western symphonic ideas: his two overtures *On Russian Themes* exploit rhythmic and harmonic ambiguities; the Symphony No. 1 in C Major of 1868 lays out overlapping patterns of exposition and development in a highly unusual way that is closer to his symphonic successor Sibelius than his model Brahms; *Tamara* (1882) is a symphonic poem evoking Oriental moods in sinuous melody and strangely slow-moving harmony.

Part of Balakirev's problem was that he wrote with glacial slowness: the symphony took more than thirty years to finish, and often his innovative ideas would first find public voice in the works of younger and more fleet-footed contemporaries acting under his influence, which lessened the impact of his own pieces when they finally emerged. His most successful work was the major exception to this habit, *Islamey, an Oriental Fantasy* for piano, composed in just a month following a visit to the Caucasus in 1869, capturing 'the majestic beauty of luxuriant nature there' through melodies played to him by 'a Circassian prince' on an instrument 'something like a violin' and another 'communicated to me in Moscow by an Armenian actor'.[55] It was long thought the most difficult piece in the piano repertoire, championed by lions of the keyboard like Franz Liszt and Nikolai Rubinstein, who gave the premiere.

César Cui was primarily a composer of opera. He was also a distinguished military engineer. Cui's reputation today is probably the slightest of The Five. His contribution to the development of Russian music included his writings (often published under the easily

A Tradition Fulfilled: Symphony, Symphonists and Sonata 325

solved cipher ***), which helped codify thinking about style and idea, turning him into a sort of semi-official spokesman (or scapegoat) for the views and aspirations of the group.

Modest Mussorgsky was a rough diamond. Balakirev said he was 'little short of an idiot';[56] Rimsky-Korsakov recoiled from his 'disconnected harmony [and] … unsuccessful scoring';[57] Tchaikovsky called him 'a hopeless case';[58] to Stravinsky he was 'a musician of genius, assuredly, but always confused in his ideas'.[59] Anatoly Lyadov, an early member of the Balakirev circle, was perhaps a little more sympathetic in remarking 'it is easy enough to correct Mussorgsky's irregularities. The only trouble is that when this is done, the character and originality of the music are done away with, and the composer's individuality vanishes.'[60] Mussorgsky was also an alcoholic of the determined Russian kind: a famous portrait, painted just a few days before his death in 1881, captures his defiant, dishevelled dissipation, like a sort of hollow-eyed Falstaff reimagined by Dostoyevsky. Many of his works were polished for the concert hall by his friend Rimsky-Korsakov, orchestrator of *Night on Bare Mountain*, composed by Mussorgsky in one night in June 1867, and the piano suite *Pictures at an Exhibition* of 1874.

By contrast, the fastidious Alexander Borodin was a physician, chemist and pioneer of medical training for women – he even has a chemical reaction named after him. His consistent fondness for abstract music such as symphonies and chamber music rather sets him apart from his fellow members of The Five: his Second Symphony, premiered in 1877, is a tidy work (is it permissible to hear the mind of a scientist in its formal logic and clarity?), weaving evocative echoes of his own and others composers' engagement with his nationalist inheritance into its montage-like structure, starting with the striking opening theme (which is inscribed on his grave in golden mosaic). His craftsmanship, creative yet respectful approach to forms like fugue and sonata, and sheer folk-like tunefulness (in all of which he can often sound agreeably like Dvořák) are on display again in his String Quartet No. 2 in D Major of 1881, home of one of the century's most famous melodies in its charming third movement, 'Notturno'.

Finally, from The Five, is Nikolai Rimsky-Korsakov, one of the great magicians of the orchestra. Two poles of his musical personality are represented by the traditional contrapuntalist and establishment conservatoire teacher characterised by Borodin as 'a German *Herr*

Professor who has put on his glasses and is about to write *Eine grosse Symphonie in C*';[61] and a more progressive side expressed in the orientalisms of many of his melodies (notably in the sensuous symphonic suite *Scheherazade* of 1888). Like Cui, Rimsky-Korsakov was a career military man, first as a naval officer then as an inspector of military bands. His charming *Chronicle of My Musical Life*, first published in 1909, provides a fascinating insight into the ever-evolving debates within his circle about style, technique and composers old and new, alongside accounts of reading over each other's scores at the piano and visiting Borodin, who had to keep hopping down to the lab to check nothing was on fire, singing 'extravagant sixths' down the corridor as he went.[62] Rimsky-Korsakov praises the talents of Mme Borodina: his own widow, Nadezhda, editor of the *Chronicle*, was herself a formidable musician, much better trained than her husband at the time of their marriage, but who, like Nannerl Mozart, Fanny Mendelssohn and Alma Mahler (but not Clara Schumann), gave up composing when she married.

The name Nikolai Rimsky-Korsakov sounds like an explosion of fireworks: in his skilful hands, so does the orchestra. The full brilliance of his example would explode in the sounds of the pupil who regarded him as a second father and wept over his grave: Igor Stravinsky.

The celebrated Five were born within little more than a decade of each other, between late 1833 and early 1844. They are buried together in the Tikhvin cemetery in St Petersburg. This may make them appear more homogeneous than they actually were: as always with a so-called compositional 'school', the differences and individualities can be as revealing as the commonalities, vividly captured in their writings and debates. These were big characters.

The Symphony in Russia: Tchaikovsky

The work and career of Pyotr Ilyich Tchaikovsky stands outside and alongside those of the Handful, for all sorts of overlapping and interlocking reasons, social, musical, geographical and professional. Relations were marked by a good deal of mutual admiration: Balakirev encouraged and received the dedication of two Tchaikovsky pieces exploring different approaches to the symphonic tradition, the fantasy overture *Romeo and Juliet* of 1880 and the large-scale 'Manfred'

Symphony of 1885; and Rimsky-Korsakov and Tchaikovsky corresponded warmly before the latter's arrival in St Petersburg in 1887, attended and promoted each other's works, and spent much time together. But relations remained ambivalent, perceptively described by Tchaikovsky's brother Modest as like 'those between two friendly neighbouring states … cautiously prepared to meet on common ground, but jealously guarding their separate interests'.[63] Stravinsky went further: '[Tchaikovsky's] musical language is as completely apart from the prejudices that characterised The Five as Glinka's had been.'[64]

In the end, Tchaikovsky was a better composer than any of The Five – the finest and most enduring nineteenth-century composer of orchestral music outside Germany.

Part of his significance lies in his substantial contribution to both sides of the Brahms/Liszt divide in instrumental music: like Elgar and Sibelius after him, he wrote symphonies and concertos in the old forms, as well as a sequence of tone poems and descriptive pieces.

Romeo and Juliet is a brilliantly put together evocation of the passion, tragedy and violence of Shakespeare's feuding houses, wholly original in form. Still with Shakespeare, *The Tempest* of 1873 is a chilly, magical piece: its opening sounds like 1980s West Coast minimalism. The *1812 Overture* contains far more subtlety and craft than might sometimes appear from behind the cannon smoke: no other composer (including Beethoven) managed to quite so convincingly stitch national anthems and marching songs into such magnificently patriotic garb.

The late symphonies are among the most personal utterances in Romantic music. All but one of Tchaikovsky's symphonies are in minor keys: all follow the established practice of ending in the tonic major, except the last, which subsides quietly back into its home key of B minor. The Fourth, Fifth and Sixth Symphonies (written over a period of about a decade and a half from 1877, which also produced the unnumbered Manfred Symphony) can be read as an exploration of his laconic comment in a letter to his patroness, Nadezhda von Meck, written while at work on the Fourth: 'You ask if I keep to established forms. Yes and no.' He goes on to tease out how he had re-evaluated sonata form and other aspects of symphonic practice in this piece – 'very freely'[65] – but barely hints at the boldness of the opening motif (often called the 'fate' motif) constantly interrupting the musical argument, both during the long, many-themed first movement and at the end of the work, contributing to the bemused, lukewarm, sometimes actively hostile reception. The Fifth opens with a brooding, low-pitched grumble, again recurring as a kind of motto, and the Sixth (the 'Pathétique') also opens quiet and low before blossoming into one of Tchaikovsky's loveliest tunes, which he repeats almost obsessively, treating accompaniment and orchestration to a series of variations before sliding back to the depths, like the Fifth.

Waltzes are never far away, though the Fourth's second theme is in a syncopated 9/8 liable to trip up the unwary, and the second movement of No. 5 goes further, waltzing lop-sidedly but deliciously in 5/4. The Fourth Symphony ends in almost manic triumph, the Fifth with a hard-won (but perhaps not entirely convincing) major inflection of the opening theme (another 'fate' motif, perhaps). The ending of the Sixth Symphony is remarkable. The third movement, with its wonderfully energetic march-like second theme, sounds like it must be the end of the symphony; then, as palms are poised to applaud, the strings come keening in on a knife-twisting chord and a melody passed bizarrely between the two violins one quaver at a time, dislocating and disturbing the very idea of what a tune is. The second theme, in D major, is one of those moments which perhaps only Verdi could also have managed to pull off, making something ultra-expressive from just a downward scale. Faster music does not so much contrast with established mood in approved sonata fashion as smash it to pieces; eventually the downward scale disappears underground in the extraordinary sound of divided low strings. There is nothing else like it.

There is rich fodder here for those who would read the life in the music. Like Mozart's, the surviving letters of Pyotr Ilyich Tchaikovsky contain elements which were long thought far too explicit and revealing for widespread publication.

Their content could hardly be more different from Mozart's childish smut. He says of a young servant, 'My God, what an angelic creature and how I long to be his slave, his plaything, his property!' Another letter records that 'Petashenka used to drop by with the criminal intention of observing the Cadet Corps, which is right opposite our windows, but I've been trying to discourage these compromising visits – and with some success'.[66] Russian officials continued to deny Tchaikovsky's homosexuality well into the twenty-first century.

The letters, and other similar documents, have only recently been published.

Key events in his emotional life included separation from his family when he was sent to boarding school 1,000 miles from home at the age of ten in 1850, the death of his mother four years later (though some accounts paint her as cold and distant), and a lasting attachment to his brothers and sister. His brother Modest was a key supporter and his last librettist. His sister Alexandra's seven children provided the closest thing he knew to real family warmth during his years of fame and international travel.

In 1877, at the age of thirty-seven, Tchaikovsky married Antonina Miliukova, a former student. The marriage was a disaster, lasting just two and a half months, and precipitating a severe crisis. Around the same time, the composer began receiving emotional and financial support from a wealthy widow, Nadezhda von Meck, which lasted for thirteen years, even though they agreed never to meet. The ending of the arrangement caused him much anxiety and grief.

In 1893, Tchaikovsky's Sixth Symphony, the 'Pathétique', was dedicated to his nephew, Alexandra's son Vladimir Davydov, known as Bob. Bob was homosexual: he and his uncle were close. Nine days after the symphony's premiere, Tchaikovsky was dead, probably from cholera picked up from drinking unboiled water.

He is buried in St Petersburg, alongside many of Russia's leading composers. But, both professionally and personally, he remained an outsider from the tradition they represented, a man apart.

But in the end this music can, must and does stand on its own: brilliantly tuneful, thrillingly rhythmic, fabulously orchestrated and intriguingly put together. Tchaikovsky's is a complex story which bears rich fruits.

Writing in the 1890s, Anton Rubinstein offered the view that the death of Schumann nearly four decades earlier had marked the end of music. In his view, the music which had followed Schumann had emphasised 'excess of colouring at the expense of drawing; of technique at the expense of thought; of frame at the expense of picture'.[67]

Rubinstein thought the Romantic symphony had gasped its last.

Rubinstein was wrong.

14

ELEPHANTS, ARIAS AND THE GODS AT TWILIGHT: OPERA

National Styles: German Romantic Opera

Towards the end of the eighteenth century, the short but brilliant compositional career of Mozart drew many historical threads of his operatic inheritance together.

The oldest, opera seria, re-emerged during the nineteenth century, first as 'grand heroic opera', then as 'grand opera'. Opera buffa, sixty or seventy years old when Mozart died in 1791, led to no real lasting tradition outside the comic operas of Rossini. The youngest of Mozart's formal models, the German Singspiel, turned out to be the most fruitful, at least in Germany. In the words of Mozart's biographer Alfred Einstein, '*Die Zauberflöte* became the starting-point of German opera; without it there would have been perhaps no *Freischütz* or *Oberon*, no *Vampyr* or *Hans Heiling*, and consequently no *Tannhäuser* or *Lohengrin* or anything else that followed these.'[1] *Die Zauberflöte* gave German Romantic opera its woodland setting, themes of magic, rescue and redemption, dark and light, and tuneful, colourful style still audible a hundred years later in the naïve charm of Engelbert Humperdinck's *Hänsel und Gretel* of 1893.

Most leading Austro-German composers attempted to tap into the popularity of opera, including a number better known for other things.

Haydn wrote lots of stage works. *L'anima del filosofo*, his account of those hardy operatic perennials Orpheus and Eurydice, contains intriguing beauties like solos flowing freely from recit to cavatina (a song-like form which came to replace the older da capo aria), and a vivid role for the chorus. Written in the same year as *Die Zauberflöte*, 1791, it had to wait 160 years for its premiere, when the lead was created by Maria Callas.

Beethoven's *Fidelio* is an essay in fidelity and political morality as much as a true work of theatre, but its long gestation wrung some superb music and perhaps surprisingly effective drama from the conventions of the prison scene, the emergence from darkness into light, *deus ex machina* and a buffa-style subplot. Beethoven is not best known as a joker (telling the opera's patient sponsor, Baron Braun, 'I don't write for the galleries'),[2] but he did apparently deliberately try to catch out the baritone Sebastian Meier, second husband of Mozart's sister-in-law Josefa Hofer, with the off-set accompaniment to one of his arias: 'my brother-in-law would never have written such damned nonsense,' snooted Meier.[3]

Schubert wrote a number of Singspiels, several left unfinished, and at least one song to be dropped into someone else's opera ('*Nein, nein, nein, nein, das ist zu viel*' for Ferdinand Hérold's *Das Zauberglöckchen* (*The Magic Bell*) of 1817 – magical musical instruments were all the rage; Schubert also wrote music for a play called *Die Zauberharfe* (*The Magic Harp*)). Operas proper include the unfinished *Sakuntala* of 1820, based on a Sanskrit story and featuring roles for fourteen sopranos, three altos, five tenors and nine basses, and, most importantly, *Alfonso und Estrella* of 1822, and *Die Verschworenen* and *Fierrabras*, both 1823. *Fierrabras* was set up as direct competition to the star appeal of Rossini at Vienna's court opera house: it never even made it through the stage door.

Mendelssohn's brief career as an opera composer left few ripples in the repertoire or his reputation. *Die Hochzeit des Camacho* is an early work even by his standards, started in 1824 when he was fifteen. Another domestic offering, *Die Heimkehr aus der Fremde*, was written for Mendelssohn's parents' wedding anniversary when he was on a visit to Wales in 1829, and includes an aria tailored to the musical abilities of his brother-in-law Wilhelm Hensel (it's all on one note). *Die Hochzeit* is a little charmer, a bit like Mozart at a similar age.

Louis Spohr put *Faust* on stage in 1813 (not, on this occasion, derived from Goethe's work of 1808, as many later operatic settings were), later replacing the spoken dialogue with recitative, turning it from a Singspiel into a grand opera, emblem of changing tastes. His other opera, *Jessonda* (1822), included ballet and spectacle from the start.

Schumann was long fascinated by the operatic potential of traditional tales and themes like the Nibelung legends, Lohengrin and

Till Eulenspiegel. The plot of his only opera, *Genoveva*, written in 1849, is a medieval tale of love and revenge containing some notably Wagnerian elements including the through-composed music and lack of vocal display.

The best, and most important, creator of German Romantic opera after Mozart was his cousin-in-law, Carl Maria von Weber. Some of the roots of his art were not German at all: his biographer John Warrack says that Weber, in his work as pioneering director of the opera in Prague, 'was in fact almost literally setting the scene for the appearance of German and Romantic opera; and to this end it was necessary to go to French opera'.[4] He staged works by Grétry, Boieldieu, Méhul and the Paris-based Cherubini, as well as the 'scale and din' of Spontini:[5] 'there was simply not enough German opera worthy of taking the centre of the stage ... until he himself had shown the way'.[6]

Regarding Italian opera, Weber thought the wildly popular Rossini was 'the sirocco wind blowing from the South, whose heat will soon be cooled',[7] and regretted the Italianisation of his friend Meyerbeer:

> [T]here must be something seriously wrong with the digestive powers of Italian stomachs for a genius of such original powers as Meyerbeer to have felt it necessary, not merely to have set nothing but sweet, luxuriantly swollen fruit on the table, but also to have sugared it over in this fashion-manner.[8]

Prophetically, Weber told his bosses at the theatre in Prague, 'The German digs deeper [than the Italian]; he wants a work of art in which all parts form themselves into a beautiful whole ... I consider nothing secondary, for art knows of no trifles'.[9] His appointment to Dresden in 1817 was part of a deliberate strategy to found a German opera, challenging the received view that only Italians could sing (Frederick the Great had said that his horse could sing an aria better than a German prima donna). Weber battled heroically against the Dresdeners' lack of taste and talent to stage seasons in which fully two-thirds of the premieres were of German operas, despite the fact that only a couple of dozen such pieces existed. He satirised operatic fads in the person of Hanswurst (Sausage Hans), the operatic ringmaster in his early autobiographical novel, started in 1809, *Tonkünstlers Leben* (*A Composer's Life*): an Italian opera opens with 'a noise made in the orchestra to shut the audience up – that's called an overture in Italian' and features a soprano who has a single facial expression and ends her aria with a ten-bar trill, bringing the house down; in French opera 'the action takes place between twelve o'clock and midday' (a dig at French adherence to the fossilised Aristotelean unities);[10] German opera is peopled with ghosts, minnesingers, hermits, robbers and a walk-on part for Brünnhilde.

Weber's own operas stand like a source book of German Romanticism: folk-like song style moving to a fully through-composed multi-sectional scena aria like Agathe's beautiful *'Leise, leise'* in *Der Freischütz* of 1821; slapstick like the Blind Man's Buff trio in the Singspiel *Peter Schmoll und seine Nachbarn*, written in 1801–2, when he was fifteen; flirtation with the exotic in *Abu Hassan* (1811) and, in 1809, the incidental music to Friedrich Schiller's *Turandot*. Orchestral innovations in *Der Freischütz* include the eerie sound of basset horns and recorders and, above all, the atmospheric evocations of the supernatural in the Wolf's Glen scene. Most striking are the many pre-echoes of Wagner, who declared over Weber's grave that 'there has never lived a more German composer than you'.[11] The critic Philipp Spitta compared Weber with his rival Spontini: 'it soon became evident that the chief effect of the latter was astonishment, while the former set the pulse of the German people beating'.[12] So it has proved. German opera owes everything to *Die Zauberflöte* and *Der Freischütz*.

The key figure in the swirling mists of German Romantic opera between Weber and Wagner was Heinrich Marschner.

In 1813 Byron wrote of a corpse that was condemned to 'ghostly haunt thy native place / And suck the blood of all thy race'.[13] Three years later Byron took part in the celebrated ghost story competition in the Villa Diodati on the shores of Lake Geneva (the event which also gave the world Mary Shelley's *Frankenstein*). His tale was published by another of those present, John William Polidori, in 1819 as *The Vampyre*, and formed the basis for Marschner's most famous opera. *Der Vampyr* was performed in Leipzig in 1828 to great success; a breathless tale of witches' sabbaths, midnight bells and virgin sacrifice full of vivid dramatic touches like spoken melodrama over orchestral backing, a spitting chorus of ghosts and 'unnatural' time signatures. *Hans Heiling* followed in 1833. Both operas featured members of the ubiquitous Devrient family, Eduard as librettist and principal baritone, delivering Hans's fine aria *'An jenem tag'* (despite Hans being dead).

Marschner was a true artist of the theatre; if not, in the high-minded Wagnerian sense, of the drama. Schumann, perceptively, accused him of 'beauty without truth'.[14] *Der Vampyr* can remind English listeners of Gilbert and Sullivan's later *Ruddigore*. Far more interesting are the links into Wagner: Wagner added an allegro to an aria from *Der Vampyr*; *Hans Heiling* places the orchestral overture second, after a sung prologue, psychologically linking the scenes as well as covering a scene change; when Hans's rival Konrad strikes him, his knife shatters mid-blow; the Queen of the Underworld's aria '*Sonst bist du verfallen*' provides a musical pre-echo of the question-and-answer scene between Siegmund and Brünnhilde in Act Two of *Die Walküre*.

Among other occasional stirrers of the bubbling cauldron of German Romantic opera, the Prussian-born, Rome-based Otto Nicolai composed several comedies in Italian and just one in German, *Die lustigen Weiber von Windsor* of 1848, and was reaching fame and position in Vienna and Berlin when he died suddenly in 1849, at the age of thirty-eight. Another border-hopper was Karl Goldmark, a Hungarian-born Jewish composer and theatre violinist based (mostly) in Vienna, composer of Brahmsian chamber music, a fine orchestrator and (briefly) Sibelius's teacher. Goldmark's *Die Königin von Saba* of 1875 is a French-style grand opera with plenty of exotic colour. Verdi greeted its popularity in Italy in the late 1870s with the comment, 'We're nearly there; another step and we shall all be completely Germanized.'[15]

Lurline of 1847 is a tale of nymphs, gnomes, Rhinemaidens and, fascinatingly, a ring with magical properties which is stolen and thrown into the Rhine, leading to mass destruction in a flood. It was composed not by a German but by a widely travelled Irishman who became known as 'the Australian Paganini', William Wallace. Described by Berlioz as 'a perfect eccentric',[16] he went whaling in the South Seas, married a Maori called Tatéa who cooked him a meal of fern roots, iguana and duck, played and conducted in South America, Mexico and the Caribbean before heading to London to stage his operas, including *Maritana* of 1845 (apparently the inspiration for Gilbert and Sullivan's *The Yeomen of the Guard*) and *The Amber Witch*, based on a popular novel about seventeenth-century witchcraft which turned out to be a Chatterton-style hoax.

Back in Germany, Peter Cornelius was the child of actors,

brought up in the same cultured circle as his older contemporary Mendelssohn in Berlin. The 1858 Weimar premiere of his *Der Barbier von Bagdad*, an unsatisfactory mixture of buffa plot and highly strung Wagnerian music, caused a rift between its conductor, Cornelius's friend Liszt, and his employers. Cornelius moved at Wagner's behest to Munich in 1864, but wisely declined Wagner's invitation to act as a sort of live-in musical amanuensis:

> Either you accept my invitation and settle yourself immediately for your whole life in the same house with me, or you disdain me, and expressly abjure all desire to unite yourself with me. In the latter case, I abjure you also, root and branch and never admit you again in any way into my life.

'I should not write a note ... I should be no more than a piece of spiritual furniture to him,' thought Cornelius.[17]

Right at the end of the Romantic century Engelbert Humperdinck looked deliberately and charmingly backwards through the woods in *Hänsel und Gretel*. Richard Strauss conducted the 1893 premiere in Weimar; it was to be German Romantic opera's last bow, tasting of gingerbread and sprinkled with sugar, before Strauss pushed on into a new, more disturbing century.

Bel Canto and Italian Opera

'Bel canto' ('beautiful singing') is one of those terms which clearly means something important, without it being entirely clear exactly what it does mean. In the hands of three composers born around the turn of the nineteenth century, Gioachino Rossini, Gaetano Donizetti and Vincenzo Bellini, the term came to encompass a vocal style which allies a whole aviary of vocal acrobatics to a basic simplicity and beauty of line: long, leisurely tunes ushering in arias fashioned in contrasting sections.

Two comments capture the contrast with the German approach. In 1824 Giuseppe Carpani said that the opera composer's 'chief duty ... is to offer *musical* delight', treating 'the *cantilena* as his primary aim, as the *sine qua non* of his science' and avoiding Germanic 'music of bumps, of clashes, of caprices ... song that is not song'.[18] Meanwhile, the German poet Heinrich Heine summed up the view that the foppish and frivolous Italian opera was not to be taken seriously when he described Bellini as 'a sigh in dancing pumps'.[19]

A symbol of the popularity of the Italian manner was the Théâtre-Italien in Paris, the latest incarnation of the venerable quarrel between native French opera and its imported southern cousin. Composers featured there included Ferdinando Paër, an Italian of Austrian descent, Domenico Cimarosa, a native of Naples whose most famous comedy, Il matrimonio segreto (1792), was seen a hundred times by Stendhal and twice in one evening by Emperor Leopold II in Vienna, and Giovanni Paisiello, favourite of Napoleon and composer of Il barbiere di Siviglia (1782), wittier and faster than Cimarosa's opera and featuring some brilliantly skilful ensemble finale writing.

An Italian with links to a different Parisian tradition was the composer whose Europa riconosciuta opened La Scala, Milan in 1778, accomplished composer of Singspiel and tragédie lyrique, who found operatic fashion leaving him behind after about 1800, devoting himself to church music, charitable causes and performing other men's music: Antonio Salieri.

Creative careers come in all sorts of different shapes. Rossini, Donizetti and Bellini died in the opposite order to that in which they were born. The oldest, Rossini, produced operas with an almost miraculous fluency up to the age of about thirty-seven, and then stopped altogether. Bellini died young, and Donizetti went mad (as, in both cases, did quite a lot of their characters).

In 1824 Stendhal hailed a new operatic hero, claiming rather breathlessly, 'Napoleon is dead; but a new conqueror has already shown himself to the world.'[20] Gioachino Rossini was born in Pesaro in 1792. His first success, a farce for Venice called La cambiale di matrimonio, staged when he was eighteen, opened an astonishing period of creativity: thirty-four operas in thirteen years, including five premieres in three cities during 1812 alone. In 1824 he turned his attentions to Paris, producing four operas all involving some kind of reworking from Italian to French, then, in 1829, his only entirely original work in French, the remarkable and groundbreaking Guillaume Tell (William Tell). Then he stopped.

Naturally, such fecundity involved a good deal of self-borrowing and some formularity – source of the term 'Code Rossini'. Rossini was a brilliant writer of overtures: a slow introduction, cantabile woodwind melody, then his trademark crescendo built on a naggingly repeated melodic motif, ending in an exhilarating pile-up. His harmonies are almost obsessively simple. Repetition is key at the local level, too: many of his faster melodies circle around a single note, like a sort of musical itch, as in the famous galloping finale of the *Guillaume Tell* overture. He specialised in the sectional cavatina aria, pure legato cantabile giving way to a dazzling display of runs and high notes known as a cabaletta (with brilliant ornamentation carefully notated by the composer, rather than added ad lib by the singer, as in previous ages). The old Metastasian model of static arias and recits advancing the action is replaced by a quick-fire succession of solos, duets and ensembles.

Rossini wrote in many operatic genres. It was comedy that suited him best. His version of *Il barbiere di Siviglia*, written in 1816 when he was just twenty-four, holds an effortless place in the repertoire with its wit, patter, variety, vivacious overture, colourful characters, great tunes, engagingly silly plot, vocal wizardry, bouncy orchestration and limitless supply of perfect cadences.

It is easy to point out Rossini's limitations. George Bernard Shaw at his most crotchety sniffed that Rossini was 'one of the greatest masters of claptrap that ever lived'.[21] Stendhal was surely overstepping to describe him as a 'revolutionary'.[22] Perhaps Europe, and Paris in particular, had had enough of revolutionaries of all kinds.

Opera didn't stop when Rossini stopped opera

Donizetti was born in 1797, Bellini in 1801, both thus reaching operatic maturity just as Rossini was staging his withdrawal in the late 1820s. Donizetti built on the success of his early, frankly Rossinian comedies by expanding his range with *Anna Bolena* of 1830 and *L'elisir d'amore* of 1832. The less prolific Bellini softened the brittle glitter of the Rossini style, but could incorporate the Rossinian brand of vocal gestures when singer and circumstance demanded (as in the complex, subtle and justly celebrated aria 'Casta diva' from *Norma*, written in 1831 for the soprano Giuditta Pasta). Bellini spent the early 1830s travelling widely and indulging in all the usual antics of operatic types, including frantic womanising, voluminous letter-writing, falling out with journalists and librettists, negotiating with managements and temperamental singers and establishing a notable reputation with works including the opera semiseria *La sonnambula* of 1831. In early 1835 both men tried their hand in the most important venue for Italian opera outside Italy, Paris's Théâtre-Italien: Bellini's *I puritani* was a big success; Donizetti's *Marin Faliero* was not. In September that year Bellini died suddenly from an infection, aged just thirty-five: days later Donizetti's *Lucia di Lammermoor* premiered in Naples, his most enduring masterpiece.

Donizetti's last active decade was marked by dramas of all kinds, on and off stage. Money worries (including having to support his ageing parents and younger brother), legal tussles and rows with promoters and dilatory librettists diluted his energy and talents. He travelled, continuing to feed the fads for operas set in Tudor England (creating a memorable, if probably not entirely authentic, dynasty of operatic queens) and Walter Scott's Scotland. In 1842, in a perhaps surprising move, he took up the old-fashioned position of Imperial Kapellmeister in Vienna, Mozart's old job. A year later the comedy *Don Pasquale* earned him what one critic described as 'one of those ovations ... which in Paris are reserved for the truly great'.[23] His personal life had some similarities with that of his younger contemporary (and a diametrically different musician), Schumann. Like Schumann, he married a younger woman, daughter of family friends, whom he first met when she was a young girl; unlike Schumann, she and their three children all predeceased him. Like Schumann, he suffered a mental and physical collapse exacerbated by syphilis, carefully cared for by his solicitous nephew as he declined into institutionalised silence and insanity. He died in Bergamo in 1848. In a little under thirty active years he had composed over seventy operas.

Rossini made a curious return to composition around 1855 with the small-scale pieces which he called *Péchés de vieillesse* (*Sins of Old Age*) for the soirées held after his return to Paris, including a charming but eccentric setting of the Mass for voices, two pianos and harmonium. Rossini died in 1868. He remains a brilliant original, injecting his unique, if limited, gestures with an unmistakable charm and vitality all his own. Giuseppe Mazzini said of him that he 'neither destroyed nor transformed the characteristics of the old Italian school, he reconsecrated them'.[24]

Another leading Italian opera composer, Saverio Mercadante, summed up his own place in operatic history in a letter written on 1 January 1838, exactly one year before the premiere of his most important opera, *Elena da Feltre*:

> I have continued the revolution I began with *Il giuramento* [his acclaimed opera of the previous year]: forms varied, vulgar cabalettas banished, crescendos out, a narrower tessitura, fewer repeats, more originality in the cadences, emphasis on the drama, orchestra rich but not so as to swamp the voices in the ensembles, no long solos, which force the other parts to stand coldly by to the detriment of the action, not much bass drum, and a lot less brass.[25]

It's a pretty good statement of developments in dramatic technique between Rossini and Verdi. Two younger composers lived to the late decades of the century but looked back to the song-like tunefulness of bel canto rather than forward into the cinematic splash and colour of verismo: Amilcare Ponchielli is known today for just one opera, *La Gioconda*, which contains several memorable and well-known individual numbers; the reputation of the short-lived Alfredo Catalani rests on even narrower foundations, a single aria, '*Ebben? Ne andrò lontana*' from *La Wally*.

These men provide the hinterland for the greatest Italian of all, Giuseppe Verdi.

France: Grand Opera

Opera, like everything else in France, had to negotiate its way through the revolutionary and Napoleonic periods and everything which followed. Sometimes this shows up on stage, usually disguised in symbolic form in the plot (*Figaro* and *Fidelio* provide two examples from other parts of the operatic repertoire, with their very different critiques of arbitrary authority). More directly, political change impacted opera in terms of composers wrangling for favour within the rapidly changing courts, kings and coteries, and in the use to which their music was put off-stage.

An aria from André Grétry's 1784 opera *Richard Coeur-de-lion* was sung at a banquet given for the officers of the Versailles garrison in 1789. Grétry studied in Italy, but favoured the dramatic clarity of the French opéra comique (meaning opera with spoken dialogue rather than anything necessarily comic). He said of his opera, 'the subject as a whole does not call for music more than any other. I will go further: the drama ought really to be spoken.'[26] In a well-used operatic conceit, he allowed his troubadour Blondel to present his aria *'Une fièvre brûlante'* as a song-within-an-opera. He also experimented with exotic instruments like the tuba curva, derived from ancient Rome.

The 1790s were marked by the rivalry of three composers of historical-classical comédies and opéras comiques, many to libretti by François-Benoît Hoffman: Étienne Méhul, Jean-François Le Sueur and Luigi Cherubini. As always, the French loved their pamphlet wars: Le Sueur wrote an *Exposé* of church music in 1787 and a *Projet ... de l'instruction musicale en France* in 1802, violently criticising the Paris Conservatoire, each of which cost him his current job. Weber staged Méhul's works in Prague, including *Joseph* of 1807, which Weber considered 'a real masterpiece',[27] and *Uthal* of 1806, based on the Ossian legends, conjuring their northern gloom and misty forests through an orchestra with no violins.

The Italian Cherubini is the most substantial of the three. Born in Florence in 1760, he settled in France following a brief period in London, where several of his operas were performed. In 1790 he adopted a French version of his forenames, Marie-Louis-Charles-Zénobi-Salvador. Early successes were the highly original hybrid *Lodoïska*, a rescue opera, of 1791, and *Elisa*, in 1794, which stretches theatrical technology by having one of a pair of lovers swept away in an avalanche. Most significant were *Médée* of 1797, a gruesome tale of mythical infanticide with one of the first starring roles for a stratospherically unhinged soprano, and, in 1800, *Les deux journées*, the politically explicit story of a Savoyard water carrier who hides a parliamentarian and his wife from Cardinal Mazarin, ending with an exhortation that *'la première charme de la vie c'est de servir l'humanité'* ('the greatest joy in life is the service of humanity').[28] The influence on Beethoven is clear: Beethoven told Cherubini, 'I prize your theatrical works beyond others.'[29]

The opening of the nineteenth century saw the beginning of the taste for lighter entertainment, exemplified by the work of François-Adrien Boieldieu, to whom Berlioz ascribes the belief that 'it is always possible to be graceful',[30] and was put through what the critic John Warrack calls 'a stiff course of counterpoint' with Cherubini.[31] Boieldieu stands as heir to the tuneful style of Grétry in works like his best-known opera, *La Dame blanche* of 1825. Following the failure of his marriage (to a dancer, in true French style) in 1804, Boieldieu worked successfully for the Tsar Alexander I in St Petersburg, returning to Paris in 1810, where he died in 1834. Today, the Parisian square which hosts the gilded home of the Opéra-Comique is called Place Boieldieu.

Among emerging differences between the French and German styles were different attitudes to spoken text. German opera moved away from musical numbers linked by spoken dialogue, Singspiel-style, towards the characteristic model of through-composed, or continuous, music, with the action knitted together by passages of descriptive or psychologically pertinent orchestral music. In 1816 E. T. A. Hoffmann said that 'opera rent asunder by dialogue is a monstrous thing, and we tolerate it merely because we are used to it'.[32] French composers held on to the idea for rather longer, as late as Bizet's *Carmen* in 1875.

In 1807 the selection committee of the Paris Opéra considered a piece composed a couple of years earlier by an Italian known so far to the Parisian public for successful but conventional opera buffa written in Naples and Rome earlier in his career. The new piece was something different: a big, noisy tragédie lyrique, in French. The committee, including Cherubini, was unimpressed. The Empress Joséphine herself intervened. The result was the dazzling success of the opera which has probably suffered the biggest historical fall from triumph to oblivion: *La Vestale* by Gaspare Spontini.

Premiered in December 1807, *La Vestale* is the highly charged story of a votary of the Roman order of Vesta. Berlioz praised 'its shower of burning ideas, its heartfelt tears, its stream of noble, touching, proud, and threatening melodies, its harmonies so full of warmth and colour, its modulations never before heard on stage, its vital orchestral writing, its truth, its depth of expression', contrasting them with 'the barefacedness with which certain Italian maestros reproduce the same cadences, the same phrases and the same pieces in their countless scores' and noting the way Spontini used seemingly 'eccentric' enharmonic modulations only for 'plausible motives', unlike 'those restless, uninspired composers who, tired of uselessly worrying one key without result, shift to another in the hope of better luck'. Tellingly, Berlioz observes that 'the instruments are the actors'. Typically, he backs up his critique with carefully chosen technical examples: divided violas; weak-beat stresses; dissonances resolved in a different part; the High Priest slipping majestically from D flat major to C major on the line 'Will they plunge the world into chaos?'[33]

Such overheated enthusiasm, coupled with Spontini's histrionic character and demanding methods (he insisted on forty-two rehearsals for the Berlin production of *Olympie*, causing even the king to baulk at the expense, and delaying the premiere of *Der Freischütz*, which had to make do with a mere sixteen rehearsals), was always going to lead to an element of reaction. Meyerbeer overtook him in popularity. In the 1840s Spontini took up a post in Berlin, then returned to Italy, where he died in 1851.

La Vestale's overt Romanticism and theatrical verve were remarkable for 1807. It had over 200 performances by 1830, including in Sweden, Italy and America. Wagner conducted it in Dresden in 1844, with his muse Wilhelmine Schröder-Devrient in the starring role: the influence on his own ancient Roman grand opera, *Rienzi*, premiered a couple of years earlier, is clear. Back in the Marche, Spontini's home town of Maiolati was renamed Maiolati Spontini after him.

By contrast, by the early twenty-first century reputable histories of opera can go as far as not mentioning Spontini at all – not so much as a footnote or index entry. History, like opera, performs funny tricks. It can make people disappear.

Méhul's pupil Ferdinand Hérold displays a number of key themes in this story: an early winner of the Prix de Rome, he regularly collaborated with other composers, including Boieldieu, Auber and Halévy, and helped promote the ballet from operatic insert to art form in its own right with *La Fille mal gardée* of 1828.

Cherubini and Le Sueur walked warily through the shifting game of Parisian musical politics, becoming members of the Académie des Beaux-Arts and leading lights of the Paris Conservatoire, where pupils included Berlioz, Gounod and Ambroise Thomas. Outside the opera house, Le Sueur introduced an orchestra to Notre Dame; Cherubini wrote a fine Requiem in commemoration of the anniversary of the execution of Louis XVI. Le Sueur died in 1837, Cherubini in 1842. Cherubini remains one of very few composers to have matched a reputation in the opera house with substantial achievement in church and chamber music. His treatise on counterpoint and fugue, published when he was eighty, in 1841, is a model of clarity. Berlioz paints him in later life as a grumpy old pedant, and Adolphe Adam said of him, 'his temper was very even, because he was always angry'.[34] But he had many friends across the artistic spectrum, including Rossini and Chopin and the painter Jean-Auguste-Dominique Ingres. He is buried close to his friend Chopin in Père Lachaise cemetery, resting place of so many artistic ghosts of Paris's past.

Like Metastasio and Goldoni in the eighteenth century, a librettist holds the key to the next important development in French opera. Eugène Scribe perfected the idea of the *'pièce bien faite'* ('well-made play'). His words were set by Boieldieu, Auber, Rossini, Meyerbeer, Verdi, Halévy, Donizetti and many others. Like Goldoni, his plays, as well as bespoke libretti, were also set to music, including by Francesco Cilea in the early years of the twentieth century. He pioneered working with a team of writers, using specialists in jokes, arias, dialogue etc., with himself as a sort of committee chair, an influential idea. Plots typically feature a colourful fantastical or historical setting, vivid if stereotypical character types, some twist or secret leading to a moment of crisis, and maybe a convenient natural disaster or violent death: the basic ingredients of French grand opera.

Naturally, not everyone approved. Alexandre Dumas *fils* called him a *'prestidigitateur de première force'* ('a Grade A conjuror'), and Théophile Gautier described him as *'un auteur dénué de poésie, de lyrisme, de style, de philosophie, de vérité, de naturel'* ('a writer denuded of poetry, lyricism, style, philosophy, truth, and all that is natural').[35]

The German composer known to us so far as Jacob Beer had added the prefix Meyer to his surname on the death of his maternal grandfather in 1811. Mixed fortunes with his early attempts at writing opera in German convinced him that he needed to study in Italy, where he heard the music of Rossini (a year younger than him but already a star), spent his family's ample wealth soaking up the sunshine, the folk song and the culture, adopted the Italianate forename Giacomo, and wrote a series of Rossini-esque operas culminating in *Il crociato in Egitto*, first performed in Venice in 1824 and within a year across Italy and in London. For a decade Meyerbeer had been carefully cultivating contacts in the most important operatic centre of all. In September 1825 his patient preparations paid off spectacularly when Rossini organised the Paris premiere of *Il crociato* at the Théâtre-Italien.

In some important respects, *Il crociato in Egitto* marks the end of a phase. It was the last major opera with a role written for a castrato (Giovanni Battista Velluti as Armando, the eponymous crusader), and among the last to feature piano-accompanied recitative, in Rossini's Italian manner. At the same time, it looks forward with its Romantic historical setting, dramatically complex finale to Act One, and emphasis on the orchestra (with two stage bands; later he used three).

Another success of the Paris season of 1825 was *Le maçon* by Daniel Auber: light, tuneful, very French. In 1828 Auber moved towards something decidedly grander with *La muette de Portici*, featuring an explosive historical plot about a real revolt, a large chorus dramatically engaged as the incarnation of *le peuple*, stirring marches, scenic spectacle (including the onstage eruption of Mount Vesuvius) and the obligatory ballet (indeed, the lead role of Fenella, the mute, is given to a ballerina, who tells the story in dance and mime). In 1830 *La muette* was performed in Brussels. At the moment of the Act Four duet '*Amour sacré de la patrie*', with its cries of '*À la gloire! À la gloire!*' the crowd 'exploded irresistibly … they booed the fifth act in order to stop the performance' and ran 'out of the hall and into history',[36] joining another crowd outside in the riots which led to revolution and the founding of modern Belgium. (The riot, and the opera's role, had in fact been carefully planned in advance with well-placed agitation in the newspapers; there was even a poster advertising the date of the revolution.)

As always, styles and traditions overlapped. In 1831 Ferdinand Hérold diverted the Parisian public from its own revolutionary problems with *Zampa*, an opéra comique about a pirate. Hérold died in 1833. His struggles with librettists of varying quality reveal a fault line in the emerging French style: music and drama were not always well aligned. Wagner was a passionate critic of 'our modern music-maker's trick of building gaudy towers of music upon a hollow, valueless foundation, and playing the rapt and the inspired where all the poetaster's botch is void and flimsy'.[37] The new creature, French grand opera, had its own inbuilt version of this dysfunction, which led to both its colossal popular success at the time and its inevitable failure to last: it privileges spectacle and show over psychology and dramatic truth; what Wagner memorably called 'effects without causes'.[38]

French grand opera from around 1830 can justly be said to rest on three founding works (interestingly, one each by a Frenchman, an Italian and a German): Auber's *La muette de Portici* of 1828; Rossini's *Guillaume Tell* of 1829; and, in 1831, *Robert le diable* by Meyerbeer.

The genesis of *Robert le diable* itself reveals aspects of changing style and taste. Meyerbeer conceived it in 1827 as a three-act opéra comique. Two years later he reworked it in five acts. Further revisions removed all spoken dialogue and added more ballet. The premiere was a sensation, attended by Auber, Berlioz, Halévy, Victor Hugo, Alexandre Dumas and Chopin, who called it a 'masterpiece'.[39] Paris alone saw it over 470 times in Meyerbeer's lifetime. Versions were staged throughout the world. The well-connected music critic Joseph Louis d'Ortigue was one of the first to place Meyerbeer 'at the crossroads where Italian song and German orchestration have to meet'.[40]

Robert features devils, jousting, rocks, ruins, a six-fold wedding, big choral tableaux and, to the audience's deep delight, a ballet of ghostly nuns. Three further operas, *Les Huguenots* (1836), *Le prophète* (1849) and *L'Africaine*, finished the day before the composer's death in 1864, cemented Meyerbeer's vast success. Careers were made, including that of the soprano Cornélie Falcon, who was just eighteen when she created the role of Alice in *Robert*. *Les Huguenots* became the first work performed more than 1,000 times at the Paris Opéra.

Success brought its share of challenges. Meyerbeer's German wife never liked Paris, and he succeeded Spontini as court Kapellmeister in Berlin when the combustible Italian was sacked, shuttling between the two cities, but never completing a long-promised German opera. He was rich, and good at publicity: Berlioz commented neatly that 'Meyerbeer had the luck to be talented and the talent to be lucky';[41] others were simply jealous, or disapproved of the immorality of his plots.

Later French composers built on their inheritance of grand opera, opéra comique and the ballet. Daniel Auber continued to produce operas of both types on a seemingly almost naturally occurring annual cycle, like a fruit tree, such as *Gustave III ou le bal masqué* in 1833 and *Manon Lescaut* in 1856. Typically, some of his stage works were collaborations. One co-composer was a man whose life, and name, pick up a couple of notable strands of this story. Fromental Halévy's unusual forename means 'oat grass', from his birth in 1799 on the day dedicated to that plant in the French Republican Calendar. Halévy, like Meyerbeer, was Jewish: his signature work was *La Juive (The Jewess)* of 1835, widely praised. Its most famous aria, '*Rachel quand du Seigneur*', was a later favourite of the early star of the recording age, the Italian tenor Enrico Caruso, and provided the nickname of the prostitute Rachel in Proust's *À la recherche du temps perdu*.

Adolphe Adam was an Alsatian, like his friend and teacher Hérold. His musical career contains the kind of scenes pictured by

Toulouse-Lautrec, playing the violin in vaudeville and the organ in church, writing cabaret songs and copying parts for Boieldieu. His most famous stage work is a ballet, *Giselle*, of 1841. His operatic manner endures in the Christmas song '*Cantique de Noël*', known to English-speaking choristers as 'O Holy Night'.

Berlioz wrote three operas. None is remotely conventional. *Benvenuto Cellini* is an almost entirely fictionalised rewriting of the memoirs of the Renaissance sculptor Cellini. It began life as an opéra comique, was rejected, rewritten as an opéra semiseria without spoken dialogue, premiered at the Paris Opéra in 1838 where it was hissed throughout, revived (and revised) by the ever-supportive Liszt in Weimar in 1852, was badly received in London the following year, and heard again in Weimar in 1856.

In 1858 Berlioz returned to the stage with one of the most astounding operatic works of the nineteenth century, indeed ever, the five-act, five-hour *Les Troyens*, an attempt to put the *Aeneid*, no less, on stage in Shakespearean form. Berlioz wrote of an encounter with the Princess Wittgenstein, Liszt's partner (or 'devoted friend', as he tactfully called her), in which she cajoled and bullied him to 'face everything for the sake of Dido and Cassandra', despite 'the pain that such an undertaking would inevitably cause me', saying, '[I]f you are so weak as to be afraid of the work ... I do not want to see you ever again.'[42] This account reads like an operatic scene in itself, but it worked. The result was a piece so huge, so ambitious and so unusual that even the big French companies never presented it complete in its composer's lifetime, or long after. Berlioz was forced to accept Acts Three to Five being performed separately, with some alterations.

In 1862 he returned to Shakespeare with *Béatrice et Bénédict*, his own faithful translation of *Much Ado about Nothing*, like Verdi capturing Shakespeare's youthful vivacity and light comic touch despite himself being at the end of his career.

There is much opera in his other works: *L'enfance du Christ* is a rich, moving, loose-limbed psychodrama with a magnificent solo scena for Herod pondering his responsibility for the massacre of the innocents; *La damnation de Faust* is a '*légende dramatique*' which thoroughly baffled its audience at the Paris Opéra. 'Nothing in my career as an artist wounded me more deeply than this unexpected indifference,' recalled Berlioz sadly.[43]

Charles Gounod tackled Goethe's *Faust* five years after Berlioz, in 1859. The progress of his version tracks many of the forces at work on a successful opera. The original French-style spoken dialogue was replaced with recitative for a successful European tour from 1861. In Germany the work was known as *Margarethe* or *Gretchen* after the other lead (Arrigo Boito made Mephistopheles his title character). It was heard in England in 1863 (in Italian) and again in 1864 (in English), when Gounod supplied a new song based on a tune in the overture, which, translated back into French, became one of its best-known arias, '*Avant de quitter ces lieux*'. An 1869 Paris revival added what opera historians Carolyn Abbate and Roger Parker call 'the obligatory ballet and other bulk items'.[44] The slow transformation into the by-now increasingly obsolescent grand opera was complete.

But the process only emphasised that the old models of Meyerbeer were becoming an expensive thing of the past. Gounod's skill was to realise this. Scarred by the failure of his *La nonne sanglante* in 1854, he fashioned *Faust* with care and concision: a small cast, Meyerbeerian longueurs curtailed. Perhaps, above all, he put the emphasis back on the art of song, offering the age's finest singers three roles – Faust the philosopher, Méphistophélès the familiar spirit of Hell, and Marguerite at her spinning wheel – to make their own and define their careers.

One who did just that was the Swedish soprano Christine Nilsson. (Newland Archer, Edith Wharton's leisurely opera-goer in *The Age of Innocence*, notes that the 'unalterable and unquestioned law of the musical world required that the German text of French operas sung by Swedish artists should be translated into Italian for the clearer understanding of English-speaking audiences. This seemed as natural to Newland Archer as all the other conventions on which his life was moulded'.) Gounod played those conventions with skill and grace. Even in New York, 'the boxes always stopped talking during the Daisy Song [from *Faust*]'.[45] Success doesn't come much bigger than that.

The next, and last, generation of nineteenth-century French opera composers carried their tradition into *La Belle Époque*. Some tried to fossilise the old style; others introduced an exotic touch of the new.

King of the first approach was Ambroise Thomas. After some attempts at comedy, his two big successes were *Mignon* (1866) and *Hamlet* (1868), written in his mid-fifties, fairly radical adaptations of, respectively, Goethe (including an identity-defying, double-cross-dressing Mignon) and Shakespeare (with ballet).

In 1871 the elderly Auber was caught up in the violence surrounding the Paris Commune: one of his horses, Almaviva, was requisitioned and eaten by the starving Parisians; the other, Figaro, survived by being hidden in a piano shop. Auber died the same year. Thomas, himself aged sixty, volunteered for the National Guard, and later succeeded Auber as director of the Paris Conservatoire, where he fought to keep out dangerous modernists like Fauré (successfully) and Franck (unsuccessfully), and to shield his students from the music of Wagner and, oddly, Rameau. But within his conservative vision he ran an efficient faculty, employing many fine teachers who shared his outlook.

The year 1875 brought the premiere of another opera composed by a much younger fellow member of the National Guard, *Carmen* by Georges Bizet. Poor Bizet was destined to give the world some of its favourite operatic music, but never to know it. Born in 1838, he was a brilliant student, winner of the Prix de Rome, praised as a composer by Berlioz and as a pianist by Liszt. But his restless early attempts to negotiate a new way through the tastes of conservative Paris brought little but frustration and several abandoned projects. His two operas to reach the stage in the 1860s, *Les pêcheurs de perles* of 1863 and *La jolie fille de Perth* of 1867, found little popular success. His personal life was mixed: in 1863 he fathered a son with the family housekeeper, and in 1869 he married the daughter of his late teacher Halévy, Geneviève. He wrote an unsuccessful opera, *Djamileh*, in 1871, some incidental music and a long-promised completion of his late father-in-law's opera *Noé*, although it was not performed until 1885, ten years after his own death. Buffeted around France with his wife and child by the upheavals of 1870–71, Bizet was delighted once hostilities were over with a commission from the Opéra-Comique. Tussles about the subject ended with the resignation of the manager Adolphe de Leuven, and Bizet set to work on a libretto by his cousin-in-law Ludovic Halévy and Henri Meilhac based on a story of 1845 by Prosper Mérimée about a Spanish gypsy girl called Carmen. The opera included spoken dialogue, obligatory at the Opéra-Comique. It also had the Opéra-Comique's first ever tragic ending (the *crime passionnel* in which José murders Carmen out of jealousy). Rehearsals, though delayed, went well. The opera's keenly anticipated premiere in March 1875 was attended by Massenet, Offenbach, Delibes and Gounod. The first act was well received. Then things got frosty. Halévy, the librettist, recorded that the Toreador's song in Act Two was met with 'coldness'. Gounod apparently cried out 'that melody is mine'[46] when Micaëla introduced her Act Three aria (the scholar Winton Dean thinks that Bizet made better use of it than Gounod, Handel-fashion[47]). Act Four's reception was 'glacial from first to last'.[48] Reviewers disagreed about whether to disapprove more of the immorality of the plot or the 'Wagnerisms' of the orchestration. The run continued, often to half-empty houses. The other big new work heard at the Opéra that season, Verdi's Requiem, fared far better. On 3 June, his wedding anniversary, Bizet died of a heart attack. He was thirty-six. *Carmen* had had thirty-three performances.

It seems barely credible today that its first audiences failed to thrill to the tunes, the rhythms, the hot-blooded passion and the swirling dresses of Bizet's opera. But it wasn't what they were used to. Bizet's father-in-law Halévy had inserted a 'boléro' into *La Juive*, but its concessions to Iberian fire extend to little more than its 3/4 time signature. Art more widely was beginning to experiment with exotic settings: as with, for instance, Flaubert in his *Salammbô* period or the paintings of Paul Gaugin and Gustave Moreau. But opera was always uniquely vulnerable to the tussle between art and taste; and taste usually won. Poor Bizet might have agreed with Degas: 'Art is killed by taste.'[49] Success for *Carmen* came soon enough, although not, alas, soon enough for its composer.

Another composer to suffer operatic disappointment in 1875 was Camille Saint-Saëns. His *Samson et Dalila* recovered from initial indifference through the influential support of the mezzo-soprano Pauline Viardot and the ever-generous Liszt.

By 1883 taste was a little more open to the tuneful and delicately orchestrated Indian setting of Léo Delibes' opera *Lakmé* (whose most famous number, as for Bizet's *Les pêcheurs de perles*, is a duet). Delibes' principal significance lies in adding depth and variety to France's other main medium of music theatre, the ballet, particularly in *Coppélia* (1870) and *Sylvia* (1876). Tchaikovsky called *Sylvia* '[t]he first ballet in which the music constitutes not just the main, but the sole interest. What charm, what grace, what melodic, rhythmic and harmonic richness.'[50]

Delibes' last opera was finished after his death (like many others) by a friend and colleague, Jules Massenet. Massenet's large output includes over thirty operas covering a wide variety of setting and approach, but always with a well-crafted intelligence based on natural fluency and hard work (he composed from 4.00 a.m. to midday throughout his life). His most famous operas, *Manon* (1884) and *Werther* (1892), are versions of two familiar operatic standbys. Other characters he put on stage include Don Quixote, Cinderella, the Bellringer of Notre Dame and Beaumarchais' sex-crazed page boy Cherubino, in pieces he called *'conte de fées'* ('fairy story'), *'haulte farce musical'*, *'opéra Romanesque'* and all sorts of other whimsical variants. He sits happily and productively between two traditions, a sort of French verismo Wagner, the sunny face of the Belle Époque, troubled only briefly by its difficulties. The author of an enjoyably unreliable memoir and always keen to enjoy himself, he gleefully tells us that, when he won the Prix de Rome in 1863 at the age of twenty-one, Auber told one of the other judges, Berlioz, 'He'll go far, that young rascal, when he's had less experience.'[51]

It had been a long century for French opera, from the Enlightenment Classicism of Grétry, who witnessed the Revolution, through the grand opera period and the huge success of Meyerbeer, to the effervescent glitter on the surface of the Belle Époque.

Today, meanwhile, the spirit of French grand opera survives in a certain type of West End musical. Andrew Lloyd Webber's *The Phantom of the Opera* is set in (or sometimes underneath) the Paris Opéra; it even name-checks the 1831 premiere of *Robert le diable* in its opening scene. Claude-Michel Schönberg's *Les Misérables* is the authentic heir of *La muette de Portici*, the stirring mob defiantly declaiming patriotic songs from the barricades: *'À la gloire!'*; 'Can you hear the people sing?'

Geneviève Bizet, née Halévy, can, by the time of her death in 1926, stand as our long-surviving emblem of the turning times. Daughter of one favourite nineteenth-century opera composer and wife of another, she was also the model for the queenly society salon hostess Oriane, Duchesse de Guermantes, in a novel penned by a schoolfriend of her son's, Marcel Proust, a novel which concerns itself, as perhaps at times she did herself, with *'la recherche du temps perdu'*.

Opera in Russia

Court opera companies from Italy and Germany visited imperial Russia regularly in the eighteenth century. Richard Wagner conducted the Riga opera from 1837 to 1839, describing the city, then part of the Russian empire, to his wife Minna as 'the nicest place in the world – especially when it comes to earning money'.[52] Wagner valued some innovative features of the Riga opera house, including its darkened auditorium, semi-circular seating and lowered orchestra pit, and began his French-style grand opera *Rienzi* there.

Russia ground out its own craggy outcrop of Romantic opera, fashioned around its grand and bloody history and its long-established taste for strong but flawed leaders, and, like all national operatic styles, around the distinctive sound of its native singers and language: listen to recordings of the Russian bass Feodor Chaliapin singing the title role in the defining work of Russian opera, Mussorgsky's *Boris Godunov*, in the 1920s. Along with Maria Callas and Enrico Caruso, Chaliapin forms part of the great trio of Cs of twentieth-century opera singing, and takes his place in the myth of the temperamental backstage star, given to tantrums and drunken brawling (a reputation which may perhaps have been a little exaggerated in the telling).

The basic plotline of Russian Romantic opera concerns the heroic struggles against fate and destiny of some stentorian tsar or prince. Running alongside these grand works are stories derived from Russian folklore or mythology which are lighter in character, though often with darker undertones. Part of the unique contribution of Pyotr Ilyich Tchaikovsky was to embed this psychologically complex narrative element into the outwardly prettified form of the ballet. A key literary source for these works was the short-lived national poet of Romanticism Alexander Pushkin, whose stories provided the framework for operas historical and fantastical, as well as ballets, cantatas, songs and countless other musical works.

Early attempts at a national opera, unsurprisingly, borrowed much of the manner and many of the themes from familiar European models (like the 1792 melodrama *Orfey i Evridika* by Yevstigney Fomin), sometimes incorporating suitably classicised Russian folk melodies, like Haydn and Mozart in their Hungarian and Turkish moods, sometimes fashioning the score from existing popular songs, like English ballad opera. Catherine the Great wrote librettos, and imperial patronage and popular appeal led to the construction of several fine theatres. Between them, Moscow's Bolshoi (opened in 1825) and St Petersburg's Mariinsky (1860) would host Russia's most important operas.

Key themes clang like the bells of St Basil's through the works of the principal pioneers of nationalist opera: *A Life for the Tsar* (1836) and *Ruslan and Lyudmila* (1842) by Mikhail Glinka, and Alexander Dargomyzhsky's *Rusalka* (1856) and *The Stone Guest* (unfinished at his death and first performed in St Petersburg in 1872 in a version completed by César Cui and Nikolai Rimsky-Korsakov). In *A Life for the Tsar* Glinka gives us the chorus-as-the-people, the Tsar as emblem of Holy Russia rising against her oppressors (in this case, Poland), hints of Russian folk melody sumptuously clad in the garb of French grand opera, and a great lead role for the nationalist hero Ivan Susanin (memorably portrayed by the hollow-eyed, long-bearded Chaliapin). *Ruslan and Lyudmila* and *Rusalka* are both derived from stories by Pushkin: Glinka whips up a wonderful overture of Rossinian verve to open his epic tale of banquets, weddings, kidnap, battles, magic rings and talking severed heads, ending with a tableau of rejoicing in young love, the gods and the motherland. Dargomyzhsky colours his depiction of the subaqueous songstresses the Rusalki with an invention of his own, a kind of 'melodic recitative' which maintains a form of speech rhythm in the music. He took the idea further in *The Stone Guest* (the story, familiar from Mozart's *Don Giovanni*, of the statue which turns up to dinner with its murderer). The text is not a purpose-made libretto but a straight stage play (by Pushkin again), so that the dialogue consists largely of people talking to each other, one at a time, rather than overlapping in carefully crafted duets, trios and ensembles. The aim was stark realism. Dargomyzhsky said, 'I want sound directly to express the word. I want truth.'[53]

The idea was a key influence on the group of composers of the next generation (including his two sub-composers), known as The Five. The objective is strikingly similar to the ideals being sought, independently and in another country and language, by Wagner. Perhaps it was Dargomyzhsky's fate to be the prophet, not the priest: his experimental approach (which also includes things like whole-tone scales, through-composition, unconventional use of dissonance and a complete avoidance of key signatures), without Wagner's rich underpinning tapestry of leitmotif, colour and orchestral contribution to the drama, produces long passages which sound like something is about to happen but never quite does. But it provides a fascinating and necessary precursor to the operatic method not just of his countrymen but of later composers like Janáček and, in a very different way, Debussy.

In 1869 Mussorgsky brought the tradition to its full bejewelled maturity with *Boris Godunov*. This enormous opera (like its near-contemporary, Verdi's *Don Carlos*) has a composition history almost as complicated and chequered as the historical events on which it is based. Mussorgsky's first draft was rejected by the committee of the imperial theatre, partly because of the lack of a prominent female lead; in 1871, however, after much cajoling by friends, he produced a second version, which was performed, first in part, then, in January 1874, complete, scoring a triumphant success with the crowd and an almost total failure with the critics. Versions with cuts and re-orderings followed. The full originality and significance of *Boris* had to wait until 1904 for its successful revival at the Mariinsky Theatre in St Petersburg, more than two decades after Mussorgsky's death, with the inevitable Chaliapin in the title role. It is a monumental achievement. The composer fashioned the libretto himself, based on the unavoidable Pushkin, who in turn was attempting the historical sweep and epic characterisation of Shakespeare's history plays. This is all the more remarkable because, at the time of its composition, Mussorgsky was working as a civil servant (partly to finance his drinking).

Borodin's only opera, *Prince Igor*, features another medieval monarch, deflected from the pursuit of his enemies by a solar eclipse. Borodin worked on the score, alongside all his other interests and commitments, for eighteen years, leaving it unfinished at his death in 1887: the completion fell to Rimsky-Korsakov (again) and Glazunov. The music bursts with colour, including the familiar Polovtsian Dances, often performed separately. Borodin's characterful tunefulness led to the dubious posthumous distinction of his melodies turning up in 1953 in an American musical about a talking goat, *Kismet*, including the songs 'Stranger in Paradise' and 'Baubles, Bangles and Beads'.

Balakirev considered several ideas for operas (including the fantastical folk tale *The Firebird*, later memorably turned into a ballet by Stravinsky), but never wrote one, partly because he composed with decadal slowness. César Cui wrote fifteen operas, most on a notably smaller scale than his colleagues, earning a mixed reception, but praise (as ever) from Liszt. 'Music and text have equal rights,' said

Cui, and music 'should impart a more grand embossing quality to the plastic forms of a poetic composition'.[54] Intriguingly, he published a monograph on Wagner's *Ring Cycle* as early as 1876, the year of its first complete performance in Bayreuth. In keeping with the general tenor of the views of The Five he is far from uncritical of Wagner, whose ideas about word-setting, though similar to theirs, developed independently: later writers have tussled over the extent to which Cui could have known the writings, and indeed the music, of Wagner. Cui's other main footprint in operatic history could hardly be more different: children's opera. His *Puss in Boots*, first performed in 1915, became a much-loved and long-standing repertoire piece in Germany, particularly in the pre-unification GDR.

Rimsky-Korsakov's operas cover historical, fantastical and folkloristic subject matter. He said that he regarded them principally as works of music rather than drama: their colourful content is most often heard today in the form of excerpts like 'The Flight of the Bumblebee' from *The Tale of Tsar Saltan* (1900) and 'The Song of the Indian Guest' from *Sadko* (1896). His 1898 opera *Mozart and Salieri* was a key staging post in fixing the (mostly) fictional rivalry between its two title characters in popular culture. Perhaps his most important stage work, *The Golden Cockerel*, written in 1907, fell foul of the censors following the pro-democracy uprising in St Petersburg in 1905 (including demonstrations inside his own workplace, the conservatoire), apparently as a result of its satirical take on autocracy and imperialism, and was never heard in his lifetime.

Tchaikovsky's early operatic efforts included one whose half-finished, handwritten libretto he managed to lose, and, too embarrassed to admit it and ask for a replacement, finished himself. *Eugene Onegin*, based closely on a play by the inevitable Pushkin, premiered in 1879. Success was slow: the story is told in a series of episodes rather than as a continuous narrative; there are no epic sets or grand scene changes; simplicity and sincerity are favoured over spectacle and flash. In a way, the work typified Tchaikovsky's ambivalent position in European music: not French enough for the Europeans; not Russian enough for the Russian nationalists. But the support of conductors like Gustav Mahler in Germany and Henry Wood in England helped earn *Onegin* its lasting popularity, based on its emotional directness, a good story and sheer lyricism. Stravinsky has been proved right: '*Eugene Onegin* is still the opera the public loves best, the one that replenishes the till.'⁵⁵ Tchaikovsky's two last operas, *The Queen of Spades* (1890) and *Iolanta* (1891), had libretti by his brother Modest. Written in Florence in just forty-four days, *The Queen of Spades* combines a large cast partying at the court of Catherine the Great with darker, typically Russian themes, like the fate of a soul resting on the turn of a card, a vengeful ghostly countess, and the grimly laughing hero maniacally declaring that 'Life is just a game' before turning up the fateful Queen of Spades.

Tchaikovsky's other principal contribution to music theatre, and source of some of the best-loved music of all time, comes in his three ballets: *Swan Lake* (1876), *The Sleeping Beauty* (1889) and *The Nutcracker* (1892). Throughout the nineteenth century, and indeed before, ballet had been just one part of the operatic experience, dropped prettily into the piece whether it fitted the plot or not. French composers Hérold, Adam and Delibes liberated the ballet into a free-standing dramatic and narrative art form in its own right. But Tchaikovsky polished and perfected this synthesis of movement and melody, artifice and athleticism, proper acting and sheer elegance, in music perfectly placed by history and character to bring his swans, toys, snowflakes, godfathers, princesses and nutcrackers to waltzing, whirling, leaping life. No art form has ever been so dependent on, or so lavishly endowed with, the rich and simple resource of the tune. In all three cases success was far from instantaneous: ballet, perhaps even more than opera, depends on a perfect meeting of many minds (and muscles), which was not always forthcoming. But charm and a Mozartian economy has earned Tchaikovsky's ballets their sure and certain place in the world's affections (and plenty of theatres and companies a substantial chunk of their annual wage bill). But beneath the charm, as so often with Tchaikovsky, blinks that hint of darkness and danger inherited from earlier versions of the stories by Hoffmann and Grimm, never quite brushed out of sight by the gingerbread and swan feathers.

Slavic Opera

Nineteenth-century Czech opera approaches musical nationalism rather more cheerfully than its tragic-heroic Russian cousin. Its principal practitioners demonstrate once again that a sense of national cultural identity often has little to do with the random political construct called a nation: they include Czechs, Slovaks, Moravians and

Bohemians, sometime citizens of Imperial Austria-Hungary, who studied across Europe, worked in Vienna and Prague, and absorbed the main European currents exemplified by the Brahms/Wagner divide alongside their own heritage of folk tales and tunes.

Ján Bedřich Kittl and Ján Levoslav Bella shared the curious distinction of setting libretti written by (or originating with) Richard Wagner (respectively *Bianca and Giuseppe* (1848) and *Wieland the Blacksmith* (1880–90)). Zdeněk Fibich's 1884 opera *Nevěsta messinská* (*The Bride of Messina*) earned both praise and wariness of its Wagnerisms from its Prague audience. Fibich countered with his choice of the legend of the siren-like Šárka for his next stage piece in 1896. Alas for Fibich, as well as being too cosmopolitan for his contemporaries (his Act Two Amazons are decidedly Valkyrie-esque), he wasn't Czech enough to carve out a niche as a *bona fide* nationalist. A 2001 New York revival intriguingly placed his richly romantic *Šárka* alongside a concise setting of the same legend by the young Janáček, with one critic preferring the Fibich, finding it 'eminently stage-worthy', even though 'there is nothing specifically Czech about it'.[56]

If Fibich foundered on a lack of singing peasants and ululating water sprites, the same cannot be said of the two most famous Czech opera composers of the period, Bedřich Smetana and Antonín Dvořák. Smetana's *Prodaná nevěsta* (*The Bartered Bride*) of 1866 is one of the most straightforwardly big-hearted of all nineteenth-century operas. Smetana was encouraged by his mentor Liszt to pursue his objective of creating a genuinely nationalistic Czech form of opera, engaging with his native musical roots in a way which Liszt himself never did. *The Bartered Bride* succeeds to perfection, with its hokey tale of love in a village, spoken dialogue, and above all its catchy music capturing all the fun of the furiant and the polka, without, apparently, quoting real folk song.

Dvořák was a more substantial musical figure than his friend Smetana. He knew the operatic repertory from the inside (or from underneath) from his long years playing the viola in the pit in the Estates and Provisional theatres in Prague. All of his operas are in Czech (apart from the very first, *Alfred*, which tells the story of the English King Alfred the Great, in German – written in 1870 but not performed in his lifetime). They encompass comedy (*The Stubborn Lovers* (1874)), grand opera (*Dimitrij* (1881)), rustic society (*The Jacobin* (1889)) and the fairy tale (*The Devil and Kate* (1899)). His ninth and most enduring opera reaches for the same watery legend (though a different tributary of the story) as Dargomyzhsky: *Rusalka* (1900) concerns a water nymph briefly permitted to sample the joy and pain of human love. He used a very similar story from the same collection of fairy tales for the scenario of an orchestral tone poem of 1896, *The Water Goblin*. Perhaps a more natural Brahmsian than Wagnerian, Dvořák nonetheless shows a fluid and uniquely personal engagement with the narrative and pictorial elements of his native folk culture which rises, Rusalka-like, to the surface in many pieces in all sorts of different genres. Rusalka's 'Song to the Moon', her opera's lyrical standout number, shares that inclusive quality with many melodies across his versatile and varied output.

Like its west European cousins, Slavic opera is founded on its voices, historical and operatic. Its emblem is the big Russian bass: French and Italian opera composers usually thought of their hero as a tenor. One of its key innovations, a vocal style based on speech rhythm and the sound and inflection of the spoken language, found its fulfilment in the hands of perhaps the most original operatic composer of the next generation: not, this time, a Russian, but a Czech: Leoš Janáček.

The Gods at Twilight: Wagner and Verdi

Wagner

Wagner invites extremes.

In a way, he acts as a mirror for the psychology of his listeners. A contemporary music critic, Eduard Hanslick, described Wagner worship as 'incomprehensible'.[57] Nietzsche, formerly a fervent admirer, called his last work 'a secret attempt to poison the presuppositions of life – a bad work ... an attempted assassination of basic ethics'.[58] Yet the poet W. H. Auden anointed him 'perhaps the greatest genius that ever lived'.[59]

Wagner himself did nothing to rein in either his acolytes or his enemies. He was, in the words of the actor and writer Simon Callow, 'a man without boundaries'.[60] Views about him verge on the theological, even pathological: King Ludwig of Bavaria told him, 'I can only adore you, only praise the power that led you to me.'[61] Hanslick describes slighted friends, who, 'three times offended, came three

a) *The Queen of the Underworld's aria from* Hans Heiling *(1833) by Heinrich Marschner.*

b) *Carl Loewe's 1818 setting of Goethe's* Erlkönig.

c) Der erste Ton *(1808–10) by Carl Maria von Weber.*

German Romanticism. Pre-echoes of Wagner in the hinterland of his predecessors and compatriots.

times back to him',[62] as if he were a sort of inverted St Peter. The fallen angel Nietzsche, by contrast, came to believe that Wagner was 'more of a disease' than a human being.[63]

Clearly, this is a man who needs to be approached with care. Perhaps best is an approach which 'neither takes, nor attempts to take, uncritical admiration or, worse still, moral censure as a frame of reference', as the Wagner scholar Roger Allen says about one of his principal interpreters.[64]

One of the challenges for the historian is that Wagner didn't really do anything the way anybody else did. In some ways, he wasn't really a composer at all: 'more of an actor than a composer,' said

Nietzsche.[65] Some of his works were written with white-hot rapidity. Others evolved over decades. In November 1851 he described the emerging dramas which became the *Ring Cycle* in a letter to Liszt:

> My dear friend
> ... However bold, extraordinary, and perhaps fantastic my plan may appear to you, be convinced that it is not the outgrowth of a mere passing whim, but has been imposed upon me by the necessary consequences of the essence and being of the subject which occupies me wholly and impels me towards its complete execution. To execute it according to my power as a poet and musician is the only thing that stands before my eyes.[66]

His vision was achieved a quarter of a century later: 'Now you've seen what I want to achieve in Art ... If you want the same thing, we shall have an Art,' he told his audience.[67]

But every artist has a hinterland, and with Wagner that hinterland was exceptionally broad. His overriding historical significance consists partly in so many converging and conflicting traits meeting in the one composer.

Early Life and the First Three Mature Operas

Wagner was born on 22 May 1813 in Leipzig, the Saxon town most closely associated in the historical imagination with J. S. Bach. The key themes of his life appeared early: the theatrical household; ambiguous family relationships, including a passionate, almost romantic attachment to an older sister (or possibly half-sister) Rosalie, an actress ('my angel, my one and only');[68] writing plays before turning to music via a textbook which he borrowed from a library and failed to return – the first of many unpaid debts (the disgruntled Leipzig librarian was Friedrich Wieck, Schumann's future father-in-law). He was kicked out of one school and walked out of another, and he drank, fought, fornicated and strutted his way round the streets and pubs of Leipzig. He heard Wilhelmine Schröder-Devrient in *Fidelio*, later recalling her 'satanic ardour' as an actress, and transcribed Beethoven's Ninth Symphony, a work which remained an obsession for his entire life.

Wagner's artistic maturity was forged through three operas written between 1832 and 1840, which worked their way through the current styles of, respectively, Marschner, Meyerbeer and Donizetti. He gained experience as a conductor and (like Berlioz) fell for an actress, Minna Planer (later finding, like Berlioz, that her charms were not sufficient basis for a lasting marriage to a restless, ambitious and temperamental maverick).

During the 1840s he dragged Minna, his debts and his dog between Riga, Dresden and Paris, suffering intermittently from the nervous skin complaint which (partly) accounts for his lifelong fondness for wearing exotic silks, and scuttled around Paris in the dark in a desperate attempt to borrow money to promote his work and to find the dog, Robber (who eventually ran off into the fog). His writings of the period, by contrast with the later theoretical essays, can be approachable and entertaining, as well as revealing some prescient indicators of his later artistic practice: *Death in Paris* (published separately in 1841 in French and German as *Un musicien étranger à Paris* and *Ein Ende zu Paris*) is a strange autobiographical fantasy (including the dog) which ends with a Creed-like statement on his visionary deathbed: 'I believe in God, Mozart and Beethoven ... in my life on earth I was a dissonant chord ... the souls of Art's true disciples will be transfigured in a shining heavenly fabric of glorious harmony ...'[69]

The 1840s brought the first three of his ten great, mature operas: *Der fliegende Holländer* (*The Flying Dutchman*), *Tannhäuser* and *Lohengrin*.

Der fliegende Holländer of 1843 draws strongly on a stormy channel crossing he and Minna (and the smuggled dog) made from Riga to England in 1839, pursued by storms both financial and meteorological. An early conductor spoke of 'the wind that blew out at you wherever you opened the score'.[70]

Tannhäuser (1845) and *Lohengrin* (1850) extended a lifelong absorption with the stories and legends not just of Germany, told by medieval chroniclers like Wolfram von Eschenbach and modern folklorists like Hoffmann and Grimm, but of the Norse lands and Arthurian Britain, too. *Tannhäuser* was easily Wagner's most popular opera in his lifetime. Typically, the poem (never 'libretto') was written first, moulding and merging a number of sources and two quite different stories to create the duality within the title character.

Popularity brought *Tannhäuser* crashing head-on into the sort of lax performance standards and populist demands which Wagner so hated. He made several versions of the work in an attempt to get it performed adequately, and in 1852 issued a guidebook *On the Performing of Tannhäuser* (a familiar Paris practice, known as a *mise-en-scène*). Worst of all, Paris (as always) demanded a ballet. For the notorious production of 1861 he attempted a compromise. Instead of putting a ballet into Act Two, as expected, he put one in Act One (which was the wrong place for the young bloods of the Jockey Club de Paris, who wanted the ballet in the usual place so they could take the dancers from the corps out to dinner), drawing on his late harmonic style in some of the most erotically charged music he ever wrote. He thus created a stylistic fracture which has been a problem with *Tannhäuser* ever since: producers have to choose between the 1845 Dresden and the 1861 Paris versions.

Lohengrin began as a prose sketch, as usual, later worked into verse form. Musical doodlings in the prose version show ideas for themes and melodies emerging alongside the ideas and dramatic situations they represent, even before the actual words to which they are eventually sung even exist: 'I can conceive a subject,' Wagner once told a friend, 'only when it comes to me in such a form that I myself cannot distinguish between the contribution of the poet and the musician in me.'[71]

The poem of *Lohengrin* was, as usual, read aloud to friends first. Schumann, who was there, said Wagner had 'the gift of the gab ... it's impossible to listen to him for any length of time' (Wagner, for his part, complained that Schumann 'never says anything')[72] Its eclectic sources also fed into a completely different scenario, later to become *Die Meistersinger von Nürnberg*, premiered in 1868.

In musical terms, *Lohengrin* extends the process of integrating thematically rich passages of entirely orchestral music into the drama. The prelude to *Lohengrin* is the first which Wagner termed 'Vorspiel' rather than 'Ouvertüre', as in *Holländer* and *Tannhäuser*: a concentrated musical expression of the dramatic essence of the opera to follow rather than a potpourri of the main themes. This Vorspiel depicts the descent of the Holy Grail, 'like streams of gold, ravishing the senses'.[73] At the climax (placed exactly two-thirds of the way through, as Ernest Newman notes), contrary motion between melody and bass (a favourite compositional device of Wagner's, surely learnt from Beethoven) builds irresistibly to a blazing brassy climax on a dominant thirteenth chord, another sound associated with what he called 'adoring self-annihilation'[74] and which he used throughout his career, most famously and powerfully in Siegfried's funeral music in *Götterdämmerung*. Tiny fragments of sound recall (or half-recall) something heard earlier: in Act Two the character Ortrud calls out to 'Elsa!' – just two notes; but the same two notes that began the hero Lohengrin's strange imprecation to Elsa never to ask his name. Through-composition becomes ever more fluid: Wagner told Liszt, who conducted the premiere, that the singers were not to know where the recitatives were, or even that there were recitatives in it at all.

Crisis, Retrenchment, Renewal: The Mid Century

On Palm Sunday 1849, with Dresden in the grip of revolution, Wagner conducted Beethoven's Ninth Symphony in 'a state of ecstasy'.[75] He wrote a play about Jesus Christ as a social revolutionary, and spent the night of 5/6 May at the top of the Kreuzkirche Tower as Prussian bullets peppered its walls and the old opera house (where he had dutifully conducted operas by the despised Meyerbeer and fought off intrigue and indifference) went Valhalla-like up in flames. On 8 May he fled Dresden, leaving behind a tearful Minna. In Weimar, Liszt supplied him with a fake passport in the name of Dr Widmann, a Swabian (Wagner the reckless actor even attempted a Swabian accent, which fortunately for him didn't give him away). A discreet steamer took him to neutral Switzerland. Back in Dresden, the police issued a warrant: 'All police departments are to ... arrest Wagner if he is discovered ... 37–38 years old, of medium height, has brown hair and wears glasses' (the glasses, incidentally, always removed for portraits).[76] He did not set foot in Germany again until eleven years later, or in Saxony for two years after that.

Typically, Wagner saw the emerging new world order as analogous to his own artistic struggles. Practically, he didn't even see the premiere of *Lohengrin*, conducted by Liszt in Weimar in 1850. Artistically, he was at a crossroads. The manner of the three operas of his early maturity had run its course.

The result was a six-year compositional gap (and an interval of fifteen years between the first performance of *Lohengrin* and his next premiere, *Tristan und Isolde*, in 1865), during which he hammered out his ideas in a dense series of writings, chiefly *Die Kunst und die Revolution* (*Art and Revolution*) (1849), *Das Kunstwerk der Zukunft* (*The*

Artwork of the Future) (1849), *Oper und Drama* (*Opera and Drama*) (1850) and *Eine Mitteilung an meine Freunde* (*A Communication to My Friends*) (1851). He tells us that Greek ideals of drama have been lost. A new concept of a unified form of drama must give pre-eminence to the words, delivered in a new form of '*Versmelodie*', or 'poetry-melody', uninterrupted by set pieces like duets and ensembles. Music sits between, and unites, poetry and physical gesture. Harmony 'grows from the bottom up as a true column of related tonal materials'. Counterpoint, on the other hand, is 'the artificial play of art with art, the mathematics of feeling'. Musical units arising directly from the verse can echo and pre-echo ideas across the work as a whole. This art serves *das Volk* ('the people'). A new vocabulary is needed: drama, not opera; actor, not singer; poem, not libretto. Wagner saw himself as a dramatist, not a composer. Above all else, 'True drama can be conceived only as resulting from the *collective impulse of all the arts*.'[77]

This is rich stuff, proving ground of the ideas behind the *Gesamtkunstwerk*, the 'total art work', or union of all the arts, in which (in the words of the British philosopher and Wagnerian Bryan Magee) 'in the deepest sense there is only one character, the different "characters" being aspects of a single personality, so that the work is a portrait of the psyche as well as a depiction of the world'.[78]

In Zurich Wagner met Otto and Mathilde Wesendonck. Mathilde acted as his muse and willing amanuensis, inspiring some of his most passionate music and performing menial tasks like inking over the pencilled libretto of *Tristan und Isolde*. Her rich husband Otto, meanwhile, gave him much-needed financial support and a cottage, called Asyl (Sanctuary), in the grounds of their home, and also sponsored some successful performances. This period of relative calm in the mid 1850s allowed the gestation of seven great works of his later maturity: the four parts of the *Ring Cycle*, *Tristan*, *Die Meistersinger* and *Parsifal*.

The Ring Cycle *and Its Hinterland*

Typically, Wagner began work on what eventually became the *Ring* with the text. The first prose sketch is 'The Nibelungen Myth as Sketch for Drama', dated 8 October 1848. This follows the shape and general course of the dramatic events that we know from the finished work – except that the ending is radically different. The actual poems were written in reverse order, but the overall dramatic conception from the beginning to the end of the world was in its creator's mind from the very first stirrings. The complete poem was published in 1853. Between 1853 and 1857, Wagner composed the music for the first two and a half operas, then set the project aside to create *Tristan und Isolde* in just two years.

On 22 July 1860 he was granted a partial amnesty to return to Germany, though not to Saxony. In 1861 he was in Paris for the troubled revival of *Tannhäuser*. These were some of the most difficult years of his life.

In March 1864 King Maximilian II of Bavaria died and his 18-year-old son, a fanatical admirer of Wagner, became King Ludwig II. Ludwig summoned Wagner to Munich, and showered him with whatever he needed to fulfil his vision, including the promise of a purpose-built new theatre for the production of his works. Around the same time, Wagner began a passionate liaison with Liszt's daughter Cosima, wife of the pianist and conductor Hans von Bülow and mother of his two children: Wagner's own wife Minna, from whom he had been separated for some time, died in 1866. A year earlier Cosima had given birth to Wagner's child, a daughter called Isolde. Two other children, Eva and Siegfried, followed. In 1868 Cosima and Bülow divorced. Cosima told her diary, 'I had no choice.' Bülow told her, 'You are determined to devote your life to a man much greater than myself, and I must admit that your choice is right.'[79] Cosima and Wagner married in 1870.

Tristan, completed in 1859, was premiered in 1865, in Munich, conducted by Bülow. In the same year Wagner resumed work on another huge piece, *Die Meistersinger von Nürnberg*, whose story had occupied him since he began work on *Lohengrin* two decades earlier. The music, too, had been in his mind for some years. The orchestral sketch of the Vorspiel is dated 13–20 April 1862. Progress was slow due to Wagner's difficult personal circumstances and the preparations for *Tristan*: the work was finally completed at Tribschen in October 1867 and premiered to great acclaim in 1868. In March 1869 Wagner resumed work on the *Ring Cycle*. The premieres of the first two parts, *Das Rheingold* (1869) and *Die Walküre* (1870), were given by command of the king and in defiance of Wagner's wishes. He completed the vast project on 21 November 1874, some twenty-six years after its first inception. Three complete cycles were given in the newly built Festspielhaus in Bayreuth in 1876.

The Texts

'Firstly, I am a poet, not a composer, and secondly, the language that expresses the profoundest truths of the human soul is music': these are the words not of Wagner himself but a summing-up of his world view by his great interpreter, the conductor Wilhelm Furtwängler.[80]

Wagner's engagement with the source legends was long-standing: 'Evening stroll with Wagner – his Nibelung text,' noted Robert Schumann in his diary in June 1848.[81]

His deliberately archaic texts have a character all their own. He adopts a version of a technique from German medieval verse form called Stabreim, using irregular line lengths and alliteration between the starting consonants of individual words rather than rhyme, as in this passage from *Siegfrieds Tod* (helpfully marked up by Ernest Newman):[82]

Was du mir nahmst, nütztest du nicht,–
deinem muthigen Trotz vertrautest du nur!
Nun du, gefriedet, frei es mir gabst,
kehrt mir mein Wissen wieder,
erkenn' ich des Ringes Runen

This moves the vocal style further away from the artificially regular patterns of the conventional libretto, exactly as intended in *Opera and Drama*, at the local level of the single line as well as at the structural level of scene and ensemble. It also presents a series of irreconcilable problems for anyone who attempts to render Wagner in another language, from his first English translator Alfred Forman (who also supplied the animal props for the very first Bayreuth *Ring*) to Forman's more scholarly and circumspect modern descendants, including Andrew Porter, Stewart Spencer and John Deathridge, who have teased out the issues in the introductions to their respective *Rings*. (Even Cosima recorded that Forman's translation was 'very severely criticised', although to her that was 'of very little account';[83] Deathridge goes somewhat further, holding Forman guilty of 'a bad case of miscalculation and a tin ear for language'; Porter rightly but ruefully notes that 'a translator cannot do everything'.)[84]

The Music: Leitmotifs

In his 1879 essay 'On the Application of Music to Drama', Wagner mentioned that 'one of my younger friends ... has devoted some attention to the characteristics of "leitmotifs" as he calls them', the only time he used the word.[85] Leitmotifs are small snatches of melody, harmony or rhythm, each associated with a particular theme in the drama. In 1882 an English reviewer described leitmotifs as offering 'guidance through the bewildering maze of the Nibelungen story and psychological phenomena'.[86] But treating them as what Debussy satirised as 'calling cards' is far too simplistic.[87] More, any idea that their meaning can be read from their first appearance is, in Newman's words, 'pure fantasy'.[88] They emerge and evolve: in *Das Rheingold*, a two-chord motif is first heard buried in the bassoons as the dwarf Alberich attempts to lure the teasing Rhinemaidens down into the deep. He doesn't know the gold is there. Nor do we. Only later do those chords reveal their full significance. Those bassoons were telling us things we didn't know we didn't know.

Motifs can combine, as when the 'redemption' motif which ends the *Ring Cycle* in *Götterdämmerung* meets Siegfried's theme, summing up the significance of his life and death; or the passionate colloquy in Act Two of *Tristan*. They can refer backwards: in *Die Walküre* Sieglinde tells Siegmund that a mysterious stranger buried the sword stuck in the tree where she lives: the orchestra tells us, via the Valhalla motif heard a whole opera ago, that the stranger was Wotan. Motifs can display as variants of each other, like the many versions of the triads-in-thirds motif of the ring itself. Robert Donington has argued that all the motifs in the *Ring* can be traced back to the radiantly orchestrated five minutes of E flat major in the opening Vorspiel of *Das Rheingold*, a sort of *ur*-motif.[89]

There are many published guides to the motifs in the *Ring*, giving them names, and listing where they appear in the score, like a sort of glossary or index. These are extremely useful – indeed, absolutely indispensable. But they must be read with caution as, while some of the motifs can be linked explicitly to something visible like a spear, most are far more fluid in terms of meaning.

A final reflection on motifs includes a word on their character. Some can be naïve, almost comical, with one foot in the simpler world of earlier German melodrama, like the clumping figure for the giants Fasolt and Fafner – Wagner notes that this idea came to him

The Wagnerian 'leitmotif'. Three very brief moments from Alberich's exchanges with the Rhinemaidens in the opening scene of Wagner's Das Rheingold *(1854, first published 1869). The brackets show the progress of a tiny two-chord theme, or leitmotif, which finally reveals itself as the musical analogue of the hidden gold and the various characters' conflicted relationships with it.*

right at the beginning of fashioning the story. There is a distinctive breed of crawling bass tunes for sinister characters like the Dragon, sinuous, wandering, and highly chromatic.

Another musical observation concerns the way in which Wagner's own ideals evolved in practice. *Opera and Drama* militates against ensemble singing: *Götterdämmerung* (whose poem was written first, the music much later) contains, as the Wagnerian Barry Millington puts it, 'a chorus for the vassals, a conspirators' trio and an oath-swearing duet that is positively Verdian'.[90] As early as the read-through of the first poetic form of *Lohengrin* in 1845, Schumann was puzzled by the lack of obvious division into discrete 'numbers': Wagner teased him by reading out bits as if they were intended as arias and cavatinas, to his apparent satisfaction.

Tristan und Isolde; Die Meistersinger von Nürnberg; Parsifal

In 1854 Wagner read Arthur Schopenhauer's *The World as Will and Representation*, first published in 1818. He remarked that 'it had a radical influence on my whole life'.[91] The novelist Thomas Mann described the encounter as '*the* great event of Wagner's life. There is no doubt that it freed his music and gave it courage to be itself.'[92] Bryan Magee says, 'Schopenhauer was able to act as a catalyst in this extraordinary way only because the need for such a change was already there in Wagner himself.'[93]

Schopenhauer ruled, in Wagner's own words, a dividing line in the mind of the artist 'between the intuitive or impulsive part of his nature and his consciously or reasonably formed ideas'.[94] Primal energy, freely expressed, confronts and contrasts with its suppression or control (an idea earlier explored independently by the English poet William Blake). In *Tristan und Isolde* this duality is expressed as darkness and light, night and day: unlike the Enlightenment figures of Mozart's *Die Zauberflöte*, Wagner's lovers seek the dark, where their passion tears them to pieces. The opera's compositional hinterland included the four-way emotional turmoil between the Wesendonck home and Asyl (poor Minna was still around, loyally hanging on to the tatters of her marriage). He set five highly charged poems by Mathilde in music which is a frank warm-up for *Tristan*. A note to Mathilde ('Take my entire soul for a morning's greeting')[95] was interrupted by Minna, who, understandably upset, confronted the Wesendoncks and was herself sent away for a 'rest'.

Bizarrely, Wagner regarded this almost four-hour opera as an eminently practical project presenting no real difficulties beyond finding the two principals. The leads at the 1865 premiere were husband and wife Malvina and Ludwig Schnorr von Carolsfeld. Malvina caused the premiere to be delayed for almost a month due to hoarseness. Worse, Ludwig collapsed and died after singing the role just four times.

Musically, *Tristan*'s position as sort of supercharged intermezzo in the middle of the creation of the *Ring* shows Wagner developing, and moving away from, some of his own ideas expressed in *Opera and Drama*: unlike the early parts of the *Ring*, already completed, *Tristan* uses much simultaneous singing in duet. All the subsequent operas go further. Potent chromaticism is associated with heightened emotion (including a turbulent little tune in the lower strings, for Isolde's angry reaction to the song of an unseen young sailor, which is almost a twelve-tone row), common triads with reliable, safe things like honour, loyalty, and King Marke. Very little happens on stage. The drama is in the unfolding musical ideas, beginning with the famous Vorspiel, described by Wagner as 'one long succession of linked phases ... from the first timidest avowal to sweetest procrastination, through anxious sighs, through hopes and fears, laments and desires, bliss and torment, to ... the highest bliss, the bliss of dying'.[96] Tristan, suffering from one of Wagner's leitmotif unhealing wounds, invites his Isolde to follow him into the 'land unlit by the sun, the dark land from which I took my being, in which my dying mother bore me', where their innermost instincts will find their fullest, final expression, in love and in death.[97]

This is strong meat. Clara Schumann called the opera 'the most disgusting thing I have ever heard or seen in my entire life'.[98] Mark Twain, a more sober and detached observer, attended a performance in Bayreuth in 1891 which received 'absolute attention' and 'broke the hearts of all' its listeners, many of whom 'cried the night away'; for his own part, he felt 'strongly out of place here ... like the sane person in a community of the mad ... like a heretic in heaven'.[99]

Die Meistersinger von Nürnberg occupies a unique, indeed anomalous, position in Wagner's work: the only opera featuring real people in a recognisable historical setting.

The medieval 'Mastersingers', members of a guild of musical artists, and their most famous son, Hans Sachs, had long fascinated Wagner as a romanticised, idealised version of a simpler, more purely German form of art. Typically, the idea had been in his mind for decades: when he was twenty-three, he and his brother-in-law Wolfram had got into a fight in a tavern actually in Nuremberg after teasing and bullying a pompous master carpenter called Lauermann into showing off his singing, claiming that Wagner was a famous visiting musician who had heard of Lauermann's prowess. The resulting brawl involved a 'roaring crowd of several hundred men': Wagner and Wolfram strolled home 'arm-in-arm, laughing and joking, through the deserted moonlit streets'.[100] This scene turns up two decades later at the end of Act Two of *Die Meistersinger*. Not long after the Nuremberg dust-up, he worked up the first prose sketch alongside his labours on *Lohengrin*. Further drafts and the verse version followed a decade and a half later, in the early 1860s. By this time the critic Eduard Hanslick had published his *Vom Musikalisch-Schönen*

(*On the Musically Beautiful*), a rejection (among much else) of Wagner's method expressed in *Opera and Drama*. Hanslick joined the poor deluded Lauermann as joint model for the character of Sixtus Beckmesser, the pernickety town clerk in *Die Meistersinger* for whom music is all about accuracy and obeying rules.

Die Meistersinger was, astonishingly, Wagner's idea of 'a popular comic opera',[101] that is, easy to stage and well within the reach of most small companies. The work lasts about four and a half hours, requires a large cast and chorus, and places demands on the orchestra which led to a strike at the premiere led by the anti-Wagner horn player Franz Strauss, father of Richard.

Musically, it is the sunniest of Wagner's mature operas. Three years after the tonal ambiguity which begins *Tristan*, his next opera opens in a blaze of C major. A London critic in 1882 captured its character, and the residual nervousness about the nature of Wagnerian music drama, well:

> it is German to the core ... steeped in the melodies of the people ... the story of the opera is pure, homely, natural and humorous, and the music is not merely suitable, but in some instances its quality is very high indeed. Wagner does not go out of his way to force his pet theory upon the hearer, and the immense advantage of a chorus and of good concerted music gives the opera fine contrasts which in his later works are wanting.[102]

For his last opera, Wagner coined yet another new word: *Ein Bühnenweihfestspiel* ('A Festival Play for the Consecration of the Stage'). *Parsifal* was first conceived alongside *Lohengrin* as long ago as the mid 1840s. He completed a draft of the text in Zurich on Good Friday 1857. The music occupied him from 1878 until 1882, when the opera was premiered at Bayreuth in July of that year.

Parsifal goes beyond *Lohengrin* in probing the duality between the holy and profane elements in the human psyche, involving the familiar tropes of the unhealing wound, the wise fool, the Schopenhauerian conflict between the expression and repression of the will, the temptress, the pilgrims and the Holy Grail. The music is astonishing: the beat-less opening melody, like a sleeping creature breathing; the shimmering A flat major chord to which this melody leads, orchestrated like a sky painted by J. M. W. Turner; the slow, hieratic tread of a simple brass theme, endlessly transposed; the overpowering clanging of a four-note theme for bells; the visceral reliance on sheer sound. Debussy described the score as sounding as if 'lit up from behind'.[103]

Wagner died in Venice a little over six months after the premiere of *Parsifal*. His achievement, and its challenges, were well rehearsed by the time of his death. Cosima, and latterly their children and grandchildren, preserved his vision with ferocious loyalty. His musical influence appears in many different guises: the opening melody of Elgar's First Symphony; the chorale-like brass in Bruckner's Seventh; the susurrating orchestra in Debussy's only opera, *Pelléas et Mélisande*; bombast in Schoenberg's *Gurre-Lieder*; pounding low chords in Stravinsky's *The Rite of Spring*. The most intelligent writers for the musical stage have found ways of learning from his technique, too: there are linking themes in Leonard Bernstein's score for *West Side Story*, and a hint of the *Ring*'s 'redemption' motif as Maria acknowledges her love for the man who murdered her brother, surely more than a coincidence. At the same time, attempts to ape Wagner too closely were bound to founder: Debussy sneered that 'nothing was ever more dreary than the neo-Wagnerian school in which the French genius had lost its way among the sham Wotans in Hessian boots and the Tristans in velvet jackets'.[104] From 1914 the English composer Rutland Boughton attempted an 'English Bayreuth' at Glastonbury with his own Arthurian cycle, with some success, but little legacy.

Among less palatable aspects of his inheritance, the scholar Joseph Kerman speaks of 'the dross of Wagnerism',[105] the totality of his legacy, good and bad, an artistic account we are left to pay, just as Wagner left others to pay his monetary debts. The music historian Alex Ross has teased out the legacy of Wagnerism in art, thought and politics with bravery and skill.[106] The ready-made appeal of his world view to Hitler (a regular attender at Bayreuth and a close friend of the family) remains the most uncomfortable aspect of its history.

Wagner's self-constructed image placed him at the peak of what by the late nineteenth century was regarded as the cultural hegemony of the grand Austro-German tradition. He wanted to be seen as the successor to Bach, Haydn, Mozart and Beethoven. To many of his admirers he transcends even their achievement.

Verdi

Beginnings: Success and Sadness

Giuseppe Verdi was born in the same year as Wagner, 1813, in Le Roncole, a tiny village in the duchy of Parma. Links between his life story and the fluctuating fortunes of his region and country came early when his mother hid him in the belfry as Austrian troops rampaged below.

Verdi's father was an innkeeper. His education was supportive if provincial, including studies (as for many others before him) with the local church organist, and schooling in the nearest town, Busseto, where he composed voluminously for the town orchestra, rather grandly known as the Philharmonic Society. Its president was the music-loving merchant Antonio Barezzi, whose family provided Verdi with musical support and a job teaching the piano to his daughter Margherita. At the age of eighteen, Verdi headed to Milan, where he tried and failed to enter the conservatoire. But the interview led to two years of diligent study with Vincenzo Lavigna, the sort of kindly, competent contrapuntal craftsman who features in the background of so many great composers.

Back at the Barezzis', the piano duet stool performed its time-honoured office and Verdi and Margherita were married in May 1836. A growing interest in writing for the stage led to his first opera, *Oberto*, staged at La Scala in 1839 on the recommendation of an established soprano, Giuseppina Strepponi. This in turn led to a contract for two further operas. Then came a period of professional disappointment and crushing personal tragedy. His 1840 comedy, *Un giorno di regno*, was a failure. Far worse, the two children of his marriage to Margherita both died in early infancy. Margherita herself died in 1840. Depressed and ill, Verdi resolved to abandon composition.

Some key features are in place in this image of the 27-year-old Verdi. Sadly, he was to have no further children. Is there an echo of his lost hopes in the anguished father/child relationships of his middle-period pomp (as in his beloved Shakespeare)? The working pattern of an ever-deepening dramatic manner expressed in periods of intense creativity interspersed with episodes of retrenchment and melancholia, during which he would often grumpily threaten not to write any more music, had begun. Often, he was talked out of his depression by supportive colleagues, beginning with Bartolomeo

Merelli, impresario of La Scala, who refused to release him from his engagement, telling him ('like a naughty child', said Verdi later), 'Now listen to me: I cannot compel you to write; but my confidence in your talent is unshaken.'[107] Merelli was rewarded with *Nabucco*, premiered in March 1842, Verdi's first success. Key people are here, too: his father Carlo; his father-in-law Barezzi; and the remarkable Strepponi, whose starry singing career (and eventful amatory career) would soon be over, but who would support him loyally and patiently through half a century of triumph and vicissitude as his companion and, much later, as his second wife.

Nabucco *to* Macbeth

Verdi's first (or early) period works were, in the concise assessment of Abbate and Parker, 'reactionary rather than revolutionary'.[108] His national inheritance was not promising. The three great standard-bearers of early nineteenth-century bel canto, Rossini, Donizetti and Bellini, had all finished their operatic careers by the mid 1840s. But Italian opera hadn't replaced or renewed their example. Attention was moving elsewhere: Paris for grand opera and Germany for the emerging techniques and ideas of Wagner. Verdi admired his older compatriots. Many decades later he praised Rossini's *Guillaume Tell* and called his *Il barbiere di Siviglia* 'the best opera buffa in existence'.[109] He also described Bellini as 'rich in feeling and in his own peculiar, individual melancholy' (though 'poor in orchestration and harmony').[110] Bellini, for his part, praised *Nabucco*, and Rossini reportedly described Verdi as

> a composer of a serious and melancholy disposition. His ideas are sombre and thoughtful and pour out of his natural disposition with abundance and spontaneity ... But I doubt whether he can write even a semi-serious opera ... much less a comedy like *L'elisir d'amore*.[111]

(Which, given the parts of Verdi's output he lived to witness, is a reasonably fair assessment of the evidence available to him.) Relations between the two *maestri* seem to have been cordial enough: Rossini, with Mozartian humour, wrote a letter to 'M. Verdi, Célèbre Compositeur de musique, pianiste de quatrième classe', signing himself 'Rossini, ex-compositeur de musique, pianiste de cinquième classe'.[112] Verdi later agreed to contribute to a planned Requiem for Rossini, to be written jointly by twelve composers, but in the event never finished.

Artistically, this early period saw Verdi fully mastering the slightly moribund inheritance of the Code Rossini in a sustained burst of creative effort, adding aspects of the Meyerbeerian ensemble and some signatures of his own, without yet fully transfiguring those elements into something new. One of those signatures was a noble simplicity and directness of utterance, exemplified in his fondness for choruses in unison, most famously in '*Va, pensiero, sull'ali dorate*' (known in English as 'Chorus of the Hebrew Slaves') in Act Three of *Nabucco*. Another novel idea was attaching musical themes to the main characters, as in *I due Foscari* of 1844, later taken to infinitely richer dramatic extremes in instances like the fateful howl of the old man's curse in *Rigoletto* or the baleful tread of the Grand Inquisitor in *Don Carlos*. These themes are never developed symphonically in the manner of Wagner's leitmotifs, but form a key element in creating what Verdi called the '*tinta*', or colour, of a particular opera, providing a golden thread running through the drama, quite absent in Rossini.

'With *Nabucco* my career can be said to have begun,' said Verdi, adding, with his usual eye for business, 'since then I have never lacked for commissions.'[113] Three years later, in 1844, *Ernani* made him an international celebrity. He travelled widely: London excited him but, like many southern visitors, he found the fog like 'living on a steamer'.[114] His relationship with Giuseppina Strepponi, empathetic foil to his bristly creativity, deepened. In 1844 he bought a house in his home town of Busseto, followed in 1848 by an estate, Sant'Agata, just outside, where his parents settled. In 1845 he also acquired an amanuensis, Emanuele Muzio.

The most important work of the period after *Nabucco* was Verdi's first operatic entanglement with Shakespeare, *Macbeth* (1847). Verdi described Shakespeare as 'a favourite poet of mine, whom I have had in my hands from earliest youth, and whom I read and re-read constantly'.[115] In the same year as Verdi's opera the influential Italian critic Francesco de Sanctis remarked that 'Shakespeare has become the banner of the Romantic movement … in Shakespeare we find jumbled together the most varied actions, both comic and tragic … but there are those who continue to reprove him'.[116]

That element of Romantic jumble was certainly enhanced by the exigencies of translators and censors: Rossini's *Otello* of 1816 was based on a French version of the play, and has two alternative endings, one happy, one less so. Even Verdi, as the letter quoted above suggests, knew Shakespeare from reading him, rather than seeing him in the theatre. All the more notable, then, that, in the words of the scholar William Weaver, 'Verdi's *Macbeth* is the first Italian opera to make a real attempt to be Shakespearean.'[117] The attempt involved endless tussles with the librettist, Francesco Piave, who was eventually dropped altogether. The result is a thrilling staging post: musical motifs woven more deeply into the texture than in *I due Foscari*; plenty of spectacularly deranged coloratura for '*la sonnambula*' Lady Macbeth, clearly drawing on the example of Donizetti and Bellini; contrasting '*tinta*' of texture and key for the human and supernatural characters; Mendelssohnian rustlings for the fog and filthy air of the blasted heath; Wagnerian stage effects like trap doors, 'phantasmagoria' (magic lanterns), and a subterranean band ('bass clarinets, bassoons and contra-bassoons, nothing else ... mind that there are no trumpets, no trombones,' insisted Verdi) for Banquo's ghost;[118] brooding choruses more dramatically and psychologically bound into the drama than the stagey unisons of the *Nabucco* manner (though, unfortunately for Verdi's English reputation at least, not yet escaping the Meyerbeerian clichés later memorably parodied by Gilbert and Sullivan in the 'cat-like tread' chorus from *The Pirates of Penzance*).

To Verdi at the time, *Macbeth* was the opera 'which I love above all my other works'.[119] He dedicated it, touchingly, to his father-in-law Antonio Barezzi, father and grandfather of his lost 'pretty chickens and their dam', because 'you ... have been to me a father, a benefactor and a friend'.[120] In 1865 he lavished further care on his favourite work when he rewrote it very substantially for Paris, adding the inevitable ballet for the witches, who 'dominate the drama; everything derives from them'.[121]

Verdi's first period of composition was rounded with premieres in London (still stuck in its reactionary rut: 'A new opera by Signor Verdi ... the music very noisy and trivial,' sniffed the stuffed Mendelssohnian Queen Victoria),[122] Paris (*Jérusalem* (1847), a Meyerbeerianisation of *I Lombardi*), and Rome, with the appropriately patriotic and bellicose *La battaglia di Legnano* of 1849.

These works found Verdi in a curious position in relation to both his obsolescent Rossinian inheritance and developing trends elsewhere. As his biographer Julian Budden puts it, 'At a time when musical opinion started to divide between the Mendelssohnian conservatives and the partisans of the New German School of Liszt and Wagner, Verdi pleased neither one side nor the other.'[123] Hanslick refused to take him seriously. Others mistook his directness for lack of originality. Many thought his music was ruinously heavy for singers schooled in the earlier, lighter manner: Bülow, never short of a forthright opinion, called him the Attila of the throat (after his own murderous Roman title character of 1844). Of course, professional cattiness played its part, too. Otto Nicolai, who had turned down the libretto of *Nabucco* and then seen Verdi use it to thoroughly usurp his own Italian pre-eminence, said Verdi 'scores like a madman, is quite without technique and must have the heart of a donkey'.[124] (As a pleasing postscript to this petulant outburst, both composers ended their careers with successful comedies based on *The Merry Wives of Windsor*, forty-five years apart.)

Three Middle-period Masterpieces

Verdi's second (middle) period produced *Rigoletto* (1851), *Il trovatore* and *La traviata* (both 1853).

His personal engagement with mid-century political upheavals was rather more detached than those of, in their different ways, either Wagner or Chopin: 'I have to buy twenty papers a day (not to read them, please understand), but to avoid the importunities of the newsboys,' he wrote from Paris in March 1848.[125]

The depth of Verdi's political involvement has been a cause of debate. Certainly, the association of early works like *Nabucco* with the cause of Italian nationhood involves a strong element of back formation. At the same time, having the chorus in *La battaglia di Legnano*, written at the height of the upheavals of 1848, 'swear to put an end to Italy's wrongs', and having the hero expire at the end with the words 'Italy is saved' on his lips is a pretty explicit alignment with the rallying cries of the '*Cinque giornate*', the 'Five Days' of uprising which drove the Austrians out of Milan (Verdi's home capital, where *La battaglia* is set) a few weeks after the premiere. The final scene was encored at every performance. The year of revolutions affected opera as it did everything else: but the effects were largely social and practical, hastening the end of small states and courts and the rise of larger, more democratic town companies. The operas themselves were not, by and large, the medium of propaganda or politics.

Verdi spent the two years from 1847 in Paris. His relationship with Strepponi, retired from the stage at the age of just thirty-one to a successful career as a teacher, settled into cohabitation in the rue de la Victoire, close, geographically if not musically, to Liszt and Chopin (all three composers living with women to whom they were not married, in true Parisian fashion). By the time of the cholera outbreak of 1850 he was based back in Italy, though still travelling frequently.

The middle-period pieces continue the preoccupations of *Macbeth* and *Ernani*: aria forms building on and moving away from the sectional cabaletta type of Rossini; ensembles adding a new dramatic flexibility to the model derived from Mozart of a quick-fire, active start adding characters one by one, each with their own mood, succeeded by a dramatically static stretta where they all sing together; choruses more rounded and engaged than the stagey solemnity of the *Nabucco*-style unison; plenty of local colour; opening instrumental preludes feeding into the drama rather than acting as stand-alone overtures; and ever-increasing demands on the new kinds of voice – the steely soprano (notably Sophie Loewe), the high (often very high) baritone (for example, his favoured Felice Varesi), the heavy-duty tenor, the chandelier-rattling bass. It didn't matter if the singers were ugly, or even if they sang out of tune: Verdi himself demanded that certain scenes 'must not be sung: they must be acted out and declaimed'.[126] Bel canto was no longer necessarily *bel*.

Rigoletto (1851) grew out of a couple of blazing rows. In 1850 Francesco Piave worked up a libretto which he called *La maledizione* (*The Curse*) from the 1832 play *Le roi s'amuse* by Victor Hugo (fertile theatrical source of sweeping historical plots and big characters). Hugo's play had been banned in France nearly two decades before, after just one night; following suit, the Italian censors rejected the 'repellent immorality and obscene triviality' of the story of a jealous jester and his desirable daughter.[127] Worse, it openly portrayed a king as a profligate libertine. Verdi's reaction is revealing: according to him, the king (tactfully demoted to duke) must be a libertine or the jester's jealousy has no dramatic foundation; he can't prettify his title character's physical deformity because 'putting on the stage a character who is grossly deformed and absurd but inwardly passionate and full of love is precisely what I feel to be so fine'; being told that he can't put the daughter Gilda's body in a sack earns a caustic comment about who knows his business best, him or the police: 'whether my music is good or bad I don't write it at random'.[128]

Verdi was right. His art was ready for this story, with its vivid vision of human frailty and love. The patient Piave managed to satisfy the bureaucrats. The result is one of the best operas of the nineteenth century: skilfully constructed, dramatically compelling and musically thrilling.

The quartet *'Bella figlia dell'amore'* is an exquisite example of the craft of the ensemble. The drama, by a kind of musical magic trick, lets some singers hear each other while others can't, allowing layers of meaning and emotion to emerge through the melodic lines of the creepy duke manipulating events like a seductive circus master, his admirer Maddalena responding flirtatiously but nervously, both of them watched (crucially, without knowing it) from outside by a second pair of singers, the despairing Gilda and the murderously vengeful Rigoletto. Four different voice types add to the skilful separation of moods and relationships. *Rigoletto* also contains wonderful music for all the tightly organised small group of leads, none of whom dominates; thrilling finales, and a fabulous thunderstorm. It is also, appearing at the zenith of the craze for the Meyerbeerian epic, strikingly short: barely two hours of music, tautly structured and bursting with melodies.

La traviata (1853) is a very different creature, another indication of Verdi's ability to continually renew his art over his career. It was based on a brand-new play, *La Dame aux camélias* by Alexandre Dumas *fils*, derived from his own novel of 1848, which Verdi and Strepponi saw in Paris in February 1852. Setting an opera in recognisably contemporary society was a daring extension of the naturalistic acting style pioneered by Sarah Bernhardt (who created the original stage roles of both Violetta and Tosca), as Verdi well knew: 'another might have avoided it on account of the costumes, the period, and a thousand other foolish scruples, but I am delighted with the idea'.[129] (Later, the habit grew of dressing *La traviata* as if it was set in around 1700, which makes a complete nonsense of the social mores on display.) The plot, too, is no routine love story but a complex three-way power struggle involving a compromised woman (itself a striking divergence from the expected moral probity of the usual leading lady), her lover and his father. The music explores this impossible triangle with considerable intelligence, sympathy and power. Duets dominate. Sometimes, one voice will set up a mood and a melody which the other will accept and embellish (Alfredo and Violetta's carefree Act One party duet). Elsewhere, the interplay of the two voices can give the psychological drama a different turn: in Act Two, Germont *père* asks Violetta to abandon Alfredo for the sake of his other child, Alfredo's sister, in music whose four-square phrasing and regular melodic shapes ooze adamantine authority; she agrees, in a heartfelt evocation of the young girl's innocence; but, at the end of the lengthy exchange, it is Violetta who leads in music of resigned simplicity while the old man breaks down in sobs (*'piangi, o misera'* ('weep, unhappy woman')). This scene is the heart of the opera as drama. *La traviata* has been criticised for celebrating Violetta's sacrifice on the altar of patriarchal authority: here, the music suggests that something more subtle and interesting is going on.

La traviata's other beauties include the fine prelude (emphatically not just an overture in the old Rossinian sense), leeching into the decaying world of Parisian immorality through the ethereal sound of divided violins (the superficial similarity with the opening of Wagner's *Lohengrin*, premiered just three years earlier, appears to be a coincidence). There is some splendid, if a little conventional, stuff to accompany drinking, dancing, dressing up and generally having a good time. But all this activity is really just the backcloth for the real action, inside the minds and hearts of the three main characters.

The premiere, at the Teatro La Fenice in Venice, on 6 March 1853, wasn't a success. 'Is the fault mine or the singers'?' mused Verdi, mournfully.[130] The answer appears to have been a bit of both – the two leading men did not impress, and the Violetta, Fanny Salvini-Donatelli, was too old (thirty-eight) and too fat ('as double-barrelled as her name', according to one of Verdi's biographers)[131] to make a convincingly alluring courtesan. Despite this inauspicious start, *La traviata* was soon rapturously received at a revival down the canal from La Fenice at the Teatro San Benedetto. Its lasting popularity was assured.

Verdi worked with white-hot intensity in these years. *La traviata* made it from that night in the theatre in Paris when he first saw the play to curtain-up on the opera in just a year. *Il trovatore*, the third of the great trio of the period, was largely written at the same time, though begun earlier, and premiered first, in January 1853 (and other projects were in hand simultaneously, too). In many ways, *Il trovatore* represents a step backwards from *Rigoletto*: its medieval setting features gypsies, jealousy and duels. Verdi had asked his librettist, Salvadore Cammarano, to avoid conventional closed forms like cavatinas, cabalettas and choruses; but, to a large extent, that's exactly what Cammarano gave him. Opportunities to negotiate were hampered by Cammarano's sudden death in July 1852, mid-project. Verdi scholar Charles Osborne thinks that, when presented with this material and a looming deadline, Verdi 'decided to do something which he had been perfecting over the years, and to do it so beautifully that he need never do it again'.[132] His relieved public rewarded him with a huge success, furthered by a French version in 1856. Translation went the other way round for the work which ended this period, the frustrating *Les Vêpres Siciliennes*, which tangled Verdi in disputes with the dilatory Eugène Scribe and the demands of the audience at the Paris Opéra (which Verdi sniffily referred to as *'la grande boutique'*), still firmly hooked on their five acts of Meyerbeer.[133]

National Figure: The Late Period

To say that Verdi's output slowed during each of his periods of composition is true, but must be set in context. In his first period he forged reputation and career by doing what Rossini and Donizetti did: writing as fast as commissions came his way (i.e. very fast indeed), producing some fine pieces, some pieces with fine elements, and some workmanlike duds. In his second period in the early 1850s, secure in skill and career, he worked to his own timetable to create three substantial works. His third (late) period produced fewer, bigger pieces, more widely spaced, which really did seem to bring down the curtain and usher in the long-promised retirement, before the final, astonishing burst of creativity in old age.

By the mid 1850s Verdi had become a national monument. He hadn't asked to be, and he didn't want to be. But fame allowed him to settle in his estate in Busseto with Strepponi, and compose, to an extent, what and when he wanted. He wrote just seven operas after the age of forty-two, compared to nineteen before. He began contributing to his own myth, peppering articles and interviews with anecdotes and aphorisms, not all of them true. In Busseto, relations with neighbours were not helped by their small-town unwillingness to sit near the unmarried Strepponi in church (Liszt had a similar problem in Weimar regarding his sweet Carolyne). Verdi wrote rather defensively to his father-in-law: 'In my house there lives a lady, free, independent, a lover like myself of solitude ... Neither I nor she owes anyone an account of our actions ... she is entitled to as much respect as myself.'[134] Verdi himself behaved with considerable gracelessness and lack of tact over plans to build a theatre named in his honour in Busseto (as did the mayor – the difficulties were overcome and the building completed in 1868, more smoothly than the much more ambitious project being hatched to the north, in Bayreuth).

The third period has two masterpieces. Verdi became increasingly engrossed in the management of his estate. He travelled, meeting a bullish young intellectual called Arrigo Boito in Paris, probably *chez* Rossini, in 1862, when Boito managed to offend Verdi with his forthright views of current trends and of what Verdi caustically called the 'Babylonian music of the future', alongside a rather curious theory that Beethoven's music was 'spherical' and of the need to purify the altar of music 'now befouled with the filth of the brothel'.[135] Boito was not the first or the last young man to think himself wiser than his elders. Happily, the two composers later became close colleagues, if not exactly musical soulmates, with Boito providing Verdi with the libretti of three late operas. In 1859 Verdi and Giuseppina married, significantly not in Busseto, but secretly, far to the north, in Haute-Savoie. They would have no children ('God is perhaps punishing me for my sins ... I will have no legitimate joys before I die,' wrote Giuseppina, sadly),[136] but later adopted an orphaned young cousin of Verdi's, whose own family became his heirs.

The year 1859 began Verdi's most active period of political involvement. He held elected office at local, regional and national level, though this was more a result of his public status as a celebrity supporter of Italian nationhood, and the urging of the nationalist leader Cavour, whom he admired, than of any political ambitions of his own. Indeed, he was dismissive of his own contribution ('as a deputy, Verdi was non-existent'),[137] and resigned as soon as he decently could (although he enjoyed the company of some of his fellow liberal-minded senators, and on one occasion apparently amused himself by setting a fiery exchange in the assembly to music, potentially a source for the council chamber scene which he and Boito added to the opera they were writing at the time, *Simon Boccanegra*). In 1859, too, his name began to be used in the famous slogan 'Viva Verdi', pasted on the crumbling walls of Naples, in which the letters of his name serve as a coded acronym for the king, Vittorio Emanuele, Re D'Italia.

Simon Boccanegra (1857) was followed by *Un ballo in Maschera* (1859), a version of the story of Gustavus III of Sweden also set by Auber, and, in the same year, *La forza del destino*, in response to a tasty commission from St Petersburg, which (tactfully engineered by Giuseppina) eased him out of another contented but unproductive period of duck-shooting, well-digging and half threatening to give up composing. A splendid photo of 1861 shows Verdi in Russia, wrapped in furs like Boris Godunov. The trip formed part of two years of travel, taking in Spain and Paris. Italy, meanwhile, endured the antics of the '*scapigliatura milanese*', one of those self-styled radical artistic movements led by stroppy young men (in this case, Boito) which make established older artists feel that the times are leaving them behind (which is, of course, very much the point). Verdi was back in Paris in 1865 for the substantially revised *Macbeth*.

Musical features of the period include opening *La forza del destino* with a full-blown overture, unusual for Verdi. The overture's scampering opening theme is soon combined with others, later recalled in arias, mixing mood and memory into the new context. This is nowhere near the manipulation of motif practised by Wagner, but it's as close as Verdi got. Verdi wrote self-mockingly to a friend about another technical trick in *La forza del destino*:

> You will smile when you see that for the battle I have written a fugue! I who detest all that smells of the school! But I tell you that in this case the musical form fits the occasion well. The rushing to and fro of the subject and counter-subject, and the clash of the dissonances express a battle well enough.[138]

It's an interesting insight into how a dry technical formula on the page can be transfigured into life and action on the stage. Fugues also end the 1865 *Macbeth* and, gloriously, *Falstaff*.

Verdi wrote just two new operas in the quarter century following *La forza del destino*'s premiere in 1862. Revised versions of several pieces consumed much of his energy. The two huge new works, *Don*

Carlos of 1867 and *Aida* of 1871, again show Verdi's remarkable capacity to continually renew and reinvent his art.

Don Carlos was commissioned by the Paris Opéra. The Verdis had an equivocal relationship with the French capital and its operatic ways. 'Everyone wants to give an opinion,' wrote Verdi later, decrying the 'fatal atmosphere of the Opéra'. Singers bickered about the size of their roles, and in rehearsal 'the tortoises of the Opéra take four hours to decide whether Mme Sax or M. Faure should raise one finger', as Giuseppina reported – not what she had been used to in her own singing career, conducted *prestissimo e con amore*.[139] Some of the 'fatal atmosphere', as well as another bout of ill health, seemed to drain Verdi of his usual appetite for harrying and chivvying his librettists, Joseph Méry and Camille du Locle, 'one of those pairs of theatre hacks by whom Verdi, as he remarked on an earlier occasion, seemed always to be haunted in Paris', as his biographer Dyneley Hussey puts it.[140] Hussey describes *Don Carlos* as 'a true music-drama'.[141] Six leads, caught in a web of private loneliness and desire and public antagonism and cruelty, invite sympathy and revulsion as they work their way through the complex plot. There is some wonderful stagey music for the big set pieces. In the Grand Inquisitor grand opera surely gains its grandest and most villainous villain. *Don Carlos* was soon heard in Italian and later substantially revised (becoming, in both cases, *Don Carlo*).

The plot of *Aida*, by contrast, is simple enough in its essence: a love triangle with a strong element of Verdi's often-revisited father–daughter motif, and an ancient Egyptian setting ambitious even by the standards of grand opera. The commission was appropriately exotic: a huge fee from the Khedive of Egypt, Isma'il Pasha, to celebrate the opening of his new opera house in Cairo (although in the event *Rigoletto* opened the house and *Aida* was first heard in late 1871).

Writing in 1881, Verdi stressed the need for 'declamation, exact and truthful – in fact, music' in opera (choosing, perhaps surprisingly, *The Barber of Seville* as his example).[142] Aria forms in the late operas still include set pieces like Radamès's slightly generic 'Celeste Aida', but move increasingly towards the free sequence form of Eboli's 'O don fatale' and Aida's 'Ritorna vincitor'. There are hints of internal thematic correspondence: when Radamès reflects on Amneris's fury a tune we have heard before injects her anger into the accompaniment. *Aida* has some unexpectedly intimate moments for this grandest of grand operas: at the beginning, before the expected Meyerbeerian hymns and marches comes a strange, slow, other-worldly prelude, and the opera ends with a beautiful but bizarre ensemble with the entombed Aida and Radamès repeating a short, angular little tune over and over: 'O terra addio ...'

As usual, this process involved much lengthy correspondence with the librettist, a skilful newcomer called Antonio Ghislanzoni. Other key figures include leading ladies Maria Waldmann, who sang Amneris at the Italian premiere in 1872, Verdi's favourite in the role, and, even more significantly, Teresa Stolz, who took the title role on the same occasion. Her fiancé, Angelo Mariani, had been first choice to conduct the Cairo premiere, though did not in fact do so. More importantly for Verdi's personal life, he mistreated Teresa, who became a regular visitor at Sant'Agata and source, naturally, of vicious rumour and gossip, stirred by the appearance in the papers of forged letters. Stolz's 'diamond-like'[143] voice and secure technique suited Verdi's late manner perfectly, and she sang many roles for him. On a personal level, the exact nature of the relationship remains hidden. Giuseppina wrote to her husband:

> If there's nothing in it ... be calmer in your attentions ... Remember that I, your wife, while despising past rumours am living at this very moment à trois and that I have the right to ask if not for your caresses at least for your consideration.[144]

But the two good-natured women managed to remain friends with each other and with their ageing Lothario. Their co-biographer describes 'each woman [as] an essential emotional benefactor without whom Verdi's career would not have been the same'.[145] (Stolz, incidentally, had identical twin sisters, both singers, who lived openly with the same man and both had his children, one of whom later became pregnant possibly by the composer Bedřich Smetana, itself a truly operatic scenario.)

Events away from the opera house at this period included the deaths in 1867 of both Verdi's father, Carlo Verdi, and his first father-in-law, Antonio Barezzi, a last link with the early days of grief and success. In 1871 he met Giulio Ricordi, key member of one of the family publishing dynasties who would feud like the best Sicilian opera plot over the rich pickings of celebrity opera composers, and a loyal friend and recording angel of his late reminiscences. A splendid series of cartoons shows Verdi stamping his feet in rehearsal, lugubriously examining a sixteenth-century motet, and playing with his much-loved Maltese spaniel Lulu. In a less happy, but sadly not untypical incident, Verdi fell out with his long-standing friend Cesare de Sanctis, who fell victim to economic recession and was unable to repay a loan. (Giuseppina, equally typically, mediated an arrangement whereby he repaid it with a regular supply of good pasta from Naples.)

Verdi, turning sixty, really did seem to have earned his long-threatened operatic retirement. In 1873, utterly out of character, he wrote a string quartet. The following year he composed his Requiem in memory of the national poet Alessandro Manzoni (using some music from the earlier abandoned project for a jointly written Requiem for Rossini). Verdi's Requiem is a thrilling piece, rattling the walls of hell in the *Dies Irae*, plangently appealing for peace in the *Agnus Dei*. Its operatic hinterland is unmissable: it was performed in opera houses, sharing billing in Paris with Bizet's brand-new *Carmen*. Bülow dismissed it as Verdi's 'latest opera, though in ecclesiastical robes',[146] but later recanted, and even admitted he hadn't actually heard it; of which Brahms said, 'Bülow has made an almighty fool of himself. Only a genius could have written such a work.'[147] Giuseppina said that 'a man like Verdi must write like Verdi', describing him earlier as 'I won't say an atheist, but certainly very little of a believer'.[148] Boito thought 'he was a great Christian'; not 'in the strictly theological sense', but 'in the ideal, moral and social sense'.[149]

The Last Operas

Verdi's final phase of creativity is without parallel in music history. He lived 'quietly, and, if not happily, well enough'[150] through sixteen years of operatic silence (years which did, however, involve much substantial revision of earlier pieces), resisting all blandishments to appear in public to 'perform the usual pirouettes and show my beautiful snout' like the *'ours Martin'* (a famous Pyrenean bear) – 'Oh! This publicity! I hate it.'[151] Friendships which helped talk him back to his work desk included a perhaps surprising link with Ferdinand Hiller, elderly emblem of all things German but an enthusiastic supporter, and with Ricordi, who reeled him in in a series of carefully planned fishing trips over the dinner table like 'an extremely wary old trout', as Hussey puts it,[152] Boito hovering in the background with libretto and landing net, until Verdi crossly declared himself 'as good as landed ... securely hooked'.[153] The bait was his beloved Shakespeare. An operatic *King Lear* had long been an ambition. Instead, Ricordi and Boito persuaded him to give up his own Lear-like 'fast intent To shake all cares and business from our age [and] ... Unburthen'd crawl toward death', and have a crack not at *Lear* but at another tragedy in the grand style, *Othello*. Verdi found Boito's libretto 'wholly Shakespearean'.[154] In December 1886 he finished the score: 'Poor Otello! He won't come back here any more.' Boito, ever encouraging, replied, '[B]ut you will go to meet the Moor at La Scala ... The great dream has come true.'[155]

The opening alone shows an imagination still full of white-hot determination not to stand still: no overture, not even a tune; not even a major or minor chord, but a violent plunge into the noise and dissonance of a thunderstorm, with an orchestra including an organ holding the three lowest notes on the pedal for fifty pages of score. Later come Iago's thunderous anti-Creed, Desdemona's 'Willow Song', and, right at the end, Otello's despairing recollection of the 'kiss' motif ('*un altro baccio ...*')

Then came *Falstaff*. Once again, the credit for talking the composer into one last burst of energy belongs to the librettist, Boito: 'There is only one way of ending your career better than with *Otello*, that is to end it with *Falstaff*.'[156] He was right. *Falstaff*, premiered at La Scala in Milan in February 1893, is a little miracle. It is short, taut, brilliantly constructed, funny, tuneful and bursting with the same vital life force which Elizabeth I of England recognised when she asked her courtier Shakespeare to give her another play featuring her favourite fat man. It's hard to say what is most astonishing about this piece: the magical orchestral evocations of the moonlit Windsor forest; the telescoping of technique in the compression of aria and melody; the extraordinary combination of points of view in the quartet, then double quartet, in Act One; the sureness of comic touch in Verdi's only mature comedy and his first since the failure of *Un giorno di regno* almost half a century before; the emergence of a brilliant, joyously youthful and entirely new manner in a man in his eightieth year, roaring with laughter in the face of death. New names among the singers mark the turning of the times: several were to make their reputations in the brave new world of verismo, just about to burst on to the operatic world.

Verdi's last decade included some sacred choral music, still inventive but a bit eccentric, and much philanthropy, including establishing a rest home for retired musicians, the Casa di Riposo, in Milan.

Giuseppina Strepponi Verdi died after a long illness in November 1897. Teresa Stolz succeeded her as Verdi's support and companion in his last years. He died in 1901. At his funeral in Milan the young Arturo Toscanini conducted a choir of 800 in 'Va, pensiero' from Nabucco. The crowd lining the streets, numbering in the tens, perhaps hundreds of thousands, joined in in spontaneous sotto voce as its composer's cortège passed.

Verdi and Wagner

From the start, commentators have looked for links as well as the more obvious radical discontinuities between the two giant contemporaries.

Verdi worked with many librettists, Wagner with just one (himself). But Verdi took a thoroughly active part in fashioning his texts alongside his wordsmiths. One of them, Cammarano, wrote to him: 'to reach the highest possible perfection in opera one single mind ought to be responsible for both words and music ... Poetry must be neither the slave of music nor its tyrant.'[157] In 1875, Verdi, having to his annoyance often been asked for his views on Wagner, said, 'I too attempted to blend music and drama, in my *Macbeth* ... but unlike Wagner I was not able to write my own libretti.'[158] Very late in life he seems partly to have accepted Wagner's ideas about vocal line and style of declamation:

> Desdemona is a part in which the thread, the melodic line never ceases from the first note to the last. Just as Iago has only to declaim and *ricaner*, and just as Otello ... must sing and shout, so Desdemona must always, always sing.[159]

The Act Two duet between Iago and Otello approaches the Wagnerian ideal of *'unendliche Melodie'*, music in continuous motion.

Orchestral sound is fundamental to the thought of both men, but was assembled by different methods. Wagner would build up his scores in a series of iterative versions, expanding a short piano score on to several staves, separating out orchestral families before moving on to the full score. Verdi, like Wagner, conceived his ideas with their orchestral colour already clear in his mind, telling his fellow senator Quintino Sella, 'The idea presents itself complete, and above all I feel the colour ... whether it should be the flute or the violin.'[160] Posa's dead march in *Don Carlos*, the lightning flashes in *Rigoletto*, and the halo-like two solo violins in the aria *'Celeste Aida'* make the point clear: this is not music which was composed one day then orchestrated the next in an entirely separate part of the process, any more than Siegfried's horn calls or the Good Friday music in *Parsifal*. But, intriguingly, Verdi would often actually specify in his contracts that orchestration would not be done until after piano rehearsals began, the creative process continuing as he listened and reacted to his singers.[161]

Both composers absolutely insisted on high standards and respectful treatment of their works; both, inevitably, didn't always get it. One writer believes that Verdi's art was always 'primarily that of a craftsman whose duty is to supply his employer with the kind of article he has ordered', while '[the] opposite point of view found its supreme expression at Bayreuth'.[162] But both men obediently inserted ballets in inappropriate places when Paris wanted them to. Verdi firmly drew the line at cuts to accommodate incompetent singers, justly railing against the 'indecent fashion' in which *Don Carlo* was given on one occasion at Reggio, with much of it missing and an act each of *Macbeth* and Meyerbeer's *Les Huguenots* added to make up time (surely a singularly bizarre and confusing night at the opera).[163]

Their attitude towards what their art was for likewise has to be triangulated between what they said and what they did. Verdi was surely writing in one of his habitual depressions (and challenging his correspondent to disagree with him) when he said, '[I]f *Don Carlos* doesn't make money, put it aside and ask for [Massenet's] *Le Roi de Lahore* ... You will say that ... it befouls the altar; no matter, you can clean it afterwards'.[164] And surely Wagner wouldn't have dreamed of saying, as Verdi did later, 'I am writing to pass the time' (though Verdi didn't mean it either).[165] On other occasions he could approach Wagner's iron-willed insistence on art 'taking into account the character and the individuality of the author'.[166]

Both men found support and inspiration in deep if unconventional relationships with women with a musical hinterland of their own. Giuseppina always referred to her husband as 'Verdi' in her letters; Wagner's satellites habitually called him 'The Master', although Cosima usually just referred to 'R.' in her diaries, which are laconic and matter of fact, by contrast to her husband's florid writing style. Verdi in his black moods could, in Hussey's apt phrase, 'quarrel with his own shadow'.[167] It was part of Giuseppina's role to cope with the fallout: 'he sees ... lapses on the part of the servants through a magnifying glass when he's in a bad mood and these poor devils need someone to look after their interests'.[168] Both composers adored their dogs.

Verdi's public pronouncements on other composers were few and guarded. Wagner's weren't. Neither were wholly reliable, both (as always) revealing as much about the writer as about the putative object of their comments.

They could hardly ignore each other. Wagner, we are told, could barely bear to hear Verdi's name mentioned. Verdi, hearing Wagner's *Tannhäuser* overture in Paris, concluded that 'he's mad'. Cosima spoke for the Wagner camp after she and Richard attended a performance of Verdi's Requiem: 'a work of which it is better not to speak',[169] and, later, would not allow Verdi's name to be mentioned in her presence.[170] Verdi heard *Lohengrin* in Bologna in 1871: the 'Lohengrenades' of publicity (as he called them) irritated him;[171] more importantly, he took a vocal score with him and marked it up with his thoughts: '*brutto ... bello ... brutto il cigno ...*' ('ugly ... beautiful ... the swan ugly ...') Many of his comments reveal the professional at work: 'chorus out of tune'; 'why slow down here?' Most revealing is a staccato summing-up at the end:

> Impression mediocre. Music beautiful, when it is clear and there is thought in it. The action, like the words, moves too slowly. Hence boredom. Beautiful effects of instrumentation. Too many held notes, which makes for heaviness.[172]

Like those other great contemporaries, Bach and Handel, they never met. But it seems that, unlike Bach and Handel, neither of them even tried. At best their attitude to each other was, perhaps, respectful but distant. Searching for a libretto in the dark hours of 1869, Verdi sent for Wagner's prose writings in a French translation 'since I want to get to know that side of him, too'.[173] The day after

Wagner's death in February 1883 Verdi wrote to Ricordi: '*Triste. Triste. Triste. Wagner è morto!* ... Reading the news yesterday, I was, I don't know, struck with terror ... A great individual has disappeared! A name that has left a most powerful mark on the history of art!'[174] It's a curious letter, with its mixture of the conventional pieties for a high-ranking colleague, the strange three-fold repetition of '*Triste*' with its unavoidable echo of the title of Wagner's most famous and most disturbing work, the odd choice of the word 'terror' to describe his reaction, and the ambiguous searching for an instant assessment of Wagner's achievement: Verdi first wrote '*potente*' ('powerful'), then crossed it out and replaced it with '*potentissima*' ('most powerful'); but, at the same time, a powerful mark is not necessarily a benevolent one.

Much more important than personal comments is evidence of places where their musical and dramatic thinking went down similar paths, and of how, despite their mutual protestations to the contrary, they influenced each other. In 1848, just before Wagner's *Opera and Drama*, Verdi was thinking along strikingly similar dramaturgical lines, as he shows in a letter concerning a production of *Macbeth*: 'the scene must be very dark ... Lady Macbeth's voice should be hard ... the band under the stage should be strengthened ... the floor ... should have a slant up and down, so that [the characters] should appear to rise and descend'.[175] He also wanted muted strings, contra-bassoons and key trumpets for the battle fugue, not valve trumpets, which sound too nice and too in tune. All this is *echt*-Wagner. Much later, in 1871, Verdi told Ricordi that for *Aida* he should 'get rid of those stage boxes [and] take the curtain right to the footlights; and also make the orchestra invisible'. 'This idea isn't mine, it's Wagner's: and it's excellent,' he said, pointing out the difficulty of the audience fully entering 'the fictional world' when their eye-line is full of 'tired evening dress and white ties', not to mention 'the massed ranks of the orchestra' in the middle of 'Egyptian, Assyrian or Druidic costumes'.[176]

In terms of mutual musical co-influence, as early as the year of Verdi's death, 1901, the musicologist Hugo Riemann noted that 'A significant change of style separates "late" Verdi from the works of his middle period. This, quite frankly, is to be traced to the influence of Richard Wagner.'[177] Verdi would no doubt have snorted in irritated derision at such presumption, but Riemann reads his evidence

Elephants, Arias and the Gods at Twilight: Opera

a) Verdi

b) Wagner

Verdi and Wagner reaching for the same chord (the dominant thirteenth, marked with a cross), to convey emotion at the moment of two very different deaths: that of Gilda in Rigoletto (1851), and of Siegfried in Götterdämmerung (f.p. 1876).

well. We have noted Wagnerian elements in Verdi's late vocal style: and, working the other way, clear echoes of Verdi can be seen in *Götterdämmerung* and in *Parsifal*'s flower maidens. As for following their own and each other's advice: both began by writing in the inherited closed units of aria and ensemble; both stated their determination to move away from the limitations of such fixed forms; both did so up to a point; both reverted to type when it suited them.

Some specific musical moments must end this brief attempt to highlight connections between the two composers. In *Un ballo in Maschera*, and again in *La traviata*, tenor and soprano lovers tear each other apart by the force of their self-destructive passion, as they do in *Tristan und Isolde*: a similar place approached from diametrically opposite directions. Both composers reach for the plangency of the dominant thirteenth chord at climactic moments of emotion and drama: Siegfried and Gilda dying; Otello bidding farewell to love; Lohengrin's knights greeting the Grail. In *Rigoletto* Gilda's dying phrase recalls an earlier appearance – a motif, if not a leitmotif. The

Grand Inquisitor's major/minor brass chords in *Don Carlos* sound Wagnerian, as Verdi must have realised: his serpentine bass line recalls similar themes buried at the bottom of the texture for sinister characters in Wagner. Posa and Siegfried's death marches have a similar structural arc: chords, inner melodies, and a wriggly chromatic tune adding something not quite understood.

Verdi and Wagner both sprang from their own soil. As Verdi put it, 'If the Germans springing from Bach have arrived at Wagner, that is well. But if we, the descendants of Palestrina, imitate Wagner, we commit a musical crime.'[178] From the more recent past, both met the magniloquent challenge of French grand opera, itself an alloy of Italian singing and German Romantic orchestral writing, and produced from it an amalgam of more lasting resilience and worth. Their inheritors (not successors), waiting not always patiently in the wings, might have found themselves remembering the closing lines of *King Lear* (which Verdi never did set to music): 'We that are young Shall never see so much, nor live so long.'

Fin-de-siècle

Italy: Boito, Verismo, Puccini

Operatically, the nineteenth century was a *siècle* with a long *fin*.

As a composer, Verdi's librettist Arrigo Boito completed only one opera, *Mefistofele*, premiered in 1868. It was a disaster. Wisely, he altered and shortened it, and, with a fine cast and conductor, achieved success in 1875.

Verdi sent up the traditional cry of the older artist: 'I had always read and understood that the Prologue in heaven was a thing of spontaneity, of genius ... yet hearing how the harmonies of that piece are almost all based on dissonances I seemed to be ... not in heaven, certainly!'[179] Accusations of unrelieved dissonance appear unfounded to our later ears: *Mefistofele* is a big piece, with some fine tableaux and a great lead character; but it certainly lacks the element of human sympathy and subtlety which the best big opera manages to convey through the bombast.

Around the same time as his comments on Boito, Verdi let fly one of his self-pitying rhodomontades: '[Massenet's] *Le Roi de Lahore* [is] an opera of many virtues, an opera of the present without human interest, most suitable to his age of *verismo* in which there is no verity, an almost surefire opera.'[180]

Verismo literally translates as 'realism'. Like opera buffa of almost two hundred years earlier or the 'kitchen sink' TV and stage drama that came a century or so later, verismo reached for ordinary life to make theatre. It formed part of a wider movement in the arts exemplified by the realistic novels of Émile Zola and Alexandre Dumas *fils*, dealing with the squalid violence and passion of everyday behaviour rather than the sweeping historical epics of Victor Hugo. In operatic terms, it burst onto the scene in 1890 when Pietro Mascagni set a play of 1884 by the Sicilian writer Giovanni Verga, based on his own story of 1880, which he called *Cavalleria Rusticana* (*Rustic Chivalry*). Two years later Ruggero Leoncavallo composed an opera to his own libretto, based, he said, on a real-life murder trial over which his father, a magistrate, had presided (the ultimate verismo is *la verità* – real life): the leader of a troupe of travelling players discovers that his wife is unfaithful to him and stabs both her and her lover during the play in which all three appear, and leaves the stage clutching his dagger, tears smearing his face paint. The opera is called *Pagliacci* (*Clowns*). Both composers wrote many other works, some of which were successful. In both cases, these early one-acters became their calling cards, not least because companies realised early on that they made a great double bill.

The two operas known ever after as 'Cav and Pag' sum up the verismo style. They present a '*squarcio di vita*', a 'slice of life', as promised in the prologue to *Pagliacci*, in a peasant or working-class setting. A horrifying or extreme event, often a crime of passion, sits at the centre. They are short and direct: even Verdi commented approvingly that Mascagni 'has invented a most effective genre: short operas without pointless longueurs'. Big tunes emerge from a through-composed texture, rather than in clearly delineated arias. Puccini in particular perfected the practice of a melody appearing first in the orchestra, usually quietly, often counterpointed with a vocal parlando (a kind of rhythmic declamation on one or just a few notes, almost like speech), then, later in the aria, in the full-throttle vocal version, complete with muscularly athletic high notes. Orchestration is vivid and brash; vocal tone is big and dark. Singers sob, pant, sigh and laugh as well as sing. Harmony is fluid, full of ambiguous added-note chords, rarely allowed to settle. Verdi, reading a score of Mascagni, 'soon got tired of all those dissonances, false relations, interrupted cadences and so on, and all those changes of tempo at almost every bar',[181] adding, 'but I'm just an old fogey [*codino*]'.[182]

Popularity wars among the veristi were conducted under the skilled generalship of publishers like the canny Ricordi and his rival Edoardo Sonzogno, who instituted an influential prize for new opera. Mascagni won it; Puccini didn't, resulting in Puccini being snapped up by Ricordi – which was a definite win for both. Some dodgy dealings by Sonzogno over a contract in Rome, and the publication of an inflammatory letter in, of all places, the London *Daily Telegraph*, even led on one occasion to Sonzogno challenging Boito to a duel. Fortunately, cooler heads prevailed.

Verismo's glory years were short. It was always principally an Italian affair: leading exponents included Francesco Cilea, Alfredo Catalani and Umberto Giordano, among many others. Composers from other countries who bought into aspects of its brightly coloured emotional style included the Frenchmen Jules Massenet and Gustave Charpentier and, perhaps surprisingly, an English composer, Henry Cowen. Its best and most lasting exponent was a composer who in some works took its innate theatricality to new levels, in others wasn't a veristo at all, and whose own life sometimes mirrored the emotional turmoil of some of his characters: Giacomo Puccini.

Puccini's reputation has occupied a curious dual position from the very start. There is something about his work which riles a certain kind of critic like no other. At the same time, music-lovers and theatre-goers flock to him.

The drama first: Puccini described the sections of *La bohème* (1896) as tableaux, not acts. His drama moves in a series of blocks. This happens within the sections, and in terms of the psychological action, too: in Act One Mimì appears at Rodolfo's door; after a minute or two they are in love. There is no negotiation, no '*Là ci darem la mano*', no getting to know you. It's like the composer has simply switched on a light. They remain in this happy state for Act Two. Then, at the opening of Act Three, without warning or explanation, Rodolfo is tormented by jealousy of a 'young rascal of a Viscount' with whom Mimì is involved. We do not meet him, nor do we find out how she got to that point. There is none of the slow, careful investigation of human motivation which makes Act Two of *La traviata* so rewarding. Puccini can portray emotional states, but he cannot make his characters change.

For the careful listener, this invisible viscount is a frustrating missing link. We either have to accept his absolutely game-changing, but missing, effect on the drama, or we ignore it. Tellingly, the libretto supplied to Puccini by Giuseppe Giacosa and Luigi Illica originally contained another act which charts how this new relationship, and with it Rodolfo's jealousy, progresses. Puccini didn't set it. Was it because, as one writer claims, 'Puccini felt it would be too similar in texture to the Café Momus scene' (which became Act Two)?[183] Or was it because his art was not up to the subtle shifting of emotions which turns Mimì's drinking glass at an *al fresco* party into an object through which '*vi agonizza l'amor implacata becchino*' ('implacable love agonises like the bringer of death')? If so, does it matter?

This tableau-like approach to emotional drama had other manifestations, too. The four acts of *Manon Lescaut* (1893) add up to what Abbate and Parker call a 'blatant discontinuity'. Each act is, in a way, an individual drama in its own right. This was Puccini's choice: while many composers harried their librettists to refine and improve the drama which they then revealed through their music, Puccini drove his wordsmiths to distraction by doing rather the opposite: as Abbate and Parker put it, he 'bullied and overrode them because he knew instinctively that modern opera didn't rely on such trivial narrative coherence'.[184]

The music, too, comes in slabs. Verdi noted the changing of the guard in a generous and perceptive comment of June 1884:

> I have heard the composer Puccini highly spoken of ... He follows modern tendencies, which is natural, but he keeps to melody which is neither ancient nor modern. However, the symphonic vein appears to predominate in him. No harm in that, but one needs to tread carefully here. Opera is opera and symphony symphony and I don't think it's a good thing to put a symphonic piece into an opera merely to put the orchestra through its paces.[185]

Leaving aside the fact that at this stage the 26-year-old Puccini had only completed one opera, the one-act *Le Villi* of 1883, and that Verdi hadn't yet heard a note of the younger man's music, the use of the slightly ambiguous term 'symphonic vein' is interesting. It could be taken as a warning shot about the effects of too much Wagner.

Puccini's early operas, understandably, contain much Wagner. In the three great successes of Puccini's middle-aged maturity, *La bohème*, *Tosca* (1900) and *Madama Butterfly* (1904), Wagner's harmonic and melodic style is largely absent, but there is a strikingly theatrical version of the principle of recurring motifs. In *Tosca*, for example, the blaring, tri-tonal opening chords recur as an emblem of the villain Scarpia's cruelty. More interestingly, in a long duet between Tosca and her ultimately doomed lover Cavaradossi in Act One, the orchestra quietly introduces one of Puccini's trademark cantabile melodies, almost in the background, with the singers conversing in a sort of parlando over the top, as if the full emotional force of their relationship and situation has not yet dawned on them. Only later in the act do they get to sing the tune, in full orchestral colour and in a different key, remembering, for themselves and the listener, its earlier associations. The whole work is made up of this sort of free-flowing, overlapping patchwork of theme and colour.

One of the key gripes of his critics is that Puccini sometimes uses his motifs with insufficient regard to dramatic and structural rigour, or even simple logic. At the end of *La bohème* Mimì, like all good operatic heroines, dies of consumption. As Rodolfo is left rueing his jealous possessiveness, the orchestra closes the drama with three chords. These chords have been heard before, at the moment when Colline, one of Rodolfo's bohemian chums, bade farewell to his manky old overcoat. Why? What do those chords have to do with Mimì's death? Similarly, Tosca chucks herself off the battlements of the Castel Sant'Angelo to a swirling burst of the tune of Cavaradossi's aria '*E lucevan le stelle*', which she didn't hear, wasn't about her, and anyway he's dead. Is this a failure on Puccini's part? Or is he just associating the moment more broadly with an emotion, allowing Tosca to echo Cavaradossi's final words, '*non ho amato mai tanto la vita*': that he never loved life so much as in what, unbeknown to him, were its last seconds? Or is his musical scheme, like his plots, sometimes as full of holes as Colline's coat?

One of Puccini's most impressive contributions is his tableau scenes. These great musical collages do not display the forensic skill of a Mozartian finale or the large-scale structural engineering of a Verdian concertato; nor do they need to. They are often constructed with extra-musical sound. The second act of *La bohème* bombards the audience with a constantly shifting kaleidoscope of children's songs, marching bands and street cries. It's more like being at the circus than the opera. The main characters are glimpsed and heard here and there through the melee. Many critics complained about the use of what they regarded as unmusical 'noise'.[186] But it cost its composer-architect considerable pains and great care. Puccini travelled to Rome to note down the notes of the bells of St Peter's and the Castel Sant'Angelo, fashioning their actual pitches into the great, clangorous passacaglia at the end of Act One, and got a poet friend to find (or write) a song in Roman dialect for a shepherd boy to sing off-stage as the waking city is sleepily summoned to Matins at dawn at the opening of Act Three. This lengthy, painstaking labour is key to the urgent immediacy of his art. *Tosca* took four years to compose from the moment he acquired the rights to Victorien Sardou's play (which was itself six years after he'd seen it). He produced no fewer than five versions of *Madama Butterfly* in the three years following its premiere.

Another part of the Puccini problem for the puritan-minded critic, whether they admit it or not, is that the emotions on display are often loud rather than deep. Benjamin Britten spoke for many when he said, '[A]fter four or five performances I never wanted to hear *Bohème* again. In spite of its neatness, I became sickened by the cheapness and emptiness of the music.'[187] In this reading, lovers are sickly and sentimental, and baddies are just bad: Scarpia has none of the redeeming grandeur of Verdi's Iago or the captivating and courageous self-confidence of Mozart's Don Giovanni. Certainly Puccini's private life had plenty of the destructive self-indulgence which he visited on many of his victims on stage: a serial womaniser, he married a woman whose husband was murdered by the husband of one of his own mistresses; she in turn accused Puccini of having an affair with their maid, who took poison and died slowly and in agony, in their house (and, tragically, turned out to be guiltless: Puccini was actually having an affair with her cousin, who bore his child). Many have linked this unhappy episode to the fate of Liù, a slave girl in his last, unfinished opera *Turandot*, who escapes from torture by suicide (both depicted voyeuristically on stage). A similarly broad-brush vein of exploitative cruelty is applied to another suicide, Madama Butterfly herself, Cio-Cio-san, seduced and abandoned by a cynical, self-serving older man: Butterfly is just fifteen years old.

The literary critic F. R. Leavis taught us that the moral outlook of a work of art is a measure of its value. Is he right? Yes. Does Puccini fail that test? Probably. Does it matter? Not really. Art is big enough to cope. In the words of the wise critic Ernest Newman: '[Puccini's] operas are to some extent a mere bundle of tricks, but no one else has performed the same tricks nearly as well.'[188]

National Styles and Language

Opera was uniquely placed to ally itself to national characteristics, through its plots and, crucially, its language.

Russian composers of the mid nineteenth century had featured peasants alongside princes, a practice which finds some echoes in the low-life settings of verismo. More influentially, works like Mussorgsky's *Boris Godunov* moved away from the stylised formality of Tchaikovsky's settings of Pushkin to something more closely aligned to the rhythms of spoken Russian, building on the practice of his compatriots Dargomyzhsky and Cui. The concept found fertile ground in various outposts of operatic Europe.

Debussy composed just one opera, *Pelléas et Mélisande*, written over several years and premiered in 1902. This wasn't for want of trying: lengthy early labour on a standard-issue libretto by the establishment writer Catulle Mendès went nowhere because the conservative conventions of French opera were far removed from the kind of drama which Debussy instinctively knew was within his grasp (and which, as he also knew, would baffle the comfortable reactionaries among Parisian opera-goers). He found what he was looking for in the dramas of Maurice Maeterlinck, focusing on the inner psychology of the characters rather than on outward action. There are clear echoes of Wagner here. To the Symbolist movement, symbols functioned a little like Wagnerian motifs, and Debussy fashioned his own version of the technique in music which, like Wagner, places much importance on the orchestra (including in orchestral linking passages, though these came about partly because the stage machinery at the Opéra-Comique worked more slowly than expected, requiring more music to cover scene changes). At the same time, Debussy deliberately distanced himself from his Wagnerian model, rewriting some passages which he thought sounded too much like Wagner.

The result is a unique and precious amalgam. One early critic, writing in 1908, talked perceptively of the work's use of 'intensified speech occasionally resembling plain or Gregorian chant'.[189] Another made a similar assessment a year earlier: 'virtually a chant; an opera in which there is no vocal melody whatsoever, and comparatively little symphonic development of themes in the orchestra'.[190] The strange, floaty, disembodied mood of the music is enhanced by the almost total lack of action on stage – a slow-burn love triangle in an indeterminately medieval setting. The vocal writing is shaped by the comparative lack of stresses in French declamation, as in much French vocal music. Despite many early difficulties, the work made a big impact, influencing composers like its champion and first conductor André Messager and Debussy's friends Vincent d'Indy and Paul Dukas, and inspiring a cult following among the rather tiresome aesthetes who gathered around the Symbolist poets Jean Lorrain and Robert de Montesquiou, as well as the inevitable criticism from old-school Brahmsians like Saint-Saëns, who apparently deliberately cancelled his summer holiday so he could stay in Paris and 'say nasty things about *Pelléas*'.[191] Debussy tried hard to write more operas, working up treatments of two stories by Edgar Allan Poe, but, perhaps partly because of the challenges presented by *Pelléas*, never succeeded. Maeterlinck's play, meanwhile, inspired music from very different musical minds, including Fauré, Sibelius and Schoenberg.

Poor old England hardly raised a ripple on the swirling seas of Romantic opera. Although he is best remembered now for his church music, Sir Charles Villiers Stanford spent much of his career conducting and composing opera. Frederick Delius wrote several operas, all of which were premiered in Germany, and were often criticised for a wafty lack of tension. His contemporary Isidore de Lara, born Isidore Cohen in 1858, was a singer and composer of operas including *Amy Robsart*, about a still-unexplained intrigue at the court of Elizabeth I. In a sign of the mongrel quality of native English opera, it was sung at Covent Garden in 1893 in French. De Lara spent much of his later career trying to establish a national opera company in England: one of those bold ideas which found fruition after its early pioneers had left the scene. One of the most striking English operas of the period is *The Wreckers* by Ethel Smyth, a stormy tale of shipwreck and plunder on the Cornish coast, encompassing a knowledge of Strauss and Wagner and notably pre-echoing aspects of Britten's *Peter Grimes*. Gustav Mahler considered giving the opera its premiere at the Vienna State Opera, but sadly lost his post there before he could bring the idea to fruition – 'one of the small tragedies of my life,' said Smyth.[192]

In the event it was heard first in Leipzig in 1906. Beecham included it in his first Covent Garden season in 1910. Another of Smyth's operas, *Der Wald*, remained the only opera composed by a woman to be staged at the New York Met for over a century following its American premiere in 1903.

Like Debussy, Béla Bartók wrote only one, highly distinctive opera. *Bluebeard's Castle* was composed in 1911, with a revised ending added in 1917, but was not heard until 1918. It is a work of extraordinary boldness, matching a minimum of stage action with an intense, Expressionist psychological drama for its two characters, wringing powerful music from the declamatory style fashioned around its Hungarian text, and brilliantly written for the orchestra. The mood is unique: as if Bartók, who could create such fizzing energy elsewhere in his music, is somehow trying to drain both characters and audience of sensory input, wandering around the darkened castle which bleeds and sighs, as the heroine Judith cajoles Bluebeard in spare, unadorned vocal phrases which barely overlap to reveal the secrets he has hidden behind seven locked doors: blood, tears and, finally, his former wives, representing dawn, midday and dusk, inviting Judith to join them as the fourth and final wife of the night. It is a disturbing and compelling piece, resisting easy interpretation.

Drama sounds different sung in different languages: the big, open vowel sounds of Italian for the big, open emotions of verismo; the lilting rhythms of French for something subtler and more self-regarding; the earthier sounds of Hungarian, Russian and Czech somehow closer to the soil.

Janáček

Leoš Janáček came late to opera. Like a much earlier operatic innovator, Jean-Philippe Rameau, he was over fifty when his first opera in his fully mature style was staged, 1904's *Jenůfa*. He wrote six further operas, completing the last, *From the House of the Dead*, in 1928, the year of his death. Their verbal and musical manner is utterly distinctive.

Janáček was born in 1854, the son of a village schoolmaster in rural Moravia. A scholarship to the choir school in Brno at the age of eleven relieved his parents of the expense of housing and feeding at least one of their children in the damp schoolhouse. Further studies followed in Prague, where, too poor to afford a piano in his lodgings, he practised by drawing a keyboard onto a table. A marked, and occasionally perverse, vein of individualism surfaced in his attitude to some of his teachers and colleagues: he was expelled for publicly criticising his professor's style of performing Gregorian chant (though subsequently reinstated), and later took to writing caustic articles and reviews in journals, accusing fellow Czech composer Karel Kovařovic of writing an operatic comedy in which 'the music and the libretto aren't connected to each other'.[193] He studied further in Leipzig and Vienna before heading back to Brno, armed with a newly internationalist outlook, a deep love of his native roots and a fierce work ethic. He married, founded an organ school and composed in a style loyal to the example of his compatriots Smetana and Dvořák, a friend from the mid 1870s.

In 1885 Janáček paid a visit to his home village and, like other composers across Europe and beyond, heard its folk music as if for the first time. Not for him was the absorption of folk style into symphonic form, as practised by Max Bruch, Brahms and back to Haydn. Nor did he anticipate the later approach of Hungarians Bartók and Zoltán Kodály by accentuating the exhilarating polyrhythms of folk song. His method was glued to the speech patterns of his native Czech language, and in particular to the vocal inflections which could give the same words, even simple greetings, different shades of meaning in different contexts. Character and mood are captured by reproducing this rise and fall accurately: an 'entire being in a photographic instant,' said Janáček.[194] His vision had found its method. Nor was this melodic manner limited to music with words: he carries its clarity and concision into his instrumental music, too, with its sparse textures, high and low sounds without the stodgy filling of the traditional Straussian 'horn sandwich', brittle fanfares, triadic harmony emerging like the sun rather than being constructed like a kit and, above all, tunes in short, bird-like bursts.

Like some other notable operas of the period, Janáček's stage works break with convention by setting existing prose plays rather than old-style poetic librettos. He favoured a kind of folksy Dostoyevskian pessimism surely partly traceable to his love of Russian music and literature: Smetana's cheery peasants would never have buried a baby under the ice of a frozen river or thrown themselves into the Volga to get away from a moralising mother-in-law, as in Janáček's *Jenůfa* and *Káťa Kabanová* respectively.

Jenůfa finds love only by accepting her stepmother's cruelty and the loss of her child. In *The Cunning Little Vixen*, woodland animals invite an old forester to reflect on life, death, good, evil and the turning of time only after Vixen Sharp-Ears is shot by a poacher. *The Makropulos Affair* of 1925 is another study in time passing, featuring a singer who lives for 300 years but comes to realise that satisfaction exists within the limits of a natural lifespan: a reflection perhaps encouraged by Janáček's late, lengthy, lifelong but unrequited infatuation with a much younger woman, Kamila Stösslová.

The Operas of Richard Strauss

After Wagner, German opera looked both forwards and backwards. One composer did both.

Richard Strauss began as an anti-Wagnerian, loyal to the opinions of his Classically inclined father Franz (who nonetheless played the horn in the premieres of no fewer than four of Wagner's operas and the viola in the Munich premiere of another). As a young conductor Richard became the bearer of the Bayreuth flame as one of Wagner's principal advocates and best interpreters, christened 'Richard III' by Hans von Bülow (apparently nobody could directly succeed Wagner as 'Richard II'). Strauss's early attempts at writing opera foundered, as for Debussy, on the usual obstacles of stifling operatic convention and dull libretti: his narrative and theatrical flair instead found expression in the brilliantly colourful orchestral tone poems of the last years of the nineteenth century. The new century saw him hailed as king of the modernists, then a strange regression back to the manners and sounds of the eighteenth century, then a lengthy and conservative (and controversial) late period, closed by a rich Indian summer in which he turned back (or is that forward?) to the lush gestures of nineteenth-century Romanticism. Musically, his was a life lived in the wrong order.

Strauss's operatic voice spoke with many different accents. *Salome* (1905) and *Elektra* (1909) pursue a kind of violent decadence, but were followed by the sumptuous Romanticism of *Der Rosenkavalier* (1911) and the neo-Mozartian *Ariadne auf Naxos* (1912). Of his nine further operas written over the next thirty years, *Die Frau ohne Schatten* (1919) is often cited as his finest operatic score, in spite of its ridiculous story. *Intermezzo* (1924), *Arabella* (1933) and *Capriccio* (1942) each take a new look at an old form, challenging and full of beauties.

Salome sets a play by Oscar Wilde, originally written in French. In the brief gospel accounts of the death of John the Baptist, Salome isn't even mentioned by name. Wilde drenched this bare outline in all the decadence of a dying decade: Herod lusts uncontrollably for his 16-year-old stepdaughter, who, egged on by her mother, agrees to dance for him in return for serving up the Baptist's head on a platter, which he does. Young Salome slavers over the Baptist's unattainable body both before and after his execution. Strauss's music adds lashings of hysteria to Wilde's excesses.

In *Der Rosenkavalier* Strauss and his librettist, Hugo von Hofmannsthal, who supplied texts for the four middle-period operas starting with *Elektra*, take us explicitly into the world of Mozartian opera buffa; indeed, in Hofmannsthal's initial sketches the characters who become Ochs, the Marschallin and Octavian are archetypes, referred to simply as 'the buffo', 'the Lady' and 'the Cherubino'.[195] Poet and composer added richness to these stock types: Strauss's Ochs has elements of a predatory Don Giovanni as well as the blustery old buffo; 'the Lady' ages like an antique portrait into a vision of the countess in later life, faded, satiated, sad and alone, letting her young lover go as she knows she must; Octavian is Cherubino transformed from a young blood who longs to have sex with every woman he meets into one who actually does: *Der Rosenkavalier* even begins with Octavian and the Marschallin in bed.

Opera's great century, the age of the suspension of disbelief, celebrated and summated in the closing pages of *Der Rosenkavalier*, was over.

Part Seven

THE AGE OF ANXIETY (1888–1975)

INTRODUCTION

The nineteenth century sought to view the world as a whole. The twentieth century was compelled to deconstruct it again.

Music followed suit. Where Romantic musical thought had merged and combined forms and techniques towards an organic unity, new styles deliberately took elements out: twelve-tone music removed tonality; Neoclassicism removed Romantic gesture; minimalism removed melody. Analyses of musical works began to begin by explaining the ways in which they weren't, in fact, in sonata form.

As always, music mirrored changes in society. Music about nature gave way to music about cities and trains. In France, 'the world of opera houses and fashionable restaurants' known as the Belle Époque hid 'an age of neurotic, even hysterical national anxiety, filled with political instability, crises and scandals'.[1] Other countries had their equivalents.

Styles and schools could be local, focused on a particular country, city or individual: German Expressionism, American jazz, Parisian Neoclassicism, Schoenbergian serialism. They could even be hyperlocal: English pastoralism grew not just from a nation but largely from a single county, Gloucestershire. Some schools served to obscure rather than illuminate the ideals of their originators: Schoenberg had limited patience with what he called the 'Schbrg clique'.[2]

Choices

All of this presented composers with choices. Are you a modernist or are you a populist? How do you confront the looming shadow of the past? What counts as a great work? What is progress? Do you believe in tonality? What, and who, is your music actually for?

Music as an artistic philosophy had, as always, to take account of the work of other thinkers, including the analyses of Freud and Jung, a profound and acknowledged influence on composers as different as Elliott Carter and Michael Tippett. Music drew on trends in other arts as varied as the Viennese Secessionists, the eclectic optimism of the Blaue Reiter artists, the gloomy depression of the Brücke group, French Impressionists, the architecture of Gropius, Goldfinger and Le Corbusier, the woodcuts of William Morris and the typefaces of Art Nouveau.

Changes in society surface, too, in the way the people in these chapters lived their lives: the story begins to feature a large number of homosexual men, and some women, and a more or less infinite variety of domestic and family arrangements. Works for children provide an intriguing subtext. Many of these musicians also did other things, often to a high level: there are composers here who were also painters, economists, inventors, novelists, engineers, insurance brokers, architects, poets and mathematicians, as well as performers, academics, lyricists, free thinkers, eccentrics and Morris dancers. A perhaps surprisingly small number were politically active, although many were caught up in political situations not of their choosing.

Politics

This raises the troublesome question of the extent to which the music itself can be held to be political. Some pieces ally themselves explicitly with historical events or ideas through their text or title (sometimes after they were composed). Others were appropriated to do so, as with the 'diverse and contradictory theories' of the Bolsheviks, as Stravinsky called them,[3] which turned Beethoven's 'Eroica' Symphony into the hymn of the warrior people to their leader, and changed the plot of *The Nutcracker* to make it less 'foreign'. New works deliberately written to fit Soviet ideology, Stravinsky tells us, included mass-opera, plotless opera and Soviet realist works such as Vladimir Deshevov's *Ice and Steel* of 1929, based on a real anti-Bolshevik uprising. Living composers were told what their pieces meant, what they'd done right and wrong, and what to do next. Some did: in 1944 Aram Khachaturian composed the official *Anthem of the Armenian Soviet Socialist Republic*, served as a Soviet deputy, and is quoted as stating that 'if I have really grown into a serious artist, then I am indebted only to the people and the Soviet Government'.[4] He remained an enthusiastic communist throughout his life, the only composer of substance to have emerged from the Soviet project. Less willingly, Heitor Villa-Lobos arranged music sung by 30,000 schoolchildren for Brazil's Independence Day in 1939, and chaired a committee to produce a definitive version of the Brazilian national anthem following the Vargas coup of 1937. Sibelius used his art to promote his own vision of his nation against a controlling regime, in the process producing national songs and melodies much more authentic than the official ones (as, in their different ways, did Parry, Elgar and Irving Berlin).

In Germany, music trod a complicated path through the Nazis' attempts to pervert the course of music, historical and contemporary. The conductor Wilhelm Furtwängler defended the composer Paul Hindemith against the charge of being *'nicht tragbar'* ('not acceptable') in his 1934 essay *'Der Fall Hindemith'* ('The Case of Hindemith'), though he later turned against the music. Hindemith followed many others into exile in Switzerland and the US. His fellow composer Carl Orff stayed. Richard Strauss greeted the election of Hitler in 1933 with the words, 'At Last! A chancellor who believes in the arts', and, naively or otherwise, allowed his work and reputation to be annexed into the Nazi project.[5]

Others used musical style as a coded flag against totalitarianism: the Austrian composer Ernst Krenek took up writing twelve-tone music because, he said, 'My adoption of the musical technique that the tyrants hated most of all may be interpreted as an expression of protest.'[6]

Ideas of nationalism in music have to be set against the experience of exile (internal and external, voluntary and involuntary) and the end of old empires. Very many composers ended up in different countries from the ones they started their lives in, even if, in some cases, they remained in the same place: it was the borders that moved, not them. For music, a key question was who decides what the nation, and therefore nationalism, is, and stands for. In 1938 the Nazis mounted an exhibition showcasing what they characterised as *Entartete Musik*: degenerate (meaning mostly Jewish) music. Mendelssohn, Mahler, Schoenberg and Kurt Weill featured on the list alongside unwholesome modernists like Stravinsky and Hindemith. Musicologist Friedrich Blume delivered his paper *'Musik und Rasse'* ('Music and Race') at the exhibition: 'German music history portrays a string of invasions ... [but] somehow remains thoroughly German ... the foreign can be absorbed, without diluting core racial stock.'[7]

Blume tussled inconclusively with the same idea in *Das Rasseproblem in der Musik* ('The Racial Problem in Music') (1939). His student Wolfgang Steinecke stated that all music must be 'in the first place national' and could never be 'an Esperanto born of something other than the spirit of the nation ... bound up with no racial conditions and laws'.[8] However, all this has to be read in the context of Nazi expectations of content and style: Steinecke went on to lead the groundbreaking Darmstadt International Summer Courses after the war, inspiring perhaps the first genuinely stylistically 'international music' from his disparate group of displaced modernists.

France stood at a crossroads, artistically and militarily. Gounod added a few patriotic songs to his huge output in the post-Commune period. Debussy contributed to a 1914 *Tribute to the Belgian King and People*, and in 1916 he published a little *Noël des enfants qui n'ont plus de maison* (*Noël for Children Who Have No Homes*), in which he asked Christ to bring them bread and keep away the German invaders. His work served, he said, 'to offer proof, small as it may be, that 30 million Boches cannot destroy French thought ... I think of the youth of France, senselessly mowed down by those merchants of "Kultur" ... What I am writing will be a secret homage to them.'[9]

In Italy, Luigi Dallapiccola wove his anti-fascist views into protest works like *Canti di prigionia* (*Songs of Imprisonment*) of 1938–41: 'in a totalitarian regime, the individual is powerless. Only by means of music would I be able to express my indignation.'[10] Dallapiccola spent some time in hiding from Mussolini's forces. The Jewish Polish-born Soviet composer Mieczysław Weinberg left Poland on foot before the advancing German army in 1939, walking the 300 miles east to Minsk. His sister turned back; Weinberg never saw her or his family again. Manuel de Falla fled Spanish fascism to Argentina; Mario Castelnuovo-Tedesco escaped Italian fascism to California. Erich Korngold exchanged writing opera and concert works in Hamburg and Vienna for film scores for Errol Flynn in Hollywood, almost single-handedly transplanting the Romantic tunefulness and rich orchestration of the central European symphonic tradition into the lifeblood of the American film industry, where it emphatically remains to this day.

Alex Ross, leading chronicler of twentieth-century music, states that music itself is 'neither guilty nor innocent'.[11] A hundred years earlier, the German novelist Thomas Mann claimed that 'German culture resists being politicised. The political element is lacking in the German concept of culture.'¹² Mann was writing in 1918. Even if his statement can be historically defended in the nation of *Figaro*, *Fidelio* and the 'Eroica', the years that followed would test its conclusion severely.

Performance style wore a national aspect, too, gradually smoothed out as recording spread sound around the world and orchestras hired internationally trained players, gradually pushing into the past the Russian orchestras with their vibrato brass, the old English orchestras with their wooden flutes, the French with their bitey wind, all with swoopy strings.

Folk music has a political side, too. It might be hard to spot socialistic undertones beneath the tweeds and fol-the-diddle-ay of the folklorism of Vaughan Williams and Butterworth, but it is there in the Fabian socialism of the most influential (and, sometimes, controversial) English folklorist, Cecil Sharp, derived from the views of William Morris about the role of art in society. In 1916 Gustav Holst organised one of the first community music festivals around the parish church in the Essex village of Thaxted, home to Reverend Conrad Noel, known as the 'Red Vicar', given to communistic rants from the pulpit. The American composer and novelist Paul Bowles found an urgent, direct political resonance in the folk music of his adopted city of Tangier, in Morocco: 'Instrumentalists and singers have come into being in lieu of chroniclers and poets, and even during the most recent chapter in the country's evolution – the war for independence and the setting up of the present regime – each phase of the struggle has been celebrated in song.'¹³ Historian Ted Gioia reminds us of one of the key musical roots of jazz:

> The griots [storytellers and keepers of the oral traditions] of West Africa aim to preserve their musical tradition as it is handed down to them. This is not a mere aesthetic choice, but a cultural imperative: they are the historians of their society and must maintain the integrity of their precious musical heritage ... music partakes of a quasi-sacred efficacy.¹⁴

Jazz turned that tradition into something quite different, speaking for another country and another age.

As in every age, alongside music as politics sits musical politics, in many ways a fallout from the choices facing composers with which we began this brief survey of twentieth-century music: tonal vs atonal, modern vs reactionary, uptown vs downtown, cloistered academia vs the rhythm of the street, classical vs pop; all surrounded by their baggage of snobbery, clique-ism, reputation, money and career.

None of this helps us to see the music for what it is. A hundred years on, it should be possible to tell whether Schoenberg or Cole Porter can be said to stand as the more authentic chronicler of their age. Is it?

Technique, Style, Example

The multiplicity of musical styles on display in the first half of the twentieth century resembled the 'menagerie' to which the audience is summoned by the animal tamer at the beginning of Alban Berg's 1935 unfinished nightmare opera *Lulu*. So do the words used to describe them: secessionism, expressionism, futurism. Above all, the supreme umbrella term modernism recurs throughout these chapters, constantly changing nuance and context 'as the front of what is old and new advances continually', in the words of scholar Richard Langham Smith.[15] A scatter-gun of examples, by theme and technical features, will help launch a difficult century.

Among words not used by Schoenberg, 'atonal' means 'without a key'; 'serialism' refers to treating musical objects such as notes as elements within a 'series', or 'set', then manipulating that series according to certain formal procedures. Schoenberg devised the principle of using each of the twelve pitches in the chromatic scale once each before any can be repeated, forming a 'row', or 'Basic Set'. This can then be treated to a number of formal processes, principally: 'Inversion' (start on the same note and keep the same melodic intervals but go up instead of down and vice versa); 'Retrograde' (start on the last note of the Basic Set and play it backwards); and 'Retrograde Inversion' (do both). None of this was new (Bach wrote twelve-tone tunes and then played them backwards and upside down); systematising it over a whole piece was. Many composers took the Schoenbergian row and used it in a tonal context, which was not the original idea at all (described by one commentator as 'so-called free twelve-tone composers – composers who are, as it were, just a little bit pregnant').[16]

The blues turned the simplicity of call and response into a sophisticated, regular pattern that turns up everywhere. Neoclassicism recreated the old as 'music to the second power',[17] and allowed itself a splash of bitonal jazz. Scales, harmony and rhythm made interesting new sounds from old materials.

French music in particular made a feature of added note chords which do not resolve (not so much smashing up tonality altogether as setting it vaguely adrift with a Gallic shrug and puff of smoke from a Gauloise), and a sort of rolling structure where phrases follow each other like waves; tightly organised but eschewing any kind of technical developmental procedure.

Other early twentieth-century sounds include the strikingly prophetic collages of Erik Satie and the babbling vocal *Ursonate* (1932) by Kurt Schwitters (an artist reduced to making sculptures out of *papier mâché* when he couldn't get plaster of paris in the prisoner-of-war camp in which he was interned on the Isle of Man); the violent, screaming Expressionism of the young Hindemith; Rachmaninoff obsessing over the plainsong motif of the *Dies Irae*; Jewish music in Mahler, Ernest Bloch and Irving Berlin; and the last gasp of lush Romanticism led by Richard Strauss, feeding fundamentally tonal chords with ever fatter added notes, like a German hausfrau drowning a mushroom in cream.

Light music, too, evolved from its nineteenth-century origins to catch the mood and manner of a challenging new world. In England the Victorian parlour song fed into music hall: the visiting Debussy much preferred to go slumming in a music hall than sit through a Wagner opera. Paris high-kicked its way from the frothing skirts of the Can-Can towards sardonic, intellectual cabaret, hinterland of Poulenc and his fellow members of Les Six. Kurt Weill did something similar for nervy Weimar Berlin. Iberian folk styles fado and flamenco were strongly allied to working-class repression in the era of Salazar and Franco. In Britain, two world wars launched songs of an unrepeatable emotional directness: 'Keep the Home Fires Burning' and 'The White Cliffs of Dover'. Albert Ketèlbey and Eric Coates fashioned irresistible orchestral light music from Edwardian Elgariana.

For the composer, the choices on offer were bewilderingly wide.

Right in the middle of the twentieth century, in 1949, Leonard Bernstein confronted his confused and confusing world in a symphony which was not a symphony. His model was W. H. Auden's virtuoso poem about identity in the modern world, set in a New

York bar and written in an imitation of Anglo-Saxon verse. Poem, and symphony, are called *The Age of Anxiety*.

Styles and processes

a)

Schoenberg: Wind Quintet, op 26. Thematic material, with main variants:

Part Seven: Introduction

Fourth movement (Rondo); bars 117-122:

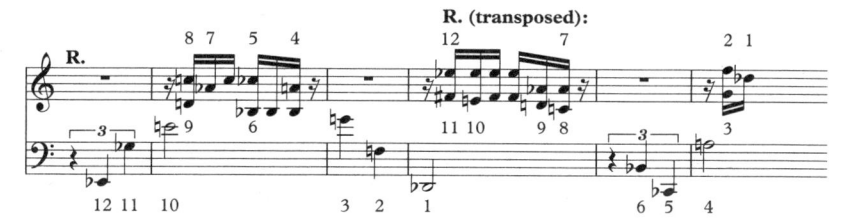

A schematic description of Schoenberg's processes in his Wind Quintet *(1923–4), one of the first works to fully use his 'Method of Composing with Twelve Tones' (taken from Schoenberg's own essay describing the method). The opening staves show the Basic Set of twelve pitches, numbered 1–12; then the Retrograde (12–1); and the Inversion. Two extracts from the* Quintet *show these forms of the set in context, used to make both melodies and chords.*

b)

An example of Neoclassicism: the opening of Stravinsky's Concerto in E flat 'Dumbarton Oaks' *(1937).*

c)

Folk-type scales in no. 58 of Béla Bartók's many-faceted piano work, Mikrokosmos.

15

A TRADITION RENEWED: MAHLER AND SIBELIUS

Meetings, Motives and Motifs

In 1907 Gustav Mahler paid a visit to Jean Sibelius while on a conducting tour of Finland.

'Mahler and I spent much time in each other's company,' recorded Sibelius later:

> When our conversation touched on the essence of the symphony, I said that I admired its severity of style and the profound logic that created an inner connection between all the motifs. This was the experience I had come to in composing. Mahler's opinion was just the reverse. *'Nein, die Symphonie muss sein wie die Welt. Sie muss alles umfassen'* ['No, a symphony must be like the world. It must embrace everything'].[1]

Sibelius's words later took their place as a classic statement of two very different answers to the same question: what did the symphony have left to say in the twentieth century?

But, as always, evidence must be placed in context. Sibelius recorded his account of the conversation nearly three decades after it took place, and almost a quarter of a century after Mahler's death. More important is the evidence of the music: Mahler's huge spans are underpinned by plenty of 'logic' and 'connection' – in 1900 the Classically minded critic Eduard Hanslick spoke of the 'puzzling coherence' of the 1888 First Symphony,[2] and Mahler himself said that his 1896 Third Symphony's opening 'has the same scaffolding, the same basic groundplan that you'll find in the works of Mozart and … Beethoven'.[3] Few pieces embrace 'the world' quite as completely as Sibelius's first, huge, symphonic utterance, the choral and orchestral

Kullervo of 1892, which, in the words of the Sibelius scholar Glenda Dawn Goss, 'swirled a world of folk song, mythic archetypes, Finland's male-choir traditions, and Freudian conflict into a Germanic symphonic structure'.[4] It seems Sibelius was a Mahlerian before Mahler.

Sibelius's seven symphonies were written between 1898 and 1924. That rugged Sibelian 'logic' manifests itself in an extreme and highly personal version of the principle of the organic development of motif historically associated more with the tone poem than with the traditional idea of the symphony. In a sense, Sibelius marks the point at which the two genres meet.

The Second Symphony (1902) opens with a rising chord figure which features throughout the work. The other of his most often performed symphonies, the Fifth, features one of the most famous endings in the symphonic repertoire. During its composition in April 1915 Sibelius told his diary:

> Today at ten to eleven I saw 16 swans. One of my greatest experiences! Lord God, what beauty! They circled over me for a long time. Disappeared into the solar haze like a gleaming silver ribbon. Their call the same woodwind type as that of cranes, but without tremolo. The swan-call closer to the trumpet ... A low refrain reminiscent of a small child crying. Nature mysticism and life's angst! The Fifth Symphony's finale-theme: legato in the trumpets!![5]

Here is Mahler's '*die Welt*' in full finery. In the end, the magnificent hymn-like closing melody is given principally to the horns rather than the trumpets, completing a process of presenting versions of theme in rotation, combination and different speeds which began right at the beginning of the work – the whole becoming clear at the moment of completion. And what a moment: energy dissolves in a final nine bars made up mostly of silence. Sibelius revised the work twice after its premiere (on his fiftieth birthday, a national holiday, for which it was commissioned by the Finnish government), as if even he was trying to find out where its formal innovations were trying to go: 'It is as if God Almighty had thrown down pieces of a mosaic for heaven's floor and asked me to find out what was the original pattern.'⁶ Other symphonies go in other directions: the Fourth is melancholy and strange; the Sixth defies traditional forms altogether; the Seventh is a single movement, organic, fluid, entirely original. None of these fascinating statements has approached the popularity of the Second and Fifth, or other equally striking approaches to tradition like the Violin Concerto (whose second, successful premiere was conducted in 1905 by Richard Strauss).

Influences: *Wunderhorn* and *Kalevala*

Early in his creative career, Gustav Mahler discovered *Des Knaben Wunderhorn* (*The Boy's Magic Horn*), the collection of German folklore assembled at the beginning of the nineteenth century by Clemens Brentano and Achim von Arnim. It stands in a slightly similar relation to his work as the *Kalevala* does to that of Sibelius: fertile source of tales, words, themes and ideas throughout their lives. A key difference is that Sibelius set the actual words of the *Kalevala* relatively rarely and mostly at the beginning of his career, later drawing extensively on its store of legends for his purely orchestral tone poems. Mahler composed mainly in two genres, symphony and song. His habit of reusing music from one piece in another means that the two often intersect and overlap, and poems from *Des Knaben Wunderhorn* feature regularly in both.

This cross-pollination between song and symphony is most prevalent in his first compositional period. As well as poems from the *Wunderhorn* collection and lyrics by Friedrich Rückert and others, Mahler also followed Wagner in sometimes writing his own words, as in his first major song cycle *Lieder eines fahrenden Gesellen* (*Songs of a Wayfarer*) of 1883–5. From 1887 to 1888 he fused some of its music into his First Symphony. Nothing could symbolise the turning of the spheres more potently than the appearance of this work just four years after the premiere of Brahms's Fourth. Musically, we are on a different planet. As well as the *Wayfarer* songs the symphony gives us a peculiar funeral march based on a minor key version of the popular round '*Bruder Jakob*' (or '*Bruder Martin*', better known in England in a French variant, '*Frère Jacques*'), and music originally written for a play. However, Mahler dropped this later (early evidence of a habit of constant revision which has left performers and editors with choices almost as multifarious as the jigsaw pieces of the Bruckner problem), giving the symphony its four-movement form. While the mood and manner of the songs was carried into the symphony but without their words, the distinctive orchestration given to their melodies in the symphony was carried back into the orchestral version of the song cycle, originally just for voice and piano, only after the appearance of the symphony: echoes and resonances between the works are rich and strange.

In the huge Second Symphony Mahler goes even further in drawing on extra-musical material (a little as Puccini did in his operatic tableau scenes): the sprawling last movement contains a strange, freely notated passage where individual instruments hover around the note C sharp, marshalled by the conductor like a police officer directing traffic; then the movement is battered by a long, sinister, growing, growling, unstoppable drum roll, coming from nowhere. The Fourth Symphony exemplifies Mahler's unique take on the art of orchestration, often treating his orchestra like a big chamber ensemble, painting subtle combinations of individual sounds, using effects like sleigh bells and asking the leader to turn up with two violins, one tuned a tone higher than normal so the second movement solo sounds 'wie eine Fidel' ('like a folk fiddler') and asking the clarinets to play 'Schalltrichter auf' (instrument sticking up in the air), before a soprano soloist joins in for a lyrical depiction of the pantheistic joys of the heavenly life as depicted in Des Knaben Wunderhorn, involving asparagus, ox meat, wine served by saints and 11,000 dancing virgins. This really is music which treats 'die Welt' as its source material.

During these years the young Mahler blazed a trail from his native small-town Bohemia to studies at the Vienna Conservatory, then forged a reputation as one of the finest, and most demanding, conductors in Europe, holding posts in a succession of increasingly prestigious opera houses in Austria, Prague, Leipzig, Budapest and Hamburg. Composition was of necessity a part-time activity. His personal and professional relationships were often far from straightforward. In 1888 in Leipzig he scored a notable success with his completion of Carl Maria von Weber's unfinished opera Die drei Pintos (Mahler's only operatic venture, despite his considerable immersion in the repertoire at this time) at the urging of his friend Captain Carl von Weber, the composer's grandson, but at the same time developed an intense attachment to the captain's wife. He was sacked from both Prague and Budapest (in the latter instance apparently deliberately).

A Hamburg acquaintance, Ferdinand Pfohl, described him as 'one of the most unsympathetic people of all times. And yet he awoke an interest in me, just as a snake or fruit might, while one is still uncertain whether or not it is poisonous.'[7] His family life took a Beethovenian turn in his thirtieth year, 1889, when both of his parents and one of his sisters died, leaving him in charge of four younger siblings. (In another sad echo of Beethoven's family troubles, Mahler's younger brother Otto later committed suicide.) In Hamburg, between 1891 and 1897, he conducted 744 performances of sixty-four operas, most of them new to him, succeeded Bülow, an admirer, as conductor of the orchestral subscription concerts (though he was later forced to resign), and earned both respect and resentment for his high standards and autocratic style. In 1892 he paid his only visit to England. In 1893 he acquired the first of an eventual series of three composing huts, small buildings overlooking lakes, away from the distractions and bustle of city life, where he established a lifelong routine of writing music in the summer months. The first complete performance of the Second Symphony, in Berlin in December 1895, consolidated his fame as a composer alongside his established reputation as a conductor. In 1897 his manoeuvrings to obtain a post in Vienna (which included converting to Catholicism to overcome the ban on jobs going to Jews) yielded success with his appointment as director at the prestigious Vienna Hofoper (now Staatsoper).

Mahler: Vienna and New York, Triumph and Tragedy

Vienna afforded Mahler a mixed reception. Viennese cab drivers would point him out to their passengers as *'der Mahler'*.[8] The author Stefan Zweig said that to have seen him on the street was an event to be reported with pride to friends 'as if it were a personal triumph'.[9] As in Hamburg, Mahler combined his operatic duties with leadership of the Vienna Philharmonic subscription concerts (though he resigned in 1901 after three seasons). Even a friend like Natalie Bauer-Lechner referred to 'the need to recover from the constant inner and outer excitement and tension that surrounds him', commenting that living alongside Mahler was 'like being on a boat that is ceaselessly rocked to and fro on the waves'.[10]

Performances, and premieres, of his own music became increasingly regular events: the Fourth Symphony in 1901, the first complete performance of the Third in 1902, notable song cycles in 1905. Meanwhile, the summer composing routine had allowed him to venture into a new, post-*Wunderhorn* phase, producing the Fifth, Sixth, Seventh and Eighth Symphonies in hut no. 2, at Maiernigg on the shores of the Wörthersee, between 1901 and 1905, the last in just eight weeks. In November 1901 he met Alma Schindler, a vivacious young pupil of (and admired by) fellow composer Alexander Zemlinsky. By the time Alma and Mahler married the following March she was already pregnant with their first child, a daughter. A second daughter followed soon after, in 1904.

The three middle symphonies, the Fifth, Sixth and Seventh, are purely instrumental, lacking the shattering choral finales (complete with organ) of the Second before them and the Eighth (a cosmic meditation on creation which moves from the Christian hymn '*Veni, Creator Spiritus*' to words from Goethe's *Faust*) after. But his unmistakable song style, expressively if not always easily written for the voice, is carried over into his increasingly deft instrumental writing, most notably in perhaps his most famous movement, the Adagietto from the Fifth Symphony, scored for harp and strings alone, a Wagnerian '*unendliche Melodie*' ('infinite melody') whose phrases lead to pungent appoggiaturas which take ages to resolve, culminating in the almost infinite last note. Romantic yearning has reached (and possibly passed) satiety: ripeness is all. Here, too, is the Sibelian revisiting of themes between movements and across works.

Meanwhile, reactionary Vienna, scared of change, scared of youth, scared of Jews, glared at by the Emperor Franz Joseph from every café wall, threatened from within by the probings of Sigmund Freud and the artistic innovations of Gustav Klimt and the Secessionists, took out its fears in a relentless campaign against its bullish opera director, who had the temerity to be talented, Jewish, barely forty and not even German, never mind Austrian. Stagehands and singers rebelled: one said Mahler treated them like a lion tamer treats his animals. In May 1907 the composer negotiated a new contract to conduct in New York. He pinned his farewell message to the company on a noticeboard: it was taken down and shredded onto the floor.

Worse, in summer 1907, he took his young family to Maiernigg to escape the febrile plotting in Vienna. Both his young daughters fell ill with scarlet fever and diphtheria. The younger, Anna, recovered, but 4-year-old Maria died on 12 July. Shortly after, Mahler learnt that he suffered from a debilitating heart condition which could severely limit physical exertion. Maiernigg, where he had built a villa on land adjacent to his composing hut, was shut up and never visited again.

Three seasons of conducting at New York's still-new Metropolitan Opera, with summers devoted to composing at a third and final hut back in the Austrian Tyrol, followed. A brief, autumnal third compositional period in 1909–10 brought *Das Lied von der Erde* (*The Song of the Earth*) and the Ninth and incomplete Tenth Symphonies, each ending quietly. He heard none of them. September 1910 brought the premiere of the Eighth Symphony in Munich, his biggest success. The same year he discovered that Alma was having an affair with the influential modernist architect Walter Gropius. Greatly distressed, Mahler visited the psychoanalyst Sigmund Freud: the content of their discussion is unknown. In late 1910 he began a demanding schedule of engagements in New York. He battled through persistent illness to conduct a concert at Carnegie Hall in February 1911, but was afterwards confined to bed. In April he and Alma travelled first to Paris and then Vienna, where he died on 18 May.

Sibelius: Fame and Silence

Sibelius long outlived Mahler. He didn't really deserve to: sociable and gregarious, he knew many leading figures and travelled and conducted widely; he also drank too much, and he often left his wife and five daughters (a sixth, in a sad parallel with Mahler, died in early childhood) in their rural home while he enjoyed himself in the city. He did well financially but managed money badly, and nearly died from a tumour in the throat caused by excessive smoking (happily, operated on with complete success). Late in life he is said to have remarked that 'all the doctors who wanted to forbid me to smoke and drink are dead'.[11]

Sibelius's last period is one of the oddest in musical history. In 1919, at the age of fifty-three, like Brahms he embraced a middle-aged change of image (though, unlike Brahms, his involved less hair, not more, shaving his head to produce the familiar gloomy dome of his later decades). Composition got harder, increasingly helped along by a glass of wine stationed on the composing desk. Following the Seventh Symphony in 1924 he produced just one more major work, the tone poem *Tapiola* of 1926. Apart from a few arrangements in

1929, he wrote nothing more. His last three decades became known as 'The Silence of Järvenpää', after the location of the beautiful house built by Sibelius and his wife Aino in the woods north of Helsinki and named after her, *Ainola*. In 1940 he burned a large collection of manuscripts, including sketches for an abandoned Eighth Symphony. Nazi enthusiasm for his Aryan credentials bothered him, but he managed to stay separate, through age, geography and a well-advised avoidance of public utterance. He died in 1957, lucky to have made it to the age of ninety-one.

Reputations

In the first half of the twentieth century people took sides. Sibelius was an easy target for Schoenbergian modernists and mercurial self-appointed neologists like Stravinsky. The American composer Virgil Thomson called Sibelius's Second Symphony 'vulgar, self-indulgent, and provincial beyond all description'.[12] In 1955 another composer, the Schoenbergian proselyte René Leibowitz, wrote a pamphlet entitled *Sibelius: The Worst Composer in the World*. More than one tendentious history of twentieth-century music dismissed him even more thoroughly by not mentioning him at all (history up to its old tricks again – the book which pointed that out doesn't mention a single work by Vaughan Williams). Another critic said, 'If Sibelius's music is good music, then all the categories by which musical standards can be measured – standards which reach from a master like Bach to most advanced composers like Schoenberg – must be completely abolished.'[13] (This comment conclusively proves the limitations not of Sibelius's music but of a certain kind of prescriptive criticism: if our critic's standards don't encompass Sibelius then, yes, they must be abolished – or, more constructively, revisited and allowed to evolve. It's the same kind of critical voice that tells people to stop listening to Rossini, Puccini and Rachmaninoff, composers who have little in common except their huge and enduring popularity.)

Sibelius's sound world is unique. His use of thematic material is compact and terse, though capable of blossoming into long-breathed melody (as in the oboe and cello exchange in the beautiful slow middle section of the Second Symphony's fast third movement). Structures move with monumental Brucknerian slowness (like the almost infinite repetition of the up and down scale figure in D minor right at the end of the Second Symphony, emerging eventually into a sunburst of D major). His orchestral writing is exhilarating: listening to it close up can be like standing outside in a high wind. Sibelius managed to pull off the historically difficult trick of approaching inherited material in new, intelligent and coherent ways: a modern, not a modernist.

Mahler's reputation has probably reached both higher and lower than any other composer with the possible exception of Bach. He was much better known in his lifetime as a conductor than as a composer (and paid for the premiere of his First Symphony himself). English reviews of his symphonies were typical: 'frankly ugly ... inartistic as well as painful';[14] 'simple to the verge of being childish';[15] 'a paucity of genuinely original matter'.[16] The puzzled *Guardian* reviewer of Thomas Beecham's performance of the Fourth Symphony in December 1907 at least has the virtue of being honest: 'I am not sure whether I liked it or not, but I was quite sure that on better acquaintance I should either admire it immensely or cordially detest it.'[17]

There were occasional triumphs, like the premieres of the Second and Eighth Symphonies, but these were the exceptions. After his death, aged just fifty, performances of his works became less frequent. But he was never without prominent champions, like Leopold Stokowski in America, Henry Wood and Adrian Boult in England, and people he had worked with like Willem Mengelberg in the Netherlands and Otto Klemperer and Bruno Walter (who once said that 'Mahler appeared to me as both a genius and a demon: life itself had all of a sudden become romantic')[18] in Germany and Austria. His standing in the Nazi period was mixed: championed by the Nazis in Austria in the late 1930s as a sort of Austrian Wagner, he joined the list of 'degenerate' (often meaning Jewish) artists proscribed by Hitler. After the war his visibility benefited massively from the spread of the long-playing record, allowing his spacious symphonic spans to be heard complete. His elevation into the pantheon was only completed in the 1960s, largely through the efforts of Leonard Bernstein. Today he is among the biggest box-office draws in the concert repertoire.

His influence was varied and widespread. Aaron Copland battled critical indifference in America to argue Mahler's case as a genuine progressive. Benjamin Britten's adolescent awakening to Mahler came at a Prom concert he went to when he was sixteen: 'not what I had expected ... the scoring startled me ... entirely clean and transparent ... wonderfully resonant ... above all, the material was remarkable, and the melodic shapes highly original'.[19] He called Mahler's *Kindertotenlieder* (*Songs on the Death of Children*) 'little miracles', while the Fifth Symphony's Adagietto left 'a nice (if erotic) taste in my mouth'.[20] (The symphony's first movement blows unmistakably through the 'storm' interlude in Britten's opera *Peter Grimes*.) Much later, in 1967, Britten conducted the modern premiere of the discarded 'Blumine' movement of Mahler's First Symphony. Britten noted Mahler's influence on Schoenberg, calling Schoenberg's *Suite for Strings* of 1934 'a Hommage to Mahler both in matter and manner'.[21] Schoenberg's *Gurre-Lieder* of 1911 has plenty of the chamber-like orchestration of Mahler's Fourth Symphony in its last movement. Schoenberg was himself admired and defended by Mahler in volatile Vienna, and repaid the debt in a thoughtful essay in which he recounted his own Pauline conversion from anti-Mahlerian to enthusiastic advocate, stoutly defending Mahler against an often-repeated charge: '*his themes are actually not banal* [his italics]'.[22] *Drei Orchesterstücke* (*Three Pieces for Orchestra*) (1915) by Schoenberg's pupil Alban Berg even include a hammer in their battery of homage, a clear echo of Mahler's Sixth.

Reading his symphonies remains a complex task. They are not programme music in the manner of the tone poems of Strauss; but the narrative, even autobiographical, element is there in the rapid swings of mood and manner and juxtaposition of funeral marches, children's songs, sleigh bells and klezmer music. Mahler would move movements around between pieces, and sometimes give them titles and then remove them. Perhaps his 'world' philosophy, referred to in the famous remark to Sibelius, can be glimpsed in the words of one of the *Rückert-Lieder* of 1901–2: '*Ich bin der Welt abhanden gekommen*' ('I am lost to the world').

Mahler scholar Seth Monahan says: 'Since it is beyond anyone's reach to fix Mahler's meaning in perpetuity ... perhaps the best tribute we can pay him is to keep asking new questions.'[23]

Schoenberg found himself emotionally overwhelmed by Mahler's Second Symphony, but warned that '[t]he intellect is skeptical; it does not trust the sensual, and it trusts the supersensual even less'.[24] Those who, like Schoenberg, seek a counterbalance to the 'supersensual' in their musical experience will find their reward in a bracing blast of northern brass from Mahler's near-contemporary and rugged equal in integrity and originality, Jean Sibelius.

16

THE CHALLENGE OF MODERNISM: SCHOENBERG, STRAVINSKY AND HOW TO AVOID THEM

The One True Way: Schoenberg

Arnold Schoenberg was born in 1874 into a Jewish family in the Viennese suburb where his father kept a shoe shop. He had little formal musical education beyond counterpoint lessons with the composer, conductor and teacher Alexander Zemlinsky, meanwhile gaining experience by orchestrating operettas and playing and studying chamber music. Works of his mid-twenties like the lush *Verklärte Nacht* (*Transfigured Night*) for strings and the huge *Gurre-Lieder* (*Songs of Gurre*) earned the approbation of both Mahler and Strauss. Strauss later turned against Schoenberg as the two composers pursued different paths, but Mahler remained a loyal, sometimes fierce, supporter even as Schoenberg's style began to move in difficult directions. Schoenberg, for his part, moved from finding Mahler's music 'unoriginal' to regarding him as 'one of the greatest men and artists'.[1]

His spiritual and personal life mirrored the restless seeking of his intellectual journey: he converted to Lutheran Christianity in 1889, then, after a long struggle against the backdrop of gathering anti-Semitism, re-embraced his Jewish heritage in 1933. He married twice, first to Mathilde Zemlinsky, sister of his admired teacher, with whom he had two children. A brief separation from Mathilde in 1908 coincided with a significant shift in his music. Following her death in 1923 Schoenberg married Gertrud Kolisch, who published and promoted his works after his death; their daughter Nuria married the Italian avant-garde composer Luigi Nono.

In 1918, after army service during the war, Schoenberg founded the *Verein für musikalische Privataufführungen* (Society for Private Musical Performance) in Vienna, at which modern works were presented without an audience, allowing concentrated rehearsal and performance away from the pressures of taste and box office. To begin with, his own works were not included, and the society's repertoire instead focused on those of leading figures like Debussy, Scriabin, Mahler, Reger, and his pupils Webern and Berg. It lasted until 1921. In 1924, as his style moved into its fully atonal phase, Schoenberg was appointed to run a composition class in Berlin following the death of Ferruccio Busoni, taking up the post in 1926. In 1933, fearing the rise of the Nazis, he tried to move to Britain without success, travelling instead with his family to the USA, where he taught first in Boston and then in Los Angeles. Still restless, he applied for a job at the conservatory in Sydney, Australia, but was turned down by its director, Edgar Bainton (himself an immigrant from the north-east of England), for being 'dangerous' and 'modernist' (not something of which Bainton's own Victorian melodiousness can be accused).[2] A well-paid job at UCLA allowed Schoenberg to buy a house in the salubrious Los Angeles suburb of Brentwood Park, where he established a salon of friends, neighbours and pupils, including George Gershwin (his regular tennis partner), former child actor Shirley Temple, fellow European refugees including the conductor Otto Klemperer and the composer Darius Milhaud, Hollywood luminaries like Harpo Marx and Peter Lorre, and American composition students including Edgard Varèse and John Cage (but not Stravinsky, who was close geographically but maintained his distance professionally and, at least to begin with, stylistically). His last phase of compositions featured some large-scale works including the Violin Concerto of 1936 and the Piano Concerto of 1942, and a partial return to the principles of tonality. He died in 1951.

Schoenberg was a writer and teacher as well as a composer and painter. Chief among his writings are *Harmonielehre* (usually translated as *Theory of Harmony*), written in 1910, the collection of essays written between 1909 and 1950 and published as *Style and Idea*, and three practical textbooks arising from his university teaching.

Three key themes can be teased from his writings.

First, his analysis of harmony is immensely thorough and thoroughly traditional. *Harmonielehre* approaches its task with the zeal of a medieval treatise and the hands-on practicality of countless earlier teaching methods, and then simply keeps going, pursuing history into Schoenberg's own ideas about what happens next. He saw himself as part of a tradition.

Second, his writings are shot through with statements like 'Great art ... presupposes the alert mind of an educated listener' who 'enables a musician to write for upper-class minds'. Conversely, 'Popular music speaks to the unsophisticated, to people who love the beauty of music but are not inclined to strengthen their minds.'[3] He is writing for an initiated elite.

Third, and most important of all, his theoretical writings provide a detailed and coherent explanation of the technical and philosophical foundations of easily his most significant testament and legacy: his music.

Schoenberg called his procedure his 'Method of Composing with Twelve Tones Which are Related Only with One Another', the title of a detailed account of the subject which he delivered as a lecture in 1941 and later published in English in the collection *Style and Idea*. He said that 'composition with twelve tones has no other aim than comprehensibility', achieved because 'the main advantage of this method of composing with twelve tones is its unifying effect' (in which he compares it to Wagner's use of leitmotifs). Historically, he explained, tonality led to extended tonality, which in turn led to 'the emancipation of the dissonance': dissonance no longer exists in relation to resolution back into a key, but as a free-standing object in its own right, equal and equivalent to consonance – 'A style based on this premise treats dissonances like consonances and renounces a tonal centre.'

An early problem was that the lack of tonal direction made the first pieces to essay the new method vanishingly short (like the *Sechs Kleine Klavierstücke* (*Six Little Piano Pieces*) of 1911). Using a poem as an underlying structural guide helped: it took him twelve years to formulate the full method (not, note, a system; a nice but significant distinction, as a system implies one correct outcome, while a method allows a degree of choice and creativity about how it is applied). According to Schoenberg's process, the twelve-tone set can be arranged 'in the accompaniment or the melody', in a clear distinction from the world view of contemporaries like Debussy, to whom the division of music into melody and accompaniment was becoming increasingly blurred. Another division with the practice of Debussy and Ravel is that in Schoenberg's music the sensual appeal of orchestral sound and colour is flatly rejected: 'mature minds resist the temptation to become intoxicated by colours, and prefer to be coldly convinced by the transparency of clear-cut ideas'. Rhythm is not systematised, but left to the composer. Orchestration forbids doublings. An interesting offshoot of his ideas about orchestration is the concept of *Klangfarbenmelodie* (literally, 'sound–colour–melody'), where a melody is passed one note at a time between different instruments.

It's easy to agree with Schoenberg's own assessment that his approach often 'seems to increase the listener's difficulties'. His predictions that '[t]he time will come when the ability to draw thematic material from a basic set of twelve tones will be an unconditional prerequisite for obtaining admission into the composition class of a conservatory',[4] not to mention that 'grocers' boys would whistle serial music in their rounds',[5] have not come to pass.

But an overview of his output as a whole reveals colossal intelligence and integrity, white-hot creativity, constant enquiry and a striking variety. *Gurre-Lieder* is unforgettable. *Verklärte Nacht*, his string sextet of 1899, is beautiful. In the String Quartet No. 2 in F Sharp Minor of 1908 a soprano soloist joins in to declare, 'I feel air from another planet.' His melodrama *Pierrot lunaire* (1912) changed the way we think about singing, and about psychology in music. The 1947 cantata *A Survivor from Warsaw* is a powerful testament to the horror of war. The two Chamber Symphonies, composed over the course of most of his active career, carry a traditional form into new territories, bracketing his mid-career innovations with a late return to earlier preoccupations. His last piece was a setting of his own text which he called *Moderner Psalm* (*Modern Psalm*). It was left unfinished.

Schoenberg wrote:

> unfortunately our historians are not satisfied with rearranging the history of the past; they also want to fit the history of the present into their preconceived scheme ... One should never forget that what one learns in school about history is the truth only insofar as it does not interfere with the political, philosophical, moral or other beliefs of those in whose interest the facts are told, coloured or arranged. The same is true with the history of music.[6]

In his analysis of the historical inevitability of his methods and their legacy, Schoenberg can stand accused of doing exactly that himself. A hundred years on from his most important innovations, his lasting place both in the long-term evolution of compositional practice and in the affections of actual listeners is still not settled. But, in passing judgement, start with the music.

A Game of Cards: Stravinsky

Stravinsky also said 'it seems to me the new music will be serial'.[7] But his commitment was different, part of a mercurial, transient, multi-coloured journey through style, language and form.

Igor Stravinsky was eight years younger than Schoenberg, born in 1882, the third of four sons of a bass singer at the St Petersburg opera. Early supporters in his rather slow start as a composer were Rimsky-Korsakov and the impresario Sergei Diaghilev, who commissioned the work which made his name on its premiere in Paris in 1910, *L'Oiseau de feu* (*The Firebird*). A second ballet, *Petrushka*, about the love affair between two puppets, followed in 1911. With his wife and young children, Stravinsky settled into a routine of summers in Russia and winters in Switzerland which would last until 1914.

The third Diaghilev ballet, *Le Sacre du printemps* (*The Rite of Spring*), sparked the most famous riot in musical history at its premiere in May 1913. It remains unclear whether parts of the audience were objecting to the choreography, the brutal scenario about primitive ritual and a young girl dancing herself to death as a sacrifice, or the music with its pounding rhythms, lack of conventional melody, block-like construction with no discernible development, and distorted versions of Latvian folk songs. The dramatist Jean Cocteau was there that night in the theatre in the Avenue Montaigne:

> A practised eye could discern there all the material for a scandal ... the 'feverish' school, a handful of *'moutons de Panurge'* [a French insult derived from Rabelais referring to lemming-like followers of fashion], [and] ... the thousand varieties of snobbism, super-snobbism, anti-snobbism ... The audience behaved as it ought to – it revolted straight away. People laughed, booed, hissed, imitated animal noises ... [while] the crowd of aesthetes and a handful of musicians [were] carried away by their excessive zeal ... the uproar degenerated into a free fight ...

Meanwhile, 'old Countess P. flourished her fan' and complained loudly that this was '"the first time for sixty years that anyone's dared make a fool out of me"'.⁸

Stravinsky wrote later: 'I was made a revolutionary in spite of myself.'⁹ *Le Sacre du printemps* unleashed a 'tumult of contradictory opinions'.¹⁰ They would not be the last.

Stravinsky's works to around 1919 are characterised as his 'Russian' period, though with a pronounced French accent. Each does something new: the delicate opera *Le Rossignol* (*The Nightingale*) of 1914 disappointed bellicose Parisians who fancied another riot; *Les Noces* (*The Wedding*) of 1923 was another Diaghilev ballet for the Bartókian forces of voices, percussion and four pianos, mining the possibilities of word stress (Stravinsky's collaborator Robert Craft later said that the composer always thought in Russian); *L'Histoire du soldat* (*The Soldier's Tale*) of 1918 is a theatrical piece for actors, dancers and instrumentalists about a soldier, his lover, the devil and his violin, like a sort of polyrhythmic medieval morality play.

Debussy encouraged him to '[b]e with all your strength a great Russian artist'.¹¹ Support came from colourful Parisian salon hostesses like Winnaretta Singer and Coco Chanel, the piano firm Pleyel and mysterious cheques from an anonymous patron in the US. In 1921 he began an affair. In 1924 he rediscovered his Christian faith. In 1934 he and his wife became French citizens. Their daughter died of tuberculosis in 1938, her mother of the same disease three months later. Unlike some, his private life left no imprint in his music.

The early 1920s began Stravinsky's so-called Neoclassical period, a catch-all title covering a huge range of influence and output (satirised by Prokofieff as 'Bach with wrong notes', to his irritation):¹² the Baroque, ragtime, Greek mythology; the *Concerto for Piano and Wind Instruments* of 1924 which he played himself; the hieratic *Symphony of Psalms*, written in 1930 for the Boston Symphony Orchestra, with its slow-turning melodies frozen in time like Byzantine chant; the strange chorale which ends the *Symphonies of Wind Instruments* (1920); the *'Dumbarton Oaks' Concerto*, a sort of jazzed-up Brandenburg Concerto written in 1938 for a wedding anniversary; actual Baroque music rewritten in *Pulcinella* (1920); a Symphony in C, a Violin Concerto in D, an opera in Latin (*Oedipus Rex*) (1927), a Lord's Prayer in Russian, a tango and a 'ballet in three deals' called *Jeu de cartes* (*Game of Cards*) (1935). Much later he said that 'refitting old ships is the real task of the artist'.¹³ The element of play is never far away. So is the visual element: 'I have always had a horror of listening to music with my eyes shut.'[14] He encountered jazz, but from sheet music, not performance. The only Stravinsky you know you won't get is the one you were expecting.

In 1939–40 Stravinsky delivered the Charles Eliot Norton Lectures at Harvard University. Discussing dissonance, he sounds like Schoenberg on the same topic: 'Having become an entity in itself, it frequently happens that dissonance neither prepares nor anticipates anything ... Of course, the instruction and education of the public have not kept pace with the evolution of technique.' However, he arrives at a different place: 'The function of tonality is completely subordinated to the force of attraction of the pole of sonority.'[15] He has moved beyond key; but, unlike Schoenberg, he needs an audible analogue to replace it: 'we no longer believe in the absolute value of the major–minor system', but, if 'an as yet un-oriented combination has been found, I shall have to determine the centre towards which it should lead'.[16] On the opera stage, 'we are still staggering under the rubbish and racket of the music drama!'[17] He hails the composer as an 'artisan', not an 'artist',[18] and believes that 'Modern man is progressively losing his understanding of values'.[19] He has no use for the concept of modernism, calling it an 'abortive neologism ... It would be so much simpler to give up lying and admit once and for all that we call anything modern that caters to our snobbishness', adding, '[t]he term modernism is all the more offensive in that it is usually coupled with another whose meaning is perfectly clear: I speak of academicism.'[20] In his view, 'the public always shows itself more honest in its spontaneity than do those who officially set themselves up as judges as works of art'.[21] There are rich reflections on Russian history and the perversions of Soviet artistic policy, which have 'nothing to do ... with music'.[22]

Schoenberg ungenerously satirised Stravinsky's habit of sloughing off his musical skin on a regular basis as *der kleine Modernsky* ('the little Modernsky').[23] Stravinsky for his part once drew up an ironical check-list comparing himself with Schoenberg. He summed himself up in his Harvard lectures with typical ambiguity: 'I am no more academic than I am modern, no more modern than I am conservative. *Pulcinella* would suffice to prove this. So you ask just what I am? I refuse to expatiate upon the subject.'[24]

Stravinsky and his second wife Vera moved to America

permanently in 1945, becoming naturalised American citizens (his third nationality) the same year. His librettist C. F. Ramuz told him, 'You never were, and never could be a foreigner anywhere.'[25]

The American end of the long, (very broadly) Neoclassical period produced the Mass (1948), giving a twist to the contrapuntal sound-world of Palestrina and the brass-accompanied seconda pratica of Gabrieli in its brief utterances, drained of emotion and display; and the opera *The Rake's Progress* (1951), to a libretto by W. H. Auden and Chester Kallman, based on a series of eighteenth-century engravings by William Hogarth and borrowing the scale, sound and shapes of a Mozartian number opera, complete with arias, ensembles and harpsichord-accompanied recitatives: Stravinsky contrasted his 'opera in verse' with Schoenberg's *Erwartung*, an 'opera in prose'.[26]

In the early 1950s, turning seventy, Stravinsky surprised his friends (again) with a series of works which came to thoroughly embrace Schoenberg's twelve-tone method. Many also reflect an increasing attachment to the beliefs and artefacts of Christianity: Old Testament stories in *Abraham and Isaac* (1963) and *The Flood* (1962), the *Canticum Sacrum* (1955) in honour of St Mark, patron saint of his beloved Venice, liturgically derived texts in the *Requiem Canticles* (1966) and *Threni* (1958), a short English anthem setting a passage from T. S. Eliot's *Little Gidding* about the incandescent descent of the dove at Pentecost. These pieces offer a curious amalgam of what he called 'a kind of *triadic* atonality',[27] Schoenbergian angularity challengingly transcribed for voices, and a sort of consciously faded Baroque splendour. Stravinsky specifically stated that aspects of his compositional technique were drawn from something he called the 'parallelism',[28] which he observed in the magnificent gold mosaics in the basilica of Torcello, in the Venetian lagoon; *Threni* was first performed in the sumptuous Scuola San Rocco, also in Venice. He arranged and completed works by the stylistically adventurous sixteenth-century madrigalist Carlo Gesualdo. The element of distancing remains: a solo in *Canticum Sacrum* is marked to be sung '*quasi rubato, con discrezione e non forte*' ('as if in free time, with discretion, and not loud'), which tells you more about how not to sing it than about what the composer actually wants.

Other features of his last years were many arrangements of his earlier works, designed partly to enable him to earn copyright income in the West, an eightieth birthday dinner with President Kennedy at the White House (at which he got drunk) and lengthy interviews with his friend and amanuensis, the conductor Robert Craft, collected and published in 1959 as *Conversations with Igor Stravinsky*. They include touching recollections of friends and events of many decades before like his admired teacher Rimsky-Korsakov, his parents' praise of Mussorgsky ('a frequent guest in our house'),[29] Glazunov playing the piano ('already a cut and dried academician'),[30] meetings with Max Reger ('he and his music repulsed me')[31] and Alfredo Casella (who made him feel 'like a poor little child'),[32] and Mahler conducting ('a triumph').[33] There were precise responses to questions about the composers in his lifetime he considered important (Webern) and which younger musicians he admired: 'I like to listen to Boulez'[34] (but was cattily dismissive of avant-garde modernism later in life, calling Stockhausen 'boring').[35] Elsewhere in his writings, in his 1936 autobiography *Chronicles of My Life* he set a tenacious hare running with the declaration, 'I consider that music is, by its very nature, essentially powerless to *express* anything at all, whether a feeling, an attitude of mind, a psychological mood, a phenomenon of nature, etc. *Expression* has never been an inherent property of music.'[36]

Stravinsky was the most intellectually organised of the great composers. He was an inventor, designing a device for ruling stem lines which he called the Stravigor. Sitting down to compose (in a daily routine) he would use the music of Beethoven or others 'to put myself in motion', like a clock.[37]

In 1962 Stravinsky visited Russia for the first time in almost half a century. Craft wrote that Stravinsky regretted 'his uprooting and exile more than anything else in his life'.[38]

He died in 1971 at the age of eighty-eight. At his own request, he was buried in the Russian section of the island cemetery of San Michele, Venice, near to the grave of Serge Diaghilev, his collaborator of six decades earlier: an exile to the end.

Prophets and Disciples

The great causes of twentieth-century music were lined up in the lists, their banners run up the flagpole, their champions massing below: serialism, Neoclassicism, folkloristic nationalism, impressionism. Others stood poised to enter the ring: minimalism (already hinted at in the rhythmic patterns of the *Rite*), jazz (again already on parade in the syncopations and dance rhythms of Stravinsky's bouncy little symphonies, the added-note harmonies of Scriabin and the non-standard scale patterns being investigated by Bartók and Messiaen), electronics (reporting for duty in the compositions of Edgard Varèse and the sparky inventions of Leon Theremin, Maurice Martenot, Laurens Hammond and Robert Moog), and self-absorbed probings into the very nature of composition and performance which came to be known as experimental music. From these spawned a whole ecosystem of avant-garde modernists, Dadaists and surrealists, songwriters, symphonists, composers of smoky subterranean cabaret and fragrant Cotswold cowpats, brittle ironists, Neoromantics and passionate polemicists, all nudged and buffeted by the politics, economics and aesthetics of a difficult century. The only thing you couldn't be was ordinary.

The most important twelve-tone and serial composers were Schoenberg's own pupils, and two in particular: Alban Berg and Anton Webern.

The links and dissimilarities can be charted in three works with similar names, written close together. Schoenberg based his *Fünf Orchesterstücke* (*Five Pieces for Orchestra*) of 1909 on a single chord of five pitches, presented without development in different instrumental colours, ultra-precise dynamic markings and chromatic derivations: 'There are no motifs in this piece.'[39] The same year, Webern's *Sechs Stücke für grosses Orchester* (*Six Pieces for Large Orchestra*) pursue Schoenbergian avoidance of motivic development with the scary logic of a bad dream: 'No motif is developed; at most, a brief progression is immediately repeated. Once stated, the theme expresses all it has to say; it must be followed by something fresh.'[40] The Funeral March in the *Six Pieces* is Mahler in a black hole, sucked down to its essentials, painfully following the stages of Webern's grief for his recently deceased mother. One critic has described their 'flickering nightmares, with vagrant touches of breathtaking beauty'.[41] Berg's *Drei Orchesterstücke* (*Three Pieces for Orchestra*) of 1913–15 put the Mahler back in: waltz, ländler, march and a grotesque synthesis of popular style and lush, impressionistic orchestration sit alongside chromatic chords borrowed as much from the over-ripe tonality of Strauss as the intellectual truth-seeking of Schoenberg.

Berg's work is dedicated 'to my teacher and friend Arnold Schoenberg in immeasurable gratitude and love'. Berg's contribution to twelve-tone music was to find a way of using a tone row within the context of inherited musical forms. Two fine pieces show the principle at work.

His Violin Concerto was composed in memory of Manon Gropius, the daughter of Mahler's widow Alma and her second husband Walter Gropius, who died of polio at the age of eighteen. Not only does it include recognisable elements like Viennese waltzes, a Carpathian folk song and time-honoured harmonic features like sequences, the row itself is structured around a series of triads, which themselves begin on the notes of the open strings of the violin, the soloist's first utterance. The last few notes of the row, left over from the triads, form a brief whole-tone scale which becomes the theme of a strangely chromatic Bach chorale, quoted at the end: '*Es ist genug! So nimm, Herr, meinen Geist*' ('It is enough! Lord, take my spirit'). All is linked, in the progress from life, through death, to transfiguration. The concerto has an elegiac quality comparable to, though stylistically utterly different from, a concerto by a composer who died the year before Berg wrote it, the Cello Concerto of Edward Elgar.

Berg's opera *Wozzeck*, first performed in 1925, is in three acts, each consciously fashioned in a five-movement form overlaid on its five scenes: a group of 'Five Character Pieces'; a 'Symphony in Five Movements' (including a Sonata, Fantasia and Fugue, and Rondo); a set of inventions, though not necessarily on a theme but on things like a rhythm, a chord, or even a single note. There are leitmotifs, and musical *objets trouvés* like a military band and an on-stage out-of-tune piano. The story, taken from a play by Georg Büchner about a real historical soldier who murdered the woman he was living with, is pure verismo in its low-life setting, shocking violence and casual sadism; the music is not. The orchestration is masterly, deploying its big forces with Mahlerian subtlety and skill. The dramatic instinct is unerring: Marie's child hopping off stage on his hobby horse at the end to join his friends peering at the newly discovered body of his mother is heartbreaking. Berg's second opera, *Lulu*, an even more intense exploration both of musical structure and the psychology of violence, was left incomplete at the time of his death in late 1935 (like Mahler, aged just fifty). Berg's masterpieces remain perhaps the only works of the Schoenberg school to have earned a place in the repertoire out of love.

If Berg expanded the Schoenbergian credo, Webern did exactly the opposite. From the intense concentration of the *Six Pieces for Orchestra* he compressed even more intently in the *Five Pieces for Orchestra* of 1911, most lasting less than a minute, the fourth containing no more than fifty notes. Schoenberg said of Webern's works of this period:

> One has to realize what restraint it needs to express oneself with such brevity. Every glance can be expanded into a poem, every sigh into a novel. But to express a novel in a single gesture, joy in a single breath; such concentration can only be found where self-pity is lacking in equal measure ... It was incredibly difficult.[42]

Like his leader Schoenberg he fully assimilated twelve-tone technique in the 1920s, first in songs often with colourful chamber accompaniments allowing raindrops of instrumental colour to hang and drip from his settings of perhaps slightly surprising texts like *Three Traditional Rhymes* (1924–5) and poems by the Romantics' favourite Goethe (*Zwei Lieder*, 1926), then in more expected (if shorter than expected) things like a symphony in 1928, a string quartet in 1937 and late essays in variation form for both piano and orchestra (variations on what? Analysts have pored over their inversions, rows and internal references). As a person, Webern was monkish and disciplined where Berg was sensual and worldly. As a performer, he insisted on passion, expression and rubato, even (indeed especially) in his own spare, enigmatic scores. As a public man, he was sadly willing to sign up to the hazardous myth of the innate superiority of pan-German culture, and was openly, if naively, welcoming of the rise of the Nazis and allied himself with anti-Semitic comments. His only son Peter, a Nazi, was killed in an Allied strafing attack on a military train in February 1945. Webern himself was shot and killed by an American soldier in September the same year when he stepped out of his house during a curfew to enjoy a cigar without disturbing his grandchildren.

Webern soon gained a deserved reputation as the most intense and cerebral scion of the Schoenberg school, which both largely kept his works off regular concert lists and also earned the awestruck devotion of later avant-garde modernists. His music takes concentration to extremes. It makes you want to hold your breath so you don't miss anything. It might help to approach him in the knowledge that he was the man who wrote a PhD on the music of the sixteenth-century

Austrian contrapuntalist Heinrich Isaac, and hear his own music in the context of the spare, dry, bony, brainy strain of Renaissance counterpoint. Webern's arrangements of Bach provide another way in: his orchestration of the six-part *Ricercar* from the *Musical Offering* is perhaps the best example of *Klangfarbenmelodie*, passing Bach's angular little tune between different sounds like a pathologist brandishing a scalpel.

Webern distils thought into utterances which Stravinsky characterised as 'dazzling diamonds'.[43] His brilliance can perhaps be obscured by later composers who used his aphoristic gestures without his fastidious concision. Webern and Berg took the example of their teacher Schoenberg (who was only a decade or so older than his two star pupils and outlived both of them) in completely different directions, both rich and strange, valid and rewarding.

Among other important names often mentioned in Schoenberg's orbit, his teacher and brother-in-law Alexander Zemlinsky set German translations of the poems of the Bengali poet Rabindranath Tagore to music in his *Lyrische Symphonie* (*Lyric Symphony*) of 1923, lost the love of Alma Schindler to Mahler, and was the dedicatee of Berg's similarly titled *Lyrische Suite* (*Lyric Suite*), which quotes Zemlinsky's symphony.

Zemlinksy's 1910 setting of Psalm 23 was conducted by a composer whose operatic popularity in the early Weimar years was second only to that of Richard Strauss, thanks to his stylistically pluralistic, time-travelling 1912 dream opera *Der ferne Klang* (*The Distant Sound*): Franz Schreker. Like Hans Pfitzner's near-contemporary opera *Palestrina*, *Der ferne Klang* uses the central character of a composer as an emblem of the difficult search for artistic truth. Zemlinsky's *Kammersymphonie* (*Chamber Symphony*) of 1916 concentrates Mahlerian form and sound into something small and dense, a solo flute floating high over the quiet flutterings of harp harmonics, harmonium, piano, celeste and divided strings, ending on a rich chord of D major. A rapid decline in his fortunes was propelled by changing tastes and anti-Semitism.

Egon Wellesz picked rather confusedly among his compositional inheritance, left Europe for England in the wake of the Anschluss in 1938, and studied ancient Byzantine music in Oxford. In around 1912 he was the first to describe the group of composers around Schoenberg as the 'Viennese School', a term which soon became 'Second Viennese School' (implying Haydn and Mozart as the 'First').

Hanns Eisler was wounded in the First World War, studied with Schoenberg from 1919, became a communist in Berlin, collaborated with his lifelong friend Bertolt Brecht on plays and songs which looked at life from street level, pioneered a collage style of musical composition in his song cycle *Zeitungsausschnitte* (*News Clippings*) (1926), was banned by the Nazis and wandered Europe before finally joining Brecht in California in 1938, where he wrote music for films before being deported by Senator Joseph McCarthy's House Un-American Activities Committee in 1948. His compositions included the national anthem of the former GDR.

The life and work of Ernst Krenek read like a one-man history of twentieth-century mid-European music. A pupil of the stylistic pluralist Schreker, he wrote a study of the music of the Flemish Renaissance composer Johannes Ockeghem, married Mahler's daughter Anna (very briefly) and composed in an atonal style before turning to his hugely successful 1926 opera about a Black jazz musician, *Jonny Spielt Auf* (*Johnny Strikes Up*), a parody of whose poster formed the centrepiece of the Nazis' exhibition of *Entartete Musik* ('Degenerate Music') in 1938. Having been persecuted for being Jewish (he wasn't), he followed many musical colleagues to America in 1938, where he taught in a variety of universities and married for a third time. He died in 1991 at the age of ninety-one. Few composers have travelled so far, from the marriage of twelve-tone technique and the principles of Renaissance modal counterpoint in *Lamentatio Jeremiae Prophetae* (*Lamentations of Jeremiah the Prophet*) of 1941 to the Mahlerian *Symphonic Elegy for String Orchestra* ('in memoriam Anton Webern') of 1946, and the use of chance as a compositional tool (also known as 'aleatoric' music), as well as electronics and tape recordings.

A complex century had its casualties. Schoenberg considered Norbert von Hannenheim 'one of the most interesting and talented pupils ... I think, confidently, that he will have a word to say in the development of music'.[44] A sufferer from depression, he entered a German psychiatric hospital in 1945, dying shortly afterwards, aged forty-seven, in what was described as a 'euthanasia hospital' in Poland. It was long thought that all his music was lost in a bombed-out Berlin bank vault; remarkably, individual items began to resurface some fifty years after his death, notably works for viola which apply Schoenberg's serial principles to themes of thirty, sometimes fifty-four pitches, rather than just twelve, and adding polyrhythmic elements from his native Transylvania in a way which echoes the practice of Bartók: a sad glimpse of lost promise.

Typically, the term Second Viennese School came to stand for an idea more than an entity. It sometimes takes in figures who predate its innovations but prefigure them, like Zemlinsky, as well as some who studied with Schoenberg in Berlin, not Vienna, like the Greek Nikolas Skalkottas, and others who added folkloristic elements from their own native traditions like the Catalan Roberto Gerhard: it tends not to include later inheritors like Schoenberg's American pupils or the post-Second World War modernists (including those stylistically and intellectually most loyal to the flame); but does take in pupils of pupils like Webern's English acolyte Humphrey Searle and the Polish-French René Leibowitz (who may have studied with Webern but complicated his legacy by regularly reinventing his own past), co-coiners of the word serialism.

Modernism and Folk Music: Bartók and Kodály

When Ferruccio Busoni heard Béla Bartók's *Fourteen Bagatelles* for piano in 1908, he exclaimed, 'At last something truly new!'[45] Few shared Busoni's prescience. In his lifetime, at least until towards its end, Bartók was better known as a pianist and collector of folk song than as a composer.

Béla Bartók was born in 1881, moving in childhood between towns then in the kingdom of Hungary, now in various parts of Romania, Slovakia and Ukraine. An early show of talent at the piano took him to Budapest in 1899, where he met Richard Strauss at a performance of *Also Sprach Zarathustra*, which 'stimulated the greatest enthusiasm in me; at last I saw the way that lay before me',[46] and fellow Hungarian Zoltán Kodály, who was to become a lifelong friend and colleague. In 1904 he experienced the kind of musical epiphany described in strikingly similar terms by other folk-influenced composers like Vaughan Williams and Janáček, when he heard a young Transylvanian nanny called Lidi Dósa singing folk songs to her young charges. Another profound influence was the music of Claude Debussy. Bartók's early adulthood was taken up with touring and teaching as a pianist, getting married, collecting folk songs with Kodály and helping to blow away the rather vague concept of 'gypsy' music in the works of Liszt and others by methodically and meticulously noting the technical characteristics of different regions and peoples. Small-scale pieces came easily to him, but finding his true voice proved hard. In 1911 his opera *Bluebeard's Castle* was rejected by the Hungarian Fine Arts Commission. His mature style was reached in the late 1920s, with the third and fourth of his six string quartets. Later he increasingly wrote in larger forms, including concertos for piano and violin, though never quickly. In 1923 he married for a second time. An outspoken opponent of his country's alliance with Nazi Germany, he followed many European musicians to America in 1940, becoming a US citizen in 1945. The conductor Serge Koussevitzky commissioned the *Concerto for Orchestra*, a rare public success, in 1944. Another presiding patron of stray geniuses, the pianist Elizabeth Sprague Coolidge, commissioned the Fifth Quartet of 1934.

Bartók never really felt at home in America. Already ill with leukaemia when Koussevitzky provided him with his first and last burst of genuine popular acclaim, he died in New York in September 1945. Forty years later his two sons from his two marriages arranged his reinterment at a state funeral in Budapest.

Bartók's orchestral music is brilliantly imaginative, often making distinctive use of the percussive (rather than lyrical or virtuosic) potential of the piano, as well as batteries of real percussion, including Hungarian elements like the cimbalom, featured in his 1928 *Rhapsody No. 1* for violin and orchestra. A distinctive feature is his hazy, floaty 'Night Music' slow movements, as in the *Sonata for Two Pianos and Percussion* of 1937 (later orchestrated as a concerto), premiered and regularly played by the composer and his second wife, Ditta Pásztory-Bartók. Ditta contributed to a lightening and lyricism in his later works: the Third Piano Concerto, not quite finished at the time of his death, was written as a surprise birthday present for her, containing allusions to Beethoven, Wagner, birdsong and insect calls in an almost Neoclassical frame. His music for young players includes the six volumes of *Mikrokosmos*, written between 1926 and 1939 and covering the whole gamut of piano technique and pedagogy from simple exercises to virtuoso concert works, the first two dedicated to his son Peter.

His six string quartets are the finest and most important essays in the form after Beethoven. As with Beethoven, they are spaced across the whole of his mature career. String Quartet No. 5 (1934) is in his favoured arch form, pairing the surprising, beautiful, calm chorale chords of the second movement with its chattering echo in the fourth, with a scherzo *Alla bulgarese* placed in the middle as the third movement , itself a palindrome with outer sections in a wonderfully lop-sided 4+2+3/8 time signature, like the spikiest and most *recherché* modern jazz. The first movement's scales, cross-rhythms and whooping glissandos are recalled in the whirlwind last movement, getting faster and faster until it subsides into a bizarre and grotesque circus version of its tune, marked *con indifferenza* and played in two keys at the same time. String Quartet No. 3 (1927) uses scale and chord patterns which tease and defy, builds to a roller-coaster fugato in scratchy *sul ponticello*, and treats its four instrumentalists like an orchestra, regularly asking them to play three or four notes at once, sometimes *arco* and *pizz* (maybe with a harmonic thrown in just to give all ten fingers something to do) at the same time. The sheer energy of this music is mind-blowing: gypsy rock in bow ties. String Quartet No. 6 (1939) has four movements each beginning with a variant of the same wanderingly lyrical melody, marked *mesto* (sad), each leading somewhere different: the second movement's dotted-note march is perhaps the closest this music gets to its hovering angel, the late quartets of Beethoven.

Folk song underpins Bartók's creative career. His many sets of Hungarian, Romanian, Transylvanian and other dances, as well as descriptive pieces like *Village Scenes* of 1924 and the late *A férj keserve* (literally, 'The Bitter Husband', although the given English title is 'Goat Song') (1945) revel in complex polyrhythms, expressive modal melodies and the swagger of a village violin, with no attempt to prettify these farmyard creatures for the concert hall, as others did.

Bartók described the three ways of incorporating folk music into art music clearly and revealingly:

> The question is, what are the ways in which peasant music is taken over and becomes transmuted into modern music? We may, for instance, take over a peasant melody unchanged or only slightly varied, write an accompaniment to it and possibly some opening and concluding phrases. This kind of work would show a certain analogy with Bach's treatment of chorales … Another method … is the following: the composer does not make use of a real peasant melody but invents his own imitation of such melodies. There is no true difference between this

method and the one described above ... There is yet a third way ... Neither peasant melodies nor imitations of peasant melodies can be found in his music, but it is pervaded by the atmosphere of peasant music. In this case we may say, he has completely absorbed the idiom of peasant music which has become his musical mother tongue.[47]

Bartók and his almost exact contemporary Zoltán Kodály shared much. Twice-married (to two women with a seventy-seven-year age difference between them), Kodály was not as wide-ranging or original a composer as his friend Bartók, though *Háry János*, his 1926 folk opera (in this case, a spoken play with songs, like the older German Singspiel) and the orchestral *Dances of Galánta* (1933) hold a worthy place in his nation's heritage. His tuneful, dramatic *Missa Brevis* was premiered in the cloakroom of the Budapest Opera House during the siege of the city in February 1945. Unlike Bartók's wider-ranging activities and sympathies, his folk roots are largely focused on their native Hungary. As he put it, 'What musical features are characteristic of Hungarian music? In general, it is active rather than passive, an expression of will rather than emotion. Aimless grieving and tears of merriment do not appear in our music.'[48] He comes nearest to Bartók in modernist muscularity in the bracing and brilliant Sonata in B Minor for Solo Cello (1915), using scordatura, or retuning, of two of the instrument's strings, a common feature of earlier pieces such as Bach's Cello Suite No. 6 in D Major: one scholar judges it 'the only unaccompanied work able to stand next to Bach'.[49] Kodály's other principal contribution to music history is the teaching method for children which bears his name, based on hand signals as indicators of pitch (an ancient idea with roots in the medieval treatises of Guido and others). Fittingly, Kodály's statue in the Hungarian city of Pécs faces not the cathedral but a children's playground.

Other twentieth-century modernists had less patience with folk influence in art music: in 1947 Arnold Schoenberg wrote an essay on 'Folkloristic Symphonies' in which he said, 'I cannot remember a single case of deriving subordinate ideas from a folk song', and, further, stated that Bach did not 'produce new material, contrasts, subordinate themes etc' from chorale melodies (both highly questionable statements).[50] Mahler, following a visit to Sibelius in Helsinki in 1904, spat: '*Pui Kaki!* They are everywhere, these national geniuses.

You find them in Russia and Sweden – and in Italy the country is overrun by these whores and their ponces.'[51] Schoenberg summed up his defence of what he calls the 'real composer' against the folklorist: 'Put a hundred chicken eggs under an eagle and even she will not be able to hatch an eagle from these eggs.' Both protest too much.

Some Other Folklorists, and Musical Nationalism

Leoš Janáček learnt to value his native heritage by leaving rural Moravia and returning with new ears. Like his near-contemporary Elgar, his major works date from a late maturity in the first years of the twentieth century. Many show a unique take on ideas of nationalism in music: descriptive piano pieces, dances arranged for orchestra and folk songs for chorus, a Mass in Old Slavonic suggested partly as a commemoration of Czech independence, a piano sonata marking the death of a student in a protest in Brno (its two movements are entitled *Předtucha* ('Foreboding') and *Smrt* ('Death')). His organ piece for Saint Wenceslas (founder and patron of Prague) is more authentic than the English carol singer's pretty Victorian folderol. Like Vaughan Williams and Holst in England, Bartók and Kodály in Hungary and Cecil Sharp in Appalachia, Janáček collected folk songs in the field and published his findings as well as using them in his own work (though Vaughan Williams never found a piece called *Music for Club-Swinging Exercises* in leafy Surrey, as Janáček did in 1893).

Latin and Mediterranean nationalism often drew on folk traditions, with an element of political protest, which developed and matured during the nineteenth century: the Portuguese fado, tango in Argentina and flamenco in Spain, nurtured into a national art from its regional roots by the Escuela Bolera. Its finest synthesis for the concert hall is the relatively small output of Manuel de Falla, notably the orchestral *Noches en los jardines de España* (*Nights in the Gardens of Spain*) of 1915 and the ballet *El amor brujo* (*Love, the Magician*) of 1925. His compatriots Isaac Albéniz and Joaquín Turina joined him in Paris from around 1907, in the heady company orbiting around Stravinsky, Debussy and Diaghilev. George Enescu arrived in Paris from Romania in 1895, aged fourteen, to study composition, piano and violin, going on to add conducting to an enormously successful international career and a reputation as his country's finest musician. His associates ranged from his teachers Massenet and Fauré to the classical Indian musician Uday Shankar (brother of Ravi) and pupils Yehudi Menuhin, Arthur Grumiaux and many others. Enescu's 1940 *Impressions d'enfance* (*Impressions of Childhood*) for violin and piano is one of the most compelling and muscular examples of Bartók's 'third way' outside Bartók's own music: like Ravel's *Tzigane* in its long, gypsy-ish solo introduction, but less mannered, more modern and more convincing. Popular music in Paris often came close to its Classical cousin in theme and manner: musicians like the *chansonniers* of Montmartre (Édith Piaf, Yvette Guilbert) and songwriters such as Charles Trenet and the Sœurs Étienne carried a defiant underground element of protest in their music.

Italy, Germany, England

There were other paths on (or around) the modernist pilgrimage.

Ferruccio Busoni set out a thoughtful analysis of style and idea in his essay *Entwurf einer neuen Ästhetik der Tonkunst* ('Sketch of a New Esthetic of Music') of 1907, welcoming the use of electronics in composition, advocating the subdivision of the octave other than just into twelve equal semitones, and reflecting on how the reception of a work changes as social circumstances also change. He addressed what it means to be modern:

> ephemeral qualities give a work the stamp of 'modernity'; its unchangeable essence hinders it from becoming 'obsolete' ... There is nothing properly modern ... the Modern and the Old have always been.[52]

Ten years later, the self-styled anti-modernist composer Hans Pfitzner responded in an ill-tempered article called '*Futuristengefahr*' ('The Dangers of Futurism'), misrepresenting Busoni, muddling dates by accusing him of supporting the Italian Futurists (whose first manifesto only appeared in 1909, two years after Busoni's essay) and sailing nastily close to blatant racism: 'Eskimos, Papuans, Swahili Negroes probably cannot distinguish major and minor either.'[53] As so often, the music is more illuminating than the verbal sparring: in practice, Busoni largely declined to follow his own avant-garde prospectus; Pfitzner's ideas about historical integrity and style are expressed much more eloquently in his 1917 opera *Palestrina*, an account of how the Renaissance master, and by association Pfitzner himself, found the true path.

The Italian 'generation of the eighties' (born in the 1880s) comprised the post-Puccini composers of well-crafted ballet and symphonic suites: Alfredo Casella, Ottorino Respighi, Ildebrando Pizzetti. Futurists Francesco Balilla Pratella and Luigi Russolo wrote *L'Arte dei Rumori* ('The Art of Noises') in 1913. It builds on the ideas of the influential Futurist Manifesto of 1909, arguing for a new art for the machine age based on the sounds of mechanisation and industry. Russolo's ideas were an important step in the evolution of electronic instruments: photographs show his work room filled with oversized speakers and phonograph horns in pursuit of what he called Bruitism.

German Expressionism dealt in the brutal, the violent, the extreme. It touched many musical styles. Paul Hindemith shocked his way to prominence in the early 1920s with pieces like *Sancta Susanna* (1921), an opera about the descent of a group of nuns into a sexual frenzy, conveyed in a fragmented libretto made up more of stage directions than speech, before retrenchment into a more conservative style later in his career.

A release from tortured Teutonic introspection came in the arts, as in so much else, in the brief gaiety of the Weimar Republic of the early 1920s. Restless and much-theorised artistic experimentation met real life as workers spent their wages on fun before their banknotes lost their value the next day. The playwright Bertolt Brecht captured this artificiality in the concept of *Verfremdungseffekte* ('estrangement effect'): the artist must constantly remind the audience that they are watching a fiction. The musical analogue is imported song style; the most polished exponent Brecht's collaborator Kurt Weill. Weill's music takes the harmonies of George Gershwin and adds a layer of irony and of theatrical and musical sophistication. The hugely successful 1928 Brecht/Weill collaboration *Die Dreigroschenoper* (*The Threepenny Opera*) is a version of John Gay's 1728 *Beggar's Opera*, parodying all sorts of styles and periods in numbers with titles like 'Das Lied von der Unzulänglichkeit menschlichen Strebens' ('The Song about the Insufficiency of Human Endeavour'). *Aufstieg und Fall der Stadt Mahagonny* (*Rise and Fall of the City of Mahagonny*) is a brittle satire on a society based on pleasure, charting the fate of a posse of fugitives including Fatty the Bookkeeper at the hands of townsfolk led by Bank-account Billy. The complete work premiered in 1930, was banned by the incoming Nazis in 1933, and was fully revived only thirty years later.

Schoenberg never did get grocers' boys to whistle his tunes. Weill's smoky, ironic melodies, including 'Alabama Song' ('Show me the way to the next whisky bar …'), 'Surabaya Johnny' and 'Mack the Knife' have been sung by artists as diverse as the dancer and actress Lotte Lenya (Weill's wife), the Welsh Wagnerian soprano Dame Gwyneth Jones, musical theatre singer Patti LuPone, jazz artists Bobby Darin and Ella Fitzgerald and rock stars David Bowie and Jim Morrison (who included an enigmatic version of 'Alabama Song' on his band's breakthrough first album *The Doors* in 1967).

Early twentieth-century England, ruled until recently by Queen Victoria, personal friend of Mendelssohn, did things differently, as always. Most visiting Continental composers continued to comment on the fog. Fauré thought England's choral tradition was a product of the weather:

> these black skies cause people to gather together and to create amateur choirs of an unrivalled standard above anything we know in France … If only our climate weren't so good![54]

Ralph Vaughan Williams was born in 1872. A descendant of both Josiah Wedgwood and Charles Darwin (whom his mother called 'Great Uncle Charles'), he studied at Cambridge, then with Parry and Stanford at the Royal College of Music in London, made a living playing the organ, editing Purcell and serving as musical editor of the 1906 *English Hymnal*: 'two years of close association with some of the best (as well as some of the worst) tunes in the world was a better musical education than any amount of sonatas and fugues'.[55] He studied with Ravel ('exactly the man I was looking for'),[56] heard Mahler conduct *Tristan und Isolde* ('staggered home in a daze and could not sleep for two nights'),[57] sat next to a nervous young Herbert Howells at a performance of Elgar's *Dream of Gerontius* in Gloucester cathedral in 1910 (the first time that masterpiece had been heard in an English cathedral with its original, avowedly Catholic text), and served in the First World War. RVW (as he was always known) taught in his turn at the Royal College, gave groundbreaking performances of the *St Matthew Passion*, became a respected establishment figure, married twice (sharing a bedroom with both his ailing wife and much younger then-partner during air raids in the Second World War, all three holding hands for comfort), wrote music for the coronation of Queen Elizabeth II in 1953, and died at the age of eighty-five in 1958.

His music is instantly recognisable and hugely popular. Modal harmonies and folk-like melodies underpin lyrical works like the early song 'Linden Lea' of 1901, *The Lark Ascending* of 1914 and the *Fantasia on a Theme by Thomas Tallis* of 1910. The Concerto in F Minor for Bass Tuba and Orchestra (1954), one of several serving instruments generally less well-off for solo repertoire, sounds like a steam train puffing through a wheat field. The *Serenade to Music* of 1938 moved Rachmaninoff to tears. That Vaughan Williams's style has certain limitations was noted at the time. Reviewing the Fourth Symphony in 1935, the critic Eric Blom called him 'one of the most venturesome composers in Europe', as daring as 'the youngest adventurer'.[58] Twenty years later Blom reviewed the opera *The Pilgrim's Progress* (actually written around the same time as the Fourth Symphony): 'That there is a certain sameness about the work is undeniable, but it is due to consistency of style, not to lack of invention or limited imagination.'[59] Britten was less forgiving, finding his music 'technically inefficient … [it] didn't seem to hang together'.[60] Fellow composer Constant Lambert complained that in Vaughan Williams's Third Symphony (the 'Pastoral' (1922)) the 'creation of a particular type of grey, reflective, English-landscape mood has outweighed the exigencies of symphonic form'.[61] Another composer, Peter Warlock, went further, saying this aspect of Vaughan Williams 'is all just a little too much like a cow looking over a gate'.[62]

But there is much more to Vaughan Williams than this version of pastoral. Choral works like the *Three Shakespeare Songs* (1951) and Mass in G Minor (1921) are challenging, original and hard. Above all, the nine symphonies range from the pastoral mood of numbers Two and Five to the dissonance and violence of the Fourth and Sixth, with its almost Shostakovich-like searing opening and the strange, frozen stillness of the all-quiet last movement, composed in the aftermath of war. Victorian sentimentality is long gone.

Vaughan Williams said of his Fourth Symphony, 'I don't know whether I like it, but it's certainly what I meant.'[63] He wrote with bulldog-like integrity and a stubborn loyalty to his own vision. He remains a huge figure in the history of English music.

Vaughan Williams shared much with his close friend Gustav

Holst (originally von Holst), including an interest in folk song and composing music for amateurs and music for teaching alongside symphonic and choral works. To this, Holst added the element of his own enquiring sympathies: the evergreen *Planets Suite* of 1916 was originally called *Seven Pieces for Large Orchestra*, partly under the influence of Schoenberg's *Five Pieces for Orchestra*. To the Elgarian breadth of his sumptuous 'Jupiter' melody Holst adds the Mahlerian rattle and Straussian crescendo of 'Mars', and mystic echoes of Debussy in the closing pages of 'Neptune', with its women's chorus placed off-stage, singing behind a door which is gradually closed, fading to silence ('unforgettable,' commented Holst's daughter Imogen).[64] Holst's Englishness is set in context, too, by his interest in Eastern art and philosophy in pieces like the *Choral Hymns from the Rig-Veda*, which he translated himself from the ancient Vedic Sanskrit between 1908 and 1912, and by a stubborn unwillingness to be typecast as a standard issue English pastoralist, contributing to some notably dissonant harmony and angularly polyphonic later music more akin to Hindemith than his friend Vaughan Williams. Like Parry with his experimental 'ethical cantatas', Holst was more of a radical free thinker than his most popular pieces may sometimes suggest.

Another in-outsider was the composer visited by Vaughan Williams on his student trip to Europe, an Englishman who spent most of his life in France but never lost his Yorkshire accent, especially when discussing cricket with his amanuensis Eric Fenby (to the puzzlement of his German wife): Frederick Delius. Delius makes some of the defining sounds of early twentieth-century English music: the tone poem *On Hearing the First Cuckoo in Spring* (1910), the part songs *Two Songs to be Sung of a Summer Night on the River* (1917), 'The Walk to the Paradise Garden' and *Sea Drift*, his 1904 setting of Walt Whitman for baritone, chorus and orchestra; but they are often criticised for a tendency to drift themselves, their downward-spiralling harmonies very beautiful but a bit aimless. His chords have something in common with what Schoenberg called 'vagrant harmonies', which can't be linked to a key:[65] as a composer, Vaughan Williams had little time for this species of chromaticism.

Beneath the spreading branches of the leading figures of early twentieth-century English music flourished a whole copse of composers, miniaturists in scale and concentrated emotion, drawing on the rich resource of the English language in the lyrics and sonnets of

Shakespeare, the religious and love poetry of seventeenth-century Metaphysical poets like John Donne and George Herbert, and the nostalgic Victoriana of Thomas Hardy and A. E. Housman: George Butterworth, killed at the Somme at the age of twenty-one; Ivor Gurney, poet and musician of precious gifts lost to mental suffering; Britten's teacher John Ireland ('a strong personality but a weak character', according to Britten);[66] elegant songwriters such as Roger Quilter and Robin Milford; composer and educator Freda Swain, whose *Airmail Concerto* was sent to her pianist husband in instalments when he was stuck in South Africa in the 1940s; Philip Heseltine, an erratic and drunken Celt who changed his name to Peter Warlock as a reflection of his interest in witchcraft; Warlock's friend E. J. Moeran, Britten's early Suffolk neighbour and supporter; the church musician Herbert Howells, whose *Hymnus Paradisi* of 1935 is the great oratorio of the English pastoral school and whose arching structures fill the spaces of the Anglican choral tradition with his big, occasionally blues-tinged phrases, hung to the wonderful words of the *Book of Common Prayer*; and a musician of delicate, introspective sensitivity who devoted much of his time and energy to growing rare apples in his orchard on the Berkshire Downs, Gerald Finzi. These composers are the best of an aspect of England: rooted in her language and landscape, small-scale, subtle and sensitive, a million miles from German angst and French irony. If they dealt with the challenge of how to build large structures and of how to be new by largely ignoring it, that is part of their legacy: polishers of jewels rather than builders of castles.

Mid-century British music found some colourful influences: Celtic culture in Arnold Bax's windswept *Tintagel* (1919); Scriabin-like associations of sound and colour in Arthur Bliss's *A Colour Symphony* of 1922 (its movements are entitled Purple, Red, Blue, Green); and, as always, her maritime setting in Frank Bridge's *The Sea* of 1911. Granville Bantock attempted an English Bayreuth at Glastonbury with his cycle of operas on the Arthurian legends. Cyril Scott captured his interest in the occult in his exotic harmonies. John Foulds was perhaps the ultimate eclectic original, self-taught, successful in light music, drawing on Indian culture and everything else in his colossal *A World Requiem*, premiered on Armistice Night 1923, Mahlerian in its scale and ambition. The indomitable Ethel Smyth once conducted her 'The March of the Women' (1910) with a toothbrush from her cell window in Wormwood Scrubs as her fellow suffragettes marched round the prison yard below. Gordon Jacob and his younger contemporary Malcolm Arnold contributed characterful and conservative instrumental pieces in a wide variety of genres.

The generation of composers born in the first five years of the century helped establish English music as a newly vital and outward-looking creative force.

Constant Lambert was born in 1905. Prodigiously gifted, he was a significant figure in the establishment of classical dance in England, as founding Music Director of the Royal Ballet. Lambert is known today almost entirely for his brilliant 1927 setting of Sacheverell Sitwell's poem *The Rio Grande* for voices, orchestra and a virtuoso solo piano, like a sort of rumba-style mixture of Beethoven's *Choral Fantasia* and Gershwin's *Rhapsody in Blue*.

Three years older than Lambert was a composer who moved late in life to the island of Ischia in the Bay of Naples, fulfilling his role as a rather semi-detached member of the British musical establishment, William Walton. Walton's musical signatures include tonal harmonies which pile thirds and fourths into big, unstable chords; lyrical melodies which can also tip over into angularity; brittle, fizzing orchestration; and a strain of cynical worldly wit as well as something darker. The First Symphony in B Flat Minor, finished in 1935, bears the influence of Sibelius in the rhythmic build-up of the first movement and the lyricism of the second; the last movement presented him with some structural problems which he did not, perhaps, quite solve. It is a compelling and original piece: Adrian Boult conducted it but decided, 'I couldn't face all that malice a second time, and said so.'[67] In 1931 *Belshazzar's Feast* exploded the staid English oratorio tradition into something loud and modern; the Viola Concerto (premiered by Paul Hindemith in 1929) is the best of his three string concertos, with its long, unusual orchestral passage without soloist in the last movement. In 1923 *Façade – An Entertainment*, in which he set Sacheverell's sister Edith's poems to music, put the spoken text about 'Old Sir Faulk, Tall as a stork' and 'Lily O'Grady, Silly and shady' against jaunty, pattering melodies, French-style, and captures perfectly the carefree *beau monde* of the Sitwell family, who took him in as a gauche northern lad emerging from his early training as a choirboy at Christ Church, Oxford, and housed him in their attic in Chelsea ('I went for a few weeks and stayed for about fifteen years').[68] His wartime work as a film composer shows up in the stirring marches 'Orb and Sceptre' and

'Crown Imperial', outranked only by Elgar in the puffed-up parade up the aisle at coronations and royal weddings. Aaron Copland called Walton 'a child of the hectic twenties who has been turned into a pillar of British musical society'.[69]

As an 11-year-old prep schoolboy Michael Tippett wrote an essay denying the existence of God, and later got into the Royal College of Music despite his lack of the necessary qualifications, taught at prep schools, ran a community choir, met Auden and Eliot and flirted with communism. During the war he taught at Morley College in London, and went to prison following his registration as a conscientious objector.

Between 1939 and 1941 he composed his genre-challenging oratorio *A Child of Our Time*, to his own text based on the murder of a German diplomat in Paris in 1937 by a 17-year-old Jewish refugee, brilliantly using American spirituals to fill the role of the chorales in Bach's Passion settings. A distinct lyricism pervades works of the period like the *Concerto for Double String Orchestra* of 1938–9, the 1952 opera *The Midsummer Marriage* and the 1953 *Fantasia Concertante on a Theme of Corelli*. Vivid madrigalian rhythms dance through works like the 1952 song 'Dance, Clarion Air' and the String Quartet No. 2 (1942). Some later works are more challenging: an astringent musical language in post-war operas like *The Knot Garden* (1969), a gay kiss in *The Ice Break* (1976), big pieces like the 1982 oratorio *The Mask of Time*. Tippett's hinterland is broad and varied, his music constantly revealing and rewarding.

Finally in this group is an English composer with a French accent, who attended Gresham's School in Holt, Norfolk, ten years before Benjamin Britten and later fell in love with him ('we have come to an agreement on that subject,' wrote Britten in his diary).[70] Having secured a fourth-class degree in French from Merton College in his home city of Oxford and studied with Nadia Boulanger in Paris, where he met Poulenc and Ravel, Lennox Berkeley became a composer of much attractive, often small-scale, mildly astringent but defiantly tonal and decidedly French music. There is no single standout work by Berkeley: his suave style and careful craftsmanship can be heard equally in the easy-going one-act opera *A Dinner Engagement* (1954), Poulenc-flavoured symphonic works like the Concerto for Two Pianos and Orchestra (1948), and a relatively small output of songs and chamber music.

France

French music approached the modernist century in its own way, breaking with the dominant Austro-Germanic tradition and looking further afield for inspiration. Ravel's *Boléro* of 1928 completes a chain of Spanish-inspired pieces leading from Bizet's *Carmen* through Emmanuel Chabrier's *España* (1883) and other works. Jacques Ibert wrote distinctively for flute, Paul Dukas brilliantly for piano and orchestra, drawing Ravel-like on the past for his 1902 *Variations, interlude et finale sur un thème de Rameau* (*Variations, Interlude and Finale on a Theme by Rameau*). Albert Roussel was the most refined of the French Neoclassicists; André Jolivet experimented with acoustics, atonality and ancient instruments; Joseph Canteloube collected and arranged folk songs like a French RVW. A number of distinguished female composers lived across the turn of the new century, including Mélanie-Hélène Bonis, the Spanish-descended Pauline Viardot and the French-Irish Augusta Holmès, and, most popular of all, Cécile Chaminade. Possibly the most naturally gifted was Lili Boulanger. Fauré spotted her perfect pitch when she was two and in 1913, aged nineteen, she became the first female winner of the Prix de Rome, but died of tuberculosis in 1918 at the age of just twenty-four. Her *Nocturne pour violon et piano* of 1911 captures her compelling, restless harmonies perfectly. Her older sister Nadia, later a hugely influential teacher, sat alongside her in Fauré's composition class: their father Ernest, who was seventy-seven when Lili was born, had himself won the Prix de Rome as long ago as 1835.

Fauré

Gabriel Fauré views his hinterland with a largely untroubled gaze. His music is lyrical, subtle, elusive, with a highly personal approach to harmony and melody, borrowing the unbumpy nature of the French language.

Camille Saint-Saëns taught Fauré the piano as a child: 'from this time dates the almost filial attachment … the immense admiration, the unceasing gratitude I [have] had for him, throughout my life,' wrote Fauré later.[71] One of his most characteristic church pieces, the beautiful *Cantique de Jean Racine*, first performed in 1866, was written when he was nineteen, fruit of his early career as a church organist which survived a minor ripple when he was sacked for turning up to

Mass still in the evening dress he had worn to an all-night ball. In 1871, aged twenty-six, he took up a post at the grand Parisian Église Saint-Sulpice, where he and the *titulaire* organist, Charles-Marie Widor, would improvise at the church's two organs, trying to catch each other out across the nave with sudden changes of key without attracting the attention of the priests below. Also in 1871 Fauré joined some fellow composers in founding the Société Nationale de Musique to perform new music. In 1874 he swapped organ benches, moving to the Madeleine. The year 1877 saw the premiere of his first Violin Sonata, a promotion to choirmaster at the Madeleine, and a passionate, short-lived romance which may be reflected in three songs of the period including the gorgeous, unhurried '*Après un rêve*' ('*After a Dream*'). He went with Saint-Saëns to Weimar to add his name to Liszt's visitors' book, and to Bayreuth to hear the music of Wagner, writing home that the *Ring* was 'not very amusing … the work amounts to the most noble form of repentance, it is almost a kind of contrition'.[72] The food at Madame Wagner's horrified his Parisian palate. Back home, the two Frenchmen wittily parodied themes from the *Ring* in their *Souvenirs de Bayreuth* of *c*.1888 for piano, four hands.

In 1883 he married Marie Fremiet. Two sons followed. But an innate '*horreur du domicile*' led him to continue to travel, working in hotels and boarding houses, and pursuing many affairs. Throughout, he wrote to Marie:

> Yes, I am happier in Paris, but when actually I am in Paris I'd rather be anywhere in the world … senseless man that I am … how often I have wondered what music is for! What is it? And what am I trying to express? What are my feelings? What are my ideas? How can I express that of which I am not aware myself?[73]

A round of musical chairs from 1892 saw the director of the Paris Conservatoire, Ambroise Thomas, threaten to resign if Fauré got the job of Professor of Composition, which he eventually did after Thomas's death in 1896, presiding, like Stanford in England, over a well-stocked and influential composition class.

Late in life Fauré wrote reflectively of 'the most satisfying assurance of all, of the complete forgetfulness of self, the Nirvâna of the Hindus, or our own *Requiem aeternam*'.[74] His setting of the Catholic Requiem Mass was begun in the late 1880s, and revised and expanded over the following years. Catholic liturgical usage allowed composers a degree of choice over the exact text of a Requiem setting: not for Fauré the thunder of the last trumpet, dwelling instead on rest and last things.

In 1905 Fauré became Director of the Conservatoire as part of the fallout from the minor scandal caused by his pupil Ravel being passed over for the Prix de Rome: Fauré revitalised the curriculum with new music by Wagner and Debussy and old music by Rameau, exactly as Thomas had feared. Composition, as ever, was done largely on trips away ('I am exhausted by the Germans,' he told Marie on one jaunt, 'and I'm really suffering from musical indigestion').[75] Feted and famous, he met everyone from Elgar and Strauss to Copland, Albéniz and the young lions of Les Six. Sadly, he suffered from increasing deafness, remarking, 'I am horror-stricken by this trouble with just that faculty that I prize most highly.'[76] In 1922 the French state honoured him with an unprecedented public *hommage*.

His late letters have a valedictory quality: he recalls that the loyal Saint-Saëns always chastised him for his lack of ambition; reputation came too late, when it was no longer of interest or value to him; he is proud of the 'naivety' which led to him 'championing the cause of people who were looked askance at'; he had been 'a man of few words ... even as a child';[77] he sends the long-suffering Marie a kiss. He died in 1924, aged seventy-nine.

In 1906 Fauré described his compositional method as follows:

> a kind of rhythmical theme in the style of a Spanish dance took shape in my mind ... this theme developed of itself, became harmonised in many different ways, changed and underwent modulations, in fact it germinated by itself ... how strange is this unconscious functioning of the mind, this precise working out of an idea in this way![78]

Nothing could be further from Brahmsian process or Schoenbergian control: when his son Philippe sent him a narrative analysis of his Violin Sonata No. 1 in A Major (1876), he found the results 'charming' but said of the analysis, 'I must confess ... that I thought of nothing of the sort and that in fact I was concerned with no exterior thoughts of any kind.'[79]

His technical hallmarks are a shifting, drifting tonality (the

Requiem), smoothly encompassing modes (the song 'Lydia'), and melody which unfurls at an untroubled pace. Of Wagner's innovations he said, 'I am absorbed by them in the way that water seeps through sand.'[79] He was the gentlest of a gentle generation, a calm voice in stormy times.

Debussy

In an interesting little coincidence (and somehow very French), Fauré and Debussy wrote charming piano pieces for two young girls, known respectively as Dolly and Chouchou: the girls were half-sisters, daughters of the same mother, Emma Bardac. A photograph shows Fauré sharing the piano stool with Dolly in the kind of elegant Parisian drawing room where music was made, tea taken, affairs begun and politics discussed, the tall wooden door ready to admit a fabled princess, a nervous American heiress seeking a husband or a middle-aged matron trying to escape one, the looming troubles of the Dreyfus affair and the Great War hidden behind the heavy curtains.

Claude Debussy rarely spoke of his childhood, which was poor and erratic. He spent some time in the south of France with his aunt Clémentine and her married lover: Debussy recalled 'a Norwegian carpenter who sang from morning to night – some Grieg, perhaps?'[80] Piano lessons led him to the Paris Conservatoire in 1872, where he stayed for twelve years, gaining early praise for his playing ('a budding virtuoso'),[81] less for his harmony exercises ('muddled'; 'scatter-brained').[82] In 1879 he secured a strange job playing the piano for a married lady (and mistress of the French president) at the chateau of Chenonceau. A similar job followed in the opulent and artistic household of the Russian widow Nadezhda von Meck, Tchaikovsky's patroness. An association with the Vasnier family included giving lessons to the two young children ('an appalling teacher,' recalled Marguerite, then aged eleven)[83] and becoming the lover of the mother, Marie. He absorbed art and ideas, earned mixed reviews from his teachers ('bizarre, but intelligent'),[84] and got bored with bad teaching. 'The best thing one could wish for French music,' he wrote in 1902, 'would be to see the study of harmony abolished as it is practised in the conservatoires.'[85] He studied with Franck (with mixed success) and admired Lalo (Debussy was kicked out of a performance of Lalo's ballet *Namouna* for his 'noisy but forgivable enthusiasm').[86]

He was less keen on the music of Massenet, then at the height of his prestige, or the venerable Gounod, who was nonetheless an influential supporter. Debussy entered the Prix de Rome (whose second round, rather bizarrely, involved all selected candidates setting the same text while shut away in a building with bars on the windows, like 'wild beasts', as he told Marguerite Vasnier) three times.[87] When he won in 1884 he commented, 'My heart sank. I had a sudden vision of boredom, and of all the worries that inevitably go together with any form of official recognition. I felt I was no longer free.'[88]

Like another winner before him, Berlioz, Rome bored him. 'You speak of the tranquillity the Villa [Medici, where the winner lived and worked] has to offer,' he wrote in a letter home; 'God knows, I could do with a bit less of it.'[89] In the piece he wrote there, *Printemps*, Debussy 'wanted to express the slow and languid genesis of beings and things in nature, then their flowering – concluding with a dazzling delight at being reborn to a new life'.[90] The shocked prize committee gave it what Debussy's biographer Eric Frederick Jensen describes as 'one of the most famous criticisms in the history of music', saying that it had 'a vague impressionism which is one of the most dangerous enemies of truth in works of art'.[91] The word has turned into one of the least useful of all such musical terms; 'what imbeciles call impressionism', as Debussy once said.[92]

Back in France, Debussy's associates among composers included the solid, conservative Vincent d'Indy; Paul Dukas, composer of *L'Apprenti sorcier* (*The Sorcerer's Apprentice*) (1897) and sorcerer of the orchestra in his own right; Ernest Chausson, with whom he played through Mussorgsky's *Boris Godunov* at the piano; and his best friend among his fellow composers, Erik Satie. 'We never had to explain things to each other,' Satie later recalled. 'Half a sentence was enough, because we understood each other and, it seemed, had always done so.'[93]

In the late 1880s Debussy travelled to Bayreuth, and heard Javanese gamelan music and new music from Russia at the Paris Exposition of 1889. In 1890 he saw Maurice Maeterlinck's Symbolist play *Pelléas et Mélisande* and met the poet Stéphane Mallarmé. In 1894 he recast one of Mallarmé's dreamily Symbolist poems as the short orchestral piece *Prélude à l'après-midi d'un faune* (*Prelude to the Afternoon of a Faun*). Mallarmé told him, 'I wasn't expecting anything like that! The music prolongs the emotion of my poem and conjures up the scenery more vividly than any colour' and sent the composer a copy of the poem with an inscription praising 'the light which Debussy has breathed here'.[94]

For Debussy, the last years of the nineteenth century were spent writing and refining his opera based on Maeterlinck's *Pelléas*. It was a time of struggle and experiment: 'a period when I wasn't yet badgered and bothered with "Debussysme"'.[95] Like Berlioz, he began working as a music critic largely for the money and, like Berlioz, found he was good at it, adopting the occasional *nom de plume* M. Croche, a crotchety character not unlike his friend Satie. He made friends with a writer of exotic musical and sexual tastes, Pierre Louÿs. He lived with a green-eyed beauty called Gabrielle (Gaby) Dupont, then 'literally stupefied' his friend Chausson by getting engaged to a 'drawing-room singer' (in Louÿs's description) called Thérèse Roger.[96] His attempts to lie his way out of the ensuing muddle ended badly: when he tried something similar in 1896, Gaby left him in a scene like 'third-rate literature', as he described it to Louÿs.[97] In 1899 Debussy told Louÿs, 'My old liaison with Music prevents me from marrying.'[98] So, with typically consistent inconsistency, he did exactly that a few months later: 'Mademoiselle Lilly Texier has exchanged her inharmonious name for that of Lilly Debussy, much more euphonious as I'm sure everybody will agree.'[99]

The orchestral works *Nocturnes*, premiered incomplete in 1902, and *La Mer* (*The Sea*) (1905) began to earn an appreciative reception. *Pelléas* had a difficult premiere in 1902, but '[t]he little group of admirers … grew day by day,' recalled its conductor, André Messager.[100]

Like Fauré, Debussy was not noted for his devotion to domesticity. He began an affair with Emma Bardac, once Fauré's mistress, and began divorce proceedings from Lilly in 1903. In 1904 poor Lilly attempted suicide by shooting herself in the stomach.

Friends turned against him. Dukas called him 'heartless, an egoist, a trifler with the feelings of others'.[101] Debussy declared self-pityingly, 'I have seen desertions taking place around me … was there some forgotten debt to life I had to pay?'[102] He retreated into bitter cantankerousness. Zoltán Kodály wanted to meet him but was advised not to try. Another composer, the Italian Alfredo Casella, perceptively diagnosed 'an almost incredible shyness which he disguised under a show of paradox and often sarcastic and unkind irony.'[103] Debussy composed little: 'I feel nostalgia for the Claude Debussy who worked so enthusiastically on *Pelléas* – between ourselves, I've not found him since,' he told Messager.[104]

Meanwhile, he and Emma settled in a neat, comfortable house, had a daughter, Claude-Emma, known as 'Chouchou', and married. He was soon back to justifying his regular absences:

> an artist by definition is a man accustomed to dreams ... How could it be expected that this same person would be able to follow in his daily life the strict observance of traditions, laws and other barriers erected by a hypocritical and cowardly world.[105]

From Vienna he sent his daughter a little story 'which would make a goldfish weep'[106] on the back of six postcards, and from St Petersburg teased her about her piano practice: 'How is Monsieur Czerny getting on – the composer of such genius?'[107]

Jeux (*Games*) is a ballet about a game of tennis, premiered in 1913 by Diaghilev's Ballets Russes. Unfortunately, it was completely overshadowed just two weeks later by Diaghilev's next commission, Stravinsky's *Le Sacre du printemps*. Debussy expressed admiration for Stravinsky, telling him 'you are a great artist' and praising the 'sonorous magic' of *Petrushka* and the 'beautiful nightmare' of *Le Sacre*.[108] In private, he acknowledged a degree of alarm, too, calling Stravinsky a 'spoilt child' and a 'young savage'.[109] Schoenberg's music he found 'empty, pretentious and stupefyingly Germanic', as his biographer Jensen puts it,[110] though he knew little of it and Schoenberg's fully mature method emerged only after Debussy's death.

The outbreak of war in 1914 confused and depressed him. He willingly accepted the use of a small, secluded villa by the sea at Pourville. A late burst of composition included a turn to Classical models like the sonata, taking the word back to its eighteenth-century French roots, recast for unusual and fragrant combinations of solo instruments, although only three of a projected set of six were completed. Debussy died in 1918 after a slow decline from cancer.

Debussy's music remains unique. It emerges from an instinctive impatience with the past: 'You know how little respect I have for the parasite development which has too long bolstered up the glory of the Masters.'[111] When he tried, early in his career, to meet the demands of a standard issue operatic libretto, the result drew the revealing comment, 'I'm afraid I may have won victories over my true self.'[112] A 1910 article, '*M. Claude Debussy et le snobisme contemporain*', simplistically set up his friends d'Indy and Dukas as rivals and alternatives. Debussy advised Emma's son Raoul to '[g]ather impressions ... music has this over painting, that it can bring together all manner of variations of colour and light'.[113]

He had no use for thematic development: 'That's architecture, not music,' he told another composer, Charles Koechlin.[114] Jensen says, 'In *La Mer* there is no set form, like ABA or sonata. The structure itself is unique and is generated in a continuous and unpredictable manner by a succession of musical ideas ... Like the ocean's waves, Debussy's musical phrases are never identical.'[115] Debussy himself described the effect he was after in his *Prélude à l'après-midi d'un faune*: 'Is it perhaps the dream left over at the bottom of the faun's flute? ... together with the humanity brought to it by thirty-two violinists who have got up too early.'[116] But the absence of formalism must not be read to imply formlessness: the piano *Préludes* are tightly and innovatively organised, the *Études* layered in complex strata.

Blocks of contrasting tonality are often set alongside each other, separate and distinct. Modes feature in many of the piano pieces. There are plenty of extended scale patterns like whole-tone and octatonic ('*Feuilles mortes*' ('Dead Leaves')). The style can take in the simple charm of '*Clair de Lune*' ('Moonlight') and '*La Fille au cheveux de lin*' ('The Girl with the Flaxen Hair'), with its distinctive seventh chords, revolving, not resolving. The titles of the *Préludes* are placed at the end, in brackets, after ellipses, telling you what you've just played, like a memory: (... *Des pas sur la neige*), (... *et la lune descend sur la temple qui fût*); ('... footsteps in the snow'), ('... and the moon descends on the temple which was'). Instructions to the player include playing a rhythm 'like the sad and icy background to a journey through a landscape'. Often three, sometimes four, staves are needed to notate Debussy's precise but veiled pianism ('to the left of Schumann, or to the right of Chopin', as he put it).[117]

Orchestration is lush but clear. Harmony and melody become one. 'A musical idea contains its own harmony (or so I believe): otherwise the harmony is merely clumsy and parasitical.'[118] Visual and other stimuli hover in the background: Debussy hung the painting *The Hollow of the Wave off Kanagawa* by the Japanese artist Hokusai on his study wall and used part of it as the title page of the published score of *La Mer*. Orientalism, Spanish rhythms, ancient Greek artefacts and English eccentrics strut through his music like Rimbaud's *'parade sauvage'*.[119]

But Debussy's compelling and utterly original visions are imagined, not lived. He visited Spain for a single afternoon. He saw pagodas not in Japan but in Paris. *'Poissons d'or'* ('Goldfish') (1907) is an evocation not of real goldfish but of an enamelled plate or piece of embroidery. *La Mer* evokes the distinctly unromantic waters of the English Channel as seen from hotel rooms in Normandy and Eastbourne. There is something telling in the detail that a composer who wrote so immersively about the sea couldn't swim.

Ravel

Claude Debussy and Maurice Ravel used to be bracketed together under the vague umbrella of Impressionism.

Many of Ravel's compositions have titles which bear witness to their roots as a rehearing of something else: Madagascan songs, Hebrew songs, *Asie*, *Boléro*, *La Valse*, *Rapsodie Espagnole*, *Tzigane*, *Le Tombeau de Couperin*. He is sometimes characterised as a watchmaker, or an illusionist: one set of piano pieces is called *Miroirs* (Mirrors). Debussy exclaimed irritatedly that 'what annoys me is the attitude he adopts of being a "conjuror", or rather a Fakir casting spells and making flowers burst out of chairs'.[120]

Ravel's father was an inventor, pioneer of an early internal combustion engine and a circus rollercoaster called the Whirlwind of Death. His mother was illegitimate and barely literate at the time of her marriage, but a free thinker and proud of her Basque-Spanish heritage. Their son grew up loving machines (he said of a field of windmills in Amsterdam: 'you begin to feel like an automaton yourself at the sight of this mechanical landscape'),[121] and the otherness of foreign styles of music, whether from another country or another age.

A happy childhood in the Basque region led in 1889 to piano studies at the Paris Conservatoire. But his progress at the Conservatoire was chequered: expelled, re-admitted, expelled again, pupil of Fauré, friend of Satie, re-expelled. He wrote one of his most recognisable early pieces, the *Pavane pour une infante défunte* (*Pavane for a Dead Princess*) (1899), to a commission from the ever-encouraging Winnaretta Singer, Princesse de Polignac; joined one of those fluidly stroppy groups of young artistic types, Les Apaches; and attended every performance of a run of Debussy's *Pelléas et Mélisande*. His debt to Debussy is clear in works like *Jeux d'eau* (*Games of Water*) for piano (1901), and the String Quartet of 1903, closely modelled on the four-movement form of Debussy's only quartet of ten years before, though with a firmer nod in the direction of Classical manners and structure: both beautiful and unusual additions to a by-then slightly lost-looking repertoire. Personal relations were not helped when Ravel took Lilly's side in the painful scandal surrounding her divorce from Debussy.

In the first five years of the twentieth century Ravel entered the unavoidable Prix de Rome five times, but failed to win. He was a painstakingly slow composer. He would often write a piece first for his own instrument, the piano, then make an orchestral version. Purely orchestral works include ballets and orchestrations of music by other composers.

Ravel is arguably the most accomplished and complete orchestrator of all, his scores a miracle of detail, throwing in a touch of harp harmonic and a dash of tam-tam like some secret ingredient in a favourite Basque recipe. Fine examples of his art are the perfectly paced build-up of *Boléro* and the best sunrise in all music, 'Lever du jour' at the beginning of Suite No. 2 of *Daphnis et Chloé* (1912), with its two harps tuned to different scales, string mutes removed one by one, and glorious burst of light at the discovery of the sleeping Chloé, the birds chattering away in Messiaen-like abundance in honour of returning life.

Like his orchestration, Ravel's piano writing bears genuine comparison with Debussy's, though Ravel went further in his technical demands: *Gaspard de la nuit* (*Gaspard of the Night*) of 1908, based second-hand on pictures by Rembrandt and written for his Conservatoire friend Ricardo Viñes, was designed to be harder than the so-far unchallenged hardest piece in the repertoire, Balakirev's *Islamey*.

Ravel never taught in a conservatoire or presided at a fashionable organ console, but he did take on a few private pupils. He told Manuel Rosenthal not to study Debussy's music because 'only Debussy could have written it',[122] and declined to accept George Gershwin as a student because he feared the experience might deprive him of his spontaneous gift for melody, advising him, 'Why become a second-rate Ravel when you're already a first-rate Gershwin?'[123] Another, very different pupil, Ralph Vaughan Williams, was 'the only one who does not write my music',[124] and hosted Ravel's first concert outside France, in London in 1909. In 1910 Ravel helped found a new Paris concert society. Stage works include the one-act comic opera *L'Heure espagnole* (*The Spanish Hour*) in 1911, and ballets including *Daphnis et Chloé* for Diaghilev in 1912.

The war challenged Ravel's precarious psychological stability severely. He worked hard to find an active role, facing considerable personal danger as a driver near the front lines, disguised in his letters home behind the soldier's habitual matey banter: 'Before we go to bed we watch the fireworks. The cannon-fire rocks us to sleep ...'[125] His health was not good. Worse was separation from his ailing mother. On the very day war broke out, 4 August 1914, he wrote to a friend, 'If only you knew what I'm going through. All day long, without a moment's respite, the same terrifying obsession: if I had to leave my poor old mother it would surely kill her.'[126] Marie Ravel died in January 1917. 'I am still all right physically,' wrote Ravel shortly afterwards,

> but mentally I'm in a frightful state. It seems only yesterday that I was writing to her or that I received one of her dear letters, and how happy I was ... I didn't imagine it would come so quickly. Now I am in a state of terrifying despair and anxiety ... I feel more alone here than anywhere.[127]

Unsurprisingly, the war years yielded little music. His most significant work of this period is the archly nostalgic piano suite *Le Tombeau de Couperin* (*Couperin's Tomb*) (1917), typically using the form and manner of an antique eighteenth-century musical memorial for distancing effect, each of the suite's six movements simply and movingly dedicated to a friend lost in the war.

The 1920s brought public recognition and an inevitable element of reaction against Ravel's style from a new generation of composers. Satie noted in 1920, 'Ravel refuses the Légion d'honneur, but all his music accepts it.'[128] *La Valse* (*The Waltz*) of 1920 was originally written as a ballet for Diaghilev, who rejected it with the revealing remark, 'It's not a ballet. It's the portrait of a ballet.'[129] In 1921 he moved to the countryside. In 1925 the opera *L'Enfant et les sortilèges* (*The Child and the Charms*), a childhood fantasy with elements of ballet and American-style revue, was successfully produced in Monte Carlo, to the delight and relief of its librettist, the novelist Colette, who had waited seven years for Ravel to finish it. In 1928 he made a hugely successful trip to North America, handsomely paid in the form of a fat fee and unlimited Gauloise cigarettes, appearing with many leading orchestras, feted and applauded. He was captivated by the vitality of North American life (if not the food), visiting Canada, New York, Niagara Falls and the Grand Canyon, Edgar Allen Poe's house in Baltimore, Denver ('Wonderful air. Glorious sunshine'), Minneapolis (whose downtown Schmitt building is splendidly decorated with a huge, three-storey-high mural of part of the score of his piano suite *Gaspard de la nuit*), and a stop at a city he refers to in a letter as 'Ohama' to change trains and hear 'the famous Ohama jazz'.[130] In 1928 he fulfilled the latest ballet commission with *Boléro*, easily his most famous piece (somewhat to his chagrin).

The early 1930s produced two piano concertos. The first is for left hand alone, written for the Austrian pianist Paul Wittgenstein, who lost his right arm early in the war and commissioned one-handed works from many composers. The more conventional Piano Concerto in G Major of 1931 is jazzily Neoclassical in its outer movements, Poulenc-ly lyrical in the middle.

In 1932 Ravel was involved in a taxi accident in Paris. He wrote little more, and died in December 1937 at the age of sixty-two. An atheist, he was buried without religious ceremony. A curious reflection on his intense privacy and lack of close family is that nobody seems to know who received his royalties after his death.

Ravel's harmony lets triads drift around in parallel motion, sometimes, like Debussy's, with added notes such as sevenths adding unresolved pungency, as in the scrunchy chords ushering in the repeat of the main tune of the elegant, early *Pavane pour une infante défunte*. He is more ready to incline towards simple diatonicism than Debussy, sometimes with a hint of antique irony (like the lovely slow movement of the G major piano concerto, a sort of dreamy, slowed-down Chopin waltz). A favourite trick is presenting a tune in octaves at the top and bottom of the texture, with the harmony in between, like the first of the *Trois Chansons* of 1915. The words of these choral works, which he wrote himself, show him hiding again behind a borrowed mask, this time a pastiche of medieval French love poetry (another half-link with Debussy, who had set real fifteenth-century lyrics to music in his *Trois Chansons de Charles d'Orléans* (known in English as *Three Songs*)). Ravel's poem in the second chanson hints sadly at their subtext: '*Mon ami z-il est à la guerre*' ('My beloved is gone to the war'). Further layers of separation surface in the list of characters in *L'Enfant et les sortilèges*: a clock, a teapot, a fire in the grate, a princess torn from a storybook, a bird, a tree and a frog, who come to life to scold the only human character, a child, for mistreating them before helping him back to his mother (represented, like the unseen adults in *Tom and Jerry*, by an enormous skirt).

Boléro doesn't bother with development, or any other kind of form: a sixteen-bar tune, repeated, then another, also repeated, then both pairs repeated, eighteen times in all, with no change of key, speed, notes, rhythm, or accompaniment, just 'one long, very gradual crescendo … altogether impersonal', as Ravel himself said.[131] Ravel famously told fellow composer Arthur Honegger, 'I've written only one masterpiece – *Boléro*. Unfortunately there's no music in it.'[132] When one audience member shouted, 'Rubbish!' at a performance at the Opéra, he agreed with her: 'That old lady got the message.'[133]

Was he joking? Is *Boléro* an elaborate, brilliantly executed windup? As with much else in his life, Ravel doesn't tell us. In 1906 he wrote to a critic thanking him for a review: 'Delicate, refined, quintessential … Rats! I couldn't believe that this was the kind of impression I was making.'[134] Perhaps that is what remains: an impression of something just out of reach, beautiful, skilful, subtle, elusive and unique.

Jazz, Irony and 'Les Six': The Rebellious Animateurs

On 10 December 1896 the title character in Alfred Jarry's new play *Ubu Roi* (*King Ubu*) walked onto the stage of the Théâtre de l'Oeuvre in Paris and spoke the opening word, '*Merdre*', a sort of mispronounced version of the French word for 'shit'. In France, as in Germany, the post-nineteenth-century generation was about to get its comfortably upholstered backside thoroughly kicked.

The key figure in the next wave of the *nouvelle vague* was a playwright, designer, artist, critic, novelist and film-maker who referred to himself simply as a 'poet', knew everyone from Proust to Diaghilev and Nijinsky to Picasso, and worked with musicians from Erik Satie to Édith Piaf: Jean Cocteau. A few key events helped a group of composers coalesce around his ideas as France emerged from the pain and hardship of war, keen to forget and move on.

In 1917, with concert halls still closed, a series of concerts was held in the studio of the painter Émile Lejeune on the rue Huyghens, the walls hung with works by Picasso, Matisse, Léger and Modigliani. Satie had the idea of convening a group of composers, including some of those featured at the rue Huyghens events, his friends Arthur Honegger, Georges Auric and Louis Durey. Like lots of other such clubs of Young Turks, they gave themselves a name: Les Nouveaux Jeunes. Shortly afterwards, in 1920, the critic Henri Collet published an article called 'The Russian Five, The French Six, and M. Erik Satie'. The idea of Les Six was born. In order to give substance to his comparison with the Russian Five (and to justify his snappy headline), Collet appointed three more members to the gang: Darius Milhaud, Francis Poulenc and Germaine Tailleferre, names chosen, according to Milhaud, 'for no other reason than that we knew each other'.[135] In the same year the group published the only work on which they all collaborated, the six-movement *L'Album des Six*, for piano. Also in 1920, the Théâtre des Champs-Élysées put on an evening of modernist music including Auric's *Adieu New York*, *Cocardes* by Poulenc, *Trois petites pièces montées* (a typically ambiguous title which could be translated as something like *Three Little Assembled Pieces*) by Satie, and a surrealist ballet by Milhaud, based on Brazilian music, called *Le Boeuf sur le Toit* (*The Ox on the Roof*). When La Gaya, the bar which had become the headquarters of Cocteau and his acolytes, moved to bigger premises, the new establishment took its name from Milhaud's ballet, becoming a meeting place of musical minds and a leading centre of the new, exciting, street-level art form, cabaret.

Musical talk at *Le Boeuf* took as its starting point Cocteau's 1918 publication *Le Coq et l'Arlequin*, dedicated to Auric. It's a manifesto:

> This book is not concerned with any existing school, but with a school to whose existence nothing points – were it not for the first-fruits of a few young artists, the efforts of the painters, and the tiredness of our ears … The musician opens the cage-door to arithmetic … With us, there is a house, a lamp, a plate of soup, a fire, wine and pipes at the back of every important work of art … In music, line is melody.

The Challenge of Modernism

The reigning deities are routinely dismissed: 'There are certain long works which are short. Wagner's works are long works which are long ... Wagner, Stravinsky and even Debussy are first-rate octopuses'; Schoenberg is 'a blackboard composer'.[136]

Les Six were never a coherent single entity. Durey has lasted least well. Tailleferre composed fluently in largely traditional forms throughout her long life (notably *La Cantate du Narcisse* (*The Cantata of Narcissus*) (1938) with poet Paul Valéry), film scores and pieces for children. Auric became a revolutionary leftist and pursued a highly successful career writing for films, from Cocteau's *Le Sang d'un Poète* (*The Blood of a Poet*) in 1930 to *Roman Holiday* (1953) with Audrey Hepburn and Gregory Peck, and the extremely un-French Ealing comedies like *Passport to Pimlico* (1949), *The Lavender Hill Mob* (1951) and *The Titfield Thunderbolt* (1953).

Arthur Honegger's most famous work shares its name with a steam train: *Pacific 231* of 1923. He said, 'I have always loved locomotives passionately. For me they are living creatures and I love them as others love women or horses.'[137] His 1921 'dramatic psalm' for chorus, *Le Roi David* (*King David*), and *Jeanne d'Arc au bûcher* (*Joan of Arc at the Stake*) of 1935 gave new impetus to the oratorio, with characteristic roles for a '*diseuse*', or speaker. Like Auric, he wrote for film, notably Abel Gance's epic *Napoléon* of 1927. He showed loyalty to a version of the symphonic tradition: his Symphony No. 3, the 'Symphonie Liturgique', of 1946 borrows titles from the Requiem Mass for its purely instrumental movements, like Britten's *Sinfonia da Requiem*, written a few years earlier (Honegger said it described 'the catastrophe in which we are living').[138] His reflective Fourth Symphony of 1946 is a tribute to the city of Basel, in a nod to his Swiss origins.

Darius Milhaud was a fluent and prolific composer. After the Great War he went to Brazil as secretary to the French ambassador and poet Paul Claudel, his collaborator on many projects. *Le Boeuf sur le Toit* is one of several works to carry a vivacious Brazilian accent. Milhaud was an eclectic consumer of musical styles: his Fifth String Quartet of 1912 is dedicated to Schoenberg, and he conducted both the French and British premieres of Schoenberg's *Pierrot lunaire*, painstakingly prepared. The 1922 ballet *La Création du monde* (*The Creation of the World*) draws on jazz which he heard in Harlem in 1920: his 'Creator' was clearly a Gershwin fan, and could whistle up a decent jazz fugue on the face of the waters, too.

In 1940 Milhaud and his wife, both Jewish, fled Paris in the face of the impending German invasion, arriving, like so many, in California, via Lisbon. He secured a teaching position at Mills College in Oakland, and later worked in Aspen, Colorado, in the early years of the Aspen Music Festival and School, still held high up in the Rockies among the gently whispering trees and cool-aired mountain meadows. After the war he alternated teaching in the US with giving classes at the Paris Conservatoire, until his long struggle with arthritis (he used a wheelchair for many decades) made travel impossible. Milhaud died in 1974 at the age of eighty-one.

The eclecticism of his sympathies is hinted at by the famous names among his students, including the jazz pianist Dave Brubeck (who named his son Darius) and the songwriter Burt Bacharach ('Close To You', 'Raindrops Keep Fallin' on My Head', 'Magic Moments'), to whom he said, 'Don't be afraid of writing something people can remember and whistle.'[139] Milhaud's wife Madeleine, a specialist in the spoken *diseuse* roles favoured by many of Les Six and librettist of several of her husband's operas, died in 2008 at the age of 105, having returned to the flat in the boulevard de Clichy where she and her husband first moved in 1925.

The most musically substantial member of Les Six was a Catholic who lost his faith in the hedonistic Paris of the 1920s cabaret scene, then found it again following the death of a friend in a car crash; a gay man who survived suspicion of his sexuality from the occupying Nazis in the early 1940s; a composer whose music moves from the circus to the choirstall in melodies of almost Gounod-like sweetness, nagging rhythms, short phrases, small forms, highly seasoned harmony, an ironic take on the manners and ideas of Neoclassicism, and a fondness for the flute: Francis Poulenc. Critic Claude Rostand summed him up: '*y a en lui du moine et du voyou*' ('half monk, half guttersnipe').[140]

Poulenc was born in Paris in 1899. From his mother he inherited an inclusive love of music of all kinds, from his father piety and lots of money from the family pharmaceuticals business. Influential friends included his piano teacher Ricardo Viñes ('a most delightful man ... I owe him everything'),[141] the harpsichordist Wanda Landowska, for whom he wrote his brilliantly brittle *Concert champêtre* in 1929, and the baritone Pierre Bernac, an inseparable performing partner until Bernac's retirement in 1959. His early compositions wore 'the ironical outlook of Satie adapted to the sensitive standards of the current intellectual circles', in the words of another leading pianist, Alfred Cortot.[142]

Bothered by his lack of formal training, Poulenc had some intermittent instruction with the polymath and pupil of Fauré, Charles Koechlin: but, perhaps ironically, it is this naïf lack of formal sophistication which gives his music much of its character. He served in the French army from the last days of the First World War, went to England in 1921, and to Vienna in 1922 with Milhaud to meet Schoenberg and his students, whom he admired but who left no trace on him, and scored a big success when his card turned up in the regular game of getting asked to write a ballet for Diaghilev, 1924's *Les Biches* (*The Hinds*, or *The Darlings*); sadly the cause of a falling-out with Satie.

The death of his friend Pierre-Octave Ferroud in 1936 and a visit to the ancient shrine of Rocamadour led to his reconversion to Catholicism and some wonderful music, including *Litanies à la Vierge noire* for women's voices, written that year and inspired by Rocamadour's black sculpture of the Virgin, and the sublime Mass in G Major of 1937. During the Second World War he remained in Paris, burying anti-German songs in his compositions and setting to music words by poets active in the resistance, including his friend Paul Éluard. His 1943 setting of Éluard's *Figure humaine* remains one of the most extraordinary choral works of the century. It was premiered (in English) in a BBC broadcast from London in 1945. Poulenc introduced it on the Third Programme in stilted but moving English, praising the RAF for dropping leaflets with the printed poem. The transmission never reached France as the lines were too busy with military operations. The work ends with the word '*liberté*' on a soprano high E. The critic of the London *Times* noted perceptively that *Figure humaine* 'removes Poulenc from the category of *petit maître* to which ignorance has generally been content to relegate him'.[143] The work wasn't heard in Paris until 1947. On the same London visit in 1945 Poulenc gave a performance of his Concerto for Two Pianos at the Royal Albert Hall, with himself and Britten as soloists. Next in his all-embracing composing career came music for the French children's favourite *Babar, le petit éléphant*, and a short opéra bouffe based on a story by a friend from his teenage years, the poet Guillaume Apollinaire, about a woman who tires of her submissive life, sets her breasts free and turns into a man, *Les Mamelles de Tirésias* (1917).

Publicly, Poulenc was secure and successful, increasingly so in the US. Polemically, he bravely took what was becoming a rather isolated stand against the carved commandments of Schoenberg, earning the enmity of the latest corps of Young Turks, led by his compatriot Pierre Boulez. Personally, he had a number of stable romantic relationships, and fathered a child, who grew up thinking he was her godfather. Stylistically, he was wittily dismissive of fashion, calling Schoenberg's twelve-tone method '*dodécaca*',[144] which translates as something like 'twelve shades of shit', and referring to the *Turangalîla-Symphonie* by his compatriot Messiaen as halfway between the urinal and the holy water stoup ('*urinoire et bénitoire*').[145]

His last decade began with another serious bout of depressive anxiety precipitated by the illness of his long-term partner, Lucien Roubert, and problems around a large-scale opera, *Dialogues des Carmélites* (*Dialogues of the Carmelites*), about a group of nuns martyred for their beliefs during the French Revolution – a striking meeting of his theatrical and religious personas which makes much of its many high-voiced roles and ends with an intensely dramatic and moving procession to the guillotine, complete with orchestral sound effects. *Dialogues des Carmélites* was finished 'at the very moment' Roubert died in October 1955, at the age of forty-seven.[146] Among other late works is the *Gloria* of 1961, bringing the fairground into the church (like the 1938 Organ Concerto, which he referred to as his 'bestseller'),[147] and three sonatas for wind instruments, of which the Flute Sonata of 1957 is the most characteristic and, somehow, the most French (Debussy before him and Messiaen after him both wrote distinctive solos for the instrument). The last of his three operas was the very different *La Voix humaine* (*The Human Voice*), a one-hander in which a woman talks despairingly to her former lover on the telephone, the day before his marriage to someone else. It was composed in 1958, almost thirty years after his old friend Cocteau wrote the play on which it is based. Poulenc died of a heart attack in 1963. Shortly after his death his last partner, Louis Gautier, went to prison for drug-smuggling and receiving stolen goods.

The composer who ties all this Frenchness together is the one who is probably best known for the fewest notes, Erik Satie. His is a sad and strange story. He studied piano but was no good at it, and fell in love with an artist's model who initially lived next door but then left, leaving him with 'nothing but an icy loneliness'.[148] He made money as a cabaret pianist, became the founder and only member of the Metropolitan Art Church of Jesus the Conductor, scored success with his humorous miniatures for piano but resented the lack of attention to his other works, and sat at the centre of avant-garde polemics but always lost when he played at its politics. He lived in chaos and squalor in a small apartment in Arcueil, a distant suburb of Paris, visited by nobody in the twenty-seven years he spent there up to his death in 1925, after which friends found a large collection of umbrellas, two grand pianos stacked on top of each other, the upper one full of papers, and scores he had thought lost or left on trains stuffed into coat pockets.

Among Satie's important early pieces is the ballet *Parade*, conceived with Cocteau for Diaghilev in 1917, with designs by Picasso. Cocteau recorded that the intended Braque-like sonic collage of the sounds of sirens, typewriters, aeroplanes and dynamos was never achieved, leading critics to misunderstand the 'absolute simplicity of the score'.[149] It would be left to later experimentalists to claim credit for inventing this all-inclusive approach. Today, Satie is known almost entirely for his *Gymnopédies* for piano, works of an almost absurdist simplicity, the first two written as early as 1888. Other pieces include *Musique d'ameublement* (*Furniture Music* (1917) – another title and idea picked up by later experimentalists and minimalists), and *Trois Morceaux en forme de poire* (*Three Pieces in the Form of a Pear*) (1903). Cocteau said, 'Each of Satie's works is an example of renunciation.'[150] Roger Shattuck called this period of French decadence and absurdism *The Banquet Years*. Of its most influential but least successful exponent he says: 'Greatness was not a quality Satie valued, and he was not a "great" musician. For being singular, for being humble and joyous and wise, both man and work are unforgettable.'[151]

Latin America

If the Frenchman Milhaud brought a Brazilian accent to European music, the Brazilian composer Heitor Villa-Lobos did exactly the opposite, at least to begin with. Influenced initially by the European mainstream, he turned back to his national inheritance from about 1918, a process given an uncomfortable nationalist twist by the Vargas revolution of 1930, after which he was required to write patriotic pieces and was prevented from undergoing all foreign travel until 1945. His mature style mixes the European and South American traditions:

Chôros of 1920–29 turn the sounds of Brazilian street musicians into concert works for the great Spanish guitarist Andrés Segovia; *Bachianas Brasileiras*, the title of a series of suites composed over a period of fifteen years from 1930, means 'Brazilian Bach pieces'. Each individual piece itself has two titles, one drawn from European Baroque music, the other from Brazilian folklore (The last movement of No. 2 is called both *Toccata* and *The Little Train of the Caipira*). The soberly titled *Nonet* sounds like a sensible bit of chamber music, but gives the game away with its subtitle *'Impressão rápida de todo o Brasil'* ('A Brief Impression of the Whole of Brazil'). It requires ten (not nine) players and a chorus.

Milhaud and Villa-Lobos crossed the Atlantic in opposite directions. Another South American in Paris was Reynaldo Hahn, composer of a small number of archly exquisite *mélodies* for voice and piano who left his native Venezuela for France at the age of three, and went on to hold a central place in the fragrant, shadowy *beau monde* immortalised by the man who became his lover, wrote to him as *'mon petit Reynaldo'*,[152] but never told their love: Marcel Proust. Hahn's most famous (and perfect) song is a pale, still setting of Verlaine, fixing a moment of tenderness in a frozen moment of delicious time: *'L'Heure exquise'* ('The Exquisite Hour') (1892).

Alberto Ginastera echoed Bartók's prescription for how to use folk music in art music in the phases he identified in his own output: 'Objective Nationalism' uses the folk song of his native Argentina more or less straight, while 'Subjective Nationalism' treats it to more abstract development.[153] His *Danzas Argentinas* of 1937 are a cheerful and undemanding exploration of things like bitonality and a twelve-tone ostinato, adding lively character to the whip-cracking high plains dance steps of a herdsman, a beautiful maiden, and his favourite, the gaucho, the 'Outlaw Cowboy'. Mexican Carlos Chávez laced his 1931 ballet *H.P.* (for Horse Power) with the energy of the sandunga, huapango and foxtrot, and much else in his eclectic six symphonies, music described by his friend Aaron Copland as 'profoundly non-European … like the bare wall of an adobe hut'.[154]

Even more distinctive use of South American street music was made by a composer who tried to find his voice by ignoring his Argentinian heritage and travelling to Paris to study with Nadia Boulanger, who (typically) told him he would actually find it by turning straight round and looking back home (which he did): Astor Piazzolla.

Piazzolla turned the smoky, sexy tango of the bars of Buenos Aires into his own brand of *nuevo tango*, tinged with jazz, Neoclassicism and a little bit of Bach. Perhaps nothing sums up the mongrel vitality of early twentieth-century music so well as the image of Piazzolla as a small boy limping home through the tough streets of Little Italy and Greenwich Village in New York, listening to jazz on a wind-up gramophone and playing Bach on the bandoleon bought for him by his father in a pawn shop, which he was taught to play by a Hungarian pianist who had herself studied with an immigrant from Russia, Sergei Rachmaninoff.

Two Czechs

Bohuslav Martinů was born in a church tower in Polička, in Bohemia, near the border with Moravia, in 1890. Training in the Romantic musical style of his compatriot Josef Suk, Dvořák's son-in-law, gave way to rapid stylistic experimentation when he headed (like everybody else) to Paris in the 1920s. His opera *Juliette* (or *Julietta*), performed in 1938, is in some ways a sequel to Debussy's *Pelléas*, with his own libretto (in French), after which he switched to a kind of Stravinskian Neoclassicism around the age of fifty. Following the German invasion of France in May 1940, he was helped to flee by the conductor Charles Munch and the influential musical patron Paul Sacher, reaching America in 1941. An enormously prolific composer, his works, often in traditional form like the six symphonies, were given by many leading US orchestras. In 1942 he composed the orchestral *Památník Lidicím* (*Memorial to Lidice*), in remembrance of the village destroyed by the Nazis in reprisal for the assassination of Reinhard Heydrich. The next year brought the opera *The Greek Passion*, about a village passion play interrupted by the arrival of a group of refugees. The end of the war found Martinů, a quiet, introverted man, caught uncertainly between Europe and America, and between two women, one on either side of the Atlantic. War divided more than countries. At least in his case the music gives the impression of trying to bridge, not widen, the sense of dislocation and divide.

An altogether sadder story is the fate of Martinů's compatriot Vítězslava Kaprálová, born in Janáček's home city of Brno in 1915. A prolific composer of piano and orchestral scores of Prokofieffian jaggedness and Bartókian lyricism, she conducted her own Military

Sinfonietta of 1937 with leading orchestras in Prague and London, studied in Paris, and died of tuberculosis at the age of twenty-five.

The Early Twentieth-century Neosymphonic Style

Three Russian composers were once discussing the notion of keys having colours. Rachmaninoff pointed out that the other two disagreed about the colour of D major: Scriabin thought it was golden yellow, Rimsky-Korsakov said it was blue. Scriabin countered by pointing to a moment in one of Rimsky-Korsakov's operas where D major accompanies the discovery of a hoard of golden coins.

Rachmaninoff was the lushest of the new-old Romantics: tall, lugubrious, with enormous hands and a fund of lyricism in his music, if not his conversation. Stravinsky recalled Rachmaninoff as 'a six-and-a-half-foot-tall scowl'.[155]

Stravinsky described the older man's progress as a composer:

> I remember Rachmaninov's earliest compositions. They were 'watercolours', songs and piano pieces freshly influenced by Tchaikovsky. Then at twenty-five he turned to 'oils' and became a very old composer indeed. Do not expect me to spit on him for that, however. He was, as I have said, an awesome man, and besides, there are too many others to be spat upon before him. As I think about him, his silence looms as a noble contrast to the self-approbations which are the only conversations of all performing and most other musicians.[156]

It's a pity that Stravinsky regarded his fellow composers as creatures 'to be spat upon', but his placing of Rachmaninoff as part of an 'old' tradition is apt, from the rhythmic rattle and Chopinesque melodiousness of the piano *Preludes* to the world's favourite works for piano and orchestra. His *Rhapsody on a Theme of Paganini* of 1934 turns its much-varied theme upside down for its sumptuous slow movement: the process, though certainly not the sound, shared with his contemporary Schoenberg.

Like that of other Russian composers before and after him, Rachmaninoff's church music drops his central European costume altogether and relishes the language and sounds of Orthodox Christianity: chant, big choirs, richly mature voices (completely different from sweet English trebles or wobbly French sopranos), low basses, no organ or other instruments. Rachmaninoff's *All-Night Vigil* of 1915 (also known as the *Vespers*) is a slow, sonorous successor to Tchaikovsky's setting.

An early attempt to fuse sacred and symphonic elements led to a crisis. Rachmaninoff's First Symphony, based on church chants, was finished in 1897 following a period of some hard-won early progress interrupted by gloom at the unexpected death of Tchaikovsky in 1893. The symphony's premiere was conducted by Glazunov, who may or may not have been drunk, but certainly hadn't rehearsed it properly. César Cui wrote that the work would appeal to the inmates of a music conservatoire in hell. A period of creative block followed, during which Rachmaninoff took up a successful sideline as a conductor, ended by a course of hypnotherapy and psychotherapy with the physician Nikolai Dahl in 1901.

The darker side resurfaces in works like the tone poem *Isle of the Dead* (1908) and in his almost obsessive return to the plainsong melody of the day of judgement and anger, *Dies Irae*, from the Requiem Mass, blazed by the brass in the whirling second movement scherzo of the Second Symphony, and featured in many other works.

From 1906 Rachmaninoff and his wife travelled, settling in Dresden and performing in Diaghilev's concert season in Paris. The year 1909 brought his first trip to America. In 1917 he gave his last concert in Russia, travelled perilously to Finland by train, crossing the border in an open sledge during a blizzard clutching 500 roubles and a small suitcase of scores. The following year he emigrated to the US, where he lived in some style on the proceeds of a gruelling concert schedule. Between his emigration in 1918 and death in 1943 he completed just six new works, devoting much of his time to recording. In 1942 he moved on doctor's advice to California, where he died in March 1943, just before his seventieth birthday.

The prediction in *Grove's Dictionary* a decade or so after his death that Rachmaninoff's music was 'not likely to last' has not, so far, proved prescient.[157] If his lyricism is perhaps a little less sophisticated than that of his great predecessor as a poet of the keyboard, Chopin, his sheer melodiousness will hold his popularity deservedly secure.

Rachmaninoff's friend Nikolai Medtner took a different route out of Russia, ending up in Golders Green in north London and then rural Warwickshire. Medtner's piano music, particularly the fourteen piano sonatas, do most of the things the twentieth century could do with a piano, from long, difficult four-movement pieces to short, difficult, one-movement pieces, many with evocative titles, some with a restrained lyricism, like the opening of the Sonata No. 10 'Sonata Reminiscenza' in A Minor of 1922, and the Interludium, marked *lugubre*, of Sonata No. 5, 'Sonata Tragica' in C Minor, of 1920. He was supported in exile by an English pupil, Edna Iles, and by an Indian prince, the Maharajah of Mysore. His music remains something of a specialist interest; it deserves more.

Another Russian, who inherited the forms of Chopin and added coloured lights and the visionary ecstasies of theosophy, was Alexander Scriabin. Scriabin pursued adding extra notes to functional chords such as sevenths, to the point at which they start to exist as free-floating dissonances in their own right (a different route from Schoenberg out of Wagner's example in the 'Tristan' chord). The end point was his 'mystic chord', an unstable heap of fourths. Like many others, he discovered the destabilising effect of non-standard scale patterns like the whole-tone and octatonic scales. The *Poem of Ecstasy* (1908) was influenced by Nietzsche's philosophy of the *Übermensch* ('Superman') and the ideas of theosophy, as well as his own version of the principle of associating certain keys with colours, taken further in *Prometheus: The Poem of Fire* of 1910, with its part for a 'keyboard of lights', which projects colours onto a screen during the music. (A vivid, in every sense, performance given at Yale University on the work's centenary in 2010 can be found on YouTube.)

Lavish Russian Romanticism had not quite bloomed its last. The symphony carried some of its nineteenth-century habits deep into the brave new world of the twentieth in the hands of composers of traditionalist, anti-modernist leanings. Alexander Glazunov fashioned a synthesis of nationalist elements and Tchaikovskian lyricism, and felt no need to react to the innovations of Schoenberg or his compatriot Stravinsky (who said, 'It is not without reason that Glazunov has been called the Russian Brahms'),[158] though he did allow hints of new sounds in his last completed work, the Saxophone Concerto of 1934. Aram Khachaturian gave the world tunes which could have poured from the pens of Tchaikovsky and Saint-Saëns in his ballets *Spartacus* (1956) and *Gayane* (premiered in 1942) with its whirling 'Sabre Dance'. In its twisted way, Soviet ideology, led by Andrei Zhdanov, found his music 'formalist' and 'fundamentally incorrect' in

1948 (alongside the works of contemporaries including Shostakovich, Prokofieff, Kabalevsky and Myaskovsky).[159] Unlike some of his colleagues, Khachaturian was able to earn restoration to favour through a fulsome apology, a return to his natural, folk-influenced style, and a well-received score for a film biography of Lenin.

Sergei Prokofieff brought his fluency and skill to the ballet and the big tune, too, in 1938, giving those perennial favourites Romeo and Juliet a dramatic and beautifully orchestrated evocation, relishing the violence of the death of Tybalt and the clash of the warring families as much as the allure of young love. Enormously prolific, Prokofieff took the symphonic idea in directions which encompass some of the brittle vitality of Bartók, especially in his five piano concertos, with some of the inner drive, though little of the anguish, of his friend Shostakovich.

The early twentieth-century symphonic style found a feisty champion in the Danish composer Carl Nielsen. His hard-won mature style effectively missed out late nineteenth-century Romanticism altogether, matching a Classical instinct for formal clarity with modernist ideas about a kind of progressive tonality. His songs were an important emblem of nationhood during the German occupation of Denmark a decade or so after his death in 1931: with the ebullient opera *Maskarade*, first performed in 1906, they have made him a national figure in his home country. His take on the symphony is utterly original: Symphony No. 4, 'The Inextinguishable', of 1916, places two sets of timpani on opposite sides of the stage in a kind of duel; Symphony No. 5 of 1922 asks a snare drummer to interrupt and disrupt the music by improvising out of time, to extraordinary effect. The *Helios Overture* of 1903 is an expansive orchestral hymn to the rising sun. His biographer Daniel Grimley has hailed Nielsen as 'one of the most playful, life-affirming, and awkward voices in twentieth-century music'.[160]

In the heartlands of the Germanic symphonic tradition, Paul Hindemith rigorously worked his own system of tonal but non-diatonic music not just into works like the appropriately named *Ludus Tonalis* (*Games with Sounds*, or possibly *Harmony*) of 1942, a set of fugues rooted in Bach, or the *Symphonic Metamorphosis of Themes of Carl Maria von Weber* of 1943, exploring a different strand of inherited technique, but also into a textbook of his own language, *The Craft of Musical Composition* (1941). Hindemith was a great believer in professionalism and practicality, writing a new piece for the London Proms on the day King George V died in time for the premiere the next day, and another during a recording session when it turned out that a side of a '78 needed filling. He gave neglected instruments like the double bass a solo repertoire of their own, and pioneered the idea of *Gebrauchsmusik*, or 'Music for Use', including community pieces and pieces for children. Hindemith moved a long way from his earlier late Romantic and Expressionist phases and the 'New Objectivity' of the Weimar period; but perhaps the listener to the later works can sometimes hear the textbook hovering drily open on the work desk just a little too much: the conservative's modernist; the modernist's professional.

Hindemith's long-lived contemporary Carl Orff also contributed ideas about music in education in the concept of *Schulwerk*, which combines music, movement, drama and speech into lessons based around a child's intuitive instinct for play. Orff is the ultimate example of a one-work composer: even in his lifetime the enormous popularity of his 1936 cantata *Carmina Burana*, settings of poems from the medieval collection known by the same name, caused him to withdraw everything else he had written to that point.

The strange journey of the symphonic idea took several significant steps in the stylistic progress of Polish composer Karol Szymanowski. Early piano music, some for his friend and compatriot Arthur Rubinstein, and songs in Polish, in a post-Straussian late Romantic style, gave way in the years around the First World War (in which he was medically unfit to serve) to a second period inspired by an immersion in Mediterranean culture and acknowledgement (if not completely in public) of his homosexuality. He wrote a homoerotic novel (at around the time that more or less cautious contemporaries like E. M. Forster, E. F. Benson, Radclyffe Hall and Colette were doing the same) and drew on highly charged Persian poetry in *Des Hafis Liebeslieder* (*The Love Songs of Hafiz*) (1911) and his Symphony No. 3 'Song of the Night' (1916). The 1924 opera *Król Roger* (*King Roger*) mines an eclectic and stylised repertoire of musical traditions for its ecstatic account of the spiritual struggle between a king and a shepherd, ending in a blaze of C major. The Fourth Symphony, written in 1932, sixteen years after the Third, can't decide if it is a piano concerto, a cyclic manipulation of a minor third, a folkloristic fantasy whipping up the traditional Polish *oberek* dance in an 'almost orgiastic' way in the third movement (in the words of its composer),[161] or all of these and more. (Its opening is echoed in Bartók's Third Piano Concerto; its type of formal eclecticism can be heard in Bernstein's 'Kaddish' Symphony.) In his third and last compositional phase Szymanowski moved away from all this mixed-up mystical eclecticism to concentrate on the cultural heritage of the Polish highland people, the Gorals, building their tonal language and rhythmic and melodic style into mazurkas for piano and songs for children.

The International Post-Stravinsky Neoclassical Style

The manner known as the Neoclassical took in many things, too. If Stravinsky gave it the neo, and Milhaud the jazz, it was Prokofieff who made it most manifestly Classical with his Symphony No. 1, the 'Classical Symphony' of 1917. His aim was 'precisely Mozartian classicism' in 'happy and uncomplicated'[1] music,[162] partly in reaction to a friend's statement that 'there is no true joyfulness to be found in Russian music'.[163] His medium was a Mozart-sized orchestra, formality lightly worn, little more than fifteen minutes of music, and tunes.

Neoclassicism spoke with many national accents in the mid century, often coupled with an active creative engagement with older music. The guitar music of Joaquín Rodrigo and Mario Castelnuovo-Tedesco (an Italian, despite his important contribution to the repertoire of Spain's national instrument, mostly written in California) draws on the forms and sounds of the Baroque. The Italian composer Alfredo Casella (alongside the American poet Ezra Pound) virtually invented Vivaldi for the modern age through his editions and 'Vivaldi Weeks' in Venice from 1939. Gian Francesco Malipiero produced a complete edition of Monteverdi. In England, Gerald Finzi edited eighteenth-century English string concertos for the Newbury String Players: a distinctive vein of mildly astringent contrapuntalism hums gently through much of his writing for strings.

Ideas, like people, travelled a long way in a fast-changing world. The house built by Schoenberg and Stravinsky turned out to have many mansions.

17

AMERICA AND THE JAZZ ERA

Give Me Your Poor …

America offered a welcome to wandering musicians of all kinds from the dark days of tsarist Russia to the last gasp of European fascism.

The challenge inherent in all this inherited diversity was for musical America to find an authentic way of looking at itself. It needed, in the words of Aaron Copland, a 'usable past'.[1]

Classical music struggled to find a voice. Many composers stayed loyal to the European tradition. Dvořák offered one version of a vernacular. The poems of Walt Whitman, Henry Wadsworth Longfellow and Robert Frost suggested another; in time, a rich resource. Earlier American musical objects like shape-note and Sacred Harp singing, camp meeting songs and the Grand Ole Opry provided a kind of primitive native vocabulary, though they were little known in serious circles. Folk music began to emerge from the woods of Appalachia and elsewhere through the work of Cecil Sharp and John Jacob Niles. But how did the serious American composer get past the gods across the water? How do you move from an old European aristocracy to a new American democracy? What does that sound like? Do you dare cross the tracks from classical to jazz? What, exactly, was the American composer supposed to do?

Popular music did better. Within a generation of 5-year-old Israel Beilin peering up at the Statue of Liberty over the balustrades of the Ellis Island immigration centre in September 1893, the piano-pounding hacks of Tin Pan Alley and the kids on the sidewalk outside the barbers' shops pocketing a penny for a song had turned the sounds around them into one of the greatest and most distinctive of all national styles: the Great American Songbook. Little Izzy Beilin had become Irving Berlin. God Bless America.

Finding the Future in the Past: Looking to Europe

Looking back at his country's musical development in 1952, Aaron Copland traced a wise path through his its musical history, from the arrival in the sixteenth century of a Franciscan friar and pioneer of musical education called Pedro de Gante, to the contributions of puritan pilgrims, Cuban farmers, Handel and Haydn societies, and the one-eyed hymn-writer and snuff addict William Billings.

An early generation of American-born symphonists largely borrowed the forms and manner of their European models. The oldest, William Henry Fry, wrote a 'Santa Claus' Symphony in 1853 and a remarkable orchestral evocation of the sound of Niagara Falls in 1854 (as well as a book on *Artificial Fish-Breeding*). Louis Gottschalk was born to an English Jewish father and French Creole mother in New Orleans, was turned away from piano studies at the Paris Conservatoire because the directors refused to believe anything good could come out of the 'land of steam engines',[2] but was hailed by both Chopin and Liszt. Early pieces like *Bamboula (Danse des Nègres)* of 1848 and *La Savane* (1836) are among the very first to fuse Creole and slave music into a Romantic context.

An important group coalesced around Boston, and Harvard University in particular, at the turn of the twentieth century: John Knowles Paine, Edward MacDowell, Horatio Parker (teacher of Charles Ives), and the pianist, composer and educator Amy Beach, who wrote a symphony and a piano concerto in a late Romantic manner as well as much church music. In her later pieces she experimented with whole-tone scales. Professionally, Beach struggled with both her mother and her husband for control of her musical activities (although she long outlived both of them), promoted music education for children at her 'Beach Clubs', supported young professionals and in 1918 wrote a newspaper article addressed 'To the Girl Who Wants to Compose'.

MacDowell is best remembered for 'To a Wild Rose', a charming piano piece of 1896 which would have done credit to any tinkling parlour in the Old World. Perhaps of more lasting importance, he and his wife, the pianist Marian MacDowell, founded the MacDowell colony in New Hampshire, where artists in a variety of disciplines could – and still can – work in peace. This idea of a self-contained community of like-minded thinkers has a particular place in American social history, traced through experiments like the Brook Farm community, sponsored by Nathaniel Hawthorne and others, back to Robert Owen and the Chartists in England, and further back still to dissident communities like the seventeenth-century Diggers. Several works with a central place in American music were written, or partly written, at the MacDowell colony, including Copland's *Appalachian Spring*, Leonard Bernstein's *Mass* (a theatre, rather than liturgical, piece), Virgil Thomson's *Mother of Us All*, plays which later inspired music like Thornton Wilder's *Our Town*, and *Porgy and Bess* by DuBose and Dorothy Heyward, source material respectively for Copland and Gershwin, as well as important novels by James Baldwin, Willa Cather, Alice Walker, Alice Sebold and, most recently, Jonathan Franzen.

Inheritors and continuers of the broadly European approach in the next generation included Roy Harris, who was brought up on an Oklahoma farmstead and worked as a truck driver to fund musical ambitions which took him to Paris and the inevitable Nadia Boulanger. He combined an interest in American folk music with the symphonic principles of Sibelius, wrote many works on American subjects, including the first American symphony to be commercially recorded and his signature work, the Symphony No. 3 of 1937–9, and occupied a leading place in American musical life alongside his wife, the pianist Johana Harris.

Another to pass through Boulanger's class was a composer who wrote in a similar 'big sky' style to his on-off friend/rival Aaron Copland (and could be excoriatingly dismissive of anyone who didn't): Virgil Thomson, composer of the innovative 1928 opera *Four Saints in Three Acts* with a libretto by Gertrude Stein, which used an all-Black cast to portray about twenty European saints (in four acts), and host with his partner Maurice Grosser of an influential gay salon at their home in the Chelsea Hotel in New York, frequented by figures like Leonard Bernstein, Tennessee Williams and composers Ned Rorem, Paul Bowles and John Cage.

An utterly different character was Ernest Bloch, born in Switzerland, who knew Debussy and corresponded with Mahler before settling in the US in 1916, and going on to achieve a distinguished academic career and fame for orchestral works which fuse the sounds of his Jewish heritage into a European symphonic model.

Aaron Copland drops us a couple of unfamiliar names who made an honest attempt to move away from 'the sure values of the academic world', without getting past a '*fin-de-siècle* tendency' to make their music 'a mere exercise in polite living': Charles Martin Loeffler and, particularly, Charles T. Griffes. Copland comments poignantly:

> No one can say how far Griffes might have developed if his career had not been cut short by death in his thirty-sixth year, in 1920. What he gave those of us who came after him was a sense of the adventurous in composition, of being thoroughly alive to the newest trends in world music and to the stimulus that might be derived from such contact.[3]

The composers noted so far were born in the nineteenth century. The stylistic European flag continued to be flown by two Americans born about a decade into the new century whose names need to be taken together. Samuel Barber and Gian Carlo Menotti were partners. They met as students at the Curtis Institute in New York, in a class also numbering Bernstein among its alumni, and went on to share a house called Capricorn in Mount Kisco, New York State, for over forty years.

Samuel Barber was a native of Pennsylvania and a talented singer and pianist. His tuneful, well-crafted scores earned early success which, unlike many, never really diminished (though his last years brought sadness, separation from Menotti and struggles with depression and alcoholism). His *Adagio for Strings*, arranged from a movement of a string quartet in 1938, earned the approving comment *'semplice e bella'* from its first conductor, Arturo Toscanini, qualities which have kept it firmly among classical favourites ever since.[4] The *Adagio* is frankly Mahlerian: 'Dover Beach' of 1931 finds him in a more English mood, setting a melancholy Victorian poem by Matthew Arnold to music with more than a hint of the tremulous cadences of Vaughan Williams – he sang it himself for an RCA recording in 1937, which shows off his silky baritone, a key factor in the natural lyricism of his writing for voices and instruments. He applies the same skills to an American landscape in *Knoxville: Summer of 1915* (1948).

Barber's 1958 opera *Vanessa* has a libretto by Menotti. Menotti himself specialised in opera, perhaps naturally for the sixth of the eight children of a coffee merchant from Cadegliano-Viconago near Lake Maggiore, whose mother brought the family from Italy to America (via Colombia) when he was a teenager. His style comes straight out of the street-level verismo of Puccini and Mascagni (his first opera was written in his mother tongue, Italian), with all that implies for singable lines, vivid emotions, brash harmony and orchestration and the capacity to irritate and wind up highbrow critics from the first visitation of the Magi to the little boy on crutches or appearance of the stigmata of Christ in a New York tenement. This is sentimentality in spades, often mixed with a plaster saint religiosity: not, certainly, to everyone's taste. Fluent and prolific, he was one of the few composers to make a success of writing opera for television. In the late 1950s he founded the Festival of the Two Worlds in Spoleto, Italy, because 'I became so completely disenchanted with the role of the artist in contemporary society. I felt useless ... I wanted to feel needed.'[5] The two worlds were Italy and the US; Spoleto USA followed in the 1970s, followed by an Australian outpost in Melbourne. In later life, after the break-up of his relationship with Barber, Menotti and his adopted son and young grandsons presided as perhaps unlikely lairds of a magnificent Palladian mansion in south-east Scotland, purchased apparently for the acoustics of its ballroom.

Finding the Future in the Future: Two Modernists

So far, the American musicians in this chapter have answered one aspect of 'the choice' in twentieth-century music by looking back across time and east across the Atlantic for their style and manner. Others took a different route. Two names in particular define American modernism.

Edgard Varèse was French. His was the kind of restlessly inventive mind unwilling to be satisfied with anything handed to him as established musical fact: instruments, a scale made of twelve equal semitones, buildings, even sound itself. He once said, 'I am not a musician. I work with rhythms, frequencies and intensities. Tunes are the gossips in music.'[6] There are no tunes in Varèse. His tiny output of compositions includes: *Ionisation* (1933), the first avant-garde work entirely for percussion; *Amériques* (1918–21), which hews huge blocks of sound from its massive orchestral forces (including sirens and, in a version written in 1927 after a return visit to Paris, the early electronic keyboard the ondes Martenot), and places them next to each other according to his own doctrine of 'sound-masses' rather than anything as limiting as logical development of theme; and the *Poème Electronique*, written to be heard in the Philips Pavilion at the 1958 World Fair in Brussels, using the same mathematical shape of the hyperbolic paraboloid which the designer of the pavilion, architect and fellow composer Iannis Xenakis, used to make the distinctive flowing shapes of its sail-like curves. Sound, space, proportion, movement and mass become one. Listening to this powerful, challenging brutalist vision, it seems barely possible that its long-lived creator was a student of the agreeable old antique Saint-Saëns. No wonder Varèse called Saint-Saëns 'an old powdered wig'.[7]

The other key American modernist could hardly be more different. Charles Ives was an insurance salesman (one of his clients was the family of the young Elliott Carter, later a long-lived and influential figure in American modernist music). Copland described Ives's contribution as 'surely unique not only in America but in musical history anywhere'.[8] As a boy he heard three village bands playing different pieces on three street corners at the same time, their music overlapping in bizarre lack of coordination, creating an effect which thrilled and captivated him. He loved the day-to-day musical sounds of the New England townscapes where he grew up: church choirs, wheezy harmoniums, barn dances. As a composer he explored innovative ways of recreating the idea of separate musical spaces going on simultaneously. In one of his most famous works, 1906's *Central Park in the Dark*, a string ensemble is placed behind a velvet screen, playing Bartók-like night music to evoke the dark, while in front of the screen a group of wind instruments makes the noises of the park. Foreground and background are concurrent, but not contiguous. *The Unanswered Question* of 1908 is for the strange combination of trumpet, four flutes and string quartet, derived in part from his interest in the work of transcendentalists like Henry David Thoreau and Ralph Waldo Emerson: *Three Places in New England* (1910–14) is one of many pieces to set vernacular quotations, sometimes several piled on top of each other, alongside avant-garde techniques like tone clusters. Largely ignored in the years they were composed, his works gradually earned the attention and respect of influential supporters and, later, a wider public. Like Sibelius, he stopped composing altogether for the last thirty years of his life. Like Borodin and Xenakis, he was also successful in his non-musical career, writing a well-received guide to *Life Insurance in Relation to Inheritance Tax* in 1918, and engaging in a lively debate as a member of the First World War committee on war bonds with the committee chairman, Franklin D. Roosevelt, over the optimum minimum value for the bond. Ives also generously supported many young composers (like Liszt before him), often anonymously.

Admiration of Ives remains compulsory for musical innovators in all parts of the musosphere, from Frank Zappa to John Adams and The Grateful Dead. Leonard Bernstein borrowed the title *The Unanswered Question* for his influential Harvard lectures of 1971. Perhaps Ives himself never answered the question articulated by his admirer Copland, of how to achieve 'formal coherence in the midst of so varied a musical material'.[9] Perhaps he never meant to. Perhaps that was the point.

Some Other Approaches

One of the great joys of Ives's vision is that it sucks the authentically American sounds of John Philip Sousa and William Billings into a recognisably modern way of looking at the world. Another who hammered ideas from elsewhere into his own shape was a rough-edged, racist loudmouth who was rudely dismissive of everyone except Ives, proudly claimed never to have studied music theory or analysed anyone else's scores, and wrote in a kind of post-Schoenbergian style christened 'dissonant counterpoint' by his friend Charles Seeger: Carl Ruggles.[10] Ruggles wrote slowly and destroyed many of his early works: fewer than twenty works represent his long life. The best-known is the orchestral *Sun-Treader* of 1931. His style takes elements of Schoenberg's ideas but applies them in his own ways, for example avoiding repetition of a pitch within eight, rather than twelve, notes. Mathematical analysis of chords by counting semitones, and building 'waves' of sound from repeating patterns based on fractals, have elements in common with later ideas like the technique of 'pitch multiplication' of Boulez.

Despite his deliberate cigar-chomping anti-Semitic cantankerousness, Ruggles earned himself some important admirers, including Varèse, the Seegers and Henry Dixon Cowell. Cowell, the Californian son of an Irish father who taught him folk music on the fiddle and an American mother who wrote an early feminist novel, became a leader of the rather vaguely named 'Ultramodernists', alongside his friend the maverick composer of virtuoso music for player piano, Conlon Nancarrow. Early piano works using full-arm clusters and notes depressed silently influenced John Cage in the development of the 'prepared piano'; Cowell's 1919 book *New Musical Resources* was, for Nancarrow, 'the most influence [sic] of anything I've ever read'; Virgil Thomson, hardly a musical soulmate, called Cowell and his crew the 'rhythmic research fellows'.[11] Cowell pioneered an early form of electronic rhythm machine. His outspoken radicalism was severely limited in 1936 by his imprisonment on a 'morals' charge around sexual relations with a 17-year-old boy: in San Quentin State Prison he composed, conducted the prison band, and developed a flexible method of composing 'modular' ballet music which allowed the choreographer to make a passage longer or shorter at will. His release and subsequent pardon were the result of efforts by loyal friends, including the woman he later married, folk music scholar Sidney Robertson. Unlike Ruggles, Cowell wrote quickly and prolifically: his output includes twenty-one symphonies. His music contains immense variety, and many rewarding surprises.

One of Cowell's students was Lou Harrison. Harrison also studied with Schoenberg in California in the 1940s, and followed the Canadian composer Colin McPhee in studying Indonesian and Javanese music, particularly the gamelan. *Genesis of a Music*, the 1946 book on tuning by the composer, inventor and railroad-riding hobo Harry Partch, nudged Harrison's style towards adopting the just intonation and microtonality of non-Western music. Many composers over the ages have taken odd jobs to keep themselves in manuscript paper and sharpened pencils: Harrison was at various times a forestry firefighter, an animal nurse, a record salesman and a florist. He and his long-term partner, William Colvig, built several gamelans, two of which were named after Darius Milhaud and his wife Madeleine, and a house made of straw bales at Joshua Tree, California. His politics and sexuality are prominently celebrated in his work, including pieces for the non-profit liberal radio network the Pacifica Foundation and the Portland Gay Men's Chorus.

Another key member of the Ultramodernists and graduate of the MacDowell colony was Ruth Crawford. Influenced by Scriabin, she journeyed to Vienna and Budapest to seek the guidance of Berg and Bartók, but pursued a modernist agenda of her own, characterised by her biographer Judith Tick as 'post-tonal pluralism'.[12] A middle period in the 1930s brought her under the influence of the 'dissonant counterpoint' of Charles Seeger, whom she married in 1932. As Ruth

Crawford Seeger, her last period of activity centred around an interest in folk music through an association with singers John and Alan Lomax: her family, including her stepson Pete and children Mike and Peggy, went on to become central figures in the world of folk music, but knew little of their mother's earlier incarnation as a pioneer of American modernism.

Crawford Seeger succumbed to cancer in 1953 at the sadly early age of fifty-two. A striking feature of the musicians around her is that many lived to a great age: Varèse and Harrison were both in their eighties when they died, Aaron Copland was ninety, Charles Seeger ninety-two and Gian Carlo Menotti ninety-five. Elliott Carter was still composing shortly before his death at the age of not quite 104 in 2012 (and gave an interview, available online, only a few weeks earlier). History doesn't record if the insurance policy sold to his family by Charles Ives a hundred years earlier was still valid.

An honoured place in the history of American music must go to a small group of wealthy and influential patrons and promoters. Between them, the singer Alice Tully, the pianist Elizabeth Sprague Coolidge, the Russian immigrant conductor Serge Koussevitzky and Mr and Mrs Robert Woods Bliss oversaw the creation of many of the twentieth century's greatest masterpieces, from Stravinsky's *'Dumbarton Oaks' Concerto* to Britten's *Peter Grimes*, and many others.

Finding the Future within: Black and Vernacular American Classical Music

Charles Ives taught American music that, when it looked within its own shores instead of out across the Atlantic, there was plenty to look at. The marches of John Philip Sousa are among the best and jauntiest of their kind, quite different in character from the *Radetzky* style of Johann Strauss or Elgar in his *Pomp and Circumstance* moods. African-American spirituals provided a rich, deep library of bitter experience and beautiful tunes, ably captured and transfigured in the songs of Stephen Foster, together with a cheerful strain unknown in real spirituals in songs like 'Camptown Races' and 'Oh! Susanna'. Dvořák urged his fellow American composers to use spirituals as the basis of 'any serious and original school of composition in America';[13] his pupil William Arms Fisher wrote the words 'Goin' Home' to the tune of the slow movement of the *New World Symphony*, following

Foster in fashioning art music out of the mood and manner of the spiritual. Foster and Fisher were white: the singer and actor Paul Robeson trod the uncomfortable path of a Black artist negotiating his way through expectation and stereotype in his long career, which included the defining version of the role of Joe in Jerome Kern and Oscar Hammerstein's 1927 musical *Show Boat*, whose immortal signature song 'Ol' Man River' draws so beautifully on the pentatonic mode of much folk music and the subdominant-facing harmonies favoured by Dvořák. He also played Othello opposite Peggy Ashcroft in 1930 (and had an affair with her), became involved in political activism during the Spanish Civil War, and in 1957 defied US government restrictions on his freedom of movement due to alleged left-wing sympathies by singing to an audience in St Pancras Town Hall in London over the new trans-Atlantic telephone cable: 'As an artist, I come to sing, but as a citizen, I will always speak for peace, and no one can silence me in this.'[14]

Arguably the most important and influential Black musician in late nineteenth-century American music was Scott Joplin. The son of a former slave, his name is forever associated with a musical development which took the simple rhythmic patterns and regular phrase lengths of conventional Western music, then fragmented and rejoined them by placing ties across strong beats to produce a grid of syncopated groups overlaying the main pulse, creating something completely new and instantly recognisable which would soon feed into all sorts of popular styles: ragtime. Joplin didn't invent ragtime, but his 'Maple Leaf Rag' of 1899 became the flagship for the style, hungrily assimilated by musical omnivores like Poulenc, Satie (whose 'Ragtime Parade' of 1919 isn't actually a ragtime) and Debussy (who wrote several pieces based on the cakewalk, a two-step derived from nineteenth-century 'prizewalks', which shares some rhythmic features with ragtime). Sadly, Joplin was one of those composers who was hugely successful in one thing but wished it had been something else: he made repeated attempts to cross over into the mainstream with his 1911 opera *Treemonisha*, but met only disappointment. *Treemonisha* contains some pleasant enough music, but it's not great theatre: Joplin's genius lay elsewhere.

Jazz: Prehistory and Three Cities

Of all the things America gave the musical world, the most important were jazz and the blues.

Jazz went through a speeded-up version of the process of finding, formalising, then deconstructing a musical language in response to artistic imperatives and external circumstances. Art mirrored life, and vice versa: George Gershwin based the role of Sportin' Life in his 1935 opera *Porgy and Bess* on the flamboyant bandleader Cab Calloway; later, Calloway played the role on stage.

Black African music gave American music some of its founding gestures: remarkable rhythmic sophistication (superior to 'the best composers of today', as one American critic put it in 1893);[15] Sunday gatherings in Congo Square, New Orleans, to sing and dance the semi-ritualistic 'ring shout' and other patterns; and psalms and sacred songs sung in a collective, improvised 'river-like style of polyphony', in the words of music historian Alan Lomax.[16] The early blues of Robert Johnson, Blind Lemon Jefferson and Leadbelly (recorded by Lomax in prison in 1933) used a hypnotic AAB pattern based on question–question–answer and irregular line lengths determined by the words, a much freer precursor of the later, formalised twelve-bar pattern. In New Orleans pianists and straggly collections of instruments played ragtime-inflected rhythms in church, in brothels, at fish fries, and on the streets. Charles 'Buddy' Bolden pushed at boundaries with 'Buddy Bolden's Stomp', also known as 'Funky Butt': 'The police put you in jail if they heard you singing that song,' recalled reed player Sidney Bechet.[17]

Money and commerce took the booze-fuelled blues style of singers Ma Rainey and Bessie Smith into the homes of white people who owned a phonograph (Bessie Smith's 1923 hit 'Down Hearted Blues' saved Columbia Records), and out on the road through the Theater Owners Booking Association or TOBA (also known as Tough on Black Artists, or Asses). Their music was about poverty, illiteracy and abuse, but also about sex and fun. Sister Rosetta Tharpe, born to cotton-pickers in Arkansas in 1915, later notably prefigured rock'n'roll with her guitar style on gospel-derived blues songs like 'This Train'.

The New Orleans diaspora spread north, most importantly to Chicago: the Original Dixieland Jazz Band, King Oliver, Kid Ory, and the 'consummate craftsman of the traditional New Orleans style' and the first genuine jazz composer, Jelly Roll Morton.[18] Morton modestly declared, 'New Orleans is the cradle of jazz, and I myself happened to be the creator.'[19] Jazz produced its first great soloists in Sidney Bechet ('an artist of genius', according to the conductor Ernest Ansermet, who called Bechet's playing style 'perhaps the highway the whole world will swing along tomorrow')[20] and trumpeter Louis Armstrong, who led the famous Hot Fives and Hot Sevens sessions in Chicago in 1925. Like so many jazz musicians, Armstrong's biography is full of hazy details and baroque embellishments around a tough outline, which in his case began with him selling coal to prostitutes at age seven and getting sent to New Orleans' Colored Waifs Home for Boys aged twelve for firing his stepfather's gun. Armstrong also claimed to have invented the wordless style of jazz singing known as 'scat' when he dropped a lyric sheet during a recording session: true or not, his pioneering vocal style remains hugely influential. Armstrong went on to bestride the jazz world, living long enough to knock the Beatles out of the US charts in May 1964 with his version of 'Hello, Dolly!'

Just as New Orleans had synthesised Spanish, African, Creole and gospel music into jazz, Chicago blended 'Black jazz, white jazz, hot jazz, sweet jazz, New Orleans jazz, Dixieland jazz', in a list assembled by jazz historian Ted Gioia.[21] The term also began to take in popular music and classical-style sweet jazz in the manner of Gershwin and bandleader and arranger Paul Whiteman, exemplified by the first talking picture, 1927's *The Jazz Singer*. Singers as varied as Jack Teagarden, Bing Crosby and Fats Waller pursued a simplified form of vocal delivery. Outliers among the jazz fraternity included the intellectual trumpeter Bix Beiderbecke, and his close colleague and co-pioneer of 'cool jazz', trombonist Frank Trumbauer, who, unlike Beiderbecke, drank little and after a gig would pack up and go home to his family.

The third key city in the history of jazz is New York. Harlem rent parties hosted music to raise cash, but this world was hidden from the mainstream: 'Those of us in the music and entertainment business were vaguely aware that something exciting was happening,' said Cab Calloway, 'but we weren't directly involved.'[22] The composer of the Charleston, James P. Johnson, pioneered 'stride' piano, which came out of ragtime and was a key component in the careers of his students Duke Ellington and Fats Waller and stride virtuoso Art Tatum. Ellington and the pianist and arranger Fletcher Henderson skilfully worked the music up into a version of orchestral form, adding singers like

Ella Fitzgerald and the dancers of the Cotton Club: Harlem created the big band.

The big band turned jazz into swing. Bandleaders who rode the wave included Harry James and the pugnacious Dorsey brothers, who gave early career impetus to perhaps the biggest star of all, Frank Sinatra, and one of the most all-embracing, wide-reaching, hard-working musicians in the whole of this history, a clarinettist who recorded Mozart, commissioned Bartók, the King of Swing, Benny Goodman.

There was life away from the principal centres, too. Kansas City produced the pianist and composer Mary Lou Williams and another musician to elect himself to the jazz peerage, William 'Count' Basie. Basie's vocalist in the late 1930s was a feisty, vulnerable, throaty singer from Baltimore whose autobiography opens with the classic lines 'Mom and Pop were just a couple of kids when they got married. He was eighteen, she was sixteen, and I was three', Billie Holliday.[23] Christened Lady Day by her mother's former lodger, the saxophonist Lester Young (whom she in turn called 'Prez'), Holliday caught the pain of a difficult childhood and even more difficult adulthood in songs like 'Strange Fruit', released in 1939, the haunting account of a lynching.

Even further away, Paris, melting pot of Neoclassical jazz, hosted the Quintette du Hot Club de France in the mid 1930s, led by Stéphane Grappelli's jazz violin and the guitar of Django Reinhardt, a virtuoso despite having largely lost the use of two fingers in a caravan fire.

The Great American Songbook

The place where jazz met Tin Pan Alley pop was Broadway. Four great names define the repertoire known to history as the Great American Songbook: Irving Berlin, George Gershwin, Jerome Kern and Cole Porter.

Irving Berlin was the longest-surviving of the four, dying in 1989 at the age of 101. His art emerged from his early days as an immigrant scraping a living in Tin Pan Alley, the cheerful bounce of earlier songwriters like George M. Cohan ('Over There') matched with a sweet melodiousness ('When I Lost You', written on the death of his first wife in 1912 from typhoid contracted on their honeymoon), the barest hint of his Jewish heritage, the styles around him on the street ('Alexander's Ragtime Band', his huge breakthrough hit), and an understated sophistication ('Puttin' On the Ritz' is one of the only songs of the period with the verse in a major key and the chorus in the minor). Irving Berlin never learnt to read music.

Berlin wrote his own words. George Gershwin (born Gershwine) collaborated with his brother Ira on songs with a remarkable range of harmonic invention ('The Man I Love') as well as a perfect jaunty streak ('They Can't Take That Away from Me'), and simple tunefulness ('Someone to Watch Over Me'). Gershwin went furthest of the four in taking his art into the classical arena with works like his Piano Concerto in F Major of 1925, concert pieces like *An American in Paris* (1928), the opera *Porgy and Bess* and, above all, *Rhapsody in Blue* (1924) for piano and orchestra (originally scored for Paul Whiteman's band).

Jerome Kern was a few years older than Berlin. Like Gershwin a second-generation immigrant of German-Jewish ancestry, he was born in New York in 1885. Kern's mature musical signatures mark him as perhaps the most European of the quartet: 'Smoke Gets in Your Eyes' takes a harmonic turn straight out of Schubert for its middle eight, and 'Ol' Man River' is no thing for a whispery crooner or Broadway belter – its nearly two-octave range (in Frank Sinatra's recording, not just nearly) requires a real operatic technique. Kern worked with all sorts of wordsmiths, from Oscar Hammerstein to Gertrude Stein and P. G. Wodehouse. He could do Gershwin-esque directness, too, as in the breezy 'Can't Help Lovin' Dat Man' (though he can't quite resist a delicious twist to the flat sixth to finish).

Last comes the only genuine American among these giants of American music. The scion of a wealthy Indiana family, who studied at Yale, struggled as a songwriter in Europe but maintained a lavish and exotic artistic milieu in Paris, married a rich divorcée eight years his senior despite his entirely open homosexuality (an arrangement which suited them both perfectly), had his first Broadway hit at the age of thirty-six in 1928 with the appropriately named musical *Paris*, and went on to write some of the best-known and best-loved songs and shows of all time ('Anything Goes', 'I Get A Kick Out of You', 'Night And Day', 'Just One of Those Things' and *Kiss Me, Kate*): Cole Porter.

Cole Porter's melodies manipulate music and words with a skill equal to any songwriter, any time. 'So in Love' starts with his trademark circling around a single note (see also 'Every Time We

Say Goodbye' and 'Night and Day'), builds through a phrase whose highest note is raised in each of its three repetitions (see also 'Begin the Beguine'), then subsides in a phrase which teases more syllables out of the opening line in its sad, obsessive ecstasy: 'So in love ... so in love ... So in love with you, my love ... Am I'. The technical skill was not lost on Porter's inheritors like Noël Coward, himself a master of the art of three-fold repetition ('If Love were All'). In another echo far away, Ivor Novello (a Welshman schooled in that most musical of English counties, Gloucestershire) provided England with her scratchy 78 rpm soundtrack to the sadness and nostalgia of war ('We'll Gather Lilacs', 'Keep the Home Fires Burning'), adding the harmonies of *Hymns Ancient and Modern* to a noble simplicity and directness.

A notable subset of these artists wrote their own words (Berlin, Porter, Coward). The stage works in which the songs were heard varied enormously in seriousness and scope. For Berlin, the medium was essentially the revue; a series of unconnected sketches. Jerome Kern's *Show Boat* of 1927 is a much more challenging piece of theatre, Oscar Hammerstein's dramatisation turning Edna Ferber's novel of 1926 into a searing, serious, challenging and coherent drama. The musicals of Cole Porter sometimes give the impression of great songs dropped with a gleeful lack of logic anywhere in the plot they sort of fit: in *Kiss Me, Kate* (1948), a couple of actors, on tour in 'Philly, Boston or Baltimo'', reminisce about a long-ago trip to Austria. Cue a Viennese operetta waltz. And why not?

Beyond these four, Richard Rodgers and Oscar Hammerstein took the stage musical to new levels of dramatic truth and seriousness in *Carousel* (1945), with its verismo-like story of low-life love, loyalty, cruelty and death, and built innovative forms like a spoken monologue to music and free-standing instrumental items (the Tchaikovsky-like 'March of the Siamese Children' from *The King and I* (1951)) into their scores. 'You'll Never Walk Alone' is one of the richest, and simplest, of all show songs; 'If I Loved You', one of the truest and saddest. Among many, many other notable songwriters, Vernon Duke was born Vladimir Dukelsky, played Poulenc's Concerto for Two Pianos with the composer in Europe, and penned an elegant song which joins two worlds, 'Paris in New York'.

The songs of the Great American Songbook, written for the stage or films, went on to become jazz standards, picked up by jazz musicians who made them into their own and formed the core of their repertoire.

Films and Shows

Writing musicals for the stage met up with another new thing for the composer to do, writing music for films. Early film songwriters included Sigmund Romberg (*Desert Song* (1929)) and Victor Herbert. Irving Berlin wrote the songs for *Top Hat*, starring Fred Astaire and Ginger Rogers, in 1935. By the mid 1940s Hollywood was feeding public demand for the glitzy fantasies of Busby Berkeley and similar fare at a rate approaching one movie musical a week. Many films featuring the great songbook composers were made after the war, for example 1956's *High Society*, matchlessly pairing Bing Crosby and Frank Sinatra with the wordy, worldly wit of Porter's lyrics and tunes. Stage musicals came to the screen in the 1950s and 1960s, too, notably Rodgers and Hammerstein's *The Sound of Music* in 1965. Jerome Kern's *Show Boat* was filmed twice, in 1936 and 1951.

New kinds of show, and new technologies, required new kinds of performers. The first popular singers of the age of broadcast, recording and the talkies, like Al Jolson, essentially sang as they would on a stage. Rudy Vallée became the first crooner to induce mass hysteria. Bing Crosby, another of the first generation to learn how to croon into a microphone, lasted a good deal longer. Frank Sinatra effortlessly did both, fronting a big band, and carrying on an intimate dialogue with a microphone as if it were a tumbler of whisky on a polished late-night bar. Nat King Cole (initially a fine jazz piano player) smoothed all the remaining rough edges out of jazz singing with his trio in the 1940s, the laid-back singer's laid-back singer, sometimes leaving the beat whole bars behind: the sort of 'easy listening' jazz now associated with singers like Diana Krall and Michael Bublé.

Yes, We'll Gather at the River: Meeting Points

There were points of meeting across the tracks between classical and jazz from the beginning. James P. Johnson followed Gershwin's lead with his Piano Concerto in A Flat Major, played at Carnegie Hall in 1928 with Fats Waller as soloist. Duke Ellington's 1941 suite *Black, Brown and Beige* folds a whole world of themes and styles into instrumental form, like a sort of jazz Mahler (if not entirely convincingly). Florence Price was the first African-American woman to make a major impact as a composer of symphonic music, drawing on her Southern roots, religious traditions and a tuneful vernacular style. The English pianist Billy Mayerl, product of the very different tradition of the music hall and that peculiarly English creature, light music, turned jazz into genuinely idiomatic piano music, well written and good to play. Europeans Darius Milhaud and Constant Lambert attempted a similar synthesis as Gershwin. Stravinsky wrote his 1945 'Ebony' Concerto for Woody Herman (but drew the line when told by an American promoter that one of his works had been a 'great success' but could do with some 'touch up orchestration' from 'our arranger' who 'does arrangements even for Cole Porter': Stravinsky apparently replied that he would 'settle for great success').[24] Influence went the other way, too: there's lots of Debussy and Ravel in the music of later jazz giants such as Bill Evans and Miles Davis.

Traditional music histories can get in a tangle when composers inconveniently do more than one thing, especially if they do both well. There are plenty of books which mention the concert hall Gershwin of *Rhapsody in Blue* and the Piano Concerto, but not his songs and shows. Similarly, songwriter composers get a pat on the back for trying their hand at oratorio or symphony. Neither approach will do. Jazz historian Ted Gioia is right:

> accepted discourses relating to 20th-century music are poorly equipped to deal with figures who straddle different idioms. For example, most chronicles of musical activity in the 1920s will draw an implicit delineation between popular music, jazz, and classical composition ... Such categorizations may make the narrative structure of a music history book flow more smoothly, but much is lost in the process ... Perhaps this would not be so much of a problem if genres rarely crossed paths, but – for better of worse – the modern age is marked by the tendency for different styles to coalesce and cross-fertilize. In music, purity is a myth, albeit a resilient one.[25]

In the middle of the century composer Aaron Copland mused about allowing improvisation into classical performance: 'Perhaps Mr Stravinsky and those who support his view of rigorous control for the performer have been trying to sit on the lid too hard. Perhaps the performer should be given more elbow room ...'[26]

Perhaps. But Stravinsky never followed his suggestion. Nor did Copland himself.

The most successful attempt to challenge the myth of stylistic purity came to fruition in the years around and after the Second World War, in the work of the composer with the richest roots in both traditions, who conducted the Berlin Philharmonic and sat in with Ornette Coleman, Leonard Bernstein.

18

WAYS AHEAD: BRITTEN, MESSIAEN, COPLAND, SHOSTAKOVICH AND THEIR WORLD

There's no reason why you shouldn't find musical genius in the household of a dentist from Lowestoft, but it might not be the first place you'd look.

This chapter invites four composers to sit back in the chair and open wide: a Russian, a Frenchman, an Englishman and an American; one Jewish, one Anglican (tepid), a reluctant atheist and a devout Catholic; two gay (one openly, one less so), two married (one twice, the other four times, though to only three women). Between them they found four entirely different ways of interpreting the century they shared. Among the challenges presented by that century were what do about war, how music fitted into society, the long shadow of Schoenberg, the tricky allure of the triad, the fickle demands of the public, and those old standbys sex, money, religion and politics.

Aaron Copland (1900–1990)
Dmitri Shostakovich (1906–75)
Olivier Messiaen (1908–92)
Benjamin Britten (1913–76)

The backgrounds and childhoods of all four bear comparison: happy, secure, surrounded by sympathetic siblings, their fathers of sound professional and trading stock (an engineer, a storekeeper, a teacher and translator of Shakespeare, and one, as noted, of dental extraction), mothers who sang to them, gave them piano lessons, and, in Messiaen's case, wrote him a wistful Baudelairean poem on his birth, regretting the end of her relationship with her unborn child: 'He is born, I have lost my young best-beloved'.[1] Copland's immediate ancestry had details in common with many other founding fathers of twentieth-century American music like Irving Berlin, Al Jolson and George Gershwin: immigrant Jewish families from imperial Russia whose names were anglicised, sometimes in two stages, either at the Ellis Island immigration centre in New York harbour or somewhere else on the voyage; Copland's parents never told him that their surname had been Kaplan, and, when he did find out late in life, he never knew if the change occurred in America or on an extended layover in Scotland where they worked to earn the boat fare.

The young Copland raided the Brooklyn Public Library for scores from the dusty upstairs shelves and wrote seven bars of an opera when he was eleven. Around the same age, transplanted by his mother to Grenoble when his father went off to the front in the First World War, Messiaen made a toy theatre out of cellophane wrappers and recited Shakespeare to his brother. In St Petersburg, Shostakovich, aged twelve, wrote a funeral march for two constitutionalists murdered by Bolshevik sailors, and would catch out his mother during piano lessons by playing pieces back to her by ear instead of reading from the score in front of him. At home by the sea in Suffolk the cherubically curly-haired boy Britten wrote 'elaborate tone poems usually lasting about twenty seconds, inspired by terrific events in my home life', including one called '*DO YOU NO THAT MY DADDY HAS GONE TO LONDON TODAY*' when he was about six. He also wrote a hundred opus numbers' worth of juvenilia which filled 'an old cupboard' before leaving the flannelled world of prep school and cricket for big school (Gresham's in Norfolk) at the age of thirteen, and got to know orchestral music by reading the scores, a skill learnt from a 'reprobate old uncle' called Willie.[2]

Each young composer worked and studied with and alongside well-established and traditionally minded older musicians, which, naturally, they chafed against, but which without doubt provided precious practical and professional grounding: Copland with Rubin Goldmark; Messiaen with Jean Gallon and organists Marcel Dupré and, a little later, Charles-Marie Widor and Charles Tournemire; Britten with John Ireland; Shostakovich with Alexander Glazunov (who received a very mixed press from the many young musicians he knew at this time, but seems to have been supportive of Shostakovich). Each also encountered, at various points in their development, teachers and patrons they found more congenial: Copland, on the obligatory dip in the heady artistic waters of 1920s Paris with Nadia Boulanger, the teacher who, with her uncanny gift for finding and bringing out inner talent, he called an 'Intellectual Amazon';[3] Messiaen with Paul Dukas at the Conservatoire there; Britten as an almost-adoptive house guest of the composer Frank Bridge and his family, poring over technique and style, studying older music by day and attending concerts in the evenings – in perhaps the nearest thing the twentieth century had to the kind of full-time immersively musical upbringing enjoyed by the sons of professionally musical families like Henry Purcell; Shostakovich (in very different circumstances) taken up by the conductors Bruno Walter and Leopold Stokowski for his First Symphony, written when he was nineteen, a work which also earned the approbation and important support of the Soviet military leader Mikhail Tukhachevsky.

Steps, mis-steps and non-steps on the road to stylistic self-fulfilment included: an abortive proposal for Britten to study with Berg in Vienna; Shostakovich resisting an attempt by his teacher Maximilian Steinberg to fit him into the Russian Romantic symphonic tradition; Copland travelling widely in Europe and taking up criticism; and Messiaen making his first forays into the use of the scale and rhythm patterns which he called, respectively, modes of limited transpositions and non-retrogradable (or palindromic) rhythms. In 1931 Messiaen also heard a gamelan for the first time, a sound and technique later to influence Britten.

All, with the exception of the culturally isolated Shostakovich, confronted, assimilated and rejected aspects of modernism. Britten's friend (and Schoenberg's pupil) Erwin Stein detected the influence of Schoenberg's Chamber Symphony No. 1 in Britten's assured, mildly serial *Sinfonietta* of 1932. Copland's *Symphonic Ode* of 1929 and *Short Symphony* of 1933 tended similarly in an abstract direction. Both consciously decided to take a different route. In the mid 1920s Copland fell under the influence of the ideas of the photographer and cultural thinker Alfred Stieglitz, who believed that American art should reflect the character of American democracy. While jazz musicians and song-makers like Gershwin, Bessie Smith and Benny Goodman were forging an American musical vernacular, only Charles Ives and Carl Ruggles among serious composers of an older generation offered anything distinctly American. The dilemma precipitated a change in style for Copland, towards something accessible in manner and American in accent. The predictable reaction followed: 'By having sold out to the mongrel commercialists half-way already,' the composer David Diamond told him, tendentiously, 'the danger is going to be wider for you, and I beg you, dear Aaron, don't sell out [entirely] yet.'[4] Copland gathered around him a group of contemporaries – Roger Sessions, Virgil Thomson, Roy Harris and Walter Piston – known as the 'Commando Squad', acting as their intelligent and articulate spokesman:[5] 'Composers of abstruse music thought they were under attack ... others took my meaning to be a justification for the watering down of their ideas ... As I see it, music that is born complex is not inherently better or worse than music that is born simple.'[6] Messiaen's main flirtation with modernism came later, when his own style was already fully formed, in works including the densely serial *Mode de valeurs et d'intensités* (*Mode of Durations and Intensities*) of 1950 and the electronic *musique concrète* piece *Timbres-durées* (*Timbres-Durations*) of 1952, written in response to the innovations of the post-war avant-garde. He came to reject both: 'it is not necessary to fly to the moon in order to learn something new.'[7] Modernism's most urgent precepts and most precipitous ways ahead would be left to others.

The views and characters which shaped their lives evolved alongside their musical style. Copland was an early enthusiast for the ideals of the Russian Revolution. Shostakovich, who lived through it, was not, and in 1926 failed an exam in Marxist methodology. Britten became a pacifist (rather less ideologically driven than his friend Michael Tippett), under the influence of two important relationships: with the tenor Peter Pears, his life and musical partner from the mid 1930s, and with the poet W. H. Auden. Auden went to America with his friend Christopher Isherwood; Britten and Pears followed in 1939, meeting up with Auden, with whom Britten had worked on films like *Night Mail* (1936), and Copland, a friend since Britten had heard and admired his music at a festival in London in 1938. In 1931 Messiaen made the traditional Parisian career move of succeeding as *titulaire*, or senior organist, at the Église de la Saint-Trinité, a post he would hold for sixty-one years.

Works and events from the mid 1930s reflected the combined pressures of finding a style, making a living and dealing with external forces like love and war. Messiaen's music had grown into the pattern of capturing religious feeling in ecstatic or reflective evocations of religious images or ideas, like a stained-glass window; for example, the sequence of nine 'meditations' for organ on events and ideas surrounding *La Nativité du Seigneur* (*The Birth of the Lord*) (1935) and *L'Ascension* (*The Ascension*) (written for orchestra in 1932/3 with an organ version a year later). In this abstract, instrumental approach to religious emotion he stands as the successor to Liszt: for him, the actual liturgy of church music held no appeal. Works reflecting events in his personal life include *Pièce pour le tombeau de Paul Dukas* of 1935, using the traditional French title for a musical memorial of his late teacher, and several works marking his marriage to the violinist Claire Delbos in 1932, including a song cycle borrowing his nickname for her for its title: *Poèmes pour Mi* (*Poems for Mi*). Shostakovich's Second and Third Symphonies were more experimental and less successful with the public than the First: a satirical opera of 1930, *The Nose*, also earned incomprehension for its bizarre story about a severed nose which becomes a state councillor, with elements of gruesome Guignol and Cocteau-esque absurdism in its plot derived from Gogol. His next opera, 1934's *Lady Macbeth of the Mtsensk District*, won official praise as representing 'the result of the general success of Socialist construction, of the correct policy of the Party', which 'could have been written only by a Soviet composer brought up in the best tradition of Soviet culture'.[8]

In 1932 Shostakovich married Nina Varzar, a physicist. They divorced in 1935, but remarried soon after in time for the birth of their first child. In January 1936 Stalin and his entourage attended a performance of *Lady Macbeth*, openly mocking the music, leaving its composer 'white as a sheet' as he took his bow[9] Two days later the state newspaper *Pravda* attacked the opera as 'deliberately dissonant'.[10] A concerted campaign against Shostakovich followed. Critics who had praised him realised they had been wrong and recanted. The Fourth Symphony, written under the revelatory influence of Mahler, was withdrawn. He wrote film music, which Stalin liked, and was safer. In 1937 the Fifth Symphony, searing, dramatic, formally more conservative, swung the public pendulum fully back the other way. Fellow composer Dmitri Kabalevsky, who had joined the earlier chorus of denunciation, shuffled Shostakovich back into the fold with a nervous pat on the back for abandoning his 'erroneous' ways.[11] A newspaper article appeared under Shostakovich's name entitled 'A Soviet Artist's Creative Response to Just Criticism'. The strange, slippery game of trying to work out who said what and why, who told them to say it and what they meant, and, even more fundamentally, what the music itself is trying to say – such a crucial factor in trying to unravel Shostakovich's intentions, personality and meaning from inside the mirrors and mantraps of Soviet falsification, duplicity and cruelty – was well underway.

On the other side of the world (in more senses than just the geographical), Copland was emerging as the musical voice of Roosevelt's New Deal America, rooted in 'my old interest in making a connection between music and the life about me'. He added revealingly: 'Our serious composers have not been signally successful at making that kind of connection.'[12] Copland refers to the motivation behind some of the tuneful, spacious scores which exemplified these ideals: 'It is a satisfaction to know that in the composing of a ballet like *Billy the Kid* or in a film score like *Our Town*, and perhaps in the *Lincoln Portrait*, I have touched off for myself and others a kind of musical naturalness that we have badly needed along with "great" works.'[13] We can hear philosophies dividing in the ironic shrug of those quote marks around the word 'great'. Copland's friend Britten found his voice in the years of travel to and from the US, too, in some important early orchestral works including the *Sinfonia da Requiem* of 1940, the first of many song cycles for Pears, the wonderful *Serenade for Tenor, Horn and Strings* (1943), an early example of his gift for anthologising disparate texts into a mysterious but coherent whole, and three choral works written in 1942–3 in a form and manner wholly new, *A Ceremony of Carols*, *Rejoice in the Lamb* and *Hymn to Saint Cecilia*. The last sets a specially written poem by Auden, wordily lecturing his precocious and impressionable young friend not to content himself with enjoying the 'gaucheness' of the 'adolescent state' of an 'impetuous child', but to 'weep, child, weep, O weep away the stain. Lost innocence who wished your lover dead.' Innocence corrupted becomes a persistent and disturbing trope in Britten's work. His life, too, is littered with people he called his 'ghosts': colleagues easily persuaded to feed his musical, artistic or psychological needs while it suited him, then dropped. Setting out for England in 1942, US customs officials impounded Britten's manuscript because they thought it contained secret messages in code; perhaps, in the inner meaning of this poem and its setting, they were right, in ways they couldn't possibly imagine.

Britten's most significant works during this period were his first two operas: *Paul Bunyan*, an apprentice work written with Auden in 1941, and, in 1945, *Peter Grimes*. *Grimes* presented a fully mature new voice to a startled and admiring world: the musical language rooted in tonality but with a peculiar personal poetry; a sensitivity to setting the English language not heard since Purcell; immensely assured writing for both voices and orchestra; skilful technique; the East Anglian setting with its complicated nostalgia; the sea; and the plot line twisted around a skewed and perilous power relationship between a man and a boy. Britten's art was rooted in opera: the remaining three decades or so of his relatively short active life would see a new stage work every couple of years, with a wide variety of librettists; at its height, almost every year.

In a curious coincidence, both Messiaen and Shostakovich tried to enlist on the outbreak of war but were turned down for the same reason: poor eyesight. Messiaen became a medical auxiliary, Shostakovich a fireman: a famous photograph shows him peering from under his tin helmet with the unreadable expression always imparted by his thick spectacles. Messiaen was captured and held in POW camp Stalag VIII-A in Silesia.

Britten's encounters with the inmates of concentration camps, and the music that flowed from them, was entirely different. In July 1945 he accompanied the violinist Yehudi Menuhin on a concert tour playing to camp survivors, travelling 'in a small car over bad roads [through] destroyed towns', as he told Pears,[14] visiting Belsen and playing to people in 'appalling states', described by Menuhin as 'desperately haggard' and 'dressed in blankets'.[15] Two years earlier, just before embarking on *Grimes*, Britten had dashed off 'a short choral work for a prison camp in Germany' called Oflag VII-B, where an incarcerated musical friend, Richard Wood, had managed to set up a series of improvised concerts.[16] Similarly, in Stalag VIII-A, Messiaen discovered a few skilled musicians among his fellow inmates: a violinist, a cellist and a clarinettist, and wrote them a work 'which they played to me in the lavatories, for the clarinettist had kept his instrument with him, and someone had given the cellist a cello with three strings ... I was the music stand ...'[17] These unpromising circumstances produced one of the most remarkable works of twentieth-century music, the *Quatuor pour la fin du temps* (*Quartet for the End of Time*). Instruments patched, poster produced, the premiere took place, outside, in the rain, to 400 freezing prisoners, on 15 January 1941. Typically, the quartet's eight movements, some rearranged from earlier works, are headed by visionary, apocalyptic phrases about rainbows, birds and angels announcing the end of days. The music vividly shows all of Messiaen's most important compositional preoccupations, from the vitality of the varied, unpredictable rhythmic patterns derived from Indian *ragas* and fashioned into his own versions of rhythmic modes, to the many kinds of scale and chord based on his 'modes of limited transposition', meticulously notated birdsong as a fully integrated feature of the language (praising God in Nature in a very different musical accent from Britten's 'Cat Jeoffry' and flowers which are 'peculiarly the poetry of Christ' in *Rejoice in the Lamb*), and the long, long melodies of praise for cello and violin, the first marked 'infinitely slow' – time suspended. Britten's POW piece, *The Ballad of Little Musgrave and Lady Barnard* of 1943, is a well-mannered, beautifully executed setting of an English folk text. The contrasting responses to similar circumstances show two young composers in full control of very different visions and technical equipment.

Shostakovich's response to war, if indeed that is what his works of this period are, define his achievement, and his ambiguity, at least as far as anything can be said to be definitely 'defined' in relation to this most enigmatic of geniuses and his puzzling, troubling working and psychological environment. The key work is the Seventh Symphony. Originally conceived as a sort of Russian psalm-based Requiem, it was mostly written during, though probably planned before, the German invasion of Russia in 1941. The fourth movement was finished in Samara, in south-western Russia, in late 1941 following his family's evacuation there from Leningrad. Events around its various premieres are part of history, and not just musical history. Russian premieres were held in Kuybyshev and Moscow in March 1942. Meanwhile, the score was microfilmed and smuggled out of Russia via Tehran and Cairo: Henry Wood gave the European premiere in London in June, Toscanini in New York in July. Most famous was the Leningrad premiere on 9 August. The regular orchestra was reduced to just fifteen players by absence on active service and the tragic effects of the terrible siege of the city by the Germans from the south and the Finns to the north. Conductor Karl Eliasberg advertised for anyone who could play (a similar problem beset the premiere of *Grimes* in London four years later, through far less severely). The score was flown in by night, to dodge the blockade, and parts prepared. The performance was broadcast, not just on the radio but on loudspeakers throughout the city. Many wept. The Soviet authorities, their habitual authoritarian instincts caught off-guard by their lack of control of the besieged city, and prompted by a favourable review by the influential Alexei Tolstoy, elected to hail the work as a symbol of heroic resistance (an added layer of complication being that the despised decadent and barbarous Western powers were now Stalin's allies). The Seventh Symphony acquired the subtitle 'Leningrad', and was widely performed and thunderously received all over Russia. Opinion in the West, meanwhile, subsided from the initial sensation into puzzlement and hostility. The length, rattling repetition of the first movement's 'invasion' theme, long passages of frozen, developmentless passages for not very pretty sounding instruments, the simplistic marches, bombastic fanfares, the inclusion (as what? Parody? Socialist realism? Jokes?) of melodies from an operetta aria by Lehár and a bit of the German national anthem baffled many listeners and polarised opinion. Copland's composer colleague and fellow accessibilitarian Virgil Thomson thought the work would 'disqualify him for consideration as a serious composer'. Bartók quoted the 'invasion' theme in his 1943 *Concerto for Orchestra*.

The Seventh Symphony is a powerful, puzzling piece. Shostakovich's musical signatures are all here. So is the impossible task of trying to align his symphonies accurately with events both outside the concert hall and inside his own mind. His next symphony, the Eighth, also gained a nickname from the defining Russian events of the war, the 'Stalingrad'. Like the middle symphonies of Vaughan Williams, their exact relationship with war was, is and will remain unexplained. That is part of their power: a true and lasting testimony to something important, even if it remains unclear exactly what.

Aaron Copland said that 'the cold war is almost worse for art than the real thing'.[18] In 1953 he found himself accused of associating with imaginary communist bogeymen almost as insidious as the real ones still persecuting Shostakovich, when he was called to testify before Senator Joseph McCarthy's paranoid, self-serving fantasy, the notorious House Un-American Activities Committee. Copland calmly held his nerve in the face of McCarthy's mendacious probing:

The Chairman: 'Answer my question. Do you know anything about the Communist movement?'
Mr Copland: 'I know what I read in the newspapers.'

> The Chairman: 'Did you ever attend a Communist meeting?'
> Mr Copland: 'I am afraid I don't know how you define a Communist meeting.'[19]

Transcripts of the testimony were only released in 2003. The sinister pantomime had little effect on Copland's career (though it did on others').

McCarthy never pretended to know anything about music. Actual communists flexed their cultural muscles and sunk their revisionist claws into the notes once again in Russia in 1948 in the form of the Zhdanov Decree. Soviet composers, including Shostakovich, were denounced (again) as formalists. Only genuinely proletarian music was acceptable. Shostakovich lost his conservatory job and most of his income. His works were banned, privileges for himself and his family denied. Worse could be expected. A friend recalled that the composer 'waited for his arrest at night out on the landing by the lift, so that at least his family wouldn't be disturbed'.[20]

The feared night-time knock never came. But a bizarre pantomime was played out the following year in New York. Shostakovich was sent by Stalin as part of a delegation to the Cultural and Scientific Conference for World Peace. At a press conference he was handed a prepared speech to read out. Nervous, short-sighted, his English stumbling, he stopped midway. The speech was finished by an actor. In the audience sat the influential Russian-American émigré composer and skilled musico-political operator Nicolas Nabokov. Determined to trap Shostakovich into demonstrating that he was unable to speak freely but instead had to parrot official policy, Nabokov asked him if he supported the Russian condemnation of Stravinsky's music. Shostakovich greatly admired Stravinsky. But he couldn't say so. Nabokov had humiliated him into lying. Outside the hall, crowds clutched banners demanding he defect, recommending a route recently used by others: 'Shostakovich! Jump thru the window!'

Messiaen's engagement with active musical polemics was largely limited to founding the group La Jeune France back in 1936, an explicit reaction against the frivolity of the Cocteau of *Le Coq et l'Arlequin*. He was, by nature and circumstance, a conservative: a married, modernist, Catholic conservatoire professor and church organist. He visited the influential Darmstadt summer schools after the war, but did not buy into the modernist agenda promoted by his bullish young compatriot Pierre Boulez, prophet of a new direction and generation. Flirtations with electronics left little imprint on his music beyond a fondness for the clear, swoopy sounds of the ondes Martenot: his second wife, Yvonne Loriod, was one of its leading players, often taking the ondes part in works by her husband like the huge and hugely colourful *Turangalîla-Symphonie* of 1946–8.

Britten, too, felt a little of the chill wind of modernism leaving him out in the conservative cold as taste turned, symbolised by the reign of William Glock, dedicated defender of the avant-garde, as new music supremo at the BBC. But Britten's reputation, skill and sheer audience appeal was always enough to allow him to tread his own artistic path, led, as always, by opera: deliberately smaller-scale operas like *The Rape of Lucretia* (1946) and *The Turn of the Screw* (1954), as well as larger pieces like *Billy Budd* (1964), hailed by some as his finest opera. The *War Requiem*, first performed in 1962, focuses on the horror and pity of war in its settings of poems by Wilfred Owen inserted between the movements of the Requiem Mass; solo voices moving to individual experience from the corporate, collective statements of the chorus and a distant boys' choir, to unforgettable effect. The work was performed in the striking new Coventry cathedral, built alongside the bombed-out shell of the medieval building, which was left standing as a memorial. Copland's politics, unsurprisingly in the light of his experiences at the hands of Senator McCarthy, moved away from early leftist sympathies. The left-leaning International Congress of Composers held in Prague in 1948 echoed Zhdanov in its analysis of the alienating effect of elitist experimental music; by now, Copland shared its analysis, if not its politics or stylistic direction. He travelled in Europe to hear new Polish and Russian music, encountered and admired the work of Tōru Takemitsu in Japan, thought that electronic music exhibited a 'depressing sameness of sound' and that aleatoric (chance-based) composing left the composer 'teetering on the edge of chaos'.[21] He updated his 1941 book *Our New Music*, a thoughtful survey of the contemporary scene, slightly altering the title to *The New Music*.

Among later musical preoccupations, Copland and, less obviously, Shostakovich explored Jewish musical themes. Shostakovich made much use of a musical cipher based on the letters of his name, like Bach, in his case spelling out the notes D, E flat, C and B natural. Copland experimented with serialism in his *Piano Fantasy*, written in 1951–7, regarding its technicalities not as scientific gospel but as 'nothing more than an angle of vision. Like fugal treatment.'[22] For Copland, a twelve-tone row was just another resource of melody, capable of being used in a tonal context; Britten and Shostakovich adopted a similar approach in, respectively, *The Turn of the Screw* and the Fourteenth Symphony, a Mahlerianly death-laden song cycle completed in 1969 and dedicated to Britten. (The two composers met in 1960 through their mutual friend, the cellist Mstislav Rostropovich, finding an instinctive friendship despite only being able to communicate in 'Aldeburgh Deutsch'.) Britten's engagement with religion remained to a large extent that of the paid professional: composing a commissioned Te Deum was 'like setting the phone book to music'.[23]

Shostakovich's political prestidigitations had a couple more cards to play. When Stalin died in 1953, many pieces emerged from the desk drawer where they had remained hidden. In 1960 he joined the Communist Party. Why? Blackmail? Pressure? Cowardice? Commitment? The offer of the post of General Secretary of the Composers' Union from the less repressive Khrushchev? The motives of the nervous, obsessive and highly strung Shostakovich are as difficult to read as his expression seen through the shape-shifting lenses of his thick specs. In 1962 he married his third wife, Irina, three decades his junior, the happiest of his marriages.

Later life held the usual highlights of honours, illness, retrospectives and critical evaluation. (Britten told his friend Michael Tippett the whole business made him feel like he was already dead and the musicologists were busy with the corpse.) Health problems dogged both Britten and Shostakovich; Messiaen managed to compose fluently to the last; Copland found his ideas drying up, 'exactly as if someone had simply turned off a faucet',[24] and turned increasingly to conducting.

What remains is the music. Each composer left a distinctive body of work, capturing four different personalities through a range of technical and artistic choices forged through observing the same century from different standpoints.

Like Mozart and Verdi, Britten's vision was essentially dramatic, his medium words and the human voice, most often and importantly the voice of his partner, muse and interpreter, Peter Pears. He once said, 'My struggle all the time was to develop a consciously-controlled professional technique.'[25] The song '*Veggio co' bei vostri occhi un dolce lume*' ('I See a Sweet Light with Your Beautiful Eyes'), Sonnet XXX, from the *Seven Sonnets of Michelangelo* of 1940, gives a clear insight into a particular way in which he fashioned that control. Many passages in Britten's music are structured around ostinato patterns of some kind. Here, a simple repeated G major triad has flowing triplet melodies added both above and below. Then a second triadic element is carefully introduced: F sharp major. The repeated chord begins to move out from its G major anchor, briefly putting down roots in B major. When the composer leads us back to G major and, at the same time, the two triplet melodies briefly coincide, the destination of the opening material is revealed. At the same time, music and words tell us that sun and moon, melody and harmony, G and F sharp, voice and piano, singer and player, Britten and Pears, have come together as one. That is what the most impeccably 'controlled' of any 'technique' of the century can do. And it is a very beautiful song.

Shostakovich leaves us guessing. There is something obsessive in his music, as in his character (he would apparently often send himself letters to test the efficiency of the postal service). The Eleventh Symphony of 1957 opens with discomfiting bits of folk song played in odd areas of the orchestra – flute, bass, timpani – but they give the strange and unsettling impression of moving separately, like slow-moving glaciers which never meet. Structure gives way to an inexorable sequence of events, leading to a cataclysmic conclusion. In the long series of string quartets, the most simplistic rhythms can alternate with frozen fugues, grotesque melodies, twelve-tone tunes simply told, and his personal D. S. C. H. motto repeated like the pulsing voice of something unseen. Death, perhaps?

Messiaen's technical preoccupations are quite different but equally compelling. He helps us understand those processes by having done us the enormous favour of writing them down in detail in a textbook of his early development and style, *La Technique de mon langage musicale* (*The Technique of My Musical Language*), in 1944. Chapters on rhythm take us through his investigations of Indian music to 'added values' (irregular mixings of groups of two and three units, which Tippett called 'additive rhythms') and 'non-retrogradable rhythms' (i.e. ones which are the same backwards as forwards, or palindromes). Melodies and scales are categorised under his 'Theory of the Modes of Limited Transpositions' (scales which only exist in a limited number of versions: transposing a whole tone scale up by semitones, for example, will give only two different versions before the first one is repeated: the octatonic scale, comprising alternating tones and semitones, has three possible transpositions). His chapter on chords – headed, appropriately, 'Harmony, Debussy, Added Notes' – sets out exactly how his exotic piles of notes are constructed and how they fit together. It is all as clear and as detailed as the best medieval treatise. And it bears the same relation to the music: this is no mathematical formula, but complex, thrilling, instantly communicative and intensely musical artifice and artistry. Listen to the varied sounds and rhythms of the *Quatuor pour la fin du temps*, or the block-like sections of '*Dieu parmi nous*' ('God Among Us') from *La Nativité du Seigneur* (1935), arriving at its end on a glorious E major chord from fizzingly dissonant, colourful and utterly logical directions. *Turangalîla* makes sheer orchestral sound as shamelessly as anything of the century, with plenty of Hollywood kitsch, splashes of Gershwin and even a dash of MGM cartoon thrown in. *Des Canyons aux étoiles (From the Canyons to the Stars)* (1971), a sonic evocation of Bryce Canyon, Utah, conjures colours and the songs of stars and birds in its extraordinary array of percussion, piano, ondes Martenot and chattering wind instruments. Photographs show Messiaen standing among the red-gold rocks of the canyon, manuscript and pencil in hand, trademark beret droopily perched on his head, carefully cocked like the golden oriole or *moqueur polyglotte* whose song he is straining to hear and transfigure into music of unique colour, personality and power.

Copland's moment comes from the wide spaces of America, too, but his is a Midwest of people, not birds or angels: *Rodeo*, *Appalachian Spring*, *Billy the Kid* and cheerful arrangements of *Old American Songs* (1950 and 1952) like 'At the River', 'Ching-a-Ring-Chaw', 'I Bought Me a Cat' and 'Simple Gifts'. One of the most instantly recognisable of all twentieth-century compositions is his *Fanfare for the Common Man*, which he wrote in 1942 to honour the ordinary American at income tax time, as he told conductor Eugene Goossens. He disagreed with Stravinsky about emotion in music, calling composition 'the product of the emotions',[26] and agreed with Britten about the importance of a 'consciously-controlled technique': 'I've spent most of my life trying to get the right note in the right place.'[27] It's a gift to be simple.

Composers often act as unreliable guides to their own art. History is full of signposts pointing the wrong way and dense thickets, some planted deliberately. Shostakovich even managed a posthumous layer of obfuscation when the book *Testimony* by Solomon Volkov appeared in 1979, four years after his death, claiming to be based on conversations with him: even his son Maxim gave contradictory assessments of its authenticity at different times. Britten spoke little about music in public; comments in private letters always have to be read in the context of the relationship between writer and reader and the composer's needs and preoccupations at the time. Messiaen enjoyed the occasional metaphor drawn from his background in a family of poets and Shakespeareans, on one occasion saying about his use of rhythm: 'Remember the witches in Macbeth: "'til Birnam wood remove to Dunsinane ..." – The miracle arrives: the forest is on the march!'[28] The preface to *La Technique de mon langage musical* begins with the guarded statement: 'It is always dangerous to speak of oneself.'[29]

Copland was perhaps the most articulate and willing to speak about music of the four. Perhaps it is to him, then, that we can leave a couple of reflections which find different resonance in the life and work of each, and by doing so say something about the century they reflected so faithfully: 'You cannot make art out of fear and suspicion ... I must believe in the ultimate good of the world and of life as I live it in order to create a work of art.'[30]

Part Eight

STOCKHAUSEN AND *SGT. PEPPER*
(1945–2000)

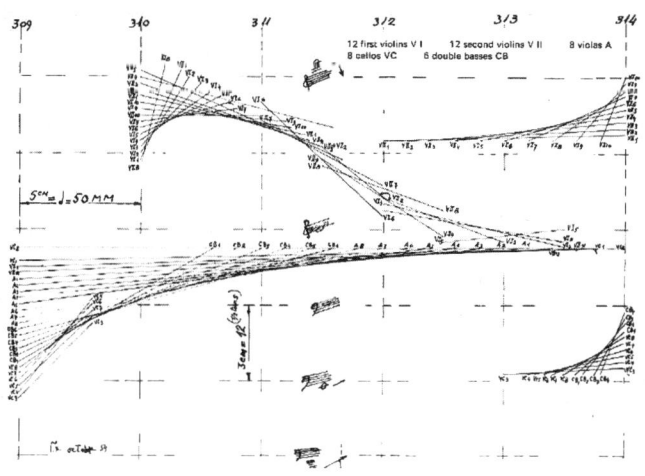

INTRODUCTION

As a young man in the 1940s, the modernist composer Pierre Boulez declared that opera houses were 'full of dust and shit' and should be 'burned down'.[1] The irony is that Boulez was part of a musical generation whose identity was forged, like Blake's Tyger, in a cosmic, pan-Continental immolation which succeeded in achieving exactly that.

All across Europe, concert halls and theatres had been blown away. In London, the Proms were forced to flee their bombed-out home at the BBC's Queen's Hall in Langham Place and find refuge in the Royal Albert Hall. In the flattened heart of Germany, the Berliner Philharmoniker gave its concerts in a cinema. Composers put up their own monuments, too: *A Child of Our Time* and the *War Requiem* by Tippett and Britten, friends and pacifists; *A Survivor from Warsaw* and a *Threnody for the Victims of Hiroshima* by Schoenberg and Krzysztof Penderecki, modernists from different generations and different corners of Europe; the eerie turbulence of Vaughan Williams's middle symphonies and the duplicitous abstractions of Shostakovich's Seventh.

For the younger generation of composers, it wasn't just the concert halls and opera houses that had gone up in flames. The old musical certainties, evoked with such desire and longing in the late works of Richard Strauss, were gone, too. Partly this was just the natural turning of the generations; but it was given immediacy and urgency by the physical and political circumstances of musical Europe, and indeed by the composers' own experiences of war. Many of the most militant modernists of the generation born in the mid 1920s saw unspeakable horrors first hand in early adulthood. They believed that they had not just an opportunity, but also a duty, to create the world all over again. 'The "tabula rasa" was something of my generation,' said Boulez; '[but] it was not tabula rasa for pleasure. It was necessity, because this generation had, for us, failed.'[2] The music forged in the furnace of that failure isn't always comfortable or likeable. It wasn't meant to be. It had no business, no right to be.

The period, like all others, produced its own peculiar mix of music and politics and musical politics. To some, the inevitable return of tradition seemed conservative and dull. 'Musical life is now quite normal,' wrote Paul Hindemith to the BBC music supremo William Glock after the war, 'with Furtwängler playing Brahms and Bruckner in the same way as [if] nothing happened in the past. All the hopes that something is changed since '45 are gone.'³ Real politics intruded on composers' lives, too. It assumed some ugly shapes: while Shostakovich and Copland were harried by communists and communist-haters respectively, the Greek composer Iannis Xenakis got a British tank shell in the face.

It was different being left wing in England. Alan Bush was a lifelong and committed communist, as well as an influential teacher, professor of composition at the Royal Academy of Music in London for over fifty years, author of a first-rate textbook on Palestrina counterpoint and president of the Workers' Music Association. His pro-Soviet views caused him some difficulty in the Second World War and in the Cold War that followed – his four large-scale operas of 1950–70 were all premiered in East Germany.

Taking totalitarianism out of music was as delicate as putting it in was brutal. In 1948 an American former classmate of Leonard Bernstein, a pianist from Mississippi called Carlos Moseley, took part in American efforts to undo the Nazi version of history. Moseley was chilled by a visit to Bayreuth during which Winifred Wagner, the composer's daughter-in-law, reminisced fondly about Hitler and talked of 'our Blitzkrieg'.⁴ The Americans wisely avoided letting the pendulum swing too far the other way: 'we should not give the impression of trying to regiment culture in the Nazi manner'.⁵ But their efforts did have some unintended consequences: the rule of having to include at least one piece formerly banned by the Nazis in every concert led to most programmes beginning with a Mendelssohn overture, which soon became 'ridiculous', according to an official report.⁶ Composers too tainted with ideas of Germanic nationhood to be allowed straight back into the fold included Strauss and Pfitzner, arguably understandably, but also Sibelius, whose *Finlandia* was deemed off limits. Strauss responded in 1948 with the faux innocent lushness of the *Four Last Songs*: the sound and sensuality from before the First World War run up the stylistic flagpole after the end of the Second; an extraordinary act of historical illusionism. A key step was the success of Bernstein's conducting in Munich in 1948, demonstrating that a young American could know and love German music as much as the Germans themselves, and that, therefore, this music belonged to the world.

As always, composers continued to negotiate their way through societal norms. The century continues to carry a particular narrative around the position of gay musicians. There were many ways of living a life successfully, and many found them. Others were not so fortunate: the American composer Marc Blitzstein was murdered by three sailors he had picked up in a bar in Martinique in 1964. Stockhausen's pupil Claude Vivier met a similar fate at the hands of a male prostitute in 1983, an event hauntingly prophesied in his last work, left unfinished and found on his desk.

Music continued to wrestle with the question of how, or even whether, to seek its audience's approval. In a classic essay of 1958, the modernist composer Milton Babbitt pushed his idea of 'the composer as specialist', deliberately isolated from his listener, who required training to be allowed in. The essay was published under the title 'Who Cares If You Listen?' (to Babbitt's irritation – 'of course I care if you listen,' he said).[7] The formidable American modernist Elliott Carter abandoned his earlier Neoclassical populist style:

> Before the end of the Second World War, it became clear to me, partly as a result of rereading Freud and others and thinking about psychoanalysis, that we were living in a world where this physical and intellectual violence would always be a problem and that the whole conception of human nature underlying the neoclassic aesthetic amounted to a sweeping under the rug of things that, it seemed to me, we had to deal with in a less oblique and resigned way.[8]

Critic and Schoenbergian proselyte Theodor Adorno spoke of music which 'has taken upon itself all the darkness and guilt of the world ... New music spontaneously takes aim at that final condition which mechanical music lives out hour by hour – the condition of absolute oblivion.'[9] Others found this dogma too limiting: composer György Ligeti believed that 'We must find a way of neither going back nor continuing the avant-garde. I am in a prison: one wall is the avant-garde, the other wall is the past, and I want to escape.'[10] Jazzman Thelonious Monk sat and stared at his piano, not moving for twenty minutes after the rest of his band had left the stage, addressing his own inner demons by playing to himself in his restless, pared-back style.

Complexity vs directness is itself far too simple a formulation. But, very broadly speaking, most composers plumped for one side or the other. Some intriguing individuals managed a partial mid-career clamber over the barricades, usually from dense modernism to something softer, setting to music the traditional midlife shuffle from bearded radical to comfortable conservative. Others somehow managed to do both while still maintaining a fierce integrity ('I've been called a prostitute – well, fine. In that case, so was Mozart,' said Peter Maxwell Davies on one occasion, no doubt with the familiar impish twinkle in his piercing blue eyes).[11] In any case, the composer is not always the most reliable witness to what is actually in the music. Many listeners have found elements of emotion or echoes of the past in modern music even when its composers have emphatically denied that they are there. The thoughtful and well-informed critic Donald Mitchell, reviewing writings about composers' approaches to inviting in the past, concluded that 'Boulez, in saying No, was really saying Yes'.[12]

Conscious rejection of the past found an analogue in technical process. Stockhausen said that his music permitted 'no recapitulation, no variation, no development. All that presupposes "formal procedures" – themes and motives that are repeated, varied, developed, contrasted, worked out ... All that I have abandoned' (the complete opposite of Schoenberg's version of modernism).[13] Ligeti said of the modernist aesthetic that 'to write melodies, even non-tonal melodies, was absolutely taboo. Periodic rhythm, pulsation, was taboo, not possible.'[14] Chuck Berry put it more simply: 'Roll Over Beethoven.'

Technology played its familiar role as leveller and equaliser. The key technology was electronics in all its forms. New sounds, and new ways of manipulating sound, emerged alongside the ability to amplify, record and broadcast them. A kaleidoscopic cornucopia of styles climbed out of the electronic chrysalis.

Society teemed with culture of all kinds. The classical Indian sitar player Ravi Shankar sat alongside both the Beatles and leading experimental modernists of the avant-garde. His influence can clearly be heard in both. Styles, people and ideas travelled, as they always have. American composer Paul Bowles travelled in the opposite direction to many, settling in North Africa.

Within the ambit of the classical tradition, things like the symphony and opera sought new ways to address their times. Compositional techniques included 'total serialism', applying Schoenberg's ideas of putting musical objects into sets and rows to other elements than just the notes, for example duration, dynamic and articulation. 'Punctualism' treats the individual sound as a 'point', sufficient in itself and unrelated to anything around it – like many other musical descriptors, the analogy with the term 'pointillism' in the visual arts is both useful and potentially misleading.

It is hardly a surprise that one of the effects of all this turbulence was a series of attempts at synthesising a mixed kind of style. Luigi Dallapiccola in Italy and Frank Martin in Switzerland picked up Berg's invitation to romanticise twelve-tone music. In Germany Hans Werner Henze went further. Many composers used twelve-tone rows within the context of a tonal composition.

There are several intriguing ways in which modernist composers of the post-war generation seem uncannily similar to their medieval forebears. One is an obsession in some quarters with maths. Graphs, ratios and patterns could generate sound, structure and notation. 'Magic squares', number grids with strict rules around things like repetition of integers and the sum of numbers in a row, could be used to generate patterns of pitch and rhythm by following a sequence around the square. Chance becomes an element in composition. This is another very ancient idea, exemplified by the Chinese *I Ching* (*Book of Changes*), a profound influence on John Cage in particular. Other mathematical approaches relate music to architecture, particularly in the striking music and writings of Iannis Xenakis, himself an architect as well as a composer. Boulez used maths to devise the concept of 'pitch multiplication', a way of making chords by combining the distance between notes, measured in semitones, according to pre-decided formulae. Boulez's methods actually borrow technical terms from the densely mathematical medieval practice of isorhythm: 'talea' and 'color' for the repeating patterns of, respectively, rhythm and pitch. Composers like the American La Monte Young went back to analysing pitch and tuning systems in microscopic detail, just as Pythagoras did.

Experiments with rhythm included much investigation of irregular, or 'additive', patterns, used in many different ways, often with exhilarating results. Harmony recovered from its post-Schoenberg ban, championed by tonalists like Britten, Bernstein and Hindemith, who called tonality 'the subtlest form of the earth's gravity'.[15] Writing in 1963, Donald Mitchell found this development 'explicitly out of historical true';[16] though Mitchell, by contrast with the teleological certainties of Adorno, had the grace and good sense to conclude that 'presented with the *fait accompli* of genius, history must take second place'.[17]

The welcome and always surprising voice of the individual speaks through the joyous Babel of sounds in these chapters, as it has in all musical ages.

Part Eight: Introduction

a)

[musical notation: Presto, Vln II, pp molto leggieramente e stacc., mp, pp]

b)

[I Ching hexagram table]

c)

[musical notation: Moderato ♩ = 92, Vln I, Vc, p, cresc.]

d)

[graphic score notation]

Tools from the toolbox, toys from the toybox:

a) Rhythm: the third movement of Michael Tippett's String Quartet No. 2 (1941–2) uses the irregular alternation of different groups of quavers that he called 'additive rhythms'.

b) Numbers and Chance: a hexagram from the I Ching, a classic Chinese text used by John Cage to determine pitch, rhythm, volume and other elements of his 1951 piano composition Music of Changes.

c) Melody and Harmony: Shostakovich's String Quartet No. 12 *(1968) opens with a Schoenbergian 'row' of all twelve chromatic pitches, but then turns immediately to the diatonic key of D flat major: Schoenberg's building block, assembled not in Schoenberg's way.*

d) Notation: part of the graphic score of Actions *(1971) by Krzysztof Penderecki.*

19

MODERNER THAN THOU: DARMSTADT, ELECTRONIC AND EXPERIMENTAL MUSIC, AND THE LEGACY OF SCHOENBERG

Several places played midwife to the rebirth of European modernism immediately after 1945: Donaueschingen, Munich, and the city flattened in an Allied bombing raid in September 1944, whose deputy mayor said, '[I]t will take us many years to rebuild homes, but we cannot leave people for that length of time without sustenance for the spirit and its cultural needs': Darmstadt.[1] Civic cultural advisor Wolfgang Steinecke gathered the free musical spirits of Europe like Aeolus stabling the winds. The Americans contributed money and practical help like carting a Steinway up to the castle in the back of a jeep. The Seventh Day Adventists provided another venue (once they'd been persuaded to drop their ban on booze and cigarettes).

The Darmstadt International Summer Courses for New Music began in the uncertain summer of 1946. Over the next couple of decades, they became the principal forum for the key debates about the direction of musical modernism. Participants gathered to talk, smoke, listen and make music – their own, but also plenty by earlier masters like Bartók, Stravinsky, Hindemith and Kodály, hearing much of it for the first time. Over time they were joined by critics, stage directors, electronics specialists, instrumentalists, poets and new kinds of virtuoso intellectual performers like the pianist David Tudor and the soprano Cathy Berberian.

The 'Darmstadt School'

The significance and legacy of Darmstadt centres around a small inner core of composers born in the 1920s, most of them too young to have fought in the Second World War but old enough to have witnessed its worst horrors at the most impressionable of ages.

The Italian Luigi Nono coined the term 'Darmstadt School'. His unswerving Marxism runs through his immersive style, and his work produced its share of riots and stink bombs, both verbal and actual. His *Prometeo* (*Prometheus*) of 1984–5 is subtitled 'the tragedy of listening'. In the late 1950s, Nono fell out badly with another key member of the inner circle, the German composer Karlheinz Stockhausen (which was not difficult to do), over certain musical processes in Nono's *Il canto sospeso* (*The Suspended Song*) of 1955–6, a post-Webernian take on letters written by executed victims of fascism.

Stockhausen didn't do compromise. His Darmstadt years were a period of fearsome experimentation in all the main forms and styles emerging from the modernist furnace. His later vision grew ever more grandiose: a piece for three orchestras; a string quartet requiring four helicopters; a ninety-minute meditation on a single six-note chord; a late cycle of operas which out-Wagners Wagner over its twenty-nine hours of Eastern-tinged musings on the theme of light.

Of the others in the classroom, the Frenchman Pierre Boulez pursued a somewhat contradictory career as an established and renowned conductor inside the concert halls and opera houses he claimed to want to burn down, and as a composer who found it difficult to compose (or at least to finish anything). One writer commented about him exasperatedly, 'There is always the promise of a major piece, rarely the fulfilment of it. Composing, when all is said and done, ultimately must depend on compositions.'[2] He was, perhaps, a man more written about than writing. *Le Marteau sans maître* (*The Hammer without a Master*) (1954) moved away from his total serialist self of the early 1950s ('I am trying to rid myself of my thumbprints,' he wrote to Cage),[3] setting French Expressionist poetry to music for contralto and a small ensemble containing a xylorimba, like a kind of Oriental-tinged *Pierrot lunaire*, using his signature 'pitch multiplication' technique. It remains one of his most approachable pieces. *Pli selon pli* (*Fold by Fold*) (1962) is a seventy-minute portrait of Symbolist poet Stéphane Mallarmé for soprano and orchestra, the words eventually subsumed from meaning into structure. It took thirty years to finish.

Perhaps the most conventionally musical of the school was the Italian Bruno Maderna. Maderna is less well known today than some of his more bullish contemporaries. Partly this is because he died at the age of just fifty-three (Boulez, Berio and Donatoni all wrote musical memorials for him). Partly it is because, like Boulez, he conducted and recorded a great deal. Perhaps it is partly because he often gave his pieces conventional titles like Concerto for Oboe (No. 2 is a thing of magic). His output reads as a personal path through modernism, but in traditional forms: an early Requiem and a Bartókian piano concerto, the almost Webernian *Quartetto per archi in due tempi* (*String Quartet in Two Speeds*) of 1955, electronic pieces, some serialism and an opera. But somehow, through it all, Maderna couldn't stop himself writing well-crafted, carefully heard music. One polyglot commentator on YouTube has said of his reputation: 'Maderna should be nesting like a god-hen among Beethovens, but he isn't.'[4] Surely the presiding genius of modernism would have approved of that strange and beautiful image.

The pan-national elements in Mauricio Kagel's name hint at the musical contradictions he embodied. The son of a German-Russian Jewish family who emigrated to Argentina in the decade before he was born, he once said, 'Actually, I feel a little foreign everywhere.' Pierre Boulez, on tour in Buenos Aires in 1954 with Jean-Louis Barrault's theatre company, told him, 'You have to leave: for Europe.' So he did. His journey took in Darmstadt and electronic music. Hearing klezmer music in Europe was, for him, 'a matter of rehearing melodies, and re-experiencing moods that I would never have thought could be recalled', part of 'a very remote but not forgotten world that I knew well, and that rose up again from its acoustic submersion' (rather as Vaughan Williams said about English folk song). He was wary of the avant-garde with its 'bizarre yearning for cult figures and leaders that always reminds me a bit of the infamous Führer principle' (though at times he was, and wanted to be, one of its leaders himself), and criticised its deliberate provincial narrowness: 'the avant-garde kept its ancestral gallery small out of ignorance, and was afraid of being contaminated'. He was well aware of the communication problem in modern music: 'the ivory tower has acquired some pretty audible gaps'.[5]

His own approach showed a rare consistency: 'contrary to many others, I was never subjected to any "shock" which would have caused a total change from one minute to the next'.[6] Drama and theatricality in music were constants. One piece is a tennis match for two cellists with a percussionist as umpire (we're back with Berlioz – 'the instruments are the actors').[7] He was a film-maker as well as a composer: *Ludwig van* (1970) finds Beethoven examining his own historical legacy through a wobbly hand-held camera, entering his own work room 150 years after he left it, discovering every surface covered with manuscripts, the soundtrack playing the music written on them as the camera pans across, the notes and phrases distorted by the curves and corners of the chairs and table edges over which they are draped and scattered.

This concept of 'Music Theatre' (emphatically not in the Broadway sense) was an important post-war genre also explored by Peter Maxwell Davies, Maurice Ohana, Claude Prey, Luciano Berio, Georges Aperghis and others. Like many avant-garde trends, it both created and depended on a new type of performer, in this case singers and vocal actors including Cathy Berberian and Roy Hart and their modern successors Jane Manning, Barbara Hannigan and others.

Kagel's music can do charm alongside its intellectual rigour: happier in its skin than some of its more muscularly aggressive contemporaries. Kagel said: 'Cultural osmoses that arise from mixtures always seem much more interesting to me' – a truth hard-won in his times.[8]

The year 1958 saw the explosive arrival at Darmstadt of a composer who once wrote, 'I have come to the conclusion that much can be learned about music by devoting oneself to the mushroom', John Cage.[9]

Cage studied and travelled widely and voraciously before turning to music under the guidance of Schoenberg ('a magnificent teacher … an extraordinary musical mind').[10] His restless mission was to take apart the whole idea of composition and performance. Cage's work is often characterised as 'experimental' music, a term he initially rejected but came to accept. His insights, innovations and inventions include the 'prepared piano', a kind of one-man band of screws, nuts, bolts, felt pads, scraps of paper and pieces of rubber placed on the piano strings (invented when he found he couldn't fit his battery of percussion instruments into a room booked for a performance by his dance company); the 'happening', like the piece in which an assistant shampooed his hair and cut off his tie while he played the piano; pieces where the 'score' is a verbal instruction ('perform a definite action'); the Ives-like 'musicircus' of lots of unrelated pieces going on at once; Beckett-like writings about music in his 1961 book *Silence* (as much a work of art in its own right as anything as conventional as a book about music); a question and answer session in which he said he would give the same four answers in rotation irrespective of the questions; later pieces like *Music of Changes* of 1951, devised from the chance-led reading of the *I Ching*; and, famously, in 1952, *4' 33"*, a work in three movements for any combination of instrumentalists, who sit in silence and don't play, inviting the audience to hear the room around them – notated nothingness ('I don't need sound to talk to me,' said Cage).[11]

Boulez was not the only one to have reservations about the Cageian aesthetic. Darmstadt's director Wolfgang Steinecke detected a touch of 'childish sensationalism' in some of Cage's tricks.[12] A two-piano recital at Donaueschingen featured two completely different pieces played simultaneously: critics were reminded of Charlie Chaplin and Buster Keaton playing their 'wild musical duet of broken strings and frantic chords' in the 1952 movie *Limelight*.[13] Donaueschingen's director described these events as 'a demonstration of what is possible and hardly as artistic performances in the true sense of the word'.[14]

Schoenberg famously said Cage was his only American student of any interest, adding, 'Of course, he's not a composer, but he's an inventor – of genius.'[15] This is neat, but incomplete. Cage's *Sonatas and Interludes* for prepared piano of 1946–8 and the *String Quartet in Four Parts* of 1950 are emphatically the work of a composer.

And the mushroom? Cage was a skilled mycologist, and once wrote that, in his experience, a sound, like a mushroom, must be approached afresh and treated with the respect due to its particular properties. He has, he tells us, created many delicious and tantalising experiences over the years, and also succeeded on occasion in giving both himself and others a nasty bellyache. Perhaps the comparison is apt.

Some Key Works

Total serialist pieces like Messiaen's *Mode de valeurs et d'intensités* (composed at Darmstadt in 1949) and (to an even greater extent) Boulez's *Structures I and II* of 1951 and 1961, both for piano, out-Schoenberg Schoenberg in an attempt 'to eliminate completely from my language all trace of heritage … in particular, stylistic reminiscence', as Boulez said, and 'to unify all aspects of the language' around the idea summed up in his title: structure.[16] Messiaen's piece is on three staves, with the slowest note version of the theme on the lowest, like a medieval tenor. Total serialism didn't really work. Iannis Xenakis called the effect *'un non-sens auditif et idéologique'* ('an auditory and ideological absurdity' or, more literally, 'non-sense'),[17] and the critic Donald Mitchell noted that 'the ear in performance longs for more organisation, not less'.[18] Messiaen, too, came to reject it. Perhaps serialism needed pushing up to and beyond its limits to find out where those limits lay.

Stockhausen called his 1952 orchestral piece *Punkte* (*Points*) (though the name, typically, was added later): 'music that consists of separately formed particles – however complexly these may be composed – [is called] **punctual** music, as opposed to linear, or group-formed, or mass-formed music [his bold]'.[19] Composer and Stockhausen biographer Jonathan Harvey explains: 'the musical idea ... *is* the process employed – as opposed to its being a statement that arises *within* the process [his italics]'.[20]

Maderna's *Improvvisazione No. 1* (*Improvisation No. 1*) of 1951–2 uses maths and magic squares to derive shapes which he called 'arrays'. The result, perhaps surprisingly, is a translucent and exquisitely orchestrated piece of music (perhaps less surprising in a composer who first conducted the orchestra of La Scala, Milan, at the age of seven), building to a jazzy climax which sounds like 'The Rumble' from *West Side Story*. Like Berg, Maderna organised his row into shapes you can actually hear: as with any computational process, what you get out depends on what you put in.

Cage's experiments with chance were echoed by, among others, the American composer Morton Feldman, in his works for several pianos, notated without indication of rhythm. Cage told Boulez that chance allowed 'the obtaining of oracles'.[21] Boulez sniped back in his 1957 Darmstadt lecture 'Aléa': 'Several composers of our generation show currently a constant preoccupation with chance – you might even say they are obsessed by it.'[22] For Boulez, 'aleatoric' music was like 'the plan of a city. One does not change its design ... One can choose one's own way through it, but there are certain traffic regulations'[23] (an echo of film-maker Jean-Luc Godard's observation that 'a story should have a beginning, a middle and an end, but not necessarily in that order').[24] Boulez's Piano Sonata No. 3 of 1948 explores this idea (and others), accompanied by an allusive essay borrowing its title from the Enlightenment intellectual Bernard Le Bovier de Fontenelle: *'Sonate, que me veux-tu?'* ('Sonata, What Do You Want from Me?') The piece was eternally revised and revisited, but never formally finished.

Electronics

The development which had the most far-reaching influence on late twentieth-century music (though in ways which the Darmstadters could not possibly have predicted) was electronics.

Pieces like the serialist piano sonatas, for all their avowed intent to do away with things past, still relied on the same disobedient little squiggles that all past music also relied on: notes. And not just notes, but notes of an equally tempered scale, played on a piano, in groups of quavers and semiquavers. As early as 1913 the Italian Futurist Luigi Russolo demanded that

> We must replace the limited variety of timbres of orchestral instruments by the infinite variety of timbres of noises obtained through special mechanisms ... For years, Beethoven and Wagner have deliciously shaken our hearts. Now we are fed up with them.[25]

Edgard Varèse echoed this complaint in 1939: 'We composers are forced to use ... instruments that have not changed for two centuries', and began to sketch an alternative: 'I need an entirely new medium of expression: a sound-producing machine.'[26]

As so often, Varèse's tragedy was that he was ahead of his time. His impassioned pre-war plea has a whiff of H. G. Wells about it: worlds await us, if we can only build a machine to take us there. The writer of a 1931 article headed 'Electricity, a Musical Liberator' in the New York magazine *Modern Music* agreed: 'The growth of musical art in any age is determined by the technological progress which parallels it.'[27]

That progress produced a marvellous menagerie of musical beasts: the Telharmonium (1897); the ondes Martenot (much loved by Messiaen) and Theremin (played by moving the hands without touching it) in the 1920s. In the 1930s the Hammond organ brought fully polyphonic electronic sound into home and church (and provided a kind of cut-price substitute jazz orchestra for virtuosos like 'The Incredible' Jimmy Smith), courtesy of inventor Laurens Hammond, pioneer of (among other things) 3-D glasses, the automatic gearbox and a self-shuffling bridge table. Advances in magnetic tape allowed composers and engineers to quite literally chop sound up and stick it back together. Sampling advanced through the 1950s, noted by Dr Werner Meyer-Eppler, chief scientist to the Darmstadt court, in his 1950 lecture 'The Sound World of Electronic Music'.

The year 1951 saw the first known recordings of music made entirely by a computer. Seven hundred miles north-west of Darmstadt, in Manchester, a BBC *Children's Hour* presenter called Auntie heard a computer called Baby stumble its way through 'God Save the King', 'Baa Baa Black Sheep' and part of 'In the Mood'. The programming manual was written by no less a figure than the great Alan Turing. Operator Christopher Strachey, a talented pianist, stayed up all night 'in front of this enormous machine with four or five rows of twenty switches and things, in a room that felt like the control-room of a battleship', ploughing through Turing's labyrinths of code. By the time Turing strolled in the next morning the exhausted but elated Strachey had Baby gurgling its way through its limited repertoire. 'Good show,' said Turing.[28]

Robert Moog achieved mass sales for his synthesised version of a perhaps unlikely composer with the album *Switched-on Bach* of 1968, played one line at a time onto tape by the composer, scientist and musician Wendy Carlos. The 1970s and 1980s replaced analogue synthesisers with digital and brought innovations like the MIDI interface, which allowed electronic musical devices to talk to each other, and ubiquitous irritations like 'chip' music, the chirpy voice of the early 1980s Pac-Man machine in the corner of the pub.

Composers played with their new toys from the first squeaks and sparks, like the medieval mason pondering his pointed arch. Percy Grainger and Darius Milhaud mucked around with the playing speeds of gramophone records as far back as the 1920s and 1930s. Paul Hindemith put an electronic instrument in a conventional setting with his *Concerto for Solo Trautonium and Orchestra* of 1931. In 1939 John Cage dreamed of an *Imaginary Landscape*, which is 'not a physical landscape. It's a term reserved for the new technologies. It's a landscape in the future.'[29]

Electronic composition really took off alongside rapid advances in technology in the 1950s. Maderna and Varèse combined tape with live instruments in *Musica su due dimensioni* (*Music in Two Dimensions*) (1958) and *Déserts* (1954) respectively. Luciano Berio got his wife Cathy Berberian to read James Joyce's *Ulysses* into a microphone in *Thema (Omaggio a Joyce)* (*Theme (Hommage to Joyce)*) of 1958, claimed as the first piece to use live electronic manipulation of the human voice.

Experiment centred in cities with the right facilities: Stockhausen at the studios of Westdeutscher Rundfunk in Cologne; Boulez, Messiaen and Xenakis at Radiodiffusion-Télévision Française in Paris (home from 1970 to the futuristic IRCAM studios next to the Centre Georges Pompidou); Nono, Maderna and Berio in Milan (Cage, visiting in 1958, renamed one of his pieces after his Italian landlady, Signora Fontana). London housed a studio in a converted Edwardian roller-skating rink, the BBC Radiophonic Workshop, where Ron Grainer and Delia Derbyshire used multiple reel-to-reel recordings of sounds made on hand-operated oscillator and a bass line sampled from a single note to create one of the most iconic of all electronic pieces, the 1963 theme to the time-travelling TV show *Doctor Who*.

The geographical separation between Cologne and Paris symbolised a philosophical divide between the German concept of *elektronische Musik*, which favoured pure electronically generated sounds, and the French ideas of *musique concrète* and *objets sonores*, which used 'found sounds' from the real world – footsteps, voices, a bus going past – as the basis for manipulation and composition. Stockhausen married the two in *Gesang der Jünglinge* (*Song of the Youths*) of 1956. The voice of the machine interweaves with the eerie sound of a boy's voice, part singing, part speaking. The Old Testament story is deconstructed by linking the components of vocal production (plosives, fricatives, sibilants) to electronic sound to make scurrying, chattering patterns of other-worldly coloratura. Five-track recording creates spatial effects, so that the music seems to run around the room. It's a fascinating piece, a mixture of the fiercely modern and the unimaginably ancient, the voice of a child and the sounds of outer space – compelling, startling and strangely musical. Berio's *Visage* takes apart Berberian's voice, piling tears and terror onto pure electronic sound, settling on a moment of stillness for the only complete word in the piece: '*parole*' ('word').

Electronic pieces don't really need a score, because nobody has to play from one. Sometimes, however, a graphic 'realisation' would be added later as part of the artwork. In 1970 the graphic designer Rainer Wehinger made a 'listening score' to go with Ligeti's tape piece *Artikulation*, composed twelve years earlier: multi-coloured blobs, swirls and comb-like objects provide a mildly hallucinogenic visual echo of the sounds on the tape, giving the eye something to follow.

A key concept is electro-acoustic music, involving manipulation of acoustic sound, from the experiments of Karel Goeyvaerts in the early 1950s through Alvin Lucier's repeatedly layered *I Am Sitting in a Room* of 1969, the ambient pop of Jean-Michel Jarre in the 1970s, and Phil Kline's 1992 *Unsilent Night* for cassettes in boomboxes.

The legacy of these electronic experiments is everywhere, perhaps more outside the concert hall than in.

Ligeti, Berio and Some Contemporaries

These ideas and innovations went forth and reacted with the rest of the remarkable generation born in the 1920s. Sparks were bound to fly.

György Ligeti was one of the most original creators in all music. Chance survivor of the hideous violence and repression which engulfed his native Transylvanian region of Hungary, and his family, in the years around the war, his stylistic journey was a kind of speeded-up personal history of Western thought: enforced pre-enlightenment isolationism (the 'prehistoric Ligeti')[30] in politically isolated provincial Hungary, where modernism was a kind of musical Schrödinger's cat – he had no way of knowing that it actually existed; folk music absorbed from his teacher Kodály; Stravinskian modernism in the manic *Six Bagatelles for Wind Quintet* of 1953 (like Bartók on speed); Darmstadt and dodecaphony after he fled Hungary for Vienna in 1956 in the wake of the Soviet crackdown following the Hungarian Uprising; avant-garde electronica like *Artikulation* (1958); the traditional falling-out with Stockhausen at Cologne *circa* 1960 ('there were [sic] a lot of political infighting because different people, like Stockhausen, like Kagel wanted to be first. And I, personally, have no ambition to be first or to be important');[31] a unique and brilliant synthesis in pieces like the two sets of *Aventures (Adventures)* for voices and instruments of 1962–6 and an eclectic 'non-atonal' theatrical goulash of quotations and pastiche in later works like the foul-mouthed opera *Le Grand Macabre* (1977) – Bruegel in the Big Top (the title is usually left untranslated in English references, but might come out as something like *The Big Horrible*). He wrote a prelude for car horns and a symphony for metronomes. Ligeti was the Pagliaccio of the modernists, a brilliant clown whose Puckish fireworks deepen the darkness behind.

The Italian composer Luciano Berio was born, like Ligeti, in the mid 1920s and, also like Ligeti, felt the effects of the war when an accident with a gun on his very first day as a young conscript into Mussolini's army ended his aspirations as a pianist. His *Sinfonia* of 1968–9 is a work of cultural theory as much as a musical composition: in a brilliant piece of performance art, which is both intellectual and entertaining, singers chat to each other to a pattering backing track of Mahler and much else, paired with a slow elegy for Martin Luther King. The long sequence of pieces, written from 1958 to 2002, called *Sequenza*, each for a different solo instrument, pushes the potentialities of performance to acrobatic and sometimes seemingly physically impossible extremes.

Hans Werner Henze joined the Hitler Youth at the insistence of his father. He denied that the bursts of 'late Romantic exuberance' in his music sound like pumped-up Richard Strauss, but they do;[32] the generous outpourings for soprano voice in *Nachtstücke und Arien* of 1957 sound as if Strauss's *Four Last Songs* weren't quite the last after all. In his search for a 'living, modern music in all its baroque opulence', the dinner-jacketed Marxist deliberately distanced himself from his Darmstadt contemporaries:

> It may seem far-fetched, but I have often thought that their attempt to make music non-communicative had something to do with the ruling class's belief that art is a thing apart from life, better kept that way, and without any social dimension. The reason why this non-communicative tendency, which possessed a mystical, indeed expressly Catholic element, was so vigorously promoted was, I think, the desire to prevent people from seeing music as a simple, concrete and comprehensible communication between human beings.[33]

Elsewhere he put it more bluntly: 'ugly people get ugly music'.[34]

These debates about doctrinal disputes in music make these musicians sound like their Renaissance forebears. Music was their vocation, modernism their theology, Darmstadt their Council of

Trent. The problem was that they could never quite agree which of them was St Paul.

Iannis Xenakis trained as an engineer and fled his native Greece under sentence of death after fighting the British on the streets of Athens,

> tormented by guilt at having left the country for which I'd fought. I left my friends – some were in prison, others were dead, some managed to escape. I felt I was in debt to them and that I had to repay that debt. And I felt I had a mission. I had to do something important to regain the right to live. It wasn't just a question of music – it was something much more significant.[35]

Alongside voracious musical studies he worked as an architect with two modernist greats, Ernö Goldfinger and Le Corbusier. Messiaen declined to teach him, saying, 'You are almost thirty, you have the good fortune of being Greek, of being an architect and having studied special mathematics. Take advantage of these things. Do them in your music.'[36]

Le Corbusier believed that 'Architecture is judged by eyes that see, by the head that turns, and the legs that walk. Architecture is not a synchronic phenomenon but a successive one, made up of pictures adding themselves one to the other, following each other in time and space, like music.'[37] Xenakis designed the windows for Le Corbusier's priory of Sainte Marie de La Tourette near Lyons, using what one observer has called 'a sort of vertical polyphony'.[38] 'Polytopes' are buildings which use speakers and lights to embed sound and colour into their design. He used the naturally occurring mathematical phenomenon of the hyperbolic paraboloid in both the Philips Pavilion, designed for the Expo '58 exhibition in Brussels, and the graphic score of *Metastasis* (1955), for orchestra. He placed performers around halls and among audiences, because 'space first and foremost has the task of allowing sound to be heard properly'.[39] His two books about what he calls 'stochastic music', *Musique Architecture* (1971) and *Musiques formelles* (1963), contain more algebra than conventional musical analysis.

Xenakis's music is physical rather than emotional: '[T]he idea of sound as beautiful or ugly makes no sense ... the level of intelligence carried by sounds must be the true criteria for the validity of such music'; 'to make music is to express human intelligence through the medium of sound'.[40]

Of course, there were as many ways through the modernist dialectic as there were composers. The Belgian Henri Pousseur began his opera *Votre Faust* (*Your Faust*) (1960–68) with a character saying he has an idea for an opera. The Italian Sylvano Bussotti draped musical staves on the page in overtly sensual human or other form, like the fourteenth-century ars subtilior, and booked a well-known prostitute to give the opening speech at the 1991 Venice Biennale, where he was director (though not for much longer), as if life was a scene from Ligeti's *Le Grand Macabre*. His fellow Italian Franco Donatoni saw himself as 'not an artist but an artisan',[41] writing witty, carefully crafted pieces with undemonstrative titles like *Small; Short; Sweet Basil (for Trombone and Big Band)*, and tottering around Verona on a bicycle.

The German Bernd Alois Zimmermann described himself as 'the oldest of these young composers'.[42] Like Donatoni, he suffered terribly from depression. A highly personal technique of layering music of many kinds on top of gesture and action embodied his idea of the 'spherical shape of time', in which all time periods can be experienced simultaneously. His huge 1965 opera *Die Soldaten* (*The Soldiers*) is played out concurrently on three stages. Zimmermann took his own life in August 1970, shortly after finishing *Ich wandte mich und sah an alles Unrecht, das geschah unter der Sonne* (a setting of Martin Luther's scriptural paraphrase, rendered in the English King James Bible as 'So I returned, and considered all the oppressions that are done under the sun'), which ends (like Berg's Violin Concerto) with Bach's setting of Christ's plea for an end to his earthly suffering: '*Es ist genug*' ('It is enough'). Perhaps, if the Classical ideal was the balancing of contrasting elements in the human psyche, the tragedy of twentieth-century art was facing up to what happened when that was no longer possible.

Some Trends in Europe and Elsewhere

As in the medieval period, ideas and influences made their way around Europe in the later twentieth century, interacting with the traditions and character of the countries where they found themselves.

Modernism was always rather under the radar in conservative England, but it found some powerful advocates like Schoenberg disciple Humphrey Searle, Marxist Alan Bush and the eclectic former choirboy Cornelius Cardew, who moved from the complexity of the Webernian ideal to simple songs in praise of Chairman Mao, and was killed in a still-unexplained hit and run car accident in north London in 1981.

Polish symphonists Witold Lutosławski and Andrzej Panufnik found distinctive ways of negotiating both their musical inheritance and state intervention in the arts, Lutosławski in the 'post-tonal' pitch organisation of the *Concerto for Orchestra* of 1950–54, Panufnik in many works for leading orchestras written after a dramatic defection to London in 1954. Their younger contemporary Henryk Górecki took Polish symphonism away from his earlier Webernian manner to something simple and direct, in works like the celebrated *Symphony of Sorrowful Songs* of 1976, and Catholic works, many associated with the election of Karol Wojtyła as pope in 1978, like the contemplative motet *Totus Tuus* of 1987. Poland specialised in building elements of chance in performance into big acoustic scores, for example, Krzysztof Penderecki's searing *Threnody for the Victims of Hiroshima* of 1960 for strings, which uses a form of graphic notation: single lines instead of staves; time measured out in seconds not beats; pitch and vibrato indicated in blocks of inky black and wandery, wavy lines.

Ligeti approaches the same aim by diametrically opposite means. In the haunting *Lux Aeterna* (*Eternal Light* – words extracted from the Requiem Mass) of 1966 (memorably used by director Stanley Kubrick in the film *2001: A Space Odyssey*), rhythm is notated in microscopic detail to make music without audible rhythm, a technique he called 'micropolyphony'. The conductor beats four (including for several bars after the singers have stopped), but you can't hear it.

In both cases, the composer sacrifices audible rhythm and individual pitch to the sheer quality of sound, or timbre. Penderecki achieves this by abrogating some decisions about what noise his performers make and when; Ligeti by controlling those decisions in forensic detail.

This privileging of timbre found its ideal technological tool in the rapid advances in computing into the 1970s. A musical score, as musico-engineer David M. Koenig points out, is 'a plot of frequency vs. time'.[43] Koenig pursued the logic of this insight by transcribing part of Louis Armstrong's 'West End Blues' as a bar graph. Turning this rise and fall into shapes on a computer screen means sound can be seen, analysed, deconstructed and moved around like smoke in a bell jar. Shapes emerge and morph like the graphic scores of Penderecki or Xenakis. Composing by analysing and manipulating the full spectrum of sound became known as 'spectralism'. The Brahms/Schoenberg tradition of valuing the function of a note over its sound is bypassed (or ignored). It's an aural philosophy which can be quite easily traced back through the simple harmonies and lavish orchestral detail of Ravel's sunrise in *Daphnis et Chloé* or the Vorspiel to *Parsifal*, and forward to the work of French composers Tristan Murail and Gérard Grisey in landmark works like *Gondwana* (1980) and *Les Espaces acoustiques* (*Acoustic Spaces*) (1974–7).

One of the most striking pieces to fuse electronic and acoustic elements is *Cantus Arcticus*, subtitled 'Concerto for Birds and Orchestra', written in 1972 by the Finnish composer Einojuhani Rautavaara, layering tape recordings of birdsong from the Arctic north onto live orchestral sound. In a shrinking world, French influences show up as far away as Japan in the works of Tōru Takemitsu, fused with native traditions in a technique he called a 'sea of tonality', a somehow appropriately French image.[44]

In the folk-flavoured centre of musical Europe the Romanian-born György Kurtág found his voice, after much study and struggle, in miniature piano pieces (often played by himself alongside his wife, Márta), like the ongoing almost-autobiographical ten volumes of *Játékok* (*Games*), a sort of Pepys' diary for piano, and much Bach, exquisitely arranged. Elsewhere in eastern Europe, the Czech Petr Eben took some aspects of modernism up the stairs to the conservative Catholic organ loft, although in a less obviously experimental way than his contemporary Messiaen.

Some ideas end up facing in completely the opposite direction from where they started. *Musique concrète instrumentale* ought to be a contradiction in terms. Helmut Lachenmann, born a decade or so after Stockhausen, in 1935, makes unconventional noises from conventional sources: playing without mouthpiece or reed; pinching a string between the fingers; turning a timpani upside down and whacking it on its metal bottom. One critic has described Lachenmann's source material as 'sounds that were marginal and overlooked, sounds with a lot of noise in them'.[45] Lachenmann himself has written widely about his aesthetic and technical preoccupations.

Lachenmann, now in his ninth decade, and Kurtág, now in his tenth, bring very different aspects of the *zeitgeist* of the 1950s avant-garde banging and whispering into the twenty-first century. It can be a bit confusing. That *zeitgeist* always carried with it a sense of cultural and historical dislocation. It still does.

The US, of course, did things its own way. Minimalism solves the challenge of what to do with outdated, inherited things like tunes by paring music back to its simplest component elements, presented in hypnotic, repeating patterns. The problem is that if you deliberately remove the things which composers have always used to create interest (structure, melody, changes of texture and harmony), then you have to replace them with something else. The best minimalists do this through complex, carefully controlled, shape-shifting patterns of rhythm, and an old-fashioned ear for the beauty of sheer sound. Less successful minimalists don't. There is a lot of dull minimalism; and it's a style which can do dull numbingly successfully.

West Coast minimalism is different from East Coast minimalism. Classic works of the former are *In C* by Terry Riley (1968) and Steve Reich's *Clapping Music* (1972) and *Electric Counterpoint* (1987), beguiling steps along the road of playing with patterns falling in and out of phase. The East Coast variety has a little more of the arty indulgence of the New York loft. La Monte Young has called himself 'the most important composer since the beginning of music', too famous even to allow actual performances of his works.[46] Philip Glass's operas have chugged around the world, spreading the iconic sounds of minimalism without always overcoming its inherent limitations.

At its best, the style is inclusive and wide-reaching. In Reich's *Different Trains* (1988) it movingly commemorates the Holocaust by placing recorded speech against a live string quartet. It can make genre, and even history, seem to disappear: Young and Reich incorporated their investigations of rhythmic patterns in Indian and African music; *Electric Counterpoint* (1987) was written for the jazz guitarist Pat Metheny. In a strange time-travelling trick which tells us something about how this music works, much earlier pieces can sound oddly minimalist when the composer sets an accompaniment jogging before bringing in the tune: try the beginning of Tchaikovsky's overture *The Tempest*, or even parts of the opening movement of Beethoven's 'Pastoral' Symphony.

Another group of Americans remained committed to the ideals of post-Webernian modernism: Morton Feldman, Milton Babbitt and the ageless Elliott Carter, who heard the US premiere of *The Rite of*

Spring as a teenager in 1924, and was still composing fluently shortly before his death in 2012 at the age of 103.

'Call That Going? Call That On?'[47]

Of course, 'the choice' has other answers. Orchestral craftsmen like the Frenchman Henri Dutilleux and the BBC's Robert Simpson loyally pursued the example of, respectively, Debussy and Nielsen in symphonies and concertos. Dutilleux's friend and fellow conservative Maurice Ohana's 1988 opera *La Célestine* was performed at the Paris Opéra. Even church music found a way to be new(-ish) in the hands of practitioners from different sides of the Reformation divide, like the Parisian Maurice Duruflé and Herbert Howells, son of that most musical of English counties, Gloucestershire, allowing just a hint of blues harmony and mildly astringent melody to mingle with the incense. The American Ned Rorem wrote art songs and short operas, French-style, and the notorious *Paris Diary* of 1966 describing his sexual encounters in the early 1950s with many celebrated men of music, outing some of them in the process. England produced the fearsome 'New Complexity' of Brian Ferneyhough and Michael Finnissy, and the remarkable creative achievement of the group loosely known as the Manchester School, especially, perhaps, in their stage works: Harrison Birtwistle being the most visceral; Alexander Goehr the most loyally Schoenbergian/intellectual; and Peter Maxwell Davies the most eclectic and wide-ranging. Maxwell Davies's operas remain among the most dramatic and theatrically gripping examples of the genre, including *Eight Songs for a Mad King* of 1969 and 1979's chilling *The Lighthouse*.

Then there are the outsiders. Harry Partch built instruments with up to forty-three pitches per octave and rode the railroads as a hobo. Conlon Nancarrow spent his days punching holes in card to create his inhumanly virtuosic (and thrilling) *Studies for Player Piano*, composed between 1948 and 1992. Kaikhosru Shapurji Sorabji lived quietly in Dorset, writing vast piano works which he refused to allow anyone to play. Moondog was a skilled contrapuntalist, blinded in a farm accident at the age of sixteen, friend of Benny Goodman and Arturo Toscanini, who invented tuning systems and instruments including the 'oo', a kind of harp, and spent his days standing on the corner of 53rd Street and 6th Avenue in New York wearing a Viking helmet. It is surely not wrong to find aspects of the psychologically extreme in the way these men used music in lives they shared with farmhands and street-dwellers rather than concert-goers and college professors.

The Great Communicator

The last word belongs to the composer who perhaps came closest to unifying the multifarious strands of influence, inheritance and technique of the twentieth century into something coherent: Leonard Bernstein. Like his century and his nation, Bernstein was made of contradictions: a married, gay, Jewish, Catholic jazz musician who knew the European classics better than anyone else who had conducted the Bavarian State Opera Orchestra (or so they told him). The elements don't always mix: his 'Kaddish' Symphony of 1963 juxtaposes hard atonality with lush tunes in a way which even its composer didn't find entirely convincing; as a conductor his wallowing in Mahler succeeds, but his Elgar can sound mannered. He tried to pretend that, in *West Side Story* (1957), he had written a grand opera. He hadn't.

What he had written was simply the greatest musical of all time (and it does no harm to have Stephen Sondheim, Arthur Laurents and Jerome Robbins as your co-creators, not to mention John Kander, later to write *Cabaret* and *Chicago*, as your rehearsal pianist). It is otiose to talk about the best tune of the century, but the 7/4 theme from the overture to *Candide* (1956) must (to paraphrase the football manager Brian Clough) be in the top one. He wrote about music with the same inclusive generosity with which he wrote and made the music itself, defending tonality with the same theological intensity as those who rejected it: 'I believe that from the Earth emerges a musical poetry, which is by the nature of its sources tonal ... idioms can all merge into a speech universal enough to be accessible to all mankind.' After Gershwin, he was the only composer to seriously attempt to bring the benefits of a classically trained technique to bear on a popular style, an idea which has not yet been sufficiently picked up by any possible successors.

His achievement, and his ambiguities, are perhaps best summed up in his own concluding words to the series of lectures he named after a work by an earlier giant of American music: 'I believe that ... Ives' *Unanswered Question* has an answer. I'm no longer quite sure what the question is, but I do know that the answer is Yes.'[48]

This has been a chapter of many colours. Not everybody liked the other guy's colour scheme: Luigi Nono apparently once smashed an expensive dinner plate on the floor at the mere mention of Hans Werner Henze's name.

The post-war avant-garde asked questions which demanded to be asked, without perhaps always answering them. Writing in 1965, Donald Mitchell said, '[W]hat the avant-garde needs is a composer.'[49] Has there been one? Who was it?

Perhaps modernism worked best when it allowed itself to move outside the demands of dogma and make music, as Maderna did. His legacy is that composers today don't have to worry about doing things that would have made Nono chuck an entire dinner service on the floor. Nono was wrong – it isn't a sin to seek beauty in past models: nor to seek to look forward; or indeed to do both.

Equally, experimental modernism created sounds for the world to sing. John Cage and his aunt Phoebe made music by hitting radiators with sticks: Leroy Anderson wrote a concerto for typewriter. Electronic *musique concrète* influenced everything from R2-D2 to the Clangers. Spectralism shows up in *Sgt. Pepper's Lonely Hearts Club Band* and *The Dark Side of the Moon*.

It was an age of getting sound to perform.

20

INDUSTRY AND ARTISTRY: POP MUSIC

Popular music has hummed and strummed its way through the whole of this story. But its fundamental form hasn't really changed in all that time – the song.

'Popular' means 'of the people', rather than of an educated elite. In musical terms, that translates into a basic simplicity and directness: a tune, supporting the mood and meaning of words through its rise and fall, with or without harmony which can be added by any instrument to hand.

In the middle of the twentieth century a combination of forces took popular music in new directions, without fundamentally changing its role and meaning. Technology allowed it to project beyond its local context. Money, marketing and media found and fed a mass audience. Perhaps above all, social changes spawned a whole interlocking ecosystem of groups, subgroups, troupes, tribes, cliques, clubs and classes, each with its own identity and achingly nuanced badges of authenticity. Music, as always, allowed them to code and communicate this information (and annoy their parents). Popular became pop.

Two Nations Divided by a Common Language: UK and USA

Music historian Colin Larkin explains how popular music emerged from its pre-war antecedents on both sides of the Atlantic: 'Rock'n'roll, jazz, blues, R&B, soul and country music emanated from the USA, and consequently America "invented" Muddy Waters, Hank Williams, Louis Armstrong, Elvis Presley, Frank Sinatra, Billie Holliday, Ella Fitzgerald, Patsy Cline and Bob Dylan. The UK comes a strong second with the Beatles, Rolling Stones, Cream, Queen, the Kinks, Oasis, Rod Stewart and Elton John.'[1]

Like its avant-garde cousin (and indeed everything else), pop emerged from, and had to deal with, the war.

In February 1944 2nd Lieutenant Eric Waters of the 8th Battalion, Royal Fusiliers, was killed at the battle of Anzio, prompting his widow to move to Cambridge with her two young sons, including five-month-old Roger. Roger's Cambridge schoolfriends included Syd Barrett and David Gilmour; later, once out of short trousers, Pink Floyd. Roger Waters unveiled a memorial in Anzio to all the casualties of the battle on the seventieth anniversary of his father's death.

Almost exactly eight months after the death of 2nd Lieutenant Waters, a small plane carrying band leader and US Army Major Glenn Miller disappeared in bad weather over the English Channel. His legacy of meticulously disciplined big band swing continued in the work of Englishman Ted Heath and others, keeping the dance halls swaying well into the 1950s.

Meanwhile, elsewhere, swing became something more modern. In 1944 *Collier's* magazine proclaimed: 'You can't sing it. You can't dance it. Maybe you can't even stand it. It's bebop.'[2] Leading the stylistic leap into the unconventional scales, altered chords and lightning fast solos of bebop was alto sax player Charlie Parker, with trumpeter John 'Dizzy' Gillespie. Parker's mid-1940s sessions for the Dial label produced just four pieces, including classics 'A Night in Tunisia' (1942), 'Yardbird Suite' (1946) and 'Ornithology' (1946), the last two named in honour of Parker's nickname, 'Bird': hard, fast music with whirlwind solos, mixing up the harmonies with extra notes and non-standard resolutions. Later, Gillespie added Cuban influences to the style to make 'Cubop'.

Present at the Dial sessions was an aloof, well-educated 19-year-old who would succeed to Gillespie's trumpet crown, Miles Davis. Davis was full of contradictions: a graduate of the elite Juilliard School who spent his years of study in jazz clubs, he became a mainstay of bebop before turning to a new, pared-back style known as the cool, later experimenting with modal, impressionist, hard bop, quasi-free jazz and, eventually, jazz-rock fusion. Davis's 1959 album *Kind of Blue* features his classic sextet, including sax players John Coltrane and Julian 'Cannonball' Adderley, and pianist Bill Evans, whose playing underpinned the ensemble's laid-back modal style.

Singer and trumpeter Chet Baker became 'The Prince of Cool', his smooth style a reaction against busy, fast, difficult bebop in favour of simplicity, lyricism and sweet sound. Elsewhere, Earl Hines and Art Tatum pushed jazz in new directions at the piano, vocalists the

'Divine' Sarah Vaughan and Etta James sang jazz and the blues, Mahalia Jackson and Aretha Franklin belted out gospel, and Nina Simone added a touch of Bach in her skilful, well-crafted piano accompaniments.

Blue Note Records was founded by two Jewish immigrants from Germany in New York in 1939. Crucially, they were fans, not businessmen: Alfred Lion said, 'We were never really figuring on a hit ... I feel the music,'[3] and artists came to know they'd cut the final take when co-founder Francis Wolff started dancing round the studio. Blue Note saved and preserved the unstable, unpredictable and uncommercial pianist Thelonious Monk. Its distinctive album covers launched historic LPs by Miles Davis, John Coltrane (1958's *Blue Train*), and the fast, hard bop of Art Blakey, notably a live album from New York jazz club Birdland. Producer Don Was said, 'The Blue Note sound broke the rules of bebop the way bebop broke the rules of whatever came before – ... adding backbeats which you weren't supposed to do – it became hard bop.'[4]

Sax player Wayne Shorter recalls Miles Davis asking him, 'Do you ever feel like you want to play like you don't know how to play? Do you ever get tired of playing music that sounds like music?'[5] Art Blakey believed that 'you can't hide behind your instrument'.[6] Sheer sound had always been a key ingredient of the jazz player's expressive armoury. Trumpeter Clifford Brown extended the soundworld explored by Gillespie and Davis. Poet Philip Larkin described Sidney Bechet's horn as sounding 'like an enormous Yes'.[7] Sax player Joe Henderson begins *Mode for Joe* (1966), his fifth and last studio album for Blue Note, with noises like an animal moaning.

Folk and other popular styles met other influences, musical and political. White men like Woody Guthrie learnt to sing the blues, and used it to carry social and political messages in songs like 1940's 'This Land is Your Land'. In London, Lonnie Donegan added a Cockney twist to make skiffle. White R&B prospered in parallel on both sides of the Atlantic. Paul Butterfield, a trained classical flautist, added the plangent sound of the harmonica to the folk idiom. All this led to Bob Dylan. Folk music permeated pop as it had classical music, using the same source material for very different effect, in the direct, from-the-heart singing styles of Joan Baez, Peter, Paul and Mary, the English singer Linda Peters, and one of the most far-ranging of all musical families, the Seegers.

Another very different ingredient in this gumbo of musical influences came from another part of the US, the land of farms, railroads and big skies: country and western. Its stars made their names sleeping in pickup trucks between small-town gigs and radio stations before graduating to the brave new world of television. In 1956 Johnny Cash sang 'I Walk the Line' to reassure his wife and kids back home that he wasn't straying from the straight and narrow on the road (although he was, of course). Patsy Cline escaped from an abusive father, auditioned for the iconic Nashville country venue the Grand Ole Opry at the age of fifteen, won $100 in a talent contest, successfully crossed over into pop with the huge hit 'Crazy', and died in a plane crash in 1963 at the age of thirty – the complete country and western CV.

Rock'n'roll

And then Elvis thrust his crotch through the whole musical edifice.

Elvis Presley didn't invent rock'n'roll. If that accolade belongs to anyone, it goes to Chuck Berry. The reasons why Elvis, not Berry, gained global super-stardom are linked uncomfortably with racial attitudes, social mores and later ideas around cultural appropriation (as well, of course, as Presley's sheer talent, star quality and sex appeal). Inclusive, liberal-minded later musicians like the Beatles learnt from listening to Chuck Berry and Blind Willie Johnson. But, as one writer reminds us, 'Blind Willie is still running an elevator in Jackson, Mississippi.'[8]

Bill Haley rocked the twelve-bar blues around the clock in 1955. The next year Presley slowed the harmony down as he sexily slobbered and mumbled his way around 'Heartbreak Hotel', and Carl Perkins speeded it up again in his 'Blue Suede Shoes'. The short-lived bespectacled rocker Buddy Holly, Jerry Lee Lewis, Chuck Berry and Little Richard, a camp, charismatic, swivelling showman who kept performing into his eighties, gave the world, respectively, 'That'll Be the Day', 'Whole Lotta Shakin' Goin' On', 'Johnny B. Goode' and 'Good Golly, Miss Molly' in the frantic last couple of years of the first complete decade since the war. Cliff Richard heard Elvis on a passing car radio and brought a polite, well-behaved rock'n'roll to England; others were not so polite or so well-behaved. The style that began in pumped-up boogie-woogie and the harmonic pattern of the blues was about to usher in the era that changed everything: the 1960s.

It was a London decade. The Beatles and the Rolling Stones took the basic model of the guitar group and turned up the volume. By the time Mick Jagger told the world that '(I Can't Get No) Satisfaction' over a pounding electronic riff in 1965, rock'n'roll had dropped the roll.

The Beatles changed music and society. Their innovations included the narrative element linking songs on the 1967 album *Sgt. Pepper's Lonely Hearts Club Band*, precursor of the 1970s concept album, and techniques borrowed from the experimental avant-garde, like the partly notated *ad lib* crescendo and the electronically manipulated decay in 'A Day in the Life', straight out of Penderecki and Stockhausen (whose face appears in homage on the album cover). Much subtlety permeates the harmony and rhythm of 'Lucy in the Sky with Diamonds' and many other songs. Modal melodies are a constant, from the skiffle-ish 'Love Me Do' in the early days to the later reflective 'Strawberry Fields Forever' and 'Eleanor Rigby'. This effortless sophistication fascinated musical theorists from the start, even though, intriguingly, it was entirely instinctive and untaught: when the musicologist Wilfrid Mellers praised the Beatles' use of an Aeolian cadence, John Lennon turned it into a running joke within the band, because none of them had the slightest idea what an Aeolian cadence was. Words can range from the weirdly hallucinogenic ('I Am the Walrus') and the frankly childlike ('Yellow Submarine') to the perfect simplicity of 'Yesterday', and somehow get away with all of it. The question of which came first, the music or the words (and, in the Beatles' case, who wrote what), becomes redundant, like asking if a composer writes the crotchets first or the quavers.

And yet there is so much more to the Beatles than this. They moved on from the standard issue macho rocker image to something more fluid, flared and long-haired, subtly capturing a kind of coy femininity. 'She Loves You' brilliantly inverts convention by borrowing the voice of a woman taking the lead in the muddle of young love, slyly inviting in the teeming legions of that brand-new creature, the teenage girl, by secretly eavesdropping on their bedroom conversations. They responded in their screaming millions.

Elsewhere in the multi-coloured 1960s the Kinks sang about Lola, who 'walked like a woman but talked like a man', and how they 'don't want to die in a nuclear war'. London hosted many of the most flamboyant (literally) antics of the self-destructive, left-handed electric guitar genius Jimi Hendrix before his death in 1970: his house was next door to Handel's. On the other side of the Atlantic Baez, Dylan and others joined hands to sing 'We Shall Overcome', a new-found voice standing up to a terrible decade of violence, Vietnam and the struggle for civil rights. Reggae emerged out of the Caribbean and its roots in ska, articulating an aspect of the African-Caribbean experience in music of an infectious, chugging rhythm and instrumentation drawn from street bands, parades and a rich mixture of religious traditions.

Among technological changes, television affected pop far more than it did classical music, just as the 45 rpm record had in the 1950s and 1960s. Like classical, popular music fractured into many shards. These divisions were fostered and massaged by press and promoters, forming sects among the drugs and rock'n'roll.

Songs, Cabaret, the Musical

Other tributaries of the great, wide-spreading river of popular music nourished some notable flowerings. The wordy, world-weary cabaret style of Noël Coward and Kurt Weill found its international descendants in performer composers like the sadly short-lived Belgian singer songwriter Jacques Brel, *doyen* of a whole generation of smoky French *chanteurs*. In England, the very different voice of Jake Thackray emerged from the northern clubs, his witty songs peopled by the Widow of Bridlington and Old Molly Metcalfe. Their songs talk of love and childhood, family and death: to Brel, '*La mort m'attend comme une princesse/ À l'enterrement de ma jeunesse*' ('Death awaits me like a princess at the funeral of my youth' (in a song badly covered by David Bowie in the Ziggy Stardust tour).[9] There is wit and wisdom among the whimsy.

On the musical stage, Frank Loesser's *Guys and Dolls* of 1950 remains unequalled for sheer good fun and great songs among the wise-cracking, lovestruck gamblers of Damon Runyon's New York. In 1959 Richard Rodgers and Oscar Hammerstein completed the canon of swoony Golden Age musicals with *The Sound of Music* (even more so in the famous 1965 movie version), which typically touched on a serious theme amid the generous melodies and stagey ensembles. John Kander and Fred Ebb peered more closely at the recent Nazi past in the spiky 1972 film *Cabaret*, again a (fairly substantial) reworking of an earlier stage piece. The same pairing apotheosised the jazz age with *Chicago* in 1975, complete with the indispensable choreography of Bob Fosse. The 1960s, meanwhile, battered down the doors of Broadway as it had everything else with *Hair* in 1967, full of attitude, nudity and rock.

The musical embraced much innovation in dramatic technique. Marvin Hamlisch's *A Chorus Line* of 1975 used taped interviews with aspiring Broadway dancers to create a show about Broadway dancers. Stephen Sondheim graduated from young lyricist of the immortal *West Side Story* to composer and wordsmith of a whole series of clever, subtle shows from the early 1970s – the Henry James of musical theatre, obsessing over the minutiae of relationships, feeling, communication and social mores. There is a show told backwards (*Merrily We Roll Along* (1981)), another based on a painting (*Sunday in the Park with George* (1984)), and one about presidential assassins (*Assassins* (1990)). There are some of the finest show songs of all ('Losing My Mind') and some of the wittiest, and cattiest, patter songs ('The Story of Lucy and Jessie'). His craftsmanship has earned him rightful and lasting esteem, if not the same global box-office appeal as some of his noisier contemporaries.

The 1980s ushered in the mega-musical, complete with helicopter (Claude-Michel Schönberg and Alain Boublil's *Miss Saigon* (1989)) or falling chandelier (Andrew Lloyd Webber's *The Phantom of the Opera* (1986)). Lloyd Webber's best wordsmiths are his first, Tim Rice, who wrote the joyfully unpretentious *Joseph and the Amazing Technicolor Dreamcoat* (1968) and the theatrically inventive *Evita* (1978), and Don Black, who penned the almost Sondheim-esque one-hander *Tell Me on a Sunday* (1977), a witty and poignant account of the bumpy road to love in the big city. Each showcases Lloyd Webber's gift for taking the art of song-writing back to its simplest and most direct utterance, in songs like 'I Don't Know How to Love Him' from *Jesus Christ Superstar* and 'Any Dream Will Do' from *Joseph*, and the skilfully crafted, moving title song from *Tell Me on a Sunday*.

Modern Jazz, Soul, post-1960s Pop, Hip Hop

Jazz in the 1960s splintered into bewildering and contradictory variety, 'like light emerging from a prism', in the memorable words of one commentator.[10] As with classical music in the early twentieth century, some musicians stayed loyal to standard and traditional forms (some big bands continued to carry the names of their fabled leaders long after they were dead), others tried to update them, mixed them with other things like Latin American music or rock, or experimented with 'free' jazz. The jazz fusion sounds of Pat Metheny, Herbie Hancock and Weather Report just hint at the diversity on offer. Meanwhile, survivors like Basie and Ellington carried on playing and composing through the 1960s and 1970s, Ellington increasingly turning to sacred music. Ellington's works in extended form don't always convince. But, as the composer Gunther Schuller rightly said, 'before we judge Ellington too harshly, we might do well to remember that the whole question of large forms in jazz has not been satisfactorily answered by anyone else'.[11] Perhaps John Coltrane's 1965 suite *A Love Supreme* comes as close as any work to making the attempt.

In 2009 Aretha Franklin belted out 'America (My Country, 'Tis of Thee)' at Barack Obama's inauguration as president, drawing on forty years in soul. Soul music was about raw emotion and, specifically, sex: the 'Godfather of Soul', James Brown, set his 'Sex Machine' in motion to a raunchy, funky beat in 1970; Marvin Gaye urged his audience 'Let's Get It On' in 1973 and in 1982 offered them 'Sexual Healing'; in 1979 Teddy Pendergrass sang 'Come Go with Me' and 'Turn Off the Lights' to women-only audiences in performances so physical the sweat would steam from his face and neck like smoke; Barry White, by contrast, barely moved – his deep baritone was enough. It wasn't just male singers who mined this particular approach: Millie Jackson became the Queen of Raunch. Other 1970s soul was more polished, polite and produced: Luther Vandross was making a living as a backing singer when Roberta Flack told him 'I'm lovingly firing you' so he could pursue a solo career.[12] Motown made African-American soul pop mainstream, and millions of dollars. Into the 1980s, the evolution of R&B into hip hop and the advent of MTV rather left soul behind, until Lionel Richie turned it into pop, complete with the now-obligatory video, when he went 'Dancing on the Ceiling' in 1986. Early soul was built around great singers; its later incarnations added great production and arrangements: Aretha Franklin partnered bouffant British-Cypriot disco darling George Michael in 'I Knew You Were Waiting (for Me)' in 1987.

Into the 1980s BBC TV's long-running *Top of the Pops* showcased a kind of family-friendly pop, with balloons and a Christmas special. Bucks Fizz won the Eurovision Song Contest in 1981 with 'Making

Your Mind Up', which is a twelve-bar blues recast as a chirpy, pastel-coloured kids' song, about as far from Bessie Smith and Sister Rosetta Tharpe as you could get. *Sic transit harmonia mundi.* Disco stuck sequins onto everything and hung a glitter ball from the ceiling; punk smashed it to the floor. Clean-cut Britpop and US post-punk rockers such as Green Day rediscovered the art of song-writing in response to the darker US grunge and shoe-gazing late-1980s alternative indie pop. Mega-artists and events filled ever-bigger venues, from Abba, Queen, Elton John and Live Aid in the 1980s through to Oasis, Iron Maiden and the boy and girl bands of the 1990s (some of them memorialised in 'juke-box' musicals, a fun if not always entirely satisfying afterword). Among survivors, clean-imaged singers like Tom Jones and Cliff Richard simply kept on doing what they do (and still are). The Stones, amazingly, have chalked up fifty-nine years of live performance, still going strong.

Other forces at work within the pop counterculture were less benign. Producer Joe Boyd, who worked with many leading acts including Dylan, Pink Floyd, the influential folk rock group Fairport Convention and singer songwriter Nick Drake, says in his 2006 memoir of the 1960s, *White Bicycles*, '[t]he *agape* spirit of '67 evaporated in the heat of ugly drugs, violence, commercialism and police pressure',[13] and ends his elegy for the electrifying era with a moving litany of the dead, free spirits whose openness to new experiences and defiance of rules proved too open – Drake, Jimi Hendrix, Devon Wilson. It's a sad list that can, of course, carve many more talented names on its drug-spattered plinth: Jim Morrison, Janis Joplin, Kurt Cobain, Amy Winehouse (all dead at the age of twenty-seven).

Some bands were made up: The Blues Brothers, The Monkees, Spinal Tap, The Commitments. Later, canny pop promoters designed a concept and then advertised for performers to bring it to life, most famously the Spice Girls in the early 1990s.

Hip hop came out of the Bronx in 1973, a reaction against the blandness of disco and an attempt to capture the percussive drive of soul singers like James Brown through novel use of an easily accessible technology, the record deck. Former head of Def Jam Records Lyor Cohen comments that 'it should be noted that early hip hop stood against the violence and drug culture that pervaded the time'.[14] Improvised 'rap battles' became part of the performance. Cohen quotes Kurtis Blow, one of the first commercially successful rappers:

'On one side of the street, big buildings would be burning down ... while kids on the other side would be putting up graffiti messages like, "Up with Hope. Down with Dope", "I Will Survive" and "Lord, Show Me the Way!" The messages of resilience unified a community of people and were the backdrop of hip hop's beginnings.'[15] Veteran jazz label Blue Note reinvented itself as the home of creative mid-1980s hip hop, fusing funk and modern jazz into the breakbeat of interlocking record decks placed side by side and played like an instrument. Jazz drum tracks by Lou Donaldson became the most frequently sampled sounds in the Blue Note catalogue on tracks by artists from De La Soul to Eminem, rooting hip hop back in its jazz, funk and R&B hinterland.

In one respect, this chapter takes its place in this book because of the fascinating cross-pollination between pop and the classical avant-garde. Some examples were noted at the end of the last chapter. There are many others: Kraftwerk and elevator music wouldn't exist without Stockhausen, and Frank Zappa remains a fascinating maverick. Such cultural references extend beyond so-called music, too, into other areas of the manipulation of sound for artistic effect: the theme to the 1970s BBC TV sitcom *Are You Being Served?* recalls the Ligeti-like symphony for cash registers which opens Pink Floyd's rhythmically irregular 'Money'.

But it is quite wrong to view any kind of music simply in its relation to another. There is a special pleasure and intensity in experiencing a well-made pop song, something more highbrow arts cannot do. As Aaron Copland reminded us, inherently complex music is not innately superior to music which is inherently simple. Doing a simple art well requires the ultimate in sophistication; and it's very difficult.

Jazz and pop did in around a hundred years what their classical cousin took five hundred and more to do. Reviewing the field in 1997, the music historian Ted Gioia noted, 'Only in the last few years, visitors to jazz record stores have encountered a novel situation in which most of the music for sale is by artists who are no longer alive ... As a result, any new artist ... must compete not just with other young talents, but with the entire history of the music. This is a heavy burden indeed!'[16] Indeed it is, and one long familiar to the classical world (whose history is yet longer and more burdensome). But Gioia sees grounds for optimism: 'The role of extended composition in jazz remains to be developed', and 'above all, there are the rapidly evolving technologies of music'.[17]

Music comes in an infinite variety of different kinds.

And, in the words (or notes) of the immortal Miles Davis:

So what?

Part Nine

THE WAY WE LIVE NOW (2000–∞)

21

WORLD MUSIC, GIRL POWER AND WHITE MEN IN WHITE TIES

One of the lessons of compiling a history like this is that writing about your own times is, frankly, a mug's game.

If we still find it difficult to assess the lasting value of trends and styles of a hundred years ago, what possible chance do we have with the music of today?

The multiplicity of styles only makes judgement harder. There are plenty of examples in this book of posterity changing its mind (and, increasingly, of changing it back again). Connected to this, the internet, home recording and desk-top publishing make everything available instantly, everywhere. Rules, styles and limitations merge and disappear. The composer can do anything.

But if you're told you can do anything you like, what, exactly, do you do? How do you know?

Stravinsky identified the problem half a century ago:

> I experience a sort of terror when, at the moment of setting to work and finding myself before the infinitude of possibilities that present themselves ... I have the feeling that everything is permissible to me ... Will I then have to lose myself in this abyss of freedom? To what shall I cling in order to escape the dizziness that seizes me before the virtuality of this infinitude? ... However, I shall not succumb. I shall overcome my terror ...[1]

HIP, Hip Hop, the Museum and the Canon

Stravinsky also felt that 'epochs which immediately precede us are temporarily further away from us than others which are more remote in time'.[2] In all styles and ages, the prevailing attitude to the past is a key ingredient in the creative processes and priorities of the present. Today that attitude is scholarly, inquiring and respectful. This has opened up whole worlds of wonderful music previously hidden by neglect, fashion, ignorance, prejudice and taste, and allowed us to hear it with new/old ears. This is very much not just about old music as a discrete genre, but about how we engage with the continuing progress of the musical arts. The scholar John Butt says, 'H[istorically] I[nformed] P[erformance] is an essential part of contemporary culture, and ... contributes to the continued survival and flourishing of western music.'[3]

At the same time, it has thereby added more galleries to what another scholar calls 'The Imaginary Museum of Musical Works',[4] presenting a more or less agreed canon of great works against which any attempt to say something new (or even get a new piece on the programme) must inevitably be judged.

The canon looms large. As well as raising difficult questions about what's in it and who decides (not to mention whether it should exist as a concept at all), it hangs over the latest incarnation of the old question of what, and who, new music is for. Today, typically, an orchestra or company may commission a new work because 'we believe we have a duty to create new works of art which will stand alongside the great works of the past' (the words here are an amalgam of more than one genuine source). Apart from handing the composer an impossible task, that is historically a very odd place for music to be. And, anyway, who wants to listen to a piece of music written out of a sense of duty?

This ambiguous status of the new has led to a delicate and not always happy balancing act between the artistic impulse to find something different to say and the demands and expectations of the listening public. It's a curious fact that a programme of deliberately challenging 'modern' music put on today could well include works written thirty, sixty, even a hundred years ago by, say, Ferneyhough, Stockhausen and Schoenberg, while today's new music can, in the hands of Arvo Pärt or Max Richter, pare musical style back to an almost reductivist simplicity. Valuing music on its own terms has got harder. A recent headline in a national newspaper stated boldly that one of our leading contemporary composers 'is the equal of Elgar. So why isn't he better known?' That headline raises more questions than it answers: why would he want to be compared to Elgar? What does the word 'equal' possibly mean in this context? And, not least, the composer in question is in fact hugely successful with an established reputation, a large body of work and a substantial international career dating back over several decades. But there the headline was.

Perhaps the uncertain role of the modern reflects another theme running through this book: the attempt by music to capture prevailing ideas about society and our place in the world. Perhaps in our modern age we are unsure about what that place is, lacking the certainty and confidence of some of our predecessors. Perhaps, in all its nervous ambiguity, contemporary classical composition is in that respect capturing the *zeitgeist* well. Perhaps we don't quite know how we fit in.

Styles

And yet it must also be true that there has never been a busier age in terms of creative vitality. Particular parts of the repertoire (for example, choral music and children's opera) nurture a constant stream of new work to feed their social, community and educational objectives as much as the purely musical, as such repertoires always have. Technology hands everyone the means to be a creator, and a limitless supply of example and source material. Pop and film music is, to a large extent, newly composed. Musicals attract large audiences, on stage and film. New things for the composer to do include writing for video games, sharing some skills with the nineteenth-century ballet score.

So this review of just some of the things happening around us presents a series of snapshots, like a collage of newspaper cuttings assembled by Satie or Braque: history as a creative act in its own right.

Composer Errollyn Wallen came to England from Belize at the age of two. Her work draws on many genres and influences: she says, 'We don't break down barriers in music; we don't see any.'[5] *Photography* (2016) for strings is tonal, and rhythmically approachable, echoing earlier English string pieces like Elgar's *Serenade*. In America, Jennifer Higdon serves leading symphony orchestras and high school ensembles with pieces they like to play; Lera Auerbach was introduced in a recent article with a quote from Vinnie Mirchandani's *The New Polymath*: '[we] can no longer be just one person but a collection of many'.[6] Sally Beamish finds space for folk influences in her skilful orchestral scores, and has worked with musicians including the jazz/classical sax player Branford Marsalis. Others have found a new engagement with trends which interested their forebears: American composer Augusta Read Thomas shares a generous attitude to tonality with her earlier compatriots Samuel Barber and Leonard Bernstein; Unsuk Chin, a South Korean composer based in Germany, draws inspiration from *Alice in Wonderland*, echoing the absurdist leanings of Cage, Satie and others. Icelandic composer Anna Thorvaldsdóttir draws her ideas in pencil sketches before turning them into sound; Olga Neuwirth cites influences from the Beastie Boys to Boulez alongside maverick film director David Lynch. Finn Kaija Saariaho studied with Brian Ferneyhough and at electronic studio IRCAM in Paris leading to her nonet with electronics *Lichtbogen (Arches of Light)* in 1986. Scot Thea Musgrave seeks the consistency of 'basic human truths' in her long career as composer, performer and teacher. Roxanna Panufnik continued the 'quiet revolution' inherited from her distinguished father, composer and refugee from Poland Andrzej Panufnik, 'a revolution that is more John Lennon than John Cage',[7] especially in much singable choral music.

Elsewhere in the modern musosphere, James MacMillan has earned his claim to a lasting legacy in works which fuse his roots as a Catholic and a Scot with a deep engagement with ideas of social justice in music of skill, beauty and raw power, from his breakthrough *The Confession of Isobel Gowdie* for the 1990 Proms to profoundly personal reinventions of ancient sacred forms like the Stabat Mater and Miserere, and pieces which mix contemporary politics and religion like *Cantos Sagrados* of 1989. Another who burst early into public acclaim via the BBC Proms was George Benjamin, a student of Messiaen and the composer of orchestral works conveying densely intellectual layers of meaning and structure like *Sudden Time* (1993) and operas drawing on ancient settings and music of carefully heard sonority.

Among operas to address the challenge of putting contemporary issues and ideas on stage, the most successful include *Greek* (1988) by Mark-Anthony Turnage, with its stamping feet evoking 1980s riots, and the huge achievement of the American John Adams, the best of the minimalists, in highly inventive stage works like *Doctor Atomic* (2005), *Nixon in China* (1987) and *The Death of Klinghoffer* (1991). Englishman Thomas Adès, Australian Brett Dean and Dane Hans Abrahamsen have all put Shakespeare on stage; in 2003 Jennifer

Walshe dismembered plastic Barbie dolls in *Live Nude Girls*; in 2011 the Irish composer Gerald Barry made Oscar Wilde's Lady Bracknell a bass in his opera version of *The Importance of Being Earnest*.

Among leading US minimalists, Steve Reich reached again for the combination of recorded speech with live acoustics used memorably in 1988's *Different Trains* to reflect powerfully on the World Trade Center attack in *WTC 9/11* (2011).

An early work of Reich's, *Drumming*, draws on his studies of the rhythmic patterns of Ghanaian music. English composer Giles Swayne has made striking use of similar engagement, particularly in the perhaps unlikely context of a setting of the Latin Magnificat for unaccompanied choir, a thrilling and unusual addition to the English choral repertoire. African music helped kickstart the promotion of what became known as 'world music', following singer songwriter Paul Simon's creative engagement in *Graceland* (1986) with the singing of groups like Ladysmith Black Mambazo, contributing to the huge international reach of musicians like the Senegalese singer (and Minister of Tourism) Youssou N'Dour. Another unaccompanied vocal work to thoroughly shake up the genre is Caroline Shaw's joyful 2012 *Partita* for her eight-voice ensemble Roomful of Teeth – a mixture of *Graceland* and the Berio *Sinfonia*, with a dash of *Hymns Ancient and Modern*.

Minimalism has found some fertile ground in looped, multi-tracked single-performer works like 'Convergence' by Radiohead's Jonny Greenwood and the improvisations of jazz fusion guitarist John Etheridge. The 'holy minimalism' of John Tavener (richly rooted in Eastern orthodox ritual) and Arvo Pärt (with his distinctive, bell-like 'tintinnabulation' technique), and the 'new optimism' of Eric Whitacre and his fraternity have found large listening publics for their fragrant choral music. In other hands minimalism hasn't quite given up its ability to be a bit self-regarding and frankly rather dull.

An entirely different approach is piling styles together in a sort of polystylistic collage, as in the reimagined Baroque conjured up by Russian composer Alfred Schnittke, for example, in the multi-faceted influences on display in the six *Concerti Grossi* composed between 1977 and 1992.

Creators and Performers

Songwriters continued to explored the timeless possibilities of their craft: Billy Joel fashioned words and melody with the skill and subtlety of any of his ancestors in songs like 'She's Always a Woman' and 'Goodnight Saigon'; Bob Dylan won the Nobel Prize for Literature (and even, eventually, turned up to collect it). Another Nobel Laureate, the Irish poet Seamus Heaney, said of the white rap star Eminem that he had 'created a sense of what is possible' and 'sent a voltage around his generation'.[8]

Pop music maintained its avaricious ability to spread out: Stewart Copeland, drummer of the Police, stressed the importance of the 'backbeat', learnt from jazz. Soul music produced a rich third phase in the powerful voices of British singers Adele and Amy Winehouse. Rapper Kendrick Lamar synthesised styles in the 2015 album *To Pimp a Butterfly*.

Blue Note Records, at eighty years old, continues its founders' philosophy of the artists, not commercial imperatives, making the musical running: the sweet, soulful jazz vocals of Norah Jones from 2002; Robert Glasper taking hip hop back to its roots in funk, modern jazz and R&B. Veterans Herbie Hancock and Wayne Shorter play tunes they played with Miles Davis in the 1960s, like 'Masqualero'.

Musicals continue to do wordy wit and worldly theatre in works like William Finn and James Lapine's *Falsettos* (1992), confronting contemporary social mores head on. The modernist opera house is less good at this (and modern classical music is generally less good at having fun). Film musicals have experienced a new golden age in the brave new world of computer-generated imagery (CGI), with its big characters and images, while remaining true to the genre's roots in fantasy theatre. The music on offer is a mixture of the good, the bad and the Disney: at its best when it draws on techniques like crafting an ensemble (the duet 'Love is an Open Door' from *Frozen*), less successful when it sounds like it was designed by focus group.

The breaking-down of stylistic barriers has produced some fascinating figures like polymath jazzman Jacob Collier, collaborator with artists as diverse as Quincy Jones, Voces8, Laura Mvula, Take 6 and the Moroccan musician Hamid El Kasri, experimenter in advanced techniques like microtonal modulations (his version of 'In the Bleak Midwinter' modulates from E major to G ½-sharp major), polyrhythms, grooves and percentages of swing. Collier is perhaps the ultimate technology-driven twenty-first-century 'home' musician – his 2016 album is named in honour of the place it was made: *In My Room*.

Officium is a 1994 recording featuring jazz saxophonist Jan Garbarek playing along in the dreamy acoustic of a middle European medieval monastery to the ascetic sound of early Renaissance four-part polyphony sung by male-voice ensemble the Hilliard Ensemble, mixing modes across the millennia. It has sold over 1.5 million copies.

And music has continued to find many other important things to do, using sound and style to reach into the human soul. In church, it reflects styles of worship in its forms and ensembles, as music always has. In school, it battles along with everything else for the right to be adequately funded, constantly having to make the case that, like exercise and diet, its benefits go far beyond the immediate context. In therapy, modern practice recalls the insights of Pythagoras into the ability of music to effect 'soul-adjustments'.

Within the new lurks the old. Ralph McTell's 'Streets of London' uses the same harmonic pattern as Johann Pachelbel's celebrated *Canon in D*. Peter Maxwell Davies referenced the Golden Section, as Josquin did. Bart Howard's 'Fly Me to the Moon' is based on a cycle of fifths, like a concerto by Vivaldi.

Reasons to be Cheerful

Musical artists continue to grapple with the choices on offer. The solutions they come up with are myriad and wonderful (with the historically rather striking omission that nobody writes twelve-tone music any more). Jazz chronicler Ted Gioia reminds us that

> The historian who hopes to come to grips with the powerful currents of creativity in modern times must learn to deal with these composite art forms on their own terms or not at all. There is no high road on the postmodern map, just a myriad of intersecting and diverging paths.[9]

One of those paths must surely be the greater use of classical technique allied to a popular style for serious purpose. Leonard Bernstein showed the way; there is further to go.

As in other fields, we need to look to the next generation for insight and hope. To musical young people, artificial divisions of musical style are to a large extent meaningless: they simply don't exist any more. Presented with an example of, say, an octatonic scale in the music of Messiaen, they will readily point out a similar instance in a song by Radiohead.

They are right. Theirs is a liberal, open, tolerant, inclusive approach. Meanwhile, academia grapples with the balance between traditional skills like harmony and counterpoint and the arts as a branch of sociology. It doesn't matter: music is big enough to cope.

But the voice of the academic and the historian must always cede precedence to the insights of the creator. Stravinsky said: 'the present moment is the most exciting in music history. It always has been.'[10]

Epilogue

THE NEXT MILLION YEARS

History isn't about the past, it's about how we look at the past. In many ways, this book is the story of how each musical generation viewed and used its inheritance, and, by association, expected the future to look at its own brief candle. We are that future. But we are also the past of the future to come.

The art historian E. H. Gombrich said, 'The artist cannot start from scratch but he can criticise his forerunners.'[1] Somebody else (possibly T. S. Eliot) said something along the lines that in order to reject something one must be intimately acquainted with the thing being rejected. Schoenberg would certainly have agreed with that (and so would Monteverdi, and Beethoven).

The introduction to this volume quotes the eighteenth-century English musical historian Sir John Hawkins. In Hawkins' view, 'the natural course and order of things ... is ever towards perfection ... so that of music it may be said, that the discoveries of one age have served but as a foundation for the improvements in the next'.[2] Well, Sir John, we don't think that any more. That doesn't, of course, mean you were wrong. You were writing for your times, as we do for ours. Your idea has a comforting logic to it – that music can and will continue to find fresh woods and pastures new simply by moving forward into the future – even if that idea contains within it the chilling certainty for each generation that its work, like Prospero's, will 'dissolve And, like this insubstantial pageant faded, Leave not a wrack behind'.

But if we reject Hawkins' view of the immutability (and desirability) of progress, we have the opposite problem. If we have learnt to value the past in its own terms, then why are we writing new music? If we think Mozart, rather than moving 'towards perfection', achieved it, then what 'improvements' can we offer?

Rather to our relief, that turns out to be the wrong question. As always, the business of making music is richer and more complex than that. For a start, the idea that 'old' music and 'new' music are different, and that when we sit down at the piano we are either playing one or the other, is wrong. Our Bach is a twenty-first-century Bach, very different from his ancestor the nineteenth-century Bach, and indeed from his crotchety corporeal original in the eighteenth. We see old music from the point we happen to inhabit in time. We have to; we have no choice.

And anyway, we don't make music to try to tell some historical story (or if we do, we will fail). That story emerges later (and changes with the telling through time).

We make music because we have to. Surely, in the end, the key to this narrative is that music tells us something precious and unique about the manners, morals, ideas, character, beliefs and social mores of the times from which it emerged. In other words, about people.

Will music continue to find a way to do that? Yes.

What will it say? I don't know.

The question of what future ages will be like, how they will think and feel, how they will approach the unknown challenges which face them, and how their music will capture all of that, remains unanswered.

But there will be an answer.

NOTES

Introduction
1. Interview with Nick Kent, *New Musical Express* (25 March 1978). (Versions of the idea date back to at least 1918.)
2. See, for example, *Room-music Tit-bits Nr. 7 Arrival Platform Humlet (An Exploration with Boats and Trains)* (1908, 1910, 1912).
3. Igor Stravinsky, *Poetics of Music in the Form of Six Lessons* (Cambridge, MA: Harvard University Press, 1947), p. 53.
4. Wolfgang Amadeus Mozart, letter to Leopold Mozart from Augsburg (23–5 October 1777), in Robert Spaethling (ed. and trans.), *Mozart's Letters, Mozart's Life* (London: Faber & Faber, 2004), p. 78.
5. Charles Rosen, *The Classical Style: Haydn, Mozart, Beethoven* (London: Faber & Faber, 1971), p. 35.
6. 'Love and Marriage' (1955), lyrics by Sammy Cahn, music by Jimmy van Heusen (Barton Music Corp.).
7. Sir John Hawkins, *A General History of the Science and Practice of Music* (London: T. Payne, 1776), vol. 1, preface.
8. Cuthbert Girdlestone and Philip Gossett, *Jean-Philippe Rameau: His Life and Work* (New York: Dover Publications, 1969), p. 14.
9. Andrea Wulf, *The Invention of Nature: The Adventures of Alexander von Humboldt, the Lost Hero of Science* (London: John Murray, 2015), p. 88.
10. Widely quoted; see, for example, Howard Pollack, *Aaron Copland: The Life and Work of an Uncommon Man* (New York: Henry Holt & Co., 1999), p. 516.
11. Robert Craft and Igor Stravinsky, *Conversations with Igor Stravinsky* (1959; London: Faber & Faber, 2011), p. 92.
12. Benjamin Britten, speech, 'On Receiving the First Aspen Award' (31 July 1964).
13. Georg August Griesinger, *Biographische Notizen über Joseph Haydn* (Leipzig: Breitkopf & Härtel, 1810).
14. Igor Stravinsky, *Chronicle of My Life* (London: Victor Gollancz, 1936), p. 215.
15. Griesinger.
16. Mozart, letter to Leopold Mozart from Vienna (26 September 1761), in Spaethling (ed.), p. 285.
17. Rosen, p. 53.
18. Quoted by Richard Langham Smith in 'French Operatic Spectacle in the Twentieth Century', in Richard Langham Smith and Caroline Potter (eds.), *French Music since Berlioz* (Aldershot: Ashgate, 2006), p. 117.
19. See Guido Adler, *The Scope, Method, and Aim of Musicology* (1885).

20. Henry James, 'Browning in Westminster Abbey', in *The Speaker* (4 January 1891), reprinted in *English Hours* (1905).
21. See, for example, Hunter Davies, *The Beatles Lyrics: The Unseen Story behind Their Music* (London: Weidenfeld & Nicolson, 2014), p. 2.
22. Ted Gioia, *The History of Jazz* (New York: Oxford University Press, 1998), p. 255.
23. James Hamilton-Paterson, *Gerontius: A Novel* (London: Macmillan, 1989), Author's Note.
24. George Dangerfield, *The Strange Death of Liberal England, 1910–14* (New York: Harrison Smith and Robert Haas, 1935), p. 393.
25. Charles Jennens, letter to Lord Guernsey (19 September 1738).

Prologue: The First Million Years
1. Gary Tomlinson, *A Million Years of Music: The Emergence of Human Modernity* (New York: Zone Books, 2015), p. 52.
2. As above, p. 91.
3. As above, p. 172.
4. As above, p. 206.
5. Steven Pinker, *How the Mind Works* (New York: W. W. Norton & Co., 1997), p. 534.
6. Tomlinson, p. 286.
7. Hugh Cobbe (ed.), *Letters of Ralph Vaughan Williams 1895–1958* (Oxford: Oxford University Press, 2008), p. 217.
8. Tomlinson, p. 50.

PART ONE: MUSIC IN THE ANCIENT WORLD (40,000 BCE–500 CE)
1: Bone Flutes and Magic, Far East and Middle Earth
1. Sir William Mitchell Ramsay published widely on the history and archaeology of the region. This observation is referred to in, for example, Giorgio Guiot and Luisella Caire, *Archaeo Epitaph*, proceedings of the IMEKO International Conference on Metrology for Archaeology and Cultural Heritage, Turin, 19–21 October 2016.
2. M. L. West, *Ancient Greek Music* (Oxford: Clarendon Press, 1992), p. 225.
3. As above, p. 14.
4. Aeschylus, *The Suppliants*, line 664. See Anna Swanwick (trans.) *The Dramas of Aeschylus*, (4th edn, 1886, Bohn's Classical Library).
5. Plato, *Republic*, book 3.
6. Aristotle, *Politics*, book 3.
7. James McKinnon, 'Early Western Civilization', in James McKinnon (ed.), *Antiquity and the Middle Ages: From Ancient Greece to the 15th Century* (Basingstoke: Palgrave Macmillan, 1990), p. 4.
8. Andrew Barker, 'Public Music as "Fine Art" in Archaic Greece', in McKinnon (ed.), p. 63.
9. See, for example, Armand D'Angour, '"Old" and "New" Music: The Ideology of Mousikē', in Tosca A. C. Lynch and Eleonora Rocconi (eds.), *A Companion to Ancient Greek and Roman Music* (Hoboken, NJ: Wiley Blackwell, 2020), ch. 29.
10. West, p. 372.
11. 1 Corinthians 13:1.
12. James McKinnon, 'Christian Antiquity', in McKinnon (ed.), p. 71.
13. Diarmaid MacCulloch, *A History of Christianity: The First Three Thousand Years* (London: Allen Lane, 2009), pp. 183–4.
14. McKinnon, 'Christian Antiquity', in McKinnon (ed.), p. 81.

15. As above.
16. M. L. W. Laistner, quoted in McKinnon, 'Christian Antiquity', in McKinnon (ed.), p. 81.
17. Angelo Berardi, *Documenti armonici* (1687).
18. West, p. 218.
19. See www.armand-dangour.com

PART TWO: THE MEDIEVAL WORLD (500–1400)
Introduction
1. Umberto Eco, *Art and Beauty in the Middle Ages* (New Haven, CT: Yale University Press, 2002), p. 15.
2. Geoffrey Chaucer, 'General Prologue', *The Canterbury Tales* (1387–1400).

2: Love and Astronomy
1. Anicius Manlius Severinus Boethius, H. R. James (trans.), *The Consolation of Philosophy: Book V, Free Will and God's Foreknowledge* (Chicago, IL: Musaicum Books, 2017).
2. Dante Alighieri, *La Divina Commedia, Canto VI, Paradiso*, translated by John Caldwell (personal communication).
3. John Caldwell, *Medieval Music* (London: Hutchinson, 1978), p. 96.
4. William Shakespeare, *Twelfth Night*, Act 2, Scene 4.
5. See Andrew Ashbee, *Records of English Court Music* (Farnham: Ashgate, 1996), vol. 6, p. 45.
6. William Shakespeare, *Hamlet*, Act 3, Scene 2.

3: The Sound of the Sacred
1. The Order of St Benedict, *The Rule of Benedict*, chapter IX.
2. Cuthbert Butler, *Benedictine Monachism* (1919; 2nd edn, London: Wipf and Stock, 2005), p. 278.
3. Charles Herbermann (ed.), 'Councils of Cloveshoʼ, *The Catholic Encyclopedia* (New York: Robert Appleton Company, 1913).
4. See, for example, Claude V. Palisca and Raymond Erickson (trans.), *Musica enchiriadis and Scolica enchiriadis* (New Haven, CT: Yale University Press, 1995).
5. Hildegard, *Scivias* (c.1141–51).
6. Franco of Cologne, *Ars Cantus Mensurabilis* (c.1280).
7. Johannes de Grocheio, *Ars musicae* (c.1300).
8. Anonymous IV (c.1270–80).
9. John Caldwell, *Medieval Music* (London: Hutchinson, 1978), p. 149.
10. Quoted in, for example, C. E. H. de Coussemaker, *Mémoire sur Hucbald et sur ses traités de musique* (Paris: J. Techener, 1841). Dr Matthew Thomson has pointed out to me that the passage about hockets and minims may have been a later addition to the Papal Bull.

PART THREE: RENAISSANCE (1400–1600)
Introduction
1. David Fallows, *Dufay* (London: J. M. Dent, 1982), p. 10.
2. Peter Frankopan, *The New Silk Roads: The Present and Future of the World* (London: Bloomsbury, 2018), p. 219.
3. Tinctoris, preface to *Proportionale musices* (1472–3), quoted in R. C. Wegman, *Born for*

    the Muses: The Life and Masses of Jacob Obrecht (New York: Oxford University Press, 2003), p. vi.
4. Phrase used by George Abbot, Archbishop of Canterbury, in reference to the English composer John Bull (1613), quoted in, for example, Julie Anne Sadie (ed.), *Companion to Baroque Music* (Oxford: Clarendon Press, 1998), p. 275.
5. Quoted in Gustave Reese (ed.), *The New Grove High Renaissance Masters: Josquin, Palestrina, Lassus, Byrd, Victoria* (New York: W. W. Norton, 1984), p. 10.
6. Johann Joseph Fux, Andrew Gant (trans.), *Gradus ad Parnassum* (1725).

4: 'To Rome for Everything …'

1. Attributed to Miguel de Cervantes.
2. David Fallows, *Dufay* (London: J. M. Dent, 1982), p. 18.
3. For a discussion of modern equivalents of le Franc's poetic language in this passage, see David Fallows, 'The Contenance Angloise: English Influence on Continental Composers of the Fifteenth Century', in *Renaissance Studies* vol. 1, no. 2 (1987), pp. 189–208.
4. See Margaret Bent, *Dunstaple* (London and New York: Oxford University Press, 1981), p. 35.
5. Andrew Hughes and Margaret Bent (eds.), *The Old Hall Manuscript* (3 vols.) (Middleton, WI: The American Institute of Musicology, 1969).
6. Bent, p. 2.
7. As above, p. 4.
8. Philip Weller, 'Rites of Passage: *Nove cantum melodie*, the Burgundian Court, and Binchois's Early Career', in Andrew Kirkman and Dennis Slavin (eds.), *Binchois Studies* (Oxford and New York: Oxford University Press, 2000), p. 57.
9. John Caldwell, *Medieval Music* (London: Hutchinson, 1978), p. 238.
10. Margaret Bent, 'The Use of Cut Signatures in Sacred Music by Binchois', in Kirkman and Slavin (eds.), p. 299.
11. Fallows, p. 79.
12. As above, p. 64.
13. Andrew Kirkman and Dennis Slavin, 'Introduction', in Kirkman and Slavin (eds.), p. 4.
14. Fallows, p. 76.
15. As above, p. 1.
16. Bent, *Dunstaple*, p. 9.
17. Josquin des Prés, *Nymphes des bois* (1497).
18. Rob C. Wegman, *Born for the Muses: The Life and Masses of Jacob Obrecht* (Oxford: Clarendon Press, 1994), p. 64.
19. Caldwell, p. 251.
20. Gustave Reese, *Music in the Middle Ages: With an Introduction on the Music of Ancient Times* (New York: W. W. Norton & Co., 1940), p. 5.
21. See Jeremy Noble, 'Josquin', in *The New Grove High Renaissance Masters: Josquin, Palestrina, Lassus, Byrd, Victoria* (London: Macmillan, 1984), p. 10.
22. Wegman, p. 282.
23. As above, p. 283.
24. Gustave Reese, *Music in the Renaissance* (New York: W. W. Norton & Co., 1959), p. 246.
25. Caldwell, p. 256.
26. Peter Phillips, '"Laboravi in gemitu meo": Morley or Rogier?', in *Music and Letters* vol. 63 (January–April 1982), pp. 85–90.
27. William Byrd, *Ye Sacred Muses* (1585).

28. John Milsom, 'Analysing Josquin', in Richard Sherr (ed.), *The Josquin Companion* (Oxford and New York: Oxford University Press, 2001), p. 431.
29. Thomas Morley, *A Plaine and Easie Introduction to Practicall Musick* (1597).
30. William Byrd, *Psalms, Songs and Sonnets* (1611).
31. See, for example, Jules Declève, *Roland de Lassus, sa vie et ses œuvres 1520–1594* (Hainaut: Société des Sciences, des Arts, et des Lettres du Hainaut, 1894), p. 45.

5: Reformation

1. John Calvin, preface to the *Genevan Psalter* (1543).
2. J. A. Froude, *Life and Letters of Erasmus* (1894), quoted in, for example, Peter Le Huray, *Music and the Reformation in England, 1549–1660* (Cambridge: Cambridge University Press, 1978), p. 11.
3. Thomas Wolsey, *Regulations for the Augustinian Order in England (22 March 1519)*, quoted in Rob C. Wegman, *The Crisis of Music in Early Modern Europe, 1470–1530* (New York: Routledge, 2005).
4. Thomas Cranmer, letter (7 October 1544), in John Edmund Cox (ed.), *Miscellaneous Writings and Letters of Thomas Cranmer* (Cambridge: Cambridge University Press, 1846; reprinted Vancouver, BC: Regent College Publishing, 2001), p. 412.
5. Martin Luther, preface to Georg Rhau, *Symphoniae Jucundae* (1538).
6. As above.
7. Royal Injunctions, Article 49 (1559), quoted in, for example, Thomas Busby, *A General History of Music, from the Earliest Times to the Present* (London: G. and W. B. Whittaker, 1819), vol. 2, p. 3.
8. Luther.
9. Gustave Reese, *Music in the Renaissance* (New York: W. W. Norton & Co., 1959), p. 358.
10. Lucas Osiander the Elder, *Cantional* (1586).
11. See John Gough Nichols (ed.), *The Diary of Henry Machyn: Citizen and Merchant-taylor of London, from AD 1550 to AD 1563* (London: Camden Society, 1848).
12. Royal Injunctions.
13. Benvenuto Cellini, Thomas Roscoe (trans.), *The Autobiography of Benvenuto Cellini* (1558) (London: Henry G. Bohn, 1850), p. 7.
14. Peter Le Huray, *Music and the Reformation in England, 1549–1660* (Cambridge: Cambridge University Press, 1978), p. 80.
15. Ben Jonson, *Epitaph on S.P., A Child of Queen Elizabeth's Chapel* (1616).
16. In George Gascoigne and Francis Kinwelmershe's 1566 play *Jocasta*; see Christopher R. Wilson and Michela Calore, *Music in Shakespeare. A Dictionary* (London: Continuum, 2007), entry for 'noise'.
17. Miguel de Cervantes, *Los baños de Argel* (1615), Act 1, line 95.
18. Miguel de Cervantes, *Pedro de Urdemalas* (1615), Act 1, line 957.
19. Hugh Chisholm (ed.), *Encyclopaedia Britannica* (11th edn, Cambridge: Cambridge University Press, 1911), Meistersinger.
20. See, for example, the dedication of *Canticum Canticorum* (1584) to Pope Gregory XIII.

PART FOUR: BAROQUE (1600–1759)
Introduction

1. Tim Carter, *Music in Late Renaissance and Early Baroque Italy* (London: Batsford, 1992), p. 7.
2. Samuel Pepys, *Diary* (Sunday, 4 September 1664).
3. J. S. Bach, letter to Georg Erdmann (28 October 1730), in Hans T. David and Arthur

Mendel (eds.), Christoph Wolff (revd), *The New Bach Reader: A Life of Johann Sebastian Bach in Letters and Documents* (New York: W. W. Norton & Co., 1999).
4. Henry Purcell, *Twelve Sonatas for Two Violins and a Bass* (1683).
5. J. S. Bach, *The Musical Offering* (1747).
6. Jean-Baptiste Lully, *Armide* (1686).
7. Colley Cibber, *An Apology for the Life of Mr Colley Cibber, Comedian ... Written by Himself* (London: John Watts, 1740), p. 344.
8. Bruce Wood, *Purcell: An Extraordinary Life* (London: ABRSM, 2009), p. 68.
9. John Hervey, 2nd Baron Hervey, *Memoirs of the Reign of George the Second* (1727–37), p. 42.
10. Georg Philipp Telemann, 'Bratensymphonien' (1693–97).
11. Wood, pp. 18, 21.
12. Donald Burrows, Helen Coffey, John Greenacombe, Anthony Hicks (eds.), *George Frideric Handel: Collected Documents: Volume I, 1609–1725* (Cambridge: Cambridge University Press, 2014), p. 473.
13. George Frideric Handel, *Suites de Pièces pour le Clavecin* (1720), preface.
14. Johann Nikolaus Forkel, letter to Hoffmeister & Kühnel, publishers (16 July 1802).
15. C. P. E. Bach, letter to Johann Nikolaus Forkel (7 October 1774).
16. Lorenz Mizler, autobiographical sketch submitted to Johann Mattheson, *Ehrenpforte* (1740).
17. *London Gazette* (11 May 1693), quoted in Hugh Arthur Scott, 'London's First Concert Room', in *Music & Letters* vol. 18, no. 4 (October 1937), p. 386.
18. *Daily Post* (10 August 1704), quoted in Scott, p. 384.
19. *Dublin Journal* (10 April 1742).
20. Edward Ward, *A Compleat and Humorous Account of All the Remarkable Clubs and Societies in the Cities of London and Westminster* (London: Joseph Collier, 1745).
21. John Evelyn, *Diary* (21 December 1662).
22. Reported by Christian Gerber in 1732.
23. 'Your Unknown Correspondent', in *Universal Spectator* (19 March 1743).
24. Playbill, King's Theatre, Haymarket (2 May 1732).
25. Joshua Rifkin (ed.), *The New Grove North European Baroque Masters: Schütz, Froberger, Buxtehude, Purcell, Telemann* (New York: W. W. Norton & Co., 1985), p. 24.
26. Colley Cibber, *Love's Last Shift* (1696).
27. Cibber, *An Apology for the Life of Mr Colley Cibber*.

6: Vespers and Vivaldi
1. Denis Arnold, *Monteverdi* (London: J. M. Dent, 1963; rev. edn: Oxford: Oxford University Press, 2000), pp. 30–31.
2. Thomas Coryat, *Coryat's Crudities: Hastily gobled up in Five Moneths Travells* (1611), vol. 1, p. 353.
3. Arnold, p. 31.
4. Angelo Berardi, *Miscellanea Musicale* (1689), quoted in, for example, Manfred F. Bukofzer, *Music in the Baroque Era* (London: J. M. Dent, 1978), p. 4.
5. Quoted in, for example, Giuseppe Bertini, *Dizionario storico-critico degli scrittori di musica e de' più celebri artisti, Di tutte le nazioni sì antiche che moderne* vol. 2 (1814).
6. Coryat, vol. 1, p. 370.
7. Giulio Caccini, *Le nuove musiche* (1602), preface.
8. In the basilica of Santa Maria Novella, Florence.
9. Coryat, vol. 1, p. 390.

10. William Shakespeare, *Troilus and Cressida*, Act 5, Scene 3.
11. Federico Follino, *Compendio delle sontuose feste fatte l'anno MDCVIII nella città di Mantova* (1608), quoted in, for example, Arnold, p. 20.
12. Claudio Monteverdi, *L'Orfeo* (1607), Act 2.
13. James Grassineau, *A Musical Dictionary* (London: J. Wilcox, 1740), p. 168.
14. Alex Ross, 'Unsung: Rediscovering the Operas of Francesco Cavalli', in the *New Yorker* (18 May 2009).
15. As above.
16. Chiara Margarita Cozzolani, in the dedication to *12 Sonate A Due Violini, Violone e Organo* (1693).
17. François Maximilian Misson, account of visit in 1688, in *Nouveau Voyage d'Italie* (1724), vol. 2, part 1, p. 35, quoted and translated in, for example, Veronica Buckley, *Christina, Queen of Sweden: The Restless Life of a European Eccentric* (New York: HarperCollins, 2004).
18. Recounted in Charles Burney, Frank Mercer (ed.), *A General History of Music (1776–89)* (New York: Dover Publications, 1957), vol. 2, pp. 442–3.
19. Quoted in Ralph Kirkpatrick, *Domenico Scarlatti* (Princeton, NJ: Princeton University Press, 1983), p. 42.
20. Burney, vol. 3, p. 358.
21. Alexandre-Toussaint de Limojon de St Didier in *La Ville et la République de Venise* (1680), quoted in, for example, David Kimbell, *Italian Opera* (Cambridge: Cambridge University Press, 1991), p. 142.
22. Kirkpatrick, p. 21.
23. Charles de Brosses, *Lettres Historiques et Critiques sur l'Italie* (1739), quoted in, for example, Laurence Dreyfus, *Bach and the Patterns of Invention* (Cambridge, MA: Harvard University Press, 1996), p. 44.
24. Carlo Goldoni, *Commedie* (1761), vol. 13, p. 11.
25. Kirkpatrick, p. 29.
26. Michael Talbot, *Vivaldi* (Oxford: Oxford University Press, 2000), p. 50.
27. Edward Holdsworth, letter to Charles Jennens (13 February 1733), in Talbot, p. 60.
28. Kirkpatrick, p. 68.
29. As above, p. 72.
30. As above, p. 80.
31. As above, p. 72.
32. As above, p. 78.
33. As above, p. 91.
34. As above, p. 94.
35. Domenico Scarlatti, preface to *Essercizi per Gravicembalo* (1739).
36. Charles Burney, *Memoirs of the Life and Writings of the Abbate Metastasio* (1796), vol. 2, pp. 205–6, *n*.

7: Violins and Versailles
1. Marin Mersenne, *Harmonie universelle, contenant la théorie et la pratique de la musique* (1636).
2. Pierre Corneille, *Cinna ou la clémence d'Auguste* (1640), Act 5, Scene 3.
3. Thomas Coryat, *Coryat's Crudities: Hastily gobled up in Five Monthes Travells* (1611), vol. 1, p. 36.
4. Jean de La Brùyere, *Oeuvres de La Brùyere* (Paris: Hachette, 1865), p. 331.
5. Charles Perrault, *Parallèle des anciens et des modernes* (1688–97).

6. In a remark reported in Pierre Perrin, *Lettre écrite à Monseigneur l'archevêque de Turin* (c.1660); see Michael Klaper, 'From Ballet to *pièce à machines*: Origin, Performance and Reception of the Opera *L'Orfeo* (1647)', in *Journal of Seventeenth-century Music* vol. 13, no. 1 (2007).
7. Manfred F. Bukofzer, *Music in the Baroque Era* (London: J. M. Dent, 1978), p. 249.
8. See Wilfrid Mellers, *François Couperin and the French Classical Tradition* (London: Faber & Faber, 1987), p. 65.
9. Bukofzer, p. 13.
10. Évrard Titon du Tillet, *Le Parnasse françois* (1732), p. 196.
11. www.iremus.cnrs.fr/sites/default/files/brunet.pdf
12. Jean de La Fontaine, *Le Florentin* (1675) (pamphlet in verse form).
13. Coryat, vol. 1, p. 177.
14. Titon du Tillet, p. 665.
15. François Couperin, *Leçons de Ténèbres* (1714), preface.
16. C. P. E. Bach and J. F. Agricola, obituary of Johann Sebastian Bach (1750; published 1754), in Hans T. David and Arthur Mendel (eds.), Christoph Wolff (revd), *The New Bach Reader: A Life of Johann Sebastian Bach in Letters and Documents* (New York: W. W. Norton & Co., 1999), p. 300.
17. Charles Burney, Frank Mercer (ed.), *A General History of Music (1776–89)* (New York: Dover Publications, 1957), vol. 4, p. 622.
18. François Couperin, preface to *4ème Livre de pièces pour clavecin* (1730).
19. Mellers, p. 75.
20. Cuthbert Girdlestone and Philip Gossett, *Jean-Philippe Rameau: His Life and Work* (New York: Dover Publications, 1969), p. 6.
21. As above, p. 10.
22. Carlo Goldoni, John Black (trans.), *Memoirs* (1787; Boston: James R. Osgood, 1877), p. 363.
23. Bukofzer, p. 257.

8: Purcell, Handel, Bach and the Bachs

1. Poem signed by 'T. B.' [Tom Brown] *To His Unknown Friend Mr Henry Purcell* in the introduction to Henry Playford, *Harmonia Sacra* (2nd edn, 1693). Reproduced in, for example, Franklin B. Zimmerman, *Henry Purcell: His Life and Times* (Philadelphia, PA: University of Pennsylvania Press, 2nd edn., 1983), p. 299.
2. See Joshua Rifkin (ed.), *The New Grove North European Baroque Masters: Schütz, Froberger, Buxtehude, Purcell, Telemann* (New York: W. W. Norton & Co., 1985), p. 43.
3. Henry Purcell, dedication of *The Vocal and Instrumental Musick of the Prophetess, or, The history of Dioclesian* (1690).
4. Henry Purcell, *Twelve Sonatas of Three Parts* (1683).
5. Samuel Pepys, diary (12 February 1667).
6. John Evelyn, diary (27 January 1685).
7. Colley Cibber, *An Apology for the Life of Mr Colley Cibber, Comedian ... Written by Himself* (London: John Watts, 1740), p. 210.
8. In a soprano chorus part of the coronation anthem *My Heart is Inditing* when it was included in performances of the oratorio Esther in 1732. See Donald Burrows, *Handel and the English Chapel Royal* (Oxford: Oxford University Press, 2005), p. 293, n. 16.
9. Rifkin, p. 19.
10. See, for example, Robert Vaughan, *The History of England under the House of Stuart* (London: Baldwin and Cradock, 1840), part 1, p. 191.

11. Pepys (14 September 1662).
12. Henry Purcell, Edward Elgar (orch.), *Jehova, quam multi sunt hostes mei*, for the Three Choirs Festival (1929).
13. Hermann Mendel (1878), quoted in, for example, Richard Petzoldt, Horace Fitzpatrick (trans.), *Georg Philipp Telemann* (London: Ernest Benn Ltd, 1974), p. 12.
14. Johann Mattheson, *Grundlage einer Ehrenpforte* (1740).
15. Charles Burney, *The Present State of Music in Germany, the Netherlands, and the United Provinces* (1773), pp. 81–2.
16. Letter from Mrs Pendarves to her mother after the first rehearsal of Alcina (12 April 1735); see C. E. Vulliamy (ed.), *Aspasia: The Life and Letters of Mary Granville, Mrs Delany (1700–1788)* (London: Geoffrey Bles, 1935).
17. Aaron Hill, letter (5 December 1732); see, for example, Colin Timms and Bruce Wood (eds.), *Music in the London Theatre from Purcell to Handel* (Cambridge: Cambridge University Press, 2017), p. 62.
18. George Frideric Handel, open letter to *London Advertiser* (17 January 1745); see Timms and Wood (eds.), p. 64.
19. J. S. Bach, letter to Georg Erdmann (28 October 1730), in Hans T. David and Arthur Mendel (eds.), Christoph Wolff (revd), *The New Bach Reader: A Life of Johann Sebastian Bach in Letters and Documents* (New York: W. W. Norton & Co., 1999), p. 151.
20. Council meeting minute, Leipzig (2 August 1730), in David *et al.*, p. 144.
21. Malcolm Boyd, *Bach*, (2nd edn, London: J. M. Dent, 1990), p. 229.
22. Johann Nikolaus Forkel, *Johann Sebastian Bach: His Life, Art, and Work* (1802), chapter 5, in David *et al.*, p. 442.
23. See David *et al.*, p. 260.
24. As above, p. 379.
25. Forkel, in David *et al.*, p. 446.
26. C. P. E. Bach and J. F. Agricola, obituary of Johann Sebastian Bach (1750; published 1754), in David *et al.*, p. 305.

PART FIVE: CLASSICISM (1740–90)
Introduction

1. Anon (attrib. C. P. E. Bach), *A Comparison of Bach and Handel* (1788), in Hans T. David and Arthur Mendel (eds.), Christoph Wolff (revd), *The New Bach Reader: A Life of Johann Sebastian Bach in Letters and Documents* (New York: W. W. Norton & Co., 1999), p. 407.
2. Johann Adolph Scheibe, 'Letter from an Able Musikant Abroad' (14 May 1737), in David *et al.*, p. 338.
3. Roy Porter, *Enlightenment: Britain and the Creation of the Modern World* (London: Allen Lane, 2000), chapter title.
4. Abbé Charles Batteux, *Traité sur les Beaux-Arts réduits à une même principe* (1747), p. 268, quoted in Philip G. Downs, *Classical Music: The Era of Haydn, Mozart, and Beethoven* (New York: W. W. Norton & Co., 1992), p. 11.
5. Cuthbert Girdlestone and Philip Gossett, *Jean-Philippe Rameau, His Life and Work* (New York: Dover Publications, 1969), p. 10.
6. Leopold Mozart, letter to his daughter Maria Anna (16 February 1785): *Ich sage Ihnen vor Gott, als ein ehrlicher Mann, ihr Sohn ist der grösste Componist, den ich von Person und den Nahmen nach kenne: er hat Geschmack, und über das die grösste Compositionswissenschaft.'*

7. Franz Xaver Niemetschek, *Lebensbeschreibung des k. k. Kapellmeisters Wolfgang Amadeus Mozart* (1808).
8. Friedrich Rochlitz, *Anekdoten aus Mozarts Leben* (1798–9), in David et al., p. 488.
9. Wolfgang Amadeus Mozart, letter to Nannerl Mozart (20 April 1782), in Robert Spaethling (ed. and trans.), *Mozart's Letters, Mozart's Life* (London: Faber & Faber, 2004), p. 308.
10. Michael Kelly, *Reminiscences* (1826), vol. 2, pp. 1–2.
11. Quoted in Kelly, p. 4.
12. Giacomo Durazzo, *Lettre sur le mécanisme de l'opéra italien* (1756), pp. 64–5, in Downs, p. 85.
13. William Beckford, quoted in Ralph Kirkpatrick, *Domenico Scarlatti* (Princeton, NJ: Princeton University Press, 1983), p. 61.
14. Giacomo Casanova, *Memoirs* (1798–1808), vol. 2, ch. 7.
15. Jean-Georges Noverre, *Lettres sur la danse, et sur les ballets* (1760), quoted in Giorgio Pestelli, Eric Cross (trans.), *The Age of Mozart and Beethoven* (Cambridge: Cambridge University Press, 1999), p. 59.
16. John Brown, *Letters on the Italian Opera, Addressed to the Hon. Lord Monboddo* (1791), p. 114.
17. Mozart, letter to Leopold Mozart (12 November 1778), in Spaethling (ed.), p. 195.
18. Durazzo, p. 46.
19. Mozart, letter to Leopold Mozart (30 December 1780), in Spaethling (ed.), p. 225.
20. Mozart, letter to Leopold Mozart (14 November 1777), in Spaethling (ed.), p. 95.
21. Pierre-Augustin Caron de Beaumarchais, preface to *Tarare* (1787), quoted in Downs, p. 406.
22. Ranieri de Calzabigi, letter, *Mercure de France* (1784), quoted in Ernest Newman, *Gluck and the Opera: A Study in Musical History* (1895).
23. See Pestelli, p. 62.
24. As above.
25. Mozart, letter to Leopold Mozart (13 June 1781), in Spaethling (ed.), p. 263.
26. Mozart, letter to Leopold Mozart (17 March 1781), in Spaethling (ed.), p. 234.
27. See Jens Peter Larsen and Georg Feder, *The New Grove Haydn* (London: Macmillan, 1982), p. 20.
28. Luigi Boccherini, dedication, *Six String Quartets*, op. 2 (1761).
29. A commonly used term; see, for example, C. P. E. Bach, *Clavier-Sonaten für Kenner und Liebhaber*, Wq. 55–9, 61 (1739).
30. Domenico Scarlatti, dedication, *Essercizi per Gravicembalo* (1739), quoted in Kirkpatrick, p. 102.
31. Alfred Einstein, *Mozart: His Character, His Work* (London: Cassell, 1946), pp. 218, 265.
32. Mozart, letter to Leopold Mozart (29 March 1783), in Spaethling (ed.), p. 346.
33. Christoph Willibald Gluck, letter to the *Mercure* (October 1772), quoted in, for example, Julien Tiersot and Theodore Baker, 'Gluck and the Encyclopaedists', *The Musical Quarterly* vol. 16, no. 3 (July 1930), pp. 336–57.
34. Mozart, letter to Leopold Mozart (17 August 1782), in Spaethling (ed.), p. 326.
35. Jean-Jacques Rousseau, *Dictionnaire de musique* (1764), entry for 'fugue'.
36. Jonathan Bate, *John Clare: A Biography* (London: Picador, 2004), p. 192.
37. Charles Rosen, *The Classical Style: Haydn, Mozart, Beethoven* (London: Faber & Faber, 1971), p. 47.
38. Leopold Mozart, *Versuch einer gründlichen Violinschule* (1756).
39. C. P. E. Bach, *Versuch über die wahre Art das Clavier zu spielen* (1753 and 1762).

40. Charles Burney, *The Present State of Music in Germany, the Netherlands, and the United Provinces* (1773), vol. 2, p. 270.
41. C. F. D. Schubart, *Ideen zu einer Ästhetik der Tonkunst (Ideas for an Aesthetic in Music)* (1806), p. 368.
42. Rosen, p. 47.
43. Johann Joachim Quantz, *On Playing the Flute* (1752), p. 313.
44. Rosen, p. 49.
45. See Adolf Bernhard Marx, *Die Lehre von der musikalischen Komposition, praktisch-theoretisch* (Leipzig, 1837/38/45/47), especially vol. 4.

9: 'Bach is the Father, We are the Children'

1. Comment widely attributed to Mozart, made to Baron Gottfried van Swieten. See, for example, Johann Friedrich Rochlitz, 'Karl Philipp Emanuel Bach' in *Für Freunde der Tonkunst* (3rd edn, Leipzig: Cnobloch, 1830), p. 202, quoted in Christoph Wolff, 'C.P. E. Bach and the History of Music', in *Notes* vol. 71, no. 2 (December 2014), p. 216.
2. Wolfgang Amadeus Mozart, letter to Leopold Mozart (10 April 1782), in Robert Spaethling (ed. and trans.), *Mozart's Letters, Mozart's Life* (London: Faber & Faber, 2004), p. 307.
3. Charles Burney, *The Present State of Music in France and Italy* (1771), quoted in Ralph Kirkpatrick, *Domenico Scarlatti* (Princeton, NJ: Princeton University Press, 1983), p. 103.
4. Mozart, letter to Leopold Mozart (27 August 1778), in Spaethling (ed.), p. 182.
5. Jean-Jacques Rousseau, *Dictionnaire de musique* (1764).
6. See Giorgio Pestelli, Eric Cross (trans.), *The Age of Mozart and Beethoven* (Cambridge: Cambridge University Press, 1999), p. 32.
7. See Pestelli, p. 62.
8. Charles Burney, *The Present State of Music in Germany, the Netherlands, and the United Provinces* (1773), pp. 94–5.
9. See Pestelli, p. 33.
10. Mozart, letters to Leopold Mozart from Mannheim (14 and 20 November, 6 December 1777), in Spaethling (ed.), pp. 94, 97, 110.
11. Tobias Smollett, *The Expedition of Humphry Clinker* (1771), ch. 31.
12. Giacomo Casanova, *Memoirs* (1798–1808), vol. 3, p. 153.
13. Mozart, letter to Nannerl Mozart (16 January 1773), in Spaethling (ed.), p. 42.
14. Mozart, letter to Joseph Bullinger (7 August 1778), in Spaethling (ed.), p. 182.
15. Casanova, p. 790.
16. See Michael Talbot, *Vivaldi* (Oxford: Oxford University Press, 2000), p. 50.
17. Mozart, letter to Leopold Mozart (5 July 1783), in Spaethling (ed.), p. 359.
18. Lorenzo da Ponte, preface to *Le nozze di Figaro* (1786); see Alfred Einstein, *Mozart: His Character, His Work* (London: Cassell, 1946), p. 430.
19. Mozart, letter to Leopold Mozart (7 May 1783), in Spaethling (ed.), p. 350.
20. Mozart, letter to Constanze Mozart (8 and 9 October 1791), in Spaethling (ed.), p. 440.
21. Casanova, pp. 790, 832.
22. Kirkpatrick, p. 110.
23. Antonio Salieri, *Memoirs* (1827), quoted in Daniel Heartz, 'Coming of Age in Bohemia: The Musical Apprenticeships of Benda and Gluck', *Journal of Musicology* vol. 6, no. 4 (Autumn 1988), pp. 510–27.
24. Jean-Jacques Rousseau, *Lettre sur la musique Françoise* (1753).
25. Cuthbert Girdlestone and Philip Gossett, *Jean-Philippe Rameau: His Life and Work* (New York: Dover Publications, 1969), p. 498.

26. Ranieri de Calzabigi and Christoph Willibald Gluck, preface to *Alceste* (1767), in Pestelli, p. 274.
27. Christoph Willibald Gluck, preface to *Don Juan* (1761), in Reinhard G. Pauly, *Music in the Classic Period* (Englewood Cliffs, NJ: Prentice-Hall, 1973), p. 161.
28. See Amber Youell, *Opera at the Crossroads of Tradition and Reform in Gluck's Vienna* (2012), PhD Thesis, Columbia University.
29. Burney, *The Present State of Music in Germany*, pp. 81–2.
30. See George Grove, *A Dictionary of Music and Musicians* (1878), vol. 4, p. 382.
31. Pauly, p. 162.
32. Friedrich Nicolai, *Beschreibung einer Reise durch Deutschland und die Schweiz, im Jahre 1781* (1783–4), vol. 4, p. 527, in Pauly, p. 163.
33. Robert Browning, *A Toccata of Galuppi's* (1855).
34. Mozart, letter to Joseph Bullinger (7 August 1778), in Spaethling (ed.), p. 181.
35. Daniel Heartz, Erich Hertzmann, Alfred Mann and Cecil Bernard Oldman, 'Thomas Attwood's Studies on Theory and Composition with Mozart', *Neue Mozart-Ausgabe* (1965), vol. 114.

10: 'Let There be Light'

1. Genesis 1:3.
2. Albert Christoph Dies, *Biographische Nachrichten von Joseph Haydn nach mündlichen Erzählungen desselben entworfen und herausgegeben* (*Biographical Accounts of Joseph Haydn, Written and Edited from His Own Spoken Narratives*) (Vienna: Camesinaische Buchhandlung, 1810), p. 216.
3. Dies, p. 57.
4. Leopold Mozart, petition to Archbishop Colloredo (1 August 1777), in Robert Spaethling (ed. and trans.), *Mozart's Letters, Mozart's Life* (London: Faber & Faber, 2004), p. 58.
5. Wolfgang Amadeus Mozart, letter to Leopold and Nannerl Mozart (29 September 1777), in Spaethling (ed.), p. 63.
6. Mozart, letter to Leopold Mozart (9 May 1781), in Spaethling (ed.), p. 248.
7. Mozart, letter to Leopold Mozart (25 July 1781), in Spaethling (ed.), p. 275.
8. Mozart, letter to Leopold Mozart (26 May 1781), in Spaethling (ed.), pp. 256–7.
9. Mozart, letter to Leopold Mozart (14 February 1778), in Spaethling (ed.), p. 130.
10. See Mozart, letters to Leopold Mozart from Munich (8 November 1780–18, January 1781), in Spaethling (ed.), pp. 209–47.
11. Mozart, letter to Leopold Mozart from Paris (12 June 1778), in Spaethling (ed.), p. 158.
12. Alfred Einstein, *Mozart: His Character, His Work* (London: Cassell, 1946), p. 265.
13. As above, p. 186.
14. Giuseppe Carpani, quoted in Dies, p. 249.
15. Dies, p. 139.
16. Georg August Griesinger, *Biographische Notizen über Joseph Haydn* (Leipzig: Breitkopf & Härtel, 1810), p. 18.
17. Giorgio Pestelli, Eric Cross (trans.), *The Age of Mozart and Beethoven* (Cambridge: Cambridge University Press, 1999), p. 105.
18. C. M. Girdlestone, *Mozart and His Piano Concertos* (1964; new edn, Mineola, NY: Dover Publications, 2011), p. 207.
19. Dies, pp. 196–7.
20. Griesinger, p. 56.

Notes

21. Mozart, letter to Leopold Mozart from Vienna (26 May 1781), in Spaethling (ed.), p. 257.
22. As above.
23. Dies, p. 196.
24. Mozart, letter to Gottfried von Jacquin from Prague (15 January 1787), in Spaethling (ed.), p. 384.
25. Einstein, p. 288.
26. Mozart, letter to Leopold Mozart from Vienna (17 August 1782), in Spaethling (ed.), p. 325.
27. Mozart, letter to Leopold Mozart from Vienna (26 September 1781), in Spaethling (ed.), p. 285.
28. Mozart, letter to Leopold Mozart from Mannheim (28 February 1778), in Spaethling (ed.), p 134.
29. Mozart, letter to Aloysia Weber from Paris (30 July 1778), in Spaethling (ed.), p. 172.
30. In a letter to a number of potential subscribers. Opus 33 was printed in 1782 by Artaria in Vienna. Prior to this, Haydn had offered the new series for subscription in manuscript copies, demanding 6 ducats per copy; see Joseph Haydn, Dénes Bartha (ed.), *Gesammelte Briefe und Aufzeichnungen* (Kassel: Bärenreiter, 1965), pp. 106–7. Three copies of this letter are preserved; see Georg Feder, 'Ein vergessener Haydn-Brief', *Haydn-Studien* I (1966), pp. 114–16.
31. Dies, p. 145.
32. As above, p. 118.
33. See Griesinger, p. 23, and Dies, p. 121.
34. Mozart, letter to Anton Stoll (12 July 1791), in Spaethling (ed.), p. 438.
35. Mozart, letter to Maria Anna Mozart (sister) (26 January 1770), in Spaethling (ed.), p.8.
36. Mozart, letter to Maria Anna Thekla Mozart (5 November [sic] 1777), in Spaethling (ed.), p. 86.
37. Joseph Haydn, letter to Marianne von Genzinger (8 January 1791).
38. Haydn, letter to Marianne von Genzinger (17 January 1791).
39. Joseph Haydn, diary; see, for example, 'The Haydn Centenary', in *The Musical Times*, vol. 50, no. 795 (1 May 1909), pp. 297–300.
40. Haydn, diary, in 'The Haydn Centenary', p. 297.
41. This comment appeared in the *Österreichische Monatsschrift* in 1793, in connection with a performance of *Die Vergötterung Hercules* by Johann Baptist von Alxinger, whose text van Swieten had previously submitted to Haydn. See Edward Olleson, 'Gottfried van Swieten: Patron of Haydn and Mozart' in *Proceedings of the Royal Musical Association* 89th Sess. (1962–3), pp. 63–7.

PART SIX: THE ROMANTIC CENTURY (1770–1914)
Introduction
1. Walter Pater, *The Classic and the Romantic in Literature* (1876).
2. Immanuel Kant, *The Critique of Judgement* (1797), quoted in Philip G. Downs, *Classical Music: The Era of Haydn, Mozart, and Beethoven* (New York: W. W. Norton & Co., 1992), pp. 340–41.
3. Johann Gottfried Herder, *Kalligone* (1800), in Downs, p. 341.
4. Friedrich von Schlegel, *Das Athenäum* vol. 3, part 1 (1800), in Peter le Huray and James Day, *Music and Aesthetics in the Eighteenth and Early Nineteenth Centuries* (Cambridge: Cambridge University Press, 1981), p. 247.

5. William Wordsworth, preface to second edition of William Wordsworth and Samuel Taylor Coleridge, *Lyrical Ballads* (1801).
6. Johann Wolfgang von Goethe, David Constantine (trans.), *The Sorrows of Young Werther* (1774; Oxford: Oxford World's Classics, 2012), p. 78.
7. Wolfgang Amadeus Mozart, letter to Leopold Mozart from Vienna (26 September 1761), in Robert Spaethling (ed. and trans.), *Mozart's Letters, Mozart's Life* (London: Faber & Faber, 2004), p. 285.
8. Alexander Wheelock Thayer, *The Life of Ludwig van Beethoven* (New York: The Beethoven Society, 1921), vol. 3, ch. 3, p. 75.
9. See Downs, p. 377.
10. Gustave Flaubert, Margaret Mauldon (trans.), *Madame Bovary* (1856; Oxford: Oxford World's Classics, 2008), pp. 57, 59, 322.
11. Hector Berlioz, C. R. Fortescue (trans.), *Evenings in the Orchestra* (1852; Harmondsworth: Penguin, 1963), 'Second Evening', p. 52.
12. Berlioz, 'Twelfth Evening', p. 136.
13. Ludwig van Beethoven, letter to Louis Schlösser (1823 [full date not given]).
14. Charles Rosen, *The Classical Style: Haydn, Mozart, Beethoven* (London: Faber & Faber, 1971), p. 47.
15. Berlioz, 'Twenty-fifth Evening', p. 241.
16. *The Gentleman's Magazine*, no. 57 (4 February 1731).
17. Berlioz, 'Eighteenth Evening', pp. 188–9.
18. John Warrack, *Carl Maria von Weber* (Cambridge: Cambridge University Press, 1976), p. 110.
19. Berlioz, 'Seventh Evening', p. 105.
20. Edith Wharton, *The Age of Innocence* (1920; Oxford: Oxford World Classics, 2006) p. 4.
21. Warrack, pp. 240–41.
22. Giuseppe Verdi, letter to Clarina Maffei (November 1854); see Dyneley Hussey, *Verdi* (London: J. M. Dent, 1974), p. 98.
23. Berlioz, pp. 128, 118, 136, 124, 130, 122, 74, 305, 129, 74, 324.
24. Hector Berlioz, David Cairns (ed. and trans.), *The Memoirs of Hector Berlioz* (New York: Alfred A. Knopf, 2002), p. 510.
25. Giorgio Pestelli, Eric Cross (trans.), *The Age of Mozart and Beethoven* (Cambridge: Cambridge University Press, 1999), p. 184.
26. See Marion M. Scott, *Beethoven* (London: J. M. Dent, 1934), p. 108.
27. As above.
28. William Makepeace Thackeray, *Vanity Fair* (1847–8), ch. 29.
29. See Ernest Newman, *Wagner Nights* (London: The Bodley Head, 1949), p. 440.
30. Mark Twain, *A Connecticut Yankee in King Arthur's Court* (1889), ch. 16, p. 45.
31. Berlioz, epilogue, p. 271.
32. Quoted in Berlioz, p. 341.
33. Berlioz, 'Twenty-first Evening', p. 221.
34. Warrack, pp. 88, 90.
35. Berlioz, 'Twenty-fifth Evening', p. 240.
36. Oscar A. H. Schmitz, *Das Land ohne Musik: englische Gesellschaftsprobleme* (1904; published 1914).
37. George Eliot, *Middlemarch* (1871–2), part 2, ch. 16,
38. Michael Kennedy, *Portrait of Elgar* (3rd edn, Oxford: Clarendon Press, 1993), p. 15.
39. Berlioz, epilogue, p. 277.

40. T. S. Eliot, 'Portrait of a Lady', *Prufrock and Other Observations* (London: Faber & Faber, 1917).
41. Richard Wagner, *On Actors and Singers* (1872).
42. N. Temperley, G. Abraham and H. Searle, *The New Grove Early Romantic Masters 1: Chopin, Schumann, Liszt* (Basingstoke: Palgrave Macmillan, 1985), p. 8.
43. Franz Liszt (ed.), preface to *John Field – 18 Nocturnes* (1859).
44. Julian Budden, *Verdi* (London: J. M. Dent, 1985; rev. edn, Oxford: Oxford University Press, 2008), p. 116.
45. Charles Dickens, 'The Handel Festival', in *All the Year Round* (27 June 1874).
46. Berlioz, 'Twenty-first Evening', p. 222.

11: I, Genius: Weber, Beethoven, Schubert and Their World

1. John Warrack, *Carl Maria von Weber* (Cambridge: Cambridge University Press, 1976), p. 50.
2. As above, p. 87.
3. As above, p. 91.
4. Alfred Brendel and Martin Meyer, Richard Stokes (trans.), *The Veil of Order: Alfred Brendel in Conversation with Martin Meyer* (London: Faber & Faber, 2002), p. 116.
5. Warrack, p. 100.
6. As above, p. 201.
7. As above, p. 95.
8. Marion M. Scott, *Beethoven* (London: J. M. Dent, 1934), p. 20.
9. As above, p. 20.
10. As above, p. 21.
11. As above, p. 23.
12. As above, p. 27.
13. As above, p. 34.
14. Alexander Wheelock Thayer, *The Life of Ludwig van Beethoven* (New York: The Beethoven Society, 1921), vol. 1, ch. 9.
15. As above, vol. 1, ch. 10.
16. Scott, p. 39.
17. Thayer, vol. 1, ch. 11.
18. As above, vol. 1, ch. 20.
19. Ludwig van Beethoven, Grace Anne Wallace (ed. and trans.), *Beethoven's Letters 1790–1826* (New York: C. H. Ditson & Co., 1866), no. 26.
20. Thayer, vol. 1, ch. 21.
21. Ferdinand Ries, 'Biographische Notizen über Ludwig van Beethoven' (1838), in O. G. Sonneck (ed.), *Beethoven: Impressions by His Contemporaries* (New York: Schirmer, 1926), p. 54.
22. Correspondent in the *Freymüthige* (April 1805); see Thayer, vol. 2, ch. 3.
23. Ludwig van Beethoven, letter to Felix Radicati (1806).
24. Ries, p. 101; see Thayer, vol. 2, ch. 2.
25. Thayer, vol. 2, ch. 4.
26. As above, vol. 2, ch. 7.
27. See Friedrich Kerst and Henry Edward Krehbiel (eds.), *Beethoven: The Man and the Artist, as Revealed in His Own Words* (New York: B. W. Huebsch, 1905; reprinted New York: Dover Publications, 1964), ch. 11.
28. William Blake, *The Marriage of Heaven and Hell* (1794).
29. Thayer, vol. 3, ch. 5.

30. Max Maria von Weber, *Carl Maria von Weber: Ein lebensbild Volume 2*, (Leipzig, 1864), p. 510.
31. Thayer, vol. 3, ch. 16.
32. Beethoven, *Beethoven's Letters*, nos. 222, 296, 325, 328, 339.
33. Thayer, vol. 3, ch. 5.
34. See, for example, Laura Tunbridge, *Beethoven: A Life in Nine Pieces* (London: Viking, 2020), p. 200.
35. Beethoven, *Beethoven's Letters*, no. 96.
36. As above, no. 41.
37. Thayer, vol. 2, ch. 13.
38. Beethoven, *Beethoven's Letters*, no. 245.
39. Thayer, vol. 2, ch. 2.
40. Beethoven, *Beethoven's Letters*, no. 14.
41. As above, no. 16.
42. Quoted in Charles Rosen, *The Classical Style: Haydn, Mozart, Beethoven* (London: Faber & Faber, 1971), pp. 36–7.
43. Ernest Newman, *The Unconscious Beethoven* (1927), quoted in Scott, p. 122.
44. Scott, p. 173.
45. Comment to Myfanwy Piper, quoted in Humphrey Carpenter, *Benjamin Britten: A Biography* (London: Faber & Faber, 1992), p. 348.
46. Franz Schubert, dedication to *Eight Variations on a French Song for Piano for Four Hands* (1818).
47. Thayer, vol. 3, ch. 5.
48. Maurice J. E. Brown, *The New Grove Schubert* (London: Macmillan, 1982), p. 2.
49. As above, p. 5.
50. As above, p. 20.
51. As above, p. 23.
52. As above, p. 29.
53. Benjamin Britten, speech, 'On Receiving the First Aspen Award' (31 July 1964).
54. Brown, p. 83.
55. Brendel and Meyer, p. 119.
56. Rosen, p. 455.
57. As above.
58. Brendel and Meyer, p. 119.
59. See Robert Schumann, Herbert Schulze (ed.), *Gesammelte Schriften über Musik und Musiker: eine Auswahl Wiesbaden*, pp. 177–9, translated in Anthony Newcomb, 'Schumann and Late Eighteenth-century Narrative Strategies', *19th-Century Music* vol. 11, no. 2 (October 1987), pp. 164–74.
60. Donald Jay Grout, *A History of Western Music* (3rd edn, London: J. M. Dent, 1981), p. 594.
61. W. S. Gilbert, *H.M.S. Pinafore* (1878).
62. Grout, p. 594.

12: 1812

1. Gerald Abraham, 'Schumann', in Nicholas Temperley, Gerald Abraham and Humphrey Searle, *The New Grove Early Romantic Masters 1: Chopin, Schumann, Liszt* (Basingstoke: Palgrave Macmillan, 1985), p. 99.
2. Nicholas Temperley, 'Chopin', in Temperley *et al.*, p. 5.
3. Gerald Abraham, in Temperley *et al.*, p. 104.

4. As above.
5. Robert Schumann, review of Chopin's *Variations on 'Là ci darem la mano'*, in *Allgemeine Musikalische Zeitung* (7 December 1831).
6. Robert Schumann (April 1830); see Georg Predota, 'At the Center of the Musical Universe: Niccolò Paganini II' (27 November 2017) https://interlude.hk/center-musical-universe-niccolo-paganini-ii/
7. Hector Berlioz, C. R. Fortescue (trans.), *Evenings in the Orchestra* (1852; Harmondsworth: Penguin, 1963), 'Sixteenth Evening', p. 169.
8. Hector Berlioz (1840, quoted in Humphrey Searle, *The Music of Liszt* (London: Williams and Norgate, 1954), p. 15.
9. Temperley, p. 14.
10. Frédéric Chopin, Henryk Opieński and E. L. Voynich (eds.) *Chopin's Letters* (New York: Dover Publications, 2012), p. 171.
11. As above, p. 168.
12. Temperley, p. 17.
13. Berlioz, 'Twelfth Evening', p. 141.
14. Temperley, p. 18.
15. As above, p. 12.
16. Chopin, Opieński and Voynich (eds.), p. 90.
17. Humphrey Searle, 'Liszt', in Temperley *et al.*, p. 242.
18. Frédéric Chopin to Ferdinand Hiller, quoted in Paul Kildea, *Chopin's Piano: A Journey through Romanticism* (London: Allen Lane, 2018), p. 13.
19. See Kildea, p. 13.
20. Marquis de Custine, in Kildea, p. 13.
21. Kildea, p. 20.
22. Frédéric Chopin, letter to Julian Fontana (28 December 1838); see Kildea, p. 25.
23. William G. Atwood, *The Parisian Worlds of Frédéric Chopin* (New Haven, CT, and London: Yale University Press, 1999), p. 351.
24. Temperley, pp. 25, 21.
25. Zdislas Jachimecki, entry on Chopin in the *Polish Biographical Dictionary* (Poland: Polish Academy of Learning / Polish Academy of Sciences, 1937), p. 424.
26. George Sand, *Lucrezia Floriani* (1846), quoted in Kildea, p. 34.
27. Temperley, p. 24.
28. As above.
29. As above, p. 25.
30. Chopin, Opieński and Voynich (eds.), p. 362.
31. Abraham, p. 148.
32. Kildea, p. 121.
33. See Temperley, pp. 27–8.
34. Abraham, p. 172.
35. Mendelssohn himself referred to this nickname in letters to Devrient, who gives his explanation of the origin in *Meine Erinnerungen an Felix Mendelssohn Bartholdy* (1869), pp. 179 *n*., 181 *n*.; see R. Larry Todd (ed.), *Mendelssohn Studies* (Cambridge: Cambridge University Press, 1992), p. 229.
36. Abraham, p. 140.
37. Often-quoted remark to Queen Victoria; see, for example, Thom Braun, *Disraeli the Novelist* (Abingdon: Routledge, 2017), p. 119.
38. Searle, p. 237.
39. Chopin, Opieński and Voynich (eds.), p. 43.

40. See Andrew Gant, *Johann Sebastian Bach: A Very Brief History* (London: SPCK Publishing, 2018), p. 82.
41. Robert Schumann, 1839 review in *Die Neue Zeitschrift für Musik*; see Kildea, p. 74.
42. Kildea, p. 86.
43. George Sand, Dan Hofstadter (trans.), *The Story of My Life* (1854; London: Folio Society, 1984), p. 240; see Kildea, p. 36.
44. Felix Mendelssohn, letter to Marc-André Souchay (15 October 1842); see Todd, p. 217.
45. Sand, p. 245, in Kildea, p. 45.
46. Joseph Filtsch, letter to his parents (8 March 1842), in Kildea, p. 45.
47. Adelaide Anne Procter, 'A Lost Chord' (1858), set to music by Sir Arthur Sullivan as 'The Lost Chord' (1877).
48. Felix Mendelssohn, letter to Lea Mendelssohn-Bartholdy (24 June 1837), in Felix Mendelssohn-Bartholdy, Paul Mendelssohn-Bartholdy (ed.), Lady Grace Wallace (trans.), *Letters of Felix Mendelssohn-Bartholdy from 1833 to 1847* (London: Longman Green, 1864), p. 113.
49. Abraham Mendelssohn-Bartholdy, letter to Fanny Mendelssohn-Bartholdy (16 July 1820), in Sebastian Hensel (ed.), Carl Klingemann (trans.), *The Mendelssohn Family (1729–1847) from Letters and Journals* (London: Sampson Low, 1881), p. 82.
50. See R. Larry Todd, *Fanny Hensel: The Other Mendelssohn* (Oxford: Oxford University Press, 2010), p. 35.
51. See Sock Siang Thia, 'The Piano Sonatas of Fanny Hensel and Clara Schumann' (2011), paper given at the 10th Australasian Piano Pedagogy Conference, Charles Sturt University, Wagga Wagga, Australia. https://www.researchgate.net/publication/298721567_The_Piano_Sonatas_of_Fanny_Hensel_and_Clara_Schumann
52. Clara Schumann, dedication to Piano Sonata in G Minor (1841); see https://imslp.org/wiki/Piano_Sonata_in_G_minor_(Schumann,_Clara)
53. Clara Schumann, diary entries (June 1870).
54. Clara Schumann, letter to Johannes Brahms from Brussels (5 May 1870), in Berthold Litzmann (ed.), *Letters of Clara Schumann and Johannes Brahms, 1853–1896* (New York: Longmans, Green and Co., 1927), p. 244.
55. Litzmann, preface.
56. See, for example, Alan Walker, *Music & Letters* vol. 72, no. 3 (1991), pp. 452–6.
57. Berlioz, 'Second Epilogue', p. 298.
58. See Humphrey Searle, 'Liszt', in Temperley et al., p. 253.
59. Searle, p. 253.
60. As above.

13: A Tradition Fulfilled

1. In an interview with Philip Clark for *Gramophone* (17 March 2015).
2. See Philip Clark, 'Schumann's Symphonies – Building a Fantasy World', *Gramophone* (8 January 2016).
3. Hector Berlioz, C. R. Fortescue (trans.), *Evenings in the Orchestra* (1852; Harmondsworth: Penguin, 1963), 'Ninth Evening', p. 127.
4. E. T. A. Hoffmann, *Beethoven's Instrumental Music* (1813); see Oliver Strunk, *Source Readings in Music History: The Romantic Era* (New York: W. W. Norton & Co., 1965), p. 35.
5. Charles Rosen, *The Classical Style: Haydn, Mozart, Beethoven* (London: Faber & Faber, 1971), p. 30.

6. Alfred Brendel, 'Schubert's Last Sonatas', in *Alfred Brendel on Music* (London: JR Books, 2007), p. 129.
7. Giorgio Pestelli, Eric Cross (trans.), *The Age of Mozart and Beethoven* (Cambridge: Cambridge University Press, 1999), p. 104.
8. David Charlton, quoted in Mark Brown, 'Étienne Méhul's Lost Masterpiece', in the *Guardian* (8 November 2010).
9. Berlioz, epilogue, p. 304.
10. Clara Schumann, diary (31 May 1839).
11. David Cairns (ed.), *The Memoirs of Hector Berlioz: Including His Travels in Italy, Germany, Russia and England, 1803–1865* (London: Cardinal, 1990), p. 21.
12. Berlioz, 'Twenty-third Evening', p. 226.
13. As above, p. 227.
14. Hugh Macdonald, 'Berlioz, (Louis-)Hector', *Grove Music Online* (Oxford: Oxford University Press, 2001).
15. As above.
16. Cairns (ed.), p. 225.
17. John Warrack, *Carl Maria von Weber* (Cambridge: Cambridge University Press, 1976), p. 170.
18. Hector Berlioz, David Cairns (ed. and trans.), *The Memoirs of Hector Berlioz* (New York: Alfred A. Knopf, 2002), p. 15.
19. Nikolai Rimsky-Korsakov, *Ma Vie musicale* (1914), ch. 4.
20. See Bryan Gilliam and Charles Youmans, 'Strauss, Richard' (2001), in *Grove Music Online*.
21. *Päivälehti* (28 April 1892); see sleeve notes to *Sibelius: Kullervo, Op. 7*, Naxos CD 8.553756.
22. Jan Swafford, *Johannes Brahms: A Biography* (London: Macmillan, 1997), p. 10.
23. As above, p. 64.
24. Robert Schumann, review in *Die Neue Zeitschrift für Musik* (1853).
25. Johannes Brahms, letter to Robert Schumann (16 November 1853); see Styra Avins (ed. and trans.) and Joseph Eisinger (trans.), *Johannes Brahms: Life and Letters* (Oxford: Oxford University Press, 1997), p. 24.
26. See Berthold Litzmann (ed.), *Letters of Clara Schumann and Johannes Brahms, 1853–1896* (New York: Vienna House, 1973).
27. See Michael Musgrave, *A Brahms Reader* (New Haven, CT, and London: Yale University Press, 2000), pp. 52–3.
28. Swafford, pp. 18–90.
29. Brahms said in a letter to a friend 'und noch merkwürdiger ist, dass das jeder Esel gleich hörst', literally, 'what is even more strange is that every donkey hears it the same way'. See Edward Lockspeiser, review of *Geschichte des Begriffes Volkslied im musikalischen Schrifttum* by Julian von Pulikowski and Carl Winter (Heidelberg, 1933), in *Music and Letters* Vol XV Issue 2, April 1934.
30. Arnold Schoenberg, Dika Newlin (ed. and trans.), 'Brahms the Progressive', in *Style and Idea: Selected Writings of Arnold Schoenberg* (New York: Philosophical Library, 1950), ch. 4.
31. As above.
32. Musgrave, p. 95.
33. Quoted in, for example, Swafford, pp. 206–11.
34. As above.
35. As above.

36. See, for example, Alan Walker, *Hans von Bülow: A Life and Times* (Oxford: Oxford University Press, 2010), pp. 92–3.
37. Musgrave, pp. 96–8.
38. As above, p. 101.
39. See, for example, Davitt Moroney, entry for 'Lully' in George Haggerty (ed.) *Encyclopedia of Gay Histories and Cultures* (Routledge, 2012).
40. See sleeve notes to *Varèse: Orchestral Works, Vol. 2*, Naxos CD 8.557882.
41. 'Mea culpa' (1890); see Jean Gallois, *Charles-Camille Saint-Saëns* (Sprimont, Belgium: Éditions Mardaga, 2004), p. 262.
42. Louis Vierne, *Mes Souvenirs* (1939), p. 43, quoted in Rollin Smith, *Toward an Authentic Interpretation of the Organ Works of César Franck* (2nd edn, Hillsdale, NY: Pendragon Press, 1997), p. 24.
43. Charles Villiers Stanford, *Pages from an Unwritten Diary* (London: Edward Arnold, 1914), p. 157.
44. Donald Mitchell, *The Language of Modern Music* (London: Faber & Faber, 3rd edn, 1976), p. 132.
45. Thomas Hardy, 'A Broken Appointment' (*Collected Poems*, 1919).
46. Edward Elgar, letter to Ernest Newman (4 November 1908), reproduced in Jerrold Northrop Moore (ed.), *Edward Elgar: Letters of a Lifetime* (Oxford: Oxford University Press, 1990), p. 200.
47. Humphrey Carpenter, *Benjamin Britten: A Biography* (London: Faber & Faber, 1992), p. 69.
48. As above, p. 108.
49. Hans-Joachim Hinrichsen, '"Halb Genie, halb Trottel" Hans von Bülows Urteil über Anton Bruckner', in *IBG-Mitteilungsblatt* (2000), pp. 21–4.
50. Deryck Cooke, 'The Bruckner Problem Simplified', *The Musical Newsletter* (1 January 1975), p. 5.
51. As above.
52. Anton Rubinstein, Aline Delano (trans.), *Autobiography of Anton Rubinstein* (1890), p. 107.
53. Nikolai Rimsky-Korsakov, Carl van Vechten (ed.), Judah A. Joff (trans.), *My Musical Life* (1925; 3rd edn, New York: Alfred A. Knopf, 1942), p. 172.
54. Robert Craft and Igor Stravinsky, *Conversations with Igor Stravinsky* (1959; London: Faber & Faber, 2011), p. 45.
55. Mily Balakirev, letter to Eduard Reiss (1892).
56. M. D. Calvocoressi, 'Mussorgsky's Youth: In the Light of the Latest Information', *The Musical Quarterly* vol. 20, no. 1 (January 1934), p. 6.
57. David Brown, *The New Grove Russian Masters 1: Glinka, Borodin, Balakirev, Mussorgsky, Tchaikovsky* (New York: W. W. Norton & Co., 1997), p. 46.
58. David Brown, *Tchaikovsky: The Man and His Music* (London: Faber & Faber, 2010), p. 212.
59. Igor Stravinsky, *Poetics of Music in the Form of Six Lessons* (Cambridge, MA: Harvard University Press, 1942), ch. 5.
60. M. D. Calvocoressi, *Modest Mussorgsky: His Life and Works* (London: Rockliff, 1956), p. 219.
61. M. O. Zetlin, George Panin (trans. and ed.), *The Five: The Evolution of the Russian School of Music* (1959; Westport, CT: Greenwood Press, 1975), pp. 303–4.
62. Rimsky-Korsakov, *Ma Vie musicale*.
63. Modest Tchaikovsky, Rosa Newmarch (abbrev. and trans.), *The Life & Letters of Peter*

       Ilich Tchaikovsky (1906); as quoted in Anthony Holden, *Tchaikovsky: A Biography* (New York: Random House, 1995), p. 64.
64. Stravinsky, ch. 5.
65. John Warrack, *Tchaikovsky* (New York: Charles Scribner's Sons, 1973), p. 132.
66. Marina Kostalevsky, Stephen Pearl, Polina E. Vaidman, *The Tchaikovsky Papers: Unlocking the Family Archive* (New Haven, CT: Yale University Press, 2018), pp. 171, 137, 107.
67. Paul Kildea, *Chopin's Piano: A Journey through Romanticism* (London: Allen Lane, 2018), p. 145.

14: Elephants, Arias and the Gods at Twilight
1. Alfred Einstein, *Mozart: His Character, His Work* (London: Cassell, 1946), p. 487.
2. Alexander Wheelock Thayer, *The Life of Ludwig van Beethoven* (New York: The Beethoven Society, 1921), vol. 2, ch. 4.
3. As above, vol. 2, ch. 3.
4. John Warrack, *Carl Maria von Weber* (Cambridge: Cambridge University Press, 1976), p. 156.
5. As above, p. 158.
6. As above, p. 159.
7. As above, p. 274.
8. As above, p. 204.
9. As above, p. 171.
10. As above, p. 97.
11. As above, p. 9.
12. As above, p. 253.
13. Lord Byron, *The Giaour: A Fragment of a Turkish Tale* (1813).
14. Robert Schumann, *Davidsbündler* magazine (1835), in Oliver Strunk, Leo Treitler (ed.), *Strunk's Source Readings in Musical History* (rev. edn, New York: W. W. Norton & Co., 1998), p. 100.
15. Julian Budden, *Verdi* (London: J. M. Dent, 1985; rev. edn, Oxford: Oxford University Press, 2008), p. 122.
16. Hector Berlioz, C. R. Fortescue (trans.), *Evenings in the Orchestra* (1852; Harmondsworth: Penguin, 1963), epilogue, p. 310.
17. Ernest Newman, *Wagner as Man and Artist* (1914; reissued Cambridge: Cambridge University Press, 2014), p. 136; see also Simon Callow, *Being Wagner: The Triumph of Will* (London: William Collins, 2017), p. xii.
18. Giuseppe Carpani, *Le rossiniane ossia Lettere musico-teatrali* (1824); see Carolyn Abbate and Roger Parker, *A History of Opera: The Last 400 Years* (London: Penguin Books, 2015), p. 208.
19. Abbate and Parker, p. 239.
20. As above, p. 188.
21. As above, p. 190.
22. As above, p. 188.
23. Étienne-Jean Delécluze, quoted in Herbert Weinstock, *Donizetti and the World of Opera in Italy, Paris, and Vienna in the First Half of the Nineteenth Century* (New York: Random House, 1963), p. 194.
24. Giuseppe Mazzini, *Filosofia della Musica* (1836), in Abbate and Parker, p. 192.
25. See sleeve notes to *Saverio Mercadante: Elena da Feltre*, Naxos CD 8.225064–65.
26. Abbate and Parker, p. 156.

27. Warrack, p. 158.
28. Gerald Abraham, *The Age of Beethoven 1790–1830* (Oxford: Oxford University Press, 1982), p. 32.
29. Ludwig van Beethoven, Friedrich Kerst (ed.), H. E. Krehbiel (trans.), *Beethoven: The Man and the Artist, as Revealed in His Own Words* (1905; New York: Dover Publications, 1964), ch. 6.
30. Hector Berlioz, David Cairns (ed. and trans.), *The Memoirs of Hector Berlioz* (New York: Alfred A. Knopf, 2002), p. 123.
31. Warrack, p. 158.
32. Abbate and Parker, p. 148.
33. Berlioz, *Evenings in the Orchestra*, 'Thirteenth Evening', pp. 154–9.
34. BBC Radio 3, *Composer of the Week* (9 June 2014).
35. See Douglas Cardwell, 'The Well-Made Play of Eugène Scribe', in *The French Review* vol, 56, no. 6 (May 1983), pp. 876–84.
36. Lionel Renieu, *Histoire des théâtres de Bruxelles depuis leur origine jusqu'à ce jour*, (Paris: Duchartre & Van Buggenhoudt, 1928), p. 744.
37. Richard Wagner, William Ashton Ellis (trans.), *Opera and Drama* (1893; Lincoln, NE: University of Nebraska Press, 1995), p. 37.
38. As above. (The German is *'Wirkung ohne Ursache'*.)
39. Clive Brown, 'Giacomo Meyerbeer', in Amanda Holden (ed.), *The New Penguin Opera Guide* (New York: Penguin, 2001), p. 572.
40. Matthias Brzoska, 'Meyerbeer: *Robert le Diable* and *Les Huguenots*', in David Charlton (ed.), *The Cambridge Companion to Grand Opera* (Cambridge: Cambridge University Press, 2003), p. 192.
41. Berlioz, *The Memoirs of Hector Berlioz*, p. 513.
42. Gottfried Samuel Fraenkel, 'Berlioz, the Princess and *Les Troyens*', in *Music & Letters* vol. 44, no. 3 (July 1963), pp. 249–56.
43. Berlioz, *The Memoirs of Hector Berlioz*, p. 452.
44. Abbate and Parker, p. 280.
45. Edith Wharton, *The Age of Innocence* (1920; Oxford: Oxford World's Classics, 2008), p. 4.
46. Mina Curtiss, *Bizet and His World* (London: Secker & Warburg, 1959), p. 391.
47. Winton Dean, *Georges Bizet: His Life and Work* (London: J. M. Dent, 1965), p. 115.
48. Curtiss, p. 391.
49. See Julian Barnes, *The Man in the Red Coat* (London: Jonathan Cape, 2019), p. 28.
50. Philip Ross Bullock, *Pyotr Tchaikovsky* (London: Reaktion Books, 2016), p. 67.
51. Jules Massenet, H. V. Barnett (trans.), *My Recollections* (London: Small, Maynard, 1919), ch. 3.
52. Letter to Minna, Berlin (1837); see Richard Wagner, Stewart Spencer and Barry Millington (eds. and trans.), *Selected Letters of Richard Wagner* (London: J. M. Dent, 1987), p. 45.
53. Richard Taruskin, '*The Stone Guest* and Its Progeny', in *Opera and Drama in Russia as Preached and Practiced in the 1860s* (Rochester, NY: University of Rochester Press, 1981), p. 258.
54. Lyle K. Neff, *Story, Style, and Structure in the Operas of César Cui* (doctoral thesis, Indiana University, 2002).
55. Igor Stravinsky, *Poetics of Music in the Form of Six Lessons* (Cambridge, MA: Harvard University Press, 1947), ch. 5.

56. Derek Katz, 'Two Czech Operas, Rarely Performed', *The New York Times* (19 August 2001).
57. Bryan Magee, *Aspects of Wagner* (rev. edn, Oxford: Oxford University Press, 1988), p. 32.
58. Friedrich Nietzsche, *Nietzsche contra Wagner* (1889).
59. Magee, p. 48.
60. Callow, p. xv.
61. Magee, p. 32.
62. As above.
63. Friedrich Nietzsche, *Götzen-Dämmerung, oder, Wie man mit dem Hammer philosophiert (The Twilight of the Idols)* (1889), ch. 10.
64. Roger Allen, *Wilhelm Furtwängler: Art and the Politics of the Unpolitical* (London: Boydell Press, 2018), p. 3.
65. Callow, p. 177.
66. Richard Wagner and Franz Liszt, Francis Hueffer (trans.), *Correspondence of Wagner and Liszt, 1841–1853 Volume 1* (1888; Cambridge: Cambridge University Press, 2010), p. 175.
67. Callow, p. xx.
68. As above, p. 20.
69. As above, p. 44.
70. Franz Lachner (Munich 1864); see 'In Focus: Richard Wagner, *Der fliegende Holländer*', essay for the New York Metropolitan Opera production (March 2020).
71. Ernest Newman, *Wagner Nights* (3rd edn, London: The Bodley Head, 1968), p. 203 n.
72. Callow, p. 64.
73. Wagner's own programmatic description, quoted in, for example, Newman, p. 137.
74. See Christopher A. Reynolds, *Wagner, Schumann, and the Lessons of Beethoven's Ninth* (Oakland, CA: University of California Press, 2015), p. 80.
75. Callow, p. 77.
76. Abbate and Parker, p. 290.
77. Richard Wagner, *Das Kunstwerk der Zukunft* (1849), in Strunk, Treitler (ed.), pp. 147, 148, 160.
78. Magee, p. 15.
79. Callow, p. 154.
80. Allen, p. 68.
81. Richard Wagner, John Deathridge (trans.), *The Ring of the Nibelung* (London: Penguin Classics, 2019), p. 409.
82. Newman, p. 428.
83. Wagner, Deathridge (trans.), p. xxxvii.
84. Richard Wagner, Andrew Porter (trans.), *The Ring of the Nibelung* (London: Faber & Faber, 1977), p. xvii.
85. Abbate and Parker, p. 362.
86. W. Beatty-Kingston, 'Our Musical Box' (1 May 1882), in Clement Scott (ed.), *The Theatre* (London: Charles Dickens and Evans, Crystal Palace Press, 1882), p. 293.
87. Claude Debussy in *Le Figaro* (1902); see Emily Kilpatrick, 'The "calling cards" of L'Heure espagnole', in *The Operas of Maurice Ravel* (Cambridge: Cambridge University Press, 2015), pp. 145–71.
88. Newman, p. 8.
89. See Robert Donington, *Wagner's 'Ring' and Its symbols: The Music and the Myth* (London: Faber & Faber, 1969).

90. [Millington: verdian- NGW p 30 might yiled a diffrnt quote]
91. Magee, p. 77.
92. As above, p. 76.
93. As above, p. 76.
94. As above, p. 77.
95. Callow, p. 119.
96. Wagner's programme note for concerts in Paris (25 January, 1 and 8 February 1860), quoted in Newman, p. 219.
97. Richard Wagner, *Tristan und Isolde* (1865), libretto.
98. Nancy B. Reich, *Clara Schumann: The Artist and the Woman* (rev. edn, Ithaca, NY: Cornell University Press, 2001), p. 203.
99. Mark Twain, 'Mark Twain at Bayreuth', *Chicago Daily Tribune* (6 December 1891).
100. Newman, p. 298.
101. As above, p. 299.
102. *The Era* (3 June 1882); see Raymond Mander and Joe Mitchenson, *The Wagner Companion* (London: W. H. Allen, 1978), p. 181.
103. Robin Holloway, *Debussy and Wagner* (London: Ernst Eulenburg Ltd, 1979), p. 165.
104. Claude Debussy, writing as M. Croche the Dilettante-Hater; see *Three Classics in the Aesthetics of Music* (New York: Dover Publications, 2000), p. 76.
105. Joseph Kerman, 'Wagner: Thoughts in Season' (1959), in *Write All These Down: Essays on Music* (Berkeley, CA: University of California Press, 1994).
106. Alex Ross, *Wagnerism: Art and Politics in the Shadow of Music* (New York: Farrar, Straus & Giroux, 2020).
107. Dyneley Hussey, *Verdi* (London: J. M. Dent, 1940), p. 15.
108. Abbate and Parker, p. 242.
109. Hussey, p. 239.
110. As above, p. 33.
111. As above, p. 239.
112. Marcello Conati, *Verdi: Interviste e incontri* (Turin: EDT, 2000) p. 49.
113. Budden, p. 21.
114. As above, p. 43.
115. William Weaver, 'The Shakespeare Verdi Knew', in David Rosen and Andrew Porter (eds.), *Verdi's Macbeth: A Sourcebook* (Cambridge: Cambridge University Press, 1984), p. 144.
116. As above, p. 147.
117. As above, p. 144.
118. Hussey, p. 55.
119. Budden, p. 42.
120. Hussey, p. 56.
121. Andrew Porter, introduction to Rosen and Porter, p. xvi.
122. Budden, p. 44.
123. As above, p. 25.
124. As above, p. 26.
125. Hussey, p. 61.
126. As above, p. 54.
127. Budden, p. 56.
128. As above.
129. Hussey, p. 81.
130. As above, p. 82.

131. As above.
132. Charles Osborne, *The Complete Operas of Verdi* (New York: Da Capo Press, 1977), p. 255.
133. Abbate and Parker, p. 374.
134. Budden, p. 60.
135. As above, pp. 88–90.
136. As above, p. 82.
137. As above, pp. 84–5.
138. Hussey, p. 149.
139. Budden, p. 95.
140. Hussey, p. 150.
141. As above, p. 156.
142. Hussey, p. 184.
143. As described by the American singer Blanche Roosevelt in 1875; see John Warrack and Ewan West (eds.), *The Oxford Dictionary of Opera* (Oxford: Oxford University Press, 1997), entry for Teresa Stolz.
144. Budden, p. 121.
145. Caroline Ellsmore, *Verdi's Exceptional Women: Giuseppina Strepponi and Teresa Stolz* (Abingdon: Routledge, 2018), preface.
146. Hans von Bülow, *Allgemeine Zeitung* (28 May 1874).
147. See Gundula Kreuzer, '"*Oper im Kirchengewande*"? Verdi's *Requiem* and the Anxieties of the Young German Empire', in *Journal of the American Musicological Society* vol. 58, no. 2 (2005), pp. 399–450.
148. Hussey, p. 211.
149. Budden, p. 147.
150. Hussey, p. 235.
151. Budden, p. 142.
152. Hussey, p. 242.
153. As above, p. 243.
154. Budden, p. 133.
155. As above, p. 134.
156. Hussey, p. 286.
157. As above, p. 64.
158. Abbate and Parker, p. 252.
159. As above, p. 391.
160. Hussey, p. 125.
161. See Julian Budden, '*Macbeth*: Notes on the Instrumentation of the Two Versions', in Rosen and Porter, p. 227.
162. Hussey, p. 281.
163. As above, p. 235.
164. Budden, p. 125.
165. Hussey, p. 289.
166. Budden, p. 106.
167. Hussey, p. 237.
168. As above, p. 97.
169. As above, p. 117.
170. See Oliver Hilmes, *Cosima Wagner: The Lady of Bayreuth* (New Haven, CT: Yale University Press, 2010), p. 214.
171. Budden, p. 109.
172. Hussey, p. 244.

173. Budden, p. 104.
174. Abbate and Parker, pp. 391–2.
175. Hussey, pp. 54–5.
176. Abbate and Parker, p. 31.
177. As above, p. 391.
178. As above, p. 283.
179. Budden, p. 122.
180. As above, p. 123.
181. As above, p. 135.
182. As above, p. 295.
183. Martin Kalmanoff, 'Aria from the "Missing Act" of *La Bohème*', in *The Opera Quarterly*, vol. 2, no. 3 (Autumn 1984), pp. 121–5.
184. Abbate and Parker, p. 417.
185. Budden, p. 130.
186. Abbate and Parker, p. 423.
187. Benjamin Britten, 'Verdi – A Symposium', in *Opera* magazine (February 1951), pp. 113–14.
188. Ernest Newman, *More Opera Nights* (London: Putnam, 1954), p. 465.
189. Eric Frederick Jensen, *Debussy* (Oxford: Oxford University Press, 2014), p. 186.
190. As above.
191. Roger Nichols and Richard Langham Smith (eds.), *Claude Debussy: Pelléas et Mélisande* (Cambridge: Cambridge University Press, 1989), p. 148.
192. Norman Lebrecht, 'Ethel Smyth', in *Mahler Remembered* (London: Faber & Faber, 1987), p. 45.
193. Hans Hollander, *Leoš Janáček: His Life and Works* (London: John Calder, 1963), p. 51.
194. Michael Beckerman, *Janáček and His World* (Princeton, NJ: Princeton University Press, 2003), p. 246.
195. Abbate and Parker, p. 458.

PART SEVEN: THE AGE OF ANXIETY (1888–1975)
Introduction

1. Julian Barnes, *The Man in the Red Coat* (London: Jonathan Cape, 2019), pp. 26, 28.
2. Arnold Schoenberg, in a note to himself; see Robert Craft, *Stravinsky: Glimpses of a Life* (New York: St Martin's Press, 1993), p. 40.
3. Igor Stravinsky, *Poetics of Music in the Form of Six Lessons* (Cambridge, MA: Harvard University Press, 1947), ch. 5.
4. 'Khachaturian, Aram', *Current Biography Yearbook* (New York: H. W. Wilson Co., 1949), vol. 9, p. 345.
5. Paul Ehlers, 'Die Musik und Adolf Hitler', in *Die Neue Zeitschrift für Musik* (April 1939), p. 361.
6. Ernst Krenek, 'A Composer's Influences', in *Perspectives of New Music* vol. 3, no. 1 (Autumn–Winter 1964), pp. 36–41.
7. From a review of Blume's paper by his student Wolfgang Steinecke, '*Musik und Rasse: Vortrag Professor Blumes bei den Reichsmusiktagen*', in *Deutsche Allgemeine Zeitung* (28 May 1938), quoted in Martin Iddon, *New Music at Darmstadt* (Cambridge: Cambridge University Press, 2013), p. 11.
8. Wolfgang Steinecke, *Smetana und die tschechische Nationalmusik* (1937), programme booklet, Duisburger opera, quoted in Iddon, p. 11.

9. Claude Debussy, letter to Émile Durand (14 October 1915), quoted in Erik Frederick Jensen, *Debussy* (Oxford: Oxford University Press, 2014), p. 115.
10. Quoted by Francesco Lombardi, Gwyn Morris (trans.), in sleeve notes to *Il Prigioniero/Canti di prigionia*, Sony Classical SK 68 323.
11. Alex Ross, *The Rest is Noise: Listening to the Twentieth Century* (London: Fourth Estate, 2008), p. 307.
12. Thomas Mann, *Betrachtungen eines Unpolitischen (Reflections of a Non-political Man)* (1918)); see Mark W. Clark, *Beyond Catastrophe: German Intellectuals and Cultural Renewal after World War II, 1945–1955* (Lanham, MD: Lexington Books, 2006), p. 86.
13. See Paul Bowles (ed. and record), booklet, p. 1, with *Music of Morocco: From the Archive of Folk Song* (Washington DC: Library of Congress, 1972), AFS L63–64.
14. Ted Gioia, *The History of Jazz* (2nd edn, New York: Oxford University Press, 2011), p. 185.
15. Richard Langham Smith, personal communication.
16. Joseph Kerman, 'Wagner: Thoughts in Season' (1959), in *Write All These Down: Essays on Music* (Berkeley, CA: University of California Press, 1994), p. 267.
17. Roman Vlad, F. and A. Fuller (trans.), *Stravinsky* (Oxford: Oxford University Press, 1960), p. 197.

15: A Tradition Renewed

1. See Glenda Dawn Goss, *Sibelius: A Composer's Life and the Awakening of Finland* (Chicago, IL: University of Chicago Press, 2009), p. 346.
2. Seth Monahan, *Mahler's Symphonic Sonatas* (New York: Oxford University Press, 2015), p. 1.
3. Monahan, p. 11.
4. Goss, p. 347.
5. As above, p. 376.
6. Jean Sibelius, diary entry (10 April 1915).
7. Ferdinand Pfohl, *Gustav Mahler: Eindrücke und Erinnerungen aus den Hamburger Jahren* (1973), quoted in Peter Franklin, 'Mahleriana', *The Musical Times* vol. 126, no. 1706 (April 1985), pp. 208–11.
8. Alex Ross, *The Rest is Noise: Listening to the Twentieth Century* (London: Fourth Estate, 2008), p. 8.
9. Stefan Zweig, *Die Welt von Gestern: Erinnerungen eines Europäers* (1941), quoted in, for example, Fischer, Jens Malte (trans. Stewart Spencer), *Gustav Mahler* (New Haven, CT: Yale University Press, 2011), p. 58.
10. Natalie Bauer-Lechner, Peter Franklin (ed.), Dika Newlin (trans.), *Recollections of Gustav Mahler* (London: Faber & Faber, 1980), p. 65.
11. Widely quoted.
12. Virgil Thomson, *New York Herald Tribune* (11 October 1940), quoted in Ross, p. 173.
13. Theodor W. Adorno, 'The Sibelius Problem' (1938), in *Memorandum: Music in Radio*, pp. 59–60, Princeton Radio Research Project (Paul Lazarsfeld Papers, Columbia University); see Ross, p. 173.
14. Unsigned, 'Concerts', *The Times* (4 December 1907), p. 12. (I am grateful to Joe Davies for sharing with me his unpublished paper '"*Herr Mahler Has Little to No Creative Faculty": Gustav Mahler's Reception in Britain, 1860–1911*' from which this and the following newspaper reviews are taken.)
15. As above.

16. Unsigned, 'Mahler's Fourth Symphony', *The Musical Standard* (7 December 1907), p. 352.
17. 'A.K.', 'Music in London', the *Guardian* (4 December 1907), p. 12.
18. Bruno Walter, *Gustav Mahler*, James A. Galston (trans.) (London: Kegan Paul, Trench, Trubner, 1937), pp. 4–5.
19. Recalled in 1942; see Humphrey Carpenter, *Benjamin Britten: A Biography* (London: Faber & Faber, 1992), p. 36.
20. Carpenter, p. 73.
21. As above.
22. Arnold Schoenberg, Dika Newlin (ed. and trans.), 'Gustav Mahler', in *Style and Idea: Selected Writings of Arnold Schoenberg* (New York: Philosophical Library, 1950), ch. 2.
23. Monahan, p. 7.
24. Schoenberg, ch. 2.

16: The Challenge of Modernism

1. Arnold Schoenberg, Dika Newlin (ed. and trans.), 'Gustav Mahler', in *Style and Idea: Selected Writings of Arnold Schoenberg* (New York: Philosophical Library, 1950), ch. 2.
2. Vincent Plush, 'They Could Have Been Ours', *ABC Radio 24 Hours* (January, 1996), quoted in Peter Biskup, 'Popper in Australasia, 1937–1945', *Quadrant*, vol. 44, no. 6 (June 2000), pp. 20–28.
3. Schoenberg, pp. 71, 192.
4. See Arnold Schoenberg, 'Composition with Twelve Tones' (1941), published as chapter 5 of *Style and Idea*.
5. See, for example, Nicholas Cook, *Music: A Very Short Introduction* (Oxford and New York: Oxford University Press, 1998), p. 46.
6. Schoenberg, 'Composition with Twelve Tones', p. ??.
7. Robert Craft and Igor Stravinsky, *Conversations with Igor Stravinsky* (1959; London: Faber & Faber, 2011), p. 131.
8. Jean Cocteau, *Le Coq et l'Arlequin: Notes autour de la musique* (Paris: Éditions de la Sirène, 1918), appendix, p. 44.
9. Igor Stravinsky, *Poetics of Music in the Form of Six Lessons* (Cambridge, MA: Harvard University Press, 1947), p. 10.
10. As above, p. 17.
11. Letter (24 October 1915).
12. Quoted in, for example, Mikhail Druskin, *Igor Stravinsky: His Life, Works and Views* (Cambridge: Cambridge University Press, 1983), p. 79.
13. As above, p. 79.
14. Igor Stravinsky, *Chronicle of My Life* (London: Victor Gollancz, 1936), pp. 122–3.
15. Stravinsky, *Poetics of Music*, p. 35.
16. As above.
17. As above, p. 43.
18. As above, p. 51.
19. As above, p. 47.
20. As above, p. 81.
21. As above, p. 87.
22. As above, ch. 5.
23. Arnold Schoenberg, in the words of his *Drei Satiren für gemischten Chor* (*Three Satires for Mixed Chorus*) (1925/6).
24. Stravinsky, *Poetics of Music*, p. 85.

25. See Paul Griffiths, *Igor Stravinsky: The Rake's Progress* (Cambridge: Cambridge University Press, 1982), p. ix.
26. Igor Stravinsky and Robert Craft, *Dialogues and a Diary* (Garden City, NY: Doubleday, 1963), p. 5.
27. Igor Stravinsky and Robert Craft, *Expositions and Developments* (Garden City, NY: Doubleday, 1962), p. 107.
28. Griffiths, p. 136.
29. Craft and Stravinsky, *Conversations with Igor Stravinsky*, p. 44.
30. As above, p. 37.
31. As above, p. 38.
32. As above.
33. As above.
34. As above, p. 128.
35. Druskin, p. 171.
36. Stravinsky, *Chronicle of My Life*, pp. 53–4.
37. Craft and Stravinsky, *Conversations with Igor Stravinsky*, p. 127.
38. See Jonathan Cross, *Stravinsky Today* (2020), boosey.com
39. Arnold Schoenberg, *Five Pieces for Orchestra* (1909), note in the score.
40. Anton Webern, *Six Pieces for Orchestra* (1909), composer's note.
41. Herbert Glass, programme note to *Six Pieces for Orchestra* for the Los Angeles Philharmonic, laphil.com
42. Arnold Schoenberg, preface to Anton Webern, *Six Bagatelles for String Quartet* (1924).
43. Igor Stravinsky, in the Universal Edition house magazine *Die Reihe* (1955).
44. See sleeve notes to Norbert von Hannenheim, *Works for Viola & Piano*, Challenge Classics CC 72734 (2016).
45. Béla Bartók, János Demény (ed.), *Levelek, fényképek, kéziratok, kották (Letters, Photographs, Manuscripts, Scores)* (Budapest: Magyar Művészeti Tanács, 1948). English edition, as Péter Balabán and István Farkas (trans.), Elisabeth West and Colin Mason (rev. and trans.), *Béla Bartók: Letters*, 2 vols. (London: Faber & Faber, 1971), vol. 2, p. 83.
46. See Halsey Stevens, *The Life and Music of Béla Bartók* (2nd edn, New York: Oxford University Press, 1964), p. 15.
47. Quoted in, for example, Richard Taruskin, *Music in the Early Twentieth Century* (Oxford: Oxford University Press, 2010), p. 378.
48. Zoltán Kodály, Ferenc Bónis (ed.), *Selected Writings of Zoltán Kodály* (London: Boosey & Hawkes, 1974), p. 32.
49. Francesco Mastromatteo, 'Kodály's Sonata Opus 8: Transformation of Hungarian Lament', *International Journal of Musicology*, vol 1. (2015), pp. 101–36.
50. Schoenberg, *Style and Idea*, ch. 10.
51. See Henry-Louis de La Grange, *Gustav Mahler, vol. 3, Vienna: Triumph and Disillusion (1904–1907)* (Oxford: Oxford University Press, 1999), p. 752.
52. Ferruccio Busoni, 'Sketch of a New Esthetic of Music' (1907), p. 3.
53. Della Couling, *Ferruccio Busoni: 'A Musical Ishmael'* (Lanham, MD: The Scarecrow Press, 2005), p. 308.
54. Gabriel Fauré, letter to his wife (3 December 1908), in Edward Lockspeiser, *The Literary Clef: An Anthology of Letters and Writings by French Composers* (London: John Calder, 1958), pp. 153–4.
55. Michael Kennedy, *The Works of Ralph Vaughan Williams* (1964; 2nd edn, Oxford: Oxford University Press, 1980), p. 74.
56. As above, p. 90.

57. As above, p. 16.
58. As above, p. 244.
59. As above, p. 329.
60. John Evans (ed.), *Journeying Boy: The Diaries of the Young Benjamin Britten 1928–1938* (London: Faber & Faber, 2010), p. 138.
61. Constant Lambert, *Music Ho!: A Study of Music in Decline* (New York: Charles Scribner's Sons, 1934), p. 107.
62. Alain Frogley and Aidan J. Thomson (eds.), *The Cambridge Companion to Vaughan Williams* (Cambridge: Cambridge University Press, 2013), p. 318.
63. As above, p. 282.
64. See *The Great Composers and Their Music, vol. 50: Holst, The Planets* (London: Marshall Cavendish Ltd, 1985), p. 1218.
65. Arnold Schoenberg, *Harmonielehre* (1911).
66. Benjamin Britten in conversation with Bruce Phillips; see Lewis Foreman, *The John Ireland Companion* (Martlesham, Suffolk: Boydell Press, 2011), p. 20.
67. Adrian Boult, comment to a friend; see, for example, Michael Kennedy, *Portrait of Walton* (Oxford: Oxford University Press, 1989), p. 281.
68. Kennedy, *Portrait of Walton*, p. 16.
69. Aaron Copland, *Music and Imagination: The Charles Eliot Norton Lectures (1951–1952)* (New York: Mentor Books, 1959), p. 67.
70. Benjamin Britten, diary (30 July 1936); see Evans (ed.), p. 366.
71. Gabriel Fauré in 1922, quoted in Jean-Michel Nectoux (ed.), J. A. Underwood (trans.), *Gabriel Fauré: His Life through His Letters* (London: Marion Boyars, 1984), pp. 1–2.
72. Fauré, letter (6 August 1896), in Lockspeiser, p. 140.
73. Fauré, letter (29 August 1903), in Lockspeiser, p. 143.
74. Fauré, letter (6 April 1922), in Lockspeiser, p. 157.
75. Fauré, letter (16 January 1905), in Lockspeiser, p. 147.
76. Fauré, letter (12 August 1903), in Lockspeiser, p. 142.
77. Fauré, letter (24 March 1921), in Lockspeiser, p. 157.
78. Fauré, letter (21 September 1904), in Lockspeiser, p. 145.
79. Fauré, letter (11 September 1906), in Lockspeiser, p. 149.
80. Claude Debussy, letter (24 March 1908); see Eric Frederick Jensen, *Debussy* (Oxford: Oxford University Press, 2014), p. 5.
81. In *L'Art musical*; see Jensen, p. 11.
82. Jensen, p. 15.
83. As above, p. 21.
84. As above, p. 24.
85. See 'The Orientation of Music', in Richard Langham Smith (ed.), *Debussy on Music* (Ithaca, NY: Cornell University Press, 1988), p. 84.
86. Jensen, p. 23.
87. As above, p. 25.
88. As above, p. 28.
89. Claude Debussy, letter (16 September 1885), in Claude Debussy, François Lesure (ed.), Roger Nichols (ed. and trans.), *Debussy Letters* (Cambridge, MA: Harvard University Press, 1987), p. 11.
90. Debussy, letter (9 February 1887), in Jensen, p. 34.
91. Jensen, p. 35.
92. As above, p. 125.
93. As above, p. 41.

94. Debussy, letter to G. Jean-Aubry (25 March 1910), in Lockspeiser, p. 117.
95. As above, p. 118.
96. Jensen, p. 59.
97. As above, p. 66.
98. Debussy, letter to Pierre Louÿs (16 May 1899), in Jensen, p. 67.
99. Debussy, letter (5 January 1900), in Lockspeiser, p. 107.
100. Roger Nichols and Richard Langham Smith, *Claude Debussy: Pelléas und Mélisande* (Cambridge: Cambridge University Press, 1989), p. 147.
101. Jensen, p. 86.
102. As above, p. 86
103. As above, p. 87.
104. As above, p. 93.
105. As above, p. 105.
106. As above, p. 107.
107. Debussy, letter (11 December 1913), in Lockspeiser, p. 121.
108. Debussy, letter (24 October 1915), in Jensen, p. 112.
109. Debussy, letter (4 January 1916), in Jensen, p. 112.
110. Jensen, p. 112.
111. Debussy, letter (25 February 1906), in Lockspeiser, p. 116.
112. Debussy, letter (30 January 1892), in Jensen, p. 48.
113. Debussy, letter (25 February 1906), in Lockspeiser, p. 117.
114. Recollection of Charles Koechlin, in Jensen, p. 163.
115. Jensen, p. 200.
116. Debussy, letter (10 October 1895), in Jensen, p. 171.
117. Debussy, letter to Jacques Durand (1 September 1905); see Paul Driver, 'Debussy through His Letters', review of *Debussy Letters* in *The Musical Times* vol. 128, no. 1738 (Dec. 1987), p. 68.
118. Debussy, letter (15 September 1902), in Jensen, p. 165.
119. Referring to Arthur Rimbaud, *Les Illuminations* (1886).
120. Debussy, letter to Louis Laloy (8 March 1907); see Deborah Mawer, *The Cambridge Companion to Ravel* (Cambridge: Cambridge University Press, 2000), p. 241.
121. Maurice Ravel, letter (29 June 1905), in Lockspeiser, p. 129.
122. Mawer, p. 188.
123. Widely quoted; see, for example, David Schiff, 'Misunderstanding Gershwin', in *The Atlantic* (1 October 1998), theatlantic.com
124. Byron Adams, 'Vaughan Williams's Musical Apprenticeship', in Alain Frogley and Aidan J. Thomson (eds.), *The Cambridge Companion to Vaughan Williams* (Cambridge: Cambridge University Press, 2013), p. 40.
125. Ravel, letter (15 April 1916), in Lockspeiser, p. 137.
126. Ravel, letter (4 August 1914), in Lockspeiser, p. 135.
127. Ravel, letter (9 February 1917), in Lockspeiser, p. 138.
128. See Barbara Kelly, *Music and Ultra-modernism in France: A Fragile Consensus, 1913–1939* (Woodbridge: Boydell Press, 2013), p. 56.
129. See Arbie Orenstein, *Maurice Ravel: Man and Musician* (New York: Dover Publications, 1991), p. 78.
130. Maurice Ravel, letter (21 February 1928), in Lockspeiser, p. 138.
131. Quoted in Arbie Orenstein (ed.), *A Ravel Reader: Correspondence, Articles, Interviews* (New York: Dover Publications, 2003), p. 477.

132. Roger Nichols, *Ravel* (New Haven, CT, and London: Yale University Press, 2011), p. 301.
133. Roger Nichols, *Ravel Remembered* (London: Faber & Faber, 1987), pp. 47–8.
134. Ravel, letter (7 February 1906), in Lockspeiser, p. 131.
135. Henri Hell, Edward Lockspeiser (trans.), *Francis Poulenc* (New York: Grove Press, 1959), pp. 14–15.
136. Jean Cocteau, Rollo H. Myers (trans.), *Cock and Harlequin* (London: The Egoist Press, 1921), pp. 4, 8, 111.
137. Griffiths, p. 7.
138. See Jean Roy, *Francis Poulenc: l'homme et son œuvre* (Paris: Seghers, 1964), p. 60.
139. Mihai Cucos, 'A Few Points about Burt Bacharach', *Perspectives of New Music* vol. 43, no. 1 (Winter 2005), p. 205.
140. See Hell, pp. 3–4.
141. See Carl B. Schmidt, *Entrancing Muse: A Documented Biography of Francis Poulenc* (Hillsdale, NY: Pendragon Press, 2001), p. 182.
142. Hell and Lockspeiser, pp. 9–10.
143. William Mann, 'Poulenc's Choral Masterpiece', in *The Times* (8 March 1963).
144. Roger Nichols, *Poulenc: A Biography* (New Haven, CT, and London: Yale University Press, 2020), p. 165.
145. I am grateful to the historian of French music Richard Langham Smith for this information.
146. Christopher Moore, 'Constructing the Monk: Francis Poulenc and the Post-War Context', in *Intersections*, vol. 32, no. 1–2 (2012), pp. 203–30.
147. I am grateful to Richard Langham Smith for this information.
148. See entry for Suzanne Valadon, in *Akademiska Föreningen* (Lund University).
149. Cocteau, p. 14.
150. As above, p. 14.
151. Roger Shattuck, *The Banquet Years: The Origins of the Avant-garde in France, 1885 to World War I* (1960; Freeport, NY: Books for Libraries Press, 1972).
152. See Kim Willsher, 'Proust's Love Letters to Composer Go on Display before Paris Auction', in the *Guardian* (22 May 2018).
153. See Deborah Schwartz-Kates, 'Alberto Ginastera, Argentine Cultural Construction, and the Gauchesco Tradition', in *The Musical Quarterly*, vol. 86, no. 2 (Summer 2002), pp. 248–81.
154. Aaron Copland, Richard Kostelanetz, Steven Silverstein (eds.), *Aaron Copland: A Reader: Selected Writings 1923–1972* (New York and London: Routledge, 2004), p. 79.
155. Craft and Stravinsky, p. 41.
156. Craft and Stravinsky, p. 42.
157. Eric Blom (ed.), entry for 'Rachmaninoff' in *Grove Dictionary of Music and Musicians* (5th edn, London: Macmillan, 1954).
158. Stravinsky, *Poetics of Music*, p. 96.
159. In the musical fallout from the Zhdanov Doctrine of 1946.
160. Daniel M. Grimley, preface to *Carl Nielsen and the Idea of Modernism* (Woodbridge: Boydell Press, 2011), p. ix.
161. Quoted by, for example, Adrian Thomas in sleeve notes to *Karol Szymanowski, Symphonies Nos. 3 and 4*, Hyperion Records CD LSO0739.
162. Sergey Prokofieff, Anthony Phillips (trans.), *Diaries 1915–1923: Behind the Mask* (London: Faber & Faber, 2008), p. 196.
163. As above, pp. 207–8.

17: America and the Jazz Era

1. Aaron Copland, *Music and Imagination: The Charles Eliot Norton Lectures (1951–1952)* (New York: Mentor Books, 1959), p. 102.
2. Comment attributed to Pierre Zimmermann, piano professor at the Paris Conservatoire; see Irving Lowens, S. Frederick Starr (revd), 'Louis Moreau Gottschalk', *Grove Music Online* (2001).
3. Copland, pp. 102–3.
4. Verbal comment at a rehearsal, reported later; see, for example, Cary O'Dell, '"Adagio for Strings" – Arturo Toscanini, Conductor; NBC Symphony Orchestra (November 5, 1938)', US Library of Congress, National Registry, 2005.
5. Gian Carlo Menotti, comment to his biographer, John Gruen. See Myrna Oliver, 'Obituary, Gian Carlo Menotti', *Los Angeles Times* (2 February 2007).
6. Alan Clayson, *Edgard Varèse* (London: Bobcat Books, 2002), p. 143.
7. See, for example, the sleeve notes to *Varèse: Orchestral Works, Vol. 2*, Naxos CD 8.557882.
8. Copland, p. 104.
9. Copland, p. 105.
10. See Stephen P. Slottow, 'Carl Ruggles and Charles Seeger: Strict vs. Free Imitation in Ruggles's Canons', in *Music Theory Spectrum*, vol. 30, no. 2 (Fall 2008), pp. 283–303.
11. Virgil Thomson, Richard Kostelanetz (ed.), *Virgil Thomson: A Reader – Selected Writings 1924–1984* (New York and London: Routledge, 2002), p. 164.
12. Judith Tick, *Ruth Crawford Seeger: A Composer's Search for American Music* (Oxford: Oxford University Press, 1997), p. 65.
13. Antonín Dvořák, 'The Real Value of Negro Melodies', in the *New York Herald* (21 May 1893).
14. Widely quoted; see, for example, Columbia University, blackhistory.news.columbia.edu
15. H. E. Krehbiel (1893); see Ted Gioia, *The History of Jazz* (New York: Oxford University Press, 1998), p. 10.
16. Alan Lomax, *The Land Where the Blues Began* (New York: Pantheon, 1993), p. 81, quoted in Gioia, p. 8.
17. Julius Lester, *To Be a Slave* (New York: Dial Press, 1968), p. 36, quoted in Gioia, p. 36.
18. Gioia, p. 45.
19. As above, p. 43.
20. As above, p. 57.
21. As above, p. 75.
22. As above, p. 94.
23. Billie Holiday, *Lady Sings the Blues* (1956; London: Penguin Books, 2018), p. 1.
24. See Roman Vlad, F. and A. Fuller (trans.), *Stravinsky* (Oxford: Oxford University Press, 1960), p. 126.
25. Gioia, p. 89.
26. Copland, pp. 89–90.

18: Ways Ahead

1. Cécile Sauvage, 'Il est né' (1908), in *L'Âme en bourgeon* (Paris: Mercure de France, 1910).
2. Humphrey Carpenter, *Benjamin Britten: A Biography* (London: Faber & Faber, 1992), p. 11.
3. Howard Pollack, *Aaron Copland: The Life and Work of an Uncommon Man* (New York: Henry Holt & Co., 1999), p. 47.

4. As above, p. 190.
5. Aaron Copland in discussion with his biographer, Anthony Tommasini; see 'They Heard America Playing', *The New York Times* (13 August 2014).
6. Aaron Copland, *Music and Imagination: The Charles Eliot Norton Lectures (1951–1952)* (New York: Mentor Books, 1959), p. 108.
7. Olivier Messiaen, preface to 'Expériences musicales (musiques concrètes, électroniques, exotiques)', *La Revue Musicale* (1959), p. 5.
8. Dmitri Shostakovich, L. Grigoryev and Y. Platek (compilers), Angus and Neilian Roxburgh (trans.), *Shostakovich: About Himself and His Times* (Moscow: Progress Publishers, 1981), p. 33.
9. Elizabeth Wilson, *Shostakovich: A Life Remembered* (2nd edn, Princeton, NJ: Princeton University Press, 2006), pp. 128–9.
10. Laurel E. Fay, *Shostakovich: A Life* (Oxford: Oxford University Press, 2000), pp. 84–5.
11. Wilson, p. 152.
12. Copland, *Music and Imagination*, p. 109.
13. As above.
14. Carpenter, p. 226.
15. As above.
16. As above, p. 198.
17. Anthony Pople, *Messiaen: Quatuor pour la fin du temps* (Cambridge: Cambridge University Press, 2003), pp. 7, 8.
18. Pollack, pp. 284–5.
19. See Sheryl Gay Stolberg, 'Transcripts Detail Secret Questioning in 50's by McCarthy', in *The New York Times* (6 May 2003); full transcript is at www.senate.gov, *Historic Senate Hearings Published*.
20. Wilson, p. 183.
21. Pollack, p. 465.
22. As above, pp. 445–6.
23. Personal communication to James Bowman, to whom I am grateful for permission to share it.
24. Pollack, p. 516.
25. In 1959, in relation to criticism of Vaughan Williams; see Peter Wiegold and Ghislaine Kenyon, *Beyond Britten: The Composer and the Community* (Woodbridge: Boydell Press, 2015), p. 23.
26. Pollack, p. 11.
27. As above, p. 465.
28. Messiaen, p. 5.
29. Olivier Messiaen, preface to *La Technique de mon langage musical* (Paris: A. Leduc, 1944).
30. Copland, *Music and Imagination*, p. 111.

PART EIGHT: STOCKHAUSEN AND *SGT. PEPPER* (1945–2000)
Introduction

1. Pierre Boulez, remark from youth, widely requoted, often in slightly varying form; see, for example, 'Obituary, L'enfant terrible', in *The Economist* (14 January 2016).
2. In an interview with Jessica Duchen, 'Pierre Boulez: A Very Modern Maestro', the *Independent* (30 August 2012).
3. See Toby Thacker, *Music after Hitler, 1945–1955* (Aldershot: Ashgate, 2007), p. 119.
4. See Alex Ross, *The Rest is Noise: Listening to the Twentieth Century* (London: Fourth Estate, 2008), pp. 347–8.

5. As above, p. 348.
6. As above, p. 349.
7. Milton Babbitt, in an interview with Gabrielle Zuckermann for 'American Mavericks' on American Public Media (July 2002).
8. See Allen Edwards, *Flawed Words and Stubborn Sounds: A Conversation with Elliott Carter* (New York: W. W. Norton & Co., 1971), p. 61.
9. Theodor W. Adorno, *Philosophie der neuen Musik* (Frankfurt: Suhrkamp Taschenbuch, 1976), p. 126.
10. György Ligeti, lecture at the New England Conservatory (10 March 1993).
11. Peter Maxwell Davies, in a widely quoted interview; see, for example, 'Obituary: Sir Peter Maxwell Davies' (14 March 2016), www.bbc.co.uk
12. Donald Mitchell, *The Language of Modern Music* (London: Faber & Faber, 3rd edn, 1976), p. 167.
13. The *Observer* (11 October 1959), p. 24.
14. Ligeti.
15. Paul Griffiths, *Igor Stravinsky: The Rake's Progress* (Cambridge: Cambridge University Press, 1982), p. 132.
16. Mitchell, p. 131.
17. As above, p. 132.

19: Moderner Than Thou

1. Julius Reiber, in the *Darmstädter Echo* (16 January 1946), quoted in Judith S. Ulmer, *Geschichte des Georg-Büchner-Preises: Soziologie eines Rituals* (Berlin: Walter de Gruyter, 2006), p. 94.
2. Donald Mitchell, *The Language of Modern Music* (London: Faber & Faber, 3rd edn, 1976), p. 152.
3. Jean-Jacques Nattiez (ed.), Robert Samuels, (trans. and ed.), *The Boulez–Cage Correspondence* (Cambridge: Cambridge University Press, 1993), p. 149.
4. https://www.youtube.com/watch?v=NIipwlKojU
5. Mauricio Kagel in conversation with Max Nyffeler (23 March 2000), on his being awarded the Ernst von Siemens Music Prize, published in *Lettre*, vol. 51 (April 2000).
6. Kagel, interview given at the festival 'Il nuovo – l'antico', Bologna, October 2008. See, for example, sleeve notes to *Der Schall, Fuer Fuenf Spieler* (LP, Deutsche Grammophon Avant Garde, ct no 2543001, April 2010).
7. Hector Berlioz, C. R. Fortescue (trans.), *Evenings in the Orchestra* (1852; Harmondsworth: Penguin, 1963), 'Twelfth Evening', p. 152.
8. Kagel in conversation with Nyffeler.
9. John Cage, 'The Music Lover's Field Guide', in *United States Lines Paris Review* (1954); reprinted in John Cage, *Silence: Lectures and Writings by John Cage* (Middletown, CT: Wesleyan University Press, 1961).
10. See Dorothy Lamb Crawford, 'Arnold Schoenberg in Los Angeles', in *The Musical Quarterly* vol. 86, no. 1 (Spring 2002), pp. 6–48.
11. John Cage, in an interview with Miroslav Sebestik (1991). From *Listen*, documentary by Miroslav Sebestik (ARTE France Développement, 2003).
12. Quoted in Christopher Shultis, 'Cage and Europe', in David Nicholls (ed.), *The Cambridge Companion to John Cage* (Cambridge, Cambridge University Press, 2002), p. 31.
13. Peter Ackroyd, *Charlie Chaplin* (London: Chatto & Windus, 2014), p. 226.

14. See Martin Iddon, *New Music at Darmstadt: Nono, Stockhausen, Cage, and Boulez* (Cambridge: Cambridge University Press, 2013), p. 161.
15. See Michael Hicks, 'John Cage's Studies with Schoenberg', in *American Music* vol. 8, no. 2 (Summer 1990), pp. 125–140.
16. See Jonathan Goldman, *The Musical Language of Pierre Boulez: Writings and Compositions* (Cambridge: Cambridge University Press, 2011), p. 7.
17. Iannis Xenakis, *Musiques formelles: nouveaux principes formels de composition musicale* (1963; Paris: Stock, 1981), p. 18.
18. Mitchell, p. 128.
19. Karlheinz Stockhausen, '*Es geht aufwärts*', in *Texte zur Musik 1984–1991*, vol. 9 (Kürten: Stockhausen-Verlag, 1998), p. 452.
20. Jonathan Harvey, *The Music of Stockhausen: An Introduction* (Berkeley, CA: University of California Press, 1975), p. 13.
21. Nattiez, p. 106.
22. Pierre Boulez, 'Aléa', published in *Nouvelle Revue française* no. 59 (1 November 1957).
23. See Joan Peyser, *To Boulez and Beyond: Music in Europe since the Rite of Spring* (New York: Watson-Guptill, 1999), p. 192.
24. Widely quoted; see, for example, Fiachra Gibbons, 'Jean-Luc Godard: "Film is Over: What to Do?"', in the *Guardian* (12 July 2011).
25. Luigi Russolo, in the Futurist manifesto *L'Arte dei Rumori* (*The Art of Noises*) (1913).
26. Peter Manning, *Electronic and Computer Music* (Oxford: Oxford University Press, 2004), p. 14.
27. Joseph Schillinger, 'Electricity, a Musical Liberator', in *Modern Music* 8 (March–April 1931), p. 26.
28. B. Jack Copeland, *Turing: Pioneer of the Information Age* (Oxford: Oxford University Press, 2014), pp. 165–7.
29. See David W. Patterson (ed.), *John Cage, Music, Philosophy, and Intention, 1933–1950* (New York: Routledge, 2008), p. 105.
30. Widely quoted remark by the composer; see, for example, Paul Griffiths' sleeve notes to *György Ligeti, String Quartets Nos. 1 & 2 – Ramifications etc.*, Deutsche Grammophon 474327-2.
31. Transcript of 'The John Tusa Interview with György Ligeti' (4 March 2001), BBC Radio 3, https://www.bbc.co.uk/programmes/p00nc1k8
32. These are Henze's own words; see, for example, Paul Griffiths, 'A Bohemian Spirit Comfortable with the Classical', *The New York Times* (6 January 1999).
33. Hans Werner Henze, Peter Labanyi (trans.), *Music and Politics: Collected Writings 1953–1981* (Ithaca, NY: Cornell University Press, 1982).
34. Helmut Lachenmann, Jeffrey Stadelman (trans.), 'Open Letter to Hans Werner Henze', in *Perspectives of New Music* vol. 35, no. 2 (Summer 1997), pp. 189–200.
35. See Bálint András Varga, *Conversations with Iannis Xenakis* (London: Faber & Faber, 2003), p. 47.
36. See Nouritza Matossian, *Xenakis* (London: Kahn and Averill, 1986), p. 48.
37. Le Corbusier, *Le Modulor* (Paris: Éditions de l'Architecture d'Aujourd'hui, 1945), p. 74.
38. Carey Lovelace, 'How Do You Draw a Sound?', in Sharon Kanach, Carey Lovelace, Mâkhi Xenakis, Ivan Hewett, *Iannis Xenakis: Composer, Architect, Visionary* (New York: The Drawing Center, 2010).
39. Varga, p. 97. See also Sven Sterken, 'Interactions between Music and Architecture in the Work of Iannis Xenakis' (2006), https://musicandarchitecture.weebly.com/uploads/2/5/3/7/25377417/document_1.pdf

40. Iannis Xenakis, Sharon Kanach (ed.), *Musiques formelles* (Stuyvesant, NY: Pendragon Press, 1990), preface, p. ix.
41. See sleeve notes to *Franco Donatoni: Chamber Works*, Naxos 0015021KAI.
42. See Clemens Kühn, 'Bernd Alois Zimmermann', in *Zeitgenössische Musik in der Bundesrepublik Deutschland 3* (1982), DMR 1007–09.
43. David M. Koenig with Delwin D. Fandrich, *Spectral Analysis of Musical Sounds with Emphasis on the Piano* (Oxford: Oxford University Press, 2015), p. v.
44. Tōru Takemitsu, 'Dream and Number', in *Confronting Silence: Selected Writings* (Berkeley, CA: Fallen Leaf Press, 1995), p. 112.
45. Paul Griffiths, in the programme note to a concert at Columbia University, New York (April 2010); see Anthony Tommasini, 'In Pursuit of Sounds Delicate and Eerie', in *The New York Times* (2 April 2010).
46. See Rob Tannenbaum, 'Minimalist Composer La Monte Young on His Life and Immeasurable Influence', *New York Vulture* (2 July 2015).
47. From Samuel Beckett, *Waiting for Godot* (1953), used as part of the text of Luciano Berio, *Sinfonia* (1968).
48. Leonard Bernstein, *The Unanswered Question: Six Talks at Harvard* (Cambridge, MA: Harvard University Press, 1976), p. 425.
49. Mitchell, p. 154.

20: Industry and Artistry

1. Colin Larkin, preface to Colin Larkin (ed.), *The Encyclopedia of Popular Music* (4th edn, New York: Oxford University Press, 2006).
2. Ted Gioia, *The History of Jazz* (New York: Oxford University Press, 1998), p. 200.
3. In Sophie Huber (dir.), *Blue Note Records: Beyond the Notes* (2018).
4. As above.
5. As above.
6. As above.
7. Philip Larkin, 'For Sidney Bechet' (1954), in *The Whitsun Weddings* (London: Faber & Faber, 1964).
8. Amiri Baraka, widely quoted in the literature around the issue of cultural appropriation. See, for example, 'Kenan Malik on Cultural Appropriation', in *ArtReview* (1 December 2017).
9. Jacques Brel, 'La Mort' (1959).
10. H. Gant, personal communication.
11. See Gioia, p. 177.
12. In Olivia Lichtenstein (dir.), *Teddy Pendergrass: If You Don't Know Me* (2018).
13. Joe Boyd, *White Bicycles: Making Music in the 1960s* (London: Serpent's Tail, 2006), p. 7.
14. See Renard 'Slangston Hughes' Bridgewater, '59/50 Flow', *Medium* (12 March 2018).
15. Quotes in, for example, Timothy Holder, *The Hip Hop Prayer Book: The Remix* (New York: Seabury Books, 2008), p. xviii.
16. Gioia, p. 394.
17. As above.

PART NINE: THE WAY WE LIVE NOW (2000–∞)
21: World Music, Girl Power and White Men in White Ties

1. Igor Stravinsky, *Poetics of Music in the Form of Six Lessons* (Cambridge, MA: Harvard University Press, 1942), pp. 63–4.
2. Stravinsky, *Poetics of Music*, p. 63.

3. John Butt, *Playing with History: The Historical Approach to Musical Performance* (Cambridge: Cambridge University Press, 2007), p. xi.
4. Lydia Goehr, *The Imaginary Museum of Musical Works: An Essay in the Philosophy of Music* (Oxford: Clarendon Press, 1994).
5. See her website, www.errollynwallen.com
6. Vinnie Mirchandani, *The New Polymath: Profiles in Compound-technology Innovations* (Hoboken, NJ: Wiley, 2010), p. xxiv.
7. See Pwyll ap Siôn, *Gramophone* (6 March 2019).
8. Seamus Heaney, in a widely reported comment to journalists; see, for example, 'Heaney Calls Eminem the Saviour of New Poetry', *The Times* (1 July 2003).
9. Ted Gioia, *The History of Jazz* (New York: Oxford University Press, 1998), p. 89.
10. Igor Stravinsky and Robert Craft, *Dialogues and a Diary* (Garden City, NY: Doubleday, 1963), p. 119.

Epilogue: The Next Million Years
1. E. H. Gombrich, *Art and Illusion: A Study in the Psychology of Pictorial Representation* (Princeton, NJ: Princeton University Press, 1969), p. 321.
2. Sir John Hawkins, *A General History of the Science and Practice of Music* (London: T. Payne, 1776), vol. 1, preface.

LIST OF ILLUSTRATIONS

Prologue: Bone flute dated to the Upper Paleolithic from Geissenklösterle, a German cave in the Swabian region. Replica. Credit: José-Manuel Benito Álvarez.
Part One: Marble seated harp player, Cycladic, 2800–2700 BCE. Metropolitan Museum of Art, New York.
Part Two: Guidonian hand from a manuscript from Mantua, last quarter of fifteenth century. Oxford University MS Canon. Liturg. 216. f. 168 recto (Bodleian Library).
Part Three: Knife engraved with musical notes forming a grace and blessing to be sung before and after a meal. Italy, first half of sixteenth century. © Victoria and Albert Museum, London.
Part Four: Violinist: Caricature by Pier Leone Ghezzi (1674–1755). © Vatican Apostolic Library, Ott.lat.3119.
Part Five: Announcement for the first performance of *Le Nozze di Figaro* (*The Marriage of Figaro*), 1 May 1786 at Vienna's Burgtheater. Granger Historical Picture Archive/Alamy.
Part Six: *Idyllische Landschaft mit Tempel und Aquädukt*. Johann Sebastian Bach the Younger (1776). Hamburg Kunsthalle.
Part Seven: A caricature of Mahler conducting the first performance of Symphony No. 1 in Vienna. (*Illustriertes Wiener Extrablatt*, 25 November, 1900).
Part Eight: Expo 1958 Philips Pavilion, designed by Le Corbusier; part of the score of *Metastasis* by Iannis Xenakis. Wouter Hagens/Angeldo; Creative Commons.
Part Nine: Hands at a rock concert; silhouettes against stage lighting. Shutterstock.
Epilogue: Troubadours (l); 'Foneno' in Florence (r). iStock; 'The Florentine', issue 225, July 2016.

Extract from Shostakovich's *String Quartet No. 12* © 1973 by Boosey & Hawkes Music Publishers Ltd. Reproduced by permission of Boosey & Hawkes Music Publishers Ltd.

While every effort has been made to contact copyright-holders of copyright material, the author and publishers would be grateful for information about any illustrations and music examples where they have been unable to trace them, and would be glad to make amendments in further editions.

ACKNOWLEDGEMENTS

I would like to thank the many people who have so kindly and willingly read this text as it emerged, including Andrew Sillett, John Caldwell, Susan Rankin, James Fellowes, Henry Mayr-Harting, Joe Davies, Felix Fardell and, in particular, Roger Allen and Richard Langham Smith. I am always amazed by the readiness and generosity with which friends and colleagues share their time and very considerable expertise. I acknowledge their contribution with gratitude and admiration. Their insights are on every page: any infelicities are mine alone. At Profile, I would like to thank my editors John Davey, who initiated the project, Louisa Dunnigan, who saw it through with patient enthusiasm, managing editor Graeme Hall, and many others. My agent Ian Drury has, as always, been a model of supportive professionalism. Staff at many libraries, particularly the Oxford University Faculty of Music and the Bodleian, have been unfailingly helpful. Talking about music with generations of students, formally and informally, is always revealing and sometimes surprising. Finally, I would like to thank my family, for everything.

INDEX

Page numbers in *italics* refer to images and/or music examples

A
Abba 549
Abbate, Carolyn 347, 373, 395
Abel, Carl Friedrich 186, 199, 226
Abrahamsen, Hans 558
Adam, Adolphe 342, 345–6, 355
    'Cantique de Noël' 346
    Giselle 346
Adamberger, Valentin 223
Adams, John 486, 558
    The Death of Klinghoffer 558
    Doctor Atomic 558
    Nixon in China 558
Adderley, Julian 'Cannonball' 542
Adele (Adele Adkins) 560
Adès, Thomas 558
Adler, Guido 9
Adorno, Theodor 517, 520
Aeschylus 23, 24
Agoult, Countess Marie d' 281, 282, 283, 284, 298
Agricola, Alexander 72
Albéniz, Isaac 296, 444, 455
    Iberia 309
Albert, Prince 285
Alberti, Giuseppe 191
Albinoni, Tomaso 13, 129, 131, 158
Albrecht V, Duke 82
Albrechtsberger, Johann Georg 245
Alcuin 28
aleatoric music, see Chance in music
Alexander I, Tsar 340
Alfonso X of Castile, 40–1
Alfred, King 28
Algarotti, Francesco
    Essay on the Opera 209
Alkan, Charles-Valentin 247
Allen, Roger 358
Amati family 125
Ambrose, St 27, 45
Amenda, Carl 256
Andersen, Hans Christian 235, 293
Anderson, Leroy 540
Anerio, Felice 114
Anerio, Giovanni 114
Angiolini, Gaspari 209
Anonymous IV 51–2
Ansermet, Ernest 491
Antwerp 104
Aperghis, Georges, 525
Apollinaire, Guillaume 469
Arbeau, Thoinot 92
Arcadelt, Jacques 82, 95
architecture and music 1, 4, 65, 114, 408, 519, 533
Aristophanes 23
    The Wasps 24–5
Aristotle 20, 24, 37, 194, 333
Aristoxenus
    on 'harmonics' and 'rhythmics' 20
Armstrong, Louis 491, 541
    'West End Blues' 536
Arne family 244
Arne, Thomas
    Comus 161
Arnim, Achim von 243, 418
Arnim, Bettina von (née Brentano) 285
Arnold, Malcolm 451
Arnold, Matthew 483
ars antiqua 50–3
ars nova 53–5
ars perfecta 75

ars subtilior 6, 55, 534
Artusi, Giovanni
  L'Artusi overo delle imperfettioni della moderna musica 119
Ashcroft, Dame Peggy 489
Astaire, Fred 495
Attaingnant, Pierre 61, 92, 93
Attwood, Thomas 212, 245
Auber, Daniel 342, 343, 344, 345, 348, 350, 382
  Gustave III ou le bal masqué 345, 382
  Le maçon 344
  Manon Lescaut 345
  La muette de Portici 344, 350
Auden, Wystan Hugh (W. H.) 357, 433, 452, 503
  The Age of Anxiety 413–4
  Hymn to Saint Cecilia (for Benjamin Britten) 503
  Night Mail 501
  Paul Bunyan 503–4
  The Rake's Progress 433
Auerbach, Lera 557
Augustine of Canterbury, St 28
Augustine of Hippo, St 27–8
  De Musica 27
Auric, Georges 466
  Adieu New York 466
  Film scores:
    The Lavender Hill Mob 466
    Passport to Pimlico 466
    Roman Holiday 466
    Le Sang d'un Poète 466
    The Titfield Thunderbolt 466
Avison, Charles 131, 137, 170, 188

B

Babbitt, Milton 517, 537
  'Who Cares If You Listen?' 517
Bach, Anna Magdalena 186
Bach, Carl Philipp Emanuel 105, 138, 153, 165, 172, 185, 188, 191, 197, 198, 214, 215, 222, 243, 251, 299
  as biographer of J. S. Bach 11
Bach, Johann Christian 2, 143, 186, 187, 189, 190, 191, 194, 197, 199, 212, 216, 222, 223, 226, 299
Bach, Johann Elias 172
Bach, Johann Sebastian 11, 102, 104, 105, 107, 109, 111, 113, 117, 125, 127, 129, 131, 132, 133, 137, 147, 150, 151, 153, 154, 158, 159, 160, 162, 165, 166, 171–4, 177, 194, 197, 243, 244, 298, 315, 323, 359, 389, 411
  personal life 8, 102, 171
  lost scores 11
  antecedents 88, 171
  family 136, 186
  later reputation and influence 208, 215, 220, 221, 246, 262, 263, 276, 289, 290, 301, 320, 371, 392, 424, 431, 436, 438, 442, 443, 447, 473, 477, 536, 543, 564
  The Art of Fugue 173
  Brandenburg Concertos 150, 172, 431
  Concerto for Three Claviers 281
  'Ein feste Burg' (cantata) 172–3
  'Es ist genug' (chorale harmonisation) 436, 534
  Goldberg Variations 173
  Mass in B minor 290
  The Musical Offering 173, 438
  'Ouvertures' (Orchestral Suites) 150
  Passacaglia and Fugue in C minor 172
  St John Passion 290
  St Matthew Passion 276, 290, 447
  Suites for Solo Cello 443
  The Well-Tempered Clavier, 111
Bach, Johann Sebastian the Younger 233
Bach, Wilhelm Friedemann, 191, 197–8
  as custodian of J. S. Bach 11
Bach, Wilhelm Friedrich Ernst 186, 290
Bach, Veit 88
Bacharach, Burt 468
  'Close To You' 468
  'Magic Moments' 468
  'Raindrops Keep Fallin' on My Head' 468
Baez, Joan 543, 546
Bainton, Edgar 427
Baker, Chet 542
Balakirev, Mily 307, 323, 326, 353
  Islamey 324, 462
  Overtures *'On Russian Themes'* 324
  Symphony No. 1 324
  Tamara 324
Baldwin, James 482
ballade, medieval 32

ballet 114, 346, 349, 355, 451
 comédie-ballet 143
Banchieri, Adriano 117
Banester, Gilbert 75
Bantock, Granville 450
Barber, Samuel 483–4, 558
 Adagio for Strings 483
 'Dover Beach' 483
 Knoxville: Summer of 1915 483
 Vanessa 483
Barbi, Alice 311
Barcelona 138
Bardac, Emma (later Debussy) 456, 458, 459
Bardac, Raoul 460
Bardac, Régina-Hélène ('Dolly') 456
Bardi, Count 113
Barezzi, Antonio 372, 373, 375, 391, 384
Barrault, Jean-Louis 524
Barrett, Syd 542
Barry, Gerald
 The Importance of Being Earnest 559
Bartók, Béla 292, 401, 431, 435, 440–3, 473, 477, 485, 487, 492, 522, 524, 531
 and folk music 442–3, 444, 445
 Bluebeard's Castle 400, 441
 Concerto for Orchestra 441, 506
 Fourteen Bagatelles 440
 'Goat Song' 442
 Mikrokosmos 415, 441
 Piano Concerto No. 3 441, 479
 Rhapsody No. 1 441
 Sonata for Two Pianos and Percussion 441
 String quartets 441–2
  String Quartet No. 3 442
  String Quartet No. 5 441–2
  String Quartet No. 6 442
Bartók, Peter 441
Basie, William 'Count' 3, 492, 548
Batteux, Charles 178
Baudelaire, Charles 498
Bauer-Lechner, Natalie 420
Bax, Sir Arnold
 Tintagel 450
Beach, Amy 481
 'To the Girl Who Wants to Compose' 481
Beamish, Sally 557–8
Beastie Boys, The 558

Beatles, The 10, 491, 518–9, 541, 544
 Sgt. Pepper's Lonely Hearts Club Band 540, 545
 'A Day in the Life' 545
 'Eleanor Rigby' 545
 'I am the Walrus' 545
 'Love Me Do' 545
 'Lucy in the Sky with Diamonds' 545
 'She Loves You' 545
 'Strawberry Fields Forever' 545
 'Yellow Submarine' 545
 'Yesterday' 545
Beaumarchais, Pierre-Augustin Caron de 182, 203, 350
 Figaro plays 203
bebop 542
Bechet, Sidney 490, 491, 543
Bechstein (piano-makers) 246
Beckett, Samuel 525
Beckford, William 179
Beecham, Sir Thomas 400, 424
Beethoven, Johann (composer's brother) 254, 262
Beethoven, Johann van (father) 254
Beethoven, Karl (brother) 256, 259
Beethoven, Karl (nephew) 246, 259–60
Beethoven, Ludwig van (grandfather) 254
Beethoven, Ludwig van 5, 11, 13, 121, 178, 184, 186, 189, 191, 221, 222, 229, 230, 236, 237, 243, 246, 253, 253–66, 269, 270, 272, 273, 274, 276, 278, 281, 291, 298, 304, 305, 319, 327, 420, 563
 later reputation and influence 284, 286, 288, 292, 294, 301, 302, 311, 320, 361, 371, 381, 416, 434, 441, 442, 451, 518
 Concertos
  Piano Concerto No. 4 220, 259, 299
  Piano Concerto No. 5 ('Emperor') 265, 276, 304
 Opera
  Fidelio 259, 264, 331, 339, 359
 Sonatas
  Piano sonatas 256
  Piano Sonatas Nos. 1–3 256
  Piano Sonata No. 8 ('Pathétique') 256
  Piano Sonata No. 17 262
  Piano Sonata No. 21 ('Waldstein') 256, 264

Piano Sonata No. 29
  ('Hammerklavier') 256
Piano Sonata No. 31 300
Violin Sonata No. 9 ('Kreutzer')
  259
Violin Sonata No. 10 259
String quartets
  Quartets Nos. 1–6 265
  Quartets Nos. 7–9 ('Razumovsky')
    258, 265
  Quartets Nos. 12–16 261, 265
  Quartet No. 14 300
  Quartet No. 16 264
  Grosse Fuge 261
Symphonies
  Symphony No. 1 208, 299, 299
  Symphony No. 3 ('Eroica') 258, 408,
    411
  Symphony No. 5 240, 259, 263, 264,
    303, 303–4, 304, 312
  Symphony No. 6 ('Pastoral') 259, 537
  Symphony No. 7 259, 264
  Symphony No. 8 259, 265
  Symphony No. 9 261, 262, 265, 266,
    300, 306, 312, 315, 320, 359, 362
Sacred music
  Mass in D Major (*Missa solemnis*) 260,
    262
Bagatelle in F 265
Choral Fantasia 259, 451
The Consecration of the House 260
'Diabelli' Variations 247
Wellington's Victory 259
Beethoven, Maria Magdalena van
  (mother) 254
Beethoven, Maria (sister-in-law) 259
Beiderbecke, Bix 491
bel canto 335
Belgium 344
Bella, Ján Levoslav
  Wieland the Blacksmith 356
Bellini, Vincenzo 296, 335, 336, 375
  Norma 337
    'Casta diva' 337
  I puritani 338
  La sonnambula 337
Benda, Georg
  Ariadne auf Naxos 181
Benedict, Julius 238, 252

Benedict, St 27, 28, 45
  Rule of St Benedict 45
Benjamin, George 558
  Sudden Time 558
Bennet, John
  'Weep, O mine eyes' 95–6
Bennett, Sir William Sterndale 281
Benson, Edward Frederick (E. F.) 478
Bent, Margaret 70
Berardi, Angelo 28, 112, 113
Berberian, Cathy, 522, 525, 530
Berg, Alban, 427, 435–6, 437, 487, 500, 527
  Drei Orchesterstücke 425, 435
  Lulu 412, 436
  Lyrische Suite 438
  Wozzeck 436
  Violin Concerto 436, 534
Berio, Luciano, 524, 525, 530, 532
  Thema (Omaggio a Joyce) 530
  Sequenza (series of compositions) 532
  Sinfonia 532, 559
  Visage 530
Berkeley, Busby 495
Berkeley, Sir Lennox 452
  Concerto for Two Pianos and Orchestra
    452
  A Dinner Engagement 452
Berlin, Irving (Baline, Israel) 3, 409, 413,
  480, 492–3, 494, 499
  inability to read music 10, 493
  'Alexander's Ragtime Band' 492
  'Cheek to Cheek' 6
  'Puttin' on the Ritz' 493
  Top Hat 494
  'When I Lost You' 492
Berlioz, Hector 13, 239, 240, 243, 244, 247,
  253, 262, 277, 284, 285, 286, 301, 304–7, 323,
  342, 345, 360, 457, 458, 525
  Writings on music 236, 237, 238, 239,
    241–2, 246, 278–9, 280, 297, 303, 341–2,
    345
  Béatrice et Bénédict 346
  Benvenuto Cellini 296, 346
  La damnation de Faust 306, 346
  L'enfance du Christ 346
  Harold en Italie 306
  Roméo et Juliette 306
  Symphonie fantastique 305
  Traité de l'instrumentation 306

Les Troyens 346
Berlioz, Louis-Clément-Thomas 307
Bernardon (actor) 214
Bernhardt, Sarah 378
Bernstein, Leonard, 413–4, 482, 497, 516, 520, 539, 558, 561
   as conductor 8, 424, 517, 539
   The Age of Anxiety 413–4
   Candide 539
   Mass 482
   Symphony No. 3 ('Kaddish') 479, 539
   West Side Story 6, 371, 527, 539, 547
   The Unanswered Question (lectures) 486, 539
Berry, Chuck, 518, 544
   'Johnny B. Goode' 544
Biber, Heinrich 160
   Rosary Sonatas 160
Bigot, Marie 274
Billings, William 481, 486
Binchois (de Bins), Gilles 3, 67, 68, 69, 71, 82
   'Mon seul et souverain desir' 68
   Nove cantum melodie 68
Birnbaum, Johann Abraham 177
Birtwistle, Sir Harrison 538
Bizet, Geneviève (née Halévy) 348, 350
Bizet, Georges 309, 348–9
   Carmen 342, 348–9, 385, 453
   Djamileh 348
   La jolie fille de Perth 348
   Les pêcheurs de perles 348, 349
Black, Don
   Tell Me on a Sunday 547
Blake, William 259, 368, 515
   'Tyger Tyger' 515
Blakey, Art 543
Bliss, Sir Arthur
   A Colour Symphony 450
Bliss, Mildred Barnes 488
Bliss, Robert Woods 488
Blitzstein, Marc, 517
Bloch, Ernest 413, 482
Blom, Eric 448
Blow, John 162, 163, 164, 166
   'Club Anthem' 164
Blow, Kurtis 549–50
blues 412, 490
Blues Brothers, The 549

Blume, Friedrich 9, 409–10
   'Music and Race' 409
   'The Racial Problem in Music' 410
Blüthner (piano-makers) 246
Boccherini, Luigi 185, 196, 212, 225, 299
Boethius 37–8, 39
Boeuf sur le Toit, Le (bar) 466–7
Böhm, Georg 172
Boieldieu, François-Adrien 323, 332, 341–2, 342, 343
   La Dame blanche 342
Boito, Arrigo 248, 315, 381, 382, 385, 386, 393
   as composer
      Mefistofele 347, 392
   as librettist 386
      Falstaff 386
      Otello 386
Bolden, Charles 'Buddy' 490
   'Buddy Bolden's Stomp' ('Funky Butt') 490
Bologna 125, 127
Bonaparte, Jérôme-Napoléon 259
Bonis, Mélanie-Hélène 453
Bononcini, Giovanni 170
Borodin, Alexander 296, 323, 325, 326, 485
   Polovtsian Dances 353
   Prince Igor 353
   String Quartet No. 2 325
   Symphony No. 2 325
Borrell, Andrew 97
Boublil, Alain
   Miss Saigon 547
Boughton, Rutland 371
Boulanger, Ernest 453
Boulanger, Lili 453
   Nocturne pour violon et piano 453
Boulanger, Nadia 452, 453, 473, 483, 500
Boulez, Pierre 434, 470, 486, 508, 515, 518, 519, 523, 524, 526, 527, 530, 558
   Le Marteau sans maître 523
   Piano Sonata No. 3 527–8
   Pli selon pli 523
   Structures I and II 526–7
Boult, Sir Adrian 451
Bourgeois, Louis 88–9
   'Or sus, serviteurs du Seigneur' 89, 90
Bowie, David 298, 447, 546
   Ziggy Stardust tour 546
Bowles, Paul 411, 482, 519

Boyce, William 170, 194, 299
    Symphony No. 1 in B Flat 195
Boyd, Joe 549
    White Bicycle 549
Brahms, Johann Jacob 310
Brahms, Johanna 310
Brahms, Johannes 2, 236, 243, 247, 253, 287, 295, 296, 301, 309–14, 315, 316, 318, 321, 385, 418, 422, 516
    reputation and influence 314–22, 324, 327, 333, 356, 357, 399, 401, 455, 476, 536
    Concertos
        Piano Concerto No. 1 311
        Piano Concerto No. 2 311
    Orchestral music
        Haydn Variations 311
        Hungarian Dances 311
    Sacred music
        Ein Deutsches Requiem 311
    Sonatas
        F-A-E sonata 287
    Songs
        Vier ernste Gesänge 311, 312
    Symphonies
        Symphony No. 1 311, 312
        Symphony No. 4 312, 418
    'O Welt, ich muss dich lassen' 312
Brand X 560
Brandt, Caroline (Caroline Weber) 251
Braque, Georges 557
Brecht, Bertolt 439, 446–7
    Rise and Fall of the City of Mahagonny 446–7
    The Threepenny Opera 446
Brel, Jacques 546
    'La mort' 546
Brendel, Alfred 253, 270, 271, 303
Brentano, Clemens 243, 418
Breuning, Eleonore von 254
Breuning, Gerhard von 261
Breuning, Stephan von 261
Bridge, Frank
    as teacher 7, 500
    The Sea 450
Bridgetower, George Polgreen 258–9
Britten, Benjamin, 450, 452, 498–512, 520
    as pupil 7
    views of other composers 264, 269, 317, 397, 424, 425, 450

as conductor 425
as pianist 469
Choral works
    The Ballad of Little Musgrave and Lady Barnard 505
    A Ceremony of Carols 503
    Hymn to Saint Cecilia 503
    Rejoice in the Lamb 503, 505
    Te Deum in C 509
Operas
    Billy Budd 508
    A Midsummer Night's Dream 317
    Paul Bunyan, 503–4
    Peter Grimes 399, 425, 488, 504, 505
    The Rape of Lucretia 508
    The Turn of the Screw 508, 509
Orchestral works
    Night Mail 501
    Sinfonia da Requiem 467, 503
    Sinfonietta 500
    War Requiem 508, 515
Songs and song cycles
    Serenade for Tenor, Horn and Strings 503
    Seven Sonnets of Michelangelo 509–10
    'Veggio co' bei vostri occhi un dolce lume' (Sonnet XXX) 509–10
Britton, Thomas 106
Broadwood & Sons (piano-makers) 245, 259
Broschi, Carlo see Farinelli
Brosses, Charles de 132
Brown, Clifford 543
Brown, James 548, 549
    'Sex Machine' 548
Brown, John 181
Browne, John 75
Brubeck, Darius 468
Brubeck, Dave 468
Bruch, Max 315, 401
Bruckner, Anton 318–20, 371, 418, 423, 516
    Mass settings 318
    Symphony No. 2 319
    Symphony No. 3 319
    Symphony No. 4 318
    Symphony No. 7 320, 371
    Symphony No. 8 320
Bruegel, Pieter, the Elder 531
Bruhns, Nicolaus 160

Brumel, Antoine 72
Brunelleschi, Filippo 70
Brunet (page-boy) 145
Brunswick, Therese von 256
Bublé, Michael 495
Büchner, Georg 436
Bucks Fizz
    'Making Your Mind Up' 548–9
Budden, Julian 376
Bull, John 93, 117
    'Doctor Bull's My Selfe – A Jigge' 93
Bülow, Hans von 246, 271, 308, 313, 314, 364, 376, 385, 402, 420
Burgmüller, Norbert 301
Burgundy, 67–70
Burleigh, Harry 321
Burney, Charles 9, 128, 136, 151, 166, 188, 189, 190, 198, 200, 211, 214, 229
Burns, Robert 235
Bush, Alan, 516, 534
Busnois, Antoine 70–1
    'Missa L'homme armé' 70–1, 71
Busoni, Ferruccio 247, 427, 440, 445
    Entwurf einer neuen Ästhetik der Tonkunst (essay) 445
Bussotti, Sylvano 534
Butt, John 556
Butterfield, Paul 543
Butterworth, George 411, 450
Buxtehude, Dietrich 106, 157, 159, 160, 172
Byttering, Thomas 67
Byrds, The 13
Byrd, William 2, 13, 75, 76, 77, 78–9, 84, 88, 90, 93, 177
    as teacher 7, 78
    'captivity' motets 6, 76–7
    Mass settings 79
    Civitas Sancti Tui 79
    'Infelix ego' 79
Byron, Lord (George Gordon) 293, 333

C

Cabezón, Antonio de 93
Caccini, Francesca 115
    La liberazione di Ruggiero 116
    Primo libro delle musiche 116
Caccini, Giulio 115, 117
    Euridice 116
Le nuove musiche 115, 116
Cage, John 427, 482, 487, 519, 523, 525–6, 527, 530, 540, 558
    4' 33" 526
    Imaginary Landscape 529
    Music of Changes 526
    Sonatas and Interludes for prepared piano 526
    String Quartet in Four Parts 526
    Silence (book) 525–6
Cahn, Sammy 3
Caldwell, John 41, 53, 72
Callas, Maria 330, 351
Callow, Simon 357
Calloway, Cab 490, 491
Calvin, John (Jean) 85, 88
Calzabigi, Ranieri de 182, 209, 211
Cambert, Robert 144, 147, 165
Cammarano, Salvadore 380
Campion, Thomas 97
    'Never Weather-beaten Sail' 97
Campra, André
    Le Devin du village 156
    Les fêtes vénitiennes 180
Canaan (Syria) 22
Cannabich family 200–1, 217
    Cannabich, Christian 191, 200–1, 299
    Cannabich, Elisabetha 200
    Cannabich, Rosa 201
'canon' of musical works 10
cantata 107
Canteloube, Joseph 453
Cardew, Cornelius 535
Cares, Agnes 276
Carissimi, Giacomo 122, 145, 147
    Diluvium universale 122
    Jephte 122
Carl Theodor, Elector 200
Carlos, Wendy
    Switched-on Bach 529
Carmina Burana 38–9, 42, 87
Carpani, Giuseppe 335
Carter, Elliott 408, 485, 488, 517, 537–8
Carter, Tim 101
Caruso, Enrico 345, 351
Casaluna, Madalena 62
Casanova, Giacomo 179–80, 183, 188, 201, 202, 205, 206
Casella, Alfredo 434, 446, 458, 479

Cash, Johnny 544
   'I Walk the Line' 544
Castelnuovo-Tedesco, Mario 401, 479
Castiglione, Baldassare 73
Castil-Blaze
   Robin des Bois 239
castrati 109, 201–2, 343
Catalani, Alfredo, 394
   La Wally 329
Cather, Willa 482
Catherine the Great, Empress 351
Catherine de Valois 67
Cavaillé-Coll, Aristide 245
Cavalieri, Emilio de 116
Cavalli, Francesco 123, 142, 143, 145
   Ercole amante 123
   Giasone 123
Cavour (Count) 381
Celle, Duke of 151
Cellini, Benvenuto 91–2, 346
Cererols, Joan 138
Cervantes, Miguel de 94
Cesti, Antonio 123, 145
   Il pomo d'oro 123
Chabrier, Emmanuel
   España 309, 453
Chaliapin, Feodor 351
Chaminade, Cécile 295, 493
chance in music 508, 519, 526, 527, 535
Chanel, Coco 431
chanson
   medieval 32
   renaissance 95
Chanson de Roland, Le 44
Chapel Royal (England) 67, 75, 78, 90, 162, 167
   as theatre company 94
Chapelle Royale (Paris) 141, 148
Chaplin, Charlie
   Limelight 526
Chappell, William 235
Charlemagne 46
Charles II, King 102
Charles the Bold 70
Charlotte, Queen 199
Charpentier, Gustave 394
Charpentier, Marc-Antoine, 147–9
   Leçons de Ténèbres 149
   Le Malade imaginaire 144, 149

Messe de minuit pour Noël 148
Chatterton, Thomas 334
Chaucer, Geoffrey 32
   The Canterbury Tales 35
Chausson, Ernest 315, 457, 458
Chávez, Carlos 472
   H.P. 472
Chelerd, Adèle du, Comtesse de Laprunarède, Duchesse de Fleury 282
Cherubini, Luigi 240, 275, 278, 332, 340, 341, 342–3
   Les deux journées 340
   Elisa 340
   Lodoïska 340
   Médée 340
   Requiem 342
Child, William
   'O Lord God, the heathen are come into thine inheritance' 91
Chin, Unsuk 558
Chopin, Emilia 273
Chopin family 273
Chopin, Frédéric, 231, 244, 247, 273–298, 342–3, 345, 376, 377, 460, 464, 474, 475, 476
   as pianist 10, 245, 246
   Études 279
   Préludes 283, 284, 290
   Piano Sonata No. 3 302
Chopin, Nicolas 274
chorales 86–7
Christian church
   early church 25–8
   monasticism 26–7
   Cecilian and Oxford movements 237
   Hymn and psalm-singing 237
Christina, Queen 126, 127, 134
Chrysostom, John 28
Cibber family 244
Cibber, Colley 102, 108, 158
   Love's Last Shift 108
Cibber, Susanna 202
Ciconia, Johannes 66
Cilea, Francesco 343, 394
Cimarosa, Domenico 213, 323, 336
   Il matrimonio segreto 336
Clare, John 189, 235
Claudel, Paul 467
clausula 32
Clemens non Papa, Jacob 3, 76

Clementi, Muzio 246
Cline, Patsy 541, 544
   'Crazy' 544
Clive, Kitty 202
Clough, Brian 539
Coates, Eric 413
Cobain, Kurt 549
Cocteau, Jean 430–1, 465–7, 470, 502, 507
   Le Coq et l'Arlequin 466–7, 507
   Parade 471
   Le Sang d'un Poète 466
   La Voix humaine 470
Cohan, George M. 492
   'Over There' 492
Cohen, Lyor 549–50
Cole, Nat 'King' (Nathaniel Adams) 495
Coleman, Ornette 497
Coleridge, Samuel Taylor
   The Rime of the Ancient Mariner 245
Colette 464, 478
Collet, Henri 466
Collier, Jacob 560–1
   In My Room 561
   'In the Bleak Midwinter' 560
Colloredo, Archbishop Hieronymus von 183, 184, 216, 217
Coltrane, John 542, 543, 548
   Blue Train 543
   A Love Supreme 548
Colvig, William 487
commedia dell'arte 94
Commitments, The 549
Compère, Loyset 72
computers and music 529, 536
concerto, Baroque 131–2
Confucius 21
Constance (Konstanz), Germany, Council of 66
Constantine, Emperor 28
contrafacta 39, 63
Cooke, Deryck 319
Cooke, Henry 161, 162
Cooper, John (Giovanni Coperario) 157
Copeland, Stewart 560
Copernicus, Nicolaus 21
Copland, Aaron, 455, 482, 488, 498–512, 516
   compositional method 7
   on other composers 424, 452, 472, 482–3, 485, 486, 496–7

   on music 480, 481, 482–3, 503, 550
   Appalachian Spring 482, 511
   Billy the Kid 503, 511
   Fanfare for the Common Man 511
   Lincoln Portrait 503
   Old American Songs 511
      'At The River' 511
      'Ching-a-Ring-Chaw' 511
      'I Bought Me a Cat' 511
      'Simple Gifts' 511
   Our New Music (The New Music) 508
   Our Town 482, 503
   Piano Fantasy 508
   Rodeo 511
   Short Symphony 500
   Symphonic Ode 500
Corbusier, Le 108, 533
Corelli, Arcangelo 125, 126, 126–8, 131, 157, 158
   Christmas Concerto 134
Corneille, Pierre 140, 141, 144
Cornelius, Peter, 310, 334–5
   Der Barbier von Bagdad 296, 335
Cornyshe, William 75
Corsi, Count 113
Cortese, Paolo 73
Cortot, Alfred 468
Coryat, Thomas 114, 118, 140–1, 147
Cossel, Otto 310
Costello, Elvis 1
Cotton Club, The 492
counterpoint 63, 110
Couperin family 111, 152–3
Couperin, François ('le Grand') 111, 113, 142, 151, 152–3, 156
   Concerts Royaux 150
   Je-ne-says-quoi 153
   La Couperin 153
   L'Apothéose de Corelli 150
   L'Apothéose de Lully 150
   L'Art de toucher le clavecin 153
   Leçons de Ténèbres 149
   Les Culbutes Jxcxbxnxs 153
   Les Folies Françoises 153
   Les Goûts réunis 150
   Les Nations 150
   Les Plaisirs de Saint-Germain-en-Laye 153
   Le Tic-Toc-Choc 153
Couperin, Louis 152

Couperin, Marguerite-Louise 148
Couperin, Nicolas (I) 153
Couperin, Nicolas (II) 153
Coward, Sir Noël 494, 546
   'If Love Were All' 494
Cowell, Henry Dixon 486–7
   New Musical Resources 487
Cowell, Sidney Robertson 487
Cowen, Henry 394
Cox, Sir William 135
Cozzolani, Chiara Margarita 124
Craft, Robert 431, 434
   Conversations with Igor Stravinsky 434
Cramer, Johann Baptist 246, 254
Cranmer, Thomas, 85
   Book of Common Prayer 78
Crawford, Ruth, see Crawford Seeger, Ruth
Cream 451
Cremona 119, 125
Croft, William 164
Cromwell, Oliver 161
Crosby, Bing (Harry Lillis) 491, 495
Cui, César 323, 324–5, 352, 353–4, 398, 475
   Puss in Boots 354
Cycladic civilisation 19
Cyprian of Carthage 26
Czerny, Carl 188, 246, 247, 263, 275, 302, 322, 459

D

Dahl, Nicolai 475
D'Alembert, Jean le Rond
   Encyclopédie ou Dictionnaire raisonné des sciences, des arts et des métiers 188
Dallapiccola, Luigi 410, 519
   Canti di prigionia 410
d'Altier, Azalais 40
dance 408, 413, 472
   see also 'ballet'
d'Anduza, Clara 40
Dangerfield, George 11
d'Anglebert, Jean-Henri 150
D'Angour, Armand 28
Dante Alighieri 38
Daquin, Louis-Claude 148
Dargomyzhsky, Alexander, 352, 357, 398
   Rusalka 352, 357
   The Stone Guest 352

Darin, Bobby 447
Darmstadt 251, 522
   International Summer Courses 410, 507, 522
   Darmstadt 'School' 522–8, 532–3
Darwin, Charles 447
   theory of evolution 6
Davenant, William
   The Siege of Rhodes 161
David, Ferdinand 274
Davis, Miles 496, 542, 543, 560
   Kind of Blue 542
   'So what?' 551
Davydov, Vladimir ('Bob') 329
Day, John 61, 90
De La Soul 550
Dean, Brett 558
Dean, Winton 349
Deathridge, John 365
Debussy, Claude 253, 296, 309, 317, 353, 366, 371, 398–9, 402, 410, 413, 427, 428, 431, 440, 444, 449, 454, 456–61, 462, 482, 489
   on other composers 371
   reputation and influence 467, 496, 511, 538
   Études 460
   Images 460–1
      Et la lune descend sur le temple qui fût 460
      'Poissons d'or' 461
   Jeux 459
   La Mer 458, 460, 461
   Nocturnes 458
   Noël for Children Who Have No Homes 410
   Pelléas et Mélisande 371, 398–9, 457–8, 459, 462, 473
   Préludes 460
      'Clair de Lune' 460
      'Feuilles mortes' 460
      'La Fille au cheveux de lin' 460
      ...*Des pas sur la neige* 460
   Prélude à l'après-midi d'un faune 457–8, 460
   Printemps 457
   String Quartet 462
   Tribute to the Belgian King and People 410
   Trois Chansons de Charles d'Orléans 464
de Bussy, Clementine 456

Debussy, Emma (formerly Bardac) see Bardac, Emma
Debussy, Claude-Emma ('Chouchou') 456, 459
Debussy, Lilly (née Texier) 458, 462
de Coussemaker, Edmond 52
Degas, Edgar 349
Delacroix, Eugène 279, 283, 286, 291
Delalande, Michel Richard 6, 148, 153
Delbos, Claire (later Messiaen) 502
Delibes, Léo 349, 349–50, 355
    Coppélia 349
    Lakmé 349
    Sylvia 349
Delius, Frederick 3, 399, 449
    On Hearing the First Cuckoo in Spring 449
    Sea Drift 449
    Two Songs to be Sung of a Summer Night on the River 449
    'The Walk to the Paradise Garden' 449
de Nesle, Blondel 41
    'Mes cuers me fait conmencier' 41
Derbyshire, Delia 530
    Doctor Who (TV theme) 530
Dering, Richard 161
Deshevov, Vladimir
    Ice and Steel 408
des Prés, Josquin 63, 72, 73–5, 76, 77, 82, 85, 561
    Qui habitat 74
    Miserere 74
    Absalon, fili mi 74
    Missa L'homme armé 74
    Nimphes des bois 74–5
    Faute d'argent 95
Devrient family 244, 333
Devrient, Eduard 11, 276, 285, 288, 333
Diabelli, Anton 246
    Sonata in F Major 192–3
Diaghilev, Sergei 430, 434, 444, 459, 463, 465, 469, 470, 475
Dialer, Joseph 270
Diamond, David 501
Dickens, Charles 248, 253, 273
Diderot, Denis
    Encyclopédie ou Dictionnaire raisonné des sciences, des arts et des métiers 188
Dies, Albert 220, 225
Disraeli, Benjamin 289

Ditters von Dittersdorf, Carl, 212, 214, 225
    Doktor und Apotheker 181
Donaldson, Lou 550
Donatoni, Franco 524, 534
    Small 534
    Short 534
    Sweet Basil (for Trombone and Big Band) 534
Donegan, Lonnie 543
Donizetti, Gaetano, 296, 335, 336, 343, 360, 373, 375, 380
    Anna Bolena 337
    Don Pasquale 338
    L'elisir d'amore 337, 373
    Lucia di Lammermoor 236, 338
    Marin Faliero 338
Donington, Robert 366
Doors, The 447
Dorsey, Jimmy 492
Dorsey, Tommy 492
Dósa, Lidi 440
Dostoyevsky, Fyodor 325, 401
Dowland, John 97
    'Now, O Now, I Needs Must Part' 97
Draghi, Giovanni Battista 164
Dragonetti, Domenico 306
Drake, Nick 549
drama, medieval sacred 42–4
Dublin 105, 158
Dudevant, Maurice 282
Dufay, Guillaume 43, 59, 67, 68–70
    Missa Ave regina caelorum 69
    Missa L'homme armé 69
    Missa Se la face ay pale 69
Dukas, Paul 399, 453, 457, 460, 500, 502
    The Sorcerer's Apprentice 457
    Variations, interlude et finale sur un thème de Rameau 453
Duke, Vernon (Vladimir Dukelsky) 494
    'Paris in New York' 494
Dumas, Alexandre *fils* 343, 345, 393
    La Dame aux camélias 377
Dunstable (Dunstaple), John 3, 60, 67
    Magnificat secondi toni 67
Duparc, Élisabeth 12, 159
Dupont, Gabrielle 458
Dupré, Marcel 499
Durante, Ottavio 117
Durazzo, Count Giacomo 179, 209

Durey, Louis 466, 467
Durón, Sebastián, 138
Duruflé, Maurice 538
Dusch, Alexander von 251
Dussek, Jan Ladislav 246
Dutilleux, Henri 538
Dvořák, Antonín 292, 311, 314, 315, 319, 320–22, 325, 356–7, 401, 473, 480, 488–9, 489
  Opera 356–7
    Alfred 356
    The Devil and Kate 356
    The Jacobin 356
    Dimitrij 356
    The Stubborn Lovers 356
    Rusalka 356–7
  Symphonies and orchestral works 321–2
    Slavonic Dances 321
    Symphony No. 6 321
    Symphony No. 8 322
    Symphony No. 9 ('From the New World') 322, 488–9
    The Water Goblin 357
  Humoresques 321
  'Songs My Mother Taught Me 321
  String Quartet No. 12 ('American') 321–2
Dvořák, Otilie (Otilie Suk) 321
Dylan, Bob (Robert Zimmerman) 541, 543, 546, 549, 560

E
Ebb, Fred
  Cabaret 546–7
  Chicago 546–7
Eben, Petr 536
Eccard, Johann 82, 88
Eck, Johann 88
Eco, Umberto 31
education
  choir-schools 62
  German 'common' and parish schools 88, 101
  German Latin schools 88
  Venetian 'scuole grandi' 101
  music for children 441, 443, 456, 478, 479
Edwardes, Richard 94
Edwards, Tom 123
Einstein, Alfred 185, 219, 222
Eisler, Hans 439
  Zeitungsausschnitte 439

electronics 435, 439, 485, 508, 518, 528–31
Elgar, Alice 316
Elgar, Sir Edward 11, 162, 170, 243, 244, 247, 314, 315–8, 327, 371, 409, 449, 452, 455, 556–7
  Cello Concerto 316, 436
  The Dream of Gerontius 317, 447
  Enigma Variations 316
  Introduction and Allegro 317
  Pomp and Circumstance March No. 1 317, 488
  Serenade for Strings 557
  Symphony No. 1 316, 317, 371
  Symphony No. 2 316
  Symphony No. 3 317
  'There is Sweet Music' 316
Eliasberg, Karl 505
Eliot, George (Mary Anne Evans) 244
  Middlemarch 4
Eliot, T. S., 452, 563
Elizabeth I, Queen 85, 89, 386
Elizabeth II, Queen 447
Ellington, Edward Kennedy 'Duke' 491–2, 548
  Black, Brown and Beige 495
Elsner, Józef 275
Éluard, Paul
  Figure humaine 469
Emerson, Ralph Waldo 485
Eminem (Marshall Mathers) 550, 560
Empfindsamer Stil 189
Enescu, George 444–5
  Impressions d'enfance 445
Epigonus 23
Érard, Sébastian (piano-makers) 236, 246
Erasmus, Desiderius 73, 85
Erdmann, Georg 323
Erdödy family 255
Ertmann, Dorothea von 277
Eschenbach, Wolfram von 360
Este, d' family 95
Este, Ercole d' 72, 73
Este, Cardinal Ippolito d' 83
Esterházy family 183, 206, 215, 220, 221, 224, 225, 255, 268, 274
Esterházy, Prince Anton 183, 230
Esterházy, Prince Johann 268
Esterházy, Prince Nikolaus ('the Magnificent') 183, 225, 226

Esterházy, Prince Nikolaus II 230
Esterházy, Prince Paul Anton 225
Esterházy, Princess Maria 225
Etheridge, John 559
Eton choirbook 75
Euripides 24
Evans, Sir Arthur 19
Evans, Bill 496, 542
Evelyn, John 158
experimental music 525–6
expressionism 407, 446
Eybler, Joseph 227, 267

F
faburden 32
Fairport Convention 549
Falcon, Cornélie 345
Falla, Manuel de 410
   El amor brujo 444
   Noches en los jardines de España 444
Fallows, David 70
Farinelli (Carlo Broschi) 135–6, 137, 158, 205, 212
Farnaby, Giles 93
Farnese, Isabel Queen 135
Farrenc, Louise 294, 301–2
   Symphony No. 3 301
Faure, Monsieur (singer) 383
Fauré, Gabriel 296, 348, 399, 444, 447, 453–6, 461, 469
   'Après un rêve' 451
   Cantique de Jean Racine 453
   Lydia 455
   Souvenirs de Bayreuth 454
   Violin Sonata No. 1 454, 455
   Requiem 454–5
Fauré, Marie (née Fremiet) 454, 455
Fauré, Philippe 455
Faustina (Faustina Bordoni) 166
Fayrfax, Robert 75
Feldman, Morton 527, 537
Felipe V, King 135, 136
Fenby, Eric 449
Ferber, Edna
   Show Boat 494
Fernando, Prince (later Ferdinand II, King) 135, 136
Ferneyhough, Brian 538, 556, 558
Ferrabosco, Mrs 101

Ferrari, Benedetto 121
Ferroud, Pierre-Octave 469
Festa, Costanzo 95
Fibich, Zdeněk
   Nevěsta messinská (The Bride of Messina) 356
   Šárka 356
Field, John 246, 279, 323
Fielding, Henry 203
film music 314, 410, 495
Filtsch, Joseph 291
Finland 309
   poetic rhythm 22
Finn, William
   Falsettos 560
Finnissy, Michael 538
Finzi, Gerald 450, 479
Fisher, William Arms 488–9
   'Goin' Home' 488
Fitzgerald, Ella 447, 492, 541
Fitzwilliam, Lord 137
Flack, Roberta 548
Flaubert, Gustave
   Madame Bovary 236
   Salammbô 349
Florence 116, 129
   Camerata 113
Flynn, Errol 410
folk music 411, 413, 441–2, 480
   in Romantic music 401, 418
   in twentieth-century music 434, 436, 440, 441–2, 443–4, 444, 445, 448, 472, 478, 479, 481, 482, 489, 524, 559
   and jazz 543
Fomin, Yevstigney
   Orfey i Evridika 351
Fontana, Julian 288
Fontenelle, Bernard le Bovier de 528
Forkel, Johann Nikolaus 9, 105, 173
   Johann Sebastian Bach, His Life, Art and Work 188
Forman, Alfred 365
Forster, Edwin Morgan (E. M.) 478
Fosse, Bob 547
Foster, Stephen 488–9
   'Camptown Races' 488
   'Oh! Susanna' 488
Foulds, John
   A World Requiem 450

Franc, Martin le 67, 68
  Le Champion des Dames 67
Franck, César 314–5, 348, 456
  Panis angelicus 315
  Symphony in D Minor 315
  Trois chorals 315
  Violin Sonata in A Major 315
Franck, Salomon 107
Franco, General Francisco 413
Franco of Cologne 50–1
Franklin, Aretha 543, 548
  'I Knew You Were Waiting (for Me)' 548
Frankopan, Peter 59
Franz, Robert 313
Franz Josef, Emperor 421
Franzen, Jonathan 482
Frauenlob, Heinrich 3, 40
Frederick Augustus, King 205
Frederick, Prince of Wales 103, 200
Frederick II (the Great), King 102, 103, 251, 332
Frederick III, King 245
Freud, Sigmund 407, 417, 421, 422, 517
Fricken, Ernestine von 281
Friedrich of Württemberg, Duke 250
Frescobaldi, Girolamo 91, 117, 157, 158
  Fiori musicali 117
Froberger, Johann Jakob 109, 117, 150, 157, 160
Frost, Robert 480
frottola 95
Frozen
  'Love is an Open Door' 560
Fry, William Henry 481
  'Niagara' symphony 481
  'Santa Claus', Christmas symphony 481
fugue 110, 111
Furtwängler, Wilhelm 365, 409, 516
Futurist Manifesto 446
Fux, Johann Joseph 65
  Gradus ad Parnassum 188, 214

G

Gabriel de Borbón, Don 138
Gabrieli, Andrea 82, 88, 118, 119, 157
Gabrieli, Giovanni 2, 82, 88, 91, 114, 117–8, 157, 159, 168, 311
  In ecclesiis 118
Gade, Niels 281, 286
  Symphony No. 5 301
Gaines, James R. 11
Gainsborough, Thomas 199
Galilei, Vicenzo
  Dialogo della musica antica e della moderna 113
Gallon, Jean 499
Galuppi, Baldassare 183, 199, 212
  Il mondo della luna 202
gamelan 457, 487, 500
Gance, Abel
  Napoléon 467
Gänsbacher, Johann 251
Gante, Pedro de 481
Garbarek, Jan 561
Garner, Erroll 22
Garrick, David 208
Gasparini, Francesco 127
Gauguin, Paul 349
Gaultier, Théophile 343
Gautier, Louis 470
Gay, John
  The Beggar's Opera 156, 170, 446
Gaye, Marvin 548
  'Let's Get It On' 548
  'Sexual Healing' 548
Gebrauchsmusik 478
Geissenklösterle (Germany) 19
Geminiani, Francesco 127, 131, 158, 170, 199
  The Art of Playing on the Violin 132
Gentle Giant 560
Genzinger, Marianne von 225
George I, King (Elector of Saxony) 167
George III, King 199
George V, King 478
Gerhard, Roberto 440
Gershwin, George (Jacob Gershwine) 290, 427, 446, 462, 467, 491, 492, 496, 497, 499, 500, 539
  'Someone to Watch Over Me' 493
  'The Man I Love' 493
  'They Can't Take That Away From Me' 493
  An American in Paris 493
  Piano concerto in F Major 493, 496
  Porgy and Bess 482, 497
  Rhapsody in Blue 451, 496
Gershwin, Ira 493

Gesualdo, Carlo 96–7, 433
   'Moro, lasso, al mio duolo' 96
   Tenebrae responsoria 97
Ghislanzoni, Antonio 384
Giacosa, Giuseppe 395
Gibbons, Christopher 161
Gibbons, Orlando 92, 93, 161
Gigault, Nicolas 148
Gilbert, William Schwenk 248
   Ruddigore 334
   The Pirates of Penzance 375
   The Yeomen of the Guard 334
Giles, Nathaniel 94
Gillespie, Dizzy (John) 542, 543
Gilmour, David 542
Ginastera, Alberto 472
   Danzas Argentinas 472
Gioia, Ted 411, 491, 496, 550, 561
Giordano, Umberto 394
Girdlestone, Cuthbert 220
Girò, Anna 133, 202
Glareanus, Henricus 73
Glasper, Robert 560
Glass, Philip 537
Glazunov, Alexander 353, 434, 475, 476, 499
   Saxophone Concerto 476
Glinka, Mikhail 323, 324, 327
   A Life for the Tsar 352
   Ruslan and Lyudmila 352
Glock, Sir William 508, 516
Gluck, Christoph Willibald 143, 182, 187, 200, 208–212, 218, 220, 237, 261, 278, 305
   Alceste 209, 210
   Les Danaïdes 211
   Don Juan 209
   Écho et Narcisse 211
   Iphigénie en Aulide 210
   Iphigénie en Tauride 211
   Orfée et Euridice 210
   Orfeo ed Eurdice 209
   De Profundis 211
Göbeleki Tepe (Turkey) 15
Godard, Jean-Luc 527
Goehr, Alexander 538
Goethe, Johann Wolfgang von 235–6, 274, 277, 294, 305, 347
   Erlkönig 236, 358
   Faust 293, 331, 346, 347, 421
   The Sorrows of Young Werther 235–6

Goeyvaerts, Karel 531
Gogol, Nikolai 502
Goldfinger, Ernö 408, 533
Goldmark, Carl 334
   Die Königin von Saba 333
Goldmark, Rubin 499
Goldoni, Carlo 123, 133, 155, 183, 202, 343
   La finta semplice 202
   Il mondo della luna 202
   Statira 202
goliards 39
Gombert, Nicolas, 75–6
   Musae Jovis 73
   Triste départ 80
Gombrich, E. H. (Sir Ernst Hans) 563
Gonzaga, Ferrante 82
Gonzaga, Vicenzo 119
Goodman, Benny 492, 500, 538
Goossens, Eugene 511
Górecki, Henryk 535
   Symphony of Sorrowful Songs 535
   Totus Tuus 535
Goss, Glenda Dawn 417
Gossec, François-Joseph 184
Gostling, John 105
Gottlieb, Anna 224
Gottschalk, Louis 246, 481
   Bamboula (Danse des Nègres) 481
   La Savane 481
Gounod, Charles 294, 342, 346–7, 349, 410, 457, 468
   Faust 346–7
   La nonne sanglante 347
Grabu, Louis 165
Graf (piano-makers) 245
Grainer, Ron 530
   Doctor Who (TV theme) 530
Grainger, Percy 2, 529
Granados, Enrique
   12 Danzas españolas 309
   Goyescas 309
Grandi, Alessandro 114, 117, 120
Grappelli, Stéphane 492
Grateful Dead, The 486
Greece
   ancient 19–24
   Mycenaean civilisation 19
   Minoan civilisation (Crete) 19
   early instruments 20

poetic rhythm 21
modes 21
Arcadians 22
archaic period 22
early Classical period 22
festivals 23
drama 23–24
athletic games 24
Green Day 549
Greene, Maurice 179
Greenwood, Jonny
  'Convergence' 559
Gregory I, Pope 28, 45
Grétry, André 182, 332, 339–40, 341, 350
  Richard Coeur-de-lion 339–40
Grieg, Edvard 315, 322, 456
  Holberg Suite 322
  Peer Gynt 322
  Piano Concerto in A Minor 322
  Piano Sonata in E Minor 322
Griesinger, Georg August 8, 9
Griffes, Charles T. 483
Grigny, Nicolas de 151
Grillparzer, Franz 268, 270
Grimley, Daniel 477
Grimm, Wilhelm Carl & Carl Friedrich (Brothers Grimm) 235, 293, 355, 360
Grisey, Gérard
  Les Espaces acoustiques 536
Gropius, Manon 436
Gropius, Walter 408, 422, 436
Grosser, Maurice 482
Grout, Donald Jay 271
Grove's Dictionary of Music and Musicians 475
Grumiaux, Arthur 445
Grzymala, Wojciech 288, 291
Guadagni, Gaetano 201, 209
Guarini, Giovanni Battista
  Il pastor fido 114
Guarneri family 125
Guicciardi, Countess Giulietta 256
Guido d'Arezzo 48, 443
  Micrologus 49
  'Guidonian hand' 29, 49
Guilbert, Yvette 445
Guilhem IX, Duke of Aquitaine 39
Guise, de (family) 148
Gunpowder Plot 102

Gurney, Ivor 450
Gustavus III, King 382
Guthrie, Woody 543
  'This Land is Your Land' 543

H

Haas, Robert 318
Hair (musical) 547
Halévy, Fromental 342, 343, 345
  La Juive 345, 349
  Noé 348
Halévy, Geneviève see Bizet, Geneviève
Halévy, Ludovic 348, 349
Haley, Bill 544
Halle, Adam de la 44
Halle, Ernoul de 32
Hahn, Reynaldo 6, 472
  L'Heure exquise 472
Hamburg, 133
Hamilton-Paterson, James 11, 317
Hamlisch, Marvin
  A Chorus Line 547
Hammerstein, Oscar II
  Carousel 494
    'If I Loved You' 494
    'You'll Never Walk Alone' 494
  The King and I 494
  Show Boat 489, 494
    'Ol' Man River' 489
  The Sound of Music 495, 546
Hammond, Laurens 435, 528–9
Han, Ulrich
  Missale Romanum 60
Hancock, Herbie 548, 560
Handel, George Frideric 104, 107, 109, 123, 129, 130, 133, 137, 151, 153, 158, 165, 166, 166–70, 171, 173, 174, 183, 189, 194, 202, 205, 208, 211, 212, 290, 389, 546
  personal life 8
  employment 103, 158
  in Italy 128, 158
  Mozart orchestrations 208
  later reputation and influence 215, 221, 229, 230, 237, 263, 280, 289, 349, 481
  Operas
    Agrippina 128
    Alexander's Feast 25
    Belshazzar 12, 168, 169
    Giulio Cesare 167

Index

   Orlando 168
   Rinaldo 167
   Tamerlano 165
  Oratorios
   Esther 107, 168
   Israel in Egypt 126, 168, 189
   Jephtha 168, 183
   Joseph and his Brethren 169
   Messiah 107, 167, 168, 169, 170, 189, 208
   Ode for St Cecilia's Day 289
   Saul 168, 169
   Semele 168
   Theodora 168
  Music for the Royal Fireworks 150
  Twelve Grand Concertos, Op. 6 131
  Water Music 150
Hannenheim, Norbert von 439
Hannigan, Barbara 525
Hanslick, Eduard 318, 321, 357–8, 369–70, 376, 416
  On the Musically Beautiful 369–70
Hardy, Thomas 316, 450
harmony 32, 110, 122, 128–9, 435, 449, 464, 476, 561
Harris, Johana 482
Harris, Roy 482, 501
  Symphony No. 3 482
Harrison, Lou 487, 488
Hart, Roy 525
Harvard University 481
  Charles Eliot Norton lectures 423, 486
Harvey, Jonathan 527
Hasse, Johann Adolf 129, 166, 179, 205, 211
  Cleofide 166
Hassler, Hans Leo 88, 119, 157
Hawkins, Sir John
  A General History of the Science and Practice of Music 4, 188, 563
Hawthorne, Nathaniel 482
Haydn, Franz Josef 2, 137, 138, 177, 178, 183, 185, 187, 188, 189, 194, 196, 197, 199, 200, 207, 208, 212, 213, 214–31, 243, 255, 256, 258, 259, 261, 268, 270, 273, 278, 289, 290, 302, 310, 351, 371, 401, 438, 481
  as conductor 7
  working method 8
  personal life 8, 215
  Chamber music
   Piano Trio in F Sharp 185

   String Quartet No. 25 219–20
   'Russian' Quartets 224
   The Seven Last Words of Our Saviour on the Cross 225
  Oratorios and cantatas
   The Creation 177, 208, 230, 231, 242
   Il ritorno di Tobia 219
   The Seasons 208, 230
  Operas
   Armida 224
   Il mondo della luna 202
   La vera costanza 220
   L'anima del filosofo 220, 330
  Symphonies
   Symphonies Nos 93–104 ('London') 229
   Symphony No 92 ('Oxford') 223, 225, 299, 299
   Symphony No. 102 185
  Sacred music
   'Insanae et vanae curae' 219
   Mass No. 4 219
   Masses Nos 9–14 230
   'Emperor's Hymn' 230
Haydn, Michael 186, 212, 217
Heaney, Seamus 560
Heath, Ted 542
Heine, Heinrich 238, 335
Henderson, Fletcher 491–2
Henderson, Roy 543
  Mode for Joe 543
Hendrix, Jimi 545–6, 549
Henry, Roy (prob. Henry V, King) 67
Henry VIII, King 76, 85
Hensel, Sebastian 288
Hensel, William 331
Henze, Hans Werner, 519, 532, 540
  Nachtstücke und Arien 532
Herbert, George 450
Herbert, Victor 495
Herder, Johann Gottfried 235
Herman, Woody 496
Hermannus Contractus 48, 49
Hérold, Ferdinand 342, 343, 345, 355
  La Fille mal gardée 342
  Zampa 344
Herschel, William 229
Hervey, Lord 103
Hesse, Grand Duke of 238

Heydrich, Reinhard 473
Heyward, DuBose and Dorothy
   Porgy and Bess 482
Hidalgo de Polanca, Juan
   El Laurel de Apolo 137–8
Higdon, Jennifer 557
Hildegard of Bingen 48–9
   Lingua Ignota 49
   'O, Jerusalem' 50
   Ordo Virtutum 49
Hill, Aaron 167, 169
Hiller, Ferdinand 246, 281, 385
Hindemith, Paul 253, 409, 446, 477–8, 516, 520, 522
   Concerto for Solo Trautonium and Orchestra 529
   Ludus Tonalis 477
   Sancta Susanna 446
   Symphonic Metamorphosis of Themes of Carl Maria von Weber 477
   The Craft of Musical Composition 477
Hines, Earl 542
Hitler, Adolf 318, 371, 409, 424, 516
hocket 32, 52
Hoffmann, E. T. A. 235, 238–9, 263, 302, 342, 355, 360
Hoffman, François-Benoît 340
Hofmannstahl, Hugo von 403
Hogarth, William 203, 433
Hohle Fels (Germany) 19
Hokusai 460
Holliday, Billie (Eleanora Fagan) 492, 541
   'Strange Fruit' 492
Holliger, Heinz 301
Holly, Buddy 544
   'That'll be the Day' 544
Holmès, Augusta 453
Holst, Gustav (von) 3, 411, 444, 448–9
   Choral Hymns from the Rig-Veda 449
   Planets Suite 449
Holst, Imogen 449
Holz, Karl 255
Holzbauer, Ignaz 182
Holzer, Michael 267
Homer 19, 23
Honegger, Arthur 465, 466
   Jeanne d'Arc au bûcher 466
   Napoléon (film score) 467
   Pacific 231 466

   Le Roi David 466
   Symphony No. 3 ('Liturgique') 466
   Symphony No. 4 466
Hooper, Edmund
   'O God of Gods' 160
Housman, A. E. 450
Howard, Bart
   'Fly Me to the Moon' 561
Howard, Harlan 560
Howells, Herbert 447, 450, 538
   Hymnus Paradisi 450
Hugo, Victor 279, 345, 377, 393
   Le roi s'amuse 377
Humboldt, Alexander von
   ecological insights as musical analogue 5, 6, 7
Humfrey, Pelham 147, 162, 164
   'Club Anthem' 164
Hummel, Johann Nepomuk 246, 247, 252, 256, 261, 273, 274, 278
Humperdinck, Engelbert 330, 335
   Hänsel und Gretel 330, 335
Hunnis, William 94
Hunter, Anne 229
Hurrian songs 22
Hussey, Dyneley 383, 386, 389
Hüttenbrenner, Anselm 269

I

Ibert, Jacques 453
I Ching 519, 521, 526
Iles, Edna 476
Illica, Luigi 395
impressionism 408, 434, 457
Indy, Vincent d' 399, 457, 460
Ingegneri, Marc'Antonio 119
Ingres, Jean-Auguste-Dominique 342
instruments
   medieval 44
   electronic 435, 485, 508
   Hungarian 441, 473
   nineteenth century 245
   experimental 487, 525, 538
intermedio 97, 115
Ireland, John 450, 499
Isaac, Heinrich 72, 82, 88, 95, 438
   'Innsbruck, ich muss dich lassen' 95
Isabella of Portugal, 68
Isherwood, Christopher 501

Isma'il Pasha, Khedive of Egypt 383
isorhythm 53, 519
Ives, Charles 481, 485–6, 488, 500, 525
    Central Park in the Dark 485
    Three Places in New England 485
    The Unanswered Question 485–6, 539

J

Jackson, Mahalia 543
Jackson, Millie 548
Jacob, Gordon 451
Jacquet de La Guerre, Élisabeth 151
    Pièces de Clavecin qui peuvent se Joüer sur le Viollon 151, 152
Jacquet of Mantua, 73–4
Jagger, Sir Mick 544
James II, King 126
James VI & I, King 78
James, Etta 543
James, Harry 492
James, Henry 9, 547
Janáček, Leoš 353, 357, 400–2, 440, 444, 473
    Operas 400–2
        The Cunning Little Vixen 402
        From The House of the Dead 400
        Jenůfa 400, 401
        Kát'a Kabanová 401
        The Makropulos Affair 402
        Šárka 356
    Glagolitic Mass 444
    Music for Club-Swinging Exercises 444
    Piano Sonata 1. X. 1905 444
    St. Wenceslas Triptych for Organ 444
Jannequin, Clément, 92
    'La Guerre' 81
Jarre, Jean-Michel 531
Jarry, Albert
    Ubu Roi 465
jazz 407, 411, 432, 434, 465, 473, 480, 490–2, 542–3, 547–8, 549–50
    and classical music 495–7, 492
Jazz Singer, The 491
Jean, Ferdinand de 217
Jefferson, 'Blind Lemon' (Lemon Henry) 490
Jenamy, Victoire 185
Jenger, Johann Baptist 269
Jenkins, John 91
Jennens, Charles 12, 169

Jensen, Eric Frederick 457, 460
Jerusalem, Ignacio de 139
Jeu de Robin et Marion, Le 44
Jeune, Claude le 92, 95
Joachim, Joseph 284, 287, 296, 298, 302, 310, 312, 313
Joel, Billy 560
    'Goodnight, Saigon' 560
    'She's Always a Woman' 560
Johannes de Garlandia 50
Johannes de Grocheio 51
John XXII, Pope 54
John, Elton (Reg Dwight) 451, 549
John of Affligem 48
John Paul II, Pope 535
Johnson, James P. 491, 495
    Piano Concerto 495
Johnson, Robert (English Renaissance composer) 94
Johnson, Robert (American blues singer) 490
Johnson, Blind Willie 544
Jolivet, André 453
Jolson, Al 13, 495, 499
Jommelli, Niccolò 209, 212
    Requiem 211
Jones, Dame Gwyneth 447
Jones, Inigo 161
Jones, Norah 560
Jones, Quincy 560
Jones, Tom 549
Jonson, Ben 94, 161
Joplin, Janis 549
Joplin, Scott 489
    'Maple Leaf Rag' 489
    Treemonisha 489
José, Crown Prince 135
Joséphine, Empress 341
Joyce, James
    Ulysses 530
Julius III, Pope 83
Jung, Carl 407
Justin Martyr 26

K

Kabalevsky, Dmitri 477, 502
Kagel, Maurice 524, 531
    Ludwig van 525
Kalevala 235, 309, 418

Kalkbrenner, Friedrich 245, 247, 279
Kallman, Chester 433
Kander, John 539
   Cabaret 539, 546–7
   Chicago 539, 546–7
Kant, Immanuel 235
Kaprálová, Vítězslava 473–4
   Military Sinfonietta 473–4
Kasri, Hamid El 560
Keaton, Buster
   Limelight 526
Keiser, Reinhard 104, 165, 166
Kelly, Michael 179, 225
Kennedy, President John F. 433–4
Kerman, Joseph 371
Kern, Jerome, 492
   Show Boat 489, 494
      'Ol' Man River' 489
Ketèlbey, Albert 413
Khachaturian, Aram 408, 476–7
   Anthem of the Armenian Soviet Socialist Republic 408
   Gayane 476
      'Sabre Dance' 476
   Spartacus 476
Khrushchev, Nikita 509
Kildea, Paul 286
King, Martin Luther 532
Kinks, The 451, 545
   'Apeman' 545
   'Lola' 545
Kinsky family 255
Kirkpatrick, Ralph 135
Kittl, Ján Bedřich
   Bianca and Giuseppe 356
Klemperer, Otto 424, 427
Klimt, Gustav 421
Kline, Phil
   Unsilent Night 531
Klinger, Friedrich Maximilian 190
Klopstock, Friedrich Gottlieb 211, 235, 236
Knaben Wunderhorn, Des 235, 243, 418, 419
Knepper, Jimmy 8
Knossos (Crete) 19
Kodály, Zoltán 401, 440, 443, 444, 458, 522, 531
   teaching method 443
   Dances of Galánta 443
   Háry János 443

   Missa brevis 443
   Sonata in B Minor for Solo Cello 443
Koechlin, Charles 460, 469
Koenig, David M. 535
Korngold, Erich 410
Koussevitzky, Serge 441, 488
Kovařovic, Karel 401
Kraft, Antonín 255
Kraft, Nikolaus 255
Kraftwerk 13, 550
Krall, Diana 495
Krenek, Ernst 409, 439
   Jonny Spielt Auf 439
   Lamentatio Jeremiae Prophetae 439
   Symphonic Elegy for String Orchestra 439
Kubrick, Stanley
   2001: A Space Odyssey 535
Kuhnau, Johann 165
Kurtág, György 536–7
   Játékok 536
Kurtág, Martá 536
Kutuzov, Marshal 273

L

La Bruyère, Jean de 141
Lachenmann, Helmut 536–7
Ladysmith Black Mambazo 559
La Fontaine, Jean de 145
Lalo, Édouard 456
   Namouna 456
   Symphonie Espagnole 309
Lamar, Kendrick
   To Pimp a Butterfly 560
Lambe, Walter 75
Lambert, Constant 448, 451, 496
   The Rio Grande 451
Lambert, Michel 143
Lampe, Frederick
   The Dragon of Wantley 170
Landini, Francesco 55
Landowska, Wanda 468
Lang, Gretchen 250
Langham Smith, Richard 411
Lanier, Nicholas 97, 157
Lapine, James
   Falsettos 560
Lara, Isidore de (Cohen) 399
   Amy Robsart 399
Larkin, Colin 451

Larkin, Philip 543
Lassus, Orlande de 3, 62, 70, 74, 76, 77, 80, 80–82, 94, 95, 118
    Che più d'un giorno 80
    Madonna sa l'amor 82
    Missa Bell' Amfitrit'altera 80
    Missa Je ne menge point du porc 65
    'O quam gloriosum' 80
    Requiem 80
    Tristis est anima mea 80
    'Vere languores nostros' 80
Lasus of Hermione 21, 23
Lauermann (carpenter) 369–70
Laurents, Arthur 539
Lavigna, Vincenzo 372
Lawes, Henry
    Comus 161
Lawes, William 91, 161
Leadbelly (Ledbetter, Huddie William) 490
Leavis, Frank Raymond (F. R.) 397
Le Cerf de la Viéville, Jean-Laurent
    Comparaison de la musique italienne et de la musique française 142
Lechner, Leonhard 82
Leclair, Jean-Marie 150
Léger, Fernand 466
Legrenzi, Giovanni 123, 125
Leibowitz, René 423, 440
Leighton, William 92
Leipzig 105, 243, 359
Lejeune, Émile 466
Lenin, Vladimir 477
Lennon, John 545, 558
Lenya, Lotte 447
Leonarda, Isabella 124
    Sonata da chiesa (no. 10) 125
Leoncavallo, Ruggero
    Pagliacci 393
Leoninus (Léonin) 52
    Magnus liber 52
Leopold II, Emperor 226, 336
'Les Six' 413, 455, 465–70
Leutgeb, Joseph 184
Leuven, Adolphe de 348
Lewis, Jerry Lee 544
    'Whole Lotta Shakin' Goin' On' 544
Lichnowsky, Prince Karl Alois 255, 256, 259, 266

Ligeti, György 517–8, 518, 531–2, 535
    Artikulation 531
    Aventures 531
    Le Grand Macabre 531, 534
    Lux Aeterna 535
    Six Bagatelles for Wind Quintet 531
light music 248, 413
Lind, Jenny 284
Linley family 244
Lion, Alfred 543
Lisbon
    1755 earthquake 11, 136
Liszt, Adam 273, 289
Liszt, Blandine (later Blandine Olivier) 296
Liszt, Cosima see Wagner, Cosima
Liszt, Daniel 283, 296
Liszt, Franz (Ferencz) 150, 190, 231, 244, 246, 247, 260, 273–298, 309, 310, 312, 313, 314, 324, 327, 335, 346, 349, 353, 359, 362, 364, 376, 377, 381, 451, 486, 502
    Années de pèlerinage 296
    Bagatelle sans tonalité 297
    Harmonies poétiques et religieuses 289
    La lugubre gondola 297
    Konzertstück for two pianos on Mendelssohn's *Lieder ohne Worte* 279
    Lorelei 293
    Nuages gris 297
    Les Préludes 308
    Transcendental studies 279
Literes, Antonio de 138
    Azis y Galatea 138
Little Richard (Richard Wayne Perriman) 544
    'Good Golly, Miss Molly' 544
Lloyd Webber, Sir Andrew (Lord Lloyd Webber)
    Evita 547
    Jesus Christ Superstar
        'I Don't Know How to Love Him' 547
    Joseph and the Amazing Technicolor Dreamcoat 547
        'Any Dream Will Do' 547
    The Phantom of the Opera 350, 547
    Tell Me on a Sunday 547
        'Tell Me on a Sunday' 547
Lobkowitz, Prince Joseph Franz von 255, 258

Locatelli, Pietro 131
Locke, Matthew 161, 164
Locle, Camille du 383
Loeffler, Charles Martin 483
Loesser, Frank 546
   Guys and Dolls 546
Loewe, Carl
   Edward 245
   Erlkönig 358
Loewe, Sophie 377
Lomax, Alan 488, 490
Lomax, John 488
London 103, 105, 133, 199, 229–30, 399
   Charitable Hospitals 101
   'Prom' concerts 478, 515, 558
   BBC studios 530
Longfellow, Henry Wadsworth 480
Loriod, Yvonne 508
Lorrain, Jean 399
Lorre, Peter 427
Losius, J. C. 101
Lotti, Antonio 129
Louis XIV, King 102, 141, 142, 143, 145, 147, 149
Louis XV, King 156, 180
Louis XVI, King 203
Louis of Savoy 69
Louÿs, Pierre 458
Lübeck 106
Lucier, Alvin
   I Am Sitting in a Room 531
Ludus Danielis 42–3
Ludwig of Bavaria, King 248, 357, 364
Lully, Jean-Baptiste (Giovanni Battista Lulli) 104, 108, 123, 141, 143–7, 149, 150, 151, 156, 162, 209
   family 147
   as actor 147
   Armide 104
   Atys 143
   Isis 146
   Le Bourgeois gentilhomme 141, 144
   Le Mariage forcé 141
   Phaëton 143
LuPone, Patty 447
Luther, Martin 73, 85–7, 534
   Formula Missae et Communionis 85
   chorales 86–7

Lutosławski, Witold 535
   Concerto for Orchestra 535
Lyadov, Anatoly 325
Lynch, David 558

M

MacCulloch, Diarmaid 27
MacDowell colony 481, 487
MacDowell, Edward 481
   'To a Wild Rose' 481
MacDowell, Marian 481
Machaut, Guillaume de 53–4, 55
   Messe de Nostre Dame 54, 55
MacMillan, James 558
   Cantos Sagrados 558
   The Confession of Isobel Gowdie 558
   Miserere 558
   Stabat Mater 558
Maderna, Bruno 523–4, 530, 540
   Concerto for Oboe No. 2 524
   Concerto for piano 524
   Improvvisazione No. 1 527
   Musica su due dimensioni 530
   Quartetto per archi in due tempi 524
   Requiem 524
madrigals 94, 95–7
Maeterlinck, Maurice 398, 457
   Pelléas et Mélisande 457, 458
Magee, Bryan 363, 368
Mahler, Alma (née Schindler, later Gropius) 326, 421, 422, 436, 438
Mahler, Anna 421, 439
Mahler, Gustav 2, 237, 241, 243, 253, 301, 311, 317, 318, 354, 399, 409, 413, 416–425, 426, 434, 443–4, 447, 482
   later reputation and influence 423–5, 426, 427, 435, 436, 449, 450, 483, 496, 502, 509, 532
   Symphonies
   Symphony No. 1 (sometimes 'Titan') 416, 418, 424, 425
   Symphony No. 2 ('Resurrection') 419, 420, 421, 424, 425
   Symphony No. 3 417, 421
   Symphony No. 4 419, 420, 424
   Symphony No. 5 421, 425
   Symphony No. 6 ('Tragic') 421, 425
   Symphony No. 7 421

Symphony No. 8 ('Symphony of a Thousand') 421, 422, 424
Symphony No. 9 422
Symphony No. 10 422
Songs, song-cycles and other works
　Kindertotenlieder 425
　Lieder eines fahrenden Gesellen 418
　Das Lied von der Erde 422
　Rückert-Lieder 425
　Die drei Pintos 419
Mahler, Maria 421
Mahler, Otto 420
Mainwaring, John 128
　Memoirs of the Life of the Late George Frederic Handel 188
Malipiero, Gian Francesco 479
Mallarmé, Stéphane 457–8, 523
　Prélude à l'après-midi d'un faune 457–8
Manelli, Francesco 121
Mann, Thomas 368, 410–11
Mannheim
　orchestra 200, 216, 218
Manning, Jane 525
Mantua 119
Manzoni, Alessandro 385
Mao, Chairman 535
Marais, Marin 141, 149–50
Marcello, Benedetto, 131
　Il teatro alla moda 130
Marchand, Louis 143, 151
Marenzio 97
Maria Barbara, Princess (later Queen) 134–5, 136
Maria Casimira, Queen 134
Mariani, Angelo 384
Maria Theresa, Empress 214
Marie Antoinette, Queen 203
Marxsen, Eduard 310
Marpurg, Friedrich Wilhelm 188
Marsalis, Branford 558
Marschner, Heinrich 10, 260, 333–4, 360
　Der Vampyr 330, 333
　Hans Heiling 330, 334, 358
Martenot, Maurice 435
Martin, Frank, 519
Martines, Marianna 206
　Isacco figura del Redentore 206

Martini, Padre Giovanni Battista 134, 179, 216
　La storia della musica 188
Martinů, Bohuslav 473
　The Greek Passion 473
　Juliette 473
　Památník Lidicím (Memorial to Lidice) 473
Marx, Adolf Bernhard 195, 302
Marx, Harpo 427
Mary I, Queen 76
Mascagni, Pietro, 393, 394, 484
　Cavalleria Rusticana 393
Mass 32, 46, 54
　based on other music 65
Massenet, Jules 349, 350, 394, 444, 457
　Manon 350
　Le Roi de Lahore 388, 392
　Werther 350
maths and music 47, 484–5, 486, 519, 527, 533, 561
Matisse, Henri 466
Mattheson, Johann 9, 11, 160, 166, 170, 171, 188, 214
Maximilian II of Bavaria, King 364
Max Franz, Elector 254
Maxwell Davies, Sir Peter, 518, 525, 538, 561
　Eight Songs for a Mad King 538
　The Lighthouse 538
Mayerl, Billy 496
Mayrhofer, Johann 267
Mazarin, Cardinal Jules (Giulio Mazzarino) 142
Mazzini, Giuseppe 338
Mazzone, Marc'Antonio 96
McCartney, Paul
　inability to read music 10
McCarthy, Senator Joseph 439, 506–7, 508
McPhee, Colin 487
McTell, Ralph
　Streets of London 561
Meck, Nadezhda von 327, 329, 456
Medici family 69, 116
Medici, Giovanni de' 59
Medici, Isabella de' 62
Medici, Piero de' 59, 70
Medtner, Nicolai 475–6
　Sonata No. 5, 'Sonata Tragica' 476
　Sonata No. 10 'Sonata Reminiscenza' 476

Méhul, Étienne 240, 303, 332, 340, 342
    Symphony No. 2 303
    Symphony No. 4 303
Meier, Sebastian 262, 331
Meilhac, Henri 348
Meistersinger 40, 94–5
Mellers, Wilfrid 545
Mellone, Annibale 119
Mendès, Catulle 398
Mendelssohn, Abraham 294
Mendelssohn, Cécile (Cécile Jeanrenaud) 282
Mendelssohn, Felix 11, 212, 231, 237, 238, 241, 243, 244, 246, 273–98, 301, 311, 331, 375, 376, 447
    personality 8
    Elijah 285
    'Hear my Prayer' 289
    Hebrides Overture 276
    Die Heimkehr aus der Fremde 331
    Die Hochzeit des Camacho 331
    Lieder ohne Worte 279, 291, 292
    A Midsummer Night's Dream 293
    Octet for strings 275
    Concerto for two pianos in A Flat 276
    Piano Concerto in G minor 246
    St Paul 280
    String quartet No. 6 286
    symphonies 305
    Symphony No. 4 ('Italian') 280
    Violin Concerto in E minor 304
Mendelssohn family 273, 274, 293–5
Mendelssohn, Fanny (Fanny Hensel) 274, 286, 293
    'Easter' Sonata 294
    Italien 285
    Piano Sonata in G Minor 294
Mengelberg, Willem 424
Menotti, Gian Carlo 483–4, 488
Menuhin, Yehudi 445, 504
Merbecke, John 90
Mercadante, Saverio 10, 338–9
    Elena da Feltre 338–9
Merelli, Bartolomeo 372–3
Mérimée, Prosper
    Carmen 348
Mersenne, Marin
    Harmonie Universelle 140, 144
Méry, Joseph 383

Mesmer, Franz Anton 227
Messager, André 399, 458, 459
Messiaen, Olivier 435, 462, 498–512, 526–7, 530, 533, 536, 558, 562
    L'Ascension 502
    Des Canyons aux étoiles 511
    Mode de valeurs et d'intensités 501, 526–7
    La Nativité du Seigneur 502, 511
    'Dieu parmi nous' 511
    Pièce pour le tombeau de Paul Dukas 502
    Poèmes pour Mi 502
    Quatuor pour la fin du temps 504–5, 511
    La Technique de mon langage Musicale 510, 512
    Timbres-durées 501
    Turangalîla-Symphonie 470, 508, 511
Metastasio, Pietro (Trapassi, Pietro) 123, 129, 136, 166, 205–6, 208, 211, 337, 343
    Adriano in Siria 205
    Artaserse 206
    Attilio Regolo 205
    La clemenza di Tito 208
    Didone abbandonata 130
Metheny, Pat 537, 548
Meyerbeer, Giacomo (Jacob Beer) 10, 244, 251, 252, 278, 286, 332, 343, 343–5, 347, 350, 360, 362, 374, 375, 380
    L'Africaine 345
    Il crociato in Egitto 343–4
    Les Huguenots 345, 388
    Robert le diable 344–5, 350
    Le prophète 345
Meyer-Eppler, Werner 529
Michael, George
    'I Knew You were Waiting (for Me)' 548
Milford, Robin 450
Milhaud, Darius 427, 466–7, 469, 471, 479, 487, 496, 529
    Le Boeuf sur le Toit 466, 467
    La Création du monde 467
Milhaud, Madeleine 468, 487
Miliukova, Antonina 329
Miller, Major Glenn 542
Miller, James 169
Millington, Barry 367
Milton, John
    Comus 161
'Mimi' (singer) 202
Mingotti (theatre troupe) 208

Mingus, Charles
  temper 8
minimalism 537, 558, 559
Minnesinger 40
Mirchindani, Vinnie
  The New Polymath 557
Mitchell, Donald 315, 518, 520, 527, 540
Mizler, Lorenz 105
Modena 125
modes
  medieval rhythmic 34
  Renaissance 63
  names 65
  folk and twentieth-century 434, 448, 460, 500, 562
Modigliani, Amedeo 466
Moeran, E. J. 450
Molière (Jean-Baptiste Poquelin) 141, 143–4, 145
  as actor-manager 141, 147
  Le bourgeois gentilhomme 141, 144, 147
  Le malade imaginaire 144, 149
  Le Mariage forcé 141
  Les Précieuses ridicules 141
Monahan, Seth 425
monasticism 62, 124–5
Monk, Thelonious 518, 543
Monkees, The 549
Monte, Philippe de 62, 76–7, 95
  '*Super flumina Babylonis*' 76
Montesquieu, Baron 126
Montesquieu, Robert de 399
Monteverdi, Claudia 119
Monteverdi, Claudio 97, 103, 104, 107–8, 112, 115, 117, 119–22, 157, 159, 161, 168, 173, 227, 479, 563
  Arianna 120
  La finta pazza 123
  L'incoronazione di Poppea 121
  L'Orfeo 113, 115, 120, 159
  Il ritorno d'Ulisse in Patria 113
  Vespro della Beata Vergine 120
Monteverdi, Giulio Cesare
  Dicharitione 119
Montpensier, Mlle de 143
Monty Python, 4
Moog, Robert 435, 529
  Switched-on Bach 529

Moondog 538
Morales, Cristóbal de 76
  Emendemus in Melius (attr.) 76
More, Thomas 61
Moreau, Gustave 349
Mörike, Eduard 11
Morley, Thomas 94, 96
  as pupil 7, 78
  Laboravi 77
Morris, William 408, 411
Morrison, Jim, 549
  The Doors (album) 447
  'Alabama Song' ('Show Me the Way to the Next Whisky Bar') 447
Morton, Jelly Roll (Ferdinand Joseph LaMothe) 490–1
Morzin, Count 215
Moscheles, Ignaz 241, 247, 276, 278, 281, 286, 289
Moseley, Carlos, 516
Mouton, Jean 72
Mozart family 252
Mozart, Anna Maria 216, 217, 228–9
Mozart, Constanze (Constanze Weber) 179, 208, 221, 226, 227, 250, 256, 278
Mozart, Franz Xaver 247
Mozart, Leopold 178, 188, 189–90, 199, 203, 216, 217, 221, 223, 228–9
Mozart, Maria Anna Thekla ('Bäsle') 216, 228
Mozart, Maria Anna ('Nannerl') 186, 216, 293, 326
Mozart, Wolfgang Amadeus 2, 3, 5, 11, 12, 123, 130, 133, 138, 143, 162, 164, 177, 178, 179, 181, 182, 183, 184, 185, 186, 187, 188, 189, 194, 196, 197, 199, 200, 201, 202, 203, 208, 211, 212, 213, 214–31, 236, 241, 241–2, 244, 246, 253, 254, 261, 265, 268, 269, 270, 272, 274, 278, 301, 310, 312, 320, 328, 330, 331, 332, 338, 351, 355, 377, 396
  jokes 1, 200, 204–5, 227, 373
  on his method 2, 8
  personal life 8
  death and funeral 208, 226–7
  later reputation, reception and influence 239, 258, 259, 260, 280, 281, 286, 290, 371, 416, 433, 438, 479, 492, 509, 518, 563

Concertos
  Concerto for Clarinet 195
  Concerto for Flute and Harp 217–8
  Piano Concerto No. 19 220
  Piano Concerto No. 20 190, 222, 256
Chamber music for strings
  String Quartet No. 14 195
  String Quartet No. 15 222
  String Quintet No. 3 222
  String Quintet No. 4 222
Operas
  La Clemenza di Tito 226, 227, 255–6
  Così fan Tutte 203, 226
  Die Entführung aus dem Serail 177, 221, 223
  La finta semplice 202
  Don Giovanni 187, 203, 205, 221, 222, 223, 239, 352, 397
  Idomeneo 182, 187, 218
  Lucio Silla 187
  Le nozze di Figaro 195, 203–4, 221, 223, 225, 239, 339, 411
  Der Schauspieldirektor 182
  Die Zauberflöte 177, 202, 204–5, 212, 226, 227, 239, 330, 333, 368
Symphonies
  Symphony No. 25 218, 219
  Symphony No. 28 218
  Symphony No. 29 218, 300, 300
  Symphony No. 35 ('Haffner') 187, 221, 223
  Symphony No. 39 221–2
  Symphony No. 40 221–2, 222
  Symphony No. 41 ('Jupiter') 220, 221–2, 222, 223
Sacred music
  Ave Verum Corpus 226
  Exsultate, Jubilate 201
  Requiem 226, 231, 267
Fantasia in C minor 190
Messiah (and other Handel orchestrations) 208
'Posthorn' serenade 187
Muffat, Georg 131
Mühlfeld, Richard 311
Müller, Wilhelm
  Die schöne Müllerin 253
  Der Neugierige 249
  Winterreise 253

Munch, Charles 473
Mundy, William (I) 76
Murail, Tristan
  Gondwana 536
Musgrave, Thea 558
Musica enchiriadis 47
musica reservata 80
Musica Transalpina 96
musique concrète 530, 536, 540
Mussolini, Benito 532
Mussorgsky, Modest 323, 325, 351, 434
  Boris Godunov 351, 353, 398, 457
  Night on Bare Mountain 325
  Pictures at an Exhibition 325
Muzio, Emanuele 374
Mvula, Laura 560
Myakovsky, Nikolai 477
Mysliveček, Josef 200, 299
Mysore, Maharajah of 476

N

Nabokov, Nicolas 7, 507
Nancarrow, Conlon 486, 487, 538
  Studies for Player Piano 538
Naples 129, 133
Napoleon (Napoléon Bonaparte) 213, 230, 240, 258, 259, 273, 274, 336
Napoleon III, Emperor (Louis-Napoléon) 241
nationalism 242, 321, 321–2, 323, 409–10, 434, 444, 472, 480
N'Dour, Youssou 559
Neefe, Christian Gottlob 254
Neri, St Philip 79
Neoclassicism 407, 415, 431–2, 453, 464, 468, 473, 479, 492
Neuwirth, Olga 558
new complexity 538
Newman, Ernest 264, 361, 365, 366, 398
Newman, Cardinal John Henry 317
Newton, Isaac 21
New York, 480, 499
  opera 238, 400, 422
Nicolai, Friedrich 212
Nicolai, Otto 334, 376
  Die lustigen Weiber von Windsor 334, 376
Nielsen, Carl 477, 538
  Helios overture 477
  Maskarade 477

Symphony No. 4, 'The Inextinguishable' 477
Symphony No. 5 477
Niemetschek, Franz 178
Nietzsche, Friedrich 357, 358, 359, 476
Nijinsky, Vaslav 465
Niles, John Jacob 480
Nilsson, Christine 347
Noel, Rev Conrad 411
Nono, Luigi 426, 523, 530, 540
  Il canto sospeso 523
  Prometeo 523
notation 10, 32, 35–6,
  neumes (plainsong) 34, 36
  medieval rhythmic modes 34, 36, 53
  ligatures 34
  tablature 34–5
  Dasian 47, 48
  early staff notation 48–9
  mensural 35, 50–1
  unmeasured 152
  graphic and modernist 527, 530–1, 535, 535–6
Notker the Stammerer 46
Notre Dame school 51–2
Novak, Leopold 318
Novello, Ivor (Ivor Davies) 413, 494
  'Keep the Home Fires Burning' 413, 494
  'We'll Gather Lilacs' 494
Noverre, Jean-Jacques 181

O
Oasis 451
Obama, President Barrack 548
Obrecht, Jacob 72–3, 73
  Mass settings 72–3, 74
Ockeghem, Johannes 69, 70, 71–2, 74, 77, 439
  Missa prolationum 71
  Requiem 72, 74
Odington, Walter 51
Odo of Cluny 48
Offenbach, Jacques, 248, 349
  Les Contes d'Hoffmann 235
  Officium 561
Ohana, Maurice 525
  La Célestine 538
Old Hall manuscript 67
Oliver, Joseph Nathan 'King' 490

Ollivier, Émile 296
opera 107–9, 114–6, 122–4, 129–131, 220, 330–403
  types 6, 330, 351, 443
  ballad and vernacular 94, 109, 170, 351
  buffa 129
  seria 129
  Opéra-comique 144
  nationalism 351, 355–6, 398, 400
  French Baroque 144–5
  mid-eighteenth-century 179–183
  Classical 220
  Romantic 238–40
    German 330–5, 402–3
    Italian 335–9, 392–8
    French 339–50
    Russian 351–5, 398
  twentieth-century 432, 436, 560
  verismo 387, 392–4
  singers 201–2
  librettists 202–6, 387
oratorio 107, 122–4
Orff, Carl 409, 478
  Carmina burana 478
organs 105
  Baroque (French and German) 151
organum 32, 47, 48
Orpheus Britannicus 163
Ortigue, Joseph Louis d' 345
Ory, Edward 'Kid' 490
Osborne, Charles 380
Ottoboni, Cardinal Pietro 126, 127
Owen, Robert 482
Owen, Wilfred 508

P
Pachelbel, Johann 113, 160
  Canon in D 561
Padilla, Juan Gutiérrez de 138
Paër, Ferdinando 278, 336
Paganini, Niccolò 244, 270, 278–9, 292, 306
Paine, John Knowles 314, 481
Paisiello, Giovanni 130, 183, 212, 240, 336
  Il barbiere di Siviglia 182, 203, 336
  Il mondo della luna 202
  La serva padrona 130
Palestrina, Giovanni Pierluigi da 3, 5, 64, 70, 74, 76, 77, 79, 80, 82, 83–4, 134
  as madrigal composer 96

later influence 134, 237, 289, 392, 516
  'Ad Dominum cum tribularer' 64
  Missa Assumpta est Maria 65
  Missa brevis 84
Palladio, Andrea 64
Palladius 27
Panufnik, Sir Andrzej 535, 558
Panufnik, Roxanna 558
Paris 105, 149, 152, 342–3, 492
  Les Vingt-quatre violons du Roi 141, 143
  Versailles 143, 149
  IRCAM 530, 558
Parker, Charlie, 542
  musical innovations 5, 542
  'A Night in Tunisia' 542
  'Ornithology' 542
  'Yardbird Suite' 542
Parker, Horatio 481
Parker, Roger 347, 373, 395
Parry, Sir Charles Hubert Hastings 314, 315, 409, 447
  'ethical cantatas' 449
Parsley, Osbert
  Lamentations of Jeremiah 77
Parsons, Robert 77
Pärt, Arvo 556, 559
Partch, Harry 487, 538
  Genesis of a Music 487
Pasta, Giuditta 278, 337
Pásztory-Bartók, Ditta 441
Pater, Walter 235
Paul, Jean 235, 276, 292
Paul, St 25, 26, 533
Pavy, Salomon 94
Payne, Anthony 317
Pears, Sir Peter 501, 503, 504, 509
Peñalosa, Francisco de 72, 74
Pendarves, Mary (Mary Delany) 167
Penderecki, Krzysztof 536, 545
  Actions, 521
  Threnody for the Victims of Hiroshima 515, 535
Pendergrass, Teddy 548
  'Come Go with Me' 548
  'Turn Off the Lights' 548
Pepys, Samuel 123, 158, 162, 163
  domestic music 101–2, 123
Pergolesi, Giovanni Battista
  Il prigioner superbo 130

La serva padrona 130, 180, 208–9
Peri, Jacopo 116
  Dafne 116
  Euridice 116
Perkins, Carl
  Blue Suede Shoes 544
Perotinus (Pérotin) 52, 74
  'Viderunt omne's 52
Perrault, Charles 142
pes 52
Pestelli, Giorgio 240
Peter, Paul and Mary 543
Peters, Linda 543
Petrarch 96
Petrucci, Ottaviano 60, 73, 93
Pfitzner, Hans, 516
  Palestrina 438, 445–6
  'Futuristengefahr' (essay) 445
Pfohl, Ferdinand 420
Philip II, King 76, 79
Philip, Chancellor 39
Philip the Good 68
Philip the Handsome 72
Philolaus of Croton 21
Phinot, Dominique
  Pleurez, mes yeux 95
photography 247–8
Piae cantiones 87
Piaf, Édith 445, 465
piano 105, 245–7
Piave, Francesco 375, 377–8
Piazzolla, Astor 472
Picander 107
Picasso, Pablo 465, 466, 470
Piccinni Niccolò, 210, 212
  La buona figliuola 180, 181
Pindar 23
Pinker, Steven 15
Pink Floyd, 542, 549
  The Dark Side of the Moon 540
  'Money' 550
Pisandel, Johann Georg 131
Piston, Walter 501
Pizzetti, Ildebrando 446
plainsong 34, 45–6
  as 'cantus firmus' 31–2, 47
  regional types 45–6
  in Romantic and later music 237, 413, 432
Planer, Minna, see Wagner, Minna

Planer, Wolfram 369
Plato 20, 24, 27, 28, 37
Platonism 31, 52, 65
Plautus 25
Playford, Henry 163
Pleyel (piano-makers) 432
Pleyel, Camille 245, 281, 282, 306
Pleyel, Ignaz 229
Pleyel, Marie (Marie Molke) 245, 305
Poe, Edgar Allan 399, 464
poetry
   medieval song-forms 32, 40
   villancico 138
Police, The 560
Polidori, John William
   The Vampyre 333
polyphony
   voice-parts 32
   earliest 46–9
   nineteenth-century view of 237
Polzelli, Antonio 224
Polzelli, Luigia 224
Ponchielli, Amilcare
   La Gioconda 339
Ponte, Lorenzo da 123, 188, 203–4, 205, 221, 223, 252
   Così fan Tutte 203
   Don Giovanni 203
   Le Nozze di Figaro 203–4
pop 541–53
popular music 5, 61–2, 109, 413, 445
Porpora, Nicola 158, 206–7, 212, 214
Porter, Andrew 365
Porter, Cole 412, 492, 493–4, 495, 496
   'Anything Goes' 493
   'Begin the Beguine' 493
   'Every Time We Say Goodbye' 494
   'High Society' 495
   'I Get A Kick Out of You' 493
   'Just One of Those Things' 493
   Kiss Me, Kate 493, 494
   'Night And Day' 493, 494
   Paris 493
   'So in Love' 493–4
Porter, Walter 101, 157
Potter, Cipriani 260
Poulenc, Francis 314, 413, 452, 464, 466, 468–70, 489
   Babar, le petit éléphant 469

Les Biches 469
Cocardes 466
Concert champêtre 468
Concerto for Organ 470
Concerto for Two Pianos 469, 494
Dialogues des Carmélites 470
Figure humaine 469
Gloria 470
Litanies à la Vierge noire 469
Les Mamelles de Tirésias 469
Mass in G Major 469
Sonata for Flute 470
La Voix humaine 470
Pound, Ezra 479
Pousseur, Henri
Votre Faust 534
Power, Leonel 67
Praetorius, Michael 160
Pratella, Francesco Balilla
   L'Arte dei Rumori 446
Presley, Elvis 541, 544
   'Heartbreak Hotel' 544
Prey, Claude 525
Price, Florence 496
prima pratica 112–4
printing 60–1, 104
   woodcut 60
   movable type 60–1
   copperplate 105
Prix de Rome, 305, 342, 348, 350, 454, 457, 462
Prokofieff, Sergei 431, 473, 477, 479
   Piano concertos 477
   Romeo and Juliet 477
   Symphony No. 1 ('Classical') 479
Proust, Marcel 4, 292, 315, 345, 350, 465, 472
   À la recherche du temps perdu 345, 350
psalm-singing 87–8, 89, 90
Ptolemy 21
publishing 110–11, 133, 187, 224, 225
Puccini, Giacomo, 394–8, 419, 423, 483
   La bohème 207, 394–5, 396–7
   Madama Butterfly 396, 397
   Manon Lescaut 395
   Tosca 396, 397
   Turandot 241, 397
   Le Villi 395
Purcell, Daniel 162

Purcell, Henry 1, 2, 7, 102, 103, 104, 105, 107,
    108, 109, 113, 145, 147, 148, 157, 161, 162,
    162–5, 170, 173, 226, 227, 447, 500, 504
  personal life 8
  Dido and Aeneas 123, 163
  The Fairy Queen 163–4
  Fantazias 162
  King Arthur 146, 163
  'My Beloved Spake' 163
  Rounds, catches and canons 1, 102
  Twelve Sonatas of Three Parts 157
Purcell, Thomas 163
Purser, Mrs 22
Pushkin, Alexander 351, 351, 353, 398
  Eugene Onegin 354
Putta, Bishop 45
Pythagoras 2, 21, 27, 519, 561

Q

Quantz, Johann Joachim 188, 194, 200
Queen 451, 549
Querelle des Bouffons 209
Quilter, Roger 450
Quinault, Philippe 144

R

Raaff, Anton 218
Rabelais, François 32, 73, 430
Rachmaninoff, Sergei 253, 413, 423, 448,
    473, 474–5
  All-Night Vigil (Vespers) 475
  Isle of the Dead 475
  Preludes 474
  Rhapsody on a Theme of Paganini 474
  Symphony No. 1 475
  Symphony No. 2 475
Racine, Jean 129, 141, 144
Radclyffe Hall (Marguerite) 478
Radiohead 559, 562
Raff, Joachim 309, 310
ragtime 489, 491
Rainey, Gertrude 'Ma' 490
Rakemann, Louis 281
Rameau, Jean-Philippe 143, 147, 153–6, 178,
    209, 212, 348, 454
  Castor et Pollux 155
  Hippolyte et Aricie 155
  Trio des Parques 156
  Les Cyclopes 154

La Livri 154
Nouveau Système de musique théorique 154
Pièces de clavecin 154
Pièces de clavecin en concert 154
Platée 155
Traité de l'harmonie 154–5
Ramsay, Sir W. M. 22
Ramuz, Charles Ferdinand 433
Rastell, John 61
Rattle, Sir Simon 301
Rautavaara, Einojuhani
  Cantus Arcticus 536
Rauzzini, Venanzio 201
Ravel, Marie (née Delouart) 461, 463
Ravel, Maurice 309, 428, 445, 447, 452, 454,
    461–5, 496
  Boléro 453, 462, 464, 465
  Daphnis et Chloé 462, 463, 536
  L'Enfant et les sortilèges 463–4, 465
  Gaspard de la nuit 462, 464
  L'Heure Espagnole 463
  Jeux d'eau 462
  Miroirs 460
  Pavane pour une infante défunte 461, 464
  Piano Concerto For the Left Hand
    464
  Piano Concerto in G 464
  Rapsodie Espagnole 460
  String Quartet 462
  Le Tombeau de Couperin 461, 463
  Trois Chansons 464–5
  Tzigane 445
  La Valse 460, 463
Ravel, Pierre-Joseph 461
Razumovsky, Count 259
Rebel, Jean-Féry 151
  Les Caractères de la danse 151
  Les Élémens 151
  Le Tombeau de Monsieur de Lully 151
Recio, Marie 307
Reger, Max 427, 434
Regularis concordia 42
Reich, Steve, 537, 559
  Clapping Music 537
  Different Trains 537, 559
  Drumming 559
  Electric Counterpoint 537
  WTC 9/11 559
Reicha, Anton 314

Reichardt, Johann Friedrich
　Erlkönig 236
Reincken, Johann Adam 160
Reinecke, Carl 315
Reinhardt, Django 492
Rembrandt 462
Respighi, Ottorino 446
Rhau, Georg 88
Rice, Sir Tim 547
　Evita 547
　Joseph and the Amazing Technicolor Dreamcoat 547
Rich, John 170
Richard, Cliff (Harry Webb) 544, 549
Richelieu, Cardinal 180
Richie, Lionel 548
　'Dancing on the Ceiling' 548
Richter, Hans 318, 320
Richter, Max 556
Ricordi, Giulio 384, 385–6, 390, 394
Riemann, Hugo 390
Ries, Ferdinand 255, 258, 263, 291
Riley, Terry
　In C 537
Rimbaud, Arthur 461
Rimsky-Korsakov, Nadezhda 326
Rimsky-Korsakov, Nikolai 307, 323, 324, 325, 325–6, 327, 352, 353, 354, 430, 474
　Chronicle of my Musical Life 326
　The Golden Cockerel 354
　Mozart and Salieri 354
　Sadko 354
　　'The Song of the Indian Guest' 354
　Scheherazade 326
　The Tale of Tsar Saltan 354
　　'The Flight of the Bumblebee' 354
Rinuccini, Ottavio 114
　Dafne 116
Ritter, Alexander 308
Robbins, Jerome 539
Robeson, Paul 489
Rode, Pierre 259, 262
Rodgers, Richard 494
　Carousel 494
　　'If I Loved You' 494
　　'You'll Never Walk Alone' 494
　The King and I 494
　　'March of the Siamese Children' 494
　The Sound of Music 495, 546

Rodrigo, Joaquín 479
Roger, Estienne 133
Roger, Thérèse 458
Rogers, Ginger 495
Rogier, Philippe
　Laboravi 77
Rolland, Romain 11
Rolling Stones, The 541, 544, 549
　'(I Can't Get No) Satisfaction' 544
Roman de Fauvel, Le 44, 53
Romberg, Sigmund 495
　Desert song 495
Rome 114, 117, 126, 305–6
　ancient 25
　Etruscan instruments 25
　Vatican 134
rondeau 32, 33
rondellus 32
Ronsard, Pierre de 96
Roomful of Teeth 559
Roosevelt, Franklin D. 485, 503
Rore, Cipriano de 95
Rorem, Ned 482, 538
　Paris Diary 538
Roseingrave, Thomas 137
Rosen, Charles 3, 8, 189, 191, 194, 237, 270, 302
Rosenthal, Manuel 462
Ross, Alex 371, 410
Rossi, Luigi 122, 142, 145
Rossini, Gioachino 130, 260, 268, 278, 330, 332, 335, 336–7, 338, 339, 342, 343, 352, 373–4, 377, 379, 380, 381, 385, 423
　Il barbiere di Siviglia 203, 337, 373, 383
　La cambiale di matrimonio 336
　La gazza ladra 278
　Guillaume Tell 336, 337, 344, 373
　Otello 375
　Péchés de vieillesse 338
Rostand, Claude 468
Rostropovich, Mstislav 509
Roubert, Lucien 470
Rousseau, Jean-Jacques 188, 200, 209
　Le Devin du village 156, 209
　Lettre sur la musique Françoise 209
　Pygmalion 181
Roussel, Albert 453
Rubinstein, Anton 244, 284, 323, 329
Rubinstein, Arthur 478

Rubinstein, Nikolai 323, 324
Rückert, Friedrich 418
Rudolph, Archduke 247, 256, 259
Rue, Pierre de la 72
Ruggles, Carl 486, 487, 500
  Sun-Treader 486
Russolo, Luigi, 528
  L'Arte dei Rumori 446

S

Saariaho, Kaija 558
  Lichtbogen 558
Sacher, Paul 473
Sachs, Hans 40, 95, 369
Sacrati, Francesco
  La finta pazza 123
Saint-Saëns, Camille 296, 314, 315, 349, 399, 453, 454, 455, 485
  Danse macabre 314
  L'assassinat du duc de Guise 314
  Samson et Dalila 349
  Souvenirs de Bayreuth 454
Salazar, António 413
Salieri, Antonio 179, 183, 203, 208, 211, 230, 231, 255, 267, 275, 277–8, 336
  Europa riconosciuta 336
  Les Danaïdes 211
  Prima la musica e poi le parole 182
Salomon, Johann Peter 186, 226
Salvini-Donatelli, Fanny 379
Sammartini, Giovanni Battista 200, 208, 299
Sanctis, Cesare de 385
Sanctis, Francesco de 374
Sand, George (Dupin, Amantine Aurore, later Baroness Dudevant) 279, 282–3, 284, 285, 286, 291
Sappho 22
Satie, Erik 413, 457, 458, 461, 463, 465–6, 469, 470–1, 557, 558
  Gymnopédies 471
  Musique d'ameublement 471
  Parade 471
  'Ragtime Parade' 489
  Trois Morceaux en forme de poire 471
  Trois petites pièces montées 466
Savonarola, Girolamo 75, 79
Sax, Madame (singer) 383
Sayn-Wittgenstein, Princesse Carolyne zu 286–7, 296, 297, 346, 381

Scarlatti, Alessandro 11, 129, 134, 135, 136, 205
Scarlatti, Domenico 127, 129, 134–7, 138, 174, 185, 198, 290
  Essercizi per Gravicembalo 136
  Keyboard sonatas 136–7
  Stabat Mater 134
Scarlatti, Maria Catalina (née Gentili) 135, 136
Scheibe, Adolph 177
Scheidt, Samuel 160
Schikaneder, Anna 202
Schikaneder, Emanuel 202, 204–5, 227, 259
Schiller, Ferdinand 266
Schlegel, Friedrich von 235, 248
Schmitz, Oscar 243
Schnittke, Alfred 559
  Concerti Grossi 559
Schnorr von Carolsfeld, Ludwig 368
Schnorr von Carolsfeld, Malvina 368
Schober, Franz von 267, 268, 269
Schoenberg, Arnold 3, 399, 407, 409, 423, 426–30, 455, 563
  compositional technique 5, 412, 428
  on other composers 312, 425, 426, 432, 437, 439, 443–4
  teaching, reception, influence and legacy 409, 412, 432, 433, 435, 437, 438, 439, 440, 447, 449, 459, 467, 469, 470, 474, 476, 479, 486, 487, 500, 517, 518, 519, 520, 525, 526, 536, 538, 556
  Chamber Symphony No. 1 429, 500
  Chamber Symphony No. 2 429
  Erwartung 433
  Fünf Orchesterstücke 435, 449
  Gurre-lieder 371, 425, 426, 429
  Moderner Psalm 429
  Piano Concerto 427
  Pierrot lunaire 429, 467, 523
  Sechs Kleine Klavierstücke 428
  String Quartet No. 2 429
  Suite for Strings 425
  A Survivor from Warsaw 429, 515
  Verklärte Nacht 426, 429
  Violin Concerto 427
  Wind Quintet, 414–5
  Prose writings 427–8
    Harmonielehre 427–8
    Style and Idea 427–8

Schoenberg, Gertrud (née Kolitsch) 426
Schoenberg, Mathilde (née Zemlinsky) 426
Schoenberg, Nuria (later Nono) 426
Schönberg, Claude-Michel
   Les Misérables 350
   Miss Saigon 547
Schopenhauer, Arthur 370
   The World as Will and Representation 368
Schreker, Franz, 438, 439
   Der ferne Klang 438
Schröder-Devrient, Wilhelmine 241, 245, 342, 359
Schrödinger's cat 531
Schroeter, Rebecca 186, 229
Schubart, Christian Friedrich Daniel 190, 200
Schubert, Ferdinand 270, 281
Schubert, Franz 13, 163, 208, 211, 236, 243, 253, 260, 261, 266–272, 275, 278, 289, 294, 301, 302–3, 320
   Chamber Music
      Trout Quintet 268
      String Quartet No. 15 318
      String Cuintet 269, 271
   Opera and stage music
      Alfonso und Estrella 296
      Fierrabras 331
      Sakuntala 331
      Die Verschworenen 331
      Die Zauberharfe 331
      Das Zauberglöckchen 331
   Piano music
      Sonata in B flat, D. 960 302
   Songs and Song Cycles
      Die Schöne Müllerin 253, 269
         'Das Wandern' 271
         'Der Neugierige' 249, 271
      Schwanengesang 269
      Winterreise 253, 269
      An die Musik 271
      Der Hirt auf dem Felsen 269
      'Du bist die Ruh' 271
      'Erlkönig' 268, 271
      'Gretchen am Spinnrade' 271
      Litanei 271
      'Ständchen' (D. 597) 271
   Sacred Music
      Mass in E Flat 269
   Symphonies
      Symphony No. 8 ('Unfinished') 269, 271, 303
      Symphony No. 9 ('Great' C major) 269, 271, 281, 303
Schubert, Franz Teodor 267
Schubert, Josefa 270
Schubert, Maria Elizabet 267
Schuller, Gunther 548
Schumann, August 274
Schumann, Clara (née Wieck) 236, 280, 281, 283, 285, 292, 293–5, 302–3, 304, 310, 311, 314, 323, 326, 369
   Lorelei 293
   Piano Concerto in A Minor 294
   Piano Sonata in G Minor 294
   Twelve Rückert songs 294
Schumann family 273, 285
Schumann, Ludwig 295
Schumann, Marie 285, 295
Schumann, Robert, 231, 236, 243, 245, 271, 272, 273–298, 276, 301, 310, 314, 316, 322, 323, 329, 331–2, 334, 338, 359, 361, 365, 367, 460
   personal life 8
   Album for the Young 288
   Carnaval 278, 280, 292
   Concerto for Violin 287
   Dichterliebe 293
   F-A-E sonata 287
   Four Marches 286
   Genoveva 287, 296, 331–2
   Humoreske 293
   Intermezzo 293
   Papillons 292
   Piano Concerto in A minor 294, 301
   Symphonies 301, 305
      Symphony No. 1 ('Spring') 285, 304
      Symphony No. 4 301, 304
   Twelve Rückert songs 294
Schuncke, Ludwig 280, 301
   Piano Sonata in G Minor 301
Schuppanzigh, Ignaz 255, 261–2
Schütz, Heinrich 103, 108, 119, 157, 159–60
   Becker Psalter 159
   Dafne 116, 159
   Musikalische Exequien (German requiem) 159
   Saul, Saul was verfolgst du mich? 159

Symphoniae Sacrae 157
Schwitters, Kurt 413
  Ursonate 413
Scolica Enchiriadis 47
Scott, Cyril 450
Scott, Sir (George) Gilbert 248
Scott, Marion 264
Scott, Sir Walter 235, 338
Scriabin, Alexander 247, 427, 450, 474, 476
  Poem of Ecstasy 476
  Prometheus: The Poem of Fire 476
Scribe, Eugène 343, 380
Searle, Humphrey 440, 534
Sebold, Alice 482
seconda pratica 112–4
'Second Viennese School' 438, 440
Seeger family 486, 487–8, 543
Seeger, Charles 486, 487
Seeger, Mike 488
Seeger, Peggy 488
Seeger, Pete 488
Seeger, Ruth Crawford 487–8
Seikilos epitaph 22
Seixas, Carlos 137
Sella, Quintino 388
Seneca 28
Senfl, Ludwig
  Christ ist erstanden 88
serialism 407, 412, 414–5, 434, 508–9, 519, 526–7, 528
Sermisy, Claudin de 65, 92
Sessions, Roger 501
Sévigné, Mme de (Marie de Rabutin-Chantal, marquise de Sévigné) 143
Sforza family 73
Sforza, Ascanio 73
Sforza, Gonzago 73
Shakespeare, William 67, 94, 96, 119, 121, 141, 235, 289, 293, 305, 316, 346, 348, 353, 372, 386, 450, 498, 512, 558
  on music 23
  Hamlet 43, 293, 348
  King Lear 386, 392
  Macbeth 374–5, 512
  The Merry Wives of Windsor 376, 386
  A Midsummer Night's Dream 164
  Much Ado about Nothing 346
  Othello 386, 489
  Romeo and Juliet 306

The Tempest 563
Twelfth Night 40
Shankar, Ravi 445, 518–9
Shankar, Uday 445
Sharp, Cecil 411, 444, 480
Shattuck, Roger
  The Banquet Years 470
Shaw, Caroline 559
  Partita 559
Shaw, George Bernard 336
Shelley, Mary
  Frankenstein 333
Shelley, Percy Bysshe 245, 293
Sheppard, John 75, 76
Shorter, Wayne 543, 560
  Masqualero 560
Shostakovich, Dmitri 477, 498–512, 516
  Lady Macbeth of the Mtsensk District 502
  The Nose 502
  String quartets 6, 7
    String Quartet No. 12, 521
  Symphonies
    Symphony No. 1 500, 502
    Symphony No. 2 502
    Symphony No. 3 502
    Symphony No. 4 502
    Symphony No. 5 502
    Symphony No. 7 ('Leningrad') 505–6, 515
    Symphony No. 8 ('Stalingrad') 506
    Symphony No. 11 510
    Symphony No. 14 509
Shostakovich, Irina 509
Shostakovich, Maxim 512
Sibelius, Aino 423
Sibelius, Jean 309, 324, 327, 333, 399, 409, 416–425, 443, 485
  reputation and influence 423–5, 451, 483, 516
  Symphonies
    Symphony No. 2 417, 423–4
    Symphony No. 5 417
    Symphony No. 4 418
    Symphony No. 6 418
    Symphony No. 7 418, 422
  Other orchestral works
    Tone poems 309
    Andante festivo 309
    Finlandia 309, 516

Kárelia 309
Kullervo 309, 417
Tapiola 422
Valse triste 309
Violin Concerto 418
Siebold, Agathe von 311
Silbermann family 105
Simon, Paul 559
   Graceland 559
Simone, Nina 543
Simpson, Robert 538
Sinatra, Frank 492, 495, 541
Singer, Winaretta (Princesse Edmond de Polignac) 431, 461
Sitwell family 451
Sitwell, Edith 451
Sitwell, Sacheverell 451
Skalkottas, Nikolas 440
slave music 481
Smart, Sir George 260
Smetana, Bedřich 296, 320, 322, 356, 384, 401
   The Bartered Bride 356
   Má Vlast 322
Smith, Bessie 490, 500, 549
Smith, 'The Incredible' Jimmy 529
Smithson, Harriet 305, 307
Smollett, Tobias
   The Expedition of Humphry Clinker 201
Smyth, Dame Ethel 399–400, 450
   'The March of the Women' 450
   Der Wald 399
   The Wreckers 400
Smythson, Robert 64
Sœurs Étiennes, Les 445
Soler, Padre Antonio 138
   Llave de la Modulación 138
   Sonata in F Sharp 138
Soler, Vicente Martín y 323
   Una Cosa Rara 203
solmisation 49
sonata
   Baroque 106–7, 125, 136–7
   Classical, 192–3, 193–6, 195
   Romantic 270–1, 292, 302–303
Sondheim, Stephen 539, 547
   Shows
      Assassins 547

Merrily We Roll Along 547
      Sunday in the Park with George 547
   Songs
      'Losing my Mind' 547
      'The Story of Lucy and Jessie' 547
   As lyricist
      West Side Story 539, 547
Sonnenfels, Joseph von 209
Sonzogno, Edoardo 394
Sophia Elisabeth of Brunswick-Lüneberg, Duchess 103
Sophocles 24
Sorabji, Kaikhosru Shapurji 247, 538
Sousa, John Philip 486, 488
Spaethling, Robert 228
Spaun, Joseph von 267, 269
spectralism 536
Spencer, Stewart 365
Spice Girls, The 549
Spinal Tap 549
spirituals
Spitta, Philipp 333
Spohr, Louis 263
   Faust 331
   Jessonda 331
   Symphony No. 6 301
   Symphony No. 7 301
Spontini, Gaspare 10, 238–9, 275, 332, 333, 341–2, 345
   Olimpie 238, 342
   La Vestale 236, 341–2
Sprague Coolidge, Elizabeth 441, 488
Stadler, Anton 196, 227
Staggins, Nicholas 7
Stalin, Josef 502, 506, 507, 509
Stamitz, Carl 191
Stamitz, Johann 191, 200
Stanford, Sir Charles Villers 314, 399, 447, 454
Steele, Richard 104
Steibelt, Daniel 246, 262
Stein, Erwin 500
Stein, Gertrude
   Four Saints in Three Acts 482
Steinberg, Maximilian 500
Steinecke, Wolgang 210, 522, 526
Steinway, Henry (piano-makers) 246
Stendahl 336, 337
Stewart, Rod 451

Stieglitz, Alfred 500
stile antico 84, 112–4
Stirling, Jane 285
Stockhausen, Karlheinz 434, 517, 518, 523, 530, 531, 536, 545, 550, 556
   Gesang der Jünglinge 530
   Punkte 527
Stokowski, Leopold 424, 500
Stoll, Anton 227
Stolz, Teresa 384, 387
Storace family 244
Storace, Nancy 224
Storace, Stephen 179, 203
Stösslová, Kamila 402
Strachey, Christopher 529
Stradella, Alessandro 126
Stradivari family 125
Strauss, Franz 370, 402
Strauss, Johann I
   Radetzky march 488
Strauss, Johann II 248, 311
Strauss, Richard 13, 305, 308, 311, 317, 318, 335, 370, 399, 401, 409, 413, 426, 435, 438, 449, 478, 515, 516, 532
   Operas 402–3
      Ariadne auf Naxos 402
      Capriccio 402
      Elektra 402, 403
      Die Frau ohne Schatten 402
      Intermezzo 402
      Der Rosenkavalier 402, 403
      Salome 402–3
   Tone poems 308, 309, 402, 425
      Also sprach Zarathustra 308, 440
      Don Juan 309
      Eine Alpensinfonie 308
      Symphonia Domestica 308
      Till Eulenspiegels lustige Streiche 308
   Four Last Songs 516–7, 532
Stravinsky, Igor 2, 7, 253, 264, 324, 326, 408, 409, 423, 427, 430–4, 444, 459, 479, 496–7, 555, 562
   working method 8
   on other composers 325, 327, 354, 433, 434, 438, 474, 476
   influence and reputation 434, 435, 459, 467, 473, 507, 522, 531
   Abraham and Isaac 433
   Canticum Sacrum 433
   Concerto for Piano and Wind Instruments 431
   'The dove descending' (Eliot) 433
   'Dumbarton Oaks' Concerto 415, 431, 488
   'Ebony' Concerto 496
   The Firebird 353, 430
   The Flood 433
   Jeu de cartes 431
   Lord's Prayer 431
   Mass 433
   The Nightingale 431
   Les Noces ('The Wedding') 431
   Oedipus Rex 431
   Petrushka 430, 459
   Pulcinella 431, 432
   The Rake's Progress 433
   Requiem Canticles 433
   The Rite of Spring 371, 430–1, 434, 459, 537–8
   The Soldier's Tale 431
   Symphonies of Wind Instruments 431
   Symphony in C 431
   Symphony of Psalms 431
   Threni 433
   Violin Concerto 431
   Writing and interviews 434
      Chronicles of My Life 434
      Conversations with Igor Stravinsky (with Robert Craft) 434
Stravinsky, Vera 11, 432
Strepponi, Giuseppina (later Verdi) 372, 373, 374, 377, 378, 380–1, 382, 385, 387, 389
stride piano 491
Strozzi, Barbara 123
Strozzi, Giulio 123
   La finta pazza 123
Sturm und Drang 190, 215, 219, 303
Sueur, Jean-François Le 305, 340, 342
   Joseph 340
   Uthal 340
suite
   Baroque 150
Suk, Josef 321, 473
Sulemy, Clement (sometimes given as Clément) 230
Sullivan, Sir Arthur, 248, 291
   The Mikado 241
   The Pirates of Penzance 375
   Ruddigore 334

The Yeomen of the Guard 334
'Sumer is icumen in' 52
Susanin, Ivan 352
Susato, Tielman
   Pavane la bataille 92
Süssmayr, Franz 227
Swain, Freda 450
   Airmail Concerto 450
Swayne, Giles 559
   Magnificat 559
Sweelinck, Jan Pieterszoon 117, 159, 160
Swieten, Baron Gottfried von 197, 207–8, 221, 230
swing 492
symphony 299–329
   Classical 194–5, 200–1
   Romantic 299–302, 309
   Cyclic form 303–304
   twentieth-century 416–25, 535
Szymanowski, Karol 478
   Des Hafis Liebeslieder (The Love Songs of Hafiz) 478
   Król Roger (King Roger) 478
   Symphony No. 3 'Song of the Night' 478
   Symphony No. 4 478

T
Tailleferre, Germaine 466, 467
   La Cantate du Narcisse 467
Takemitsu, Tōru 508, 536
Tallis, Thomas 2, 43, 75, 77–8, 90, 91
   Gaude, gloriosa Dei mater 77
   'If Ye Love Me' 90
   Miserere nostri 77
   Missa puer Natus est nobis 77
   Salvator mundi (I & II) 78
   Spem in alium 77
   Tunes for Archbishop Parker's Psalter 77
Tartini, Giuseppe 131, 189
Tasso, Torquato 96
Tatum, Art 491, 542
Tavener, John 559
Taverner, John 76
Tchaikovsky, Alexandra (Alexandra Davydov) 329
Tchaikovsky, Antonina (Antonina Miliukova) 329

Tchaikovsky, Modest 327, 329, 355
Tchaikovsky, Pyotr Ilyich 315, 324, 325, 326–9, 349, 351, 354–5, 474, 476, 494
   Ballet 355
      The Nutcracker 355, 408
      The Sleeping Beauty 355
      Swan Lake 355
   Opera 354–5, 398
      Eugene Onegin 354
      Iolanta 355
      The Queen of Spades 355
   Orchestral works 326–8
      1812 overture 327
      Romeo and Juliet 326
      The Tempest 327, 537
   Symphonies 326–8
      'Manfred' symphony 326–7
      Symphony No. 4 327–8
      Symphony No. 5 327–8
      Symphony No. 6 327–8
Teagarden, Jack 491
Telemann, Georg Philipp 101, 103, 104, 105, 107, 158, 159, 165–6, 169, 171, 276
   Der Geduldige Socrates 165
   Methodical sonata 166
   Pastorelle en musique 165
   Pimpinone 165
   Tafelmusik 150
Teltscher, Josef 269
Temperley, Nicholas 284
Temple, Shirley 427
Terence 25
Texier, Lilly (see Debussy, Lilly) 458
Thackeray, William Makepeace
   Vanity Fair 241
Thackray, Jake 546
   Old Molly Metcalfe 546
   The Widow of Bridlington 546
Thalberg, Sigismond 246, 279, 281
Tharpe, Sister Rosetta 490, 549
Thayer, Alexander Wheelock 240, 255, 259, 275
theatre 94, 179, 525, 560–1
Theater Owners Booking Association 490
Themistocles 23
Theodosius 28
theory
   hexachord 49

rhythmic modes 36, 53 (see also modes; notation)
imitation 63, 64
counterpoint 63, 64, 110, 111
modes 63, 562 (see also modes; notation)
harmony and keys 109, 191
dissonance 63, 64, 428, 432
microtones 487
Theremin, Leon 435
Thomas, Ambroise 342, 347–8, 454
　Mignon 347–8
　Hamlet 347–8
Thomas, Augusta Read 558
Thomson, James 208
Thomson, Virgil, 482, 487, 501, 506
　Four Saints in Three Acts 482
　Mother of Us All 482
Thoreau, Henry David 485
Thorvaldsdóttir, Anna 558
Thurber, Jeanette 321
Tick, Judith 487
Timotheus 24
Tinctoris, Johannes 59, 68, 70, 71, 74
Tippett, Sir Michael 408, 452, 501, 509, 510
　A Child of our Time 452, 515
　Concerto for Double String Orchestra 452
　'Dance, Clarion Air' 452
　Fantasia Concertante on a Theme of Corelli 452
　The Mask of Time 452
　String quartet No. 2 521
　Operas
　　The Ice Break 452
　　The Knot Garden 452
　　The Midsummer Marriage 452
Titon du Tillet, Évrard 145, 151
Tofts, Mrs 158
Tolstoy, Alexei 506
Tolstoy, Leo
　War and Peace 241
Tom and Jerry 465
Tomkins, Thomas
　'Sad Pavan for These Distracted Times' 91
　Seventh Service 160
Tomlinson, Gary 14–16
Tone poem 307–09
Torelli, Giuseppe 131

Toscanini, Arturo 387, 483, 505, 538
Tournemire, Charles 499
Traetta, Tomasso 209
Trenet, Charles 445
Trent (Trento), Italy, Council of 66, 84, 533
Triumphs of Oriana, The 96
tropes 32
troubadours 39–41, 95
　jongleurs 40
　trobairitz 40
　trouvères 40
　Cantigas de Santa Maria 40–1
Trumbauer, Frank 491
Tudor, David, 522
Tukhachevsky, Mikhail 500
Tully, Alice 488
Turina, Joaquín 444
Turing, Alan 529
Turnage, Mark-Anthony 11, 558
　Greek 558
Turner, Joseph Malord William (J. M. W.) 370
Turner, William
　'Club Anthem' 164
Twain, Mark 241, 369
twelve-tone composition 407, 412, 414–5, 437, 439, 508–9, 519, 561
Tye, Christopher 76

U
Unger, Caroline 262

V
Valentini (Valentino Urbano) 158
Valéry, Paul 467
Vallée, Rudy 495
Vandross, Luther 548
Vanhal, Johann Baptist 212, 225, 255, 299
Varèse, Edgard 314, 427, 435, 484–5, 486, 488, 528
　Amériques 484
　Déserts 530
　Ionisation 484
　Poème Electronique 484
Varesi, Felice 377
Vargas, President Getúlio 471
Varzar, Nina (Shostakovich) 502
Vasnier family 456
Vasnier, Marguerite 456, 457

Vasnier, Marie 456
Vaughan, Sarah 543
Vaughan Williams, Ralph, 317, 411, 423,
    440, 444, 447–9, 453, 463, 483, 506, 524
  on the origins of music 15
    'All People That on Earth Do Dwell'
      89
    Fantasia on a Theme by Thomas Tallis
      448
    The Lark Ascending 448
    'Linden Lea' 448
    Mass in G Minor 448
    The Pilgrim's Progress 448
    Serenade to Music 448
    Three Shakespeare Songs 448
    Tuba Concerto 448
    The Wasps 24–5
  Symphonies 448, 506, 515
    Symphony No. 2 448
    Symphony No. 3 ('Pastoral') 448
    Symphony No. 4 448
    Symphony No. 5 448
    Symphony No. 6 448
Velluti, Giovanni Battista 343
Venice 114, 117, 121, 123, 125, 129, 433, 434,
    534
  Charitable 'ospedali' 101, 123, 132
  Parish 'scuole grandi' 101, 114, 118
  St Mark's basilica 112, 114, 120, 132
Verdelot, Philippe 75–6, 95
Verdi, Carlo 372, 373, 383
Verdi, Giuseppe 13, 227, 231, 237, 239, 241,
    247–8, 296, 311, 328, 339, 343, 346, 372–387,
    396, 509
  on other composers 334, 373, 392–3,
    393–4, 395
  and Wagner 382, 387–392
  Operas
    Aida 383, 390
    Un ballo in Maschera 382, 391
    La battaglia di Legnano 375, 376
    Don Carlos 353, 374, 382–3, 388, 392
    I due Foscari 374, 375
    Ernani 374, 377
    Falstaff 376, 382, 386
    La forza del destino 382
    Un giorno di regno 372, 386
    I Lombardi 375
    Macbeth 374–5, 377, 382, 387, 388, 390

Nabucco 372, 376
  'Va, pensiero, sull'ali dorate' 374, 387
Oberto 372
Otello 386, 387, 391, 397
Rigoletto 6, 374, 376, 377–8, 383, 388, 391,
  391
Simon Boccanegra 382
La traviata 376, 378–9, 391, 394
Il trovatore 376, 379–80
Les Vêpres Siciliennes 380
Requiem 349, 385, 389
Verdi, Giuseppina (née Strepponi), see
  Strepponi, Giuseppina
Verdi, Margherita (née Barezzi) 372
Verga, Giovanni
  Cavalleria Rusticana 393
Verlaine, Paul
  L'heure exquise 472
Viadana, Ludovico Grossi de 3, 114, 117
  Cento Concerti Ecclesiastici 117
Viardot, Pauline 349, 453
Victoria, Queen 285, 375, 447
Victoria, Tomás Luis de 77, 79–80, 84
  Missa pro Victoria 81
Vienna 133, 179, 206–8, 214, 240, 241–2,
  244–6, 420–1, 426–7
Vierne, Louis 314
Villa-Lobos, Heitor 409, 471–2
  Bachianas Brasileiras 472
  Toccata/The Little Train of the Caipira 472
  Chôros 472
  Nonet:'Impressão rápida de todo o Brasil'
    472
Vinci, Leonardo 130
  Didone abbondonata 130
  Li zite 'ngalera 130
Viñes, Ricardo 462, 468
Viollet-le-Duc, Eugène 248
Vitali, Tomaso
  Artificii musicali 125
Vittorio Emanuele II, King 382
Vitry, Philippe de 53
virelai 32
Vivaldi, Antonio 101, 123, 126, 129, 131–4,
  147, 158, 202, 479, 561
  La Candace 133
  'Gloria in excelsis' RV 588 132
  'Gloria in excelsis' RV 589 132
  Griselda 133

Vivier, Claude, 517
Vivier, Eugène Léon 306
Vogl, Johann Michael 256, 268
Vogler, Abbé Georg Joseph 238, 250, 251
Volkov, Solomon
   Testimony 511–12

W

Wagner, Cosima (née Liszt, later von Bülow) 281, 296–7, 364, 365, 371, 389, 454
Wagner, Eva 364
Wagner, Isolde 364
Wagner, Johanna (composer's mother) 273
Wagner, Johanna (niece) 245
Wagner, Minna (née Planer) 351, 360, 362, 364, 368
Wagner, Richard 13, 155, 212, 231, 236, 240, 241, 243, 244, 245, 252, 253, 281, 284, 286, 293, 296, 297, 298, 312, 313, 315, 317, 318, 320, 332, 334, 335, 342, 344, 348, 350, 351, 352, 356, 357, 357–371, 373, 375, 376, 398, 399, 402, 424
   personality 8
   and Bayreuth 238, 381
   prose writings 241, 344, 360, 362–3
      Art and Revolution 362–3
      The Artwork of the Future 362–3
      A Communication to My Friends 362–3
      'On the Application of Music to Drama' 367
      Opera and Drama 362–3, 365, 367, 368, 370, 390
   as librettist 361, 363–4, 365, 367, 387
   death 297, 320, 371
   and Verdi 367, 379, 382, 387–392,
   leitmotifs 366–7, 367, 371, 428
   later reputation and influence 371, 413, 418, 421, 428, 441, 454, 456, 467, 476, 523
   Operas
      Der fliegende Holländer 245, 360, 361
      Lohengrin 296, 330, 360, 361–2, 364, 367, 369, 379, 389, 391
      Die Meistersinger von Nürnberg 313, 361, 363, 364, 368, 369–370
      Parsifal 297, 368, 370–1, 388, 391, 536
      Rienzi 342, 351
      The Ring Cycle 354, 359, 363, 363–7, 368, 371

      Das Rheingold 364, 366, 367
      Die Walküre 313, 334, 364
      Siegfried 363
      Götterdämmerung 362, 366, 367, 391, 391, 391
      Tannhäuser 245, 246, 296, 313, 330, 360–1, 364, 389
      Tristan und Isolde 297, 362, 363, 364, 366, 368–9, 370, 391, 447, 476
Wagner, Rosalie 359
Wagner, Siegfried 364
Wagner, Winifred, 516
Waldmann, Maria 384
Waldstein, Count Ferdinand von 254–5, 256
Walker, Alice 482
Wallace, William 334
   The Amber Witch 334
   Lurline 334
   Maritana 334
Wallen, Errollyn 557
   Photography 557
Waller, Thomas Wright 'Fats' 491, 495
Walsh family 104
Walshe, Jennifer
   Live Nude Girls 558–9
Walter, Bruno 424, 500
Walther, Johann 87
Walton, Sir William 317, 451–2
   Belshazzar's Feast 451
   'Crown Imperial' 452
   Façade 451
   'Orb and Sceptre' 451
   Symphony No. 1 451
   Viola Concerto 451
Walpole, Horace 101
Warlock, Peter (Philip Heseltine) 448, 450
Warrack, John 332, 341
Was, Don 543
Waters, 2nd Lt. Eric 542
Waters, Muddy (McKinley Morganfield) 541
Waters, Roger 542
Watteau, Antoine 237
'We Shall Overcome' 546
Weather Report 548, 560
Weaver, William 375
Weber (later Lange), Aloysia 216, 221, 223
Weber, Carl von 419

Weber, Carl Maria von 155, 238, 245, 250–3, 260, 262, 269, 272, 276, 278, 281, 332–3, 340, 477
   Abu Hassan 238, 333
   Aufforderung zum Tanze (Invitation to the Dance) 251, 253
   Die drei Pintos 419
   Der Erste Ton 358
   Der Freischütz 212, 238, 251, 252, 330, 333, 342
   Oberon 330
   Peter Schmoll und seine Nachbarn 333
   Turandot 333
   Tonkünstlers Leben 251, 252, 332–3
Weber, Constanze, see Mozart, Constanze
Weber, Fridolin 216
Weber family (Mozart's in-laws) 216, 217, 221, 241, 250
Weber, Gottfried 250, 251
Weber, Max Maria von
   As biographer of C. M. von Weber 11
Weber, Josefa (later Hofer, then Meier) 221, 331
Webern, Anton 427, 434, 435, 436–8, 439, 440, 524, 535, 537
   Fünf Orchesterstücke 437
   Ricercar (from Bach's *The Musical Offering*, arr.) 438
   Sechs Stücke für grosses Orchester 435, 437
   Three Traditional Rhymes 437
   Zwei Lieder 437
Webern, Peter 437
Wedgwood, Josiah 447
Weelkes, Thomas
   'Strike It Up, Tabor' 96
   'Thule, the Period of Cosmography' 96
Wegeler, Franz 255
Wehinger, Rainer 531
Weill, Kurt 409, 413, 546
   Operas
      Rise and Fall of the City of Mahagonny 446–7
      The Threepenny Opera 446
   Songs
      'Alabama Song' 447
      'Mack the Knife' 447
      'Surabaya Johnny' 447
Weinberg, Mieczysław 410
Wellesz, Egon 438
Wells, Herbert George (H. G.) 528
Werner, Gregor 183
Wert, Giaches de 95
Wesendonck, Mathilde 363, 368
Wesendonck, Otto 363
West, M. L. 23, 28
Wharton, Edith
   The Age of Innocence 238, 347
Whitacre, Eric 559
White, Barry 548
White, Robert
   Lamentations of Jeremiah 77
Whiteman, Paul 491, 493
Whitman, Walt 449, 480
Wider family 217
Widor, Charles-Marie 454, 499
Wieck, Clara see Schumann, Clara
Wieck, Friedrich 276, 280, 283, 359
Wilde, Oscar 403
   The Importance of Being Earnest 559
Wilder, Thornton
   Our Town 482
Wilhelm, Duke 82
Wilhelmine of Prussia, Margravine of Brandenburg-Bayreuth 104
   Argenore 146
Willaert, Adrian 72, 76, 95
Williams, Hank 541
Williams, Mary Lou 492
Williams, Tennessee 482
Wilson, Devon 549
Winchester Tropers 47–8
Winehouse, Amy 549, 560
Wise, Michael 162
Witteczek, Josef 268
Wittgenstein, Paul 464
Wodzińska, Maria 282
Wolf, Hugo 6
Wolff, Francis 543
Wolsey, Cardinal Thomas 76, 85
Wood, Sir Henry 354, 424, 505
Wood, Richard 504
Worcester fragments 52, 67
Wordsworth, William 279
Wojtyła, Karol (Pope John Paul II) 535
Woyciechowski, Tytus 277, 281–2
Würtemmburg, Duke of 92

X

Xenakis, Iannis 485, 516, 519, 527, 530, 533–4, 536
  Metastasis 533
  Writings on music
    Musique Architecture 533
    Musiques Formelles 533

Y

Yale University 476, 493
Young, LaMonte, 519, 537
Young, Lester 492

Z

Zappa, Frank 486, 550
Zelter, Carl 294
Zemlinsky, Alexander 421, 426, 440
  Kammersymphonie 438
  Lyrische Symphonie 438
  Psalm 23 438
Zeno, Apostolo 129
Zhdanov, Andrei 476–7, 508
  Zhdanov decree 477, 507
Zimmermann, Bernd Alois 534
  Ich wandte mich und sah an alles Unrecht, das geschah unter der Sonne 534
  Die Soldaten 534
Zmeskall, Nicolaus 261
Zola, Émile 393
Zorzi Trombetta de Modon 60
Zumaya, Manuel de 138
Zweig, Stefan 420